GRAY'S Anatomy Review

GRAY'S Anatomy Review

Marios Loukas, MD, PhD
Associate Professor
Department of Anatomical Sciences
St. George's University School of Medicine
Grenada, West Indies

Gene L. Colborn, PhD
Professor Emeritus of Anatomy and Surgery
The Medical College of Georgia
Augusta, Georgia

Peter Abrahams, MBBS, FRCS(ED), FRCR, DO(Hon)
Professor of Clinical Anatomy
Medical Teaching Centre
Institute of Clinical Education
Warwick Medical School
University of Warwick
United Kingdom

Stephen W. Carmichael, PhD
Department of Anatomy
Mayo Clinic
Rochester, Minnesota

With illustrations from Abrahams P, Boon J, Spratt J:
McMinn's Clinical Atlas of Human Anatomy, 6th edition. St. Louis: Elsevier, 2008

1600 John F. Kennedy Blvd.
Ste 1800
Philadelphia, PA 19103-2899

GRAY'S ANATOMY REVIEW

ISBN: 978-0-443-06938-3
International ISBN: 978-0-8089-2403-6

Notice

Knowledge and best practice in this field are constantly changing. As new research and experience broaden our knowledge, changes in practice, treatment and drug therapy may become necessary or appropriate. Readers are advised to check the most current information provided (i) on procedures featured or (ii) by the manufacturer of each product to be administered, to verify the recommended dose or formula, the method and duration of administration, and contraindications. It is the responsibility of the practitioner, relying on their own experience and knowledge of the patient, to make diagnoses, to determine dosages and the best treatment for each individual patient, and to take all appropriate safety precautions. To the fullest extent of the law, neither the Publisher nor the Author assumes any liability for any injury and/or damage to persons or property arising out of or related to any use of the material contained in this book.

The Publisher

Library of Congress Cataloging-in-Publication Data

Loukas, Marios.
Gray's anatomy review / Marios Loukas, Stephen Carmichael, Gene L. Colborn.
p. ; cm.
Questions in this review are correlated with the textbook Gray's anatomy for students and with Gray's atlas of anatomy.
ISBN 978-0-443-06938-3
1. Human anatomy--Examinations, questions, etc. I. Carmichael, Stephen W. II. Colborn, Gene L. III. Gray's anatomy for students. IV. Gray's atlas of anatomy. V. Title.
[DNLM: 1. Anatomy--Examination Questions. QS 18.2 L888g 2009]

QM32.L68 2010
611.0076--dc22

2008046824

Acquisitions Editor: William Schmitt
Developmental Editor: Andrew Hall
Design Direction: Ellen Zanolle

Printed in the United States of America
Last digit is the print number: 9 8 7 6 5 4 3 2

To my daughter, Nicole, and my wife, Joanna, for their continuous support and love

Marios Loukas

To my wife and friend, Sarah

Gene Colborn

To "Lucy in the Sky with Diamonds," who puts up with my early mornings and late nights

Peter Abrahams

To Susan Stoddard and Allen Carmichael

Stephen Carmichael

PREFACE

Rote memorization of anatomic facts has been the cardinal feature of exhaustive, and exhausting, courses in human anatomy for many generations of students in medicine, dentistry, and other allied health science programs. Often, little distinction was made between the wheat and the chaff, and little attention was given to the practical, clinical application of the data. In the face of the modern explosion of information and technical advances in the medical sciences, *Gray's Anatomy for Students* was conceived and written as a clinically oriented, student-friendly textbook of human anatomy. The authors, Richard L. Drake, Wayne Vogl, and Adam W. M. Mitchell, have provided a sound base for student learning and understanding of both normal and altered human anatomy in the clinical setting.

This book, the *Gray's Anatomy Review*, was designed for use by students after they have read the textbook and is in keeping with course objectives. The questions, answers, and explanations in this book are intended to serve multiple purposes for students in various programs:

1. This review provides a thought-provoking source for study by students in preparation for examinations in various programs of gross anatomy.
2. To avoid pointless memorization by the student, all the questions are framed within clinical vignettes that guide the student toward practical applications of the textual material.
3. The multiple-choice, single-best-answer format of the questions is designed to facilitate student review in preparation for the USMLE and similar testing methods.
4. The explanations of the answers emphasize the critical importance of understanding normal and dysfunctional human anatomy.
5. Student understanding is further enhanced by critical examination of alternative, incorrect answers that students might be tempted to choose.
6. Finally, the review provides a succinct distillation of the plethora of facts in clinical anatomy, assisting the student's learning and understanding of important concepts in the practice of medicine, irrespective of the student's career choice.

The questions in this review are correlated with *Gray's Anatomy for Students* and with *Gray's Atlas of Anatomy* by Richard L. Drake, Wayne Vogl, Adam W. M. Mitchell, Richard M. Tibbitts, and Paul E. Richardson. Each answer is referenced to pages in the anatomy text (GAS) and in the atlas (GA). We have incorporated or adapted many drawings, full-color illustrations, and radiologic images in an attempt to accelerate the learning process and to enhance understanding of both the anatomy and the clinical applications. The primary sources upon which we have drawn for illustrative material are from the 6th edition of *McMinn's Clinical Atlas of Human Anatomy* by Peter H. Abrahams, Joahannes M. Boon, and Jonathan D. Spratt.

ACKNOWLEDGMENTS

A clinical review book is the work not only of the authors but also of numerous scientific and clinical friends and colleagues who have been so generous with their knowledge and given significant feedback and help. This book would not have been possible were it not for the contributions of the colleagues and friends listed below.

A very special group of medical students, members of the Student Clinical Research Society at the Department of Anatomical Sciences at St. Georges' University, helped enormously with the completion of this project through their comments and criticism.

Steven Andrade
Esther Bilinsky
Samuel Bilinsky
Julie Ferrauiola
Chris Groat
Michael Hill
Rajkamal Khangura
Alexis Lanteri
Elizabeth Lax
Gopi Maharaja
Nadine Mirzayan
Michelle Shirak
Ashley Steinberg
Darius Strike
Ashley Sullivan

The following Professors from the Department of Anatomical Sciences at St. Georges' University have also been very helpful with their comments and criticism.

Feisal Brahim, Ph.D.
Danny Burns, MD., Ph.D.
Brian Curry, Ph.D.
Robert Hage, MD., Ph.D.
Robert Jordan, Ph.D.
Vid Persaud, MD., Ph.D.
Vish Rao, Ph.D.

Dr. R. Shane Tubbs, Ph.D., Associate Professor at the University of Alabama, Birmingham, has always been a great friend and colleague. His continuous support, comments, criticism, and enthusiasm have contributed enormously to the completion of this project.

The authors thank the following individuals and their institutions for kindly supplying various clinical, operative, endoscopic, and imaging photographs:

Dr. Ray Armstrong, Rheumatologist, Southampton General Hospital, Southampton, and Arthritis Research Campaign

Professor Paul Boulos, Surgeon, Institute of Surgical Studies, University College London Medical School, London

Professor Norman Browse, Emeritus Professor of Surgery, and Hodder Arnold Publishers, for permission to use illustrations from *Symptoms and Signs of Surgical Disease,* 4th edition, 2005

Mr. John Craven, formerly Consultant Surgeon, York District Hospital, York

Professor Michael Hobsley, formerly Head of the Department of Surgical Studies, The Middlesex Hospital Medical School, London

Mr. Ralph Hutchings, photographer for Imagingbody.com

Mr. Umraz Khan, Plastic Surgeon, Charing Cross Hospital, London

Professor John Lumley, Director, Vascular Surgery Unit, St. Bartholomew's and Great Ormond Street Hospitals, London

Dr. J. Spratt, Consultant Radiologist, University Hospital of North Durham

Dr. William Torreggiani, Radiologist, The Adelaide and Meath Hospital, Tallaght, Dublin

Miss Gilli Vafidis, Ophthalmologist, Central Middlesex Hospital, London

Mr. Theo Welch, Surgeon, Fellow Commoner Queens' College, Cambridge

Professor Jamie Weir, Department of Clinical Radiology, Grampian University Hospitals Trust, Aberdeen, Scotland, and editor of *Imaging Atlas of Human Anatomy,* 3rd edition, Elsevier 2003.

CONTENTS

1

BACK

1 A 55-year-old man with severe coughing is admitted to the hospital. Radiographic examination reveals tuberculosis of the right lung, with extension to the thoracic vertebral bodies of T6 and T7, producing a "gibbus deformity." Which of the following conditions is most likely also to be confirmed by radiographic examination?

- ☐ **A.** Lordosis
- ☐ **B.** Kyphosis
- ☐ **C.** Scoliosis
- ☐ **D.** Spina bifida
- ☐ **E.** Osteoarthritis

2 A 68-year-old man is admitted to the hospital due to severe back pain. Radiographic examination reveals severe osteoporosis of the vertebral column, with crush fractures of vertebrae L4 and L5. Which of the following parts of the vertebrae are most likely to be fractured in this patient?

- ☐ **A.** Spinal process
- ☐ **B.** Vertebral bodies
- ☐ **C.** Transverse process
- ☐ **D.** Superior articular process
- ☐ **E.** Intervertebral disk

3 A 45-year-old man is admitted to the hospital because of severe pain in the back and lower limb. Radiographic examination reveals spinal stenosis syndrome. Which of the following conditions is most likely to be confirmed by MRI examination?

- ☐ **A.** Hypertrophy of supraspinous ligament
- ☐ **B.** Hypertrophy of interspinous ligament
- ☐ **C.** Hypertrophy of ligamentum flavum
- ☐ **D.** Hypertrophy of anterior longitudinal ligament
- ☐ **E.** Hypertrophy of nuchal ligament

4 A 35-year-old man is admitted to the hospital after a severe car crash. Radiographic examination reveals an injury to the dorsal surface of the neck and a fracture in the medial border of the right scapula. During physical examination the patient presents with the scapula retracted laterally on the affected side. Which of the following nerves has most likely been injured on that side?

- ☐ **A.** Axillary
- ☐ **B.** Long thoracic
- ☐ **C.** Dorsal scapular
- ☐ **D.** Greater occipital
- ☐ **E.** Suprascapular

5 A 64-year-old man arrived at the clinic with a severely painful rash and skin eruptions that are localized entirely on one side of his body, closely following the dermatome level of spinal nerve C7. The patient was diagnosed with herpes zoster virus. In what structure has the virus most likely proliferated to cause the patient's current condition?

- ▢ **A.** The sympathetic chain
- ▢ **B.** The dorsal root ganglion of the C7 spinal nerve
- ▢ **C.** The lateral horn of the C7 spinal cord segment
- ▢ **D.** The posterior cutaneous branch of the dorsal primary ramus of C7
- ▢ **E.** The ventral horn of the C7 spinal cord segment

6 A 45-year-old woman states that she has experienced moderate pain for 2 years over her left lower back, pain that radiates to her left lower limb. She states that after lifting a case of soft drinks, the pain became intense. She was admitted to the emergency department. Radiographic examination revealed disk herniation between vertebral levels L4 and L5. Which of the following nerves was most likely affected by the disk herniation?

- ▢ **A.** L1
- ▢ **B.** L2
- ▢ **C.** L3
- ▢ **D.** L4
- ▢ **E.** L5

7 A 3-year-old child is admitted to the emergency department with severe headache, high fever, malaise, and confusion. Radiographic and physical examinations reveal that the patient suffers from meningitis. A lumbar puncture is ordered. Which vertebral level is the most appropriate location for the lumbar puncture?

- ▢ **A.** T12-L1
- ▢ **B.** L1-2
- ▢ **C.** L2-3
- ▢ **D.** L4-5
- ▢ **E.** L5-S1

8 When a lumbar puncture is performed to sample cerebrospinal fluid, which of the following external landmarks is the most reliable to determine the position of the L4 vertebral spine?

- ▢ **A.** The inferior angles of the scapulae
- ▢ **B.** The iliac crests
- ▢ **C.** The lowest pair of ribs bilaterally
- ▢ **D.** The posterior superior iliac spines
- ▢ **E.** The posterior inferior iliac spines

9 A 39-year-old male presents with severe neck pain after a whiplash injury, sustained when his car was struck from behind. Radiographic studies reveal trauma to the ligament lying on the anterior surface of the cervical vertebral bodies. Which ligament is this?

- ▢ **A.** Anterior longitudinal ligament
- ▢ **B.** Ligamentum flavum
- ▢ **C.** Nuchal ligament
- ▢ **D.** Posterior longitudinal ligament
- ▢ **E.** Transverse cervical ligament

10 A 65-year-old male complains of severe back pain and inability to move his left lower limb. Radiographic studies demonstrate the compression of nerve elements at the intervertebral foramen between vertebrae L5 and S1. Which structure is most likely responsible for this space-occupying lesion?

- ▢ **A.** Anulus fibrosus
- ▢ **B.** Nucleus pulposus
- ▢ **C.** Posterior longitudinal ligament
- ▢ **D.** Anterior longitudinal ligament
- ▢ **E.** Ligamentum flavum

11 A 27-year-old man is admitted to the emergency department after a car crash. Physical examination reveals weakness in medial rotation and adduction of the humerus. Which of the following nerves was most probably injured?

- ▢ **A.** Thoracodorsal
- ▢ **B.** Axillary
- ▢ **C.** Dorsal scapular
- ▢ **D.** Spinal accessory
- ▢ **E.** Radial

12 A 39-year-old woman complains of an inability to reach the top of her head to brush her hair. History reveals that she had undergone a bilateral mastectomy procedure 2 months earlier. Physical examination demonstrates winging of both of her scapulae. Which nerves were most likely damaged during surgery?

- ▢ **A.** Axillary
- ▢ **B.** Spinal accessory
- ▢ **C.** Long thoracic
- ▢ **D.** Dorsal scapular
- ▢ **E.** Thoracodorsal

13 A 19-year-old man is brought to the emergency department after dislocating his shoulder while playing football. Following treatment of the dislocation, he cannot initiate abduction of his arm. An MRI of the shoulder shows a torn muscle. Which muscle was most likely damaged by the injury?

- ▢ **A.** Coracobrachialis
- ▢ **B.** Long head of the triceps
- ▢ **C.** Pectoralis minor
- ▢ **D.** Supraspinatus
- ▢ **E.** Teres major

14 A 1-year-old girl is brought to the clinic for a routine checkup. The child appears normal except for a dimpling of the skin in the lumbar region with a tuft of hair growing over the dimple. You reassure the mother that this condition is seen in 10% to 25% of births and normally has no ill effects. What is this relatively common condition that results from incomplete embryologic development?

- ▢ **A.** Meningomyelocele
- ▢ **B.** Meningocele
- ▢ **C.** Spina bifida occulta
- ▢ **D.** Spina bifida cystica
- ▢ **E.** Rachischisis

15 Which nerve fibers carry the sensation of a mosquito bite on the back, just lateral to the spinous process of the T4 vertebra?

- ▢ **A.** Somatic afferent
- ▢ **B.** Somatic efferent
- ▢ **C.** Visceral afferent
- ▢ **D.** Visceral efferent
- ▢ **E.** Somatic efferent and visceral afferent

16 A 15-year-old female was suspected to have meningitis. To obtain a sample of cerebrospinal fluid by spinal tap in the lumbar region (lumbar puncture), the tip of the needle must be placed in which of the following locations?

- ▢ **A.** In the epidural space
- ▢ **B.** Between anterior and posterior longitudinal ligaments
- ▢ **C.** Superficial to the ligamentum flavum
- ▢ **D.** Between arachnoid mater and dura mater
- ▢ **E.** In the subarachnoid space

17 In the event of intervertebral disk herniation in the cervical region, which of the following ligaments is in an anatomic position to protect the spinal cord from direct compression?

- ▢ **A.** Supraspinous
- ▢ **B.** Posterior longitudinal
- ▢ **C.** Anterior longitudinal
- ▢ **D.** Ligamentum flavum
- ▢ **E.** Nuchal ligament

18 In spinal anesthesia the needle is often inserted between the spinous processes of the L4 and L5 vertebrae to ensure that the spinal cord is not injured. This level is safe because in the adult the spinal cord usually terminates at the disk between which of the following vertebral levels?

- ▢ **A.** T11 and T12
- ▢ **B.** T12 and L1
- ▢ **C.** L1 and L2
- ▢ **D.** L2 and L3
- ▢ **E.** L3 and L4

19 A 22-year-old female is diagnosed with Raynaud's disease. In such a case the patient suffers chronic vasospasm in response to cold. This can lead to arterial constriction and painful ischemia, especially in the fingers or toes. Relief from the symptoms in the hands would require surgical division of which of the following neural elements?

- ▢ **A.** Lower cervical and upper thoracic sympathetic fibers
- ▢ **B.** Lower cervical and upper thoracic ventral roots
- ▢ **C.** Lower cervical and upper thoracic dorsal roots
- ▢ **D.** Lower cervical and upper thoracic spinal nerves
- ▢ **E.** Bilateral spinal accessory nerves

20 A 69-year-old female visits her physician due to severe neck pain. Radiographic studies reveal bony growths (osteophytes) in the intervertebral foramen between vertebrae C2 and C3. Which of the following muscles would be most likely affected by this condition?

- ▢ **A.** Rhomboid
- ▢ **B.** Serratus anterior
- ▢ **C.** Supraspinatus
- ▢ **D.** Diaphragm
- ▢ **E.** Latissimus dorsi

21 A 42-year-old female is diagnosed with constriction of the cervical vertebral canal. A laminectomy of two vertebrae is performed. Which of the following ligaments will most likely also be removed?

- ▢ **A.** Anterior longitudinal
- ▢ **B.** Denticulate
- ▢ **C.** Ligamentum flavum
- ▢ **D.** Nuchal
- ▢ **E.** Cruciate

22 A 28-year-old pregnant woman is admitted to the obstetrics department for delivery. In the final stages of labor a caudal anesthetic is administered via the sacral hiatus. Into which of the following spaces in the sacral canal is the anesthetic placed?

- ▢ **A.** Vertebral canal
- ▢ **B.** Vertebral venous plexus
- ▢ **C.** Epidural space
- ▢ **D.** Subarachnoid space
- ▢ **E.** Subdural space

23 A 12-year-old child was brought to the emergency department by his parents because he has been suffering from a very high fever and severe stiffness in his back. The initial diagnosis is meningitis. The attending physician orders a lumbar puncture to confirm the diagnosis. Upon microscopic examination of the cerebrospinal fluid, hematopoetic cells are seen. Which of the following ligaments is most likely to be penetrated by the needle?

- ▢ **A.** Supraspinous
- ▢ **B.** Denticulate
- ▢ **C.** Anterior longitudinal
- ▢ **D.** Posterior longitudinal
- ▢ **E.** Nuchal ligament

24 A 25-year-old male race car driver is admitted to the emergency department after a severe car crash. Radiographic studies reveal damage to the tip of the transverse process of the third cervical vertebra, with a significantly large pulsating hematoma. What artery is the most likely to have been damaged?

- ▢ **A.** Anterior spinal artery
- ▢ **B.** Vertebral artery
- ▢ **C.** Ascending cervical artery
- ▢ **D.** Deep cervical artery
- ▢ **E.** Posterior spinal arteries

25 A 79-year-old male retired military veteran presents to the outpatient clinic with an abnormal curvature of the vertebral column. He complains that it has become increasingly painful to walk around town. Upon physical examination he has an abnormally increased thoracic curvature resulting from osteoporosis. Which of the following is the most likely clinical condition of this patient's spine?

- ▢ **A.** Scoliosis
- ▢ **B.** Kyphosis
- ▢ **C.** Spinal stenosis
- ▢ **D.** Lordosis
- ▢ **E.** Herniated disk

26 A 42-year-old woman complains of pain and stiffness in her neck. She was injured sliding into second base headfirst during her company softball game. Radiographs reveal no fractures of her spine. However, upon physical examination her right shoulder is drooping and she has difficulty in elevating that shoulder. If you ordered an MRI, it would most likely reveal soft tissue damage to which of the following nerves?

- ▢ **A.** Thoracodorsal nerve
- ▢ **B.** Spinal accessory nerve
- ▢ **C.** Dorsal scapular nerve
- ▢ **D.** Greater occipital nerve
- ▢ **E.** Axillary nerve

27 A 53-year-old male was in a head-on vehicle collision that resulted in compression of the spinal cord by the dens of the axis, with resulting quadriplegia. Which of the following ligaments was most probably torn?

- ▢ **A.** Anterior longitudinal ligament
- ▢ **B.** Transverse ligament of the atlas
- ▢ **C.** Ligamentum flavum
- ▢ **D.** Supraspinous ligament
- ▢ **E.** Nuchal ligament

28 An 18-year-old female passenger injured in a rollover car crash was rushed to the emergency department. After the patient is stabilized she undergoes physical examination. She demonstrates considerable weakness in her ability to flex her neck, associated with injury to CN XI. Which of the following muscles is most probably affected by nerve trauma?

- ▢ **A.** Iliocostalis thoracis
- ▢ **B.** Sternocleidomastoid
- ▢ **C.** Rhomboid major
- ▢ **D.** Rhomboid minor
- ▢ **E.** Teres major

29 A 23-year-old male was killed in a high-speed motor vehicle collision after racing his friend on a local highway. When the medical examiner arrives upon the scene, it is determined that the most likely cause of death was a spinal cord injury. Upon confirmation by the autopsy, the medical examiner officially reports that the patient's cause of death was a fracture of the pedicles of the axis (C2). Breaking of which of the following ligaments would be most likely implicated in this fatal injury?

- ▢ **A.** Ligamentum flavum
- ▢ **B.** Nuchal ligament
- ▢ **C.** Cruciform ligament
- ▢ **D.** Posterior longitudinal ligament
- ▢ **E.** Supraspinous ligament

30 A 65-year-old male is injured when a vehicle traveling at a high rate of speed hits his car from behind. Radiographic examination reveals that two of his articular processes are now locked together, a condition known as "facet jumping." In which region of the spine is this injury most likely to occur?

- ▢ **A.** Cervical
- ▢ **B.** Thoracic
- ▢ **C.** Lumbar
- ▢ **D.** Lumbosacral
- ▢ **E.** Sacral

31 Following a car crash a 47-year-old female complains of severe headache and back pain. Radiographic examination reveals bleeding of the internal vertebral venous plexus (of Batson), resulting in a large hematoma. In what space has the blood most likely accumulated?

- ▢ **A.** Subarachnoid space
- ▢ **B.** Subdural space
- ▢ **C.** Central canal
- ▢ **D.** Epidural space
- ▢ **E.** Lumbar cistern

32 A 32-year-old male elite athlete was lifting heavy weights during an intense training session. The athlete felt severe pain radiating to the posterior aspect of his right thigh and leg. The patient was taken to the hospital where MRI revealed a ruptured L4/L5 intervertebral disk. Which nerve is most probably affected?

- ▢ **A.** L3
- ▢ **B.** L4
- ▢ **C.** L2
- ▢ **D.** L5
- ▢ **E.** S1

33 A 24-year-old patient suffered a lower back strain after a severe fall while snow skiing. MRI studies reveal injury to the muscles responsible for extending and laterally bending the trunk. What arteries provide blood supply for these muscles?

- ▢ **A.** Subscapular
- ▢ **B.** Thoracodorsal
- ▢ **C.** Anterior intercostal
- ▢ **D.** Suprascapular
- ▢ **E.** Posterior intercostal

34 A 22-year-old male soccer player is forced to leave the game following a head-to-head collision with another player. He is admitted to the hospital, and radiographic examination reveals slight dislocation of the atlantoaxial joint. As a result, he experiences decreased range of motion at that joint. What movement of the head would most likely be severely affected?

- ▢ **A.** Rotation
- ▢ **B.** Flexion
- ▢ **C.** Abduction
- ▢ **D.** Extension
- ▢ **E.** Adduction

35 A 42-year-old male is struck in the back, rupturing the internal vertebral venous plexus (of Batson). Radiographic studies reveal a hematoma causing compression of the spinal cord. When aspirating the excess blood, the physician performing the procedure must stop the needle just before puncturing which of the following structures?

- ▢ **A.** Spinal cord
- ▢ **B.** Pia mater
- ▢ **C.** Arachnoid mater
- ▢ **D.** Dura mater
- ▢ **E.** Ligamentum flavum

36 A 35-year-old male pedestrian is crossing a busy intersection and is hit by a truck. He is admitted to the emergency department, and a CT scan reveals a dislocation of the fourth thoracic vertebra. Which of the following costal structures is most likely also involved in the injury?

- ▢ **A.** Head of the fourth rib
- ▢ **B.** Neck of the fourth rib
- ▢ **C.** Head of the third rib
- ▢ **D.** Tubercle of the third rib
- ▢ **E.** Head of the fifth rib

37 A 20-year-old hiker suffers a deep puncture between the trapezius and latissimus dorsi muscles on the right lateral side of his back. Upon admission to the hospital, physical examination reveals weak adduction and medial rotation of his arm. Which of the following muscles is most probably injured?

- ☐ **A.** Teres minor
- ☐ **B.** Triceps brachii
- ☐ **C.** Supraspinatus
- ☐ **D.** Infraspinatus
- ☐ **E.** Teres major

38 A 22-year-old male is thrown through a plate glass wall in a fight. Radiologic examination reveals that the lateral border of his right scapula is shattered. He is admitted to the emergency department, and physical examination reveals difficulty laterally rotating his arm. Which of the following muscles is most probably injured?

- ☐ **A.** Teres major
- ☐ **B.** Infraspinatus
- ☐ **C.** Latissimus dorsi
- ☐ **D.** Trapezius
- ☐ **E.** Supraspinatus

39 A 24-year-old female presents with severe headache, photophobia, and stiffness of her back. Physical examination reveals positive signs for meningitis. The attending physician decides to perform a lumbar puncture to determine if a pathogen is in the CSF. What is the last structure the needle will penetrate before reaching the lumbar cistern?

- ☐ **A.** Arachnoid mater
- ☐ **B.** Dura mater
- ☐ **C.** Pia mater
- ☐ **D.** Ligamentum flavum
- ☐ **E.** Posterior longitudinal ligament

40 A 19-year-old presents at the emergency department with high fever, severe headache, nausea, and stiff neck for 3 days. The attending physician suspects meningitis and obtains a sample of CSF using a lumbar puncture. From which of the following spaces was the CSF collected?

- ☐ **A.** Epidural space
- ☐ **B.** Subdural space
- ☐ **C.** Subarachnoid space
- ☐ **D.** Pretracheal space
- ☐ **E.** Central canal of the spinal cord

41 A 38-year-old male is admitted to the emergency department after a car collision. During physical examination several lacerations in the back are discovered. Pain from lacerations or irritations of the skin of the back is conveyed to the central nervous system by which of the following?

- ☐ **A.** Dorsal primary rami
- ☐ **B.** Communicating rami
- ☐ **C.** Ventral primary rami
- ☐ **D.** Ventral roots
- ☐ **E.** Intercostal nerves

42 A 66-year-old female had been diagnosed with a tumor on her spine. She has started to retain urine and is experiencing decreased anal and rectal tone. Both of these symptoms are signs of conus medullaris syndrome. At which of the following vertebral levels is the tumor probably located?

- ☐ **A.** L3/L4
- ☐ **B.** L3
- ☐ **C.** L4
- ☐ **D.** T12 to L2
- ☐ **E.** T11

43 Examination of a 3-day-old male infant reveals protrusion of his spinal cord and meninges from a defect in the lower back. Which of the following describes this congenital anomaly?

- ☐ **A.** Avulsion of meninges
- ☐ **B.** Meningitis
- ☐ **C.** Spina bifida occulta
- ☐ **D.** Spina bifida with meningomyelocele
- ☐ **E.** Spina bifida with meningocele

44 A 32-year-old mother complains of serious pain in the coccygeal area some days after giving birth. To determine whether the coccyx is involved, a local anesthetic is first injected in the region of the coccyx and then dynamic MRI studies are performed. The MRI reveals coccydynia, which confirms that her coccyx dislocates upon sitting. The local anesthetic is used to interrupt which of the following nerve pathways?

- ☐ **A.** Visceral afferents
- ☐ **B.** Somatic efferent
- ☐ **C.** Somatic afferent
- ☐ **D.** Sympathetic preganglionic
- ☐ **E.** Parasympathetic preganglionic

45 During a routine physical examination a 65-year-old male patient is tested for ease and flexibility of the movements of his lumbar region. Which of the following movements is most characteristic of the intervertebral joints in the lumbar region?

- ▢ **A.** Circumduction
- ▢ **B.** Lateral flexion
- ▢ **C.** Abduction
- ▢ **D.** Adduction
- ▢ **E.** Inversion

46 A 72-year-old man with cancer of the prostate gland presents with loss of consciousness and seizures. A CT scan is performed and a brain tumor is diagnosed. The tumor spread to the brain from the abdomen via the internal vertebral venous plexus (of Batson). What feature of the plexus allows this to happen?

- ▢ **A.** They are the longest veins in the body.
- ▢ **B.** They have valves that ensure one-way movement of blood.
- ▢ **C.** They are located in the subarachnoid space.
- ▢ **D.** They are valveless.
- ▢ **E.** They are located in the subdural space.

47 A 26-year-old man painting his house slipped and fell from the ladder, landing on the pavement below. After initial examination in the emergency department, the patient is sent to the radiology department. Radiographs reveal that the portion of his left scapula that forms the tip, or point, of the shoulder has been fractured. Which part of the bone was fractured?

- ▢ **A.** Coracoid process
- ▢ **B.** Superior angle of the scapula
- ▢ **C.** Glenoid
- ▢ **D.** Spine of the scapula
- ▢ **E.** Acromion

48 A 43-year-old male construction worker survived a fall from a two-story building but lost all sensation from his lower limbs and was admitted to the hospital for examination and treatment. Radiographic studies revealed that he crushed his spinal cord at vertebral level C6. Which of the following muscles will most likely be paralyzed?

- ▢ **A.** Supraspinatus
- ▢ **B.** Trapezius
- ▢ **C.** Rhomboid muscles
- ▢ **D.** Latissimus dorsi
- ▢ **E.** Deltoid

49 A maternal serum sample with high alpha-fetoprotein alerted the obstetrician to a possible neural tube defect. Ultrasound diagnosis revealed a meningocele protruding from the back of the child. Which of the following is the most likely diagnosis of this congenital anomaly?

- ▢ **A.** Cranium bifida
- ▢ **B.** Spina bifida occulta
- ▢ **C.** Spina bifida cystica
- ▢ **D.** Hemothorax
- ▢ **E.** Arnold-Chiari malformation

50 A 7-year-old female who is somewhat obese is brought to the emergency department because of a soft lump above the buttocks. Upon physical examination you note the lump is located just superior to the iliac crest unilaterally on the left side. The protrusion is deep to the skin and pliable to the touch. Which of the following is the most probable diagnosis?

- ▢ **A.** Tumor of the external abdominal oblique muscle
- ▢ **B.** Herniation at the lumbar triangle (of Petit)
- ▢ **C.** Indirect inguinal hernia
- ▢ **D.** Direct inguinal hernia
- ▢ **E.** Femoral hernia

51 A 54-year-old woman is admitted to the emergency department due to increasing back pain over the preceding year. MRI reveals that her intervertebral disks have been compressed. It is common for the disks to shrink in people older than 40, and it can result in spinal stenosis and disk herniation. At which locations are the spinal nerves most likely to be compressed?

- ▢ **A.** Between the denticulate ligaments
- ▢ **B.** As they pass through the vertebral foramen
- ▢ **C.** Between the superior and inferior articular facets
- ▢ **D.** Between inferior and superior vertebral notches
- ▢ **E.** Between the superior and inferior intercostovertebral joints

52 A 37-year-old pregnant woman is administered a caudal epidural block to alleviate pain during delivery. Caudal epidural block involves injection of local anesthetic into the sacral canal. Which of the following landmarks is most commonly used for the caudal epidural block?

- ▢ **A.** Anterior sacral foramina
- ▢ **B.** Posterior sacral foramina
- ▢ **C.** Cornua of the sacral hiatus
- ▢ **D.** Intervertebral foramina
- ▢ **E.** Medial sacral crest

53 A 34-year-old pregnant woman in the maternity ward was experiencing considerable pain during labor. Her obstetrician decided to perform a caudal epidural block within the sacral canal. What are the most important bony landmarks used for the administration of such anesthesia?

- ☐ **A.** Ischial tuberosities
- ☐ **B.** Ischial spines
- ☐ **C.** Posterior superior iliac spines
- ☐ **D.** Sacral cornua
- ☐ **E.** Coccyx

54 A 22-year-old man is brought into the emergency department following a brawl in a tavern. He has severe pain radiating across his back and down his left upper limb. He supports his left upper limb with his right, holding it close to his body. Any attempt to move the left upper limb greatly increases the pain. A radiograph is ordered and reveals an unusual sagittal fracture through the spine of the left scapula. The fracture extends superiorly toward the suprascapular notch. Which nerve is most likely affected?

- ☐ **A.** Suprascapular nerve
- ☐ **B.** Thoracodorsal nerve
- ☐ **C.** Axillary nerve
- ☐ **D.** Subscapular nerve
- ☐ **E.** Suprascapular nerve and thoracodorsal nerve

55 A 5-year-old boy is admitted to the hospital because of pain in the upper back. Radiographic examination reveals abnormal fusion of the C5 and C6 vertebrae and a high-riding scapula. Which of the following conditions is characteristic of his symptoms?

- ☐ **A.** Lordosis
- ☐ **B.** Kyphosis
- ☐ **C.** Scoliosis
- ☐ **D.** Spina bifida
- ☐ **E.** Klippel-Feil syndrome

56 A 53-year-old male is admitted to the emergency department due to severe back pain. MRI examination reveals anterior dislocation of the body of the L5 vertebra upon the sacrum. Which of the following is the most likely diagnosis?

- ☐ **A.** Spondylolysis
- ☐ **B.** Spondylolisthesis
- ☐ **C.** Herniation of intervertebral disk
- ☐ **D.** Lordosis
- ☐ **E.** Scoliosis

57 A male newborn infant is brought to the clinic by his mother and diagnosed with a congenital malformation. MRI studies reveal that the cerebellum and medulla oblongata are protruding inferiorly through the foramen magnum into the vertebral canal. What is this clinical condition called?

- ☐ **A.** Meningocele
- ☐ **B.** Klippel-Feil syndrome
- ☐ **C.** Arnold-Chiari malformation
- ☐ **D.** Hydrocephalus
- ☐ **E.** Tethered cord syndrome

58 A 62-year-old woman is admitted to the hospital because of her severe back pain. Radiographic examination reveals that the L4 vertebral body has slipped anteriorly, with fracture of the zygapophysial joint (Fig. 1-1). What is the proper name of this condition?

- ☐ **A.** Spondylolysis and spondylolisthesis
- ☐ **B.** Spondylolisthesis
- ☐ **C.** Crush vertebral fracture
- ☐ **D.** Intervertebral disk herniation
- ☐ **E.** Klippel-Feil syndrome

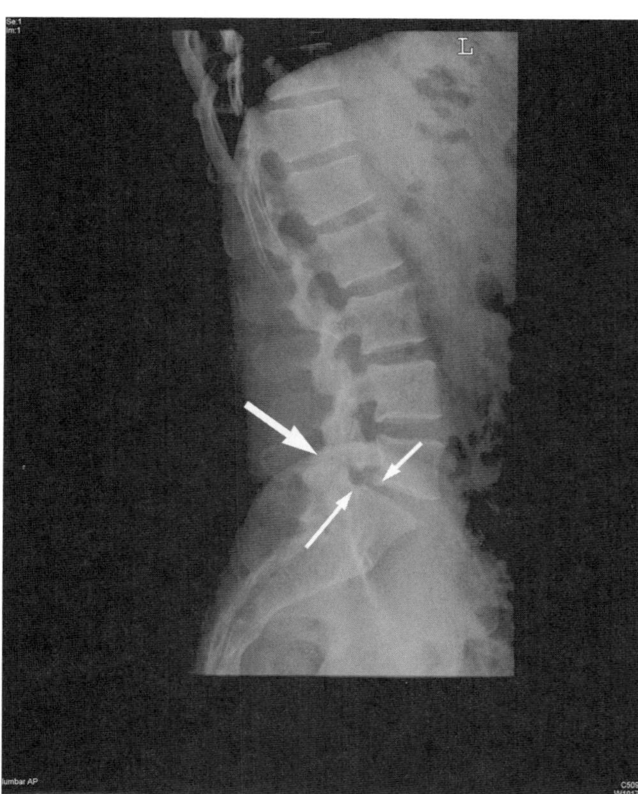

Fig. 1-1

59 A 40-year-old woman survived a car crash in which her neck was hyperextended when her vehicle was struck from behind. At the emergency department a plain radiograph of her cervical spine revealed a fracture of the odontoid process (dens). Which of the following was most likely injured?

- ▢ **A.** Anterior arch of the atlas
- ▢ **B.** Posterior tubercle of the atlas
- ▢ **C.** Atlanto-occipital joint
- ▢ **D.** Inferior articular process of the axis
- ▢ **E.** Anterior tubercle of the atlas

60 A 34-year-old woman is admitted to the emergency department after a car crash. Radiographic examination reveals a whiplash injury in addition to hyperextension of her cervical spine. Which of the following ligaments will most likely be injured?

- ▢ **A.** Ligamentum flavum
- ▢ **B.** Anterior longitudinal ligament
- ▢ **C.** Posterior longitudinal ligament
- ▢ **D.** Anulus fibrosus
- ▢ **E.** Interspinous ligament

61 A 23-year-old college student is admitted to the emergency department after jumping from a 50-foot waterfall. The MRI of his back reveals a lateral shift of the spinal cord to the left. Which of the following structures has most likely been torn to cause the deviation?

- ▢ **A.** Posterior longitudinal ligament
- ▢ **B.** Tentorium cerebelli
- ▢ **C.** Denticulate ligaments
- ▢ **D.** Ligamentum flavum
- ▢ **E.** Nuchal ligament

62 A 6-year-old boy is admitted to the hospital with coughing and dyspnea. During taking of the history he complains that it feels like there is glass in his lungs. Auscultation reveals abnormal lung sounds. The abnormal lung sounds are heard most clearly during inhalation with the scapulae abducted. Which of the following form the borders of a triangular space where one should place the stethoscope in order to best hear the lung sounds?

- ▢ **A.** Latissimus dorsi, trapezius, medial border of scapula
- ▢ **B.** Deltoid, levator scapulae, trapezius
- ▢ **C.** Latissimus dorsi, external abdominal oblique, iliac crest
- ▢ **D.** Quadratus lumborum, internal abdominal oblique, inferior border of the twelfth
- ▢ **E.** Rectus abdominis, inguinal ligament, inferior epigastric vessels

63 A 45-year-old woman is admitted to the outpatient clinic for shoulder pain. During physical examination she presents with weakened shoulder movements. Radiographic examination reveals quadrangular space syndrome, causing weakened shoulder movements. Which of the following nerves is most likely affected?

- ▢ **A.** Suprascapular
- ▢ **B.** Subscapular
- ▢ **C.** Axillary
- ▢ **D.** Radial
- ▢ **E.** Ulnar

64 A 29-year-old female elite athlete was lifting heavy weights during an intense training session. The athlete felt severe pain radiate suddenly to the posterior aspect of her right thigh and leg. The patient was taken to the hospital where an MRI was performed (Fig. 1-2). Which nerve was most probably affected?

- ▢ **A.** L3
- ▢ **B.** L4
- ▢ **C.** L2
- ▢ **D.** L5
- ▢ **E.** S1

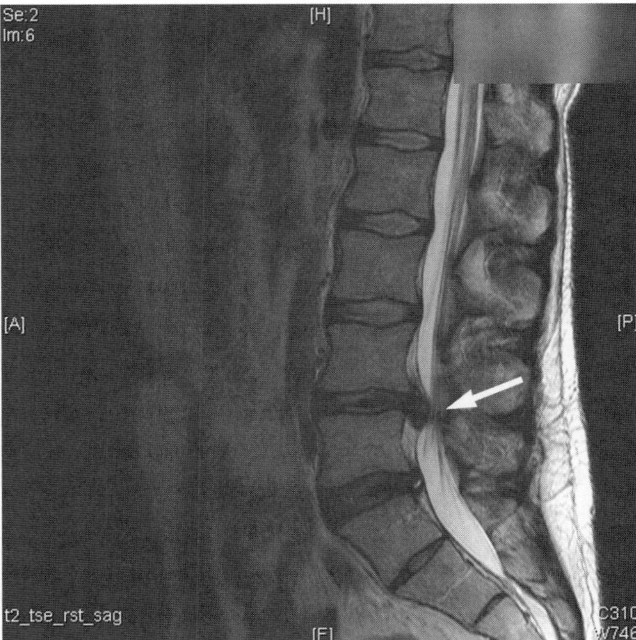

Fig. 1-2

65 A 58-year-old male in the intensive care ward exhibited little voluntary control of urinary or fecal activity following a transplant procedure of his left kidney. In addition, physical examination revealed widespread paralysis of his lower limbs. These functions were essentially normal prior to admission to the hospital. The most likely cause of this patient's problems is which of the following?

- ▢ **A.** Injury to the left vertebral artery
- ▢ **B.** Injury of the great radicular artery (of Adamkiewicz)
- ▢ **C.** Ligation of the posterior spinal artery
- ▢ **D.** Transection of the conal segment of the spinal cord
- ▢ **E.** Division of the thoracic sympathetic chain

66 A 23-year-old woman is admitted to the hospital due to back pain. Radiographic examination reveals that she suffers from a clinical condition affecting her vertebral column. Physical examination and history taking reveals that she suffered from polio and a muscular dystrophy. Which of the following conditions of the vertebral column will most likely be present in this patient?

- ▢ **A.** Lordosis
- ▢ **B.** Kyphosis
- ▢ **C.** Scoliosis
- ▢ **D.** Spina bifida
- ▢ **E.** Osteoarthritis

67 A 65-year-old patient complains of severe, chronic pain from the region of her right hip. The patient is admitted to the hospital and a decision is made to perform surgery to avoid prescribing excessive pain medication. In such a case, which would the surgeon most likely choose to perform?

- ▢ **A.** Division of the ventral primary rami of nerves supplying the affected region
- ▢ **B.** Transection of all dorsal primary rami of nerves from the hip area
- ▢ **C.** Removal of abdominal sympathetic chain ganglia on the right side
- ▢ **D.** Transection of the dorsal rootlets of spinal nerves supplying the right hip
- ▢ **E.** Division of lower lumbar and sacral ventral rootlets

ANSWERS

1 B. Kyphosis is characterized by a "hunchback" due to an abnormal increase in curvature of the thoracic region of the vertebral column. Lordosis, or "swayback," is an increase in lumbar curvature of the spine. Lordosis can be physiologic, such as seen in a pregnant woman. Scoliosis is a lateral curvature of the spine with rotation of the vertebrae. Spina bifida is a neural tube defect characterized by failure of closure of the vertebral arch. Osteoarthritis is a degenerative disorder that affects the articular cartilage of joints and is not specifically related to the thoracic region of the spine.
GAS 77; GA 2, 26

2 B. A crush fracture is characterized by compression of the entire vertebral body. The wedge fracture is similar in that it affects the vertebral bodies, but it involves small fractures around the perimeter of the vertebral body. Both of these fractures cause reductions in overall height. Fracture of the spinal, transverse, or superior articular processes can be due to an oblique, transverse, or comminuted fracture. Intervertebral disks are associated with disk herniation, not compression fractures.
GAS 84; GA 21-30

3 C. The ligamentum flavum connects the lamina of two adjacent vertebrae and forms the posterior wall of the vertebral canal. It is the only answer choice that is in direct contact with the vertebral foramen. Therefore, hypertrophy of only the ligamentum flavum would present as spinal stenosis. The supraspinous and interspinous ligaments connect spinous processes. The anterior longitudinal ligament connects the anterior portion of the vertebral bodies and intervertebral disks. Finally, the nuchal ligament is a thickened extension of the supraspinous ligament above the level of C7.
GAS 84; GA35

4 C. The dorsal scapular nerve (from the ventral ramus of C5) is responsible for innervating rhomboids major and minor. The rhomboids are responsible for medial retraction (adduction) of the scapula. Therefore, if this nerve is damaged, individuals present with a laterally displaced (abducted) scapula. In this case the levator scapular remains functional due to additional innervation provided by C3-4 spinal nerves. The axillary nerve innervates the deltoid and teres minor muscles. The deltoid muscle abducts the humerus, and the teres minor laterally rotates the humerus. The long thoracic nerve innervates the serratus anterior, which functions to abduct and upwardly rotate the scapula. The greater occipital nerve is mainly sensory and is also contributing to the innervation of the semispinalis capitis. In addition, greater occipital nerve is implicated in occipital neuralgias. The suprascapular nerve innervates the supraspinatus and infraspinatus muscles. The

supraspinatus abducts the humerus, and the infraspinatus muscles laterally rotate the humerus. Injury to any of these other nerves would not present with a laterally retracted scapula.
GAS 89, 110-111; GA 37, GA 369-371

5 B. Herpes zoster is a viral disease that remains latent in the dorsal root ganglia of sensory nerves and presents as a painful skin lesion. It is associated only with sensory nerve fibers and has no motor involvement. The only answer choice that is solely responsible for sensory innervation is the dorsal root ganglion.
GAS 110; GA 45-49

6 E. Disk herniation in the lumbar region between L4 and L5 affects the L5 spinal nerve roots. Even though the L4 spinal nerve root lies directly between the L4 and L5 vertebrae, it exits from the spinal canal superior to the intervertebral disk, whereas the L5 spinal nerve root lies directly posterior to the disk.
GAS 81; GA 32-34

7 D. A lumbar puncture is performed by taking a sample of CSF from the lumbar cistern (the subarachnoid space below the spinal cord) between vertebrae L4 and L5 or sometimes between L3 and L4. It is done in this region because the spinal cord ends at the level of L1 to L2 and the dural sac ends at the level of S2. Therefore it is the safest place to do the procedure because it lies between these areas and the risk of injuring the spinal cord is avoided.
GAS 108; GA 34, 44-49

8 B. The iliac crests are used as a landmark for locating the position of L4 to L5 for a lumbar puncture; they are identified and traced medially toward the vertebral column. The inferior angles of the scapulae lie at vertebral level T7; the lowest ribs lead one to T12; a line between the posterior superior iliac spines crosses vertebral level S2; the posterior inferior iliac spines lie below S2.
GAS 101, 106-109; GA 34, 44-49

9 A. The anterior longitudinal ligament lies anterior to the vertebral bodies along the vertebral column. The ligamentum flavum connects the lamina of two adjacent vertebrae. The nuchal ligament is a continuation of the supraspinous ligament above C7, which connects spinous processes. The posterior longitudinal ligament lies on the posterior edge of the vertebral bodies. The transverse cervical (cardinal) ligament is associated with the pelvic region of the body and not the spinal column.
GAS 82-84; GA 35

10 B. Compression of nerves at the intervertebral foramen indicates a disk herniation. A disk herniation is characterized by protrusion of the nucleus pulposus from the anulus fibrosus posterolaterally into the spinal canal or intervertebral foramen. The ligaments may be affected by the herniation but are not responsible for the compression of the spinal nerve roots.
GAS 79-81; GA 32-35

11 A. The thoracodorsal nerve innervates the latissimus dorsi, one of three major muscles that adduct and medially rotate the humerus. The axillary nerve supplies the deltoid muscle, the dorsal scapular supplies the rhomboids and levator scapulae, whereas the spinal accessory innervates the trapezius. None of these nerves medially rotates or adducts the humerus. The radial nerve is responsible for the innervation on the posterior aspect of the arm. The medial and lateral pectoral nerves and the lower subscapular nerve supply the other two medial rotators of the humerus.
GAS 89-90; GA 371

12 C. The long thoracic nerve innervates the serratus anterior, which is responsible for elevation and abduction of the scapula beyond the horizontal level while maintaining its position against the thoracic wall. Along with the thoracodorsal nerve, the long thoracic nerve runs superficially along the thoracic wall and is commonly subject to injury during mastectomy procedures. The axillary nerve, the spinal accessory nerve, and the thoracodorsal nerve supply the deltoid muscle, trapezius muscle, and latissimus dorsi muscles, respectively. The dorsal scapular nerve is responsible for innervation of the rhomboids and levator scapulae. Aside from the long thoracic and thoracodorsal nerves, the remaining nerves do not course along the lateral thoracic wall.
GAS 89-90, 139, 688-690; GA 371

13 D. The rotator cuff muscles are common sites of damage during shoulder injuries. These muscles include the supraspinatus, infraspinatus, teres minor, and subscapularis (SITS). Initiation of abduction of the humerus (the first 15°) is performed by the supraspinatus, followed by the deltoid from 15° to 90°. Above the horizontal, the humerus is abducted by the trapezius and serratus anterior. The teres major and the pectoralis major are responsible for medial rotation and adduction of the humerus. These muscles are therefore not involved in abduction at the glenohumeral joint.
GAS 674-678; GA 356-358, 362-366

14 **C.** Spina bifida is a developmental condition resulting from incomplete fusion of the vertebral arches within the lumbar region. Spina bifida occulta commonly presents asymptomatically with a tuft of hair and a small dimple in the overlying skin. More severe forms (spina bifida cystica) are categorized into three types: Spina bifida cystica with meningocele presents with protrusion of the meninges through the unfused vertebral arches. Spina bifida with meningomyelocele is characterized by protrusion both of the meninges and CNS tissues and is often associated with neurologic deficits. Rachischisis, also known as spina bifida cystica with myeloschisis, results from a failure of neural folds to fuse and is characterized by protrusion of the spinal cord or spinal nerves and meninges.
GAS 76; GA 21-35

15 **A.** Somatic afferents are responsible for conveying pain, pressure, touch, temperature, and proprioception to the CNS. Afferent fibers carry only sensory stimuli, whereas efferent fibers convey motor information. Visceral innervation is associated with the autonomic nervous system. Visceral afferents generally carry information regarding the physiologic changes of the internal viscera whereas visceral efferents deliver autonomic motor function to three types of tissue: smooth muscle, cardiac muscle, and glandular epithelium.
GAS 35-42, 40-41; GA 44-45

16 **E.** Cerebrospinal fluid is found within the subarachnoid space and is continuous with the ventricles of the brain (CSF flows from the ventricles to the subarachnoid space). The epidural space, positioned between the dura mater and periosteum, is characterized by fat deposits and contains the internal vertebral venous plexus (of Batson). The subdural space, between the arachnoid mater and dura mater, exists only as a potential space and does not contain cerebrospinal fluid. The anterior and posterior longitudinal ligaments traverse the length of the vertebral body.
GAS 106-108; GA 47-51

17 **B.** The posterior longitudinal ligament is the only ligament spanning the posterior aspect of the vertebral bodies and intervertebral disks. With intervertebral disk herniation, the nucleus pulposus of the intervertebral disk protrudes posterolaterally. The anterior longitudinal ligament traverses the anterior side of the vertebral bodies and thus would not protect the spinal cord from direct compression. The supraspinous and ligamentum flavum ligaments connect the spinous processes and the laminae of adjacent vertebrae, respectively. The nuchal ligament is a continuation of the supraspinous ligaments near the C7 vertebrae and runs to the occipital protuberance.
GAS 82-84; GA 35

18 **C.** L1 and L2. This is the location of the conus medullaris, a tapered conical projection of the spinal cord at its inferior termination. Although the conus medullaris rests at the level of L1 and L2 in adults, it is often situated at L3 in newborns. The cauda equina and filium terminale extend beyond the conus medullaris.
GAS 101-102; GA 44-51

19 **A.** Lower cervical and upper thoracic sympathetic fibers. The sympathetic division of the autonomic nervous system is primarily responsible for vasoconstriction. Separation of ventral or dorsal roots would lead to undesired consequences, such as a loss of motor or sensory activity. Similarly, surgical division of spinal nerves would also have unwanted consequences, but such are not related to the increased arterial constriction and the painful ischemia in the digits. Division of selected sympathetic chain ganglia, however, would decrease the sympathetic outflow to the upper limbs.
GAS 41-42; GA 44-45

20 **D.** The diaphragm is innervated by the phrenic nerve, which arises from C3 to C5. The rhomboid, serratus anterior, supraspinatus, and latissimus dorsi are innervated by the ventral rami of the brachial plexus (C5 to T1).
GAS 157-158; GA 110

21 **C.** The anterior longitudinal ligament runs along the anterior-most aspect of the vertebral column from C1 to the sacrum and would therefore be unaffected by laminectomy. Denticulate ligaments extend laterally from the pia mater to the arachnoid mater along the length of the spinal cord. The ligamentum flavum is one of the two ligaments found in the vertebral canal and is adherent to the anterior aspect of the vertebral arches. It is thus simultaneously removed upon excision of the lamina. The nuchal ligament is a thick longitudinal extension continuing from the supraspinous ligament at the level of C6 to the external occipital protuberance. The cruciate ligament is an incorrect answer because it is located anterior to the spinal cord, and thus would not be involved in laminectomy.
GAS 82-84; GA 21-27

22 **C.** The vertebral canal is the longitudinal canal that extends through the vertebrae, containing the meninges, spinal cord, and associated ligaments. The

vertebral venous plexus is the valveless network of veins extending longitudinally along the vertebral canal. Neither of these answer choices describes a specific space. The epidural space is found superficially to the dura mater. It is a fat-filled space extending from C1 to the coccyx. The subarachnoid space is a true space containing CSF. It is found within the CNS and extends to the level of S2. The subdural space is a potential space between the dura and the arachnoid mater. Normally these two layers are fused due to the pressure of CSF in the subarachnoid space.
GAS 106-109; GA 44-49

23 **D.** Lumbar puncture is generally performed at the level of L4, L5. The supraspinous ligament extends between spinous processes on the dorsal aspect of the vertebrae. The needle would bypass this structure. The denticulate ligaments are not correct because they terminate with the conus medullaris at the level of L2 and are located laterally. The anterior longitudinal ligament extends along the most anterior aspect of the vertebral bodies and can be reached only ventrally. The posterior longitudinal ligament is present at the correct vertebral level but will be punctured only if the procedure is performed incorrectly as in this case, where hematopoetic cells were aspirated from the vertebral body anterior to the ligament. The nuchal ligament extends cranially from the supraspinous ligament in the lower cervical region to the skull.
GAS 106-109; GA 44-51

24 **B.** The anterior spinal artery is located anteriorly along the spinal cord and is not directly associated with the vertebrae. The vertebral arteries run through the transverse foramina of cervical vertebrae C6 through C1 and are therefore most closely associated with injury to the transverse processes. The ascending cervical artery is a very small branch from the thyrocervical trunk of the subclavian artery, running on the anterior aspect of the vertebrae. The deep cervical artery arises from the costocervical trunk is also a very small artery and courses along the posterior aspect of the cervical vertebrae. The posterior spinal arteries are adherent to the posterior aspect of the spinal cord.
GAS 102-103; GA 41

25 **B.** Scoliosis is defined as a lateral deviation of the spinal column to either side. Kyphosis is an increased primary curvature of the spinal column. This curvature is associated with thoracic and sacral regions and is most likely this patient's clinical condition. Spinal stenosis is a narrowing of the vertebral canal and is not directly associated with a displacement of the spinal column. Lordosis is the increased secondary curvature affecting the cervical and lumbar regions. A herniated disk is a rupture of the anulus fibrosus of the intervertebral disk, commonly causing a posterolateral displacement of the nucleus pulposus into the vertebral canal.
GAS 77; GA 21

26 **B.** The thoracodorsal nerve innervates the latissimus dorsi, which has no action on the shoulder girdle. The spinal accessory nerve is the eleventh cranial nerve (CN XI) and innervates both the trapezius and sternocleidomastoid muscles. The loss of CN XI results in drooping of the shoulder due to paralysis of the trapezius. In addition to the clinical findings of the MRI, one can test the innervation of this nerve by asking the patient to shrug his or her shoulders against resistance (testing the trapezius), as well as turning his or her head against resistance (testing the sternocleidomastoid). The dorsal scapular nerve innervates the levator scapulae muscle, as well as the rhomboids. The greater occipital nerve is a sensory nerve innervating the posterolateral aspect of the scalp. The axillary nerve is a branch of the brachial plexus and innervates the deltoid and teres minor. It is not involved in shoulder elevation.
GAS 89-90; GA 371

27 **B.** The anterior longitudinal ligament runs on the anterior aspect of the vertebrae and is not affected. The transverse ligament of the atlas anchors the dens laterally to prevent posterior displacement of the dens. This ligament has been torn in this injury. The ligamentum flavum is found on the posterior aspect of the vertebral canal and does not contact the anteriorly placed dens. The supraspinous ligament is located along the spinous processes of the vertebrae. The nuchal ligament is a longitudinal extension of the supraspinous ligament above the level of C7.
GAS 82-84; GA 35

28 **B.** The iliocostalis thoracis muscle is found in the deep back and functions to maintain posture. It is not associated with neck flexion. The sternocleidomastoid muscle is innervated by CN XI and functions in contralateral rotation and bilateral flexion of the neck. Rhomboid major and minor are both innervated by the dorsal scapular nerve and serve to adduct the scapulae. Teres major is innervated by the lower subscapular nerve and serves to medially rotate and adduct the humerus.
GAS 95-97; GA 40-41

29 C. The pedicles are bony structures connecting the vertebral arches to the vertebral body. The ligamentum flavum runs on the posterior aspect of the vertebral canal and is more closely associated with the lamina than to the pedicles of the vertebrae. The nuchal ligament is a longitudinal extension of the supraspinous ligament from C7 to the occiput, both running on the most posterior aspect of the vertebrae along the spinous processes. The cruciform (also called cruciate) ligament is a stabilizing ligament found in C1/C2. It attaches to the pedicles and helps anchor the dens in situ, but it has been broken in this case. The posterior longitudinal ligament extends the length of the anterior aspect of the vertebral canal and is anterior to the pedicles.
GAS 72-73; GA 35

30 A. Spondylolysis, also known as "facet jumping," is the anterior displacement of one or more vertebrae. This is most commonly seen with the cervical vertebrae because of their small size and structure and the oblique angle of the articular facets. Lumbar vertebrae are somewhat susceptible to this problem because of the pressures at lower levels of the spine and the sagittal angles of the articular facets. It is much less common in the thoracic vertebrae due to the stabilizing factor of the ribs. It is never seen in the sacral vertebrae because they are fused together.
GAS 85-86; GA 21-29

31 D. The internal vertebral plexus (of Batson) surrounds the dura mater in the epidural space; hence, the bleeding would cause the hematoma in that space. The subarachnoid space, containing the CSF, is located between pia and arachnoid mater. A subarachnoid bleed would most likely result from a ruptured intercerebral aneurysm. A subdural hematoma would result most likely from a venous bleed from a torn cerebral vein as it enters the superior sagittal venous sinus within the skull. The central canal is located within the gray matter of the spinal cord. The lumbar cistern is an enlargement of the subarachnoid space between the conus medullaris of the spinal cord and the inferior end of the subarachnoid space.
GAS 106-108; GA 47

32 D. In the lumbar region spinal nerves exit the vertebral column below their named vertebrae. In an L4, L5 intervertebral disk herniation, the L5 spinal nerve would be affected as it descends between L4, L5 vertebrae to exit below the L5 level. L2, L3, and L4 spinal nerves have already exited above the level of herniation; therefore, they would not be affected by this herniation. An "L6" spinal nerve normally does not exist. (The NBME does not allow "made up" structures, but in cases of lumbarization of S1, some people recognize an L6 nerve.)
GAS 107-109; GA 44-45

33 E. Posterior intercostal arteries supply the deep back muscles that are responsible for extending and laterally bending the trunk. The subscapular supplies subscapularis muscle, the thoracodorsal supplies latissimus dorsi, the anterior intercostal supplies the upper nine intercostal spaces, and the suprascapular supplies supraspinatus and infraspinatus muscles. These muscles are not responsible for extension and lateral flexion of the trunk.
GAS 102-103; GA 46, 68

34 A. The atlantoaxial joint is a synovial joint responsible for rotation of the head, not flexion, abduction, extension, or adduction. The atlanto-occipital joint is primarily involved in flexion and extension of the head on the neck.
GAS 102-103; GA 46, 68

35 D. The internal vertebral plexus (of Batson) lies external to the dura mater in the epidural space. To aspirate excess blood, the physician must pass the needle through the ligamentum flavum to reach the epidural space wherein the blood would accumulate. The spinal cord, pia mater, and arachnoid mater are located deep to the epidural space.
GAS 103-108; GA 47

36 E. The T4 thoracic vertebra articulates with the head of the fifth rib. The head of the rib has two facets. The rib articulates with the superior facet on the body of its own vertebra (fourth rib articulates with the superior facet T4 vertebra) and with the inferior facet on the body of the vertebra above (fourth rib articulates with the inferior facet of T3 vertebra). Taking the T4 vertebra into consideration, the superior facet of this vertebra articulates with the head of the fourth rib and the inferior facet articulates with the head of the fifth rib. The head of the fourth rib has two points of articulation (a joint with the vertebral body and costotransverse joint) on T4, so when it is injured it moves as a unit, whereas the fifth rib has only one articulation with T4.
GAS 125-126; GA 57-61

37 E. Teres major is responsible for adduction and medial rotation of the humerus. Teres minor is responsible for lateral rotation of the humerus. Triceps brachii is responsible for extension of the forearm. Supraspinatus is responsible for the 0° to 15° of

abduction, and infraspinatus is a lateral rotator.
GAS 89-91; GA 364-365

38 **B.** Infraspinatus is responsible for lateral rotation (along with the teres minor, not a choice here). Teres major is responsible for adduction and medial rotation of the humerus. Latissimus dorsi is responsible for adduction, extension, and medial rotation of the humerus. Trapezius is an elevator of the scapula and rotates the scapula during abduction of the humerus above the horizontal plane. Supraspinatus is responsible for the 0° to 15° of abduction.
GAS 89-91; GA 364-365

39 **A.** When a lumbar puncture is performed, the needle must penetrate the ligamentum flavum, the dura mater, and finally the arachnoid mater to reach the subarachnoid space where the CSF is located. The lumbar cistern is a continuation of the subarachnoid space below the conus medullaris. The pia mater is adherent to the spinal cord, and the posterior longitudinal ligament is attached to the posterior aspect of the vertebral bodies.
GAS 106-108; GA 44-49

40 **C.** The subarachnoid space, containing the CSF, is located between the pia and the arachnoid mater. Neither the epidural space, the subdural space, nor the pretracheal space contains CSF. Although the central canal, contained within the substance of the spinal cord, does contain CSF, extraction of CSF from this region would result in spinal cord injury. CSF circulates in the area of the subarachnoid space and can be aspirated only from that location. The subdural space is only a potential space between the dura and arachnoid mater. The epidural space contains the epidural fat and Batson's venous plexus and is the preferred site for aspirating CSF for diagnostic purposes (and epidural anesthesia). CSF is not located in the pretracheal space.
GAS 103-108; GA 44-49

41 **A.** General somatic afferent fibers are conveyed from the skin of the back via the dorsal primary rami. Communicating rami contain general visceral efferent (sympathetic) fibers and general visceral afferent fibers of the autonomic nervous system. Ventral primary rami convey mixed spinal nerves to/from all other parts of the body excluding the back, and parts of the head innervated by cranial nerves. The ventral roots contain only efferent (motor) fibers. Intercostal nerves are the ventral rami of T1 to T11. The ventral ramus of T12 is the subcostal nerve.
GAS 39-49; GA 14-15

42 **D.** The conus medullaris is located at the L1-2 vertebral level; therefore, any choice that contains that region is the correct answer. L3-4 is a common location to perform lumbar puncture, but it is caudal to the apex of the conus medullaris. L3 and L4 are caudal to the conus medullaris. T11 is superior to the conus medullaris.
GAS 101-108; GA 44-49

43 **D.** Because the meninges and spinal cord are included in the protrusion, the patient's condition is a classic presentation of spina bifida with meningomyelocele. If the protrusion contains only meninges but no CNS tissue, it is known as spina bifida with meningocele. Meningitis is an inflammation of the meninges caused by bacteria, viral, or numerous other irritants. It does not cause deformation of vertebrae or result in protrusion of spinal cord contents. Spina bifida occulta is a normally asymptomatic condition in which the vertebral lamina fail to fuse completely during embryologic development. A tuft of hair is commonly seen growing over the affected region (usually lumbar in position).
GAS 76; GA 44-49

44 **C.** Somatic afferent fibers convey localized pain, typically from the body wall and limbs. Visceral afferents convey autonomic nervous system sensory information. Pain from these fibers will present as dull and diffuse. Somatic efferent fibers convey motor information to skeletal muscle. Sympathetic preganglionic fibers are visceral efferent fibers and do not contain sensory information. Parasympathetic preganglionic fibers are also visceral efferents and do not contain sensory information.
GAS 39-49; GA 14-19

45 **B.** Lateral flexion is the best answer because other movements of the lumbar portion of the vertebral column are very limited due to the orientation of the articular facets.
GAS 67-75, 41; GA 21-24, 35

46 **D.** Batson's venous plexus is a valveless network of veins located in the epidural space of the vertebral canal. The lack of valves can provide a route for the metastasis of cancer (i.e., from prostate or breast to brain) because the flow of blood is not unidirectional. The length of Batson's plexus is irrelevant to the question. B is incorrect because Batson's plexus does not have valves or one-way movement of blood. Batson's plexus is located within the epidural space, not the subarachnoid or subdural spaces.
GAS 102-106; GA 47

47 E. The acromion (the highest point of the shoulder) is the part of the scapula that forms the "point" of the shoulder. The coracoid process is located more medially. The superior angle of the scapula is located near the midline of the back. The glenoid of the scapula articulates with the head of the humerus to form the glenohumeral joint. The spine of the scapula is located posteriorly and separates supraspinous and infraspinous fossae.
GAS 665-673; GA 354-358

48 D. All of the spinal nerves below the C7 vertebral level will be affected. This includes the C7 spinal nerve because it exits the vertebral column above the C7 vertebra. The trapezius would be intact because it is innervated by the spinal accessory nerve. The deltoid muscles and supraspinatus muscles will be unaffected because they receive motor supply from C5 and C6. The rhomboid muscles should function normally because they are innervated by the dorsal scapular nerve (C5). The latissimus dorsi muscles would not function normally because they are innervated by the thoracodorsal nerves, which receive contributions especially from the C7 spinal nerves.
GAS 89-92; GA 34

49 C. Spina bifida cystica refers to spina bifida with meningocele and is the correct answer. Cranium bifida could present with meningocele in the skull, but it would not be located in the lower back. Spina bifida occulta is a defect in the formation of the vertebral arches and does not present with meningocele. Hemothorax refers to blood accumulation in the pleural space surrounding the lungs. Arnold-Chiari malformation is a herniation of the medulla oblongata and cerebellum through the foramen magnum and would not present with pathologies in the lower back.
GAS 76; GA 21-27

50 B. The lumbar triangle (of Petit) is bordered medially by the latissimus dorsi, laterally by the external abdominal oblique, and inferiorly by the iliac crest. The floor of Petit's triangle is formed by the internal abdominal oblique, and this is a possible site of herniation. An indirect inguinal hernia is located in the inguinal canal of the anterior abdominal wall. A direct inguinal hernia is located in the Hesselbach triangle of the anterior abdominal wall. A femoral hernia occurs below the inguinal ligament. Answer A is not the best answer because this lump is described as soft and pliable, which would not likely indicate a tumor, as tumors tend to be hard masses.
GAS 91-94; GA 37

51 D. This question tests anatomic knowledge relating to typical vertebrae and the spinal cord. Intervertebral disk herniations occur when the nucleus pulposus of the intervertebral disk protrudes through the anulus fibrosus into the intervertebral foramen or vertebral canal. The most common protrusion is posterolaterally, where the anulus fibrosus is not reinforced by the posterior longitudinal ligament. The inferior and superior vertebral notches frame the intervertebral foramen, so this is the most likely location of compression. The denticulate ligaments are lateral extensions of pia mater that anchor to the dura mater, and they hold the spinal cord in position within the subarachnoid space. The vertebral foramen is the canal through which the spinal cord passes; while this may also be a place of compression, it is not the most likely site of herniation. Articular facets are the locations where vertebral bodies articulate with each other. Intercostovertebral joints are locations where vertebral bodies articulate with ribs.
GAS 80-86; GA 32-35

52 C. Caudal anesthesia is used to block the spinal nerves that carry sensation from the perineum. This procedure is commonly used by obstetricians to relieve pain during labor and childbirth. Administration of local anesthetic to the epidural space is via the sacral hiatus, which opens between the sacral cornua. The anterior sacral foramina are located on the pelvic surface of the sacrum and are not palpable from a dorsal approach. The posterior sacral foramina and intervertebral foramina are the openings through which sacral nerves exit and are not palpable landmarks. The medial sacral crest is cranial to the injection site.
GAS 106-110; GA 44-48

53 D. The sacral cornua lie on either side of the sacral hiatus, from which one can gain access to the sacral canal. This is the best landmark for administration of anesthesia. The ischial tuberosities are more commonly used as landmarks for a pudendal nerve block. The ischial spines cannot be palpated. The posterior superior iliac spines, though palpable, are not proximal enough for an epidural block within the sacral canal. The coccyx is not part of the sacral canal.
GAS 106-110; GA 44-48

54 A. The suprascapular nerve passes through the suprascapular notch, deep to the superior transverse scapular ligament. This nerve is most likely affected in a fracture of the scapula as described in the question. The thoracodorsal nerve runs behind the axillary artery

and lies superficial to the subscapularis muscle and would therefore be protected. The axillary nerve passes posteriorly through the quadrangular space, which is distal to the suprascapular notch. The subscapular nerve originates from the posterior cord of the brachial plexus, which is distal to the site of fracture.
GAS 680-683; GA 366, 370

55 **E.** Klippel-Feil syndrome is a congenital defect in which there is a reduction, or extensive fusion, in the number of cervical vertebrae. It often manifests as a short, stiff neck with limited motion. Lordosis is an abnormal increase in lumbar curvature. Kyphosis ("hunchback") is an abnormal increase in thoracic curvature. Scoliosis is a lateral curvature. Spina bifida often presents with deformities in the lumbar region.
GAS 76-79; GA 21-33

56 **B.** Spondylolisthesis is an anterior vertebral displacement created by an irregularity in the anterior margin of the vertebral column such that L5 and the overlying L4 (and sometimes L3) protrude forward rather than being restrained by S1. Spondylolysis is a condition in which the region between the superior and inferior articular facets (on the posterior arch of the L5 vertebra) is damaged or missing, which is not the case in this example. Herniation is a protrusion of the nucleus pulposus through the anulus fibrosus, and this is not associated with vertebral dislocation. Lordosis and scoliosis are excessive curvatures that do not involve dislocations.
GAS 85-86; GA 21-33

57 **C.** Arnold-Chiari malformation results from herniation of the medulla and cerebellum into the foramen magnum. Meningocele is a small defect in the cranium in which only the meninges herniate. Klippel-Feil syndrome results from an abnormal number of cervical vertebral bodies. Hydrocephalus results from an overproduction of cerebrospinal fluid, obstruction of its flow, or interference with CSF absorption. Tethered cord syndrome is a congenital anomaly caused by a defective closure of the neural tube. This syndrome is characterized by a low conus medullaris and a thick filum terminale.
GAS 76, 294, 834; GA 21-33

58 **A.** Spondylolisthesis is an anterior displacement created by an irregularity in the anterior margin of the vertebral column such that L5 and the overlying L4 (and sometimes L3) protrude forward. Spondylolysis is a condition in which the region between the superior and inferior articular facets (on the posterior arch of the L5 vertebra) is damaged. Crush vertebral fracture is a collapse of vertebral bodies as a result of trauma. Intervertebral disk herniations occur when the nucleus pulposus protrudes through the anulus fibrosus into the intervertebral foramen or vertebral canal. The most common protrusion is posterolaterally, where the anulus fibrosus is not reinforced by the posterior longitudinal ligament. Klippel-Feil syndrome results from an abnormal number of cervical vertebral bodies.
GAS 85-86; GA 21-33

59 **A.** The odontoid process, or the dens, projects superiorly from the body of the axis and articulates with the anterior arch of the atlas. The posterior and anterior tubercles of the atlas are bony eminences on the outer surface. The inferior articular facet is where the axis joins to the C3 vertebra.
GAS 67-74; GA 21-33

60 **B.** The anterior longitudinal ligament is a strong fibrous band that covers and connects the anterolateral aspect of the vertebrae and intervertebral disks; it maintains stability and prevents hyperextension. It can be torn by cervical hyperextension. The ligamentum flavum helps maintain upright posture by connecting the laminae of two adjacent vertebrae. The posterior longitudinal ligament runs within the vertebral canal supporting the posterior aspect of the vertebrae and prevents hyperflexion. The anulus fibrosus is the outer fibrous part of an intervertebral disk. The interspinous ligament connects adjacent spinous processes.
GAS 82-86; GA 35

61 **C.** The denticulate ligaments are lateral extensions of pia mater between the dorsal and ventral roots of the spinal nerves that attach to the dura mater. These ligaments function to keep the spinal cord in the midline position. The posterior longitudinal ligament supports the posterior aspect of the vertebrae within the vertebral canal. The tentorium cerebelli is a layer of dura mater that supports the occipital lobes of the cerebral hemispheres and covers the cerebellum. The ligamentum flavum helps maintain upright posture by connecting the laminae of two adjacent vertebrae. The nuchal ligament is a thickening of the supraspinous ligaments extending from the C7 vertebra to the external occipital protuberance.
GAS 101-110; GA 48-49

62 **A.** The region bounded by the upper border of the latissimus dorsi, the lateral border of the trapezius, and the medial border of the scapula is known as the triangle of auscultation. Lung sounds can be

heard most clearly from this location because minimal tissue intervenes between the skin of the back and the lungs. The deltoid, levator scapulae, and trapezius do not form the borders of the "triangle of auscultation." The latissimus dorsi, external abdominal oblique, and iliac crest form the border of Petit's inferior lumbar triangle. The quadratus lumborum, internal abdominal oblique, and inferior border of the twelfth rib form the border of the Grynfeltt's superior lumbar triangle. The rectus abdominis, inguinal ligament, and inferior epigastric vessels form the border of the Hesselbach triangle. Petit, Grynfeltt, and Hesselbach triangles are common sites for hernias.
GAS 80-94; GA 37, 141

63 **C.** The weakness in shoulder movement results from denervation of the teres minor and deltoid by the axillary nerve, which passes through the quadrangular space. Quadrangular space syndrome happens when there is hypertrophy of the muscles that border the quadrangular space or fibrosis of portions of the muscles that are in contact with the nerve.
GAS 680-682; GA 362-366, 378

64 **D.** In this MRI a posterolateral herniation between L4/L5 exists. In the lumbar region, spinal nerves exit the vertebral column below their named vertebrae. In an L4/L5 intervertebral disk herniation, the L5 spinal nerve would be affected as it descends between L4/L5 vertebrae to exit below the L5 level.
GAS 108-110; GA 32-33, 44

65 **B.** The (great radicular) artery of Adamkiewicz is important for blood supply to anterior and posterior spinal arteries. The location of this artery should be noted during surgery because damage to it can result in dire consequences, including loss of all sensation and voluntary movement inferior and at the level of the injury. Injury to the left vertebral artery would not be likely due its superior location to the surgical site. Ligation of the posterior spinal artery would not occur because of its protected location inside the spinal column. Transection of the conus medullaris of the spinal cord would not occur as this structure is located at L1, L2 levels and is, again, protected inside the spinal column. Division of the thoracic sympathetic chain would not be likely as the symptoms described include limb paralysis, which would not be a consequence of sympathetic disruption.
GAS 102-103; GA 46

66 **C.** Scoliosis can be a secondary condition in such disorders as muscular dystrophy and polio in which abnormal muscle does not keep the vertebral column's normal alignment and results in a lateral curvature. Lordosis is increased secondary curvature of the lumbar region. It can be caused by stress on the lower back and is quite common in pregnancy. Kyphosis is increased primary curvature of the thoracic regions and produces a hunchback deformity. It can be secondary to tuberculosis, producing a "gibbus deformity," which results in angulated kyphosis at the lesion site. Spina bifida is a congenital defect and would not present as a result of muscular dystrophy or polio. Osteoarthritis most commonly presents with age from normal "wear and tear." It is not likely in a 23-year-old woman.
GAS 77-79; GA 21-30

67 **B.** Transection of all dorsal rootlets of the nerves from the hip area is also known as a dorsal rhizotomy. This type of surgical procedure is performed to eliminate pain sensation from whichever dermatome level is transected. Because dorsal rootlets contain general sensory afferent fibers, cutting these would eliminate sensation and thus pain. Division of the ventral primary rami might result in pain elimination; however, because the fibers in ventral rootlets are mixed, there would also be adverse consequences such as motor and sympathetic and even parasympathetic deficits depending on the level. Removal of abdominal sympathetic chain ganglia on the right side would not eliminate pain in the hip area since the fibers for this sensation are general somatic afferents and the sympathetic chain contains general visceral efferents and afferents. Transection of dorsal primary rami of spinal nerves would not eliminate pain in the hip because the dorsal rootlets contain mixed fibers that supply only a limited area on the back. Division of lower lumbar and sacral ventral rootlets would not eliminate pain sensation since these rootlets contain efferent motor fibers and no afferents.
GAS 36-39, 107-110; GA 45

2

THORAX

1 A 2-day-old newborn is diagnosed with transposition of the great arteries. Which structure is responsible for the division of the truncus arteriosus into the great arteries?

- ☐ **A.** Septum secundum
- ☐ **B.** Septum primum
- ☐ **C.** Bulbar septum
- ☐ **D.** Aorticopulmonary septum
- ☐ **E.** Endocardial cushions

2 A 32-year-old woman in her third trimester of pregnancy is undergoing a routine ultrasound examination. The examination of the fetus reveals enlarged and echogenic lungs, inverted diaphragm, and fetal ascites. Which condition is best characterized by these signs?

- ☐ **A.** Laryngeal atresia
- ☐ **B.** Tracheal atresia
- ☐ **C.** Polyhydramnios
- ☐ **D.** Lung hypoplasia
- ☐ **E.** Oligohydramnios

3 A 2-year-old child is seen in the pediatric cardiology unit for a congenital heart condition. Which of the following conditions occurs most often?

- ☐ **A.** Membranous ventricular septal defect
- ☐ **B.** Tetralogy of Fallot
- ☐ **C.** Muscular ventricular septal defect
- ☐ **D.** Ostium secundum defect
- ☐ **E.** Ostium primum defect

4 A 2-day-old is diagnosed with transposition of the great arteries. If this condition were to be left untreated for more than 4 months, it would be fatal. Which of the following structures must remain patent so that the infant can survive until surgical correction of the malformation?

- ☐ **A.** Ductus arteriosus
- ☐ **B.** Umbilical arteries
- ☐ **C.** Umbilical vein
- ☐ **D.** Coarctation of the aorta
- ☐ **E.** Pulmonary stenosis

5 A 2-day-old newborn female is diagnosed with pulmonary stenosis, overriding of the aorta, ventricular septal defect, and hypertrophy of the right ventricle. Which condition is best characterized by these signs?

- ☐ **A.** Tetralogy of Fallot
- ☐ **B.** Atrial septal defect

- ☐ **C.** Transposition of the great vessels
- ☐ **D.** Pulmonary atresia
- ☐ **E.** Ventricular septal defect

6 A 2-day-old newborn female is diagnosed with pulmonary stenosis, overriding of the aorta, ventricular septal defect, and hypertrophy of the right ventricle. Which of the following embryologic mechanisms is most likely responsible for the development of this cluster of anomalies?

- ☐ **A.** Superior malalignment of the subpulmonary infundibulum
- ☐ **B.** Defect in the aorticopulmonary septum
- ☐ **C.** Endocardial cushion defect
- ☐ **D.** Total anomalous pulmonary venous connections
- ☐ **E.** Atrioventricular canal malformation

7 A 5-year-old boy is admitted to the hospital with severe dyspnea. During physical examination a loud systolic murmur and a wide, fixed, split S_2 sound is noted. What is the most likely diagnosis?

- ☐ **A.** Ventricular septal defect
- ☐ **B.** Atrial septal defect
- ☐ **C.** Tetralogy of Fallot
- ☐ **D.** Transposition of the great arteries
- ☐ **E.** Aortic stenosis

8 A 3-month-old infant is diagnosed with Down syndrome. A routine cardiovascular examination reveals that the infant suffers from arrhythmias. What other cardiac conditions are most likely to occur with Down syndrome?

- ☐ **A.** Tetralogy of Fallot
- ☐ **B.** Transposition of the great arteries
- ☐ **C.** Atrial septal and ventricular septal defects
- ☐ **D.** Truncus arteriosus
- ☐ **E.** Coarctation of the aorta

9 A 3-month-old infant is diagnosed with a deletion at the 22q11 chromosome. A routine cardiovascular examination reveals severe congenital cardiac malformation. Which of the following malformations will most likely be associated with 22q11 syndrome?

- ☐ **A.** Tetralogy of Fallot and truncus arteriosus
- ☐ **B.** Transposition of the great arteries
- ☐ **C.** Atrial septal and ventricular septal defects
- ☐ **D.** Coarctation of the aorta
- ☐ **E.** Aortic atresia

10 A 28-year-old woman in her third trimester of pregnancy with a complaint of dizziness for several days is admitted to the hospital. Physical examination reveals that she has diabetes mellitus. Which of the following cardiac malformations is most likely to affect the fetus when the mother has this disease?

- ☐ **A.** Tetralogy of Fallot
- ☐ **B.** Transposition of the great arteries
- ☐ **C.** Atrial septal and ventricular septal defects
- ☐ **D.** Truncus arteriosus
- ☐ **E.** Coarctation of the aorta

11 During cardiac catheterization of a 6-year-old child, the radiologist notes that the contrast medium released into the arch of the aorta is visible immediately in the left pulmonary artery. What is the most likely explanation for this finding?

- ☐ **A.** Atrial septal defect
- ☐ **B.** Mitral stenosis
- ☐ **C.** Patent ductus arteriosus
- ☐ **D.** Patent ductus venosus
- ☐ **E.** Ventricular septal defect

12 A 3-year-old male patient presents with a clinically significant atrial septal defect (ASD). The ASD usually results from incomplete closure of which of the following structures?

- ☐ **A.** Foramen ovale
- ☐ **B.** Ligamentum arteriosum
- ☐ **C.** Ductus arteriosus
- ☐ **D.** Sinus venarum
- ☐ **E.** Coronary sinus

13 A premature infant has progressive difficulty in breathing and is diagnosed with respiratory distress syndrome. Which cells are deficient in synthesizing surfactant in this syndrome?

- ☐ **A.** Alveolar capillary endothelial
- ☐ **B.** Bronchial mucous
- ☐ **C.** Bronchial respiratory epithelium
- ☐ **D.** Type I alveolar
- ☐ **E.** Type II alveolar

14 A newborn baby was diagnosed with eventration of the diaphragm. In this condition, half of the diaphragm ascends into the thorax during inspiration, while the other half contracts normally. What is the cause of this condition?

- ☐ **A.** Absence of a pleuropericardial fold
- ☐ **B.** Absence of musculature in one half of the diaphragm

- ▢ **C.** Failure of migration of diaphragm
- ▢ **D.** Failure of the septum transversum to develop
- ▢ **E.** Absence of a pleuroperitoneal fold

15 A 35-year-old male is admitted to the emergency department because of a severe nosebleed and a headache that had become worse during the weekend. On physical examination his upper body appears much better developed than his lower body, a loud midsystolic murmur is present on his anterior chest wall and back, his lower extremities are cold, and femoral pulses are absent. Which of the following embryologic structure(s) has been most likely affected to produce such symptoms?

- ▢ **A.** Bulbus cordis
- ▢ **B.** Ductus arteriosus
- ▢ **C.** Third, fourth, and sixth pharyngeal arches
- ▢ **D.** Right and left horns of sinus venosus
- ▢ **E.** Right cardinal vein

16 After a 2-day-old newborn male swallows milk he becomes cyanotic. After 3 days he develops pneumonia. A tracheoesophageal fistula is suspected. Failure of development has occurred most specifically in which of the following structures?

- ▢ **A.** Esophagus
- ▢ **B.** Trachea
- ▢ **C.** Tongue
- ▢ **D.** Tracheoesophageal septum
- ▢ **E.** Pharynx

17 After a 2-day-old newborn male swallows milk he becomes cyanotic. After 3 days he develops pneumonia. A tracheoesophageal fistula is suspected. Which of the following conditions is most likely to be associated with a tracheoesophageal fistula?

- ▢ **A.** Oligohydramnios
- ▢ **B.** Rubella
- ▢ **C.** Polyhydramnios
- ▢ **D.** Thalidomide
- ▢ **E.** Toxoplasmosis

18 A 2-day-old newborn male develops mild cyanosis. An ultrasound examination reveals a patent ductus arteriosus. Which of the following infections will most likely lead to this congenital anomaly?

- ▢ **A.** Toxoplasmosis
- ▢ **B.** Rubella
- ▢ **C.** Cytomegalovirus
- ▢ **D.** Varicella virus
- ▢ **E.** Treponema pallidum

19 A 5-year-old boy has frequent episodes of fatigability and dyspnea. An ultrasound examination reveals an atrial septal defect, located at the opening of the superior vena cava. Which of the following types of atrial septal defects are characteristic for this description?

- ▢ **A.** Ostium secundum
- ▢ **B.** Ostium primum
- ▢ **C.** Atrioventricular (AV) canal
- ▢ **D.** Common atrium
- ▢ **E.** Sinus venosus

20 A 3-day-old newborn was born with ectopia cordis. Despite the efforts of doctors at the pediatric intensive care unit the infant died from cardiac failure and hypoxemia. Which of the following embryologic events is most likely responsible for the development of such conditions?

- ▢ **A.** Faulty development of the sternum and pericardium, secondary to incomplete fusion of the lateral folds
- ▢ **B.** Interruption of third pharyngeal arch development
- ▢ **C.** Interruption of fourth pharyngeal arch development
- ▢ **D.** Interruption of fifth pharyngeal arch development
- ▢ **E.** Faulty development of sinus venosus

21 A 2-day-old newborn male is admitted to the pediatric intensive care unit with cyanosis and tachypnea. Cardiac ultrasound and MRI examinations reveal totally anomalous pulmonary connections. Which of the following embryologic events is responsible for this malformation?

- ▢ **A.** Abnormal septation of the sinus venosus
- ▢ **B.** Abnormal development of the septum secundum
- ▢ **C.** Abnormal development of the left sinus horn
- ▢ **D.** Abnormal development of the coronary sinus
- ▢ **E.** Abnormal development of common cardinal vein

22 A 3-day-old newborn has difficulties breathing. A CT scan of his chest and abdomen reveals the absence of the central tendon of the diaphragm. Which of the following structures failed to develop normally?

- ▢ **A.** Pleuroperitoneal folds
- ▢ **B.** Pleuropericardial folds

- ▢ **C.** Septum transversum
- ▢ **D.** Cervical myotomes
- ▢ **E.** Dorsal mesentery of the esophagus

23 A 30-year-old man is diagnosed with a blockage of arterial flow in the proximal part of the thoracic aorta. Brachial arterial pressure is markedly increased, femoral pressure is decreased, and the femoral pulses are delayed. The patient shows no external signs of inflammation. Which of the following structures failed to develop normally?

- ▢ **A.** Second aortic arch
- ▢ **B.** Third aortic arch
- ▢ **C.** Fourth aortic arch
- ▢ **D.** Fifth aortic arch
- ▢ **E.** Ductus venosus

24 A 1-year-old child was admitted to the pediatric clinic due to severe dyspnea. ECG reveals cardiac arrhythmia and right ventricular hypertrophy. An angiogram reveals a patent ductus arteriosus (PDA). From which of the following embryologic arterial structures does the PDA take origin?

- ▢ **A.** Left sixth arch
- ▢ **B.** Right sixth arch
- ▢ **C.** Left fifth arch
- ▢ **D.** Right sixth arch
- ▢ **E.** Left fourth arch

25 A 4-year-old girl is admitted to the hospital with high fever. *Staphylococcus aureus* is isolated from her blood cultures and antibiotic therapy is initiated. A loud, harsh murmur is heard on auscultation. A chest radiograph shows prominent pulmonary arteries. Echocardiography shows all the valves to be normal. Which congenital heart disease most likely explains these findings?

- ▢ **A.** Atrial septal defect
- ▢ **B.** Tetralogy of Fallot
- ▢ **C.** Coarctation of the aorta
- ▢ **D.** Patent ductus arteriosus
- ▢ **E.** Aortic atresia

26 A 3-day-old infant is admitted to the cardiology unit with severe cyanosis. During echocardiographic examination a right-to-left shunt is identified. Which of the following conditions will most likely produce this type of shunt?

- ▢ **A.** Interatrial septal defect
- ▢ **B.** Interventricular septal defect
- ▢ **C.** Patent ductus arteriosus
- ▢ **D.** Corrected transposition of the great arteries
- ▢ **E.** Common truncus arteriosus

27 A 4-day-old infant was admitted to the pulmonary unit suffering from dyspnea and cyanosis. Radiographic examination revealed a left hypoplastic lung and herniation of abdominal intestines into the left thoracic cavity. Which of the following embryologic structures most likely failed to develop properly?

- ▢ **A.** Septum transversum
- ▢ **B.** Pleuroperitoneal membrane
- ▢ **C.** Tracheoesophageal septum
- ▢ **D.** Laryngotracheal groove
- ▢ **E.** Foregut

28 A 3-month-old infant is diagnosed with a ventricular septal defect (VSD) at the area of the subpulmonary infundibulum. Which of the following structures must be avoided carefully by the surgeon when the sutures are placed at the site of the defect?

- ▢ **A.** Right bundle branch
- ▢ **B.** Right coronary artery
- ▢ **C.** Tricuspid valve
- ▢ **D.** Left anterior descending coronary artery
- ▢ **E.** Aortic valve

29 A 2-day-old infant is diagnosed with incomplete division of the foregut into respiratory and digestive portions. Which is the most common congenital condition characteristic of this description?

- ▢ **A.** Esophageal atresia
- ▢ **B.** Esophageal achalasia
- ▢ **C.** Tracheoesophageal fistula
- ▢ **D.** Congenital diaphragmatic hernia
- ▢ **E.** Esophageal fistula

30 An unconscious 2-month-old infant is admitted to the emergency department after an automobile collision. An emergency tracheostomy is performed. Which of the following structures is most commonly at high risk of injury during this procedure?

- ▢ **A.** Left brachiocephalic vein
- ▢ **B.** Left common carotid artery
- ▢ **C.** Vagus nerve
- ▢ **D.** Phrenic nerve
- ▢ **E.** Thoracic duct

31 A 45-year-old female is admitted to the hospital with difficulty breathing. Radiographic examination reveals a tumor invading the lung surface anterior to the hilum. Which nerve is most likely compressed by the tumor to result in dyspnea?

- ▢ **A.** Phrenic
- ▢ **B.** Vagus
- ▢ **C.** Intercostal
- ▢ **D.** Recurrent laryngeal
- ▢ **E.** Cardiopulmonary

32 A 62-year-old male patient expresses concern that his voice has changed over the preceding months. Imaging reveals a growth located within the aortic arch, adjacent to the left pulmonary artery. Which neural structure is most likely being compressed to cause the changes in the patient's voice?

- ▢ **A.** Left phrenic nerve
- ▢ **B.** Esophageal plexus
- ▢ **C.** Left recurrent laryngeal nerve
- ▢ **D.** Left vagus nerve
- ▢ **E.** Left sympathetic trunk

33 A 39-year-old woman visits the outpatient clinic and complains of inability to reach a pantry shelf just above her head. History reveals that 2 months ago she underwent a mastectomy procedure and she did not have this complaint prior to the surgery. Which nerve was most likely damaged during surgery to result in the patient's complaint?

- ▢ **A.** Axillary
- ▢ **B.** Spinal accessory
- ▢ **C.** Long thoracic
- ▢ **D.** Radial
- ▢ **E.** Thoracodorsal

34 A 41-year-old female is admitted to the emergency department with a complaint of severe, sharp, but poorly localized pain on the chest wall. Radiographic examination gives evidence of pleural effusion. What is the location of the neuronal cell bodies responsible for the nerve fibers that carry this pain to the central nervous system (CNS)?

- ▢ **A.** Dorsal root ganglia
- ▢ **B.** Sympathetic chain ganglia
- ▢ **C.** Dorsal horn of the spinal cord
- ▢ **D.** Lateral horn of the spinal cord
- ▢ **E.** Ventral horn of the spinal cord

35 A 23-year-old man is admitted to the emergency department after an automobile collision. Physical examination reveals tachycardia. What is the location of the preganglionic neural cell bodies involved in increasing the heart rate?

- ▢ **A.** Deep cardiac plexus
- ▢ **B.** Dorsal motor nucleus of vagus
- ▢ **C.** Lateral horn T5 to T9
- ▢ **D.** Lateral horn T1 to T4
- ▢ **E.** Superior, middle, and inferior cervical ganglia

36 A 55-year-old male is admitted to the emergency department with a diagnosis of possible myocardial infarction. Which nerves carry pain fibers from the heart to the CNS?

- ▢ **A.** Vagus
- ▢ **B.** Greater thoracic splanchnic
- ▢ **C.** Least thoracic splanchnic
- ▢ **D.** Cardiopulmonary (thoracic visceral)
- ▢ **E.** T5 to T9 ventral rami

37 A 17-year-old girl is admitted to the hospital with severe dyspnea. Physical examination reveals that the patient is suffering from an asthma attack, with associated bronchospasm. Which of the following nerves is responsible for the innervation of the bronchial smooth muscle cells?

- ▢ **A.** Greater thoracic splanchnic
- ▢ **B.** Phrenic
- ▢ **C.** Vagus
- ▢ **D.** Intercostal
- ▢ **E.** Lesser thoracic splanchnic

38 A 42-year-old woman is admitted to the hospital with an inability to speak. The patient's personal history reveals that she has experienced hoarseness for the past month. A chest radiograph reveals a mass at the aortopulmonary window. Which of the following nerves is most likely compressed?

- ▢ **A.** Vagus
- ▢ **B.** Phrenic
- ▢ **C.** Left recurrent laryngeal
- ▢ **D.** Right recurrent laryngeal
- ▢ **E.** Greater thoracic splanchnic

39 Following the diagnosis of breast cancer, a 42-year-old woman underwent a total mastectomy, including excision of the axillary tail (of Spence). Postoperatively, the patient complains of dysesthesia in the inner aspect of the arm and axilla. Which of the following nerves was most likely injured during the procedure?

- ▢ **A.** Ulnar
- ▢ **B.** Long thoracic

- ☐ **C.** Intercostobrachial
- ☐ **D.** Lateral cutaneous nerve of T4
- ☐ **E.** Axillary nerve

40 A 39-year-old male is admitted to the hospital with a complaint of severe retrosternal pain that radiates to the left shoulder. The pain is relieved by leaning forward. Auscultation reveals a pericardial friction rub, leading to a diagnosis of pericarditis. Which of the following nerves is responsible for the radiating pain?

- ☐ **A.** Intercostobrachial
- ☐ **B.** Phrenic
- ☐ **C.** Long thoracic
- ☐ **D.** Greater thoracic splanchnic
- ☐ **E.** Cardiopulmonary

41 A 72-year-old male is admitted to the hospital with complaints of severe chest pain radiating to his left arm. ECG examination provides evidence of significant myocardial infarction of the posterior wall of the left ventricle. Which of the following nerves is responsible for the radiation of pain to the arm during myocardial infarction?

- ☐ **A.** Phrenic
- ☐ **B.** Vagus
- ☐ **C.** Intercostobrachial
- ☐ **D.** Greater splanchnic
- ☐ **E.** Suprascapular

42 A 43-year-old male hunter is admitted to the emergency department after falling over a barbed wire fence, as a result of which he suffered several deep lacerations along the left midaxillary line. When the patient is examined in the outpatient clinic several days later, numbness and anhydrosis are observed anterior to the area of the cuts. Which structures were most likely damaged to result in these signs?

- ☐ **A.** Dorsal roots
- ☐ **B.** Ventral roots
- ☐ **C.** Cutaneous branches of dorsal rami
- ☐ **D.** Cutaneous branches of ventral rami
- ☐ **E.** Rami communicans

43 A 62-year-old patient is admitted to the hospital with a complaint of suddenly occurring, tearing pain radiating to his back. A CT examination reveals that the patient has an aortic aneurysm. An urgent placement of an endovascular stent-graft is ordered. Which of the following nerves are most likely responsible for the tearing sensation radiating to his back?

- ☐ **A.** Somatic afferent
- ☐ **B.** Thoracic visceral afferent
- ☐ **C.** Sympathetic postganglionics
- ☐ **D.** Sympathetic preganglionics
- ☐ **E.** Parasympathetic afferent

44 A 22-year-old woman had undergone elective breast enhancement, with the insertion of 250-ml saline bags bilaterally. This resulted, unfortunately, in loss of sensation bilaterally in the nipples and areolae and some reduction of sensation of the skin from the areolae laterally to the midaxillary lines. Which of the following nerves were most likely subject to iatrogenic injury?

- ☐ **A.** Anterior cutaneous branches of second and third intercostal nerves
- ☐ **B.** Anterior and lateral cutaneous branches of the fourth intercostal nerves
- ☐ **C.** Lateral pectoral nerves
- ☐ **D.** Cutaneous branches of the second thoracic spinal nerves (intercostobrachial nerves)
- ☐ **E.** Lateral cutaneous branches of the second and third intercostal nerves

45 A 32-year-old female is admitted to the emergency department with dyspnea, dysphagia, hoarseness, and severe anxiety. Her medical history reveals that she has lived on a liquid diet for some months and has lost more than 30 lb. Over the past several weeks, she has had bloody sputum during attacks of coughing. Fluoroscopy and a barium swallow reveal a 4-cm mass associated with a bronchus and associated compression of the esophagus. Which of the following nerves is most likely to be affected?

- ☐ **A.** Right recurrent laryngeal nerve
- ☐ **B.** Left vagus nerve, posterior to the hilum of the lung
- ☐ **C.** Left recurrent laryngeal nerve
- ☐ **D.** Greater thoracic splanchnic nerve
- ☐ **E.** Phrenic nerve

46 A 35-year-old man is admitted to the hospital with pain on swallowing. Imaging reveals a dilated left atrium. Which structure is most likely being compressed by the expansion of the left atrium to result in the patient's symptoms?

- ☐ **A.** Esophagus
- ☐ **B.** Root of the lung
- ☐ **C.** Trachea

- ▢ **D.** Superior vena cava
- ▢ **E.** Inferior vena cava

47 A 32-year-old female is admitted to the hospital in a comatose state. Physical examination reveals that the patient suffers from anorexia nervosa. A nasogastric tube is ordered to be inserted. What is the last site at which resistance would be expected as the tube passes from the nose to the stomach?

- ▢ **A.** Pharyngoesophageal junction
- ▢ **B.** Level of the superior thoracic aperture
- ▢ **C.** Posterior to the aortic arch
- ▢ **D.** Posterior to the left main bronchus
- ▢ **E.** Esophageal hiatus of the diaphragm

48 A 59-year-old man is admitted to the hospital with severe chest pain. During examination a slight rhythmic pulsation on the chest wall at the left fifth intercostal space is noted in the midclavicular line. What part of the heart is responsible for this pulsation?

- ▢ **A.** Right atrium
- ▢ **B.** Left atrium
- ▢ **C.** Aortic arch
- ▢ **D.** Apex of the heart
- ▢ **E.** Mitral valve

49 A 42-year-old male was admitted to the hospital after a head-on vehicular collision in which he received severe blunt trauma to his sternum from the steering wheel. What part of the heart would be most likely to be injured by the impact?

- ▢ **A.** Right ventricle
- ▢ **B.** Apex of left ventricle
- ▢ **C.** Left ventricle
- ▢ **D.** Right atrium
- ▢ **E.** Anterior margin of the left atrium

50 A 54-year-old male is admitted to the hospital with dyspnea. Imaging and physical examination and echocardiographic studies reveal severe mitral valve prolapse. Auscultation of this valve is best performed at which location?

- ▢ **A.** Left fifth intercostal space, just below the nipple
- ▢ **B.** Right lower part of the body of the sternum
- ▢ **C.** Right second intercostal space near the lateral border of the sternum
- ▢ **D.** Directly over the middle of the manubrium
- ▢ **E.** Left second intercostal space near the lateral border of the sternum

51 A 48-year-old male patient is admitted with chronic angina. Coronary angiography reveals nearly total blockage of the circumflex artery near its origin from the left coronary artery. When this artery is exposed to perform a bypass procedure, what accompanying vein must be protected from injury?

- ▢ **A.** Middle cardiac
- ▢ **B.** Great cardiac
- ▢ **C.** Small cardiac
- ▢ **D.** Anterior cardiac
- ▢ **E.** Posterior cardiac

52 A 55-year-old patient is to undergo a coronary bypass operation. The artery of primary concern is the vessel that supplies much of the left ventricle and the right and left bundle branches of the cardiac conduction system. Which artery is the surgeon most concerned with?

- ▢ **A.** Right marginal
- ▢ **B.** Anterior interventricular
- ▢ **C.** Circumflex
- ▢ **D.** Artery to the sinoatrial (SA) node
- ▢ **E.** Posterior interventricular

53 A 58-year-old patient presents himself to the emergency department with severe angina. Upon cardiac catheterization, it is found that he has a significant occlusion in his right coronary artery, just distal to the right sinus of the aortic valve. His collateral cardiac circulation is minimal. Assuming the patient is right coronary dominant, which of the following arteries would be most likely to still have normal blood flow?

- ▢ **A.** Right (acute) marginal artery
- ▢ **B.** Atrioventricular nodal artery
- ▢ **C.** Posterior interventricular artery
- ▢ **D.** Sinoatrial nodal artery
- ▢ **E.** Anterior interventricular artery

54 A 55-year-old male is admitted to the emergency department with severe chest pain. Coronary angiography reveals that the patient's right coronary artery is free of pathology. The left coronary artery is found to be 70% to 80% occluded at three points proximal to its bifurcation into the circumflex and left anterior descending arteries. Having a left dominant coronary circulation, and without surgery, what is the most likely explanation for a poor prognosis for recovery of this patient to a normally active life?

- ▢ **A.** All the branches of the coronary artery are end arteries, precluding the chance that anastomotic connections will occur.

- ☐ **B.** It is probable that the anterior and posterior papillary muscles of the tricuspid valve have been damaged.
- ☐ **C.** The blood supply of the SA node is inadequate.
- ☐ **D.** The development of effective collateral circulation between anterior and posterior interventricular arteries will not be possible.
- ☐ **E.** The blood supply of the AV node will be inadequate.

55 A 35-year-old woman is admitted to the hospital with dyspnea. During physical examination her S_1 heart sound is very loud. Which of the following valves is most likely defective?

- ☐ **A.** Mitral valve
- ☐ **B.** Aortic
- ☐ **C.** Pulmonary
- ☐ **D.** Aortic and pulmonary
- ☐ **E.** Tricuspid

56 A 72-year-old male is admitted to the hospital with severe chest pain. ECG examination provides evidence of severe myocardial infarction of the lower part of the muscular interventricular septum. The function of which of the following valves will be most severely affected?

- ☐ **A.** Pulmonary
- ☐ **B.** Aortic
- ☐ **C.** Tricuspid
- ☐ **D.** Mitral
- ☐ **E.** Eustachian

57 A 35-year-old woman is admitted to the hospital with a complaint of shortness of breath. During physical examination it is noted that there is wide splitting in her S_2 heart sound. ECG reveals a right bundle branch block. Which of the following valves is most likely defective?

- ☐ **A.** Mitral valve
- ☐ **B.** Pulmonary
- ☐ **C.** Aortic and mitral
- ☐ **D.** Tricuspid
- ☐ **E.** Tricuspid and aortic

58 A 3-month-old infant is diagnosed with a membranous ventricular septal defect. A cardiac operation is performed, and the septal defect is patched inferior to the noncoronary cusp of the aorta. Two days postoperatively the infant develops severe arrhythmias affecting both ventricles. Which part of the conduction tissue was most likely injured during the procedure?

- ☐ **A.** Right bundle branch
- ☐ **B.** Left bundle branch
- ☐ **C.** Bundle of His
- ☐ **D.** Posterior internodal pathway
- ☐ **E.** Atrioventricular node

59 A 62-year-old male was admitted to the hospital with intense left chest pain. ECG and echocardiography reveal myocardial infarction and pulmonary valve regurgitation. Emergency coronary angiography is performed and provides evidence that the artery supplying the upper portion of the anterior right ventricular free wall is occluded. Which of the following arteries is most likely to be occluded?

- ☐ **A.** Circumflex
- ☐ **B.** Anterior interventricular artery
- ☐ **C.** Posterior interventricular artery
- ☐ **D.** Artery of the conus
- ☐ **E.** Acute marginal branch of the right coronary artery

60 A 3-month-old male infant died unexpectedly in his sleep. The pathologist examined the histologic slides of tissue samples taken from the heart of the infant and observed that a portion of the conduction tissue that penetrates the right fibrous trigone had become necrotic. As a result, a fatal arrhythmia probably developed, leading to the death of the infant. Which of the following parts of the conduction tissue was most likely interrupted?

- ☐ **A.** Right bundle branch
- ☐ **B.** The bundle of Bachmann
- ☐ **C.** The left bundle branch
- ☐ **D.** The atrioventricular bundle of His
- ☐ **E.** The posterior internodal pathway

61 A 42-year-old woman is admitted to the hospital after blunt trauma to her sternum by the steering wheel during a car crash. Radiographic examination reveals a cardiac tamponade. ECG data indicate that the heart has been severely injured. Which of the following cardiac structures will most likely be injured?

- ☐ **A.** Right ventricle
- ☐ **B.** Obtuse margin of the left ventricle
- ☐ **C.** Right atrium

- D. Left atrium
- E. Apex of the left ventricle

62 A 69-year-old male is admitted to the hospital with intense left chest pain. ECG reveals hypokinetic ventricular septal muscle, myocardial infarction in the anterior two thirds of the interventricular septum, and left anterior ventricular wall. The patient's ECG also exhibited left bundle branch block. Which of the following arteries is most likely occluded?

- A. Circumflex
- B. Proximal right coronary
- C. Proximal left coronary
- D. Proximal left anterior interventricular artery
- E. Posterior interventricular artery

63 A 49-year-old woman is admitted to the hospital complaining of severe, crushing, retrosternal pain during the preceding hour. An ECG reveals that she is suffering from acute myocardial infarction in the posterior aspect of her left ventricle and posteromedial papillary muscle. A coronary angiogram is performed and the patient is found to have left coronary dominant circulation. Which of the following arteries is the most likely to be occluded?

- A. Artery of the conus
- B. Right coronary artery
- C. Circumflex
- D. Right acute marginal
- E. Left diagonal

64 A 75-year-old man is scheduled for his routine annual medical examination. During echocardiographic examination a large, mobile structure resembling a thrombus is identified in the right atrium near the opening of the inferior vena cava. After careful examination the doctor identifies the large mobile structure as a normal component of the heart. Which of the following structures could most likely resemble a thrombus in this location?

- A. Tricuspid valve
- B. Eustachian valve
- C. Thebesian valve
- D. Septum primum
- E. Fossa ovalis

65 A 4-year-old male is operated on for a correction of a small, muscular interventricular septal defect. To access the right side of the intraventricular septum, a wide incision is first made in the anterior surface of the right atrium. Instruments are then inserted through the tricuspid valve to correct the ventricular septal defect. Which of the following structures is the most crucial to protect during the opening of the right atrium?

- A. Crista terminalis
- B. Pectinate muscles
- C. Tricuspid valve
- D. Eustachian valve
- E. Coronary sinus

66 A 52-year-old patient is admitted to the hospital with severe chest pain. ECG and radiographic examinations provide evidence of a significant myocardial infarction and cardiac tamponade. An emergency pericardiocentesis is ordered. At which of the following locations will the needle best be inserted to relieve the tamponade?

- A. Right seventh intercostal space in the midaxillary line
- B. Left fifth intercostal space in the midclavicular line
- C. Right third intercostal space, 1 inch lateral to the sternum
- D. Left sixth intercostal space, ½ inch lateral to the sternum
- E. Triangle of auscultation

67 A 55-year-old man is brought to the emergency department after his motorcycle collided with an automobile. He is hypotensive, his pulse is irregular, and he shows other signs of substantial blood loss. MRI and CT scan evaluations reveal profuse abdominal bleeding. A decision is made to enter the chest so that the descending thoracic aorta can be clamped to minimize blood loss and to preserve cerebral blood flow. After surgical entrance into the thorax, the fibrous pericardium is elevated with a forceps and punctured. A midline, longitudinal incision of the pericardium would best be made to prevent injury to which of the following structures?

- A. Auricular appendage of the left atrium
- B. Coronary sinus
- C. Left anterior descending artery
- D. Left phrenic nerve
- E. Left sympathetic trunk

68 During cardiac surgery of a 45-year-old male the cardiac surgeon can place her fingers in the transverse pericardial sinus, if necessary. This allows the surgeon to easily place a vascular clamp upon which of the following vessels?

- A. Right and left pulmonary veins
- B. Superior and inferior vena cava
- C. Right and left coronary arteries

- ▢ **D.** Pulmonary trunk and ascending aorta
- ▢ **E.** Pulmonary trunk and superior vena cava

69 A 48-year-old male patient is scheduled to have a coronary arterial bypass because of chronic angina. Coronary arteriography reveals nearly total blockage of the posterior descending interventricular artery. In exposing this artery to perform the bypass procedure, which accompanying vessel is most susceptible to injury?

- ▢ **A.** Middle cardiac vein
- ▢ **B.** Great cardiac vein
- ▢ **C.** Small cardiac vein
- ▢ **D.** Anterior cardiac vein
- ▢ **E.** Coronary sinus

70 A 54-year-old male is admitted to the hospital with severe chest pain. ECG examination reveals a myocardial infarction. If the posterior interventricular branch in the patient arises from the right coronary artery, which part of the myocardium will most likely have its blood supply reduced if the circumflex branch of the left coronary artery becomes occluded from an atherosclerotic plaque?

- ▢ **A.** Anterior part of the interventricular septum
- ▢ **B.** Diaphragmatic surface of the right ventricle
- ▢ **C.** Infundibulum
- ▢ **D.** Lateral wall of the left ventricle
- ▢ **E.** Posterior part of the interventricular septum

71 A 70-year-old male with a history of two previous myocardial infarctions is admitted to the hospital with severe chest pain. ECG reveals a new myocardial infarction and ventricular arrhythmia. Coronary angiography reveals that the right coronary artery is blocked just distal to the origin of the right marginal artery in a right coronary dominant circulation. Which of the following structures would most likely be affected after such a blockade?

- ▢ **A.** Right atrium
- ▢ **B.** SA node
- ▢ **C.** AV node
- ▢ **D.** Lateral wall of the left ventricle
- ▢ **E.** Anterior interventricular septum

72 A 43-year-old woman is diagnosed with mitral valve stenosis. During physical examination the first heart sound is abnormally loud. Which of the following heart valves are responsible for the production of the first heart sound?

- ▢ **A.** Aortic and mitral
- ▢ **B.** Aortic and tricuspid
- ▢ **C.** Tricuspid and mitral
- ▢ **D.** Mitral and pulmonary
- ▢ **E.** Tricuspid and pulmonary

73 A 75-year-old woman is admitted to the hospital with anginal pain. ECG reveals myocardial infarction and a right bundle branch block. During physical examination the patient has a loud second heart sound. Which of the following heart valves are responsible for the production of the second heart sound?

- ▢ **A.** Aortic and pulmonary
- ▢ **B.** Aortic and tricuspid
- ▢ **C.** Tricuspid and mitral
- ▢ **D.** Mitral and pulmonary
- ▢ **E.** Tricuspid and pulmonary

74 Ten days after a surgical procedure to correct her cardiac malformation, a 3-month-old infant died unexpectedly in her sleep. After an autopsy, the pathologist reported as follows: "A significant portion of the conduction tissue was found to be necrotic. The area of the necrotic tissue was located inferior to the central fibrous body, membranous septum, and septal leaflet of the tricuspid valve. Further examination revealed infarction of the surrounding tissue. The rest of the heart was unremarkable." Which of the following arteries was most likely occluded?

- ▢ **A.** Artery of the conus
- ▢ **B.** SA node artery
- ▢ **C.** AV node artery
- ▢ **D.** First septal perforator of the anterior interventricular artery
- ▢ **E.** All of the above

75 A 55-year-old male is undergoing an aortic valve replacement. During the procedure the heart is connected to the heart lung machine. As the surgeon explores the oblique pericardial sinus, which of the following is not directly palpable with the tips of the fingers?

- ▢ **A.** Inferior vena cava
- ▢ **B.** Superior vena cava
- ▢ **C.** Posterior wall of the left atrium
- ▢ **D.** Inferior right pulmonary vein
- ▢ **E.** Right atrium

76 A 42-year-old female is admitted urgently to the emergency department after suffering a penetrating wound to her chest from an ice pick during a violent domestic dispute. Physical and ultrasound examinations reveal that the patient has cardiac tamponade. Which of the following will most likely be found during physical examination?

- ☐ **A.** There will be a visible or palpable decrease in the dimensions of the external jugular and internal jugular vein.
- ☐ **B.** There will be gradual enlargement of the ventricles in diastole.
- ☐ **C.** The difference between systolic and diastolic arterial pressures will increase significantly.
- ☐ **D.** There will be diminished heart sounds.
- ☐ **E.** The pulses in the internal carotid arteries will become increasingly distinct, as detected behind the angles of the mandible.

77 During surgical repair of a congenital cardiac anomaly in a 15-year-old boy with a right dominant coronary arterial system, the surgeon accidentally injured a vessel that usually supplies part of the conduction system. This results in intermittent periods of atrioventricular block and severe arrhythmia. The injured artery was most likely a direct branch of which of the following arteries?

- ☐ **A.** Distal anterior interventricular artery
- ☐ **B.** Circumflex artery
- ☐ **C.** Left coronary artery
- ☐ **D.** Marginal artery
- ☐ **E.** Right coronary artery

78 A 42-year-old female is admitted to the hospital with dyspnea. Imaging reveals severe mitral valve regurgitation. Which of the following structures prevents regurgitation of the mitral valve cusps into the left atrium during systole?

- ☐ **A.** Crista terminalis
- ☐ **B.** Crista supraventricularis
- ☐ **C.** Pectinate muscles
- ☐ **D.** Chordae tendineae
- ☐ **E.** Trabeculae carneae

79 A 58-year-old female with cardiac arrhythmia has undergone a procedure to implant a pacemaker. The electrical conducting leads for the pacemaker must be passed into the heart from the pacemaker. Which of the following is the correct order of structures for passage of the leads into the right ventricle?

- ☐ **A.** Brachiocephalic vein, superior vena cava, mitral valve, right ventricle
- ☐ **B.** Superior vena cava, right atrium, mitral valve, right ventricle
- ☐ **C.** Superior vena cava, right atrium, tricuspid valve, right ventricle
- ☐ **D.** Brachiocephalic vein, superior vena cava, right atrium, tricuspid valve, right ventricle
- ☐ **E.** Brachiocephalic vein, superior vena cava, right atrium, mitral valve, right ventricle

80 A 68-year-old male patient in the cardiology ward complains at each mealtime of difficulty in swallowing (dysphagia). Radiographic studies reveal significant cardiac hypertrophy. A barium swallow, followed by radiographic examination of the thorax, reveals esophageal constriction directly posterior to the heart. Which of the following is the most likely cause of the patient's dysphagia?

- ☐ **A.** Mitral valve stenosis
- ☐ **B.** Pulmonary valve stenosis
- ☐ **C.** Regurgitation of the aorta
- ☐ **D.** Occlusion of the anterior interventricular artery
- ☐ **E.** Occlusion of the posterior interventricular artery

81 A 35-year-old female is admitted to the emergency department because of cardiac arrhythmia. ECG examination reveals that the patient suffers from atrial fibrillation. Where is the mass of specialized conducting tissue that initiates the cardiac cycle located?

- ☐ **A.** At the junction of the coronary sinus and the right atrium
- ☐ **B.** At the junction of the inferior vena cava and the right atrium
- ☐ **C.** At the junction of the superior vena cava and the right atrium
- ☐ **D.** Between the left and right atria
- ☐ **E.** In the interventricular septum

82 A 45-year-old female is admitted to the hospital with swelling (edema) of the lower limbs. Ultrasound examination reveals an incompetent tricuspid valve. Into which area will regurgitation of blood occur in this patient?

- ☐ **A.** Pulmonary trunk
- ☐ **B.** Left atrium
- ☐ **C.** Ascending aorta
- ☐ **D.** Right atrium
- ☐ **E.** Left ventricle

83 A 34-year-old male with a complaint of sharp, localized pain over the thoracic wall is diagnosed with pleural effusion. Through which intercostal space along the midaxillary line is it most appropriate to insert a chest tube to drain the effusion fluid?

- ▢ **A.** Fourth
- ▢ **B.** Sixth
- ▢ **C.** Eighth
- ▢ **D.** Tenth
- ▢ **E.** Twelfth

84 A 51-year-old male is admitted to the hospital with severe dyspnea. Radiographic examination reveals a tension pneumothorax. Adequate local anesthesia of the chest wall prior to insertion of a chest tube is necessary for pain control. Of the following layers, which is the deepest that must be infiltrated with the local anesthetic to achieve adequate anesthesia?

- ▢ **A.** Endothoracic fascia
- ▢ **B.** Intercostal muscles
- ▢ **C.** Parietal pleura
- ▢ **D.** Subcutaneous fat
- ▢ **E.** Visceral pleura

85 A 5-year-old boy had been playing with his little race cars. Soon after he put a wheel from one of the cars in his mouth, he began choking and coughing. Where in the tracheobronchial tree is the most common site for a foreign object to lodge?

- ▢ **A.** The right primary bronchus
- ▢ **B.** The left primary bronchus
- ▢ **C.** The carina of the trachea
- ▢ **D.** The beginning of the trachea
- ▢ **E.** The left tertiary bronchus

86 A 3-year-old child is admitted to the emergency department with a particularly severe attack of asthma. Which of the following is the most important factor in increasing the intrathoracic capacity in inspiration?

- ▢ **A.** "Pump handle movement" of the ribs—thereby increasing anterior-posterior dimensions of the thorax
- ▢ **B.** "Bucket handle movement" of the ribs—increasing the transverse diameter of the thorax
- ▢ **C.** Straightening of the forward curvature of the thoracic spine, thereby increasing the vertical dimensions of the thoracic cavity
- ▢ **D.** Descent of the diaphragm, with protrusion of the abdominal wall, thereby increasing vertical dimensions of the thoracic cavity
- ▢ **E.** Orientation and flexibility of the ribs in the baby, thus allowing expansion in all directions

87 A 54-year-old female is admitted to the hospital with a stab wound of the thoracic wall in the area of the right fourth costal cartilage. Which of the following pulmonary structures is present at this site?

- ▢ **A.** The horizontal fissure of the left lung
- ▢ **B.** The horizontal fissure of the right lung
- ▢ **C.** The oblique fissure of the left lung
- ▢ **D.** The apex of the right lung
- ▢ **E.** The root of the left lung

88 A 55-year-old female visited her doctor because of a painful lump in her right breast and a bloody discharge from her right nipple. Radiographic studies and physical examination reveal unilateral inversion of the nipple, and a tumor in the right upper quadrant of the breast is suspected. In addition, there is an orange-peel appearance of the skin (peau d'orange) in the vicinity of the areola. Which of the following best explains the inversion of her nipple?

- ▢ **A.** Retention of the fetal and infantile state of the nipple
- ▢ **B.** Intraductal cancerous tumor
- ▢ **C.** Retraction of the suspensory ligaments of the breast by cancer
- ▢ **D.** Obstruction of the cutaneous lymphatics, with edema of the skin
- ▢ **E.** Inflammation of the epithelial lining of the nipple and underlying hypodermis

89 A 58-year-old woman is admitted to the emergency department with severe dyspnea. Bronchoscopy reveals that the carina is distorted and widened. Enlargement of which group of lymph nodes is most likely responsible for altering the carina?

- ▢ **A.** Pulmonary
- ▢ **B.** Bronchopulmonary
- ▢ **C.** Inferior tracheobronchial
- ▢ **D.** Superior tracheobronchial
- ▢ **E.** Paratracheal

90 A 72-year-old patient vomited and then aspirated some of the vomitus while under anesthesia. On bronchoscopic examination, partially digested food is observed blocking the origin of the right superior lobar bronchus. Which of the following groups of bronchopulmonary segments will be affected by this obstruction?

- ▢ **A.** Superior, medial, lateral, medial basal
- ▢ **B.** Apical, anterior, posterior
- ▢ **C.** Posterior, anterior, superior, lateral

- D. Apical, lateral, medial, lateral basal
- E. Anterior, superior, medial, lateral

91 A 35-year-old woman is admitted to a surgical ward with a palpable mass in her right breast and swollen lymph nodes in the axilla. Radiographic studies and biopsy reveal carcinoma of the breast. Which group of axillary lymph nodes is the first to receive lymph drainage from the secretory tissue of the breast and therefore most likely to contain metastasized tumor cells?

- A. Lateral
- B. Central
- C. Apical
- D. Anterior (pectoral)
- E. Posterior (subscapular)

92 A 30-year-old man is admitted to the emergency department because of significant nosebleeding and a headache that has worsened over several days. He also complains of fatigue. Upon examination it is noted that brachial artery pressure is markedly increased, femoral pressure is decreased, and the femoral pulses are delayed. The patient shows no external signs of inflammation. Which of the following is the most likely diagnosis?

- A. Coarctation of the aorta
- B. Cor pulmonale
- C. Dissecting aneurysm of the right common iliac artery
- D. Obstruction of the superior vena cava
- E. Pulmonary embolism

93 A 22-year-old man is diagnosed with signs of reduced aortic flow. Upon examination it is noted that brachial artery pressure is markedly increased, femoral pressure is decreased, and the femoral pulses are delayed. The patient shows no external signs of inflammation. Which of the following conditions will most likely be observed in a radiographic examination?

- A. Flail chest
- B. Pneumothorax
- C. Hydrothorax
- D. Notching of the ribs
- E. Mediastinal shift

94 A patient who has undergone a radical mastectomy with extensive axillary dissection exhibits winging of the scapula when she pushes against resistance on an immovable object, such as a wall. Injury of which of the following nerves would result in this condition?

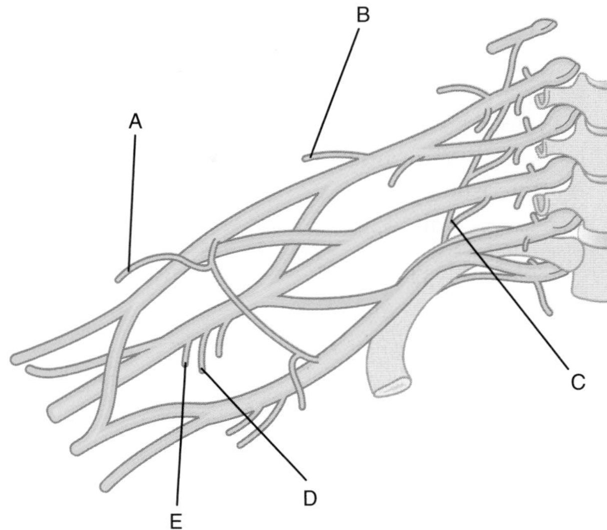

- A. A
- B. B
- C. C
- D. D
- E. E

95 A 22-year-old woman sustained a chest injury upon impact with the steering wheel during a car crash. Upon admission of the patient to the hospital, physical examination revealed profuse swelling, inflammation, and deformation of the chest wall. A radiograph revealed an uncommon fracture of the manubrium at the sternomanubrial joint. Which of the following ribs would be most likely to also be involved in such an injury?

- A. First
- B. Second
- C. Third
- D. Fourth
- E. Fifth

96 A 47-year-old male is admitted to the emergency department, due to severe dysphagia. Edema of the lower limbs is apparent upon physical examination. A barium sulfate swallow imaging procedure reveals esophageal dilation, with severe inflammation, due to constriction at the esophageal hiatus. What is the most likely cause of the severe edema of the lower limbs?

- A. Thoracic aorta constriction
- B. Thoracic duct blockage
- C. Superior vena caval occlusion

- D. Aortic aneurysm
- E. Femoral artery disease

97 In coronary bypass graft surgery of a 49-year-old female, the internal thoracic artery is used as the coronary artery bypass graft. The anterior intercostal arteries in intercostal spaces three to six are ligated. Which of the following arteries will be expected to supply these intercostal spaces?

- A. Musculophrenic
- B. Superior epigastric
- C. Posterior intercostal
- D. Lateral thoracic
- E. Thoracodorsal

98 A 10-year-old boy is admitted to the hospital with retrosternal discomfort. A CT scan reveals a midline tumor of the thymus gland. Which of the following veins would most likely be compressed by the tumor?

- A. Right internal jugular
- B. Left internal jugular
- C. Right brachiocephalic
- D. Left brachiocephalic
- E. Right subclavian

99 A 25-year-old man is admitted to the emergency department with a bullet wound in the neck just above the middle of the right clavicle and first rib. Radiographic examination reveals collapse of the right lung and a tension pneumothorax. Injury to which of the following respiratory structures resulted in the pneumothorax?

- A. Costal pleura
- B. Cupula
- C. Right mainstem bronchus
- D. Right upper lobe bronchus
- E. Mediastinal parietal pleura

100 A 51-year-old female with a history of brain tumor and associated severe oropharyngeal dysphagia develops right lower lobe pneumonia after an episode of vomiting. Which of the following is the best reason that this type of aspiration pneumonia most commonly affects the right lower lung lobe?

- A. Pulmonary vascular resistance is higher in the right lung than the left lung.
- B. The right main bronchus is straighter than the left main bronchus.
- C. The right main bronchus is narrower than the main bronchus.
- D. The right main bronchus is longer than the left main bronchus.
- E. The right lower lung lobe has poorer venous drainage than the other lobes.

101 A 41-year-old male is admitted to the emergency department with complaints of shortness of breath, dizziness, and sharp chest pain. The large arrow in his chest radiograph indicates the region of pathology (Fig. 2-1). What is this structure?

- A. Superior vena cava
- B. Right ventricle
- C. Left ventricle
- D. Arch of the aorta
- E. Pulmonary artery

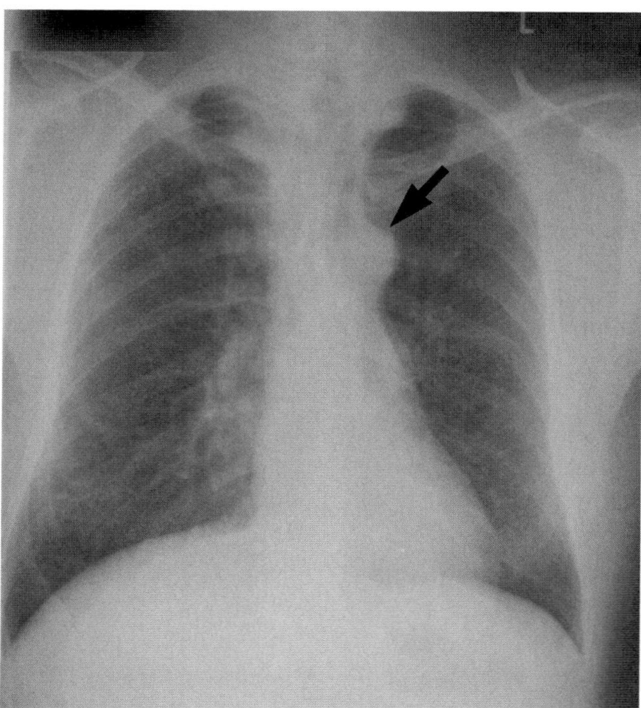

Fig. 2-1

102 A 42-year-old woman is seen by her family physician because she has a painful lump in her right breast and a bloody discharge from her right nipple. Upon physical examination it is noted that there is unilateral inversion of the right nipple and a hard, woody texture of the skin over a mass of tissue in the right upper quadrant of the breast. Which of the following conditions is most frequently characterized by these symptoms?

- A. Peau d'orange
- B. Cancer en cuirasse
- C. Intraductal cancerous tumor
- D. Obstruction of the lymphatics draining the skin of the breast, with edema of the skin
- E. Inflammation of the epithelial lining of the nipple and underlying hypodermis

103 A 25-year-old female is admitted to the hospital after a violent automobile crash. Radiographic examination reveals four broken ribs in the left thoracic wall, producing a flail chest observable on physical examination. Which of the following conditions is most likely to also be observed during physical examination?

- ▢ **A.** During deep inspiration the flail segment moves in the opposite direction of the chest wall.
- ▢ **B.** During deep inspiration the flail segment moves in the same direction as the chest wall.
- ▢ **C.** "Pump handle movements" of the ribs will not be affected by the rib fractures.
- ▢ **D.** The descent of the diaphragm will be affected on the side of the broken ribs.
- ▢ **E.** The descent of the diaphragm will be affected on the side of the broken ribs and also on the opposite side.

104 A 33-year-old male is admitted to the hospital with severe traumatic injuries. His blood pressure is 89/39 mm Hg, and a central venous line is ordered to be placed. Which of the following injuries is most likely to occur when a subclavian central venous line procedure is performed?

- ▢ **A.** Penetration of the subclavian artery
- ▢ **B.** Impalement of the phrenic nerve
- ▢ **C.** Penetration of the superior vena cava
- ▢ **D.** Penetration of the left common carotid artery
- ▢ **E.** Impalement of the vagus nerve

105 A 39-year-old man is admitted to the hospital with odynophagia. A barium swallow reveals an esophageal constriction at the level of the diaphragm. A CT scan and a biopsy further indicate the presence of an esophageal cancer. Which of the following lymph nodes will most likely be affected first?

- ▢ **A.** Posterior mediastinal and left gastric
- ▢ **B.** Bronchopulmonary
- ▢ **C.** Tracheobronchial
- ▢ **D.** Inferior tracheobronchial
- ▢ **E.** Superior tracheobronchial

106 A 42-year-old man is admitted to the hospital with retrosternal pain. Endoscopy and biopsy examinations of the trachea reveal a malignant growth at the right main bronchus. Which of the following lymph nodes will most likely be the first infiltrated by cancerous cells from the malignancy?

- ▢ **A.** Inferior tracheobronchial
- ▢ **B.** Paratracheal
- ▢ **C.** Bronchomediastinal trunk
- ▢ **D.** Bronchopulmonary
- ▢ **E.** Thoracic duct

107 A 60-year-old man is admitted to the hospital with severe abdominal pain. A CT scan reveals a dissecting aneurysm of the thoracic aorta. While in the hospital the patient's aneurysm ruptures and he is transferred urgently to the operating theater. Postoperatively, the patient suffers from paraplegia. Which of the following arteries was most likely injured during the operation to result in the paralysis?

- ▢ **A.** Right coronary artery
- ▢ **B.** Left common carotid
- ▢ **C.** Right subclavian
- ▢ **D.** Great radicular (of Adamkiewicz)
- ▢ **E.** Esophageal

108 A 47-year-old woman is admitted to the hospital with pain in her neck. During physical examination it is observed that the thyroid gland is enlarged and is compressing the trachea. A biopsy reveals a benign tumor. A CT scan examination reveals tracheal deviation to the left. Which of the following structures will most likely be compressed as a result of the deviation?

- ▢ **A.** Left brachiocephalic vein
- ▢ **B.** Left internal jugular vein
- ▢ **C.** Left subclavian artery
- ▢ **D.** Vagus nerve
- ▢ **E.** Phrenic nerve

109 A 33-year-old male is admitted to the hospital after a violent, multiple car collision. His blood pressure is 89/39 mm Hg, and a central venous line is ordered to be placed. Which of the following structures is used as a landmark to place the tip of the catheter of the central venous line?

- ▢ **A.** Carina
- ▢ **B.** Subclavian artery
- ▢ **C.** Superior vena cava
- ▢ **D.** Left atrium
- ▢ **E.** Right atrium

110 A 42-year-old male is diagnosed with liver and pancreatic disease as a result of alcoholism. During physical examination it is noted that he has abnormal enlargement of his mammary glands, as a secondary result of his disease process. Which of the following clinical conditions will most likely describe this case?

- ▢ **A.** Polythelia
- ▢ **B.** Supernumerary breast

- ▢ **C.** Polymastia
- ▢ **D.** Gynecomastia
- ▢ **E.** Amastia

111 A 21-year-old female gymnast is admitted to the hospital with severe dyspnea after a fall from the uneven parallel bars. Radiographic examination reveals that her right lung is collapsed and the left lung is compressed by the great volume of air in her right pleural cavity. During physical examination she has no signs of external injuries. Which of the following conditions will most likely describe this case?

- ▢ **A.** Flail chest with paradoxical respiration
- ▢ **B.** Emphysema
- ▢ **C.** Hemothorax
- ▢ **D.** Chylothorax
- ▢ **E.** Tension pneumothorax

112 A 34-year-old male unconscious patient is admitted to the hospital. His blood pressure is 85/45 mm Hg. A central venous line is ordered to be placed. During subsequent radiographic examination a chylothorax is detected. Which of the following structures was most likely accidentally damaged during the placement of the central venous line?

- ▢ **A.** Left external jugular vein
- ▢ **B.** Site of origin of the left brachiocephalic vein
- ▢ **C.** Right subclavian vein
- ▢ **D.** Proximal part of right brachiocephalic vein
- ▢ **E.** Right external jugular vein

113 A 28-year-old woman in the third trimester of pregnancy has experienced severe dizziness for several days and is admitted to the hospital. During physical examination her blood pressure is normal when standing or sitting. When the patient is supine, her blood pressure drops to 90/50 mm Hg. What is the most likely explanation for these findings?

- ▢ **A.** Compression of the inferior vena cava
- ▢ **B.** Compression of the superior vena cava
- ▢ **C.** Compression of the aorta
- ▢ **D.** Compression of the common carotid artery
- ▢ **E.** Compression of the internal jugular veins

114 A 17-year-old girl is admitted to the hospital with dyspnea and fever. Radiographic examination reveals lobar pneumonia in one of the lobes of her right lung. During stethoscope examination at the level of the sixth intercostal space at the midaxillary line, rales (or crackles) are heard and dull sounds are produced during percussion. Which of the following lobes is most likely to be involved by pneumonia?

- ▢ **A.** Upper lobe of the right lung
- ▢ **B.** Middle lobe of the right lung
- ▢ **C.** Lower lobe of the right lung
- ▢ **D.** Lower lobes of the right and left lungs
- ▢ **E.** Upper lobes of the right and left lungs

115 A 35-year-old man is admitted to the hospital with severe chest pain, dyspnea, tachycardia, cough, and fever. Radiographic examination reveals significant pericardial effusion. When pericardiocentesis is performed, the needle is inserted up from the infrasternal angle. The needle passes too deeply, piercing the visceral pericardium and entering the heart. Which of the following chambers would be the first to be penetrated by the needle?

- ▢ **A.** Right ventricle
- ▢ **B.** Left ventricle
- ▢ **C.** Right atrium
- ▢ **D.** Left atrium
- ▢ **E.** The left cardiac apex

116 A 45-year-old man is admitted to the hospital with severe chest pain radiating to his left arm and left upper jaw. An emergency ECG reveals an acute myocardial infarction of the posterior left ventricular wall. Which of the following spinal cord segments would most likely receive the sensations of pain in this case?

- ▢ **A.** T1, T2, T3
- ▢ **B.** T1, T2, T3, T4
- ▢ **C.** T1, T2
- ▢ **D.** T4, T5, T6
- ▢ **E.** T5, T6, T7

117 A 55-year-old woman is admitted to the hospital with cough and severe dyspnea. Radiographic examination reveals that the patient suffers from emphysema. Upon physical examination the patient shows only "bucket handle movements" during deep inspiration. Which of the following movements of the thoracic wall is characteristic for this type of breathing?

- ▢ **A.** Increase of the transverse diameter of the thorax
- ▢ **B.** Increase of the anteroposterior diameter of the thorax
- ▢ **C.** Increase of the vertical dimension of the thorax
- ▢ **D.** Decrease of the anteroposterior diameter of the thorax

- ▢ **E.** Decrease of the transverse diameter of the thorax

118 A 15-year-old male is admitted to the hospital with cough and severe dyspnea. Physical examination reveals expiratory wheezes, and a diagnosis is made of acute asthma. The expiratory wheezes are characteristic signs of bronchospasm of the smooth muscle of the bronchial airways. Which of the following nerves could be blocked to result in relaxation of the smooth muscle?

- ▢ **A.** Phrenic
- ▢ **B.** Intercostal
- ▢ **C.** Vagus
- ▢ **D.** T1 to T4 sympathetic fibers
- ▢ **E.** Recurrent laryngeal nerve

119 A 34-year-old male with a complaint of sharp, localized pain over the thoracic wall is diagnosed with pleural effusion. A chest tube is inserted to drain the effusion through an intercostal space. At which of the following locations is the chest tube most likely to be inserted?

- ▢ **A.** Superior to the upper border of the rib
- ▢ **B.** Inferior to the lower border of the rib
- ▢ **C.** At the middle of the intercostal space
- ▢ **D.** Between the internal and external intercostal muscles
- ▢ **E.** Between the intercostal muscles and the posterior intercostal membrane

120 A 42-year-old woman is admitted to the emergency department after a fall from the balcony of her apartment. During physical examination there is an absence of heart sounds, reduced systolic pressure, reduced cardiac output, and engorged jugular veins. Which condition is most likely characterized by these signs?

- ▢ **A.** Hemothorax
- ▢ **B.** Cardiac tamponade
- ▢ **C.** Hemopneumothorax
- ▢ **D.** Pneumothorax
- ▢ **E.** Deep vein thrombosis

121 A 35-year-old woman is admitted to the hospital with a complaint of shortness of breath. During physical examination it is noted that there is wide splitting in her S_2 heart sound. Which of the following valves is/are responsible for production of the S_2 heart sound?

- ▢ **A.** Mitral valve
- ▢ **B.** Pulmonary and aortic
- ▢ **C.** Aortic and mitral
- ▢ **D.** Tricuspid
- ▢ **E.** Tricuspid and aortic

122 A 35-year-old female is admitted to the hospital with dyspnea. During physical examination her S_1 heart sound is very loud. Which of the following valves is/are responsible for production of the S_1 heart sound?

- ▢ **A.** Mitral valve
- ▢ **B.** Pulmonary and aortic
- ▢ **C.** Aortic and mitral
- ▢ **D.** Tricuspid
- ▢ **E.** Tricuspid and mitral

123 A 57-year-old male is admitted to the emergency department after he was struck by a truck while crossing a busy street. Radiographic examination reveals flail chest. During physical examination the patient complains of severe pain during inspiration and expiration. Which of the following nerves is most likely responsible for the sensation of pain during respiration?

- ▢ **A.** Phrenic
- ▢ **B.** Vagus
- ▢ **C.** Cardiopulmonary
- ▢ **D.** Intercostal
- ▢ **E.** Thoracic splanchnic

124 A 62-year-old female is admitted to the hospital with severe dyspnea and also complains of pain over her left shoulder. A radiographic examination reveals an aneurysm of the aortic arch. Which of the following nerves is most likely affected by the aneurysm?

- ▢ **A.** Phrenic
- ▢ **B.** Vagus
- ▢ **C.** Cardiopulmonary
- ▢ **D.** Intercostal
- ▢ **E.** Thoracic splanchnic

125 A 62-year-old female accountant is admitted to the emergency department with severe chest pains that radiate to her left arm. ECG reveals that the patient suffers from an acute myocardial infarction. Coronary angiography is performed and a stent is placed at the proximal portion of the anterior interventricular artery (left anterior descending). Because of the low ejection fraction of the right and left ventricles, a cardiac pacemaker is also placed in the heart. The function of which of the following structures is essentially replaced by the insertion of a pacemaker?

- ▢ **A.** AV node
- ▢ **B.** SA node
- ▢ **C.** Purkinje fibers

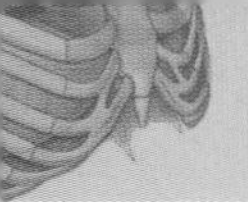

- D. Bundle of His
- E. Bundle of Kent

126 A 22-year-old marathon runner is admitted to the emergency department with severe dyspnea. Physical examination reveals that the patient is experiencing an acute asthma attack, and a bronchodilating drug is administered. Which of the following elements of the nervous system must be inhibited by the drug to achieve relaxation of the smooth muscle of the tracheobronchial tree?

- **A.** Postganglionic sympathetic fibers
- **B.** Preganglionic sympathetic fibers
- **C.** Postganglionic parasympathetic fibers
- **D.** Visceral afferent fibers
- **E.** Somatic efferent fibers

127 Radiographic examination of a cyanotic 3-day-old infant gives evidence of abnormalities within the heart. Blood tests reveal abnormally high levels of TGF-β factor *Nodal*. Which of the following conditions is most likely to be associated with these findings?

- **A.** Dextrocardia
- **B.** Ectopia cordis
- **C.** Transposition of the great arteries
- **D.** Unequal division of the truncus arteriosus
- **E.** Coarctation of the aorta

128 A 35-year-old female who was brought into the emergency department for a drug overdose requires insertion of a nasogastric tube and administration of activated charcoal. What are the three sites in the esophagus where one should anticipate resistance due to compression on the organ?

- **A.** At the aortic arch, the cricopharyngeal constriction, and the diaphragmatic constriction
- **B.** The cardiac constriction, the cricoid cartilage constriction, and the thoracic duct
- **C.** The pulmonary constriction, cricothyroid constriction, and the azygos arch
- **D.** The cardiac constriction, the azygos arch, the pulmonary trunk
- **E.** The cricopharyngeal constriction, cricothyroid constriction, thymus gland

129 A 29-year-old patient complains of severe pain radiating across her back and chest. Upon clinical examination you observe a rash characteristic of herpes zoster infection passing from her upper left back and across her left nipple. Which of the following spinal nerve roots sheds the active virus?

- **A.** Dorsal root of T3
- **B.** Ventral root of T3
- **C.** Dorsal root of T4
- **D.** Ventral root of T4
- **E.** Dorsal root of T5

130 A 3-year-old male who fell from a tree complains of severe pain over the right side of his chest because of a rib fracture at the midaxillary line. He is admitted to the hospital due to his difficulty breathing. Radiographic and physical examinations reveal atelectasis, resulting from the accumulation of blood in his pleural space and resulting hemothorax. What is the most likely the source of bleeding to cause the hemothorax?

- **A.** Left common carotid artery
- **B.** Intercostal vessels
- **C.** Pulmonary arteries
- **D.** Pulmonary veins
- **E.** Internal thoracic artery

131 A 45-year-old woman is admitted to the hospital with severe dyspnea. Radiographic examination confirms the presence of a Pancoast tumor (Fig. 2-2). Physical examination reveals that the patient has miosis of the pupil, partial ptosis of the eyelid, and anhydrosis of the face. Which of the following structures has most likely been injured?

- **A.** Sympathetic chain
- **B.** Vagus nerve
- **C.** Phrenic nerve
- **D.** Arch of aorta
- **E.** Cardiopulmonary plexus

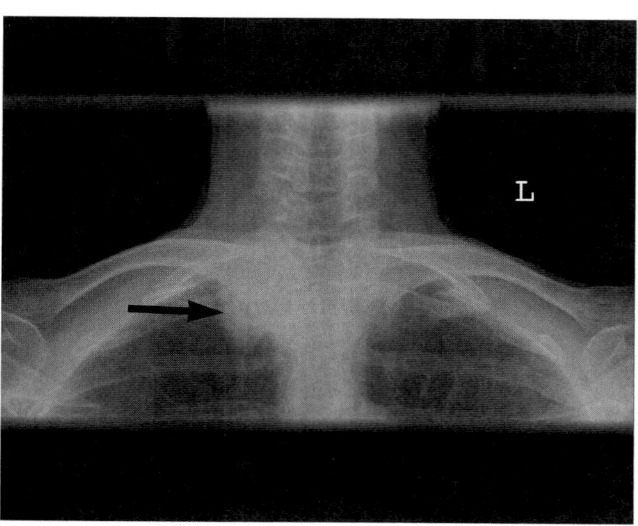

Fig. 2-2

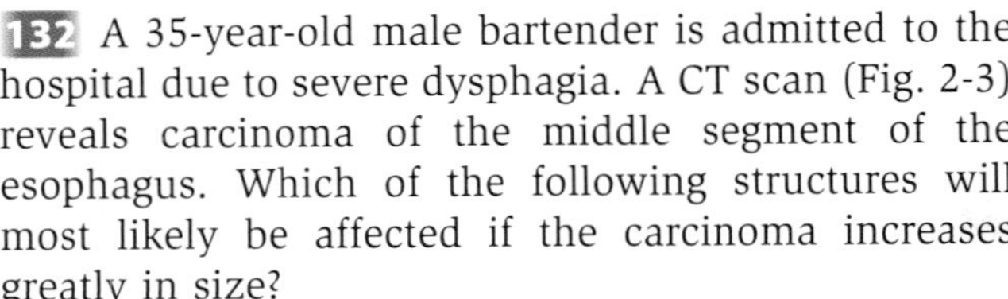

132 A 35-year-old male bartender is admitted to the hospital due to severe dysphagia. A CT scan (Fig. 2-3) reveals carcinoma of the middle segment of the esophagus. Which of the following structures will most likely be affected if the carcinoma increases greatly in size?

- ☐ **A.** Inferior vena cava
- ☐ **B.** Left atrium
- ☐ **C.** Pulmonary artery
- ☐ **D.** Left ventricle
- ☐ **E.** Vertebral body

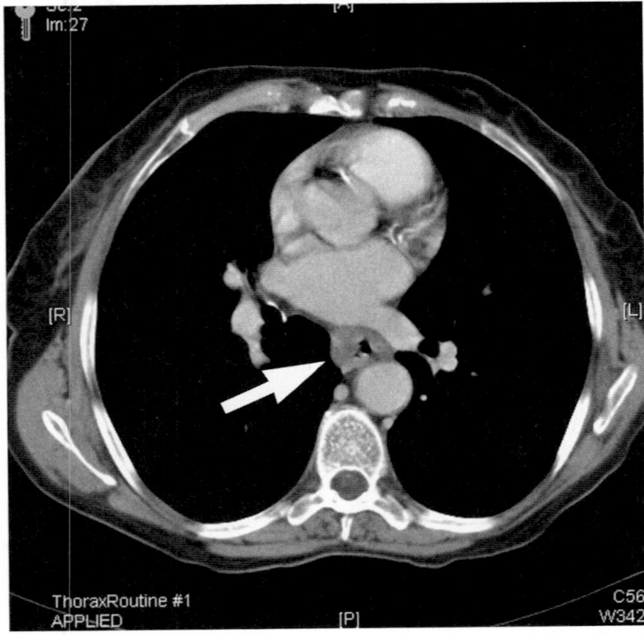

Fig. 2-3

133 A 62-year-old male internist is admitted to the emergency department with a complaint of severe chest pain. Physical examination reveals acute myocardial infarction. After the patient is stabilized, angiography is performed and the ejection fraction of the left ventricle is shown to be reduced to 30% of normal values. A cardiac pacemaker is placed to prevent fatal arrhythmias (Fig. 2-4). What is the location of the tip of the pacemaker?

- ☐ **A.** Right atrium
- ☐ **B.** Left atrium
- ☐ **C.** Right ventricle
- ☐ **D.** Left ventricle
- ☐ **E.** Superior vena cava

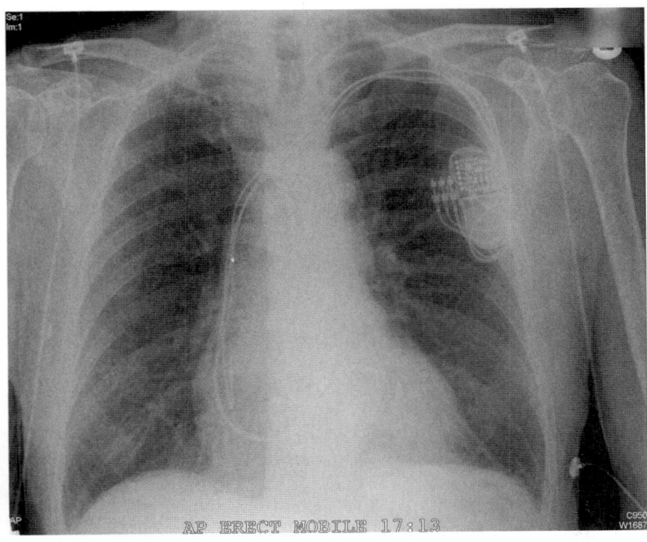

Fig. 2-4

134 Postoperative examination of a 68-year-old male who underwent mitral valve replacement demonstrates significant cardiac hypertrophy (Fig. 2-5). Which of the following structures would be most likely to be compressed?

- ☐ **A.** Esophagus
- ☐ **B.** Pulmonary trunk
- ☐ **C.** Superior vena cava
- ☐ **D.** Trachea
- ☐ **E.** Inferior vena cava

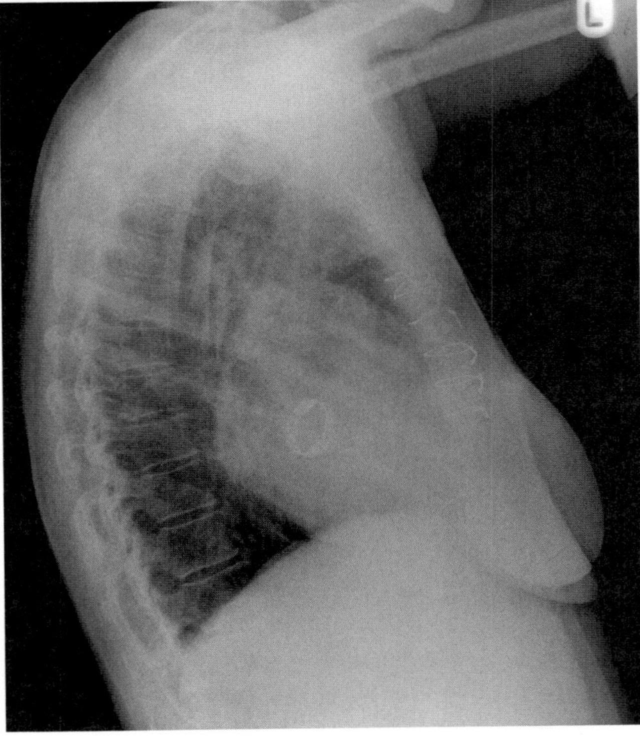

Fig. 2-5

135 A 29-year-old man is admitted to the hospital with great difficulty breathing after an automobile accident. Radiographic examination (Fig. 2-6) reveals no fractured bones or mediastinal shift. During physical examination he has no signs of external injuries, but the dyspnea becomes progressively worse. Which of the following conditions would best describe this case?

- ▢ **A.** Flail chest with paradoxical respiration
- ▢ **B.** Emphysema
- ▢ **C.** Hemothorax
- ▢ **D.** Spontaneous pneumothorax
- ▢ **E.** Tension pneumothorax

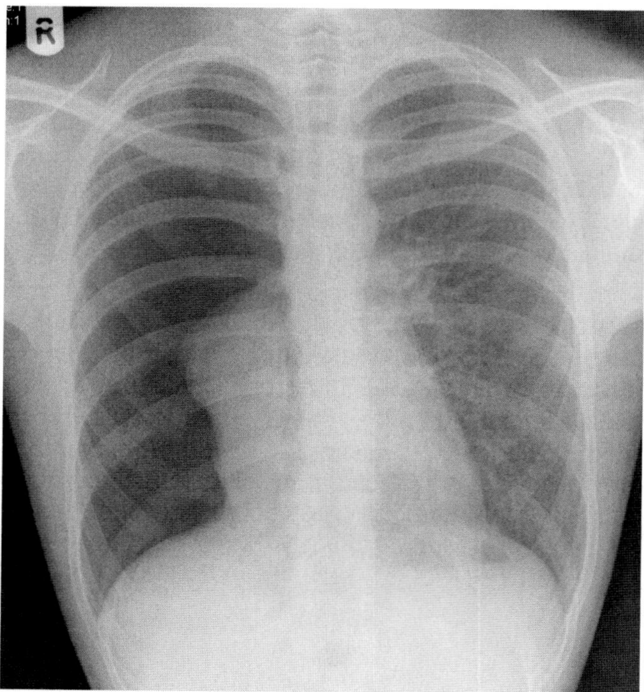

Fig. 2-6

136 A 56-year-old male swimming coach is admitted to the hospital with dyspnea, cough, and high fever. A radiographic examination reveals lobar pneumonia (Fig. 2-7). Which of the following lobes of the lung is affected as shown in the image?

- ▢ **A.** Right upper lobe
- ▢ **B.** Right middle lobe
- ▢ **C.** Right lower lobe
- ▢ **D.** Left upper lobe
- ▢ **E.** Left lower lobe

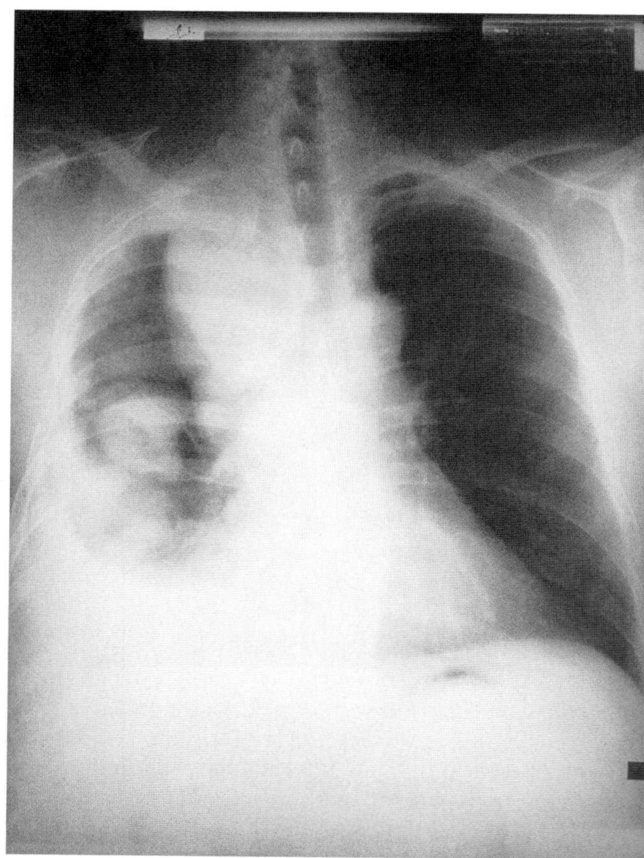

Fig. 2-7

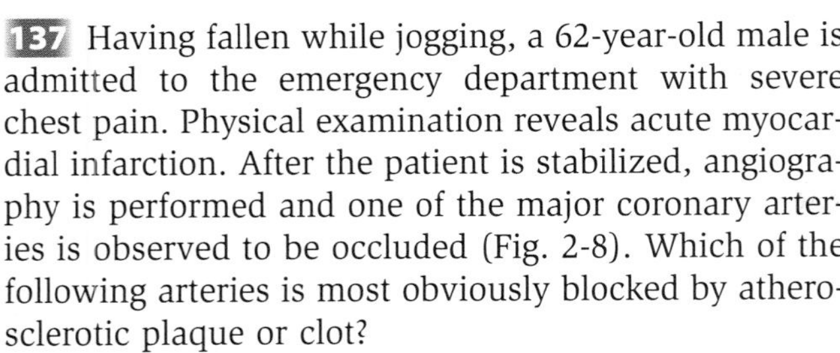

137 Having fallen while jogging, a 62-year-old male is admitted to the emergency department with severe chest pain. Physical examination reveals acute myocardial infarction. After the patient is stabilized, angiography is performed and one of the major coronary arteries is observed to be occluded (Fig. 2-8). Which of the following arteries is most obviously blocked by atherosclerotic plaque or clot?

- ☐ **A.** Right coronary
- ☐ **B.** Left anterior interventricular
- ☐ **C.** Posterior interventricular
- ☐ **D.** Diagonal
- ☐ **E.** Circumflex

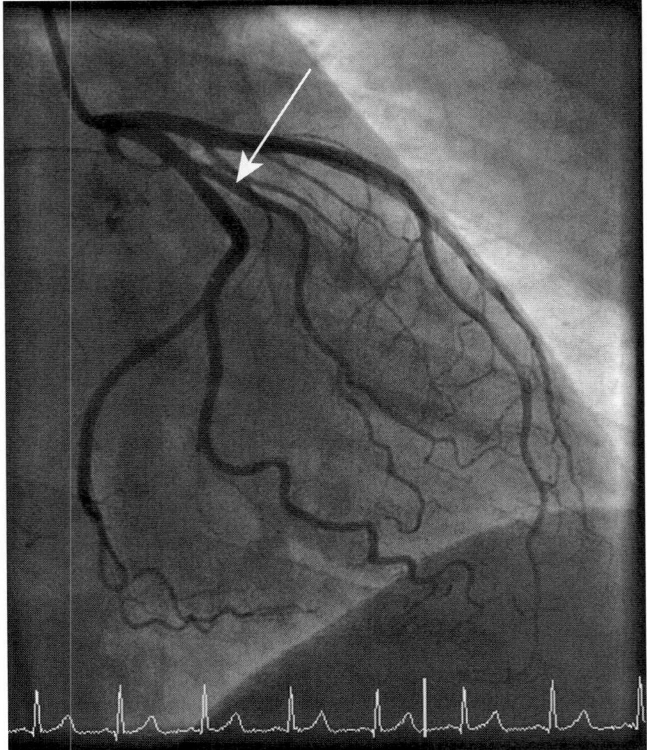

Fig. 2-8

138 A 47-year-old female patient's right breast exhibited peau d'orange characteristics. This condition is primarily a result of which of the following occurrences?

- ☐ **A.** Blockage of cutaneous lymphatic vessels
- ☐ **B.** Shortening of the suspensory ligaments by cancer in the axillary tail of the breast
- ☐ **C.** Contraction of the retinacula cutis of the areola and nipple
- ☐ **D.** Invasion of the pectoralis major by metastatic cancer
- ☐ **E.** Ipsilateral (same side) inversion of the nipple from cancer of the duct system of the breast

139 A 27-year-old male billiards player received a small-caliber bullet wound to the chest in the region of the third intercostal space, several centimeters to the left of the sternum. The patient is admitted to the emergency department and a preliminary notation of "Beck's triad" is entered on the patient's chart. Which of the following are features of this triad?

- ☐ **A.** There was injury to the left pulmonary artery, left primary bronchus, and esophagus.
- ☐ **B.** The patient has bleeding into the pleural cavity, a collapsed lung, and mediastinal shift to the right side of the thorax.
- ☐ **C.** The patient has a small, quiet heart; decreased pulse pressure; and increased central venous pressure.
- ☐ **D.** The young man is suffering from marked diastolic emptying, dyspnea, and dilation of the aortic arch.
- ☐ **E.** The left lung has collapsed, there is paradoxical respiration, and there is a mediastinal shift of the heart and trachea to the left.

140 A 34-year-old patient had been diagnosed earlier in the week with Guillain-Barré syndrome. He is now in extreme respiratory distress. His thoracic wall contracts and relaxes violently, but there is little movement of the abdominal wall. The degenerative disease has obviously affected the muscle that is most responsible for increasing the vertical dimensions of the thoracic cavity (and pleural cavities). Which of the following is the most likely cause of his disease?

- ☐ **A.** Paralysis of his intercostal muscles and loss of the "bucket handle movement" of his ribs
- ☐ **B.** Generalized intercostal nerve paralysis that resulted in loss of the "pump handle movement" of his ribs
- ☐ **C.** Paralysis of his medial and lateral pectoral nerves, interrupting the function of his pectoralis major muscles, an important accessory muscle of respiration
- ☐ **D.** Paralysis of his sternocleidomastoid muscles
- ☐ **E.** Degeneration of the myelin of his phrenic nerves

141 Two days after the patient's breathing had become assisted by mechanical ventilation, a patient with Guillain-Barré syndrome began experiencing severe cardiac arrhythmia, with perilously slow cardiac contractions, resulting in reduced cardiac output. This most likely resulted from interruption of the contractile stimulus carried by which of the following?

- ☐ **A.** Left vagus nerve
- ☐ **B.** Right phrenic nerve

- ☐ **C.** Preganglionic sympathetic fibers in upper thoracic spinal nerves
- ☐ **D.** Cardiac pain fibers carried by upper thoracic spinal nerves
- ☐ **E.** Ventral horn neurons of spinal cord levels T1 to T4

142 During transesophageal echocardiography (TEE), an ultrasound transducer is placed through the nose or mouth to lie directly behind the heart. The closer a structure is to the transducer, the better the ultrasound image that can be obtained. In TEE, which heart valve can be best visualized?

- ☐ **A.** Tricuspid
- ☐ **B.** Pulmonary
- ☐ **C.** Mitral
- ☐ **D.** Aortic
- ☐ **E.** Valve of the inferior vena cava

ANSWERS

1 D. The aorticopulmonary septum functions to divide the truncus arteriosus and bulbus cordis into the aorta and pulmonary trunk. The septum secundum forms an incomplete separation between the two atria. The septum primum divides the atrium into right and left halves. The bulbar septum is derived from the bulbus cordis and will give rise to the interventricular septum inferior to the aorticopulmonary septum, eventually fusing with it. The endocardial cushions play a role in the division of the AV canal into right and left halves, by causing the AV cushions to approach each other.
GAS 197; GA 88-89

2 A. Laryngeal atresia (congenital high airway obstruction syndrome) is a rare obstruction of the upper fetal airway. Distal to the site of the atresia, the airways dilate, lungs enlarge and become echogenic, the diaphragm flattens or inverts, and fetal ascites and/or hydrops develop. Tracheal atresia is a rare obstruction of the trachea, commonly found with a tracheoesophageal fistula, probably resulting from the unequal division of foregut into esophagus and trachea. Polyhydramnios is an excess of amniotic fluid, often associated with esophageal atresia or tracheoesophageal fistula. Lung hypoplasia is reduced lung volume, often seen in infants with a congenital diaphragmatic hernia. Oligohydramnios, or a decrease in amniotic fluid, is associated with stunted lung development and pulmonary hypoplasia.
GAS 168, 174; GA 80

3 A. Ventricular septal defects account for 25% of congenital heart defects. The most common of these are defects in the membranous portion of the interventricular septum (membranous ventricular septal defects).
GAS 197; GA 90-95

4 A. In a case of transposition of the great arteries, oxygenated blood travels from the left ventricle into the pulmonary trunk, where it will eventually reach the lungs. In contrast, the aorta would be carrying deoxygenated blood into the systemic circulation. A patent ductus arteriosus acts as a shunt between the aorta and pulmonary trunk, allowing oxygenated and deoxygenated blood to mix and therefore allowing some oxygenated blood to reach the tissues. None of the other answer choices would correct this problem; with these structures remaining patent, the body would still not receive sufficient oxygenated blood for survival to be possible.
GAS 197; GA 90-95

5 A. Tetralogy of Fallot is always characterized by four cardiac defects: pulmonary stenosis, ventricular septal defect (VSD), overriding aorta, and these in turn lead to right ventricular hypertrophy. An atrial septal defect (ASD) is characterized by the communication between the two atria. In a case of transposition of the great vessels, the aorta arises from the right ventricle and the pulmonary trunk arises from the left ventricle.
GAS 197; GA 90-95

6 A. Superior malalignment of the subpulmonary infundibulum causes stenosis of the pulmonary trunk. This leads to the four symptoms mentioned and is known as tetralogy of Fallot. A defect in formation of the aorticopulmonary septum is characteristic of transposition of the great arteries. An endocardial cushion defect is associated with membranous ventricular septal defects.
GAS 187-188, 197; GA 90-95

7 B. The murmur at S_2 localizes the defect at an atrioventricular valve. An atrial septal defect causes a diastolic murmur in the tricuspid valve, whereas a ventricular septal defect would cause a pansystolic murmur. Transposition of the great arteries and aortic stenosis will cause a murmur at S_1, and tetralogy of Fallot does not cause a murmur at S_1 or S_2.
GAS 197; GA 90-95

8 C. Down syndrome (more properly called "trisomy 21") is associated with cardiovascular abnormalities such as arrhythmias and atrial and ventricular septal defects. It is also characterized by mental retardation, brachycephaly, flat nasal bridge, upward slant of the palpebral fissure, protruding tongue, simian crease, and clinodactyly of the fifth digit.
GAS 197; GA 90-95

9 A. Tetralogy of Fallot and truncus arteriosus are associated with DiGeorge syndrome (22q11). Transposition of the great arteries is associated with maternal diabetes. ASDs and VSDs are present in individuals with Down syndrome. Coarctation of the aorta is related to Turner syndrome. Marfan syndrome is present in individuals with aortic atresia.
GAS 197; GA 90-95

10 B. Transposition of the great arteries is associated with maternal diabetes. Tetralogy of Fallot and truncus arteriosus are associated with DiGeorge syndrome (22q11). ASDs and VSDs are present in individuals with Down syndrome. Coarctation of the aorta is related to Turner syndrome. Marfan syndrome is present in individuals with aortic atresia.
GAS 197; GA 90-95

11 C. The ductus arteriosus is an embryologic structure that acts as a communication between the pulmonary trunk and the aorta. If it remains patent, the injected contrast medium would flow from the aorta through this communication and into the pulmonary artery. An atrial septal defect is a communication between the atria. Mitral stenosis is a narrowing of the AV valve between the left atrium and left ventricle. The ductus venosus transports blood from the left umbilical vein to the inferior vena cava, bypassing the liver. A ventricular septal defect is a communication between the ventricles.
GAS 197; GA 90-95

12 A. An atrial septal defect (ASD) is a communication between the right and left atria. In the formation of the partition between the two atria, the opening in the foramen secundum, also known as the foramen ovale, typically closes at birth. If it remains patent, an ASD will result. The rest of the structures are not associated with atrial septal defects.
GAS 197; GA 88-95

13 E. Type II alveolar cells are the only cells that produce surfactant.
GAS 163-164; GA 80-82

14 B. An absence of musculature in one half of the diaphragm causes it to protrude into the thoracic cavity forming a pouch into which the abdominal viscera protrude. Pleuropericardial folds are responsible for separating the pericardial cavity from the pleural cavity. Typically, the diaphragm migrates to its position with the fibrous pericardium. The septum transversum is the primordial central tendon of the diaphragm that separates the heart from the liver. The pleuroperitoneal folds form the pleuroperitoneal membranes that separate the pleural cavity from the peritoneal cavity. Absence of any of these would not have anything to do with eventration of the diaphragm.
GAS 253; GA 67

15 C. The anomalies present in this individual are all caused by a coarctation of the aorta. The portion of the aortic arch that is constricted arises from the third, fourth, and sixth pharyngeal arches. The bulbus cordis becomes part of the ventricular system. The ductus arteriosus becomes the ligamentum arteriosum.
GAS 210; GA 110

16 D. The tracheoesophageal septum is a primordial structure that separates the trachea from the esophagus. If this structure fails to develop, a tracheoesophageal fistula will result, in which event the two structures will not separate completely. When the infant attempts to swallow milk, it spills into the esophageal pouch and is regurgitated. The child becomes cyanotic because an insufficient amount of oxygen is reaching the lungs as a result of the malformed trachea.
GAS 211; GA 81-82, 106

17 C. Polyhydramnios is an excess of amniotic fluid, often associated with esophageal atresia or a tracheoesophageal fistula. This abnormality affects fetal ability to swallow the normal amount of amniotic fluid; therefore, excess fluid remains in the amniotic sac. None of the other factors listed has an association with this type of fistula.
GAS 323

18 B. Congenital heart defects are common problems that can be caused by teratogens, such as the rubella virus, or single-gene factors or chromosomal abnormalities.
GAS 197

19 E. Sinus venosus atrial septal defects occur close to the entry of the superior vena cava in the superior portion of the interatrial septum. Ostium secundum atrial septal defects are located near the fossa ovale and encompass both septum primum and septum secun-

dum defects. An ostium primum defect is a less common form of atrial septal defect and is associated with endocardial cushion defects because the septum primum fails to fuse with the endocardial cushions, resulting in a patent foramen primum. An AV canal defect is not a clinically significant type of atrial septal defect. A common atrium is an uncommon type of atrial septal defect in which the interatrial septum is absent.
GAS 186-188; GA 99

20 **A.** Ectopia cordis is a condition in which the heart is located abnormally outside the thoracic cavity, commonly resulting from a failure of fusion of the lateral folds in forming the thoracic wall. This is incompatible with life because of the occurrence of infection, cardiac failure, or hypoxemia. Faulty development of the sinus venosus is related to atrial septal defects that result from deficient absorption of the sinus venosus into the right atrium and/or unusual development of the septum secundum.
GAS 186-188; GA 99

21 **A.** The right horn of the sinus venosus has two divisions: One develops into the sinus venarum, the smooth interior aspect of the right atrial wall; the other half develops into the pulmonary veins. Abnormal septation of the sinus venosus can lead to inappropriate pulmonary connections. Abnormal development of the left sinus horn would present with abnormalities in the coronary sinus, whereas incorrect development of the septum secundum can result in an atrial septal defect but would not be involved with anomalous pulmonary veins. The left sinual horn develops into the coronary sinus, and the right sinual horn is incorporated into the right atrial wall.
GAS 186-188, 253; GA 99

22 **C.** The septum transversum is a thickened layer of mesoderm that gives origin to the central tendon of the diaphragm. It is situated between the thoracic cavity and the omphaloenteric duct. As the lungs grow into the pericardio-peritoneal canal, they give rise to two folds: the pleuroperitoneal and pleuropericardial folds. The pleuroperitoneal folds are responsible for formation of the posterolateral aspect of the diaphragm, and the pleuropericardial folds develop into the fibrous pericardium. The crura provide origin of the dorsal mesentery of the esophagus, whereas the cervical myotomes are responsible for the musculature of the diaphragm. (Note that these are cervical myotomes C3 to C5, the levels of origin of the phrenic nerve.)
GAS 253; GA 67

23 **C.** The fourth aortic arch develops into the aortic arch on the left side and the brachiocephalic and subclavian arteries on the right side of the embryo. Improper development of the arch of the aorta will cause an increased pressure in the subclavian artery and, subsequently, the brachial artery. Similarly, decreased flow through the aorta will lead to a decreased pressure in the femoral artery. The second aortic arch, specifically the dorsal aspect, develops into aspects of the small stapedial artery. The proximal part of the third aortic arch gives rise to the common carotid arteries, which supply the head. The fifth aortic arch is said not to usually develop in human embryos. The proximal part of the sixth aortic arch develops into the left pulmonary artery.
GAS 206-207; GA 106, 115

24 **A.** The left sixth aortic arch is responsible for the development both of the pulmonary arteries and the ductus arteriosus. Without regression of the ductus arteriosus, a patent connection remains between aorta and the pulmonary trunk. The ductus arteriosus often reaches functional closure within 24 hours after birth, whereas anatomic closure and subsequent formation of the ligamentum arteriosum often occur by the twelfth postnatal week.
GAS 197; GA 106

25 **D.** With a patent ductus arteriosus, an abnormal connection persists between the aorta and the pulmonary trunk. Blood leaving the left ventricle of the heart and into the aorta is reshunted back into the left pulmonary artery. This is responsible for the murmur heard during auscultation of the heart. The diversion of blood to the pulmonary arteries causes increased atrial pressure, leading to enlarged, and therefore noticeable, pulmonary arteries on the chest radiograph. The tetralogy of Fallot often presents with a right-to-left shunt of blood flow through the ventricles. It is also associated with pulmonary artery stenosis, right ventricular hypertrophy, interventricular septal defect, and an overriding of the aorta. This condition would not present with a murmur, however. Atrial septal defects are often characterized by a left-to-right shunt of blood, which often presents with dyspnea and abnormal heart sounds. A chest radiograph would not reveal prominent pulmonary arteries in such cases. Both aortic atresia and coarctation of the aorta result in a narrowing of the aorta but would not lead to noticeable prominent pulmonary arteries on the radiograph.
GAS 197; GA 106, 110

26 **E.** A common truncus arteriosus results from failure of separation of the pulmonary trunk and

aorta. Without proper perfusion of the child by oxygenated blood, severe cyanosis will result.
GAS 197; GA 106

27 **B.** The pleuroperitoneal membrane forms the posterolateral aspect of the diaphragm. A defect in this membrane would allow for communication between the upper left abdominal cavity and thoracic cavity and could result in a congenital diaphragmatic hernia. The septum transversum provides origin to the central tendon of the diaphragm but is not involved in herniation of the intestines. The tracheoesophageal septum, laryngotracheal groove, and oligohydramnios are not associated with development of the diaphragm.
GAS 253; GA 67

28 **A.** When closing a ventricular septal defect, it is important not to suture over the right bundle branch because it carries the stimulating impulse from the atrioventricular node to the apex of the heart through the right bundle of His. Following the course of the right bundle branch on the interventricular septum, the impulses travel along the septomarginal trabeculation (moderator band) and Purkinje fibers, leading to ventricular contraction. The right coronary artery passes dorsally in the atrioventricular groove; therefore, it does not pass through the interventricular septum. The anterior interventricular (left anterior descending) coronary artery is superficial to the IV septum on the anterior surface of the heart. The tricuspid valve and aortic valve are not directly associated with the interventricular septum.
GAS 187, 197; GA 91-93

29 **A.** Esophageal atresia is often the result of an incomplete division of the tracheoesophageal septum, thus causing an absence of, or blind ending of, the esophagus. Though similar to an esophageal atresia, a tracheoesophageal fistula is an atypical connection between the trachea and the esophagus.
GAS 168-171; GA 102-104

30 **A.** In a tracheotomy, an incision is made at the level of the sixth cervical vertebra, near the cricoid cartilage. The left brachiocephalic vein passes across the trachea immediately anterior to the brachiocephalic trunk. This vein is the most superficial structure and thus the most likely to be damaged. The left common carotid artery, the vagus nerve, and the phrenic nerve are not situated near the midline incision of the tracheotomy. The thoracic duct is located posterior and lateral to the esophagus and the trachea and is not likely to be damaged during a tracheotomy, other than the intentional opening made in it.
GAS 806, 1009, 1065, 1080; GA 102-104

31 **A.** The phrenic nerve has a path between the anterior medial aspect of the lung and the mediastinum. Along the path of the nerve, it courses over the hilum of the lung. The vagus nerves run posterior to the heart as they give off branches to the cardiac plexus upon the trachea near the carina. The recurrent laryngeal nerves arise from the vagus nerves before the vagus nerves pass behind the hila of the lungs.
GAS 215; GA 101, 104

32 **C.** The left recurrent laryngeal nerve passes beneath the ligamentum arteriosum and then loops superiorly toward the tracheoesophageal groove, medial to the arch of the aorta.
GAS 163-164, 211-216; GA 101, 104

33 **C.** During mastectomy procedures, three superficial nerves are susceptible to ligation or laceration: the long thoracic nerve, intercostobrachial nerve, and thoracodorsal nerve. In the event of injury to the long thoracic nerve, the patient complains of an inability to fully abduct the humerus above the horizontal. The serratus anterior (supplied by the long thoracic nerve) is necessary to elevate, rotate, and abduct the scapula, to facilitate abduction of the humerus above the shoulder. Because the patient does not indicate any loss of medial rotation or adduction of the humerus, ligation or injury of the thoracodorsal nerve can be eliminated.
GAS 175; GA 371

34 **A.** The dorsal root ganglia contain nerve cell bodies for general somatic afferent and general visceral afferent neuronal processes. Pain localized on the chest wall is transmitted back to the CNS via sensory fibers.
GAS 134-137; GA 120-121

35 **D.** The lateral horns, or intermediolateral cell columns, contain the cell bodies of preganglionic neurons of the sympathetic system. Spinal cord segments T1 to T4 are often associated with the upper limbs and thoracic organs; the autonomic neurons in spinal cord segments T5 to T9 usually correlate with innervation of organs in the abdominal cavity, specifically organs derived from the foregut.
GAS 221-222; GA 101, 120-121

36 **D.** The cardiopulmonary splanchnic (or thoracic visceral) nerves are responsible for carrying the cardiac sympathetic efferent fibers from the sympathetic

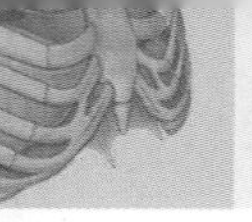

ganglia to the thoracic viscera and afferent fibers for pain from these organs. The vagus nerve is responsible for carrying parasympathetic fibers. The greater and lesser splanchnic nerves carry sympathetic preganglionic fibers to the abdomen. T1 to T4 ventral rami receive sensory fibers for pain, carried initially by the cardiopulmonary nerves, en route to their respective final destination.
GAS 221-222; GA 101, 120-121

37 **C.** The vagus nerve is the only nerve responsible for parasympathetic innervation of the lungs. The phrenic nerve and intercostal nerves are somatic nerves and are not involved in innervation of the heart or lungs. The greater thoracic splanchnic and lesser thoracic splanchnic nerves are responsible for carrying preganglionic sympathetic fibers for the innervation of the abdomen. They also carry afferents for pain from the abdomen.
GAS 211-222; GA 82

38 **C.** There is close proximity between the aortopulmonary window and the left recurrent laryngeal nerve. A mass within or adjacent to this window is thus likely to compress the left recurrent laryngeal nerve, resulting in the hoarseness for the patient. The greater and lesser thoracic splanchnic nerves arise inferior and posterior to the aortopulmonary window and are thus unlikely to be compressed. The thoracic splanchnic nerves are not involved in the innervation of the larynx. Though the vagus is responsible for innervation of the larynx, it passes dorsal to the area of the aortopulmonary window and is not likely to be compressed.
GAS 211-222; GA 101,104

39 **C.** The intercostobrachial nerve is responsible for innervation of the skin on the medial surface of the arm. The ulnar nerve is responsible for cutaneous sensation on the medial aspect of the hand, and the axillary nerve innervates the lateral aspect of the shoulder. The lateral cutaneous branch of T4 innervates the dermatome corresponding to the nipple and areola and also supplies the medial aspect of the axilla. The long thoracic nerve provides motor supply to the serratus anterior and is not involved in cutaneous innervation of the axillary region. Only the intercostobrachial nerve is responsible for sensory supply of the lateral aspect of the axilla.
GAS 703; GA 63, 70

40 **B.** Pericarditis is an inflammation of the pericardium and often causes a pericardial friction rub, with the surface of the pericardium becoming gradually coarser. Because the phrenic nerve is solely responsible for innervation of the pericardium, it would transmit the pain fibers radiating from the pericardial friction rub. The phrenic nerve contains sensory nerve fibers from C3 to C5, spinal nerve levels that also supply the skin of the shoulder area; therefore, pain carried by the phrenic nerve may be referred to the shoulder.
GAS 179; GA 86-87

41 **C.** The intercostobrachial nerve is the lateral cutaneous branch of the second intercostal nerve. It serves a sensory function both in the thoracic wall and medial aspect of the arm. The phrenic nerve arises from spinal nerves C3 to C5 and innervates the diaphragm. This nerve has no branches that pass into the arm. The vagus nerve is CN X and is a major supplier of autonomic function to the gut, up to the left colic flexure, and also provides some autonomic motor and sensory supply to organs in the head, neck, and thorax. The greater thoracic splanchnic nerve originates in the thorax from the sympathetic chain at the levels of T5 to T9 and innervates abdominal structures. The suprascapular nerve originates from the upper trunk of the brachial plexus and receives fibers primarily from C5 and C6. It innervates the supraspinatus and the infraspinatus.
GAS 213-222; GA 108-109

42 **D.** Ventral rami contain both sensory and motor fibers and also sympathetics to the body wall, supplying all areas of the body wall except for tissues of the back. In this case both sensory fibers (numbness) and sympathetics (anhydrosis) are disrupted at the midaxillary line; therefore, cutaneous ventral rami is the only correct choice. The dorsal roots carry somatic and visceral sensory information from the periphery. Because only cutaneous sensation is lost the deficit cannot be the dorsal roots. The ventral roots of the spinal cord carry only somatic and visceral efferents. Because no motor functions are disrupted, this is not the correct answer. The branches of dorsal rami provide cutaneous and postural muscle innervation to the back and thus have no relation to the midaxillary line. The rami communicans are components of the sympathetic nervous system and are not involved with general somatic afferent sensation.
GAS 63-64; GA 120-121

43 **B.** General visceral afferents are nerve fibers that carry sensation from organs, in this case pain from the abdominal aorta. These fibers get mixed with general somatic afferents in the dorsal roots. This is the phenomenon of "referred pain." The dorsal root ganglia (or their counterparts associated with sensory cranial nerves) contain the cell bodies associated with

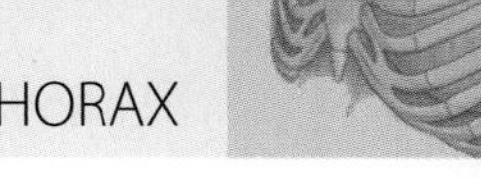

all sensory fibers from the body, including somatic and visceral sensation.
GAS 63-64; GA 120-121

44 **B.** The anterior and lateral cutaneous branches of the fourth intercostal nerves provide the sensory and sympathetic supply to the areolae and nipples. Anterior cutaneous branches of the second and third intercostal nerves innervate the skin above the nipples and areolae. Lateral pectoral nerves provide motor innervation to the pectoralis major and minor, not sensory supply. Ventral primary rami of the second thoracic spinal nerves provide muscle innervation and sensory innervation above the nipples and areolae and sensory fibers for the medial side of the arm.
GAS 130, 137; GA 63, 361, 371

45 **C.** The left recurrent laryngeal nerve passes superiorly in the tracheoesophageal groove after looping around the aorta. The compression of this nerve and compression of the esophagus against the trachea would result in the presenting symptoms. The right recurrent laryngeal nerve loops around the right subclavian artery before passing toward the larynx and therefore does not descend into the thorax. The left vagus nerve courses posterior to the hilum of the lung, after it has already given off its left recurrent laryngeal branch at the level of the aortic arch; therefore, compression of this nerve would not result in the presenting symptoms. The greater thoracic splanchnic nerve arises from sympathetic chain ganglia at levels T5 to T9 and therefore would not cause the presenting symptoms. The phrenic nerve innervates the diaphragm; compression of this nerve would not result in the presenting symptoms.
GAS 211-215; GA 108-109

46 **A.** The patient's chief complaint is pain upon swallowing. With a dilated left atrium, the most probable structure being compressed is the esophagus. The esophagus descends into the abdomen immediately posterior to the left atrium below the level of the tracheal carina. The root of the lung is the site of junction at the hilum where the pulmonary arteries, veins, and bronchi enter or leave. The lung root is not so intimately associated with the esophagus and would not be associated with pain during swallowing. The trachea ends and bifurcates above the level of the left atrium and therefore would be unaffected by a dilated left atrium. The inferior vena cava ascends from the abdomen to the right atrium and the superior vena cava is quite anterior in position. Neither of these veins is closely related to the esophagus or the left atrium.
GAS 211-215; GA 108-110

47 **E.** The esophageal hiatus in the diaphragm is one of four openings associated with the diaphragm. It is located at the level of T10 and allows the esophagus to pass through the thoracic cavity into the abdominal cavity. It is the most inferior of four esophageal constrictions. The pharyngoesophageal junction is the site at which the pharynx ends and the esophagus begins in the neck, at the level of the sixth cervical vertebra. It is the first and the most superior of the esophageal constrictions. There are no constrictions found at the level of the superior thoracic aperture; this is the opening for passage of the structures passing from the neck into the thorax. The esophagus descends posterior to the arch of the aorta. It is at this level that the second of the esophageal constrictions is found. The third constriction occurs as the esophagus passes posteriorly to the left main bronchus.
GAS 127, 211-217; GA 108-110

48 **D.** The apex of the heart is located in the left fifth intercostal space, about $3\frac{1}{2}$ inches to the left of the sternum. When this area of the heart is palpated, any pulsations would be generated by throbbing of the apex of the heart against the thoracic wall. This is also the location for performing auscultation (listening) of the mitral valve, not associated with palpation. The right atrium is located to the right of the sternum. The left atrium is located on the posterior aspect of the heart, thus no direct palpation is realized. The aortic arch would be located posterior to the manubrium of the sternum, above the second intercostal space.
GAS 180; GA 83-87

49 **A.** These components of the heart are readily viewed in a plain radiograph of the thorax. It is important to understand the spatial arrangement of the heart as it rests in the thorax. The conus region of the right ventricle is located on the most anterior aspect of the heart, thus it is the most anterior portion of the heart within the thorax. The apex of the left ventricle is also located anteriorly, but it is located lateral to the sternum and occupies little area compared with the right ventricle. The left ventricle is positioned on the left lateral side and slightly posterior position in the thorax. The right atrium is located on the right lateral side of the heart. The anterior margin of the left atrium is positioned posteriorly in the thorax.
GAS 180-185; GA 83-87

50 **A.** The left fifth intercostal space, just below the left nipple, is typically the location to listen to the mitral valve. Although the mitral valve is located at the fourth intercostal space just to the left of the sternum, the sound is best realized "downstream" from

the valve. The right lower part of the body of the sternum is the location of the tricuspid valve. The right second intercostal space near the lateral border of the sternum is the typical location of auscultation of the aortic valve. It is difficult to hear valvular sounds through bone, so auscultating directly over the middle of the manubrium is not a good choice. The left second intercostal space near the lateral border of the sternum is the site chosen typically for auscultation of the pulmonary valve.
GAS 197, 227; GA 83-87, 100

51 **B.** The great cardiac vein (anterior interventricular vein) takes a pathway initially beside the anterior interventricular coronary artery (left anterior descending: LAD) in its course, finally terminating in the coronary sinus when it is joined by the oblique vein of the left atrium (of Marshall). This vein must be protected when performing bypass procedures. The middle cardiac vein is located on the posterior aspect of the heart, but it also drains into the coronary sinus. The small cardiac vein drains blood along the same path as the right marginal branch. The anterior cardiac veins drain the blood from the right ventricle anteriorly and drain directly into the right atrium, and are not associated with the anterior interventricular artery.
GAS 198; GA 88, 91, 96

52 **B.** The anterior interventricular artery supplies the right and left ventricles and anterior two thirds of the IV septum. The right marginal artery supplies the right ventricle and apex of the heart; therefore, it does not supply the left ventricle. The left coronary circumflex artery supplies the left atrium and left ventricle; it courses posteriorly in, or near to, the coronary sulcus and supplies the posterior portion of the left ventricle and left atrium. The artery to the SA node is a branch of the right coronary artery and does not supply the left ventricle. The posterior interventricular (posterior descending) artery arises from the right coronary artery in 67% of people (this is referred to as a right dominant pattern) and supplies the posterior aspect of both ventricles and the posterior third of the interventricular septum.
GAS 192-196; GA 96-98

53 **E.** The anterior interventricular artery arises from the left coronary artery. If there is occlusion in the right coronary artery, the anterior interventricular artery will still have normal blood flow. The right marginal artery branches from the right coronary artery; therefore, if there is occlusion of the right coronary artery, flow from the marginal artery will be compromised. The AV nodal artery is supplied by the coronary artery that crosses the crux of the heart posteriorly. If this artery arises from the right coronary, supply to the AV node might be reduced, depending upon collateral supply. The SA nodal artery is supplied by the right coronary artery in 55% of the population (only 35% from the left); inasmuch as it is stated that the patient is right coronary dominant, it would be predicted that the SA nodal artery will not have normal blood flow.
GAS 192-196; GA 96-98

54 **D.** Because the patient is left coronary artery dominant, if there is 70% to 80% occlusion of the left coronary, there will be deficiencies in flow both in the anterior descending and circumflex coronary arteries. No possibility is available for collateral flow from the posterior descending interventricular artery, for it too would be derived from the left coronary, by way of the circumflex artery. If the patient does not undergo surgery to remove or bypass the occlusion, he will be unable to have any substantial type of collateral circulation between the two major branches of the left coronary. The branches of the coronary arteries are *not* end arteries, and there *are* anastomoses between them. The papillary muscles of the tricuspid valve would not be affected with left coronary artery occlusion. The blood supply to the SA node would not be inadequate. The blood supply of the region of the AV node might or might not be adequate, for it could still be supplied by a branch of the right coronary artery.
GAS 192-196; GA 96-98

55 **A.** The mitral valve corresponds to the S_1 heart sound produced during systole. The aortic and pulmonary valves correspond to the S_2 heart sound produced during diastole. The tricuspid valve also corresponds with the S_1 heart sound. The aortic valve, however, corresponds with the S_2 sound, so this answer would be incorrect.
GAS 197; GA 100

56 **C.** The interventricular septum is intimately involved with the tricuspid valve on the right side, via the muscular connections of the septomarginal trabeculum (moderator band) to the anterior papillary muscle. Therefore, if the electrical system of the heart is disrupted, as with a myocardial infarction in the upper portion of the muscular septum, the innervation of the interventricular septum will be compromised and the tricuspid valve will be directly affected. None of the other valves are directly involved with the interventricular septum.
GAS 200-202; GA 96-98

57 **B.** The pulmonary valve is associated with the S_2 heart sound produced in diastole. A splitting in the S_2 sound indicates that the aortic and pulmonary valves are not closing simultaneously and would correlate with a possible defect in this valve. The mitral valve is associated with the S_1 heart sound, produced in systole; therefore, it cannot be defective if only the S_2 sound is involved. The aortic valve is associated with the S_2 heart sound, but the mitral valve is not (as stated earlier); therefore, this answer cannot be correct. The tricuspid valve is associated with the S_1 heart sound and therefore is not associated with the occurrence of an abnormal S_2 heart sound.
GAS 197; GA 98

58 **C.** The bundle of His is a collection of specialized cardiac muscle cells that carry electrical activity to the right and left bundle branches. Because both ventricles are affected, this is the logical site of injury, for this bundle leads to the bundle branches supplying both ventricles. An injury either to the right or left bundle branch would affect only one ventricle. Terminal Purkinje fibers transmit the electrical activity to the greater sections of the ventricles, yet dysfunction in the terminal part of the conduction system would affect only a small section of one ventricle, not both. The atrioventricular node is a group of specialized cardiac muscle cells that serve to decrease the rate of conduction to the ventricles and is located in the region deep to the septal wall of the right atrium. The posterior internodal pathway is in the roof of the right atrium and is not involved here.
GAS 200-202; GA 99

59 **D.** The artery of the conus is given off from the right coronary artery and winds around the conus arteriosus. The conus region is the superior part of the right ventricle that tapers into a cone (infundibulum) where the pulmonary valve leads into the pulmonary trunk. This conus artery supplies the upper portion of the anterior right ventricle and usually has a small anastomotic connection with the anterior interventricular (left anterior descending) branch of the left coronary artery. The circumflex artery supplies the left atrium and ventricle and does not supply the right ventricle except when the posterior interventricular (posterior descending) artery arises from the circumflex, or in unusual cases in which the circumflex passes to the surface of the right ventricle. The anterior interventricular artery supplies the right and left ventricles and the anterior two thirds of the IV septum. It is given off by the left coronary artery and does not specifically supply the upper portion of the right ventricle. The posterior interventricular artery supplies the right and left ventricles and the posterior third of the IV septum. It does not supply the upper portion of the right ventricle.
GAS 192-198; GA 96-98

60 **D.** The atrioventricular bundle of His is a strand of specialized cardiac muscle fibers that arises from the atrioventricular node and passes through the right fibrous trigone. The right fibrous trigone (central fibrous body) is a dense area of connective tissue that interconnects the mitral, tricuspid, and aortic valve rings. After reaching the upper portion of the muscular interventricular septum, the bundle of His splits into right and left bundle branches. The bundle of Bachmann is a collection of fibers running from the sinoatrial node to the left atrium and is the only collection of conducting fibers to innervate the left atrium. Finally, the posterior internodal pathway, also known as Thorel's pathway, is the principal pathway of electrical activation between the sinoatrial node and atrioventricular node in humans.
GAS 200-202; GA 99

61 **A.** The sternocostal surface of the heart consists mostly of the right ventricle. Therefore, an anterior injury to the thorax would mostly likely first affect the right ventricle because it is adjacent to the deep surface of the sternum.
GAS 180-185; GA 83-86

62 **D.** The tissues affected in this case, the interventricular septum and anterior ventricular wall, are mostly supplied by the proximal portion of the left anterior interventricular artery. If the circumflex artery were blocked, the left atrium and left ventricle would be affected (in a right coronary dominant heart). If the right coronary artery were occluded, again assuming right coronary dominance, it would affect the right atrium, the sinoatrial and atrioventricular nodes, part of the posterior left ventricle, and the posterior part of the interventricular septum. If the left coronary artery (LCA) were blocked, most of the left atrium and left ventricle, the anterior two thirds of the interventricular septum, and the area of bifurcation of the bundle of His would be affected. If the posterior interventricular artery were occluded, it would affect the right and left ventricles and the posterior third of the interventricular septum. The circumflex and the anterior interventricular arteries are branches of the LCA, and the posterior interventricular artery is most commonly a branch of the terminal segment of the right coronary artery.
GAS 192-198; GA 96-98

63 **C.** A "left coronary dominant" circulation means, most simply, that the left coronary artery (LCA) pro-

vides the posterior interventricular artery as a terminal branch of the coronary circumflex. The posterior aspect of the heart is composed primarily of the left ventricle and is supplied by the posterior interventricular branch. The artery of the conus supplies the right ventricular free wall. If the right coronary artery were occluded (in a right coronary dominant heart), it would affect the right atrium, right ventricle, the sinoatrial and atrioventricular nodes, the posterior part of the interventricular septum, and part of the posterior aspect of the left ventricle. The right acute marginal artery supplies the inferior margin of the right ventricle. The left diagonal arteries arise most commonly from the anterior interventricular (left anterior descending) artery but can also arise as branches of the left coronary or the circumflex.
GAS 192-198; GA 96-98

64 **B.** The eustachian valve is an embryologic remnant of the valve of the inferior vena cava and is not a functional valve. The tricuspid valve is located below the inferior vena cava between the right atrium and right ventricle. The fossa ovalis is an embryonic remnant of the septum primum of the interatrial septum, located interatrially. The Thebesian valve is a semicircular fold at the orifice of the coronary sinus.
GAS 186-187; GA 90

65 **A.** The crista terminalis is a muscular ridge that runs from the opening of the superior vena cava to the inferior vena cava. This ridge provides the path taken by the posterior internodal pathway (of Thorel) between the sinoatrial and atrioventricular nodes. The crista also provides the origin of the pectinate muscles of the right auricle. The tricuspid valve is located below the inferior vena cava, between the right atrium and right ventricle. The eustachian valve is an embryologic remnant of the valve of the inferior vena cava. The ostium of the coronary sinus is located between the right atrioventricular orifice and the inferior vena cava.
GAS 186-187; GA 90

66 **B.** During pericardiocentesis, the needle is inserted below the xiphoid process, or in the left fifth intercostal space in the midclavicular line. The most effective way of draining the pericardium is by penetrating the thoracic wall at its lowest point anatomically, hence the third intercostal space would be too cranial in position. The sixth and seventh intercostal spaces are locations that are not used clinically because of the increased likelihood of injury to the pleura or lungs and other complications.
GAS 177-180; GA 86-87

67 **C.** The anterior interventricular (left anterior descending) artery lies anteriorly and to the left and descends vertically to the left toward the apex. It can be more easily injured by a transverse incision of the pericardium, which would cross perpendicular to this artery. The auricular appendage of the left atrium is located posteriorly; therefore, it would not be injured in an anterior longitudinal incision. The coronary sinus is between the right atrioventricular orifice and the inferior vena cava and would not be affected. The left phrenic nerve lies between the heart and the left lung and is too deep to be injured in this incision. The left sympathetic trunk is also too posterior to be injured.
GAS 176-185; GA 96-98, 108-109

68 **D.** A finger passing through the transverse pericardial sinus passes directly behind the great arteries exiting the heart, allowing the surgeon to rather easily place a vascular clamp upon the pulmonary trunk and ascending aorta. The other vessels listed are not readily accessible by way of the transverse sinus.
GAS 177-180; GA 86-87

69 **A.** The middle cardiac veins run parallel with the posterior interventricular (posterior descending) artery and drains directly into the coronary sinus. The great cardiac vein parallels the anterior interventricular artery and the small cardiac veins pass parallel with the right marginal artery. The anterior cardiac veins are several small veins that drain directly into the right atrium. The coronary sinus is a wide venous channel that runs from left to right in the posterior part of the coronary groove.
GAS 196-200; GA 96

70 **D.** The left coronary artery bifurcates into the anterior interventricular artery (left anterior descending: LAD) and the coronary circumflex branch. The circumflex branch gives off the left marginal branch, which supplies the lateral wall (obtuse margin) of the left ventricle. The anterior part of the interventricular septum is supplied by the LAD. The diaphragmatic surface of the right ventricle is supplied by the posterior descending artery and the right marginal, a branch of the right coronary artery. The infundibulum, also known as the conus arteriosus, is the outflow portion of the right ventricle. The posterior part of the interventricular septum is supplied by the posterior descending artery, in most cases a branch of the right coronary artery.
GAS 192-198; GA 96-98

71 **C.** The atrioventricular (AV) node is most commonly supplied by a branch of the right coronary artery. This branch arises at the crux of the heart (the

point of junction of all four cardiac chambers posteriorly); this is the location of the occlusion. The right atrium is supplied by the right coronary artery, which additionally supplies the sinoatrial node. The left marginal artery supplies the lateral wall of the left ventricle. The anterior portion of the interventricular septum is supplied by the anterior interventricular artery.
GAS 200-203; GA 96-98

72 **C.** The first heart sound is caused by the closure of the tricuspid and mitral valves. The second heart sound is caused by the closure of the aortic and pulmonary valves.
GAS 197, 229; GA 100

73 **A.** The second heart sound is caused by the closure of the aortic and pulmonary valves. The first sound by the heart is caused by the closure of the tricuspid and mitral valves.
GAS 197, 229; GA 100

74 **D.** The first septal perforating branch of the anterior interventricular artery (left anterior descending: LAD) is the first branch of the LAD that supplies the conducting tissue of the heart; it passes directly to the point of bifurcation of the common atrioventricular bundle of His. The other vessels listed have no anatomic relation to the area of ischemia.
GAS 192-198; GA 96-98

75 **B.** The superior vena cava empties into the right atrium on the superior aspect of the heart; it is not directly palpable from the oblique sinus. The oblique sinus is a blind cul-de-sac providing access to the inferior vena cava, the posterior wall of the left atrium, right atrium, and the right and left pulmonary veins.
GAS 176-179

76 **D.** Cardiac tamponade is characterized by hypotension, tachycardia, muffled heart sounds, and jugular vein distention. Bleeding into the pericardial cavity would muffle the heart sounds because of the increased distance between the chest wall and the heart, leading to "distant" heart sounds. When the effusion is particularly severe, the heart may take on a "water bottle" appearance on an anterior-posterior radiograph.
GAS 176-179; GA 86-87

77 **E.** "Right coronary dominant circulation" refers simply to the fact that the right coronary artery provides origin for the posterior interventricular (posterior descending) coronary artery. In such cases, it provides supply for the sinoatrial and atrioventricular nodes. It might be anticipated that right coronary blockage could result in dysfunction of the atrioventricular node, if collateral supply is poor or absent. The LAD, circumflex, and left marginal are all branches of the left coronary artery. The right marginal artery marginal is a branch of the right coronary artery.
GAS 192-198; GA 96-98

78 **D.** The chordae tendineae are fibrous cords that connect papillary muscles to valve leaflets. The restraint provided by these cords on the valve leaflets prevents the prolapse of the mitral valve cusps into the left atrium. The crista terminalis is a ridge that runs from the opening of the inferior vena cava to the superior vena cava. Trabeculae carneae are irregular ridges of myocardium that are present within the ventricles.
GAS 187-188; GA 90-93

79 **D.** The correct path that leads to the right ventricle for the lead of the pacemaker is the brachiocephalic vein (could be right or left; pacemakers are more commonly placed on the left so would be left brachiocephalic vein), superior vena cava, right atrium, tricuspid valve, and right ventricle.
GAS 179-185; GA 86-87

80 **A.** Mitral stenosis leads to left atrial dilation, which can exert a compressive effect on the esophagus. The pulmonary valve is located between the outflow tract of the right ventricle and the pulmonary trunk. The aortic valve is located between the left ventricle and the aorta. Anterior interventricular (left anterior descending) and posterior interventricular (posterior descending) arterial occlusions can cause a myocardial infarction, but not dysphagia. In the normal position of the heart the left atrium lies most posteriorly. Therefore, a stenosis of the mitral valve (atrioventricular valve between left atrium and left ventricle) would lead to enlargement of the left atrium, which would in turn impinge upon the esophagus. A stenosis of the pulmonary valve would have no effect upon the esophagus because of the anterior position of the pulmonary trunk in the thorax. Regurgitation through any valve will ultimately decrease systemic blood flow. An occlusion of a coronary artery will lead to ischemia and possibly myocardial infarction.
GAS 190-197; GA 86-87, 108, 110

81 **C.** The SA node, the primary pacemaker of the heart, is a mass of specialized cardiac cells within the myocardium at the upper end of the crista terminalis, near the opening of the superior vena cava into the right atrium. The AV node is at the junction of the coronary sinus and the right atrium upon the right fibrous trigone (central fibrous body). The eustachian

valve directs blood from the inferior vena cava and through the right atrium toward the tricuspid valve ostium. The interatrial septum is located between the left and right atria. The septomarginal trabeculum (moderator band) arises from the muscular portion of the interventricular septum and passes to the base of the anterior papillary muscle in the right ventricle. The moderator band carries the right bundle branch of the conduction system just beneath its endocardial layer.
GAS 200-203; GA 99

82 **D.** The tricuspid valve is the atrioventricular valve located between the right atrium and right ventricle. An incompetent valve would allow blood to regurgitate into the right atrium during systole and subsequently raise pressure in the venous system, increasing capillary pressure and causing edema. A regurgitation of blood into the pulmonary trunk would be a result of an incompetent pulmonary valve. Regurgitation of blood from the left ventricle back into the left atrium is a result of prolapse of the mitral valve. There is no direct anatomic relationship between the tricuspid valve and the ascending aorta. Blood would pool in the left ventricle in the event of aortic valve incompetence.
GAS 187-188; GA 90-91

83 **C.** To avoid damaging the lungs, a chest tube should be placed below the level of the lungs, in the costodiaphragmatic recess. Such a point of entrance for the tube would be the eighth or ninth intercostal space. At the midclavicular line, the costodiaphragmatic recess is localized between intercostal spaces 6 and 8, at the midaxillary line between 8 and 10, and at the paravertebral line between ribs 10 and 12.
GAS 157-167, 230-231; GA 72-75

84 **C.** The parietal pleura is innervated by the intercostal nerves and is very sensitive to pain, in this case being somatic innervation. Therefore, the parietal pleura is the deepest layer that must be anesthetized to reduce pain during aspiration or chest tube placement.
GAS 157-167; GA 108-109

85 **A.** The right main bronchus is the shorter, wider, and more vertical primary bronchus. Therefore, this is most often the location that foreign objects will likely be lodged. The left primary bronchus is not as vertical and therefore does not present the path of least resistance. (It must be understood, however, that in some cases of aspiration, the foreign body can pass into the left primary bronchus rather than the right bronchus!) The carina is a ridge separating the openings of left and right bronchi, the "fork in the road," so to speak. The trachea is a tubular structure supported by incomplete cartilaginous rings, and the likelihood that an object will be lodged there is minimal. It is unlikely that a foreign object would descend so far as to obstruct a tertiary bronchus, although this could happen.
GAS 157-172; GA 72-85

86 **D.** Contraction of the diaphragm (descent) pulls the dome inferiorly, increasing the vertical dimension of the thorax. This is the most important factor in inspiration for increasing the internal pulmonary volume and concomitantly decreasing intrathoracic pressure. The contraction of intercostal muscles is usually involved in forced inspiration, resulting in increases in the transverse and anteroposterior dimensions of the thoracic cavity.
GAS 157-160; GA 66-67

87 **B.** The horizontal fissure of the right lung is a fissure separating the superior lobe from the middle lobe. It usually extends medially from the oblique fissure at the midaxillary line to the sternum, along the lower border of the fourth rib. The apex of the right lung reaches to a level above the clavicle and is therefore superior to the stab wound in the fourth costal cartilage. The other answers are related to features of the left lung, which is not addressed in the question.
GAS 157-172; GA 74-82

88 **C.** The patient's symptoms are all indicative of inflammatory breast cancer. Common symptoms include inversion of the nipple and dimpling of the overlying skin, changes that are due to the retraction of the suspensory ligaments (of Cooper). Intraductal cancerous tumors show symptoms including breast enlargement, breast lump, breast pain, and nipple discharge. The other answers are not cancerous conditions.
GAS 138-139; GA 63

89 **C.** The inferior tracheobronchial nodes are also known as the carinal nodes and are located on the inferior aspect of the carina, the site of bifurcation of the trachea. The pulmonary nodes lie on secondary bronchi. The bronchopulmonary (hilar) nodes run along the primary bronchi. The superior tracheobronchial nodes are at the junction of the bronchi and the trachea. The paratracheal nodes run along the trachea.
GAS 138-139; GA 71

90 **B.** The superior lobar bronchus is one of the divisions of the right main bronchus. This bronchus branches into apical, anterior, and posterior tertiary bronchi.
GAS 163-171; GA 71

91 D. Lymphatic drainage of the breast is typically to the axillary nodes, more specifically to the anterior (pectoral) nodes. Lymphatic vessels from the pectoral nodes continue into the central axillary nodes, the drainage of which passes farther into the apical node, just inferior to the clavicle in the deltopectoral triangle. From these nodes lymph passes to the "sentinel," or scalene, nodes and the subclavian lymph trunk. The lateral and posterior axillary nodes do not normally receive lymph drainage from the breast but do receive lymph from the upper limb. (This is the reason for the edema of the upper limb that occurs after a mastectomy, in which there may be a total removal of axillary lymph nodes.)
GAS 138-139; GA 71

92 A. Increased arterial pressure in the upper limbs (as demonstrated in the brachial artery) and decreased pressure in the lower limbs (as demonstrated in the femoral artery) are common symptoms of coarctation of the aorta. Other symptoms include tortuous and enlarged blood vessels above the coarctation and an increased risk of cerebral hemorrhage. This condition of coarctation occurs when the aorta is abnormally constricted during development. The patient does not complain of respiratory distress, so cor pulmonale would not likely be the underlying condition. Dissection of the right common iliac artery would not result in nosebleed or headache. Obstruction of the superior vena cava would not account for decreased femoral pulse. A pulmonary embolism will not present with these findings.
GAS 210; GA 110

93 D. The diagnosis for these symptoms is coarctation of the aorta. This condition occurs when the aorta is abnormally constricted. One of the cardinal signs is a characteristic rib notching. "Notching" of the ribs is due to the reversal of direction of blood flow through the anterior intercostal branches of the internal thoracic artery, as these usually small arteries carry collateral arterial blood flow to the lower thoracic portion of the aorta inferior to the coarctation. Enlargement and vibration of the intercostal arteries against the rib results in erosion ("notching") of the subcostal grooves, which is visible on radiography.
GAS 210; GA 110

94 C. The long thoracic nerve arises from the C5, C6, and C7 spinal nerves and innervates the serratus anterior muscle. Injury of this nerve will result in a characteristic winged scapula. A is the lateral pectoral nerve, which innervates the pectoralis major muscle. B is the suprascapular nerve, which innervates the supraspinatus and infraspinatus muscles. D is the thoracodorsal nerve, which innervates latissimus dorsi. E is the lower subscapular nerve that innervates the lower part of the subscapularis muscle and the teres major.
GAS 690, 704, 768; GA 361, 370-371

95 B. The superior margin of the manubrium is characterized by the jugular notch. Laterally are the sternoclavicular joints and the articulations of the first ribs with the manubrium. The second pair of ribs articulates with the sternum at the sternal angle, the junction of the manubrium with the body of the sternum.
GAS 144-147; GA 58-61

96 B. The thoracic duct is important in lymph drainage of the entire body with the exception of the upper right quadrant. The thoracic duct ascends between the aorta and azygos vein behind the esophagus. Dilation of the esophagus here in the lower thorax can compress the thoracic duct, leading to impairment of lymphatic drainage and resultant edema.
GAS 219-220; GA 71

97 C. The anterior intercostal arteries anastomose with the posterior intercostal arteries. Ligation of the anterior arteries would not affect the supply of the intercostal spaces because the posterior arteries would provide collateral arterial supply. Branches of the musculophrenic artery provide supply for the lower seventh, eighth, and ninth intercostal spaces. The superior epigastric artery passes into the rectus sheath of the anterior abdominal wall. The lateral thoracic artery arises from the second part of the axillary artery, and the thoracodorsal artery is a branch of the subscapular artery, a branch of the third part of the axillary artery.
GAS 151-153; GA 68

98 D. The thymus lies in the superior mediastinum and extends upward into the neck, especially in the young. A midline tumor of this gland can compress the left brachiocephalic vein. The subclavian vein is distal or lateral to this location, and the thymus gland would not likely impinge upon it. The internal jugular veins are located superior and lateral to the position of the thymus gland. A midline tumor is more likely to cause compression of the left brachiocephalic vein, which crosses the midline, than the right brachiocephalic vein, which is not located in the midline.
GAS 206; GA 12, 102

99 B. The parietal pleura can be divided regionally into costal, diaphragmatic, mediastinal, and cervical portions, depending upon local topographic relations. Another name for the cervical pleura is the cupula. This forms the dome of the plura, projecting into the

neck above the first rib and corresponding to the area of injury. The costal pleura lines the internal surfaces of the ribs and intercostal spaces. The mediastinal pleura lies between the lungs and the organs in the mediastinum. The right primary bronchus and upper lobe bronchus are not in the vicinity of the right clavicle or first rib.
GAS 158-162; GA 73-79

100 **B.** The right primary bronchus is shorter, wider, and more vertical than the left main bronchus. When a foreign body is aspirated, it is more likely to enter the right main bronchus (although in some cases the foreign body enters the left bronchus). Pulmonary vascular resistance is not related to the question. The right lower lung lobe does not have poorer venous drainage than the other lobes.
GAS 168-171; GA 80-85

101 **D.** The normal position of the heart as seen in a plain radiograph has the right border of the heart formed by the superior vena cava, right atrium, and inferior vena cava. The left border is formed by the aortic arch superiorly, left pulmonary artery, left auricle, left ventricle, and the apex of the heart inferolaterally. The area indicated by the arrow is just inferior to the clavicle (on the left side), and this marks the location of the arch of the aorta. The superior vena cava and right ventricle would make up the right border. The pulmonary artery and left ventricle would be more inferior.
GAS 180-185; GA 85-88

102 **B.** All of the symptoms described in the question are indicative of breast cancer. The best choice of answers is cancer en cuirasse, a pathologic condition that presents as a hard, "woodlike" texture. Intraductal cancerous tumor is often a mild form of cancer detected by mammography. A, D, and E are all symptoms, not pathologic conditions.
GAS 139; GA 62-63

103 **A.** When multiple rib fractures produce a flail segment of the thoracic wall, paradoxical motion of the flail segment is commonly experienced upon deep inspiration; that is, the flail area is sucked in rather than expanding outward with inspiration, and the reverse movement occurs in expiration. Because the ribs are fractured, they will not be able to facilitate the normal "pump handle" motion during inspiration. The excursions of the diaphragm will not be affected by the broken ribs, except as pain restricts the breathing effort of the patient.
GAS 147-148; GA 64-67

104 **A.** The subclavian artery lies directly posterior to the subclavian vein; therefore, it is the structure that would be most vulnerable to damage when placing a central venous line in the subclavian vein. Both the phrenic and vagus nerves will be medial to the placement of the line and are not likely to be damaged. The common carotid artery is also too medial to be damaged by the line. The superior vena cava lies medial and inferior to the site of placement and is too deep to be easily damaged.
GAS 215-216; GA 108-109

105 **A.** Lymph from the lower third of the esophagus drains into the posterior mediastinal and left gastric lymph nodes. The middle third of the esophagus drains into posterior and superior mediastinal lymph nodes. The upper third of the esophagus drains into the deep cervical nodes. The other answer choices drain parts of the trachea, bronchi, and lungs.
GAS 172; GA 71

106 **A.** Lymph from the right primary bronchus would drain first into the inferior tracheobronchial nodes. The bronchomediastinal trunk and the thoracic duct are not lymph nodes, so they cannot be the correct answers to the question. The paratracheal nodes receive lymph from the superior tracheobronchial nodes. The superior tracheobronchial nodes receive lymph from the inferior tracheobronchial nodes.
GAS 172; GA 71

107 **D.** The artery of Adamkiewicz (great radicular artery) is an important artery that provides oxygenated blood to the lower portion of the spinal cord, specifically the anterior cord where lower motor neurons are located, inferior to the vertebral level of origin of the artery, and provides collateral anastomoses with the anterior spinal artery. Care should be taken during surgery to prevent damage to this artery as this can lead to paraplegia and alteration of functions of pelvic organs. The other answer choices are not likely to be damaged during the surgery and would not lead to paraplegia.
GAS 102-103; GA 46

108 **A.** A left tracheal deviation with an enlarged thyroid gland will most likely compress the left brachiocephalic vein. The other answer choices lie too far laterally to be affected by the tracheal deviation.
GAS 168-170; GA 102, 108, 110

109 **A.** The carina is the only answer listed that can easily be seen in radiograph. The carina is at the level of T4-5 (plane associated with the sternal angle of

Louis). This landmark is commonly used to guide the placement of a central venous line.
GAS 168-170; GA 108, 110

110 D. Gynecomastia is the abnormal growth of mammary glands in males. Polythelia refers to supernumerary nipples. Polymastia refers to supernumerary, or extra, breasts. Amastia refers to the absence of breasts.
GAS 129-131, 138-139; GA 62-63

111 E. A tension pneumothorax is caused by injury to the lung, leading to air in the pleural cavity. The site of the wound acts as a one-way valve, allowing air to enter the pleural cavity but not to leave the cavity. The lack of negative pressure in the pleural cavity causes the lung to collapse. Neither flail chest, emphysema, nor hemothorax will necessarily lead to the increased volume of air in the pleural cavity. The tension pneumothorax occurred during a violent fall; therefore, the clinical condition is not likely to be a spontaneous pneumothorax, in which case there is rupture of the pleura without the necessary occurrence of trauma.
GAS 234-235; GA 73-82

112 B. Chylothorax is usually caused by injury to the thoracic duct. The thoracic duct enters the venous system at the junction of the left internal jugular vein and the left subclavian vein, where they form the left brachiocephalic vein. Penetrating injuries at the beginning of the left brachiocephalic vein commonly also disrupt the termination of the thoracic duct. The other answers provided do not receive lymphatic drainage from the thoracic duct.
GAS 219; GA 71

113 A. The inferior vena cava quite likely undergoes compression by the growing fetus when the mother is in the supine position. In this case the compression led to reduced blood flow through the heart, with a resultant drop in blood pressure. The other structures listed as answers are not likely to be compressed by the growing fetus.
GAS 180-185; GA 108-110

114 C. Crackling noises in the lungs due to the buildup of fluid are referred to as rales. The fluid usually migrates to the inferior portion of the lung due to the effects of gravity. Auscultation over the sixth intercostal space at the midaxillary line would be associated with the lower lobe of the right lung. Remember that the oblique fissure runs from the level of T2 posteriorly to the sixth costal cartilage anteriorly. At the sixth intercostal space in the midaxillary line, one would be percussing below this fissure and therefore over the lower lobe. This question does not indicate any examination of the left lung.
GAS 158-175, 240-241; GA 73-82

115 A. Pericardiocentesis is usually performed through the infrasternal angle with the needle passing up through the diaphragm to the fibrous pericardium. The diaphragmatic surface of the heart is largely composed of the right ventricle and would therefore be entered if a needle is inserted too far. The other chambers of the heart would not lie in the direct path of the needle.
GAS 176-180; GA 86-87

116 B. The pain experienced by the patient travels with the sympathetic innervation of the heart, derived from spinal nerve levels T1 to T4. The pain fibers leave the heart and the cardiac plexuses via the cardiopulmonary nerves. Subsequently, the pain fibers pass through the sympathetic chain, enter the spinal nerve, and pass into the dorsal roots of the spinal nerves. The cell bodies of the pain fibers are located in the dorsal root ganglia of the spinal nerves from T1 to T4. The other levels indicated do not correspond to the typical pattern of innervation of this region.
GAS 229-230, 235-237; GA 120-121

117 A. The "bucket handle movement" of the ribs affects the transverse diameter of the thorax. Inspiration would increase the transverse diameter, whereas expiration decreases the transverse diameter. The anteroposterior diameter of the thorax is increased and decreased by the "pump handle movements" of the ribs and sternum. Vertical dimensions of the thorax would be changed by contraction and relaxation of the diaphragm.
GAS 157-158; GA 73-75

118 C. Bronchial constriction is induced by the parasympathetic innervation of the airways. This is supplied by the vagus nerves, which could be blocked to result in relaxation of the airways. The phrenic nerve provides motor and sensory innervation to the diaphragm. The intercostal nerves provide sensory and somatic motor innervation to their respective intercostal spaces. Stimulation of sympathetic innervation results in bronchodilation. The recurrent laryngeal nerve is a branch of the vagus and innervates parts of the larynx.
GAS 172; GA 108-109

119 A. The location where one is least likely to damage important structures by making an incision or pushing a chest tube into the thorax is over the upper border of the rib. At the inferior border of each

rib, one will encounter intercostal **v**ein, **a**rtery, and **n**erve, in that order (VAN structures). Entrance through the middle of the intercostal space does not eliminate the heightened possibility of piercing important structures. Neither passage between the internal and external intercostal muscles, nor between the intercostal muscles and the posterior intercostal membrane would allow entry to the pleural cavity.
GAS 147-148; GA 66-72

120 B. Cardiac tamponade is a condition in which fluid accumulates in the pericardial cavity. It can result from pericardial effusion or from leakage of blood from the heart or proximal portions of the great vessels. The increased pressure within the pericardial sac leads to decreased cardiac filling during diastole and therefore reduced systolic blood pressure. Because of the reduced pumping capacity of the heart, there is increased pressure in the venous system, leading to the distension of the jugular venous system. Deep vein thrombosis often occurs in the lower limbs and increases the risk of pulmonary embolism. The other answers listed are conditions that affect pulmonary function rather than cardiac functions.
GAS 179-180; GA 86-87

121 B. The S_2 heart sound refers to the second *(dub)* heart sound. This sound is produced by the closure of the aortic and pulmonary semilunar valves. The closure of mitral/bicuspid and tricuspid valves produce the first S_1 *(lub)* heart sound.
GAS 197; GA 100

122 E. The closure of the mitral/bicuspid and tricuspid valves produces the first S_1 *(lub)* heart sound. The S_2 heart sound refers to the second *(dub)* heart sound. This latter sound is produced by the closure of the aortic and pulmonary semilunar valves.
GAS 197; GA 100

123 D. Flail chest is characterized by paradoxical breathing movements caused by multiple rib fractures. The sensory innervation provided to intercostal spaces and to the underlying parietal pleura is supplied via the corresponding intercostal nerves. The phrenic nerve provides motor innervation to the diaphragm and sensory innervation to the diaphragmatic and mediastinal parietal pleura and pericardium. The vagus nerves provide parasympathetic innervation to the thoracic viscera, and to the gastrointestinal tract as distal as the left colic flexure. The cardiopulmonary nerves carry sympathetic innervation from T1 to T4 levels to the thoracic organs, and pain fibers from these organs. Thoracic splanchnic nerves carry sympathetic innervation to the abdomen.
GAS 213-214; GA 108-109

124 A. An aneurysm of the aortic arch could impinge upon the phrenic nerve, causing referral of pain to the left shoulder. This referral occurs because the root levels of the phrenic nerve are C3 to C5, nerve levels that are also distributed to the skin over the shoulder region. The other choices do not cause referral of pain to the left shoulder. The vagus nerve does not transmit pain sensations except from certain organs in the abdomen and pelvis. The intercostal nerves carry sensory information from the intercostal spaces and parietal pleura, pain that would not be referred to the shoulder. The thoracic splanchnics carry sympathetic innervation to the abdomen.
GAS 210; GA 108-109

125 B. The SA node functions as the primary intrinsic pacemaker of the heart, setting the cardiac rhythm. An artificial pacemaker assists in producing a normal rhythm when the SA node is not functioning normally. The atrioventricular node receives the depolarization signals from the sinoatrial node. The signal is delayed within the atrioventricular node (providing the time for the atria to contract), then propagated from the atrioventricular node through the bundle of His and Purkinje fibers.
GAS 200-203; GA 99

126 C. Postganglionic parasympathetic fibers are involved in the constriction of smooth muscle in the tracheoesophageal tree. Sympathetic fibers cause dilation of this structure. Visceral and somatic afferents are sensory fibers and therefore cannot cause dilation of muscle, as this is a motor nerve function.
GAS 172; GA 120-121

127 A. Dextrocardia is a condition that results from a bending of the heart tube to the left instead of to the right. TGF-β factor *Nodal* plays a role in the looping of the heart during the embryonic period.
GAS 197

128 A. The esophagus typically has four constrictions. In the thorax the esophagus is compressed by (1) the arch of the aorta, (2) the left principal bronchus, and (3) the diaphragm. The cricopharyngeal constriction is in the neck.
GAS 211, 215, 217, 298-299; GA 76, 82

129 C. The dermatome that encompasses the nipple is supplied by spinal nerve T4. In this case the

herpes zoster virus is harbored in the dorsal root ganglion of T4 and can be activated to cause the characteristic rash that is distributed along the dermatome including the nipple.
GAS 137-138; GA 62-63

130 **B.** Due to rib fracture, the intercostal vessels are damaged, parietal pleura is torn, and blood flows into the pleural space. The loss of negative pressure within the pleural cavity results in collapse of the lung. The carotid vessels would not be affected by the described injury. The pulmonary vessels are found within the parenchyma of the lungs and would not be injured due to an external injury such as that described. The internal thoracic artery is well protected by the sternum and is not the cause of this hemothorax.
GAS 146-148; GA 57-61, 68-71

131 **A.** Miosis, partial ptosis, and anhydrosis are a clinically important constellation of symptoms possibly indicating Horner syndrome. Horner syndrome is a lesion of the cervical sympathetic chain and sympathetic chain ganglia and is often a result of a Pancoast tumor, also known as a superior pulmonary sulcus tumor of the apex of the lung. The pupil, eyelid (superior tarsal muscle), and sweat glands are all under sympathetic nervous system control. The arch of the aorta and phrenic nerve are not part of the autonomic nervous system. The vagus nerve does carry parasympathetic fibers to muscles of the trachea, bronchi, digestive tract, and heart but not to any structure in the head and neck (laryngeal supply, and Von Ebner's glands in the tongue). A lesion to the phrenic nerve would result in paralysis of the diaphragm. The cardiopulmonary nerves are splanchnic nerves that are postganglionic and sympathetic. They originate in cervical and upper thoracic ganglia and innervate the thoracic cavity. The cardiopulmonary plexus is the autonomic supply to the heart.
GAS 888-889; GA 108-109

132 **B.** The esophagus lies posterior to the heart. Of the four chambers in the heart, the left atrium lies most posteriorly, just anterior to the esophagus when the heart is in its normal position in the mediastinum. The inferior vena cava runs on the right side within the thoracic cavity and empties its contents into the right atrium. The pulmonary arteries are too anterior to the esophagus to be affected by an esophageal tumor. The left ventricle is too anterior within the mediastinum to be affected by an esophageal tumor. Whereas the esophagus does lie against the vertebral bodies, a growing tumor would affect the esophagus first because it is a smooth muscle structure and therefore the path of least resistance, but this organ can be deviated relatively easily rather than compressed.
GAS 212-213; GA 108, 110

133 **C.** Artificial pacemakers are commonly used to treat patients who have weak or failing heart conduction systems. The electrode or "tip" of the pacemaker is threaded through the subclavian vein to the superior vena cava into the right atrium and then the right ventricle where it is used to stimulate the Purkinje fibers to result in ventricular contraction. The right atrium and left atrium do not contain Purkinje fibers and would therefore not be useful in artificially pacing the heart. The left ventricle is more difficult to access. The superior vena cava is not related to cardiac pacing.
GAS 238; GA 102-103

134 **A.** Cardiac hypertrophy is a compensatory mechanism of the myocardium in response to increasing demands on the heart due to ischemia, incompetent valves, or hypertension. The increased size of the heart muscle would most likely compress the esophagus, and due to the incompetent mitral valve, a backflow of blood into the left atrium can cause a left atrial dilation. The left atrium lies just anteriorly to the esophagus in the mediastinum. The pulmonary trunk is located superiorly and delivers blood to the lungs, so cardiac hypertrophy would not cause direct compression to this structure. The superior vena cava and inferior vena cava are vessels that deliver blood to the right atrium and are not likely to be compressed in this example of cardiac hypertrophy. The heart is inferior to the trachea.
GAS 212-213; GA 102-103, 108, 110

135 **E.** Tension pneumothorax is a progressive accumulation of air in the pleural cavity that is trapped during inspiration. The resulting increase of pressure diminishes the negative pressure required to maintain an inflated lung, resulting in a collapsed lung as seen on the radiograph. A flail chest is a result of ribs being broken in two or more locations, and no broken ribs are seen on this radiograph. Emphysema is a chronic condition in which elastic tissues and alveoli in the lungs are destroyed, reducing the surface area for gas exchange. Emphysema may result in a secondary spontaneous pneumothorax. A hemothorax is an accumulation of blood in the pleural space. On a radiograph, it is identifiable by a meniscus of fluid. Although spontaneous pneumothorax would present the same way on a radiograph, the patient's history of trauma (car crash) indicates the patient does not have a spontaneous pneumothorax.
GAS 235; GA 74-84

136 **C.** Right lower lobe. The right upper lobe extends from the apex of the lung (above the clavicle) to the fourth rib. The radiograph shows an opacity on the right side, eliminating the possibility of it being a left lung pneumonia. Opacity in the right middle lobe would extend inferiorly to the sixth rib. In the present case the opacity is inferior to the sixth rib extending to the tenth rib in the midaxillary line affecting the lower lobe of the right lung.
GAS 158-169; GA 74-84

137 **D.** In many people the anterior interventricular branch of the left coronary artery gives rise to a lateral diagonal branch that descends on the anterior surface of the heart. This branch is occluded in the radiograph. The left coronary artery arises from the left aortic sinus of the ascending aorta and passes between the left atrium and the left side of the pulmonary trunk in the coronary groove. The left coronary artery divides into two branches: an anterior interventricular branch (also known as the left anterior descending branch: LAD) and a circumflex branch. The LAD runs along the interventricular groove to the apex of the heart. The right coronary artery arises from the right aortic sinus and runs in the coronary groove. It usually gives off a sinoatrial nodal branch; it descends in the coronary groove and gives off a right marginal branch. At the crus of the heart, it gives off an AV nodal branch and a large posterior interventricular branch (in the "right dominant" pattern).
GAS 192-198; GA 96-98

138 **A.** Blockage of cutaneous lymphatic vessels results in edema of the skin surrounding the hair follicles, leading to an appearance like an orange peel (peau d'orange). Shortening of the suspensory ligaments leads to dimpling of the overlying skin, not peau d'orange. Contraction of retinacula cutis results in retraction and inversion of the nipple and/or areola. Pectoralis major involvement has nothing to do with this condition but can result in fixing the tumor firmly to the chest wall.
GAS 139; GA 62-63, 71

139 **C.** The patient is suffering from cardiac tamponade, that is, filling of the pericardial cavity with fluid. The classic signs of this tamponade are referred to as "Beck's triad." This trio, by definition, includes a small heart, from compression of the heart by the fluid-filled pericardial sac, and a quiet heart because the tamponade muffles the cardiac sounds; decreased pulse pressure resulting from the reduced difference between systolic and diastolic pressure because the tamponade restricts the ability of the heart to fill in diastole; and increased central venous pressure because venous blood cannot enter the compressed heart. None of the other answers provided includes these data to fit the definition.
GAS 179-180; GA 86-87

140 **E.** Myelin degeneration of the phrenic nerves, as can occur in Guillain-Barré, results in loss of phrenic nerve function and paralysis of the diaphragm. Diaphragmatic paralysis is predictable with lack of movement of the abdominal wall in respiratory efforts. The ribs are moving "violently" in this case; therefore, intercostal muscles and the pectoral musculature have retained their motor supply.
GAS 214; GA 108-109

141 **C.** The lost of myelin from the preganglionic (normally myelinated) sympathetic fibers in T1 to T4 results in interruption in their transmission of electrical stimulating impulses and, therefore, reduction of positive inotropic (force increasing) and chronotropic (rate increasing) stimulation of the heart. Reduction of function of the vagus nerves would not result in slowing cardiac activity; just the opposite would occur. Interruption of phrenic nerve activity has no effect on cardiac rate (as this nerve innervates the diaphragm), nor would the interruption of the thinly myelinated pain fibers from the heart. The ventral horn neurons do not innervate the heart, but rather skeletal muscle; therefore, they would not be directly affected by the disease process affecting the heart.
GAS 202-204; GA 108-109

142 **C.** The mitral valve is best visualized by TEE because the transducer within the esophagus is directly posterior to the left atrium. The physical laws that apply to ultrasound imaging dictate that the closer the structure to the transducer, the better the ability to obtain a better image. This question asks which heart valve is most directly related to the posterior aspect of the left atrium, which is the mitral valve.
GAS 181-208; GA 108, 110

3

ABDOMEN

1 A 1-year-old female is admitted to the hospital with a palpable mass within one of her labia majora. Radiographic examination reveals that a loop of intestine has herniated into the visibly enlarged labium majus. This condition is due to failure of the processus vaginalis to close off. From which of the following tissue layers is the processus derived?

- ☐ **A.** Parietal peritoneum
- ☐ **B.** Extraperitoneal tissue
- ☐ **C.** Transversalis fascia
- ☐ **D.** Dartos fascia
- ☐ **E.** Internal abdominal oblique aponeurosis

2 A 3-year-old boy is admitted to the hospital with signs of acute renal failure. Radiologic studies reveal that the boy has bilateral masses involving both kidneys. Examination of biopsy material confirms the diagnosis of Wilms tumor. Which of the following gene mutations is the most common in Wilms tumor?

- ☐ **A.** The gene responsible for *WT1*
- ☐ **B.** The gene responsible for *HGF*
- ☐ **C.** The gene responsible for *VEGF*
- ☐ **D.** The gene responsible for *GDNF*
- ☐ **E.** The gene responsible for *FGF-2*

3 Fusion of the caudal portions of the kidneys during embryonic development is most likely to result in which of the following congenital conditions?

- ☐ **A.** Bicornuate uterus
- ☐ **B.** Cryptorchidism
- ☐ **C.** Horseshoe kidney
- ☐ **D.** Hypospadias
- ☐ **E.** Renal agenesis

4 Which of the following congenital malformations will most predictably result in oligohydramnios?

- ☐ **A.** Anencephaly
- ☐ **B.** Pyloric stenosis
- ☐ **C.** Renal agenesis
- ☐ **D.** Tracheoesophageal fistula
- ☐ **E.** Urethral atresia

5 Failure to urinate during embryonic or fetal life usually causes respiratory difficulties postnatally. Which of the following relationships best describes this situation?

- ☐ **A.** Oligohydramnios linked with hypoplastic lungs
- ☐ **B.** Polycystic kidneys linked to tracheoesophageal fistula
- ☐ **C.** Polyhydramnios
- ☐ **D.** Renal agenesis linked to insufficient surfactant
- ☐ **E.** Urethral obstruction linked to ectopic viscera

6 A 4-year-old male child is admitted to the hospital with severe vomiting. Radiographic examination and history taking reveals that the boy suffers from an annular pancreas. Which of the following structures is most typically obstructed by this condition?

- ▢ **A.** Pylorus of the stomach
- ▢ **B.** First part of the duodenum
- ▢ **C.** Second part of the duodenum
- ▢ **D.** Third part of the duodenum
- ▢ **E.** Jejunum

7 A 3-year-old male child is admitted to the pediatric clinic. Diagnosis reveals that the intermediate portion of the processus vaginalis is not obliterated. Which of the following conditions will most likely result from this?

- ▢ **A.** Hypospadias
- ▢ **B.** Sterility
- ▢ **C.** Congenital hydrocele
- ▢ **D.** Ectopic testis
- ▢ **E.** Epispadias

8 Testicles are absent from the scrotum of a 1-year-old male admitted to the pediatric clinic. The pediatrician examined the infant and palpated the testes in the inguinal canal. Which of the following terms is used to describe this condition?

- ▢ **A.** Pseudohermaphroditism
- ▢ **B.** True hermaphroditism
- ▢ **C.** Cryptorchism
- ▢ **D.** Congenital adrenal hyperplasia
- ▢ **E.** Chordee

9 A 28-year-old woman who is 8 months pregnant goes to the outpatient clinic for her prenatal checkup. Ultrasound examination of the fetus reveals gastroschisis, with herniation of the small bowel into the amniotic cavity. Failure of proper formation of which of the following structure(s) has resulted in this condition?

- ▢ **A.** Head fold
- ▢ **B.** Tail fold
- ▢ **C.** Neural folds
- ▢ **D.** Lateral folds
- ▢ **E.** Amnion

10 Rotation of the stomach during development results in movement of the left vagus nerve from its original position. Through approximately how many degrees of rotation does the nerve move, and what is its final position?

- ▢ **A.** 90° to become the anterior vagal trunk
- ▢ **B.** 90° to become the posterior vagal trunk
- ▢ **C.** 270° to become the anterior vagal trunk
- ▢ **D.** 270° to become the posterior vagal trunk
- ▢ **E.** 180° to become the right vagal trunk

11 A newborn baby was diagnosed with eventration of the diaphragm, wherein one half of the diaphragm ascends into the thorax during inspiration, but the other half contracts normally. What is the most likely cause of this condition?

- ▢ **A.** Absence of a pleuropericardial fold
- ▢ **B.** Absence of musculature in one half of the diaphragm
- ▢ **C.** Failure of migration of the diaphragm
- ▢ **D.** Failure of development of the septum transversum
- ▢ **E.** Absence of a pleuroperitoneal fold

12 A 2-day-old newborn male is cyanotic after attempts to swallow milk result in collection of the milk in his mouth. After 2 days he develops pneumonia. A tracheoesophageal fistula is suspected. Which of the following structures has failed to develop properly?

- ▢ **A.** Esophagus
- ▢ **B.** Trachea
- ▢ **C.** Tongue
- ▢ **D.** Tracheoesophageal septum
- ▢ **E.** Pharynx

13 A 3-day-old male newborn has difficulties in breathing. A CT scan of his chest and abdomen reveals the absence of the central tendon of the diaphragm. Which of the following structures failed to develop properly?

- ▢ **A.** Pleuroperitoneal folds
- ▢ **B.** Pleuropericardial folds
- ▢ **C.** Septum transversum
- ▢ **D.** Cervical myotomes
- ▢ **E.** Dorsal mesentery of the esophagus

14 A 2-day-old female infant with fever is examined by the pediatric team. Imaging reveals malrotation of the small intestine without fixation of the mesenteries. The vessels around the duodenojejunal junction are obstructed and the intestine is at risk of becoming gangrenous. Which of the following has occurred to cause the obstruction?

- ▢ **A.** Diaphragmatic atresia
- ▢ **B.** Subhepatic cecum

- ☐ **C.** Midgut volvulus
- ☐ **D.** Duplication of the intestine
- ☐ **E.** Congenital megacolon

15 A 5-day-old male infant is diagnosed with Hirschsprung disease. CT scan examination reveals an abnormally dilated colon. Which of the following is the most likely embryologic mechanism responsible for Hirschsprung disease?

- ☐ **A.** Failure of neural crest cells to migrate into the walls of the colon
- ☐ **B.** Incomplete separation of the cloaca
- ☐ **C.** Failure of recanalization of the colon
- ☐ **D.** Defective rotation of the hindgut
- ☐ **E.** Oligohydramnios

16 A 1-day-old infant has a mass protruding through her umbilicus. Physical examination reveals an umbilical hernia. A CT scan reveals that part of another organ is attached to the inner surface of the hernia. What portion of the gastrointestinal tract is most likely to be attached to the inner surface of the umbilical hernia?

- ☐ **A.** Anal canal
- ☐ **B.** Appendix
- ☐ **C.** Cecum
- ☐ **D.** Ileum
- ☐ **E.** Stomach

17 A 38-year-old pregnant woman is admitted to the emergency department with severe vaginal bleeding. Ultrasound examination confirms the initial diagnosis of ectopic pregnancy. Which of the following is the most common site of an ectopic pregnancy?

- ☐ **A.** Uterine tubes
- ☐ **B.** Cervix
- ☐ **C.** Mesentery of the abdominal wall
- ☐ **D.** Lower part of uterine body overlapping the internal cervical os
- ☐ **E.** Fundus of the uterus

18 A 23-year-old woman is admitted with severe abdominal pain, nausea, and vomiting. History taking shows that the pain is acute and has been constant for 4 days. The pain began in the epigastric region and radiated bilaterally around the chest to just below the scapulae. Currently the pain is localized in the right hypochondrium. A CT scan examination reveals calcified stones in the gallbladder. Which of the following nerves is carrying the afferent fibers of the referred pain?

- ☐ **A.** Greater thoracic splanchnic nerves
- ☐ **B.** Dorsal primary rami of intercostal nerves
- ☐ **C.** Phrenic nerves
- ☐ **D.** Vagus nerves
- ☐ **E.** Pelvic splanchnic nerves

19 A 32-year-old male is admitted to the emergency department with groin pain. Examination reveals that the patient has an indirect inguinal hernia. Which of the following nerves is compressed by the herniating structure in the inguinal canal to give the patient pain?

- ☐ **A.** Iliohypogastric
- ☐ **B.** Lateral femoral cutaneous
- ☐ **C.** Ilioinguinal
- ☐ **D.** Subcostal
- ☐ **E.** Pudendal

20 A 54-year-old male is admitted to the emergency department with severe upper abdominal pain. Gastroscopy reveals a tumor in the antrum of the stomach. A CT scan is ordered to evaluate lymphatic drainage of the stomach. Which of the following lymph nodes is most likely to be involved in a malignancy of the stomach?

- ☐ **A.** Celiac
- ☐ **B.** Superior mesenteric
- ☐ **C.** Inferior mesenteric
- ☐ **D.** Lumbar
- ☐ **E.** Hepatic

21 During a scheduled laparoscopic cholecystectomy in a 47-year-old female patient, the resident accidentally clamped the hepatoduodenal ligament instead of the cystic artery. Which of the following vessels would most likely be occluded in this iatrogenic injury?

- ☐ **A.** Superior mesenteric artery
- ☐ **B.** Proper hepatic artery
- ☐ **C.** Splenic artery
- ☐ **D.** Common hepatic artery
- ☐ **E.** Inferior vena cava

22 A 45-year-old male was admitted to the hospital with groin pain and a palpable mass just superior to the inguinal ligament. The patient was diagnosed with an inguinal hernia and a surgical repair was performed. During the operation the surgeon found a loop of intestine passing through the deep inguinal ring. Which of the following types of hernia was this?

- ☐ **A.** Direct inguinal
- ☐ **B.** Umbilical
- ☐ **C.** Femoral
- ☐ **D.** Lumbar
- ☐ **E.** Indirect inguinal

23 A 55-year-old man was admitted to the hospital with severe abdominal pain. Gastroscopy and CT scan examinations revealed a perforating ulcer in the posterior wall of the stomach. Where would peritonitis most likely develop initially?

- ▢ **A.** Right subhepatic space
- ▢ **B.** Hepatorenal space (of Morison)
- ▢ **C.** Omental bursa (lesser sac)
- ▢ **D.** Right subphrenic space
- ▢ **E.** Greater sac

24 A 58-year-old male alcoholic is admitted to the hospital after vomiting dark red blood (hematemesis). Endoscopy reveals ruptured esophageal varices, resulting from portal hypertension. Which of the following venous tributaries to the portal system anastomoses with caval veins to cause the varices?

- ▢ **A.** Splenic
- ▢ **B.** Left gastroomental
- ▢ **C.** Left gastric
- ▢ **D.** Left hepatic
- ▢ **E.** Right gastric

25 A 45-year-old male entered the emergency department with a complaint of severe abdominal pain. During physical examination it is observed that his cremasteric reflex is absent. Which of the following nerves is responsible for the efferent limb of the cremasteric reflex?

- ▢ **A.** Ilioinguinal
- ▢ **B.** Iliohypogastric
- ▢ **C.** Genitofemoral
- ▢ **D.** Pudendal
- ▢ **E.** Ventral ramus of T12

26 The decision is made by emergency department surgeons to perform an exploratory laparotomy on a 32-year-old female with severe abdominal pain. Where would the incision most likely be made to separate the left and right rectus sheaths?

- ▢ **A.** Midaxillary line
- ▢ **B.** Arcuate line
- ▢ **C.** Semilunar line
- ▢ **D.** Tendinous intersection
- ▢ **E.** Linea alba

27 After a "tummy-tuck" (abdominoplasty) procedure is performed on a 45-year-old man, which of the following layers of the abdominal wall will hold the sutures?

- ▢ **A.** Scarpa's fascia (membranous layer)
- ▢ **B.** Camper's fascia (fatty layer)
- ▢ **C.** Transversalis fascia
- ▢ **D.** Extraperitoneal tissue
- ▢ **E.** External abdominal oblique fascia

28 A 49-year-old man presents with acute abdominal pain and jaundice. Radiographic studies reveal a tumor in the head of the pancreas. Which of the following structures is most likely being obstructed?

- ▢ **A.** Common bile duct
- ▢ **B.** Common hepatic duct
- ▢ **C.** Cystic duct
- ▢ **D.** Accessory pancreatic duct
- ▢ **E.** Proper hepatic artery

29 A 44-year-old man is admitted to the emergency department with excessive vomiting and dehydration. Radiographic images demonstrate that part of the bowel is being compressed between the abdominal aorta and the superior mesenteric artery. Which of the following intestinal structures is most likely being compressed?

- ▢ **A.** Second part of duodenum
- ▢ **B.** Transverse colon
- ▢ **C.** Third part of duodenum
- ▢ **D.** First part of duodenum
- ▢ **E.** Jejunum

30 During the surgical repair of a perforated duodenal ulcer in a 47-year-old male patient, the gastroduodenal artery is ligated. A branch of which of the following arteries will continue to supply blood to the pancreas in this patient?

- ▢ **A.** Inferior mesenteric
- ▢ **B.** Left gastric
- ▢ **C.** Right gastric
- ▢ **D.** Proper hepatic
- ▢ **E.** Superior mesenteric

31 A 70-year-old man is admitted to the emergency department with severe diarrhea. An arteriogram reveals 90% blockage at the origin of the inferior mesenteric artery from the aorta. Which of the following arteries would most likely provide collateral supply to the descending colon?

- ▢ **A.** Left gastroepiploic artery
- ▢ **B.** Middle colic artery
- ▢ **C.** Sigmoid artery
- ▢ **D.** Splenic artery
- ▢ **E.** Superior rectal artery

32 A 24-year-old woman has a dull aching pain in the umbilical region, and flexion of the hip against resistance (psoas test) causes a sharp pain in the right lower abdominal quadrant. Which of the following structures is most likely inflamed to cause the pain?

- ▢ **A.** Appendix
- ▢ **B.** Bladder
- ▢ **C.** Gallbladder
- ▢ **D.** Pancreas
- ▢ **E.** Uterus

33 A 35-year-old male is admitted to the hospital from the emergency department because of excruciating pain in the back and left shoulder. A CT scan reveals an abscess in the upper part of the left kidney, but no abnormality is detected in the shoulder region. The shoulder pain may be caused by the spread of the inflammation to which of the following neighboring structures?

- ▢ **A.** Descending colon
- ▢ **B.** Diaphragm
- ▢ **C.** Duodenum
- ▢ **D.** Liver
- ▢ **E.** Pancreas

34 A 62-year-old man is admitted to the hospital with dull, diffuse abdominal pain. A CT scan reveals a tumor at the head of the pancreas. The abdominal pain is mediated by afferent fibers that travel initially with which of the following nerves?

- ▢ **A.** Greater thoracic splanchnic
- ▢ **B.** Intercostal
- ▢ **C.** Phrenic
- ▢ **D.** Vagus
- ▢ **E.** Subcostal

35 A 52-year-old male with a history of smoking and hypercholesterolemia is diagnosed with severe atherosclerosis affecting the arteries of his body. Laboratory examination reveals extremely low sperm count. Which of the following arteries is most likely occluded?

- ▢ **A.** External iliac
- ▢ **B.** Inferior epigastric
- ▢ **C.** Umbilical
- ▢ **D.** Testicular
- ▢ **E.** Deep circumflex iliac

36 In a routine visit to the outpatient clinic for his annual checkup, a 42-year-old male is informed that radiographic examination has given strong evidence that he has a malignancy of his scrotum. Which of the following nodes are the first lymph nodes that drain the affected area?

- ▢ **A.** Superficial inguinal
- ▢ **B.** Internal iliac
- ▢ **C.** Lumbar
- ▢ **D.** Presacral
- ▢ **E.** Axillary

37 A 35-year-old male is admitted to the hospital with an indirect inguinal hernia. During an open hernioplasty (in contrast to a laparoscopic procedure), the spermatic cord and the internal abdominal oblique muscles are identified. Which component of the spermatic cord is derived from the internal abdominal oblique muscle?

- ▢ **A.** External spermatic fascia
- ▢ **B.** Cremaster muscle
- ▢ **C.** Tunica vaginalis
- ▢ **D.** Internal spermatic fascia
- ▢ **E.** Dartos fascia

38 A 63-year-old man with a history of alcoholism is brought to the emergency department with hematemesis (vomiting blood). Findings on endoscopic examination suggest bleeding from esophageal varices. The varices are most likely a result of the anastomoses between the left gastric vein and which other vessel or vessels?

- ▢ **A.** Azygos system of veins
- ▢ **B.** Inferior vena cava
- ▢ **C.** Left umbilical vein
- ▢ **D.** Superior mesenteric vein
- ▢ **E.** Subcostal veins

39 A 34-year-old man is undergoing an emergency appendectomy. After the appendectomy has been performed successfully, the patient undergoes an exploratory laparoscopy. Which of the following anatomic features are the most useful to distinguish the jejunum from the ileum?

- ▢ **A.** Jejunum has thinner walls compared with the ileum.
- ▢ **B.** Jejunum has less mesenteric fat compared with the ileum.
- ▢ **C.** Jejunum has more numerous vascular arcades compared with the ileum.
- ▢ **D.** Jejunum has more numerous lymphatic follicles beneath the mucosa compared with the ileum.
- ▢ **E.** Jejunum has fewer villi compared with the ileum.

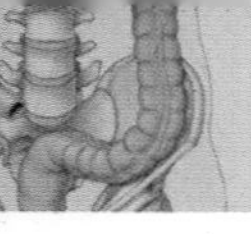

40 After a mastectomy, a musculocutaneous flap is used to restore the thoracic contour in a 34-year-old female patient. The ipsilateral (same side) rectus abdominis muscle was detached carefully from the surrounding structures and transposed to the thoracic wall. Which of the following landmarks is most often used to locate the inferior end of the posterior, tendinous layer of the rectus sheath?

- ☐ **A.** Intercristal line
- ☐ **B.** Linea alba
- ☐ **C.** Arcuate line
- ☐ **D.** Pectineal line
- ☐ **E.** Semilunar line

41 An anteroposterior radiograph is taken of the lumbar region in a 31-year-old female patient who had been treated for tuberculous spondylitis at vertebral levels T12-L1. The patient has been asymptomatic for 10 years. Which of the following is the most likely site of the calcified tuberculous abscess?

- ☐ **A.** Body of pancreas
- ☐ **B.** Cecum
- ☐ **C.** Fundus of stomach
- ☐ **D.** Psoas fascia
- ☐ **E.** Suspensory ligament of the duodenum

42 A 45-year-old female is admitted to the hospital with symptoms of an upper bowel obstruction. Upon CT examination it is found that the third (transverse) portion of the duodenum is being compressed by a large vessel. Which of the following vessels will most likely be causing the compression?

- ☐ **A.** Inferior mesenteric artery
- ☐ **B.** Superior mesenteric artery
- ☐ **C.** Inferior mesenteric vein
- ☐ **D.** Portal vein
- ☐ **E.** Splenic vein

43 A 61-year-old woman had been scheduled for a cholecystectomy. During the operation the scissors of the surgical resident accidentally entered the tissues immediately posterior to the epiploic (omental) foramen (its posterior boundary). The surgical field was filled immediately by profuse bleeding. Which of the following vessels was the most likely source of bleeding?

- ☐ **A.** Aorta
- ☐ **B.** Inferior vena cava
- ☐ **C.** Portal vein
- ☐ **D.** Right renal artery
- ☐ **E.** Superior mesenteric vein

44 A 32-year-old woman was admitted to the hospital with a complaint of pain over her umbilicus. Radiographic examination revealed acute appendicitis. The appendix was removed successfully in an emergency appendectomy. One week postoperatively the patient complained of paresthesia of the skin over the pubic region and the anterior portion of her perineum. Which of the following nerves was most likely injured during the appendectomy?

- ☐ **A.** Genitofemoral
- ☐ **B.** Ilioinguinal
- ☐ **C.** Subcostal
- ☐ **D.** Iliohypogastric
- ☐ **E.** Spinal nerve T9

45 Exploratory laparoscopy was performed on a 34-year-old male, following a successful emergency appendectomy. Which of the following anatomic relationships would be seen clearly, without dissection, when the surgeon exposes the beginning of the jejunum?

- ☐ **A.** The second portion of the duodenum is related anteriorly to the hilum of the right kidney.
- ☐ **B.** The superior mesenteric artery and vein pass posterior to the third part of the duodenum.
- ☐ **C.** The portal vein crosses anterior to the neck of the pancreas.
- ☐ **D.** The second part of the duodenum is crossed anteriorly by the attachment of the transverse mesocolon.
- ☐ **E.** The third part of the duodenum is related anteriorly to the hilum of the left kidney.

46 A 30-year-old female patient complains that she has been weak and easily fatigued over the past 6 months. She has a 3-month acute history of severe hypertension that has required treatment with antihypertensive medications. She has recently gained 4.5 kg (10 lb) and currently weighs 75 kg (165 lb). Her blood pressure is 170/100 mm Hg. Purple striae are seen over the abdomen on physical examination and she possesses a "buffalo hump." Fasting serum glucose concentration is 140 mg/dl. A CT scan of the abdomen shows a 6-cm mass immediately posterior to the inferior vena cava. Which of the following organs is the most likely origin of the mass?

- ☐ **A.** Suprarenal (adrenal) gland
- ☐ **B.** Appendix
- ☐ **C.** Gallbladder
- ☐ **D.** Ovary
- ☐ **E.** Uterus

47 An obese 45-year-old female patient with an elevated temperature comes to the physician's office complaining of nausea and intermittent, acute pain in the right upper quadrant of the abdomen during the past 2 days. She has a 24-hour history of jaundice. She has a history of gallstones. Which of the following structures has most likely been obstructed by a gallstone?

- ▢ **A.** Common bile duct
- ▢ **B.** Cystic duct
- ▢ **C.** Left hepatic duct
- ▢ **D.** Pancreatic duct
- ▢ **E.** Right hepatic duct

48 A 67-year-old man has severe cirrhosis of the liver. He most likely has enlarged anastomoses between which of the following pairs of veins?

- ▢ **A.** Inferior phrenic and superior phrenic
- ▢ **B.** Left colic and middle colic
- ▢ **C.** Left gastric and esophageal
- ▢ **D.** Lumbar and renal
- ▢ **E.** Sigmoid and superior rectal

49 A 45-year-old male is admitted to the hospital with a massive hernia that passes through the inguinal triangle (of Hesselbach). Which of the following structures is used to distinguish a direct inguinal hernia from an indirect inguinal hernia?

- ▢ **A.** Inferior epigastric vessels
- ▢ **B.** Femoral canal
- ▢ **C.** Inguinal ligament
- ▢ **D.** Rectus abdominis muscle (lateral border)
- ▢ **E.** Pectineal ligament

50 A 36-year-old man was brought to the emergency department with a bullet wound to the abdomen. The bullet penetrated the anterior abdominal wall superior to the umbilicus. If the bullet passed directly posterior in the midline, which of the following structures was most likely to have been struck first by the bullet?

- ▢ **A.** Abdominal aorta
- ▢ **B.** Transverse colon
- ▢ **C.** Stomach
- ▢ **D.** Gallbladder
- ▢ **E.** Pancreas

51 A 48-year-old man has had three episodes of upper gastrointestinal bleeding from esophageal varices. He has a history of chronic alcoholism but has recently been rehabilitated. Further evaluation shows ascites and splenomegaly. Which of the following surgical venous anastomoses is most commonly used to relieve these symptoms and signs before a liver transplant is attempted?

- ▢ **A.** Left gastric to splenic vein
- ▢ **B.** Right gastric to left gastric vein
- ▢ **C.** Right renal to right gonadal vein
- ▢ **D.** Splenic to left renal vein
- ▢ **E.** Superior mesenteric to inferior mesenteric vein

52 A 55-year-old man is admitted to the hospital with nausea, vomiting, and hematuria. A CT scan examination reveals a neoplasm in the posterior surface of the inferior pole of the left kidney that has invaded through the renal pelvis, renal capsule, ureter, and fat. To which of the following regions will pain most likely be referred?

- ▢ **A.** Skin of the anterior and lateral thighs and femoral triangle
- ▢ **B.** Skin over the gluteal region, pubis, medial thigh, and scrotal areas
- ▢ **C.** Skin over the medial, anterior, and lateral side of the thigh
- ▢ **D.** Skin over the pubis and umbilicus
- ▢ **E.** Skin over the pubis, umbilicus, and posterior abdominal wall muscles

53 A 30-year-old female patient has complained of weakness and fatigability over the past 6 months. She has a 3-month acute history of severe hypertension that has not responded to antihypertensive medications. Fasting serum glucose concentration is 140 mg/dl. A CT scan of the abdomen shows a 6-cm mass in the adrenal gland affecting the secretory cells of the adrenal medulla. Which of the following structures is most likely releasing products into the bloodstream to produce the hypertension and other signs?

- ▢ **A.** Preganglionic sympathetic axons in thoracic splanchnic nerves
- ▢ **B.** Cells of neural crest origin that migrated to the adrenal medulla
- ▢ **C.** Preganglionic parasympathetic branches of the posterior vagal trunk
- ▢ **D.** Postganglionic parasympathetic branches of the left or right vagus nerves
- ▢ **E.** Postganglionic fibers from pelvic splanchnic nerves

54 A 48-year-old man is admitted to the hospital with severe abdominal pain. Radiographic examination reveals a tumor in the tail of the pancreas. A diagnostic arteriogram shows that the tumor has compromised the blood supply to another organ. Which of the following organs is most likely to have its blood supply compromised by this tumor?

- ▢ **A.** Duodenum
- ▢ **B.** Gallbladder
- ▢ **C.** Kidney
- ▢ **D.** Liver
- ▢ **E.** Spleen

55 A 57-year-old man is admitted to the emergency department with left flank pain. Blood tests indicate hematuria and anemia. A magnetic resonance scan reveals that blood flow in the left renal vein is being occluded by an arterial aneurysm where the vein crosses the aorta. The aneurysm is most likely located in which of the following arteries?

- ▢ **A.** Celiac
- ▢ **B.** Inferior mesenteric
- ▢ **C.** Left colic
- ▢ **D.** Middle colic
- ▢ **E.** Superior mesenteric

56 A 57-year-old man is admitted to the emergency department with pain in his left flank and testicles. Laboratory tests indicate hematuria and anemia. A CT scan examination provides evidence that blood flow in the left renal vein is being occluded where it crosses anterior to the aorta. Which of the following is the most likely cause of the testicular pain?

- ▢ **A.** Compression of the testicular artery
- ▢ **B.** Occlusion of flow of blood in the testicular vein
- ▢ **C.** Compression of the afferent fibers in the lumbar splanchnic nerves
- ▢ **D.** Compression of the sympathetic fibers in the preaortic plexus
- ▢ **E.** Compression of the posterior vagus nerve

57 A 51-year-old woman is admitted to the hospital with an acutely painful abdomen. Radiographic examination reveals penetration of the fundic region of the stomach by an ulcer, resulting in intraabdominal bleeding. Which of the following arteries is the most likely source of the bleeding?

- ▢ **A.** Common hepatic artery
- ▢ **B.** Inferior phrenic artery
- ▢ **C.** Left gastroepiploic artery
- ▢ **D.** Short gastric artery
- ▢ **E.** Splenic artery

58 A 39-year-old woman is admitted to the hospital with pain radiating to her inguinal region. Radiographic and physical examination reveal a herniation. Which of the following is the most common type of hernia in a female patient?

- ▢ **A.** Femoral hernia
- ▢ **B.** Umbilical hernia
- ▢ **C.** Direct inguinal hernia
- ▢ **D.** Indirect inguinal hernia
- ▢ **E.** Epigastric hernia

59 Radiographic examination of a 42-year-old female reveals penetration of the duodenal bulb by an ulcer, resulting in profuse intraabdominal bleeding. Which of the following arteries is the most likely source of the bleeding?

- ▢ **A.** Posterior superior pancreaticoduodenal
- ▢ **B.** Superior mesenteric
- ▢ **C.** Inferior mesenteric
- ▢ **D.** Inferior pancreaticoduodenal
- ▢ **E.** Right gastric

60 A 23-year-old man is admitted to the hospital with a bulge in his scrotum. Physical examination reveals an indirect inguinal hernia. During the open hernia repair the internal spermatic fascia is identified and reflected to expose the ductus deferens and testicular vessels. Which of the following provides the internal spermatic fascial layer of the spermatic cord?

- ▢ **A.** External abdominal oblique aponeurosis
- ▢ **B.** Internal abdominal oblique aponeurosis
- ▢ **C.** Transversus abdominis aponeurosis
- ▢ **D.** Transversalis fascia
- ▢ **E.** Processus vaginalis

61 A 45-year-old woman is admitted to the emergency department with a complaint of severe abdominal pain. CT scan and MRI examinations reveal a tumor of the head of the pancreas involving the uncinate process. Which of the following vessels is most likely to be occluded?

- ▢ **A.** Common hepatic artery
- ▢ **B.** Cystic artery and vein
- ▢ **C.** Superior mesenteric artery
- ▢ **D.** Inferior mesenteric artery
- ▢ **E.** Portal vein

62 A 35-year-old obese man is admitted to the hospital with jaundice and complaints of abdominal pain. Physical examination reveals an epigastric pain that migrates toward the patient's right side and posterior toward the scapula. Radiographic examination reveals multiple gallstones, consistent with the patient's jaundice and typical pains of cholecystitis. Which of the following structures is most likely obstructed by the gallstones?

- ◯ **A.** Common bile duct
- ◯ **B.** Cystic duct
- ◯ **C.** Left hepatic duct
- ◯ **D.** Pancreatic duct
- ◯ **E.** Right hepatic duct

63 A 36-year-old woman is admitted to the hospital for the imminent birth of her baby. The decision is made to perform an emergency cesarean section. A Pfannenstiel incision is used to reach the uterus by making a transverse incision through the external sheath of the rectus muscles, about 2 cm above the pubic bones. It follows natural folds of the skin and curves superior to the mons pubis. Which of the following nerves is most at risk when this incision is made?

- ◯ **A.** T10
- ◯ **B.** T11
- ◯ **C.** Iliohypogastric
- ◯ **D.** Ilioinguinal
- ◯ **E.** Lateral femoral cutaneous

64 A 37-year-old woman was admitted to the emergency department with high fever (39.5° C), nausea, and vomiting. Physical examination revealed increased abdominal pain in the paraumbilical region, rebound tenderness over McBurney's point, and a positive psoas test. Blood tests showed marked leukocytosis. Which of the following is the most likely diagnosis?

- ◯ **A.** Ectopic pregnancy
- ◯ **B.** Appendicitis
- ◯ **C.** Cholecystitis
- ◯ **D.** Kidney stone
- ◯ **E.** Perforation of the duodenum

65 A 56-year-old male is admitted to the hospital with severe abdominal pain. The patient has a history of "irritable bowel syndrome" affecting his rectum. Which of the following nerves will most likely be responsible for the transmission of pain in this case?

- ◯ **A.** Lumbar sympathetic chains
- ◯ **B.** Pelvic splanchnic nerves
- ◯ **C.** Pudendal nerves
- ◯ **D.** Sacral sympathetic chains
- ◯ **E.** Vagus nerves

66 A 42-year-old female is admitted to the hospital due to blood in her stools. Physical examination reveals no signs of inflammation, infection, or tumor. An endoscopic examination of the distal segment of the ileum reveals a lesion of the intestinal wall. Biopsy gives histologic evidence that the lesion contains gastric mucosa. Which of the following clinical conditions will most likely explain the symptoms and signs?

- ◯ **A.** Internal hemorrhoids
- ◯ **B.** External hemorrhoids
- ◯ **C.** Diverticulosis
- ◯ **D.** Meckel's diverticulum
- ◯ **E.** Borborygmi

67 An 80-year-old male patient is admitted to the hospital with hypertension. His history includes a notation that he has had a poor appetite for some time. During physical examination it is observed that his blood pressure is 175/95 mm Hg and that he has a marked pulsation in his epigastric region. Which of the following diagnoses will most likely explain the symptoms and signs?

- ◯ **A.** Hiatal hernia
- ◯ **B.** Splenomegaly
- ◯ **C.** Cirrhosis of the liver
- ◯ **D.** Aortic aneurysm
- ◯ **E.** Kidney stone

68 A 48-year-old female is admitted to the hospital with a distended abdomen. A CT scan examination provides evidence of the presence of ascites (Fig. 3-1). In which of the following locations will an ultrasound machine most likely confirm the presence of the ascitic fluid with the patient in the supine position?

- ◯ **A.** Subphrenic recess
- ◯ **B.** Hepatorenal recess (pouch of Morison)
- ◯ **C.** Rectouterine recess (pouch of Douglas)
- ◯ **D.** Vesicouterine recess
- ◯ **E.** Subhepatic recess

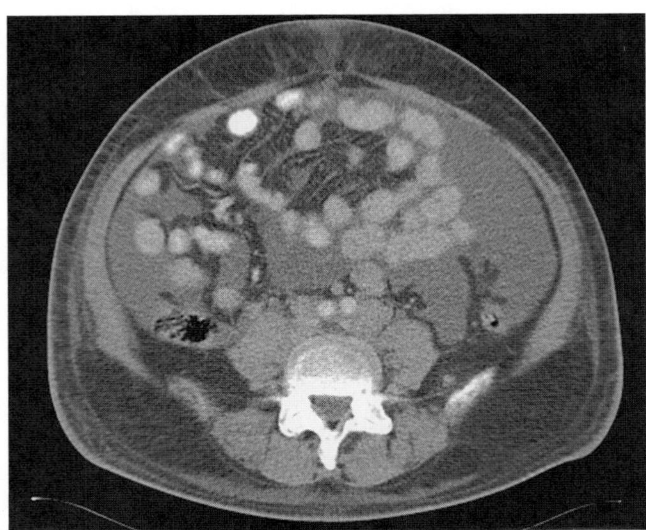

Fig. 3-1

69 A 19-year-old male is admitted to the hospital after a violent automobile collision. An MRI examination reveals that the spinal cord has been transected at the L4 cord level. Which of the following portions of the intestine will most predictably lose parasympathetic innervation from the central nervous system?

- ☐ **A.** Jejunum
- ☐ **B.** Ascending colon
- ☐ **C.** Ileum
- ☐ **D.** Descending colon
- ☐ **E.** Transverse colon

70 A 55-year-old male is admitted to the hospital because of severe weight loss over the preceding 6-month period of time. Radiographic examination and other tests provide evidence that a tumor is causing portal hypertension. Laboratory studies reveal that the patient has fatty stool, malnutrition, and liver hypoxia. At which of the following locations is the tumor most likely located?

- ☐ **A.** Right lobe of the liver
- ☐ **B.** Left lobe of the liver
- ☐ **C.** Porta hepatis
- ☐ **D.** Falciform ligament
- ☐ **E.** Hepatogastric ligament

71 During a laparoscopic cholecystectomy on a 61-year-old male, which of the following arteries must be clamped to remove the gallbladder safely?

- ☐ **A.** Common hepatic
- ☐ **B.** Proper hepatic
- ☐ **C.** Right hepatic
- ☐ **D.** Left hepatic
- ☐ **E.** Cystic

72 A 45-year-old woman is admitted to the hospital after her automobile left the highway in a rainstorm and hit a tree. She had been wearing a seat belt. On radiographic examination, it is observed that she has suffered fractures of the ninth and tenth rib on her left side and that she has intraabdominal bleeding. Physical examination reveals hypovolemic shock and progressive hypotension. Which of the following organs is most likely injured to result in these clinical signs?

- ☐ **A.** Liver
- ☐ **B.** Pancreas
- ☐ **C.** Left kidney
- ☐ **D.** Spleen
- ☐ **E.** Ileum

73 Two days after an appendectomy on a 45-year-old male patient, the patient has developed an elevated temperature (39° C), is hypotensive, and complains of abdominal pain. An exploratory laparotomy reveals large amounts of blood in the peritoneal cavity due to an injury to a vessel that occurred during the appendectomy. Which of the following vessels must be ligated to stop the bleeding?

- ☐ **A.** Right colic artery
- ☐ **B.** Right colic artery and superior rectal artery
- ☐ **C.** Superior mesenteric artery
- ☐ **D.** Ileocolic artery
- ☐ **E.** Ileocolic artery and middle colic artery

74 A 42-year-old male is admitted to the hospital with severe hematemesis. Radiographic studies reveal hepatomegaly and esophageal varices. During physical examination it is observed that the patient is icteric (jaundiced) and dilated veins ("caput medusae") are seen on his anterior abdominal wall. Which of the following venous structures is most likely obstructed for the development of caput medusae?

- ☐ **A.** Portal vein
- ☐ **B.** Inferior vena cava
- ☐ **C.** Superior vena cava
- ☐ **D.** Lateral thoracic vein
- ☐ **E.** Superficial epigastric vein

75 A 58-year-old man was admitted to the hospital with complaints of pain in the right upper quadrant and jaundice. Ultrasound examination reveals numerous large gallstones in his gallbladder. Which of the following nerves would transmit the pain of cholecystitis?

- ☐ **A.** The right vagus nerve, with referral to the inferior angle of the scapula
- ☐ **B.** Afferent fibers in spinal nerves T1 to T4
- ☐ **C.** Visceral afferent fibers in the greater thoracic splanchnic nerve, with referral to the dermatomes from T6 to T8
- ☐ **D.** Sympathetic T10 to T12 portions of greater thoracic splanchnic nerve via celiac ganglion and celiac plexus
- ☐ **E.** Afferent fibers of dorsal primary rami of spinal nerves T6 to T8, with referral to the epigastric region

76 A 15-year-old female is brought to the hospital with fever, nausea, and diffuse paraumbilical pain, which later becomes localized in the lower right quadrant. An appendectomy procedure is begun with an incision at McBurney's point. Which of the following landmarks best describes McBurney's point?

- ▢ **A.** The midpoint of the inguinal ligament in line with the right nipple
- ▢ **B.** Two thirds of the distance from the umbilicus to the anterior superior iliac spine
- ▢ **C.** A line that intersects the upper one third of the inguinal ligament
- ▢ **D.** A line that intersects the lower third of the inguinal ligament, about 2 cm from the pubic tubercle
- ▢ **E.** One third of the distance from the anterior superior iliac spine to the umbilicus

77 A 41-year-old woman is admitted to the hospital with upper abdominal pain. A gastroscopic examination reveals multiple small ulcerations in the body of the stomach. Which of the following nerves transmits the sensation of pain from this region?

- ▢ **A.** Spinal nerves T5 to T12
- ▢ **B.** Greater thoracic splanchnic nerves
- ▢ **C.** Lesser thoracic splanchnic nerves
- ▢ **D.** Lumbar splanchnic nerves
- ▢ **E.** Spinal nerves T12 to L2

78 A 68-year-old woman is admitted to the hospital with severe pain radiating from her lower back toward her pubic symphysis. Ultrasound examination reveals that a renal calculus (kidney stone) is partially obstructing her right ureter. At which of the following locations is the calculus most likely to lodge?

- ▢ **A.** Major calyx
- ▢ **B.** Minor calyx
- ▢ **C.** Pelvic brim
- ▢ **D.** Midportion of the ureter
- ▢ **E.** Between the pelvic brim and the uterine cervix

79 A 42-year-old female is admitted to the hospital after a traumatic landing while skydiving. Radiographic examination reveals a ruptured spleen. An emergency splenectomy is performed. Which of the following peritoneal structures must be carefully manipulated to prevent intraperitoneal bleeding?

- ▢ **A.** Coronary ligament
- ▢ **B.** Gastrocolic ligament
- ▢ **C.** Splenorenal ligament
- ▢ **D.** Phrenocolic ligament
- ▢ **E.** Falciform ligament

80 A 74-year-old woman is admitted to the hospital with complaints of abdominal pain. Radiographic examination reveals diverticulosis and diverticulitis of the lower portion of the descending colon, with diffuse ulcerations. It is determined that the involved area of the bowel should be removed. If the patient's anatomy follows the most typical patterns, which vessels and nerves will be cut during the operation?

- ▢ **A.** Branches of the vagus nerve and middle colic artery
- ▢ **B.** Superior mesenteric plexus and superior rectal artery
- ▢ **C.** Branches of pelvic splanchnic nerves and left colic artery
- ▢ **D.** Branches of vagus nerve and ileocolic artery
- ▢ **E.** Left thoracic splanchnic nerve and inferior mesenteric artery

81 A 15-year-old boy underwent an appendectomy procedure. Two weeks postoperatively the patient complains of numbness of the skin over the pubic region and anterior portion of his genitals. Which of the following nerves was most likely iatrogenically injured during the operation?

- ▢ **A.** Pudendal
- ▢ **B.** Genitofemoral
- ▢ **C.** Spinal nerve T10
- ▢ **D.** Subcostal
- ▢ **E.** Ilioinguinal

82 A 5-year-old boy is admitted to the hospital with projectile vomiting. Physical examination reveals severe dysphagia. Two days later the boy develops aspiration pneumonia. Esophagographic examination shows webs and strictures in the distal third of the thoracic esophagus. Which of the following developmental conditions will most likely explain the symptoms?

- ▢ **A.** Incomplete recanalization of the esophagus during the eighth week
- ▢ **B.** Tracheoesophageal fistula
- ▢ **C.** Esophageal atresia
- ▢ **D.** Duodenal atresia
- ▢ **E.** Duodenal stenosis

83 The vomitus of a 5-day-old infant contains stomach contents and bile. The vomiting has continued for 2 days. Radiographic examinations reveal stenosis of the fourth part of the duodenum. The child cries almost constantly, appearing to be hungry all of the time, yet does not gain any weight. Which of the following developmental conditions will most likely explain the symptoms?

- ▢ **A.** Patent bile duct
- ▢ **B.** Duodenal stenosis
- ▢ **C.** Hypertrophied pyloric sphincter
- ▢ **D.** Atrophied gastric antrum
- ▢ **E.** Tracheoesophageal fistula

84 A 4-day-old male infant vomits the contents of his stomach, but the vomitus does not appear to contain bile. The baby is obviously distressed and makes sucking movements of his lips in response to offerings to suckle by his mother or of the bottle, but he is failing to thrive. Which of the following conditions will best explain the symptoms?

- ▢ **A.** Duodenal stenosis
- ▢ **B.** Duodenal atresia
- ▢ **C.** Hypertrophied pyloric sphincter
- ▢ **D.** Atrophied gastric fundus
- ▢ **E.** Tracheoesophageal fistula

85 A 5-day-old female infant has emesis (vomit) containing stomach contents and bile. The vomiting continues for 2 days. Radiographic examinations reveal stenosis of the third part of the duodenum. The child cries consistently and is constantly hungry, but she does not gain any weight. Which of the following conditions will most likely explain her symptoms?

- ▢ **A.** Incomplete recanalization of the esophagus during the eighth week
- ▢ **B.** Incomplete recanalization of the duodenum
- ▢ **C.** Esophageal atresia
- ▢ **D.** Duodenal atresia
- ▢ **E.** Tracheoesophageal fistula

86 A 2-hour-old male infant had been diagnosed in utero with polyhydramnios. Now he is vomiting stomach contents and bile. The vomiting continues for 2 days. Radiographic examination reveals a "double bubble" sign on ultrasound scan. The child cries consistently and is constantly hungry but has lost 300 g in weight. Which of the following conditions will most likely explain the symptoms?

- ▢ **A.** Duodenal stenosis
- ▢ **B.** Duodenal atresia
- ▢ **C.** Hypertrophied pyloric sphincter
- ▢ **D.** Atrophied gastric antrum
- ▢ **E.** Tracheoesophageal fistula

87 A 4-year-old male child is admitted to the hospital with severe vomiting. Radiographic examination and history taking reveal that the boy suffers from an annular pancreas. Which of the following conditions will most typically explain the symptoms?

- ▢ **A.** The main pancreatic duct persisted as an accessory duct that opened at the minor papilla.
- ▢ **B.** Bile ducts failed to canalize.
- ▢ **C.** The bifid ventral bud fused with the dorsal bud.
- ▢ **D.** Only the dorsal pancreatic bud formed a ring of pancreatic tissue.
- ▢ **E.** Dorsal pancreatic bud developed around the third part of the duodenum.

88 The surgeon decided that a 35-year-old male patient must undergo an emergency appendectomy due to rupture of his appendix. A midline incision was made for greater access to the peritoneal cavity. The surgeon noted a 5-cm-long fingerlike pouch on the anterior border of the ileum about 60 cm away from the ileocecal junction. Such a pouch is a remnant of which of the following developmental structures?

- ▢ **A.** Omphaloenteric duct (yolk stalk)
- ▢ **B.** Branch of superior mesenteric artery
- ▢ **C.** Umbilical vesicle (yolk sac)
- ▢ **D.** Cecal diverticulum
- ▢ **E.** Umbilical cord
- ▢ **F.** Urachus

89 A 3-month-old boy is admitted to the hospital with an abnormal mass of tissue protruding from his abdomen. An MRI examination reveals that the mass contains some greater omentum and some small intestine. The abnormal mass protrudes when the infant cries, strains, and coughs. Which of the following conditions will most likely explain the symptoms?

- ▢ **A.** Umbilical hernia
- ▢ **B.** Omphalocele
- ▢ **C.** Gastroschisis
- ▢ **D.** Epigastric hernia
- ▢ **E.** Indirect inguinal hernia

90 Ultrasound examinations of a male fetus in the seventh month of gestation indicate a defect on his right side, lateral to the median plane, in which the viscera protrude into the amniotic cavity. Which of the following conditions will most likely explain these findings?

- ▢ **A.** Nonrotation of the midgut
- ▢ **B.** Patent urachus
- ▢ **C.** Abdominal contents have not returned from the umbilical cord

- ▢ **D.** Incomplete closure of the lateral folds
- ▢ **E.** Persistent cloacal membrane

91 A 2-hour-old male infant vomits stomach contents and bile. The vomiting continues for 2 days. In addition, abdominal distension is noted, and he is unable to pass meconium (the earliest feces to be eliminated after birth). Which of the following is the most common cause of this condition?

- ▢ **A.** Infarction of fetal bowel due to volvulus
- ▢ **B.** Incomplete closure of the lateral folds
- ▢ **C.** Failure of recanalization of the ileum
- ▢ **D.** Remnant of the proximal portion of the omphaloenteric duct
- ▢ **E.** Nonrotation of the midgut

92 A 5-year-old male infant is admitted to the hospital with signs of appendicitis. An operation is performed and an ileal (Meckel) diverticulum is discovered. Which of the following is the most common cause of this condition?

- ▢ **A.** Infarction of fetal bowel due to volvulus
- ▢ **B.** Incomplete closure of the lateral folds
- ▢ **C.** Failure of recanalization of the ileum
- ▢ **D.** Remnant of the proximal portion of the omphaloenteric duct
- ▢ **E.** Nonrotation of the midgut

93 A newborn male infant has no passage of first stool (meconium) for 48 hours after birth. Physical examination reveals that the young patient has anal agenesis with a perineal fistula. Which of the following is the most common cause of this condition?

- ▢ **A.** Incomplete separation of the cloaca by the urorectal septum
- ▢ **B.** Dorsal deviation of the urorectal septum
- ▢ **C.** Failure of the anal membrane to perforate
- ▢ **D.** Abnormal recanalization of the colon
- ▢ **E.** Remnant of the proximal portion of the omphaloenteric duct

94 A 3-month-old female infant is diagnosed with anal stenosis after several periods of stool infrequency, two of which lasted 10 days without a bowel movement. Which of the following is the most likely cause of this condition?

- ▢ **A.** Incomplete separation of the cloaca by the urorectal septum
- ▢ **B.** Dorsal deviation of the urorectal septum
- ▢ **C.** Failure of the anal membrane to perforate
- ▢ **D.** Abnormal recanalization of the colon
- ▢ **E.** Remnant of the proximal portion of the omphaloenteric duct

95 A 2-month-old male infant presents with a fecal discharge from his umbilicus. Which of the following diagnoses will best explain this condition?

- ▢ **A.** Enterocystoma
- ▢ **B.** Vitelline cyst
- ▢ **C.** Ileal (Meckel) diverticulum
- ▢ **D.** Vitelline fistula
- ▢ **E.** Volvulus

96 A 5-day-old male infant is diagnosed with anorectal agenesis. An ultrasound study reveals a rectourethral fistula. Which of the following is the most likely embryologic cause of this condition?

- ▢ **A.** Failure of the proctodeum to develop
- ▢ **B.** Agenesis of the urorectal septum
- ▢ **C.** Failure of fixation of the hindgut
- ▢ **D.** Abnormal partitioning of the cloaca
- ▢ **E.** Premature rupture of the anal membrane

97 A 12-year-old boy was admitted to the hospital with massive rectal bleeding. Upon inspection, the color of the blood ranged from bright to dark red. The child appeared to be free of any pain. Radiographic examination revealed an ileal (Meckel) diverticulum. Which of the following is the underlying embryologic cause of this condition?

- ▢ **A.** Failure of yolk stalk to regress
- ▢ **B.** Duplication of the intestine
- ▢ **C.** Malrotation of the cecum and appendix
- ▢ **D.** Nonrotation of the midgut
- ▢ **E.** Herniation of the intestines

98 A 23-year-old pregnant woman visits her gynecologist for her routine ultrasound checkup. Ultrasonographic examination reveals unilateral renal agenesis and oligohydramnios. Which of the following conditions most likely occurred?

- ▢ **A.** Polycystic kidney disease
- ▢ **B.** Degeneration of the mesonephros
- ▢ **C.** Ureteric duplication
- ▢ **D.** Failure of a ureteric bud to form
- ▢ **E.** Wilms tumor

99 A 15-year-old female was admitted to the hospital with bilateral inguinal masses. Physical examination revealed that she had not begun to menstruate but showed

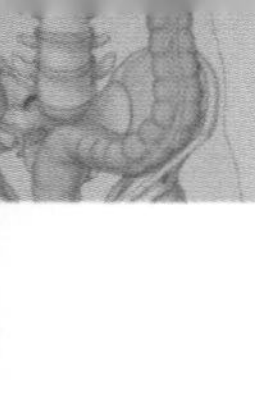

normal breast development for her age. Her external genitalia were feminine, the vagina was shallow, but no uterus could be palpated. Laboratory examination revealed that her sex chromatin pattern was negative. Which of the following is the most likely diagnosis?

- ☐ **A.** Male pseudohermaphroditism
- ☐ **B.** Female pseudohermaphroditism
- ☐ **C.** Androgen insensitivity syndrome
- ☐ **D.** Inguinal hernias
- ☐ **E.** Turner syndrome

100 An 18-year-old female gymnast is admitted to the hospital with pelvic pain. Physical examination reveals that the patient has a history of primary amenorrhea and an imperforate hymen. Which of the following is the most likely explanation for this condition?

- ☐ **A.** Failure of the vaginal plate to canalize
- ☐ **B.** Cervical atresia
- ☐ **C.** Patent processus vaginalis
- ☐ **D.** Androgen insensitivity syndrome
- ☐ **E.** Failure of the sinovaginal bulbs to develop

101 During a routine gynecologic examination, a 22-year-old female complains of dyspareunia (pain during sexual intercourse). During a pelvic examination a mass of tissue is detected on the lateral wall of the vagina. An ultrasound examination reveals that the abnormal structure is a Gartner duct cyst. From which of the following embryonic structures does this cyst take origin?

- ☐ **A.** Mesonephric tubules
- ☐ **B.** Paramesonephric duct
- ☐ **C.** Urogenital folds
- ☐ **D.** Mesonephric duct
- ☐ **E.** Sinovaginal bulbs

102 A 2-day-old male infant is hospitalized in the intensive care unit with acute respiratory distress. Radiographic examination reveals that the patient has anuria, oligohydramnios, and hypoplastic lungs. Facial characteristics are consistent with Potter syndrome. Which of the following is the most likely explanation for these initial findings?

- ☐ **A.** Multicystic dysplastic kidney
- ☐ **B.** Polycystic kidney
- ☐ **C.** Renal agenesis
- ☐ **D.** Wilms tumor
- ☐ **E.** Extrophy of the bladder

103 A 58-year-old male bricklayer is admitted to the hospital with severe pain that radiates from his lower back to the pubic region. Ultrasound examination reveals that a kidney stone is partially obstructing his right ureter; the examination also indicates the presence of a second ureter on the right side. Which of the following is the most likely cause of this latter finding?

- ☐ **A.** Failure of ureteric bud to form
- ☐ **B.** Early splitting of the ureteric bud
- ☐ **C.** Failure of urorectal septum to develop
- ☐ **D.** Persistent urachus
- ☐ **E.** Failure of ureteric bud to branch

104 A 50-year-old female with a long history of heartburn (self-treated with various over-the-counter medications) develops severe epigastric pain and is urgently admitted to the hospital. A gastroscopic examination reveals a small, perforated ulceration in the posterior wall of the stomach body. At surgery, with the patient in supine position, 150 ml of blood-tinged, frothy gray liquid is aspirated from the peritoneal cavity. Where in the peritoneal cavity would liquid most likely first collect when the patient is supine?

- ☐ **A.** Right subphrenic space
- ☐ **B.** Hepatorenal pouch (of Morison)
- ☐ **C.** Left paracolic gutter
- ☐ **D.** Vesicouterine pouch
- ☐ **E.** Rectouterine pouch (of Douglas)

105 A 43-year-old female accountant complains of severe epigastric pain and is admitted to the hospital. A gastroscopic examination reveals a small, perforated ulceration in the posterior wall of the greater curvature of her stomach. An upright chest radiograph reveals a small amount of free air in the peritoneal cavity. Where is the air most likely located?

- ☐ **A.** Right subphrenic space
- ☐ **B.** Supravesical space
- ☐ **C.** Paracolic gutters
- ☐ **D.** Vesicouterine pouch
- ☐ **E.** Rectouterine pouch (of Douglas)

106 A 25-year-old female is admitted to the hospital with sharp pain in the left lower quadrant. Patient history reveals that her last menstrual period was 10 days ago. Transvaginal ultrasound reveals a ruptured cyst on the left ovary. The sonogram also reveals approximately 100 ml of fluid in the pelvis, which is presumed to represent cyst contents and bleeding from the rupture site. Where is this fluid most likely located?

- ☐ **A.** Right subphrenic space
- ☐ **B.** Hepatorenal pouch (of Morison)
- ☐ **C.** Paracolic gutters

- ▢ **D.** Vesicouterine pouch
- ▢ **E.** Rectouterine pouch (of Douglas)

107 A 60-year-old man is admitted to the emergency department with severe abdominal pain. Physical examination reveals guarding and rigidity in the abdominal wall. An abdominal CT scan shows a thrombus in an intestinal artery supplying the ileum. Which of the following layers of peritoneum will have to be entered by the surgeon to access the affected vessel?

- ▢ **A.** Parietal peritoneum and the greater omentum
- ▢ **B.** Greater and lesser omentum
- ▢ **C.** Lesser omentum and the gastrosplenic ligament
- ▢ **D.** Parietal peritoneum and the mesentery
- ▢ **E.** Greater omentum and the transverse mesocolon

108 A 52-year-old male presents to the emergency department complaining of persistent severe right upper quadrant pain for the past 2 hours. During that period of time he felt nauseated, was sweating profusely, and also experienced pain in the posterior aspect of his right shoulder. The pain began shortly after a lunch consisting of "fast food." Ultrasound examination reveals multiple stones in an inflamed gallbladder with a normal bile duct. Which of the following spinal nerve segments are involved in the shoulder pain, associated with cholecystitis?

- ▢ **A.** C3 to C5
- ▢ **B.** C5 to C8
- ▢ **C.** T1 to T4
- ▢ **D.** T5 to T9
- ▢ **E.** T10, T11

109 During a cholecystectomy on a 64-year-old female, the right hepatic artery was accidentally injured. In addition to bleeding profusely, the lacerated artery was hidden from view by overlying connective tissue and fat. Which of the following procedures would most likely be performed by the surgeon to slow, or perhaps arrest, the blood loss?

- ▢ **A.** Pringle maneuver
- ▢ **B.** Kocher maneuver
- ▢ **C.** Valsalva maneuver
- ▢ **D.** Heimlich maneuver
- ▢ **E.** Placement of a vascular clamp on the porta hepatis

110 A 53-year-old quality control engineer is admitted to the hospital with severe abdominal pain. The patient's history and physical examination indicate chronic colonic diverticulitis, with tachycardia and hypotension at the present time. An ultrasonographic examination reveals massive bleeding from the descending colon. Which of the following arteries is most likely to be the source of the hemorrhage?

- ▢ **A.** A branch of the inferior mesenteric
- ▢ **B.** Middle colic
- ▢ **C.** Superior rectal
- ▢ **D.** Inferior rectal
- ▢ **E.** Left gastroepiploic

111 The gallbladder of a 51-year-old female patient is characterized by the presence of multiple gallstones, consistent with the diagnosis of cholecystitis. Which of the following tests would be anticipated to be positive in this patient?

- ▢ **A.** Rebound tenderness
- ▢ **B.** Iliopsoas test
- ▢ **C.** Obturator sign
- ▢ **D.** Murphy's sign
- ▢ **E.** Cough tenderness

112 A 35-year-old man is admitted to the hospital with a small-caliber bullet wound to the left upper quadrant of the abdomen. Radiographic examination reveals profuse intraperitoneal bleeding. An emergency laparotomy is performed, and the source of bleeding appears to be a vessel within the lesser sac. Which of the following ligaments would most likely be transected to gain adequate entry to the lesser sac?

- ▢ **A.** Coronary
- ▢ **B.** Gastrosplenic
- ▢ **C.** Splenorenal
- ▢ **D.** Gastrocolic
- ▢ **E.** Hepatoduodenal

113 A 45-year-old woman is admitted to the hospital with rectal bleeding. Physical examination, including a rectal examination, reveals an abnormal mass of tissue protruding below the pectinate line. Biopsy reveals the presence of an adenocarcinoma. Which of the following groups of lymph nodes would first receive lymph from the area of pathology?

- ▢ **A.** Internal iliac
- ▢ **B.** External iliac
- ▢ **C.** Middle rectal
- ▢ **D.** Superficial inguinal
- ▢ **E.** Deep inguinal

114 A 53-year-old man is admitted to the hospital with rectal bleeding. Physical examination, including a rectal examination, reveals an abnormal mass of tissue protruding from an area superior to the external anal sphincter, superior to the pectinate line. Biopsy reveals the presence of an adenocarcinoma. Which of the following groups of lymph nodes would first receive lymph from the cancerous area?

- ▢ **A.** Internal iliac
- ▢ **B.** External iliac
- ▢ **C.** Middle rectal
- ▢ **D.** Superficial inguinal
- ▢ **E.** Deep inguinal

115 A 32-year-old male is admitted to the emergency department with severe esophageal reflux. Radiographic examination reveals that the patient has a hiatal hernia, and a surgical procedure is scheduled. Which of the following landmarks would be the most useful to distinguish between sliding and paraesophageal hiatal hernias?

- ▢ **A.** Sliding hernias possess a normal gastroesophageal junction.
- ▢ **B.** In sliding hernias the gastroesophageal junction is displaced.
- ▢ **C.** Paraesophageal hernias have a displaced gastroesophageal junction.
- ▢ **D.** In paraesophageal hernias the antrum moves into the stomach corpus.
- ▢ **E.** In paraesophageal hernias the antrum and the cardia move into the body of the stomach.

116 A 43-year-old man is admitted to the emergency department with complaints of intense abdominal pain. Radiographic examination reveals a right subphrenic abscess that extends to the midline. Which of the following structures would most likely be in a position to retard the spread of the abscess across the midline?

- ▢ **A.** Round ligament
- ▢ **B.** Falciform ligament
- ▢ **C.** Coronary ligament
- ▢ **D.** Hepatoduodenal ligament
- ▢ **E.** Gastroduodenal ligament

117 A 21-year-old football player is admitted to the emergency department with intense back pain. Physical examination shows that his left lower back is bruised and swollen. He complains of sharp pain during respiration. A radiograph reveals a fracture of the eleventh rib on the left side. Which of the following organs would be the most likely to sustain injury at this site?

- ▢ **A.** Spleen
- ▢ **B.** Lung
- ▢ **C.** Kidney
- ▢ **D.** Liver
- ▢ **E.** Pancreas

118 A 46-year-old man is admitted to the hospital with a rather large but painless mass on his right groin. During physical examination it is noted that the inguinal lymph nodes are hard and palpable. A lymph node biopsy reveals the presence of malignant cells. Which of the following locations would be the most likely primary source of carcinoma?

- ▢ **A.** Prostate
- ▢ **B.** Bladder
- ▢ **C.** Testis
- ▢ **D.** Anal canal
- ▢ **E.** Sigmoid colon

119 A 54-year-old man is admitted to the hospital with vomiting and severe weight loss. Physical examination reveals that the umbilical and epigastric regions are tender and painful. A CT scan examination reveals a massive tumor originating from the third part of the duodenum. Which of the following structures is more likely to be compressed or invaded by the tumor?

- ▢ **A.** Common bile duct
- ▢ **B.** Portal vein
- ▢ **C.** Superior mesenteric artery
- ▢ **D.** Gastroduodenal artery
- ▢ **E.** Posterior superior pancreaticoduodenal artery

120 A 24-year-old woman is admitted to the hospital with lower abdominal pain. A CT examination reveals an abnormal mass occupying the left adnexa in the pelvis. During the surgical procedure the ureter and the structures immediately medial to the ureter are identified. Which of the following vascular structures crosses the ureter just lateral to the cervix of the uterus?

- ▢ **A.** Middle rectal artery
- ▢ **B.** Superior vesical artery
- ▢ **C.** Internal pudendal vein
- ▢ **D.** Uterine artery
- ▢ **E.** Gonadal vein

121 A 32-year-old woman is admitted to the hospital with cramping abdominal pain around her umbilicus and vomiting for the previous 2 days. Radiographic studies indicate numerous stones in the gallbladder and air accumulation in the gallbladder and biliary tree. At which of the following places will an obstructive stone most likely be found?

- ▢ **A.** Jejunum
- ▢ **B.** Terminal ileum

- ▢ **C.** Common bile duct
- ▢ **D.** Duodenum
- ▢ **E.** Hepatic duct

122 A 37-year-old woman is admitted to the hospital with signs of cholecystitis. A physical examination confirms the initial diagnosis and a cholecystectomy is planned. Which of the following landmarks will best describe the precise location of the gallbladder with respect to the body wall?

- ▢ **A.** The intersection of the right linea semilunaris with the ninth costal cartilage
- ▢ **B.** The intersection of the right linea semilunaris with the intertubercular plane
- ▢ **C.** To the right of the epigastric region
- ▢ **D.** Superiorly to the umbilical region
- ▢ **E.** Upper right quadrant

123 A 45-year-old male is admitted to the hospital with jaundice. This patient has a long history of alcoholism. Radiographic studies reveal ascites, portal hypertension, and liver cirrhosis. Which of the following veins are likely to be responsible for the production of ascitic fluid?

- ▢ **A.** Direct portal vein tributaries
- ▢ **B.** Anastomosing vessels between parietal veins and veins of retroperitoneal intestine
- ▢ **C.** Paraumbilical veins
- ▢ **D.** Esophageal submucosal anastomoses with azygos tributaries
- ▢ **E.** Superior rectal left gastric and middle rectal veins

124 A 45-year-old man is admitted to the hospital with a palpable and painful mass at his groin that is exacerbated when he stands erect or physically exerts himself. Physical examination indicates the probability of a direct inguinal hernia, a diagnosis that is confirmed laparoscopically. Which of the following is the most likely cause of this type of inguinal hernia?

- ▢ **A.** Defective transversalis fascia around the deep inguinal ring
- ▢ **B.** Defective peritoneum around the deep inguinal ring
- ▢ **C.** Defective aponeurosis of external abdominal oblique muscle
- ▢ **D.** Defective extraperitoneal connective tissue
- ▢ **E.** Defective aponeurosis of transversus abdominis muscle

125 A 22-year-old female is admitted to the hospital with a complaint of intense periumbilical pain. Physical examination indicates a strong possibility of appendicitis. Shortly before an appendectomy is to be performed, the inflamed appendix ruptures. In which area would the extravasating blood and infectious fluids from the appendiceal region most tend to collect if the patient was sitting upright?

- ▢ **A.** Subphrenic space
- ▢ **B.** Hepatorenal recess (pouch of Morison)
- ▢ **C.** Rectouterine recess (pouch of Douglas)
- ▢ **D.** Vesicouterine space
- ▢ **E.** Subhepatic space

126 The 22-year-old female patient cried out in agony from the pain of her burst appendix. Which of the following structures contain the neuronal cell bodies of the pain fibers from the appendix?

- ▢ **A.** Sympathetic chain ganglia
- ▢ **B.** Celiac ganglion
- ▢ **C.** Lateral horn of the spinal cord
- ▢ **D.** Dorsal root ganglia of spinal nerves T8 to T10
- ▢ **E.** Dorsal root ganglia of spinal nerves L2 to L4

127 A 30-year-old woman complains of weakness and fatigability over the past 6 months. She has a 3-month acute history of severe hypertension that has required treatment with antihypertensive medications. Radiographic examination reveals a tumor of her right suprarenal gland. The patient is diagnosed with a pheochromocytoma (tumor of the adrenal medulla) and is scheduled for a laparoscopic adrenalectomy. Which of the following nerve fibers will need to be cut when the adrenal gland and tumor are removed?

- ▢ **A.** Preganglionic sympathetic fibers
- ▢ **B.** Postganglionic sympathetic fibers
- ▢ **C.** Somatic motor fibers
- ▢ **D.** Postganglionic parasympathetic fibers
- ▢ **E.** Preganglionic parasympathetic fibers

128 A 55-year-old man is admitted to the hospital for his annual checkup. An ultrasound examination reveals a tumor that has incorporated the right common iliac artery and compressed the vein that lies posterior to it. Doppler ultrasound studies give evidence of the development of a deep venous thrombosis that could block venous return from the left lower limb, causing ischemia and pain. Which of the following vessels is most likely to be involved in the production of the deep venous thrombosis?

- A. Inferior vena cava
- B. Right renal vein
- C. Left testicular vein
- D. Left common iliac vein
- E. Right common iliac vein

129 A 48-year-old woman is admitted to the emergency department with a complaint of severe abdominal pain. Radiographic examination reveals advanced carcinoma of the head of the pancreas. A celiac plexus block is performed to relieve her pain. Which of the following best describes the nerve structures that are most likely to be present in the celiac ganglion?

- A. Preganglionic parasympathetic and somatic motor fibers
- B. Postganglionic parasympathetic and visceral afferent fibers
- C. Postganglionic sympathetic and visceral afferent fibers
- D. Pre- and postganglionic sympathetic, preganglionic parasympathetic, and visceral afferent fibers
- E. Preganglionic sympathetic, preganglionic parasympathetic, and visceral afferent fibers

130 A 21-year-old woman is admitted to the hospital with a complaint of severe pain radiating from her lower back toward and above the pubic symphysis. Ultrasound examination reveals that a kidney stone is partially obstructing her right ureter. Which of the following nerves is most likely responsible for conducting the sensation of pain?

- A. Subcostal
- B. Iliohypogastric
- C. Ilioinguinal
- D. Lateral femoral cutaneous
- E. Obturator

131 A 42-year-old woman is admitted to the hospital with an acutely painful abdomen. Radiographic examination reveals penetration of a posterior duodenal ulcer resulting in intraabdominal bleeding. Which of the following arteries is most commonly eroded by this type of ulcer?

- A. Gastroduodenal artery
- B. Superior mesenteric
- C. Posterior superior pancreaticoduodenal
- D. Posterior inferior pancreaticoduodenal
- E. Right gastric

132 A 37-year-old female court stenographer is admitted to the hospital with a complaint of intense pain in her abdomen. Radiographic examination reveals penetration of an anterior duodenal ulcer. Which of the following conditions will most probably occur?

- A. Bleeding from gastroduodenal artery
- B. Bleeding from superior mesenteric artery
- C. Bleeding from posterior superior pancreaticoduodenal artery
- D. Bleeding from posterior inferior pancreaticoduodenal artery
- E. Peritonitis

133 A 56-year-old male is diagnosed with midgut volvulus and intestinal ischemia. A laparotomy is performed to release the obstruction of the intestines. Which of the following structures is used as a landmark to determine the position of the duodenojejunal junction?

- A. Superior mesenteric artery
- B. Inferior mesenteric artery
- C. Vasa recta
- D. Suspensory ligament of the duodenum (ligament of Treitz)
- E. Ladd bands

134 A 4-month-old female infant is admitted to the hospital with cyanosis. Physical examination reveals decreased breath sounds, abdominal sounds in the thorax, and respiratory distress. A radiographic examination reveals a posterolateral defect of the diaphragm and abdominal contents in the left pleural cavity. Which of the following is the most likely cause of this defect?

- A. Absence of a pleuropericardial fold
- B. Absence of musculature in one half of the diaphragm
- C. Failure of migration of diaphragm
- D. Failure of the septum transversum to develop
- E. Failure of pleuroperitoneal fold to close

135 A 58-year-old male complains of sharp epigastric pain, most commonly felt just after a large meal. He is tender to palpation at the xiphisternal junction. Barium swallow exams and dye injections (HIDA scan) to test gallbladder functions are negative. Ultrasound reveals that a portion of the greater omentum is trapped at its entry to the thorax between the xiphoid process and the costal margin on the right. What is the most likely diagnosis of this condition?

- A. Bochdalek hernia
- B. Sliding esophageal hernia
- C. Morgagni hernia

- ▢ **D.** Cholecystitis
- ▢ **E.** Hiatal hernia

136 A 62-year-old woman is admitted to the emergency department with abdominal pains of uncertain origin. A CT scan reveals an aortic aneurysm affecting the origin of the superior mesenteric artery, resulting in ischemia to an abdominal organ. Which of the following organs is most likely affected?

- ▢ **A.** Ileum
- ▢ **B.** Transverse colon
- ▢ **C.** Spleen
- ▢ **D.** Stomach
- ▢ **E.** Duodenum

137 A 41-year-old man entered the emergency department with abdominal trauma after his motorcycle was struck by a hit-and-run automobile driver. One week following emergent surgery the patient was released from the hospital. Two months postoperatively the patient complained of abdominal pain. A CT scan examination demonstrated an internal hernia in which the hepatic flexure of the colon had herniated through the epiploic (omental) foramen (of Winslow). Gastrointestinal veins appeared to be markedly dilated, including the veins forming anastomoses between the portal and caval systems (veins of Retzius). Which of the following structures is most likely compressed?

- ▢ **A.** Portal vein
- ▢ **B.** Inferior vena cava
- ▢ **C.** Hepatic artery
- ▢ **D.** Common bile duct
- ▢ **E.** Cystic duct

138 A 48-year-old woman visited the outpatient clinic with a complaint of lower left quadrant pain that had persisted for the previous 3 months. Laboratory examinations revealed that the patient had blood in her stools. A colonoscopy gave evidence of diverticulosis that had been affecting the distal part of the descending colon. To which of the following dermatomes would pain have most likely been referred?

- ▢ **A.** T5 to T9
- ▢ **B.** T10 to L1
- ▢ **C.** L1, L2
- ▢ **D.** L1 to L4
- ▢ **E.** T10 to L2

139 A 61-year-old man is admitted to the emergency department with abdominal pain and a 2-day history of vomiting. Physical examination reveals a colicky abdominal pain in the right lower quadrant, with abdominal distention. Upon auscultation, episodes of pain were associated with rushes, gurgling, and tinkling sounds. A CT scan examination reveals a mechanical obstruction of the bowel. Which of the following parts of the gastrointestinal tract is most likely obstructed?

- ▢ **A.** Hepatopancreatic ampulla of Vater
- ▢ **B.** Duodenal bulb
- ▢ **C.** Proximal ileum
- ▢ **D.** Pyloric sphincter
- ▢ **E.** Ileocecal junction

140 A 43-year-old woman is admitted to the emergency department with esophageal pain and hematemesis after swallowing a fish bone. An endoscopic examination reveals perforation of the intraabdominal portion of the esophageal wall. Which of the following arteries is most likely injured?

- ▢ **A.** Branches of left gastric
- ▢ **B.** Bronchial
- ▢ **C.** Thoracic intercostal
- ▢ **D.** Branches of right gastric
- ▢ **E.** Right inferior phrenic

141 A 42-year-old patient is admitted to the hospital after suffering a ruptured spleen in a skiing accident. Physical examination reveals intense pain that radiates to the region of the left shoulder, presumably due to irritation of the diaphragm. Which of the following signs best describes this condition?

- ▢ **A.** Mittelschmerz
- ▢ **B.** Kerh sign
- ▢ **C.** Rovsing sign
- ▢ **D.** Psoas sign
- ▢ **E.** Obturator sign

142 A 43-year-old man is admitted to the hospital with a knife wound to the right lobe of the liver. After a laparotomy is performed, digital pressure is applied to the hepatoduodenal ligament, but brisk bleeding continues, indicating a variation in the origin of the right hepatic artery. Which of the following is the most common variation in the arterial supply to the right lobe of the liver?

- ▢ **A.** The right hepatic originates from the gastroduodenal.
- ▢ **B.** The right hepatic originates from the superior mesenteric.
- ▢ **C.** The right hepatic originates from the left gastric.

- D. The right hepatic originates from the left hepatic.
- E. The right hepatic originates directly from the aorta.

143 A 38-year-old woman is admitted to the hospital with signs of cholecystitis and gallbladder stones. During cholangiography, the catheter is inserted with difficulty into the gallbladder. Which of the following structures is most likely to interfere with the passage of the catheter into the cystic duct?

- A. Cystic duct compression by a hepatic artery
- B. Spiral valve (of Heister)
- C. Tortuosity of the cystic duct
- D. Adhesions from the hepatoduodenal ligament
- E. Portal vein compression of the cystic duct

144 A 57-year-old woman is admitted to the hospital with symptoms and signs of acute cholecystitis. Radiographic and physical examinations confirm the initial diagnosis, and a cholecystectomy is performed. On the fifth postoperative day the patient develops bile peritonitis. Which of the following conditions would most likely be responsible for such an outcome, assuming the cholecystectomy had been performed correctly?

- A. The common bile duct is leaking.
- B. The ducts of Luschka are leaking.
- C. The right hepatic duct is leaking.
- D. The cystic duct is leaking.
- E. The left hepatic duct is leaking.

145 A 64-year-old man is admitted to the hospital with intense abdominal pain from a pancreatic tumor. A neurectomy is performed to interrupt the neural fibers supplying the pancreas. Which of the following neural fibers would be the most likely objective of the neurectomy?

- A. Sympathetic preganglionic
- B. Sympathetic postganglionic
- C. Visceral afferent
- D. Postganglionic and preganglionic
- E. Postganglionic and postganglionic

146 A 54-year-old man is admitted to the emergency department with a 2-day history of mild abdominal pain, in addition to bloating, nausea, vomiting, and poor appetite. Past medical history reveals that the patient has just recovered from a pneumonia infection. Radiographic examination reveals a paralytic ileus. Which of the followings signs would most likely be found during a physical examination?

- A. Increased bowel sounds
- B. Absent bowel sounds
- C. Borborygmi
- D. Crampy abdominal pain
- E. Localized tenderness

147 A 65-year-old man is admitted to the emergency department with complaints of nonspecific abdominal pain. Physical and radiographic examinations reveal mild intestinal ischemia due to atherosclerotic occlusion of the midproximal part of the superior mesenteric artery, but collateral blood supply has delayed the onset of necrosis. What vessels provide collateral channels between the celiac trunk and the superior mesenteric artery?

- A. Superior and inferior pancreaticoduodenal
- B. Left gastric and hepatic
- C. Cystic and gastroduodenal
- D. Right and left colic
- E. Right and left gastroomental

148 A 22-year-old man is admitted to the emergency department with acute abdominal pain at his right lower quadrant. Radiographic and physical examinations provide evidence of acute appendicitis. An appendectomy is performed, beginning with an incision at McBurney's point. Through which of the following abdominal layers must the surgeon pass to reach the appendix through this incision?

- A. External abdominal oblique muscle, internal oblique muscle, transversalis fascia, parietal peritoneum
- B. Aponeurosis of the external abdominal oblique muscle, internal oblique muscle, transversus abdominis muscle, transversalis fascia, parietal peritoneum
- C. Aponeurosis of the external abdominal oblique muscle, internal oblique muscle, transversus abdominis muscle, parietal peritoneum
- D. Aponeurosis of the external abdominal oblique muscle, aponeurosis of internal oblique muscle, transversus abdominis muscle, transversalis fascia, parietal peritoneum
- E. Aponeurosis of the external abdominal oblique muscle, aponeurosis of internal oblique muscle, aponeurosis of transversus abdominis muscle, transversalis fascia, parietal peritoneum

149 A 12-year-old male is admitted to the hospital with profuse rectal bleeding but appears to be free of any associated pain. Which of the following is the most common cause of severe rectal bleeding in the pediatric age group?

- ☐ **A.** Internal hemorrhoids
- ☐ **B.** External hemorrhoids
- ☐ **C.** Diverticulosis
- ☐ **D.** Ileal (Meckel) diverticulum
- ☐ **E.** Borborygmi

150 A 48-year-old male is admitted to the hospital with abdominal distension and pain. The radiographic image is shown in Fig. 3-2. In which of the following locations will blood be detected with an ultrasound machine if the patient stands upright?

- ☐ **A.** Subphrenic space
- ☐ **B.** Hepatorenal space (pouch of Morison)
- ☐ **C.** Rectouterine space (pouch of Douglas)
- ☐ **D.** Rectovesical space
- ☐ **E.** Subhepatic space

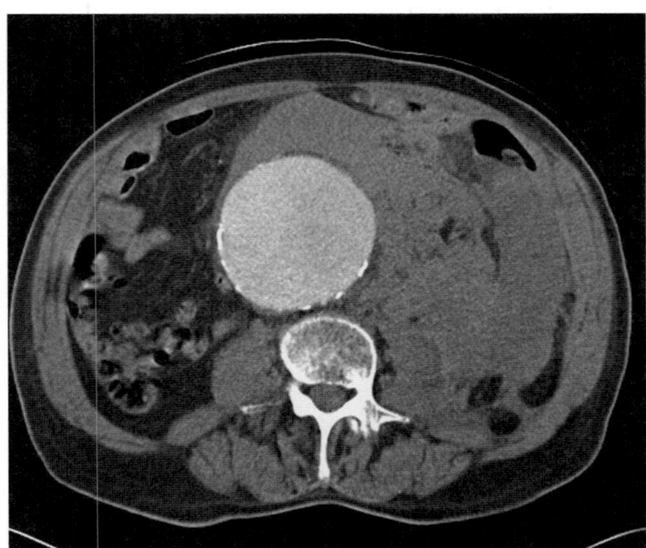

Fig. 3-2

151 A 27-year-old woman is admitted to the emergency department with markedly elevated temperature and abdominal pain. Physical examination initially indicates paraumbilical pain, but the site of origin of pain soon shifts to the right lower quadrant. A CT scan is shown in Fig. 3-3. Which of the following structures is affected?

- ☐ **A.** Right ovary
- ☐ **B.** Appendix
- ☐ **C.** Iliocecal junction
- ☐ **D.** Ascending colon
- ☐ **E.** Ileum

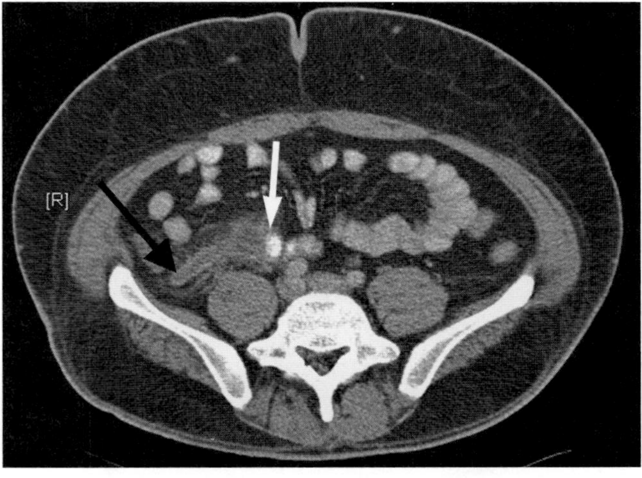

Fig. 3-3

152 A 51-year-old complains of abdominal pain of 2-month duration. A CT scan of the patient's abdomen is shown in Fig. 3-4. An angiogram indicates that several arteries of the gastrointestinal tract are occluded due to atherosclerosis, producing bowel ischemia. Which of the following arteries is most likely occluded in the CT scan?

- ☐ **A.** Middle colic
- ☐ **B.** Right colic
- ☐ **C.** Left colic
- ☐ **D.** Iliocolic
- ☐ **E.** Marginal

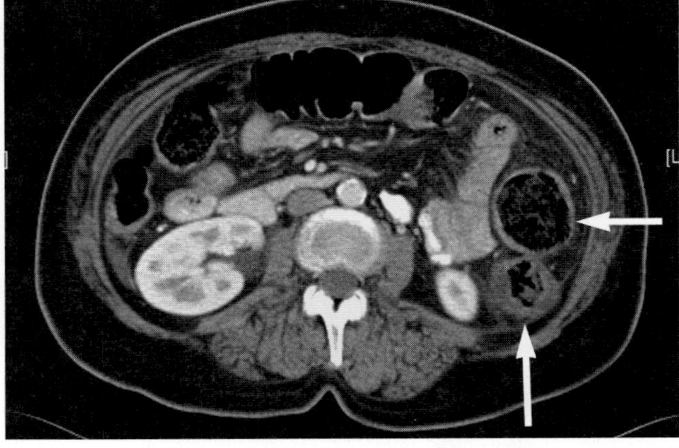

Fig. 3-4

153 A 53-year-old man visits the outpatient clinic because of an abnormal mass developing in his anal canal. An image from the physical examination is seen in Fig. 3-5. A biopsy of the tissue reveals squamous cell carcinoma of the anus. Which of the following lymphatics will most typically first receive cancerous cells from the anal tumor?

- ☐ **A.** Deep inguinal lymph nodes
- ☐ **B.** Superficial inguinal lymph nodes

- ▢ **C.** Internal iliac nodes
- ▢ **D.** External iliac nodes
- ▢ **E.** Paraaortic nodes

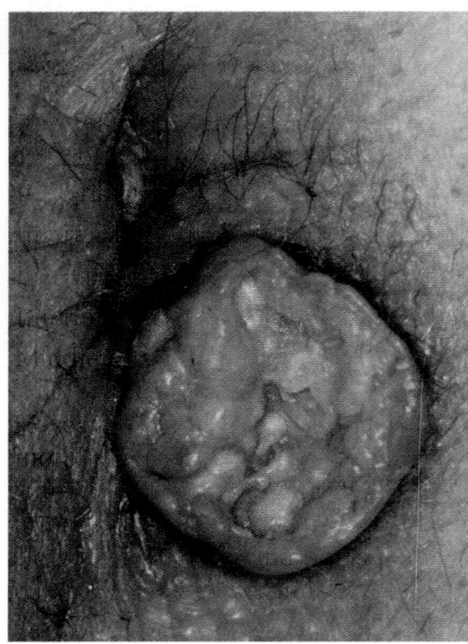

Fig. 3-5

154 A 49-year-old man comes to the outpatient clinic with complaints of bloating, gas, and a sense of fullness for the preceding 2 years. A CT scan examination is shown in Fig. 3-6. Which of the following structures is affected?

- ▢ **A.** Spleen
- ▢ **B.** Stomach
- ▢ **C.** Duodenum
- ▢ **D.** Pancreas
- ▢ **E.** Descending colon

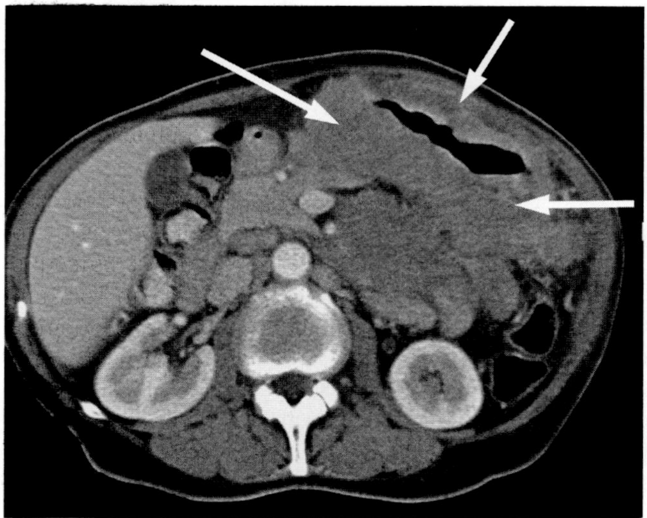

Fig. 3-6

155 An endoscopic examination is performed on a 49-year-old patient with a preliminary diagnosis of a gastrointestinal cancer, and a tissue sample is sent for histopathologic examination. Biopsy reveals a gastric adenocarcinoma, and a total gastrectomy is performed. Which of the following lymph nodes will most likely first receive metastatic cells?

- ▢ **A.** Celiac
- ▢ **B.** Splenic
- ▢ **C.** Suprapancreatic
- ▢ **D.** Right gastric
- ▢ **E.** Cisterna chyli

156 A 28-year-old female visits the outpatient clinic to receive the required physical examination for an insurance policy. Physical and laboratory examinations give evidence that she is probably a normal, healthy woman. A radiograph of the patient is shown in Fig. 3-7. Which of the following is the most likely diagnosis?

- ▢ **A.** Cholecystitis
- ▢ **B.** Carcinoma of the liver
- ▢ **C.** A caudal extension of the right hepatic lobe (Riedel lobe)
- ▢ **D.** Pancreatic carcinoma
- ▢ **E.** Carcinoma of the stomach

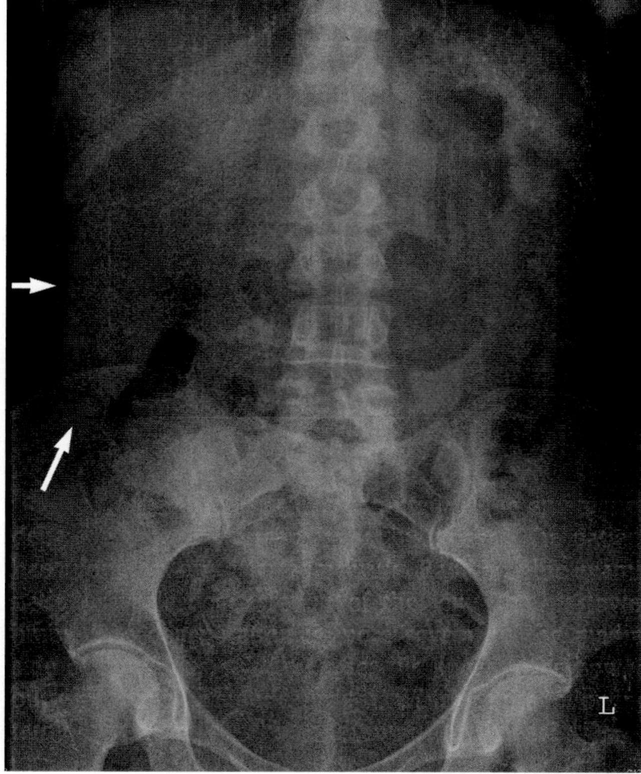

Fig. 3-7

157 A 35-year-old woman is admitted to the hospital with a mass protruding through her skin at the right lower quadrant. Physical examination reveals intestinal herniation, as shown in Fig. 3-8. Which of the following is the most likely diagnosis?

- ▢ **A.** Richter hernia
- ▢ **B.** Spigelian hernia
- ▢ **C.** Paraumbilical
- ▢ **D.** Incisional hernia
- ▢ **E.** Ventral hernia

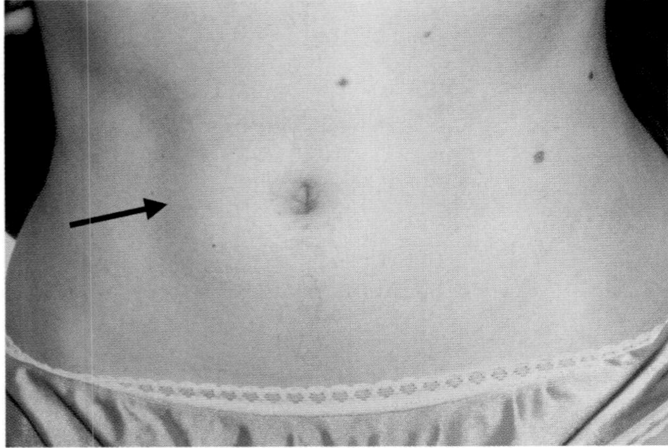

Fig. 3-8

158 A 3-year-old male is admitted to the pediatric clinic with a palpable mass in the right side of his scrotum, and a preliminary diagnosis is made of a congenital, indirect inguinal hernia. Which of the following is the most likely cause of an indirect inguinal hernia in this patient?

- ▢ **A.** The deep ring opens into an intact processus vaginalis.
- ▢ **B.** Congenital hydrocele
- ▢ **C.** Ectopic testis
- ▢ **D.** Epispadias
- ▢ **E.** Rupture of the transversalis fascia

159 A 43-year-old woman visits the outpatient clinic with complaints of chronic dysphagia and gastroesophageal reflux. An endoscopic examination reveals achalasia of the cardia of the stomach. Which of the following is the most likely cause of this condition?

- ▢ **A.** Failure of relaxation of the lower esophageal sphincter
- ▢ **B.** Dyspepsia
- ▢ **C.** Gastritis
- ▢ **D.** Gastroparesis
- ▢ **E.** Peptic ulcer

160 A 21-year-old male is admitted to the hospital with periumbilical pain. A CT scan examination reveals internal bleeding about 2 feet proximal to the ileocecal junction. Which of the following is the most likely diagnosis?

- ▢ **A.** Ruptured appendix
- ▢ **B.** Volvulus
- ▢ **C.** Diverticulosis
- ▢ **D.** Ileal (Meckel) diverticulum
- ▢ **E.** Borborygmi

161 A 45-year-old man is admitted to the hospital with pain in the right upper quadrant, with radiation to the tip of his scapula. Radiographic examination reveals gallbladder stones, with associated cholecystitis. An open cholecystectomy is performed, using a Kocher incision (along the right costal margin). Which of the following nerves are most likely at risk during this incision?

- ▢ **A.** T5, T6
- ▢ **B.** T6 to T8
- ▢ **C.** T7, T8
- ▢ **D.** T9 to L1
- ▢ **E.** T5 to T9

162 A 3-year-old female is admitted to the pediatric clinic because of a palpable right inguinal mass. An open surgical procedure is performed. Digital pressure is used to return organ contents of the hernia to the abdomen. A sac of peritoneum can be seen clearly, protruding from the internal ring. Which of the following terms is most accurate for the origin of this structure?

- ▢ **A.** A patent processus vaginalis (canal of Nuck)
- ▢ **B.** Congenital hydrocele
- ▢ **C.** Ectopic uterus
- ▢ **D.** Femoral hernia
- ▢ **E.** Rupture of the transversalis fascia

163 A 48-year-old female was scheduled for radiographic examination because of severe abdominal pain. The imaging gave evidence of a pancreatic pseudocyst. Which of the following is the typical topographic location for this type of pseudocyst?

- ▢ **A.** Right subhepatic space
- ▢ **B.** Hepatorenal space
- ▢ **C.** Omental bursa
- ▢ **D.** Right subphrenic space
- ▢ **E.** Greater sac

164 A 38-year-old male is examined in the outpatient clinic because of his complaint of mild abdominal pain of 2 years' duration. Upon examination, it is observed that the pain is dull and located principally in the left upper quadrant around the xiphoid process. An endoscopic examination reveals that the patient suffers from a gastric ulcer. At which of the following spinal nerve levels are the neuronal cell bodies located for the sensory fibers in such a case of gastric ulcer?

- ▢ **A.** T5, T6
- ▢ **B.** T6 to T8
- ▢ **C.** T7, T8
- ▢ **D.** T9 to L1
- ▢ **E.** T5 to T9

165 A 43-year-old man is admitted to the hospital with abdominal pain and vomiting. A CT scan examination reveals that the patient has an internal hernia involving his duodenum. An exploratory laparotomy reveals a paraduodenal hernia. Which of the following arteries is most at risk during the repair of this hernia?

- ▢ **A.** Middle colic
- ▢ **B.** Sigmoidal
- ▢ **C.** Ileocolic
- ▢ **D.** Ileal
- ▢ **E.** Ascending branches of left colic

166 A 42-year-old male patient with jaundice is admitted to the hospital with severe pain that radiates to his back. A CT scan examination reveals a tumor at the neck of the pancreas. Biopsy reveals a ductular adenocarcinoma. Which of the following structures will first receive metastatic cells?

- ▢ **A.** Stomach
- ▢ **B.** Spleen
- ▢ **C.** Duodenum
- ▢ **D.** Liver
- ▢ **E.** Vertebral column

167 A major vessel appears to be nearly occluded in a 42-year-old male patient diagnosed with ductular adenocarcinoma. A CT scan examination has clearly demonstrated the tumor is at the neck of the pancreas. Which of the following vessels would be the most likely to be obstructed?

- ▢ **A.** Inferior mesenteric vein
- ▢ **B.** Portal vein
- ▢ **C.** Superior mesenteric artery
- ▢ **D.** Posterior superior pancreaticoduodenal artery
- ▢ **E.** Greater pancreatic artery

168 A 49-year-old woman is admitted to the hospital with abdominal pain. Physical examination reveals an epigastric pain that migrates toward the patient's right side and posteriorly toward the scapula. Radiographic examination reveals cholecystitis with a large gallstone and no jaundice. In which of the following structures is it most likely the gallstone will be located?

- ▢ **A.** Common bile duct
- ▢ **B.** Hartmann pouch
- ▢ **C.** Left hepatic duct
- ▢ **D.** Pancreatic duct
- ▢ **E.** Right hepatic duct

169 A 47-year-old female is admitted to the hospital with jaundice and epigastric pain that migrates toward the patient's right side and posteriorly toward the scapula. Radiographic examination reveals cholecystitis with a large gallstone. Which of the following is the most likely site for a gallstone to lodge?

- ▢ **A.** Common bile duct
- ▢ **B.** Hepatopancreatic ampulla
- ▢ **C.** Left hepatic duct
- ▢ **D.** Pancreatic duct
- ▢ **E.** Right hepatic duct

170 A 40-year-old male with nine children is urged by his wife to have a vasectomy. During the operation the urologist separates the layers of the spermatic cord to expose the ductus deferens so that it can be ligated and cut. From what structure is the internal spermatic fascial covering derived?

- ▢ **A.** Internal oblique muscle
- ▢ **B.** Cremaster muscle
- ▢ **C.** External abdominal oblique muscle fascia
- ▢ **D.** Transversus abdominis aponeurosis
- ▢ **E.** Transversalis fascia

171 A 26-year-old female patient has a nonpainful hernia in the midline of the abdominal wall, several inches above the level of the umbilicus. Which of the following hernias will most likely characterize this condition?

- ▢ **A.** Umbilical hernia
- ▢ **B.** Spigelian hernia
- ▢ **C.** Epigastric hernia
- ▢ **D.** Femoral hernia
- ▢ **E.** Omphalocele

172 A 23-year-old male suffered a knife wound to the epigastric region. At laparotomy, when the abdomen is opened for inspection, it is seen that an injury to the liver occurred between the bed of the gallbladder and the falciform ligament, and the wound is bleeding profusely. The Pringle maneuver is performed with a nontraumatic vascular clamp, but blood continues spurting from the surface of the liver. Which part of the liver and which artery is most likely injured?

- ☐ **A.** Lateral segment of the left lobe and the left hepatic artery
- ☐ **B.** Caudate segment of the liver, with injury both to right and left hepatic arteries
- ☐ **C.** Anterior segment of the right lobe, with injury to the right hepatic artery
- ☐ **D.** Medial segment of the left lobe, with injury to an aberrant left hepatic artery
- ☐ **E.** Quadrate lobe, with injury to the middle hepatic branch of the right hepatic artery

173 A 47-year-old male patient had undergone bilateral vagotomy, with division of both vagus trunks at the esophageal hiatus, to relieve his chronic difficulty with peptic ulcers. Which of the following conditions will most likely occur?

- ☐ **A.** Parasympathetic supply to the descending colon is lost.
- ☐ **B.** The patient would no longer have contraction of the urinary bladder.
- ☐ **C.** The patient would become impotent.
- ☐ **D.** The patient would be sterile because of paralysis of the ductus deferens and ejaculatory duct.
- ☐ **E.** Parasympathetic supply to the ascending colon would be reduced or absent.

174 A 35-year-old male, an accountant, was brought to the emergency department with the complaint of intense abdominal pain of one-hour duration. His abdomen was distended, rigid, did not move in respiration, and was painful to palpation. He had adynamic (paralytic) ileus resulting from a peptic ulcer, although there was very little bleeding into the peritoneal cavity. He complained that he had pain in his right shoulder. Which of the following conditions will most likely occur?

- ☐ **A.** Radiographs would not reveal the presence of air under his diaphragm.
- ☐ **B.** Borborygmi would be decreased in frequency and amplitude.
- ☐ **C.** He probably suffered from a posterior penetrating ulcer rather than from an anterior perforating ulcer.
- ☐ **D.** The patient's ulcer probably occurred in the second part of the duodenum.
- ☐ **E.** The patient probably had acute appendicitis.

175 A 68-year-old woman had been suffering long-term effects of diverticulosis and inflammation of the transverse colon. To permit operating on a patient with severe diverticulosis of the transverse colon, it would be necessary to first ligate (tie off) or clamp the source of arterial supply. Which of the following arteries will most likely be ligated?

- ☐ **A.** Middle colic
- ☐ **B.** Right colic
- ☐ **C.** Superior mesenteric
- ☐ **D.** Ileocolic
- ☐ **E.** Left colic

176 A hard mass (a fecolith) in the ostium of the 27-year-old patient's appendix had led to a local infection (appendicitis) with a slightly elevated temperature and a moderate increase in WBC count. The initial pain from the infection was dull and difficult to localize, but the patient placed his hand in the periumbilical area to indicate the general area of discomfort. The region of the umbilicus receives its sensory supply, classically, from which of the following spinal nerves?

- ☐ **A.** T7
- ☐ **B.** T8
- ☐ **C.** T10
- ☐ **D.** T12
- ☐ **E.** L1

177 A 55-year-old male had been unsuccessfully treated for alcoholism for 3 years. He was admitted to the hospital for emergency medical treatment for severe portal hypertension. Which of the following is a feature of the development of severe portal hypertension?

- ☐ **A.** Esophageal varices—from increased pressure in the right gastric vein
- ☐ **B.** Ascites—from effusion of fluid from the inferior mesenteric vein
- ☐ **C.** Internal hemorrhoids—from increased pressure within the superior mesenteric vein and its tributaries
- ☐ **D.** Expansion of veins within the falciform ligament, which anastomose with veins of the umbilical region
- ☐ **E.** Recanalization and expansion of the vessels within the medial umbilical ligaments

178 In performing a laparoscopic hernia repair on a 24-year-old female gymnast, the surgical resident observed the bright reflection provided by the tissues of the iliopubic tract. The iliopubic tract could be traced medially to the site of the femoral herniation. The ilio-

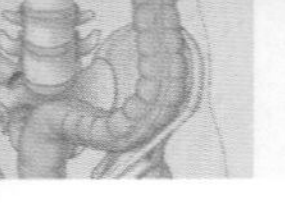

pubic tract is characterized by which of the following statements?

- ▢ **A.** The iliopubic tract represents the aponeurotic origin of the transversus abdominis.
- ▢ **B.** The iliopubic tract forms the lateral border of the inguinal triangle (of Hesselbach).
- ▢ **C.** The iliopubic tract forms the lateral border of the femoral ring.
- ▢ **D.** The iliopubic tract is the part of the inguinal ligament that attaches to the pectineal ligament.
- ▢ **E.** The iliopubic tract is the lateral extension of the pectineal ligament.

179 A 47-year-old male had been scheduled for an appendectomy. During the open operative procedure it was discovered that atypical embryologic rotation of the intestine, adhesions, and adipose tissue made it somewhat difficult to find the appendix. Most commonly, the vermiform appendix is best located by locating and tracing which of the following?

- ▢ **A.** Anterior cecal artery
- ▢ **B.** Descending branch of the right colic artery
- ▢ **C.** Ileum to the ileocecal juncture
- ▢ **D.** Posterior cecal artery
- ▢ **E.** Taeniae coli of the ascending colon

ANSWERS

1 A. The processus vaginalis (meaning sheathlike process) is composed of parietal peritoneum that precedes the testis as it "migrates" from a position in the upper lumbar wall to a position outside the abdomen. This process usually obliterates, leaving only a distal portion that surrounds most of the testis as the tunica vaginalis. Whereas these features are typical of development in the male, females also have a processus vaginalis that extends into the labia majus, although congenital inguinal hernias are more common in males than females. The other listed structures are not involved in congenital inguinal hernias.
GAS 283; GA 140

2 A. Wilms tumor is a kidney malignancy that usually occurs in children. It has recently been shown that it can be caused by mutations in the *WT1* gene, behaving according to Knudson's two-hit model for tumor suppressor genes.
GAS 355; GA 147

3 C. During development, the kidneys typically "ascend" from a position in the pelvis to a position high on the posterior abdominal wall. Although the kidneys are bilateral structures, occasionally the inferior poles of the two kidneys fuse. When this happens, the "ascent" of the fused kidneys is arrested by the first midline structure they encounter, the inferior mesenteric artery. The incidence of horseshoe kidney is about 0.25% of the population.
GAS 355; GA 147

4 C. In normal kidney development the kidneys function during the fetal period with the resulting urine contributing to the fluid in the amniotic cavity. When the kidneys fail to develop (renal agenesis), this contribution to the fluid is missing and decreased amniotic fluid (oligohydramnios) results.
GAS 355; GA 147

5 A. There is some evidence that oligohydramnios is linked to hypoplastic lungs. This is apparently not a genetic link but rather related to the importance of adequate amniotic fluid in normal lung development.
GAS 163, 355; GA 76, 147

6 C. In normal pancreatic development a bifid ventral pancreatic bud rotates around the dorsal side of the gut tube and fuses with the dorsal pancreatic bud. Rarely, a portion of the ventral bud rotates around the ventral side of the gut tube, resulting in an annular pancreas. The portion of the gut tube is the same where the main pancreatic duct enters the second part of the duodenum (along with the common bile duct). The incidence of annular pancreas is about 1 in 7000.
GAS 322; GA 167

7 C. The distal portion of the processus vaginalis contributes to the tunica vaginalis that is related to the testis. If an intermediate portion of the processus vaginalis persists, it often fills with fluid, creating a hydrocele. If the entire processus vaginalis persists, the patient is likely to develop a congenital inguinal hernia.
GAS 260; GA 225

8 C. Cryptorchism, often called an undescended testis, is the result of incomplete migration of the gonad from the abdomen to a location in the scrotum where it is exposed to temperatures slightly lower than core body temperature. This is important for spermatogenesis and testicular function. A testis that cannot be surgically relocated into the scrotum is usu-

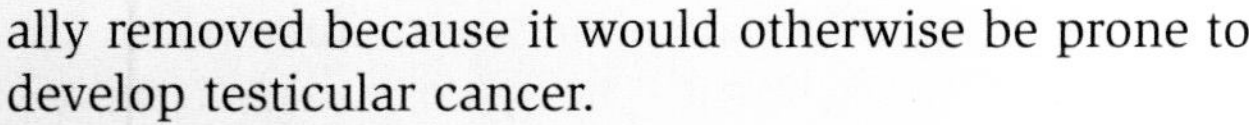

ally removed because it would otherwise be prone to develop testicular cancer.
GAS 283; GA 137

9 D. The lateral folds are key structures in forming the muscular portion of the anterior abdominal wall. Failure of the lateral folds can cause a minor defect, such as an umbilical hernia, or a major defect, such as gastroschisis.
GAS 256, 299; GA 154

10 A. Rotation of the gut tube is a major event in the development of the gastrointestinal system. Parts of the tube rotate 270°, but the proximal foregut, specifically that portion that forms the esophagus, rotates only 90°. Looking from below (the standard CT or MRI view), this rotation is counterclockwise. This brings the left vagus nerve onto the anterior surface of the esophagus as it passes through the thorax.
GAS 256, 345; GA 190

11 B. The diaphragm develops from several components. Initially, the septum transversum (which will become the central tendon) forms in the cervical region, gaining innervation from C3, C4, and C5. Later, myoblasts migrate in from the body wall to form the muscular part of the diaphragm, often considered to be two bilateral hemidiaphragms. These muscles are innervated by the phrenic nerves. Eventration of the diaphragm occurs when one muscular hemidiaphragm fails to develop. With positive pressure in the abdominal cavity, and low or negative pressure in the thoracic cavity, abdominal organs are pushed into the thorax. The pleuroperitoneal folds contribute to a portion of the diaphragm posteriorly.
GAS 353; GA 67

12 D. The tracheoesophageal septum is the downgrowth that separates the ventral wall of the foregut (esophagus) from the laryngotracheal tube. The presence of a fistula would result in passage of fluid from the esophagus into the trachea and could cause pneumonia. If the esophagus did not develop correctly, as in esophageal atresia, it would end as a blind tube. This kind of defect, although associated with tracheoesophageal fistula, is not the result of an opening into the trachea, and pneumonia would not result. Abnormal tracheal development can be associated with tracheoesophageal fistula, therefore, but it is not the direct cause of it. Abnormal tongue development does not result in a tracheoesophageal fistula. Abnormal development of the pharynx is not associated with a tracheoesophageal fistula.
GAS 168; GA 87

13 C. The septum transversum forms the central tendon of the diaphragm. The pleuroperitoneal folds form the posterolateral part of the diaphragm. The pleuropericardial folds separate the pericardial cavity from the pleural cavity and form the fibrous pericardium. The cervical myotomes form the musculature of the diaphragm. The dorsal part of the dorsal mesentery of the esophagus forms the crura of the diaphragm.
GAS 156; GA 67

14 C. Midgut volvulus is a possible complication of malrotation of the midgut loop without fixed mesentery. The small intestines twist around the vasculature that is providing support for them. This can result in ischemic necrosis of the intestine. Diaphragmatic atresia is not a cause of volvulus. Subhepatic cecum is due to failure of the descent of the cecal bud and results in the absence of an ascending colon. Duplication of the intestine would not cause volvulus because there would still be a fixed mesentery and no free movement of the intestines. Congenital megacolon is due to faulty migration of neural crest cells into the wall of the colon, which causes a lack of parasympathetic postganglionic neurons.
GAS 299; GA 154

15 A. Congenital megacolon (Hirschsprung disease) results from the failure of neural crest cells to migrate into the walls of the colon. Incomplete separation of the cloaca would result in anal agenesis either with or without the presence of a fistula. The failure of recanalization of the colon results in rectal atresia, wherein both the anal canal and rectum exist but are not connected due to incomplete canalization or no recanalization. Defective rotation of the hindgut can cause volvulus or twisting of its contents. Oligohydramnios is a deficiency of amniotic fluid, which can cause pulmonary hypoplasia but would not cause Hirschsprung disease.
GAS 311; GA 192

16 D. The ileum is the best answer choice here because it is the most common site of Meckel diverticulum. This outpouching is a persistence of the vitelline duct and it can be attached to the umbilicus. The other answer choices are not correlated with the vitelline duct and therefore will not result in the condition discussed here.
GAS 291; GA 155

17 A. The most common site of ectopic pregnancy is in the uterine tubes. Implantation in the internal os of the cervix can result in placenta previa, but the internal os of the cervix is not the most common site.

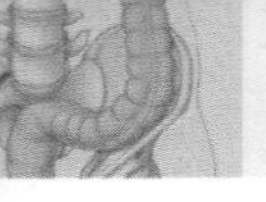

The other choices listed are not the most common sites of ectopic pregnancy. The fundus of the uterus is the normal site of implantation.
GAS 456, 512; GA 228

18 A. The greater splanchnic nerve carries general visceral afferent fibers from abdominal organs and can be involved in the occurrence of referred pain. The dorsal primary rami of intercostal nerves carry general somatic afferent fibers. Pain from these fibers would result in sharp, localized pain not dull and diffuse as occurs in referred pain. Although the phrenic nerve carries visceral afferent fibers, it does not innervate the gallbladder. The vagus nerve carries visceral afferent fibers that are important for visceral reflexes, but they do not transmit pain. The pelvic splanchnic nerves are parasympathetic nerves from S2 to S4 and contain visceral afferent fibers that transmit pain from the pelvis but not from the gallbladder.
GAS 319-342; GA 191

19 C. An indirect inguinal hernia occurs when a loop of bowel enters the spermatic cord through the deep inguinal ring (lateral to the inferior epigastric vessels). The ilioinguinal nerve runs with the spermatic cord to innervate the anterior portion of the scrotum and proximal parts of the genitals and could readily be compressed during an indirect inguinal hernia. The other nerves listed are not likely to be compressed by the hernia. The iliohypogastric nerve innervates the skin of the suprapubic region. The lateral femoral cutaneous nerve innervates the skin over the lateral thigh. The subcostal nerve innervates the band of skin superior to the iliac crest and inferior to the umbilicus. The pudendal nerve innervates the musculature and skin of the perineum.
GAS 290; GA 140

20 A. The celiac lymph nodes receive lymph drainage directly from the stomach before they drain into the cisterna chyli. The superior and inferior mesenteric lymph nodes receive drainage below the stomach and not from the stomach itself. The lumbar lymph nodes receive drainage from structures inferior to the stomach and not the stomach directly. Hepatic lymph nodes are associated with liver drainage and not drainage from the stomach.
GAS 342; GA 188

21 B. The proper hepatic artery is the only artery typically within the hepatoduodenal ligament and therefore would be occluded. This artery lies within the right anterior free margin of the omental (or epiploic) foramen (of Winslow). The superior mesenteric artery branches from the abdominal aorta inferior to the hepatoduodenal ligament. The splenic artery runs behind the stomach and is not located in the hepatoduodenal ligament. The common hepatic artery gives origin to the proper hepatic artery but does not run within the hepatoduodenal ligament. The inferior vena cava is located at the posterior margin of the omental foramen and therefore would not be clamped.
GAS 331; GA 164

22 E. Indirect hernias commonly result from herniation of the intestines through the deep inguinal ring. Direct hernias penetrate the anterior abdominal wall medial to the inferior epigastric vessels through the inguinal triangle (of Hesselbach) and do not penetrate the deep inguinal ring. Umbilical hernias exit through the umbilicus, not the deep inguinal ring. Femoral hernias exit through the femoral ring inferior to the inguinal ligament. Lumbar hernias can penetrate through superior (Grynfeltt) or inferior (Petit) lumbar triangles.
GAS 290; GA 140

23 C. The omental bursa is located directly posterior to the stomach and therefore would be the most likely space to develop peritonitis initially. The right subhepatic space (also called the hepatorenal space, or pouch of Morison) is the area posterior to the liver and anterior to the right kidney. This space can potentially accumulate fluid and may participate in peritonitis but primarily when the patient is in the supine position. The right subphrenic space lies just inferior to the diaphragm on the right side and is not likely to accumulate fluid from a perforated stomach ulcer. Peritonitis could develop in this area only when the patient is in the supine position. Fluid from a perforated ulcer on the posterior aspect of the stomach is not likely to enter the greater sac.
GAS 295; GA 144

24 C. The left gastric vein carries blood from the stomach to the portal vein. At the esophageal-gastric junction the left gastric vein (portal system) anastomoses with esophageal veins (caval system). High blood pressure in the portal system causes high pressure in this anastomosis, causing the ruptured esophageal varices. The splenic vein and its tributaries carry blood away from the spleen and do not form a caval-portal anastomosis. The left gastroomental vein accompanies the left gastroomental artery and joins the splenic vein with no direct anastomosis with caval veins. The left hepatic vein is a caval vein and empties into the inferior vena cava. The right gastric vein drains the lesser curvature of

the stomach and is part of the portal system but does not have any caval anastomosis.
GAS 265, 337; GA 172

25 C. The genitofemoral nerve originates from the ventral rami of L1 and L2. The femoral part supplies skin to the femoral triangle area, whereas the "genito" part in males travels with the spermatic cord and supplies the cremaster muscle and scrotal skin. The ilio-inguinal nerve arises from L1 and supplies the skin over the root of the penis and upper part of the scrotum in the male. The iliohypogastric nerve arises from L1 (and possibly fibers from T12) and supplies skin innervation over the hypogastric region and anterolateral gluteal region. The pudendal nerve provides innervation to the external genitalia for both sexes but does not innervate the cremaster muscle in males. The ventral ramus of T12 is also associated with the lower portion of the anterior abdominal wall and the iliohypogastric nerve; it does not contribute to the cremasteric reflex.
GAS 288; GA 187

26 E. The linea alba is formed by the intersection of aponeurotic tissues between the right and left rectus abdominal muscles. It contains the aponeuroses of the abdominal muscles and is located at the midline of the body. The midaxillary line is oriented vertically in a straight line inferior to the shoulder joint and axilla. The arcuate line (of Douglas) is a curved horizontal line that represents the lower edge of the posterior tendinous portion of the rectus abdominis sheath. An incision at this line will not separate the rectus abdominis sheaths. The semilunar line is represented by an imaginary vertical line below the nipples and usually parallels the lateral edge of the rectus sheath. The tendinous intersections of the rectus abdominis muscles divide the muscle into sections and are usually not well defined. An incision along these intersections would not divide the two rectus sheaths.
GAS 272; GA 128

27 A. Scarpa's fascia is the thick, membranous layer deep to the Camper's adipose fascia in the anterior abdominal wall (subcutaneous). Because of the relatively thick, tough nature of connective tissue that makes up Scarpa's fascia, this layer is typically the site to maintain sutures. Camper's fascia is a fatty layer (subcutaneous) and tends not to hold sutures as well, due to the increased cellular content versus the connective tissue found in the Scarpa layer. Transversalis fascia is located deep to the abdominal musculature and associated aponeurosis. Extraperitoneal fascia is the deepest layer, adjacent to the parietal peritoneum of the anterior abdominal wall. The anterior wall of the rectus sheath is the layer just deep to Scarpa's fascia and superficial to the rectus abdominis muscle anteriorly. The latter three layers are not considered to be superficial fascia.
GAS 271; GA 126

28 A. The common bile duct is located at the head of the pancreas and receives contents from the cystic duct and hepatic duct. An obstruction at this site causes a backup of bile back through the common bile duct and hepatic duct, with resulting pain and jaundice. The common hepatic duct is located more superior to the head of the pancreas and leads into the cystic duct. The cystic duct allows bile to enter the gallbladder from the common bile duct (draining the liver) and releases bile to the common bile duct. The accessory pancreatic duct is not affected by an obstruction of the common bile duct due to a lack of any connections between the two ducts. Hepatic veins will not be obstructed, for it carries blood from the liver to the inferior vena cava.
GAS 286; GA 167

29 C. The third part of the duodenum takes a path situated anterior to the abdominal aorta and inferior to the superior mesenteric artery (a major ventral branch of the abdominal aorta). Because the third part of the duodenum lies in the angle between ("sandwiched") these two structures, constrictions of this portion of the duodenum can occur readily. The second part of the duodenum lies parallel with, and to the right of, the abdominal aorta and is not normally in close proximity to the superior mesenteric artery. The transverse colon takes a horizontal path through the anterior abdominal cavity but travels superior or anterior to the superior mesenteric artery. The first part of the duodenum continues from the pylorus, flexing to lead to the second part of the duodenum; thus, it is not located near the superior mesenteric artery or abdominal aorta. The jejunum is an extension of the small intestine after the duodenum and is further removed from the superior mesenteric artery.
GAS 331; GA 161

30 E. The superior mesenteric artery will supply the pancreas if the gastroduodenal artery is ligated. It arises immediately inferior to the celiac trunk from the abdominal aorta. Its first branches are the anterior and posterior inferior pancreaticoduodenal arteries, which aid the superior pancreaticoduodenal arteries (which take origin from the gastroduodenal branch of the celiac trunk) in supplying the pancreas with oxygenated

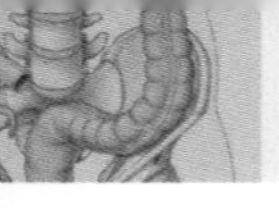

blood. The inferior mesenteric artery is the most inferior of the three main arterial branches supplying the gastrointestinal tract. It supplies the hindgut from the left colic flexure to the rectum. The left gastric artery is the smallest branch of the celiac trunk and supplies the cardioesophageal junction, the inferior esophagus, and the lesser curvature of the stomach. The right gastric artery arises from the common hepatic artery, which is a branch from the celiac trunk. It supplies the lesser curvature of the stomach and anastomoses with the left gastric artery. The proper hepatic artery arises from the common hepatic artery and ascends to supply the liver and gallbladder. It is one of three structures forming the portal triad and is found in the free edge of the hepatoduodenal ligament.
GAS 333, 336; GA 169

31 B. The middle colic artery can provide collateral supply to the descending colon when the inferior mesenteric artery is blocked or ligated. It is one of the first branches of the superior mesenteric artery and supplies the transverse colon. It provides collateral blood supply both to the ascending colon and descending colon by anastomosing with the right colic branch of the superior mesenteric artery and with the left colic artery, a branch from the inferior mesenteric artery. The left gastroepiploic artery, also known as the left gastroomental artery, is a branch of the splenic artery and supplies the greater curvature of the stomach along with the right gastroomental branch of the gastroduodenal artery. The sigmoid arteries are branches from the inferior mesenteric artery and supply the inferior portion of the descending colon, the sigmoid colon, and the rectum. The sigmoid arteries have no contributing branches to the foregut or midgut. The splenic artery is the largest artery arising from the celiac trunk. It supplies the spleen and the neck, body, and tail of the pancreas and also provides short gastric branches to the stomach. It supplies no structures in the midgut or hindgut. Finally, the superior rectal artery is the terminal branch of the inferior mesenteric artery and supplies only the rectum.
GAS 333; GA 160

32 A. The appendix is the most likely structure that is inflamed. It lies in the right lower quadrant, and of the choices provided, it is most closely associated with the umbilical region by way of referral of pain. The patient also exhibited a positive psoas sign when flexion of the hip against resistance was attempted. This is because the iliopsoas muscle group lies directly beneath the appendix, and upon flexion of this muscle group, contact and direct irritation to the appendix can occur. The bladder lies inferior to the umbilicus within the pelvis and is not related to the site of pain or with a positive psoas sign. The gallbladder lies inferior to the liver and is positioned in the upper right abdominal quadrant, which is superior to the umbilicus. It is not associated with a positive psoas sign. The pancreas lies behind the stomach and is positioned between the spleen and the duodenum. It therefore lies in the upper left quadrant and is superior to the umbilicus. The uterus is located within the pelvis and is positioned anteflexed and anteverted over the bladder. It lies inferior and medial to the iliopsoas group and would not be affected by flexion of these muscles.
GAS 310, 395; GA 154

33 B. The abscess may have spread to the diaphragm and be causing the referred shoulder pain. This is because the diaphragm lies in close proximity to the superior poles of the kidneys. The diaphragm is innervated by the phrenic nerves, bilaterally, which descend to the diaphragm from spinal nerve levels C3, C4, and C5. It is probably at the spinal cord that the referral of pain occurs between the phrenic nerve and somatic afferents entering at those levels. The descending colon is innervated by parasympathetic nerves from S2 to S4 and visceral afferents, which do not carry pain. The duodenum is innervated by the vagus nerve, which innervates the gastrointestinal tract to the left colic flexure. The liver is innervated sympathetically from the celiac ganglion; the parasympathetic nerves to the liver are by the vagus nerve. Neither of these two sources of innervation enters the spinal cord at the level of the shoulder and therefore could not cause referred pain to the shoulder. The pancreas is innervated by the vagus nerve, branches from the celiac ganglion, and the pancreatic plexus. None of these nerves enters the spinal cord at the level of the shoulder and therefore cannot facilitate referral of pain to the shoulder.
GAS 355; GA 150

34 A. The afferent fibers mediating the pain from the head of the pancreas run initially with the greater thoracic splanchnic nerves. The greater splanchnic nerves arise from sympathetic ganglia at the levels of T5 to T9 and innervate structures of the foregut and thus the head of the pancreas. Running within these nerves are visceral afferent fibers that relay pain from foregut structures to the dorsal horn of the spinal cord. Also entering the dorsal horn are the somatic afferents from that vertebral level, which mediate pain from the body wall. Intercostal nerves

T1 to T12 provide the terminal part of the pathway to the spinal cord of visceral afferents for pain from the thorax and much of the abdomen. Therefore, pain fibers from the pancreas pass by way of the splanchnic nerves to the sympathetic chains and then, by way of communicating rami, to ventral rami of intercostal nerves, finally entering the spinal cord by way of the dorsal roots. The phrenic nerve innervates the diaphragm and also carries visceral afferents from mediastinal pleura and the pericardium, but it does not carry with it any visceral afferent fibers from the pancreas. The vagus nerve innervates the pancreas with parasympathetic fibers and ascends all the way up to the medulla where it enters the brain. It has no visceral afferent fibers for pain. The subcostal nerve is from the level of T12 and innervates structures below the pancreas and carries no visceral afferents from the pancreas.
GAS 318-319, 342; GA 191

35 **D.** The testicular artery originates from the abdominal aorta and travels with the spermatic cord, leading to the testes in the male. The external iliac artery is located "downstream" to the origin of the testicular artery from the aorta and would not cause any problems in sperm count. The inferior epigastric artery originates close to the deep inguinal ring (spermatic cord exit) as a branch of the external iliac artery and is not associated with the testicular production of sperm. The umbilical artery originates from the internal iliac artery and is divided in adults: one part is obliterated (medial umbilical artery), and the other part gives origin to superior vesical arteries to the urinary bladder. The umbilical artery plays no role in sperm production.
GAS 367; GA 183

36 **A.** The lymph drainage of the scrotum is into the superficial inguinal nodes. The internal iliac lymph nodes drain the pelvis, perineum, and gluteal region. The lumbar nodes drain lymph from kidneys, the adrenal glands, testes or ovaries, uterus, and uterine tubes. They also receive lymph from the common internal or external nodes. Axillary lymph nodes drain the anterior abdominal wall above the umbilicus.
GAS 494; GA 254

37 **B.** The contents of the spermatic cord include ductus deferens; testicular, cremasteric, and deferential arteries; the pampiniform venous plexus; the genital branch of the genitofemoral nerve; the cremasteric nerves; and the testicular sympathetic plexus and also lymph vessels. The cremaster muscle and fascia originate from the internal abdominal oblique muscle. The external spermatic fascia is derived from the aponeurosis and fascia of the external oblique muscle. The tunica vaginalis is a continuation of the processus vaginalis (from parietal peritoneum) that covers the anterior and lateral sides of the testes and epididymis. The internal spermatic fascia is derived from the transversalis fascia. The dartos tunic consists of a blending of the adipose (Camper) and membranous (Scarpa) layers of the superficial fascia, with interspersed smooth muscle fibers.
GAS 285; GA 128

38 **A.** Esophageal varices are dilated veins in the submucosa of the lower esophagus. They often result from portal hypertension due to liver cirrhosis. The left gastric vein and the esophageal veins of the azygos system form an important portal-caval anastomosis when pressure in the portal vein, and in turn the left gastric vein, is increased. None of the other choices forms important portal-caval anastomoses.
GAS 265, 337; GA 172

39 **B.** The jejunum makes up the proximal two fifths of the small intestine. There are several ways in which the ileum and jejunum differ. During surgery the easiest way to distinguish the two based on appearance is the relative amount of mesenteric fat. The jejunum has less mesenteric fat than the ileum. Although the jejunum does have thicker walls, more villi, and higher plicae circulares compared with the ileum, these distinctions are not visible unless the intestinal wall is incised. The jejunum has fewer vascular arcades in comparison with the ileum. Lymphatic follicles are visible, usually only histologically, in the ileum.
GAS 300; GA 155

40 **C.** The arcuate line is a horizontal line that demarcates the lower limit of the posterior aponeurotic portion of the rectus sheath. It is also where the inferior epigastric vessels perforate the sheath to enter the rectus abdominis. The intercristal line is an imaginary line drawn in the horizontal plane at the upper margin of the iliac crests. The linea alba is a tendinous, median raphe running vertically between the two rectus abdominis muscles from the xiphoid process to the pubic symphysis. The pectineal line is a feature of the superior ramus of the pubic bone; it provides an origin for the pectineus muscle of the thigh and medial insertions for the abdominal obliques and transversus muscles. The semilunar line is the curved, vertical line along the lateral border of the sheath of the rectus abdominis.
GAS 276; GA 126

41 D. The psoas muscles (covered in psoas fascia) originate from the transverse processes, intervertebral disks, and bodies of the vertebral column at levels T12 to L5. In the image, this fascia contains a calcified tuberculous abscess. The pancreas is an elongated organ located across the back of the abdomen, behind the stomach. The tapering body extends horizontally and slightly upward to the left and ends near the spleen. The cecum is the blind-ending pouch of the ascending colon, lying in the right iliac fossa. The fundus of the stomach lies inferior to the apex of the heart at the level of the fifth rib. The suspensory ligament of the duodenum is a fibromuscular band that attaches to the right crus of the diaphragm.
GAS 353; GA 186

42 B. The superior mesenteric artery arises from the aorta, behind the neck of the pancreas, and descends across the uncinate process of the pancreas and the third part of the duodenum before it enters the root of the mesentery behind the transverse colon. It can compress the third part of the duodenum. The inferior mesenteric artery passes to the left behind the horizontal portion of the duodenum. The inferior mesenteric vein is formed by the union of the superior rectal and sigmoid veins and it does not cross the third part of the duodenum. The portal vein is formed by the union of the splenic vein and the superior mesenteric vein posterior to the neck of the pancreas. It ascends behind the bile duct and the hepatic artery within the free margin of the hepatoduodenal ligament. The splenic vein is formed by the tributaries from the spleen and is superior to the third part of the duodenum.
GAS 331; GA 161

43 B. The omental (epiploic) foramen (of Winslow) is the only natural opening between the lesser and greater sacs of the peritoneal cavity. It is bounded superiorly by the visceral peritoneum on the caudate lobe of the liver, inferiorly by the peritoneum on the first part of the duodenum, anteriorly by the free edge of the hepatoduodenal ligament, and posteriorly by the parietal peritoneum covering the inferior vena cava. Therefore, the inferior vena cava would be the most likely source of bleeding. The aorta lies to the left of the inferior vena cava in the abdomen. The portal vein, right renal artery, and superior mesenteric vein are not borders of the epiploic foramen.
GAS 368; GA 150

44 B. The ilioinguinal nerve, which arises from the L1 spinal nerve, innervates the skin on the medial aspect of the thigh, scrotum (or labia majora), and the mons pubis. It has been injured in this patient. The genitofemoral nerve splits into two branches: The genital branch supplies the scrotum (or labia majora) whereas the femoral branch supplies the skin of the femoral triangle. The subcostal nerve has a lateral cutaneous branch that innervates skin in the upper gluteal region, in addition to distribution over the lower part of the anterior abdominal wall. The iliohypogastric nerve innervates the skin over the iliac crest and the hypogastric region. Spinal nerve T9 supplies sensory innervation to the dermatome at the level of T9, above the level of the umbilicus.
GAS 378; GA 186

45 D. The second part of the duodenum is crossed anteriorly by the transverse mesocolon, a relationship that can be seen when the beginning of the jejunum is exposed by lifting the transverse colon superiorly. The posterior relationships of the second part of the duodenum and the portal vein cannot be seen without some dissection. The third part of the duodenum is not related anteriorly to the hilum of the left kidney.
GAS 300; GA 154

46 A. The right adrenal gland is a retroperitoneal organ on the superomedial aspect of the right kidney, partially posterior to the inferior vena cava. The appendix is a narrow, hollow tube that is suspended from the cecum by a small mesoappendix. The gallbladder is located at the junction of the ninth costal cartilage and the lateral border of the rectus abdominis, quite anterior to the pathologic mass. The ovaries and uterus are both inferior to the confluence of the inferior vena cava.
GAS 368; GA 174

47 A. The symptoms of yellow eyes and jaundice would be caused by reversal of flow of bile into the bloodstream. The common bile duct, if obstructed, allows no collateral pathway for drainage of bile from the liver or gallbladder. The cystic duct, if obstructed would block gallbladder drainage but allow for bile flow from the liver. Obstruction of either the right or left hepatic duct would still allow for drainage from the liver, as well as the gallbladder. The pancreatic duct is not involved in the path of bile flow from the liver to the duodenum. It drains pancreatic enzymes from the pancreas to the duodenum.
GAS 318; GA 153

48 C. Cirrhosis of the liver would lead to inability of the portal system to accommodate blood flow. Blood backs up toward systemic circulation, draining

to the inferior vena cava, with pooling at areas of portal-caval anastomoses. The left gastric vein (portal) meets the esophageal vein (caval) and enlarges or expands in instances of cirrhosis. The left colic and middle colic veins are both simply tributaries to the portal system, excluding this as the correct answer. The inferior phrenic and superior phrenic veins are both systemic veins and would not be affected by portal hypertension. The same can be said for the renal and lumbar veins, both components of the caval-systemic venous system. The sigmoidal and superior rectal veins are both components of the portal venous system and would not engorge due to the portal-caval bottleneck experienced in cirrhosis. (The anastomoses between the superior rectal veins and middle or inferior rectal veins can expand in portal hypertension as hemorrhoids.)
GAS 396-397; GA 172

49 A. The key distinguishing feature of a direct inguinal hernia is that the direct hernia does not pass through the deep inguinal ring; it passes through the lower portion of the inguinal triangle (of Hasselbach). This triangle is bordered laterally by the inferior epigastric artery and vein; medially, it is bordered by the lateral edge of rectus abdominis; inferiorly, it is bordered by the iliopubic tract and inguinal ligament. An indirect hernia passes through the deep inguinal ring and into the inguinal canal. It often descends through the superficial ring into the scrotum or labium, a feature less common in a direct inguinal hernia. If the tip of the examiner's little finger is inserted into the superficial ring, and the patient is asked to cough, an indirect inguinal hernia may be felt hitting the very tip of the little finger. A direct inguinal hernia will be felt against the side of the digit. Both types of inguinal hernias occur above the inguinal ligament, and both are present lateral to the lateral border of the rectus abdominis. The pubic symphysis, a midline joint between the two pubic bones, provides no information for distinguishing types of hernias. The femoral canal, a feature of the femoral sheath, passes beneath the inguinal ligament into the thigh, providing the pathway taken by a femoral hernia. The pectineal ligament lies behind, or deep to, the proximal end of the femoral canal.
GAS 288; GA 140

50 B. The bullet would probably first penetrate the transverse colon because it is the most superficial structure located slightly superior to the umbilicus. The abdominal aorta is located deep, on the left side of the vertebral column, and would not be encountered first. The stomach is located more superior, to the left, and posterior to the transverse colon and would not be affected by the anterior-posterior trajectory of the bullet. The pancreas is located deep to the stomach and duodenum. The gallbladder is located superiorly in the upper right quadrant of the abdomen, largely under cover of the liver. This would exclude its possibility of being penetrated by the midline bullet.
GAS 268; GA 143

51 D. Surgical anastomoses to alleviate symptoms of portal hypertension are rooted in the premise that connection of a large portal vein to a large systemic vein allows for collateral drainage of the portal system. The splenic vein, a component of the portal venous system, and the left renal vein, a component of the caval-systemic venous system, are ideally located to allow for a low-resistance, easily performed anastomosis. Anastomosing the left gastric vein to the splenic vein, the right gastric vein to the left gastric vein, or the superior mesenteric vein to the inferior mesenteric vein would all be ineffectual because each of these veins is a component of just the portal venous system. In addition, the right renal and right gonadal veins are both tributaries of the caval system, and surgical connection would provide no benefit.
GAS 288; GA 140

52 B. Visceral pain from the kidneys and the ureter at the point of the neoplasm is mediated via T11 and T12 spinal cord levels. Therefore, pain is referred to these dermatomes leading to pain in the upper gluteal, pubic, medial thigh, scrotal, and labial areas (from subcostal and iliohypogastric nerves, in particular). In contrast, the umbilical region, the T10 dermatome, is supplied by the T10 spinal nerve, excluding it from being the correct answer. The dermatomes of the anterior and lateral thighs are supplied from nerves of upper lumbar origin and would not receive pain referred from the kidneys.
GAS 361; GA 195

53 B. The mass leads to increased stimulation and secretions of the chromaffin cells of the adrenal medulla. These cells are modified postganglionic sympathetic neurons of neural crest origin, and the epinephrine (adrenaline) and norepinephrine (noradrenaline) released by these cells passes into the suprarenal (adrenal) veins. The adrenal medulla receives stimulation from preganglionic sympathetic fibers carried by the thoracic splanchnic nerves. Parasympathetic neurons are not found in the adrenal medulla and would have no participation in the effects of the tumor. In addition, the pelvic splanchnic nerves are parasympathetic and do not travel to the adrenal medulla.
GAS 362; GA 194

54 **E.** The splenic artery lies adjacent to the superior border of the pancreas. The organ it principally supplies is the spleen, which is located at the termination of the pancreatic tail. Blood supply to the spleen can therefore be affected in the event of a tumor in the tail of the pancreas. The duodenum receives blood from the gastroduodenal artery, located near the head of the pancreas. The gallbladder is supplied by the cystic artery, a branch of the hepatic artery and is not in contact with the pancreas. The liver is also supplied by the hepatic artery. The kidneys are supplied by the right and left renal arteries. The left renal artery lies deep and medial to the pancreatic tumor, and blood supply would proceed uninterrupted.
GAS 323; GA 166

55 **E.** The superior mesenteric artery lies just superior and anterior to the left renal vein as the vein passes to its termination in the inferior vena cava. The celiac artery is located superiorly and would not compress the left renal vein. The inferior mesenteric artery and its left colic branch are located too inferiorly to occlude the left renal vein. The middle colic artery arises from the anterior aspect of the superior mesenteric artery inferior to the position of the left renal vein. An aneurysm of the superior mesenteric artery would therefore be most likely to occlude the left renal vein.
GAS 359; GA 174

56 **B.** Blood flow would be impeded or greatly reduced in the left testicular vein because of the occlusion of the left renal vein—into which the left testicular vein drains. This would result in pain as the testicular venous vessels become swollen. The testicular artery originates from the abdominal aorta more inferiorly and is not being compressed. Pain mediated from the renal organs would pass to the T11 and T12 spinal cord levels via the thoracic splanchnic nerves. There would be no compression of lumbar splanchnic nerves in this case. Compression of the preaortic sympathetics would not produce pain, nor would it cause referral of pain. Visceral afferents for pain terminate at the T7 level of the spinal cord. The vagus, a parasympathetic nerve, does not carry visceral pain fibers in the abdomen; pain is mediated by branches of the sympathetic chains.
GAS 474-475; GA 138

57 **D.** The most likely candidate for bleeding from the fundic region of the stomach in this case would be either the short gastric or dorsal gastric branches of the splenic artery. The short gastric arteries pass from the area of the splenic hilum to the fundus, supplying anterior and posterior branches to this part of the stomach. The dorsal gastric artery, which arises from the midportion of the splenic artery, passes to the dorsal aspect of the fundus. The main stem of the splenic artery would pass somewhat inferior to the location of the ulceration. The common hepatic artery and inferior phrenic artery are quite removed from the area of the ulcer. The left gastroepiploic artery courses along the greater curvature of the body of the stomach, distal to the fundus.
GAS 329; GA 150

58 **D.** Indirect inguinal hernia is the most common groin hernia in females. Although femoral hernias occur more commonly in females than in males, the occurrence of indirect inguinal hernias in women is greater. Inguinal hernias are much more common in males than in females. Epigastric and umbilical hernias would not present with pain to the inguinal region. Direct inguinal hernias, while exhibiting equal incidence in both sexes, are not the most common female hernia.
GAS 290-291; GA 140

59 **A.** The posterior superior pancreaticoduodenal artery arises from the gastroduodenal artery and travels behind the first part of the duodenum, supplying the proximal portion, with branches to the head of the pancreas. Duodenal ulcers commonly arise within the first portion of the duodenum, thus making the posterior superior pancreaticoduodenal artery one of the more frequently injured vessels. The superior mesenteric artery supplies derivatives of the midgut from the distal half of the duodenum to the left colic flexure. It lies inferior to the region of ulceration. The inferior pancreaticoduodenal artery arises from the superior mesenteric artery and supplies the distal portion of the second part of the duodenum, with anastomoses with its superior counterparts. The inferior mesenteric artery is responsible for supplying most of the hindgut derivatives, generally supplying intestine from the left colic flexure to the superior aspect of the rectum. The right gastric artery is responsible for supplying the pyloric portion of the lesser curvature of the stomach.
GAS 303; GA 150

60 **D.** The transversalis fascial layer is the source of the internal spermatic fascia. The walls of the spermatic cord consist of three layers: external spermatic fascia, cremaster muscle, and the internal spermatic fascia. The external spermatic fascia is an extension of the external oblique fascia and aponeurosis. The cremaster muscle is a derivative of the

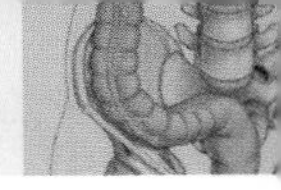

internal oblique abdominal muscle and its fascia. The processus vaginalis is a pouch of peritoneum that precedes the testis as it descends through the deep inguinal ring and inguinal canal in the seventh month of development. That portion of the processus that is normally retained forms the tunica vaginalis of the testis. Retention of the proximal part of the processus provides a pathway for a congenital indirect inguinal hernia. If a portion of the intermediate part of the processus remains, it can form a fluid-filled hydrocele.
GAS 288; GA 139

61 **C.** The superior mesenteric artery arises from the aorta, deep to the neck of the pancreas, then crosses the uncinate process and third part of the duodenum. An uncinate tumor can cause compression of the superior mesenteric artery. The common hepatic artery arises superior to the body of the pancreas and is unlikely to be affected by a tumor in the uncinate region of the pancreas. The cystic artery and vein, supplying the gallbladder, are also superior to the pancreas. The inferior mesenteric artery arises at the level of L3, which is thus situated deep to and inferior to the head of the pancreas. The portal vein, formed by the confluence of the superior mesenteric vein and splenic vein, passes deep to the neck of the pancreas.
GAS 331; GA 154

62 **A.** The common bile duct is occluded. The pattern of pain of cholecystitis (and other signs), combined with jaundice, indicates blockage of release of bile into the duodenum. The cystic duct joins the common hepatic duct to form the common bile duct. Bile is released from the gallbladder into the cystic duct in response to cholecystokinin. From the cystic duct, bile flows normally through the common bile duct and the hepatopancreatic ampulla (of Vater) to enter the descending duodenum. Patients will often present with multiple gallstones. Cholecystitis is an inflammation of the gallbladder, most frequently in association with the presence of gallstones, and often resulting from a blocked cystic duct. Increasing concentration of bile in the gallbladder can precipitate a bout of inflammation. Blockage of the cystic duct, with concomitant cholecystitis, is not necessarily associated with jaundice. An obstruction in the common hepatic duct and subsequently the common bile duct would thus prevent communication between the duodenum and the liver, causing obstructive jaundice. An occlusion in either the left or right hepatic duct might cause mild jaundice; however, gallstones might not be present. An occlusion in the pancreatic duct would result in neither gallstones nor jaundice but may cause pancreatitis.
GAS 326; GA 168

63 **C.** The anterior cutaneous branch of the iliohypogastric nerve is responsible for the innervation of the skin above the mons pubis. This nerve arises from the T12 and L1 spinal nerves and runs transversely around the abdominal wall and over the lowest portion of the rectus sheath. It is the first cutaneous nerve situated superior to the mons pubis. Nerves from the T11 and the T12 ventral rami terminate below the umbilicus but superior to the mons pubis. The ilioinguinal nerve courses through the inguinal canal, commonly on the lateral side of the spermatic cord and is therefore typically inferior to the incision. The lateral femoral cutaneous nerve travels lateral to the psoas muscle and emerges from the abdomen about an inch medial to the anterior superior iliac spine, passing thereafter to the lateral aspect of the thigh.
GAS 378; GA 134

64 **B.** Appendicitis is often characterized by acute inflammation and is indicated with both a positive psoas test and rebound pain over McBurney's point. McBurney's point lies 1 inch lateral to the midpoint of an imaginary line in the right lower quadrant, joining the anterior superior iliac spine and the umbilicus. In patients with appendicitis, rebound tenderness may be felt over McBurney's point after quick, deep compression of the right lower quadrant. An ectopic pregnancy would be associated with generalized abdominal pain instead of the localized pain felt over McBurney's point. Cholecystitis results from an inflammation of the gallbladder and would result in pain over the epigastric region shifting to the right hypochondriac region. Kidney stones result in referred pain to the lumbar or possibly inguinal regions. Perforation of the duodenum could result in pain to palpation of the abdomen, together with adynamic (paralytic) ileus, rigidity of the abdominal wall, and referral of pain to the shoulder.
GAS 311; GA 154

65 **B.** The visceral afferent innervation of the rectum is transmitted by way of the pelvic splanchnic nerves, which also provide the parasympathetic supply to this organ. The lumbar sympathetic chain receives sensory fibers from the fundus and body of the uterus. The pudendal nerve provides origin for the inferior rectal nerve, the perineal nerve, and the dorsal nerve of the penis. The inferior rectal nerve supplies somatosensory fibers to the anal canal below the

pectinate line and the perianal skin; the perineal nerve and dorsal nerve of the penis innervate structures of the urogenital region. The vagus nerve provides parasympathetic supply and afferent innervation (excluding pain) to the intestine proximal to the left colic flexure. The lumbar and sacral sympathetic chains contribute sympathetic fibers for innervation of smooth muscle and glands of certain pelvic viscera, but not sensory fibers for the rectum.
GAS 468; GA 189

66 D. Meckel diverticulum is a fingerlike projection of the ileum that is generally remembered by the "rule of 2s": It occurs in about 2% of the population, is approximately 2 feet proximal from the ileocecal junction, is about 2 inches long, occurs 2 times as often in males as in females, may contain 2 types of ectopic tissue, and may be confused often with 2 different clinical conditions. The two types of ectopic tissue are gastric mucosa and pancreatic tissue. These, along with bleeding and pain, may give indications of peptic ulcer or appendicitis. Internal and external hemorrhoids involve the rectoanal area, not the ileum, in addition to which biopsy of hemorrhoids would not reveal the presence of gastric mucosa. Borborygmi are bowel sounds that occur with the passage of gas and bowel contents through the intestines. Diverticuloses are outpouchings of the colon and would therefore be lined with colic mucosa.
GAS 306; GA 159

67 D. The aortic aneurysm often occurs between L3 and L4, below the bifurcation of the aorta, resulting in significant increase in pressure, creating the marked abdominal pulsation. The remaining answer choices would be associated with referred pain and would not be likely to result in elevated blood pressure.
GAS 368; GA 133

68 B. In a supine patient, fluid accumulation will often occur in the pouch of Morison, which is the lowest space in the body in a supine position. The hepatorenal space is located behind the liver and in front of the parietal peritoneum covering the right kidney. The vesicouterine and rectouterine spaces are also potential areas of fluid accumulation; however, fluid accumulation in these spaces occurs when the patient is in an erect position rather than a supine position.
GAS 307; GA 144

69 D. Descending colon. Below the left colic flexure, innervation of the gastrointestinal tract is supplied by parasympathetic fibers of the pelvic splanchnic nerves. The parasympathetic innervation of the midgut up to the descending colon is supplied by the vagus nerve. A hematoma occurring below L4 would affect innervation of the descending colon because the pelvic splanchnic nerves arise from spinal nerve levels S2 to S4. The jejunum, ascending colon, ileum, and transverse colon are all innervated by the vagus nerve.
GAS 307; GA 156

70 C. The porta hepatis (transverse fissure of liver) transmits the proper hepatic artery, portal vein, common hepatic duct, autonomic nerves, and lymph vessels. A tumor in this region would be most detrimental because of its abundance of vessels and lymphatics that could lead to all of these symptoms when they are compromised functionally. A tumor in either the right or left lobes would not be as serious because it would not completely obstruct all of these vessels. The falciform ligament does not carry any vessels, so a tumor in this area would not lead to the symptoms described. The hepatogastric ligament is the bilaminar peritoneal connection between the liver and the lesser curvature of the stomach and is unrelated to the symptoms and signs here.
GAS 318; GA 163

71 E. The cystic artery is the only artery listed that goes directly to the gallbladder. It is often a branch of the right hepatic artery and must be clamped before the gallbladder is cut free from its attachments. The common hepatic artery provides origin to the proper hepatic artery, which divides into right and left hepatic arteries supplying the liver, gallbladder, and biliary tree.
GAS 331; GA 169

72 D. The spleen is a large lymphatic organ that rests against the diaphragm and ribs 9, 10, and 11 in the left hypochondriac area. A laceration of the organ is often associated with severe blood loss and shock. Almost all of the liver is located in the right hypochondrium and epigastrium, although some protrudes into the left hypochondrium below the diaphragm. The left kidney lies retroperitoneally approximately at the level of the T11 to L3 vertebrae on the left side of the body. The ilium is the upper portion of the hip bone and contributes to the bony pelvis. Ileum is the distal portion of the small intestine and is pronounced the same as "ilium."
GAS 327; GA 149

73 D. The ileocolic artery is the only artery listed that directly supplies the appendix. The superior mesenteric artery gives origin to the ileocolic, right colic,

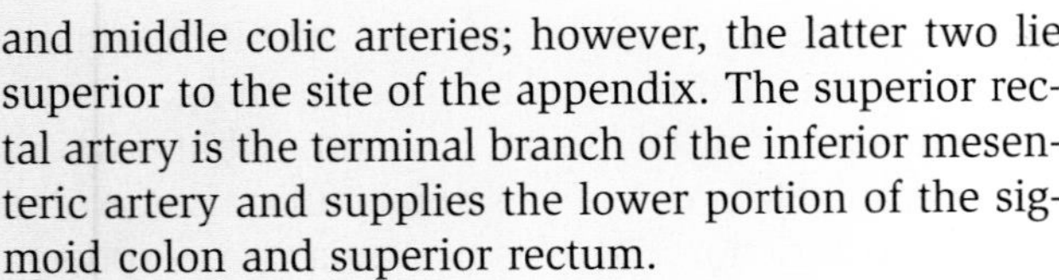

and middle colic arteries; however, the latter two lie superior to the site of the appendix. The superior rectal artery is the terminal branch of the inferior mesenteric artery and supplies the lower portion of the sigmoid colon and superior rectum.
GAS 333; GA 160

74 A. Caput medusae (referring to the head of Medusa, whose hair was formed by snakes) is caused by severely elevated portal pressure, with venous reflux from the liver to the periumbilical veins, by way of the usually collapsed veins in the ligamentum teres. The presence of caput medusae is usually associated with end-stage disease. Caput medusae is identified by the appearance of engorged veins radiating toward the lower limbs. The portal vein is the central connection of these anastomoses. Obstruction of the inferior vena cava, superior vena cava, and lateral thoracic vein do not cause portal hypertension and would not produce these symptoms. The superficial epigastric vein also is not associated with the development of portal hypertension but could provide a collateral channel for venous drainage.
GAS 266; GA 152, 164

75 C. Cholecystitis is an inflammation of the gallbladder due to increased concentration of bile or obstruction of the cystic duct by gallstones. Pain is ultimately felt in the right hypochondriac region, which corresponds to the T6 to T8 dermatomes. Sensory afferents from the viscera carry pain fibers as they travel with sympathetic axons in the greater thoracic splanchnic nerves. Pain cannot be felt in the viscera and is therefore referred to the body wall. The vagus nerve carries visceral sensory fibers from the head, neck, and trunk, but these do not include pain fibers. Spinal nerves of T1 to T4 receive afferents for pain from thoracic viscera, including the heart, but not abdominal organs. Sympathetic neurons are autonomic motor nerves and therefore do not carry sensory information. Afferent fibers of the dorsal primary rami of spinal nerves T6 to T8 convey sensory fibers from the back but not from internal organs.
GAS 342; GA 190

76 B. McBurney's point usually corresponds to the location of the base of the appendix where it attaches to the cecum. It is found on the right side of the abdomen, about two thirds of the distance from the umbilicus to the anterior superior iliac spine. The inguinal ligament is localized lateral and inferior to the appendix and hence would not be used as a landmark.
GAS 309; GA 125

77 B. The greater thoracic splanchnic nerves arise from the levels of the T5 to T9 thoracic sympathetic ganglia and are responsible for carrying general visceral afferents from upper abdominal organs and, therefore, from the body of the stomach. The pain fibers pass from the sympathetic chain to spinal nerves T5 to T9, thereafter to the spinal cord. Spinal nerves T1 to T5 do receive sensory afferents for pain but from thoracic organs. The vagus nerves do not carry afferents for pain. The lumbar splanchnic nerves are associated with the lower portion of the abdominopelvic area.
GAS 342; GA 190

78 C. The ureter is normally constricted to some degree as it crosses the pelvic brim from major to minor pelvis. The minor and major calyces are proximal to the ureter and not typical sites for obstruction by kidney stones. The midportion of the ureter is not a typical site for obstruction. The site of oblique entrance of the ureter into the urinary bladder is a common site for obstruction because it is compressed by bladder contents and the muscular wall. There are no common sites of obstruction between the pelvic brim and the uterine cervix.
GAS 360; GA 219

79 C. The splenorenal ligament is the attachment of the spleen to the left kidney and is the only ligament that contains the major branches of the splenic artery to the spleen and greater curvature of the stomach. The coronary ligament is the peritoneal reflection from the diaphragmatic surface of the liver onto the diaphragm that encloses the bare area of liver; it is not attached to the spleen. The falciform ligament is a peritoneal fold in contact with only the diaphragm and the liver. The gastrocolic ligament contains branches of the gastroomental vessels but should not be a factor in the splenectomy.
GAS 329; GA 149

80 C. Pelvic splanchnic nerves and the left colic artery supply the descending colon. The vagus nerve supplies the bowel only to the left colic flexure, and the middle colic artery supplies the transverse colon. The superior rectal artery supplies the lower sigmoid and rectum. The ileocolic artery supplies the cecum and ascending colon. The left thoracic splanchnic nerve has nothing to do with the descending colon.
GAS 335; GA 147, 189

81 E. The ilioinguinal nerve is a terminal branch of spinal nerve L1. It innervates the skin overlying the iliac crest; the anterior portion of the urogenital

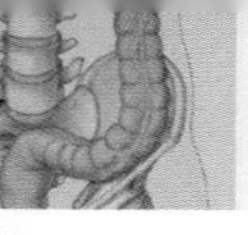

region; and the upper, inner thigh. Its pathway takes it below the typical site of McBurney's point, but it can be injured with extension of an appendectomy incision. Spinal nerve T10, the genitofemoral nerve, and the pudendal nerve are not located in the area of the incision; what is more, the area of sensory deficit does not correlate well with their injury. The genitofemoral nerve leaves the body wall at the superficial inguinal ring, well below the appendectomy incision. The pudendal nerve is both motor and sensory to the perineum. The genitofemoral nerve provides motor supply to the cremaster, sensory fibers to the scrotum, and a femoral branch innervating only the skin over the femoral triangle. Spinal nerve T10 innervates the umbilical region. The subcostal nerve innervates the skin at the level of the costal margin and the lower portion of the abdominal wall above the pubic region.
GAS 280; GA 138

82 A. Esophageal stenosis results from a failure of esophageal recanalization in the eighth week of development, which may also cause esophageal atresia. Webs and strictures are found in an examination of the esophagus in cases of stenosis, but they are not noticed in cases of atresia. A tracheoesophageal fistula is an abnormal passage between the trachea and the esophagus and is associated with esophageal atresia; therefore, webs and strictures would not be seen. Duodenal atresia and stenosis occur in the small intestine and would not cause aspiration pneumonia, and clinical manifestations would not be seen in the esophagus.
GAS 215; GA 106

83 B. Duodenal stenosis is caused by incomplete recanalization of the duodenum. The vomit contains bile in addition to the stomach contents because of the location of the occlusion, distal to the ampulla of Vater (hepatopancreatic ampulla), where the common bile duct enters the small intestine. Lack of weight gain is due to constant vomiting. A patent bile duct would not cause vomiting with bile. A hypertrophied pyloric sphincter would cause projectile vomiting without the presence of bile. An atrophied gastric antrum is caused by the removal of the membranous lining of the stomach and occurs proximal to the site of the entrance of the bile duct; therefore, the vomit would not contain bile. A tracheoesophageal fistula would not cause vomiting of stomach contents and bile because it is a defect of the respiratory system and occurs proximal to the site at which bile is added to stomach contents.
GAS 300; GA 152

84 C. With hypertrophy of the pyloric sphincter and the associated narrowing of the opening, there is projectile vomiting of stomach contents, but without bile, because bile enters the duodenum distal to the pyloric constriction. Duodenal atresia, like duodenal stenosis, causes vomiting of stomach contents and bile. Vomiting begins soon after birth in cases of atresia; vomiting due to stenosis does not begin necessarily immediately after birth and can occur days after delivery. Lack of weight gain is due to constant vomiting. An atrophied gastric fundus would not produce the signs seen here. A tracheoesophageal fistula would not cause vomiting of stomach contents and bile because it is a defect of the respiratory system and occurs proximal to the site at which bile is added to intestinal contents.
GAS 299; GA 159

85 B. Incomplete recanalization of the duodenum is caused either by duodenal stenosis or partial occlusion of the lumen of the duodenum and usually occurs in the distal third portion of the duodenum. This occlusion often results in vomiting of stomach contents plus bile later in life and is the reason the child was constantly hungry but did not gain weight. Incomplete recanalization of the esophagus during the eighth week of development causes esophageal stenosis and presents as webs and strictures. Esophageal atresia is generally seen with a tracheoesophageal fistula because it is caused by the tracheoesophageal septum deviating in the posterior direction. In some cases, it may result from a failure of recanalization during the eighth week of development and presents as a fetus with polyhydramnios due to an inability to swallow amniotic fluid. Duodenal atresia is the result of a failed reformation of the lumen of the duodenum and is associated with vomiting within the first few days of birth, polyhydramnios, and the "double bubble" sign. Tracheoesophageal fistula is an abnormal passage between the trachea and esophagus and would not be a cause for vomiting because it is associated with the respiratory system and also occurs proximal to the site of the defect.
GAS 256; GA 152

86 B. Duodenal atresia is the result of a failed reformation of the lumen of the duodenum and is associated with vomiting within the first few days of birth. Polyhydramnios is seen due to abnormal absorption of amniotic fluid by the intestines. Finally, radiographic or ultrasound examination would review the "double bubble" sign because of distended, gas-filled stomach. Duodenal stenosis is caused by incomplete recanalization of the duodenum and often results in

vomiting of stomach contents plus bile later in life. Hypertrophied pyloric sphincter would cause projectile vomiting. An atrophied gastric antrum is caused by the removal of the membranous lining of the stomach and occurs proximal to the site of the entrance of the common bile duct; therefore, vomit would not contain bile. Tracheoesophageal fistula is an abnormal passage between the trachea and esophagus and would not be a cause for any of symptoms cited in the question.
GAS 300; GA 152

87 **C.** Annular pancreas causes duodenal obstruction due to the thick band of pancreatic tissue that surrounds and constricts the second part of the duodenum. This obstruction can be found shortly after birth or much later. Annular pancreas can result from the bifid ventral pancreatic bud wrapping around the duodenum during development and fusing with the dorsal pancreatic bud, thereafter forming a ring. Both the dorsal and bifid ventral pancreatic buds are involved in this process; therefore, answers A, D, and E cannot be correct because they refer to either the dorsal or ventral buds, not both. This anomaly is not involved with lack of canalization of the bile ducts.
GAS 322; GA 166

88 **A.** A remnant of the omphaloenteric duct generally presents as an ileal (Meckel) diverticulum in the proximal portion of the omphaloenteric duct. It normally arises as a fingerlike pouch about 3 to 6 cm long from the antimesenteric border of the ileum and 40 to 50 cm from the ileocecal junction. The umbilical vesicle normally turns into a pear-shaped remnant about 5 mm in diameter by week 20. The cecal diverticulum is the primordium of the cecum and appendix. The Meckel diverticulum is not a remnant of the umbilical cord.
GAS 302; GA 158

89 **A.** An umbilical hernia results when the body wall does not close appropriately at the site of attachment of the umbilical cord. In such cases, part of the greater omentum and small intestine can herniate from the abdomen. Umbilical herniation differs from omphalocele. In congenital omphalocele, there is a failure of intestine to return to the abdominal cavity so that there is an apparent herniation of abdominal viscera into the proximal portion of the umbilical cord, without a covering of the hernia by skin. In umbilical hernia, the herniating structures are covered by subcutaneous tissue and skin. Gastroschisis is incomplete closure of the lateral folds, resulting in an epigastric hernia, in which the viscera protrude into the amniotic cavity, surrounded by amniotic fluid. An epigastric hernia occurs through a defect in the linea alba superior to the level of the umbilicus and occurs far more commonly in adults. An indirect inguinal hernia is when the communication between the tunica vaginalis and the peritoneal cavity do not close, and a loop of intestine or a portion of another organ such as the cecum herniates through the deep inguinal ring into the inguinal canal, with possible further descent through the superficial inguinal ring into the scrotum or labium majus.
GAS 291; GA 155

90 **D.** Gastroschisis results from an incomplete closure of the lateral folds during the fourth week of development from a defect in the medial plane of the abdominal wall. This results in an epigastric hernia, with viscera that protrude into the amniotic cavity without a peritoneal covering into the amniotic cavity and are covered by amniotic fluid. Nonrotation of the midgut results in the lower portion of the loop returning to the abdomen first, the small intestine passing to the right side of the abdomen, and the large intestine lying entirely on the left. Most cases are asymptomatic; however, obstruction of the superior mesenteric artery can cause infarction and gangrene of the part of the intestine it supplies. An umbilical hernia results when an abdominal organ herniates through an umbilical ring that does not close perfectly. Such a hernia often contains part of the greater omentum and small intestine. The cloacal membrane usually ruptures during the eighth week of development, creating a communication between the anal canal and the amniotic cavity.
GAS 256; GA 154

91 **A.** The inability to pass meconium denotes an obstruction of the fetal bowel. Midgut volvulus results in the twisting of the intestines and ultimately obstruction of the small and/or large intestines. Gastroschisis results from an incomplete closure of the lateral folds during the fourth week of development from a defect in the medial plane of the abdominal wall. This results in an epigastric hernia, with viscera that protrude into the amniotic cavity and are covered by amniotic fluid. Failure of recanalization of the ileum is seen with 50% of obstructive lesions of the intestine. This obstruction is caused by stenosis or atresia of the intestines. A remnant of the omphaloenteric duct generally presents as an ileal (Meckel) diverticulum in the proximal portion of the omphaloenteric duct. It normally arises as a fingerlike pouch about 3 to 6 cm long from the antimesenteric border of the ileum and 40 to 50 cm from the ileocecal junction. Nonrotation of the midgut results in the lower portion

of the loop returning to the abdomen first, the small intestine sitting on the right side of the abdomen, and the large intestine lying entirely on the left. Most cases are asymptomatic; however, obstruction of the superior mesenteric artery can cause infarction and gangrene of the part of the intestine it supplies.
GAS 313

92 D. A remnant of the proximal portion of the omphaloenteric duct generally presents as an ileal (Meckel) diverticulum. It normally arises as a finger-like pouch about 3 to 6 cm long from the antimesenteric border of the ileum and 40 to 50 cm from the ileocecal junction. Midgut volvulus results from a twisting of the intestines and, ultimately, obstruction of the small and large intestines. Infarction of fetal bowel is seen and would not be the cause of the signs of appendicitis. Gastroschisis results from an incomplete closure of the lateral folds during the fourth week of development from a defect in the medial plane of the abdominal wall. This results in an epigastric hernia, with viscera that protrude into the amniotic cavity and are covered by amniotic fluid. Failure of recanalization of the ileum is seen in 50% of obstructive lesions of the intestine. This obstruction is caused by stenosis or atresia of the intestines. Nonrotation of the midgut results in the lower portion of the loop returning to the abdomen first so that the small intestine becomes fixed on the right side of the abdomen, with the large intestine lying entirely on the left. Most cases are asymptomatic; however, obstruction of the superior mesenteric artery can cause infarction and gangrene of the part of the intestine it supplies.
GAS 302; GA 158

93 A. Incomplete separation of the cloaca by the urorectal septum results in anal agenesis. Dorsal deviation of the urorectal septum would result in anal stenosis. Failure of the anal membrane to perforate results in imperforate anus, not anal agenesis. Abnormal recanalization of the colon results in rectal atresia, in which there is no connection between the rectum and anal canal. Remnants of the proximal portion of the omphaloenteric duct would result in a Meckel diverticulum, not anal agenesis.
GAS 480; GA 210

94 B. Dorsal deviation of the urorectal septum results in anal stenosis. Incomplete separation of the cloaca by the urorectal septum results in anal agenesis. Failure of the anal membrane to perforate results in imperforate anus. The anal canal exists but is obstructed by a layer of tissue. Abnormal recanalization of the colon results in rectal atresia, in which there is no connection between the rectum and anal canal. Remnants of the proximal portion of the omphaloenteric duct would result in a Meckel diverticulum, not anal stenosis.
GAS 462; GA 210

95 D. A vitelline fistula is caused by the persistence of the vitelline duct, which can, by its connections with the umbilicus, cause the symptoms described. An enterocystoma is a tumor and would not result in the symptoms described. A vitelline cyst is a persistence of the vitelline duct; however, it would not open directly to the outside so would not cause the symptoms. Meckel diverticulum can result in a vitelline fistula, but it is simply the persistence of the vitelline duct that can appear in different forms (such as cyst or fistula). Volvulus is the twisting of the small intestines around their suspending vasculature. It can result from malrotation of the midgut loop and would not result in the symptoms described.
GAS 302; GA 155

96 D. Anorectal agenesis is due to abnormal partitioning of the cloaca and is often associated with a rectourethral, rectovaginal, or rectouterine fistula. Failure of fixation of the hindgut can result in volvulus. Failure of the proctodeum to develop will result in an imperforate anus. Agenesis of the urorectal septum would most likely lead to a fistula but would not cause anorectal agenesis. Premature rupture of the anal membrane would not cause anorectal agenesis.
GAS 462; GA 210

97 A. Meckel's diverticulum is a remnant of the yolk stalk. It is usually 2 inches long and 2 feet proximal from the ileocecal junction. Meckel's diverticulum is prone to ulceration (possibly leading to perforation) that can result in gastrointestinal bleeding. Duplication of the intestine does not predispose the patient to GI bleeding. A subhepatic cecum and appendix is due to failure of the cecal bud to form and results in the absence of an ascending colon. Nonrotation of the midgut could lead to volvulus but is not the most likely cause for GI bleeding. Herniation of intestines can exist without any symptoms; however, if the loop of intestine becomes strangulated, it can lead to gangrene.
GAS 306; GA 159

98 D. Failure of the ureteric bud to form results in renal agenesis and oligohydramnios, that is, deficient production of amniotic fluid. Polycystic kidney disease is an autosomal recessive disease characterized by spongy kidneys with a multitude of cysts. Degeneration of the mesonephros occurs during normal development; however, a small portion of the meso-

nephric tubules may go on to form parts of the urogenital system. Ureteric duplication occurs due to premature division of the ureteric bud and can result in either a double kidney or a duplication of the ureter. Wilms tumor is a malignancy of the kidney that is more common in children than it is in adults; it does not cause renal agenesis.
GAS 355; GA 180

99 **C.** Androgen insensitivity syndrome involves the development of testes and female external genitalia, with a blind-ending vagina and absence of the uterus and uterine tubes. This is consistent with the presenting symptoms. Male pseudohermaphroditism and female pseudohermaphroditism have different presentations from those described and result from 46XY and 46XX genotypes, respectively. Inguinal hernias have nothing to do with absence of the uterus and a negative sex chromatin pattern. Turner syndrome results from a 45X genotype and presents with short stature, webbed neck, congenital hypoplasia of the lymphatics, and shield chest—among other symptoms—and is not consistent with the symptoms described.
GAS 454; GA 228

100 **A.** The vaginal plate, which arises from the sinovaginal bulbs, undergoes canalization during embryonic development. Failure of canalization results in a persistent vaginal plate and thus imperforate hymen. The hymen is a fold of mucous membrane that covers the opening of the vaginal canal. It is often torn early in life. The processus vaginalis is a tubelike projection of the peritoneum into the inguinal canal that precedes the descent of the testis or round ligament. Both cervical atresia and androgen insensitivity syndrome would result in amenorrhea; however, neither disorder would present with an imperforate hymen because the vaginal canal would still undergo canalization. The sinovaginal bulbs are responsible for the development of the vaginal plate. Failure of development would result in complete absence of the vagina.
GAS 458; GA 210

101 **D.** Gartner ducts cysts, which often appear in the lateral wall of the vagina, are the result of remnants of the mesonephric (wolffian) duct. The mesonephric duct gives rise to a variety of structures, including the ureter and collecting tubules. In males, the duct eventually forms the ductus deferens and ejaculatory ducts, whereas it often disappears in females. The only remaining traces of the mesonephric ducts are the epoophoron, paroophoron, and Gartner cyst; thus, persistence of this duct can result in formation of these cysts. The mesonephric tubules are elongations of the mesonephric vesicles. These tubules are subsequently invaginated by the glomeruli to form a component of the renal corpuscle. The paramesonephric ducts are responsible for formation of the uterus, cervix, and uppermost aspect of the vagina. The urogenital folds form the labia minora in females and the spongy urethra in males. Sinovaginal bulbs are responsible for the development of the vaginal plate in embryonic development.
GAS 458; GA 210

102 **C.** Potter sequence, or Potter syndrome, is a rare autosomal recessive trait and is associated with renal agenesis or hypoplasia. Altered facial characteristics include flattened nasal bridge, mandibular micrognathia, malformed low-set ears, etc. Absence or lack of proper development of the kidneys causes oligohydramnios, or possibly anhydramnios. Multicystic dysplastic kidney and polycystic kidney are usually secondary to Potter sequence and are therefore not the cause of Potter sequence or oligohydramnios. Wilms tumor is a relatively common renal tumor that presents in children; it is not associated with oligohydramnios and Potter sequence. Extrophy of the bladder is a congenital defect that exposes the posterior surface of the bladder on the exterior of the abdominal wall; there is no indication of this defect in the patient.
GAS 355; GA 147

103 **B.** The ureteric bud is responsible for the development of the ureter, and thus an early splitting of the ureteric bud would result in formation of a second ureter on the ipsilateral side. Failure of the ureteric bud to form would cause a complete absence of the ureter, whereas failure of the ureteric bud to branch occurs normally during embryonic development and results in one ureter joined to each kidney. The urorectal septum is a section of tissue of mesenchymal origin that develops between the allantois and hindgut. Failure of this structure to develop would not result in an additional ureter. Finally, a persistent urachus acts as an abnormal fistula that runs from the bladder to the umbilicus, resulting in urine leaking from the external abnormal wall.
GAS 355; GA 180

104 **B.** The hepatorenal pouch (or recess or space) is situated between the liver and both the parietal peritoneum covering the right kidney and suprarenal gland. This recess is the lowest space in the peritoneal cavity in supine patients. Accumulation of fluid in the peritoneal cavity will ordinarily collect in this pouch. The right subphrenic space is located between the liver and diaphragm. Although this recess is positioned in the

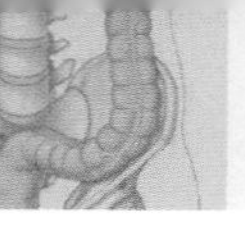

appropriate abdominal quadrant, it is not the deepest space within the peritoneal cavity. Fluid may reach the right subphrenic space, but it will not accumulate in this region. The paracolic gutters are grooves lateral to the ascending and descending colons. Though these recesses are potential spaces for fluid accumulation, they are located inferior to the hepatorenal recess and would not collect fluid while the patient is supine. The vesicouterine and rectouterine pouch would not be potential spaces for fluid accumulation in a supine patient, although they provide predictable sites when the patient is upright or ambulating.
GAS 395-396; GA 144

105 **A.** The right subphrenic space is located between the inferior aspect of the diaphragm and the superior surface of the liver. An ulceration in the posterior stomach wall would allow the passage of air from the stomach into the right subphrenic space through an open communication in the omental bursa. The remaining answer choices are located inferior to the site of ulceration and would not accumulate air. The paracolic gutters traverse lateral to the ascending and descending colons. The vesicouterine and rectouterine pouches are located in the pelvic cavity; air would not accumulate in these spaces.
GAS 395-396; GA 144

106 **E.** The most likely location of fluid to accumulate is the pouch of Douglas because it is the lowest point in the pelvis when a patient is standing erect. Additionally, fluid would accumulate here because the mesoovarian ligament causes the ovary to be located on the posterior aspect of the board ligament. This allows for communication between the fluid of the ovary and the rectouterine pouch. The right subphrenic space is located inferior to the right side of the diaphragm and superior to the liver. The paracolic gutters are located lateral to the ascending and descending colons. Neither of these locations is a likely site of fluid accumulation when the patient is standing. The hepatorenal recess is situated between the liver and both the right kidney and suprarenal gland. This recess, also known as the Morison pouch, is the deepest space in the peritoneal cavity in a supine patient but not when the patient sits or stands. The vesicouterine pouch is located between the bladder and uterus and is separated from the ovaries by a double layer of visceral peritoneum also known as the broad ligament of the uterus.
GAS 460; GA 210

107 **D.** Parietal peritoneum and "the mesentery." The parietal peritoneum lines the abdominal wall, whereas the visceral peritoneum is in intimate contact with organs. The greater omentum extends from the greater curvature of the stomach and covers the midgut. Access to the ileum would require penetration of the parietal peritoneum to enter the peritoneal cavity and interruption of the visceral peritoneum of "the mesentery" covering the thrombosed vessel. Although it would probably be necessary to reflect the greater omentum for adequate exposure, it would not ordinarily require incision.
GAS 366; GA 154

108 **D.** Referred pain from cholecystitis is generally referred to the region of the inferior angle of the right scapula. These fibers are generally from T5 to T9. These sensory fibers for pain are stimulated by the gallbladder inflammation because of the proximity of the adjacent structures. C3 to C5 sensory fibers innervate the shoulder area. The distribution of C5 to C8 is primarily to the upper limb, to the level of the hand; T1 to T4 distribution is to the upper thoracic wall and medial upper arm; T10 and T11 distribution is to the thoracic and abdominal wall, T1 to T4 visceral fibers for pain are generally associated with referred pain from the heart.
GAS 342; GA 190

109 **A.** The Pringle maneuver is a surgical technique employed when the hepatic artery has been accidentally ligated. The hepatoduodenal ligament is clamped off to prevent the passage of blood flow through both the hepatic artery and the portal vein. The Kocher maneuver, in which the ascending colon and descending duodenum are reflected to the left, is often employed to expose and arrest a hemorrhage from the inferior vena cava. The Valsalva maneuver involves stopping the passage of air with the vocal folds to build up intrathoracic pressure, as for coughing or vocalization. The Heimlich maneuver involves sharp, rapid compressions of the xiphisternal region to expel foreign bodies from the trachea. Putting a clamp on the porta would not stop the bleeding but could certainly produce major injury to the numerous vascular elements there.
GAS 295-296; GA 164

110 **A.** The most likely source of this hemorrhage is from the left colic artery. Colonic diverticular disease is the development of blind end sacs from the wall of the colon. Of the selected choices the left colic artery is the only artery supplying a portion of the descending colon. The superior and inferior rectal (hemorrhoidal) arteries supply the rectum and anal canal. The left

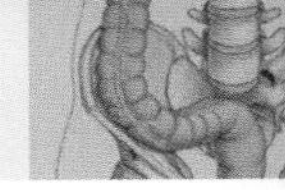

gastroepiploic artery arises from the splenic artery and supplies the greater curvature of the stomach.
GAS 335; GA 147

111 D. Murphy's sign is a specific test designed to detect and diagnose problems in the upper right abdominal quadrant. It is classically used to diagnose problems of the gallbladder by pressing deeply under the right costal margin and asking the patient to breathe deeply. This causes sharp pain in the patient with cholecystitis. Rebound tenderness is pain experienced when applied pressure is removed quickly from a location on the body. It is not specific to areas of the body and is not indicative of problems in the upper right quadrant. The iliopsoas test is generally used to diagnose appendicitis because flexing the iliopsoas muscle group applies pressure to the ascending colon and appendix. When the appendix is inflamed, this pressure elicits pain. The obturator sign is used to diagnose irritation of the obturator internus muscle and would not elicit a positive test with the patient's current symptoms. Finally, cough tenderness would not be present because it is generally associated with hernias and problems associated with rises in intraabdominal pressure.
GAS 319; GA 125

112 D. The lowest point of the lesser sac occurs at the intersection of the gastrocolic ligament and transverse colon. Bleeding would travel to the lowest point of the lesser sac. Access to this area would require entry through the gastrocolic ligament, which extends from the greater curvature of the stomach to the transverse colon. The hepatogastric and hepatoduodenal ligaments attach between the liver and the lesser curvature of the stomach and the first part of the duodenum, respectively. Dividing the hepatogastric ligament provides entry into the lesser sac, but this is not the most efficient access point because it does not provide the best exposure of the inferior aspect of the lesser sac.
GAS 298; GA 144

113 D. Superficial inguinal nodes. The external anal sphincter is skeletal muscle of the anal canal. This suggests that the carcinoma is originating from the anal canal. The results of the biopsy support the finding that the carcinoma most likely occurred below the pectinate line where you would find squamous cells of the anal canal. The anal canal primarily drains to the superficial inguinal lymph nodes. The inferior rectum above the pectinate line drains into the internal iliac. The superior aspect of the rectum drains into the middle rectal lymph nodes. The external iliac nodes primarily drain lower limb, pelvic, and deep peritoneal structures. The deep inguinal lymph nodes drain the glands of the clitoris and penis and the superficial inguinal nodes.
GAS 496; GA 255

114 A. The lymphatics of the inferior rectum above the pectinate line drain into the internal iliac nodes. Below the pectinate line, lymphatics of the anal canal will primarily drain into the superficial inguinal (horizontal) nodes. The external iliac nodes primarily drain lower limb, pelvic, and deep peritoneal structures. The deep inguinal lymph nodes primarily drain the glands of the clitoris and penis, receiving lymph also from the superficial inguinal nodes. The superior aspect of the rectum is drained by the middle rectal nodes, lymph from which eventually flows into the lumbar nodes.
GAS 496; GA 255

115 B. In sliding hernias the gastroesophageal junction is displaced. Diaphragmatic hernias of the esophagus can be characterized by analyzing the gastroesophageal junction. In sliding hernias the gastroesophageal junction is displaced anteriorly into the mediastinum. The paraesophageal hernia is generally characterized by herniation of the stomach into the mediastinum; however, the gastroesophageal junction remains fixed. In paraesophageal hernias the fundus herniates into the stomach, but the antrum does not.
GAS 215; GA 159

116 B. The falciform ligament separates the subphrenic spaces into right and left recesses and extends between the liver and the anterior abdominal wall. Because of its location and attachments, it would serve to stop the spread of such an abscess from one side to the other. The location of the other answer choices makes them insufficient in limiting the spread of an abscess. The round ligament of the liver is the obliterated remains of the umbilical vein and lies in the free margin of the falciform ligament ascending from the umbilicus to the inferior surface of the liver. The coronary ligament encloses the bare area of the liver and forms the triangular ligaments. The hepatoduodenal and hepatogastric ligaments attach the liver to the duodenum and stomach, respectively. Together they form the lesser omentum.
GAS 317; GA 141

117 C. The kidney lies at the twelfth rib, and problems with pain associated with respiratory processes

would result from the ribs being injured. The spleen lies under the left side of the liver superior to the kidneys, adjacent to ribs 9 to 11. The lungs are located completely within the thoracic cavity above the level of the twelfth rib. The liver is located on the right side of the body and lies around the level of the fifth to tenth ribs. The pancreas is predominantly located in the middle of the body more medial to the kidneys at the level of the eleventh to twelfth ribs.
GAS 355; GA 177

118 D. A malignancy of the anal canal would drain into the inguinal lymph nodes, specifically the superficial lymph nodes. The internal iliac lymph nodes receive drainage from the rectum, the uterus, the prostate gland, and the bladder. The testes, though located in the scrotum, external to the abdominopelvic cavities, drain into the lumbar nodes located on the anterior aspect of the aorta. The sigmoid colon drains into the inferior mesenteric lymph nodes.
GAS 496; GA 255

119 C. The superior mesenteric artery arises from the aorta, behind the neck of the pancreas, at the level of L1 within the abdominal cavity, and traverses inferiorly across the anterior surface of the third part of the duodenum. As it crosses the uncinate process of the pancreas and duodenum, this artery could readily be affected by a tumor in the immediate area. The common bile duct and the portal vein course anteriorly from the head of the pancreas and therefore are associated with the first part of the duodenum. The gastroduodenal artery supplies the duodenum, the head of the pancreas, and the greater curvature of the stomach and is a branch of the common hepatic artery. This artery does not cross the third part of the duodenum. The posterior superior pancreaticoduodenal courses posteriorly over the head of the pancreas and supplies both the head of the pancreas and the second portion of the duodenum. It is therefore more associated with the second part of the duodenum.
GAS 300; GA 153

120 D. Vascular structures situated immediately medial to the ureter are often subject to ligation during surgical procedures. The ureter is crossed by the uterine artery an inch or so lateral to the cervix and must be identified and avoided, in ligating the uterine vessels. The middle rectal artery arises from the internal iliac artery and passes dorsal to the uterus and the rectum. The superior vesical artery arises from the umbilical artery anteriorly in the pelvis. The internal pudendal vein enters the pelvis through the greater sciatic foramen and terminates in the internal iliac vein, laterally at the pelvic wall. The gonadal vein in the female passes to the ovary by way of the infundibulopelvic ligament, near the pelvic brim.
GAS 365; GA 234

121 B. Pain in the umbilical region can be indicative of referred pain from the large intestine. Gallstones can ulcerate through the wall of the fundus of the gallbladder and into the transverse colon, or through the wall of the body of the gallbladder into the duodenum. The stone would then most likely be entrapped at the ileocecal junction, possibly leading to an intestinal obstruction. This could lead predictably to the pain, cramping, and vomiting experienced by the patient. The radiographic results suggest that the biliary trees are clear (indicated by the presence of air) and rule out the common bile duct or hepatic duct as potential sites of gallstone obstruction. Because the gallstones would pass thereafter through the duodenum, this would not be the site of blockage. Because the gallstones could pass freely through the intestine as far distally as the ileocecal junction, it would be unlikely that they would accumulate in the jejunum.
GAS 322; GA 154

122 A. The intersection of the right linea semilunaris with the ninth costal cartilage in the right upper quadrant is associated typically with the point of contact of the gallbladder fundus with the anterior abdominal wall. The anatomic quadrants provide a useful tool for understanding the location of various anatomic structures and viscera located within the body. The linea semilunaris runs parallel with the lateral border of the rectus sheath and is a prominent landmark for surface anatomy. The upper right quadrant is the correct anatomic region for the location of the gallbladder as mentioned earlier; however, this choice is too general and would not be the best answer choice. Similarly, the intersection of the right semilunaris with the right intertubercular plane is situated in the upper right quadrant; however, this is not the most precise location of the gallbladder. The epigastric region is located superior to the umbilical region. The contents of the epigastric region are the left portion of the liver and a portion of the stomach. The right hypochondriac region, the anatomic region situated to the right of the epigastric region, is located superior and lateral to the gallbladder and would thus not be the appropriate answer choice.
GAS 388; GA 125

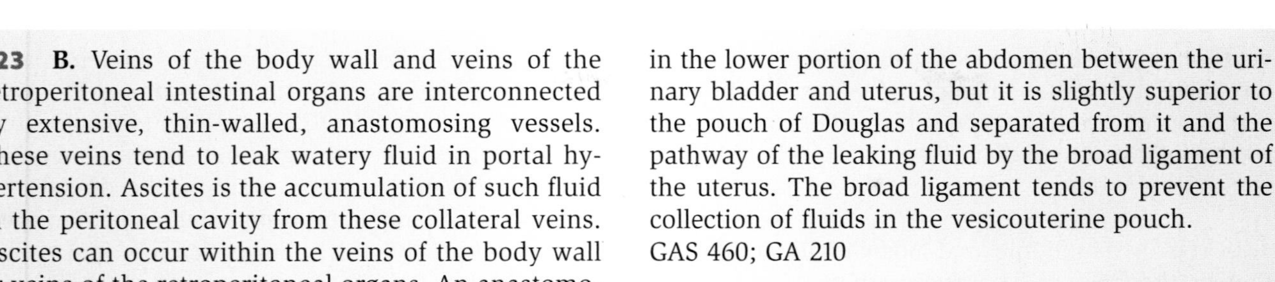

123 B. Veins of the body wall and veins of the retroperitoneal intestinal organs are interconnected by extensive, thin-walled, anastomosing vessels. These veins tend to leak watery fluid in portal hypertension. Ascites is the accumulation of such fluid in the peritoneal cavity from these collateral veins. Ascites can occur within the veins of the body wall or veins of the retroperitoneal organs. An anastomosis between the epigastric veins and the paraumbilical veins would lead to possible contribution to caput medusae but would not likely result in significant ascites. Esophageal varices are due to expansion of submucosal esophageal veins from portal hypertension, resulting from anastomoses between the left gastric vein and the esophageal veins. These anastomoses would produce varices, perhaps with profuse bleeding, rather than ascites. Further, ascites occur within the peritoneal cavity. Superior rectal, left gastric, and the middle rectal veins all contribute to the portal-systemic anastomoses, but these anastomoses form varices or hemorrhoids, not ascites. The portal vein would not lead to ascites because it is not involved directly with any caval anastomoses.
GAS 339, 392; GA 172

124 E. The transversus abdominis aponeurosis and transversalis fascia form a significant portion of the posterior wall of the inguinal canal and the lower part of the inguinal triangle (of Hesselbach). Gradual weakness or attrition of tissues in the posterior wall provides the likelihood of egress of a direct inguinal hernia. A patent processus vaginalis at the deep inguinal ring, or expansion of the deep inguinal ring, with stretching of the transversalis fascia there, can contribute to the formation of indirect inguinal hernias. Weakness of the transversalis fascia by itself is not a key feature of inguinal herniation, nor is weakness of the peritoneum, or defects in the aponeuroses of the external or internal oblique muscles.
GAS 290-291; GA 140

125 C. The rectouterine pouch (of Douglas) is the lowest recess of the female abdominopelvic cavity when the woman is standing or sitting upright. Any fluid accumulation in this cavity will settle in the rectouterine pouch due to it being the most dependent or inferior space. The subphrenic space would likely not collect fluid because of its location in the superior abdominal cavity, which does not tend to collect fluid from the pelvis. The hepatorenal pouch (of Morison) is located in the right posterosuperior aspect of the abdominal cavity, far from the pelvic cavity. The vesicouterine space is a recess that is similarly located in the lower portion of the abdomen between the urinary bladder and uterus, but it is slightly superior to the pouch of Douglas and separated from it and the pathway of the leaking fluid by the broad ligament of the uterus. The broad ligament tends to prevent the collection of fluids in the vesicouterine pouch.
GAS 460; GA 210

126 D. The dorsal root ganglia contain all cell bodies of sensory neurons from the body wall and limbs. Afferent fibers from the appendix travel in T8 to T10. The sympathetic chain contains postganglionic sympathetic cell bodies that are targeted to smooth muscle and glands of the viscera and heart muscle. The greater splanchnic nerve (T5 to T9) carries preganglionic sympathetic axons to the celiac ganglion, which is formed by postganglionic sympathetic neurons. The lateral horn of the spinal cord is found in levels T1 to L2 and contains preganglionic sympathetic cell bodies.
GAS 302; GA 191

127 A. The preganglionic sympathetic fibers running to the adrenal gland would be cut during adrenalectomy for they synapse on catecholamine-secreting cells within the adrenal medulla. Unlike the normal route of sympathetic innervation, which is to first synapse in a sympathetic ganglion and then send postganglionic fibers to the target tissue, the chromaffin cells of the adrenal gland are innervated directly by preganglionic sympathetic fibers. This is because the chromaffin cells are embryologically postganglionic neurons that migrate to the medulla and undergo differentiation. The adrenal gland receives no other recognized types of innervation; therefore, the remaining answer choices are all incorrect.
GAS 374; GA 194

128 D. The left common iliac vein lies posterior to the right common iliac artery. Compression of the vein in this location is a frequent cause of deep venous thrombosis of the left lower limb; that is, the venous drainage of the lower limb is obstructed. This can cause extreme pain, together with ischemia of the limb that, in some untreated cases, can lead to amputation of the limb or death. The inferior vena cava would not be compressed, for it has branched superior to the location of the tumor. The renal veins would not be compromised because these veins extend from the kidneys to the inferior vena cava quite far above the blockage. The testicular veins pass lateral to the area of obstruction, with the right gonadal vein passing superiorly to join the inferior vena cava, and the left gonadal vein terminating in the left renal

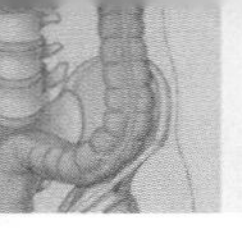

vein. The right common iliac vein passes freely about the pelvic brim after taking origin from the inferior vena cava and would not be subjected to compression by the right common iliac artery.
GAS 264; GA 180

129 D. Preganglionic and postganglionic sympathetics, preganglionic parasympathetic, and visceral afferent fibers are present within the celiac ganglion. The cell bodies of postganglionic sympathetic fibers are contained within the celiac ganglion and their axons pass to upper abdominal organs. Preganglionic parasympathetic nerves also run through the ganglion but do not synapse within the ganglion; therefore, there are no postganglionic parasympathetic nerves in the ganglion. The preganglionic parasympathetic fibers are extensions from the right vagal trunk and run within the preaortic plexus. No somatic motor fibers are present within this ganglion. Running through all of the abdominal ganglia are also visceral afferent fibers passing superiorly to reach the spinal cord at spinal nerve levels T5 to L2. Answer B is incorrect because there are no postganglionic parasympathetic fibers running within the ganglion or the celiac plexus. Postganglionic parasympathetic nerves arise from terminal ganglia located upon, or within the wall of, target organs. Answers C and E are incorrect because they do not include postganglionic sympathetic cell bodies and their axons, which also run though the celiac ganglion.
GAS 342; GA 191

130 B. The ureter is innervated by sympathetic and parasympathetic fibers in the ureteric plexus. General visceral afferent fibers in the ureteric plexus follow sympathetic fibers from spinal cord levels T11 to L2; therefore, pain from these fibers will be referred to nerves at these levels. The iliohypogastric nerve receives fibers from T12 and L1 and innervates the skin over the pubic symphysis. The ilioinguinal nerve receives fibers from L1 and innervates the skin from the iliac crest to the upper portions of the labia. The subcostal nerve innervates skin at the T12 dermatome level. The lateral cutaneous branch of the iliohypogastric nerve contains fibers from T12-L1 and supplies the anterior superior gluteal skin. The lateral femoral cutaneous nerve contains fibers from L2 and L3 spinal cord levels and innervates the skin over the lateral thigh. The obturator nerve contains fibers from L2 to L4 spinal cord levels and innervates the major adductors of the thigh.
GAS 279; GA 53, 134, 186, 283

131 C. Perforation of a posterior duodenal ulcer most commonly damages the posterior superior pancreaticoduodenal artery. This artery branches from the inferior aspect of the gastroduodenal artery. The superior mesenteric artery does not lie directly beneath the duodenum and is not likely to be damaged. The posterior inferior pancreaticoduodenal artery branches from the superior mesenteric artery and lies too far inferior to be damaged. The right gastric artery branches from the proper hepatic artery and runs along the pyloric portion of the lesser curvature of the stomach.
GAS 331; GA 150, 163

132 E. A perforating ulcer in the anterior wall of the duodenum is likely to cause peritonitis. The duodenum is covered anteriorly by a layer of peritoneum. The gastroduodenal and posterior superior pancreaticoduodenal arteries lie posterior to the duodenum and are not likely to be damaged. The posterior inferior pancreaticoduodenal artery is a branch of the superior mesenteric artery and neither of these arteries is likely to be damaged because they lie inferior to the duodenum. Perforating ulcers pierce the duodenum or stomach anteriorly; penetrating ulcers pierce the duodenum or stomach posteriorly.
GAS 303; GA 210

133 D. The suspensory ligament of the duodenum (ligament of Treitz) originates from the right crus of the diaphragm and is attached to the fourth part of the duodenum at the duodenojejunal junction. This ligament is commonly used as a palpable landmark during abdominal surgeries. The superior and inferior mesenteric arteries and the vasa recta are highly variable and cannot be used as reliable landmarks. Ladd bands connect the cecum to the abdominal wall and can obstruct the duodenum in cases of malrotation of the intestine. These bands can be surgically divided to treat malrotation of the intestine, but Ladd bands are not used as a common landmark.
GAS 301; GA 153

134 E. Failure of fusion of the pleuroperitoneal folds can cause herniation of abdominal contents into the thorax (congenital diaphragmatic hernia), most commonly on the left side. This defect can impair lung function, causing respiratory distress and cyanosis. The absence of the pleuropericardial fold would cause communication between the pericardial sac and the pleural cavity and would not lead to the symptoms described. The musculature of the diaphragm is derived from the third to fifth cervical myotomes. Absence of musculature in one half of the diaphragm

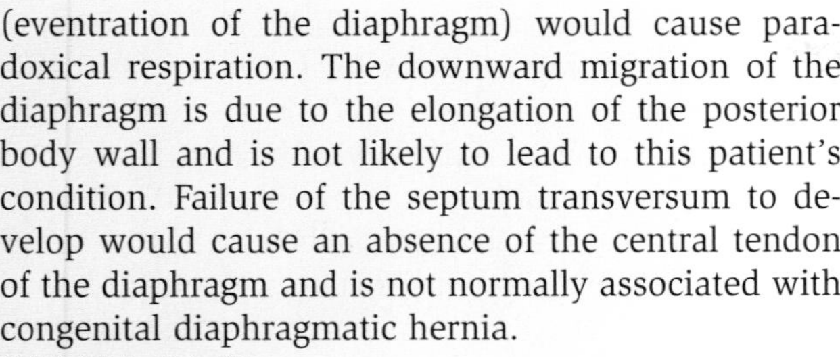

(eventration of the diaphragm) would cause paradoxical respiration. The downward migration of the diaphragm is due to the elongation of the posterior body wall and is not likely to lead to this patient's condition. Failure of the septum transversum to develop would cause an absence of the central tendon of the diaphragm and is not normally associated with congenital diaphragmatic hernia.
GAS 354; GA 67

135 C. Both Morgagni and Bochdalek hernias are due to defects in the pleuroperitoneal membrane. Morgagni hernia is normally found retrosternally just lateral to the xiphoid process and, if severe, can cause respiratory distress. More commonly, it is perceived as a sharp, epigastric pain that can be confused with several other maladies. In this case, the barium test rules out esophageal problems; the HIDA scan injection to study the gallbladder and biliary apparatus is negative also. Bochdalek hernia can cause similar symptoms but is due to a posterolateral herniation and would not be near the xiphoid process. A congenital hiatal hernia occurs when part of the stomach herniates into the thoracic cavity and can be caused by a shortened esophagus. This type of hernia would not present between the xiphoid process and costal margin.
GAS 354; GA 67

136 A. The ileum can become ischemic when arterial supply from the superior mesenteric artery is compromised. The superior mesenteric artery arises from the aorta posterior to the neck of the pancreas. It descends across the third part of the duodenum and enters the root of the mesentery behind the transverse colon. This artery gives origin to the following branches: inferior pancreaticoduodenal artery, middle colic artery, ileocolic artery, right colic artery, and intestinal arteries. The ileocolic artery descends behind the peritoneum toward the right and ends by dividing into the ascending colic artery, anterior and posterior cecal arteries, the appendicular artery, and ileal branches. The ileum is supplied by the ileal branches, which do not have any anastomoses with another major source vessel. The transverse colon is supplied by the marginal artery, which possesses anastomoses of the right colic artery arising from the superior mesenteric artery, and the left colic artery arising from the inferior mesenteric artery. The spleen, stomach, and duodenum are all supplied by branches of the celiac trunk, which arise from the abdominal aorta just below the aortic hiatus of the diaphragm.
GAS 302; GA 154

137 A. The portal vein is compressed in its passage through the hepatoduodenal ligament, the anterior border of the omental (epiploic) foramen (of Winslow). The veins of Retzius are located along the sides of the abdominal walls and communicate between tributaries of retroperitoneal parts of the gastrointestinal tract and veins of the body wall. In portal hypertension the portal blood cannot pass freely through the liver, and the portal-caval tributaries and their anastomoses become dilated. The inferior epigastric veins anastomose with the paraumbilical veins, which is the first branch off the hepatic portal vein. These would be the first affected in portal hypertension. The inferior vena cava is the main route of blood return to the right atrium and is posterior to the omental (epiploic) foramen (of Winslow); it would not likely be compressed due to herniation through the foramen. Compression of the proper hepatic artery in the hepatoduodenal ligament would not result in dilation of veins of Retzius but could conceivably diminish blood supply to the gallbladder and liver. Common bile duct compression would result in jaundice and increased serum bilirubin. The cystic duct joins with the hepatic duct to form the common bile duct. Compression of this would lead to an inflamed gallbladder (cholecystitis).
GAS 337-339; GA 172

138 C. A dermatome is an area of skin that is supplied by a single spinal nerve. The descending colon receives its visceral sensory supply for pain from spinal segments L1 and L2. Injury to the descending colon can cause referral of pain to the corresponding dermatomes. Spinal segments T6 to T10 supply upper abdominal organs, including the pancreas and the duodenum. L1 to L4 supply the rectum, bladder, and uterus. T6 to L2 supply portions of all abdominal viscera.
GAS 389; GA 191

139 E. A gallstone ileus occurs when a gallstone (cholelith) ulcerates through the wall of the body of the gallbladder and into the duodenum. In this case, gallstones became lodged in the ileocecal region. Obstruction in the ileocecal junction can produce pain that mimics appendicitis. However, bowel sounds will be exaggerated above the obstruction and absent distal to the obstruction. This obstruction would require surgical correction. The hepatopancreatic ampulla (of Vater) is the location where the pancreatic and bile ducts join before entering the duodenum. An obstruction here would cause jaundice, and radiating pain would be localized into the right upper quadrant, with referred pain to the scapula. The duodenal cap, or bulb, is

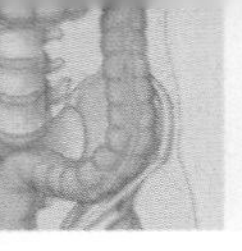

proximal to the entrance of the common bile duct, and any obstruction would be distal to this point. The ileum is not a likely site for gallstone obstruction. The pyloric sphincter surrounds the pyloric orifice and controls the rate of emptying of the stomach contents into the duodenum. This location is proximal to the entrance of gallbladder contents into the small intestine.
GAS 303, 308-309; GA 158

140 **A.** The upper and intermediate portions of the esophagus receive blood supply from three branches of the aorta: the inferior thyroid, bronchial, and esophageal arteries; the lower portion of the esophagus is supplied by the inferior phrenic and left gastric arteries. The lowest part of the esophagus, below the diaphragm, is supplied by the left gastric artery. Perforation to this area could easily injure this artery. The bronchial artery supplies a small section of the esophagus inferior to the level of the carina (T4). The thoracic intercostal arteries supply intercostal spaces and do not contribute to esophageal arterial supply. The right gastric arises from the common hepatic artery and supplies the pyloric part of the lesser curvature of the stomach. The inferior phrenic supplies the portion of the esophagus just superior to the diaphragm.
GAS 329, 330; GA 150

141 **B.** Kerh sign is a clinical indication of a ruptured spleen and is characterized by intense radiating pain to the top of the left shoulder. Mittelschmerz can occur in the middle of a woman's menstrual cycle when the graafian follicle ruptures and the ovum is released from the ovary. Rovsing sign is a clinical indicator of gallbladder inflammation and pain referred to the right shoulder, also owing to diaphragmatic irritation. The iliopsoas muscle has clinically important relations to the kidneys, ureters, cecum, appendix, sigmoid colon, pancreas, lumbar lymph nodes, and nerves to the posterior abdominal wall. If any of these structures is diseased, a positive psoas sign will be observed. The obturator sign may cause painful spasms of the adductor muscles of the thigh and sensory deficits in the medial thigh.
GAS 326; GA 191

142 **B.** The most common variation in hepatic artery supply to the right lobe of the liver is the right hepatic artery originating from the superior mesenteric artery, in approximately 18% of cases.
GAS 331; GA 147, 169

143 **B.** The gallbladder consists of a fundus, body, and neck. The fundus is the rounded, blind end that comes in contact with the transverse colon. The body is the major part and rests on the upper part of the duodenum and transverse colon. The neck is the narrowest part and gives rise to the cystic duct. This duct contains the spiral valve (of Heister), which is a redundant mucosal fold that maintains patency of the duct. This is not actually a valve and does not determine the direction of flow of bile. This could potentially be a point of constriction that could present difficulty with insertion of a catheter. The cystic duct comes into contact only with the cystic artery and is not particularly tortuous. The hepatoduodenal ligament is the thickened free edge of the lesser omentum, and it conducts the portal triad (portal vein, hepatic artery, and bile duct) and encloses structures that pass through the porta hepatis. This ligament is unlikely to compress the cystic duct. Though the cystic duct is in close relation to the portal vein and the hepatic artery, the most likely cause of difficulty would be potential constriction by the spiral valve.
GAS 322; GA 168

144 **B.** The ducts of Luschka are accessory biliary ducts that are not present in all individuals. During a cholecystectomy the cystic duct and cystic artery are ligated and the gallbladder is removed, using sharp dissection to separate the gallbladder from the liver. Routinely, the right hepatic duct and left hepatic duct are not encountered directly. If the surgeon was unaware that ducts of Luschka were present in the patient, they would not have been ligated or clipped and their leakage would result in bile peritonitis. The common bile duct and hepatic ducts are left intact during the surgery and should not leak. The cystic duct is ligated during the surgery and with proper ligation would not produce bile peritonitis.
GAS 317-319; GA 167

145 **C.** Visceral afferents are nerve fibers that transmit the sensation of visceral pain. The target of the neurectomy would be to eradicate visceral pain. One would not want to interfere with sympathetic and parasympathetic nerves, as these provide motor innervation to viscera.
GAS 374; GA 192

146 **B.** Adynamic ileus is essentially paralysis of the bowel. It can result from many causes, including kidney stone, spinal injury, peritonitis, etc. Typically, bowel obstruction is characterized initially by increased borborygmi (bowel sounds). Mechanical obstruction can be caused by blockage within the bowel or compression of the bowel from an external source. Increased borborygmi usually follow such obstructions immediately. As the bowel muscle tires, however, bowel sounds can become reduced or absent. Although this patient might have peritonitis, with an

abdomen tender to palpation, the data simply indicate generalized abdominal pain. Crampy pain has not been noted.
GAS 296; GA 154

147 A. Blood supply from the inferior pancreaticoduodenal artery via the superior mesenteric artery can provide collateral blood supply to the head of the pancreas and the first part of the duodenum in situations when the celiac trunk is occluded. Such anastomoses occur between the superior pancreaticoduodenal branches of the gastroduodenal artery (a derivative of the common hepatic branch of the celiac trunk) and the inferior pancreaticoduodenal. The left gastric artery and hepatic artery are derivatives of the celiac trunk and do not anastomose with the superior mesenteric. The cystic artery and the gastroduodenal artery are derivatives of the common hepatic from the celiac trunk. They would not typically provide an anastomosis between the celiac trunk and superior mesenteric artery (unless there is an aberrant right hepatic branch from the superior mesenteric artery). The right colic artery and left colic artery anastomose via the marginal artery of the colon, but this provides collateral supply of the inferior mesenteric artery. The right and left gastroomental arteries anastomose and provide collateral supply to the greater curvature of the stomach but are derived from the celiac trunk and thus do not provide communication between the celiac trunk and superior mesenteric artery.
GAS 331; GA 150

148 B. The incision and tissue separation at McBurney's point to reach the appendix will usually encounter the aponeurosis of the external abdominal oblique muscle, internal oblique muscle, transversus abdominis muscle, transversalis fascia, and peritoneum. Muscle fibers of the internal oblique and transversus can be separated bluntly, without cutting them. The appendix is located intraperitoneally within the abdomen, thus it is covered with visceral peritoneum. The transversalis fascia separates the internal surface of the transversus abdominis from the parietal peritoneum. Thus, five layers must be penetrated to access the inflamed appendix.
GAS 279; GA 131

149 D. Ileal (Meckel) diverticulum, which is an outpouching of the distal ileum, is twice as prevalent in males as in females. The diverticulum is clinically important because ulceration of the diverticulum with pain, bleeding, perforation, and obstruction is a complication that may require emergent surgery. Signs and symptoms frequently mimic appendicitis or peptic ulcer. Internal hemorrhoids are thrombosed tributaries of the middle rectal vein, which can prolapse into the anal canal. External hemorrhoids are thromboses in the veins of the external rectal venous plexus. Diverticulosis is ordinarily an outpouching of the wall of the large intestine. This primarily affects the aged and does not cause bleeding in most cases. Borborygmi are sounds created by gas and intestinal contents as they pass through the gastrointestinal tract.
GAS 306; GA 131

150 D. Fig. 3-2 is a CT scan that reveals an aortic aneurysm with hemorrhage. If the man stands in an erect position, the blood will be detected in the rectovesical space, which is a peritoneal recess between the bladder and the rectum in males. The subphrenic space is a peritoneal pouch between the diaphragm and the anterior and superior part of the liver. The hepatorenal space (pouch of Morison) is a deep peritoneal pocket between the posterior surface of the liver and the right kidney and suprarenal gland. The rectouterine space (pouch of Douglas) is a sac in females formed by a peritoneal-lined recess between the rectum and uterus. Although this is a logical answer choice, the rectouterine space is found only in women. The subhepatic space is between the liver and the transverse colon.
GAS 458; GA 208

151 B. Paraumbilical pain progressing into the right iliac fossa is a sign of appendicitis. The CT scan is one of an inflamed appendix. The structures in the scan that lie to the right of the vertebral body are part of the psoas muscle. Transverse section of this muscle signifies that it is a cut from the lumbar region.
GAS 388; GA 158

152 C. The arrows in the CT scan point to the descending colon. Therefore, the left colic artery, which supplies the descending colon, is the one most likely occluded in the CT scan. The middle colic, right colic, and ileocolic artery supply the ascending colon, and the marginal artery provides an anastomosis between branches of the superior mesenteric artery and inferior mesenteric artery.
GAS 336; GA 147, 160

153 B. The superficial inguinal lymph nodes are the first drainage site for superficial perineal structures like the skin of the perianal region, prepuce of penis, scrotum, and anal canal inferior to the pectinate line. The superficial inguinal nodes also drain structures of the inferolateral quadrant of the trunk,

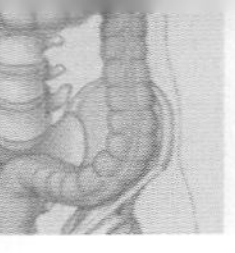

including the anterior abdominal wall inferior to the umbilicus, gluteal region, and the lower limb. The deep inguinal lymph nodes drain the glans of the penis and the distal spongy urethra and receive drainage from the superficial inguinal lymph nodes. The common iliac nodes drain the external and internal iliac lymph nodes. The internal iliac lymph nodes drain inferior pelvic structures and deep perineal structures and receive drainage from the sacral nodes. The para-aortic nodes are the final drainage site for all the above lymph nodes before they drain to the thoracic duct by way of the lumbar lymph trunks.
GAS 372-375; GA 345

154 **B.** The white arrows in the CT scan in Fig. 3-6 point to the stomach. The spleen would not be in this CT slice because it is located more superiorly in the body than this section. Also, note that the psoas muscles are seen lying on the sides of the vertebral body, meaning that the section is in the lumbar region of the body. The duodenum is the structure located to the right of the stomach in the scan and is posterolateral to the aorta.
GAS 294; GA 148

155 **A.** Cancerous cells in the stomach would metastasize first to the celiac nodes. The splenic nodes are located along the splenic artery and are related to drainage from the pancreas; therefore, they will not be the first to receive metastatic cells from a stomach cancer. The suprapancreatic nodes would be associated with pancreatic carcinoma. The right gastric lymph nodes may receive metastatic cells but would not be the first to receive this lymph because they are located along the lesser curvature of the stomach. The cisterna chyli, the proximal expanded portion of the thoracic duct, receives lymph drainage from the entire abdomen; therefore, it would not be first to receive cancerous cells.
GAS 341; GA 188, 254-255

156 **C.** Because physical and laboratory tests show a normal, healthy woman, the anomaly of the radiograph would be expected to be benign. Riedel's lobe is a normal variation of the liver, often an inferior extension of the right lobe of the liver, lateral to the gallbladder that extends about 4 or 5 cm below the rib cage. Carcinomas would present with abnormal laboratory examinations, and cholecystitis would present with an abnormal physical examination, as when the gallbladder is inflamed.
GAS 316-317; GA 142-143, 162

157 **B.** A Spigelian hernia occurs along the semilunar line below the umbilical region and can protrude through the skin. A Richter hernia is a hernia that presents as a strangulated segment of part of the wall of an intestinal loop through any hernial opening. A paraumbilical hernia occurs at the level of the umbilicus, near the midline. An incisional hernia occurs with dehiscence (breakdown and reopening) of an operative incision after surgery. A ventral hernia is a type of incisional hernia located on the ventral surface of the abdomen, occurring only after surgery.
GAS 276; GA 126

158 **A.** Congenital inguinal hernias occur when a large patency of the processus vaginalis remains so that a loop of intestine herniates into the inguinal canal. A congenital hydrocele is also caused by a patent segment of a processus vaginalis filled with fluid, but it does not cause an indirect hernia. Ectopic testes occur when the gubernaculum does not migrate correctly during development and the testis does not reach the scrotum, but this does not cause a hernia. Epispadias occurs when the external urethral orifice opens onto the dorsal surface of the penis and is generally associated with exstrophy of the bladder. A rupture, or tear, of the transversalis fascia would not cause the intestines to herniate through the deep inguinal ring and therefore would not cause an indirect inguinal hernia.
GAS 260; GA 255

159 **A.** Failure of relaxation of the lower esophageal sphincter (also known as the cardiac sphincter) causes an accumulation of food in the esophagus. Achalasia is the failure of motility of food through the esophagus into the stomach. A constricted lower esophageal sphincter is the cause of these conditions. Dyspepsia is chronic pain or discomfort in the upper abdomen. This usually accompanies problems with digestion and is not associated with difficulty swallowing. Gastritis is inflammation of the mucosal lining of the stomach and would also not contribute to dysphagia. Gastroparesis is defined as delayed stomach emptying due to stomach paralysis, which would reveal chyme overloading in the stomach and esophagus (achalasia involves only the esophagus). Peptic ulcers mostly result in pain in the stomach, more commonly the duodenum, due to erosion of the mucosal lining.
GAS 297-298; GA 148

160 **D.** Meckel diverticulum is an embryologic remnant of the vitelline duct in the embryo located on the distal ileum and proximal to the cecum. If this diverticulum becomes infected, it produces pain in the umbilical region of the abdomen, in addition to possible bleeding. A ruptured appendix usually presents

with pain in the lower right quadrant of the abdomen, when the infective processes come in contact with adjacent parietal peritoneum. A volvulus is characterized by a twisted bowel, which causes obstruction of the bolus and/or ischemia as the blood supply is occluded. Diverticulosis is a condition that causes outpouchings of the wall of the gut tube, usually found in the sigmoid colon. Pain from this condition would usually present in the lower left quadrant. Borborygmi are sounds produced from gas and other contents moving through the bowels. This would not cause pain in one specific area because peristaltic activity moves the length of the GI tract.
GAS 306; GA 131

161 C. Pain from the gallbladder is sent to the spinal cord by visceral afferents and also is mediated (referred) by nerve fibers that provide pain sensation to the scapula. Open cholecystectomy would cause a risk to the T7 and T8 spinal nerves due to their close proximity to the gallbladder. These nerves are located below the associated rib and along the same horizontal plane as the gallbladder. T5 and T6 nerves are located superior to an incision and thus are not affected. For the same reason, nerves from T6 to T8 would not be the right choice due to T6 not being at risk during this procedure. Nerves from T9 to L1 are located inferior to the incision during this procedure. T5 to T9 is a broad range answer that includes many nerves that would not be affected by the incision.
GAS 279; GA 135

162 A. The processus vaginalis is formed as the parietal peritoneum layer of the abdominal wall (inguinal region) evaginates through the deep inguinal ring and continues through the superficial inguinal ring. Normally, this evagination or outpouching is obliterated during development. A cyst can develop in a segment of the processus (which is also referred to as the canal of Nuck) if this processus is not obliterated. Congenital hydrocele would present at the base of the canal; in this case, the swelling would be in the labium majus. An ectopic uterus would present as a mass in the pelvis and not the inguinal region. A femoral hernia would be palpated below the inguinal ligament (usually) just medial to the femoral triangle. A defect of the transversalis fascia could result in inflammation in a specific area but would not be located along the inguinal ligament because this fascial layer is located deep to the inguinal ligament.
GAS 260; GA 255

163 C. The most likely place that a pancreatic pseudocyst will be formed is in the floor of the omental bursa, deep to the stomach. The omental bursa is a potential space behind the stomach and directly anterior to the pancreas. Pancreatic extravasations will fill this space. The right subhepatic space is the space in the peritoneal cavity between the inferior visceral surface of the liver and the transverse colon. The hepatorenal space of the subhepatic space, also known as the pouch of Morison, is located between the right lobe of the liver and the parietal peritoneum covering the superior pole of the right kidney and suprarenal gland. The right subphrenic space is the space directly inferior to the diaphragm and above the diaphragmatic surface of the liver. It is above the pancreas; therefore, fluid from the pancreas could not accumulate there. Finally, the greater sac is the general peritoneal cavity of the abdomen. The greater sac communicates with the omental bursa (lesser sac) by way of the omental (epiploic) foramen (of Winslow). The peritoneal cavity contains nothing except a very thin film of serous fluid that allows the organs to slip around relatively freely against one another and on the body wall.
GAS 295; GA 142

164 C. The spinal cord levels containing the soma of the sensory fibers transporting the sensation of pain are more than likely at the level of T7 and T8. This is because the xiphoid process is at these dermatome levels for somatic sensations of pain, and these same spinal nerves receive visceral afferents from the stomach.
GAS 341; GA 192

165 E. The ascending branches of the left colic artery are at risk during repair of a paraduodenal hernia because the location of this hernia is in the upper left quadrant, adjacent to the junction of the terminal duodenum and the jejunum. The ascending branches of the left colic artery supply the upper segment of the descending colon and the splenic flexure of the transverse colon. The middle colic artery arises from the superior mesenteric artery and supplies the ascending colon and the transverse colon and anastomoses with the left colic artery. The right colic artery is a more inferior branch of the superior mesenteric artery and supplies the proximal ascending colon. The ileocolic artery supplies the ileum and large intestine in the area of the ileocecal junction. Finally, the ileal arteries are the small terminal branches of the superior mesenteric artery supplying blood to the ileum.
GAS 336; GA 147, 160

166 D. The liver would be the first structure to receive these metastatic cells because they would flow

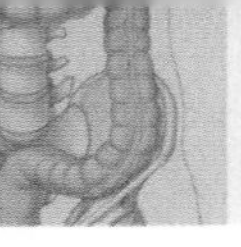

through the portal venous system from the pancreas to the liver. The stomach would not receive these cells because there is no communication between the stomach and pancreas through circulatory or ductal pathways. The spleen also does not have direct communication with the pancreas and would not receive metastases first. The duodenum is the site for pancreatic emptying, but as these metastases pass through venous circulation they would not pass into the duodenum. The vertebral column would not receive the metastases because they would not enter the vertebral venous plexus.
GAS 322; GA 163

167 **B.** The portal vein is the most likely structure to be occluded by a large tumor at the neck of the pancreas. The pancreas is drained via the splenic vein and empties into the portal vein. It directly enters the liver through the portal vein. The superior mesenteric vein drains the small intestines and the proximal part of the large intestine. The posterior superior pancreaticoduodenal artery would not be obstructed, nor would the greater pancreatic artery.
GAS 322; GA 167

168 **B.** The Hartmann's pouch is located in the gallbladder at the junction of the neck and the cystic duct. When a gallstone is located in this area, the patient will present with pain but usually no jaundice due to no occlusion of the cystic duct. A common bile duct and/or left and right hepatic duct obstruction would cause posthepatic jaundice due to bile obstructed in the duct system. Obstruction of the pancreatic duct would cause pain in the umbilical region, not in the right upper quadrant.
GAS 326; GA 167

169 **B.** The hepatopancreatic ampulla is also known as the ampulla of Vater and is located at the junction of the pancreatic duct and common bile duct. It is the narrowest part of the ductal system. The common bile duct, left hepatic duct, pancreatic duct, and right hepatic duct all have larger diameters than the ampulla of Vater.
GAS 322; GA 167

170 **E.** The innermost covering of the spermatic cord is the internal spermatic fascia. It originates from the transversalis fascia. The internal oblique muscle provides origin for the cremaster layer of the cord. The external spermatic fascia is continuous from the external oblique aponeurosis and its fascia. The transversus abdominis aponeurosis plays no part in the formation of the spermatic cord.
GAS 286-288; GA 139

171 **C.** An epigastric hernia is formed by a weakness in the intersecting fibers of the linea alba superior to the umbilicus. In most cases, herniation of fat and other tissue through the defect causes a palpable, but painless, mass. If a nerve branch also passes through the defect, it can be associated with local pain. Umbilical hernias are common in newborn babies and pregnant females in the third trimester of pregnancy. This kind of hernia usually represents a weakness in the wall structure at the level of the umbilicus. Omphaloceles are a more serious (but less common) defect, representing failure of intestines to return to the abdominal cavity, associated with lack of proper growth of the body wall. Spigelian hernias occur through the semilunar lines, lateral to the rectus sheath. Femoral hernias pass through the femoral canal, deep to the inguinal ligament.
GAS 389; GA 125

172 **D.** The knife injured the medial segment of the left lobe of the liver, located between the falciform ligament and the gallbladder. This area of the liver is usually supplied by the left hepatic artery. If this were the case, the Pringle maneuver (compression of the hepatoduodenal ligament) would slow or stop the bleeding. An aberrant, left hepatic branch of the left gastric artery does not pass through the hepatoduodenal ligament, however, and is therefore not compressed in a Pringle maneuver; thus, the bleeding is not reduced by that technique. The lateral segment of the left lobe is located to the left of the falciform ligament. The caudate segment of the liver is located in the inferior aspect of the upper portion of the liver, well above the site of injury. The anterior segment of the right lobe is located to the right of the gallbladder. The right lobe receives its arterial supply from the right hepatic artery.
GAS 331; GA 164

173 **E.** Interruption of both vagus nerves would deprive the abdominal viscera of parasympathetic supply, that is, to the level of the splenic flexure of the colon. Distal to the splenic flexure, the colon receives parasympathetic nerve from S2-S4 fibers and not from vagus nerve. Pelvic splanchnic nerves supply the descending colon, the urinary bladder, and the erectile tissues of the penis. The innervation of the ductus deferens and ejaculatory duct is carried by sympathetic nerve supply through the pelvic plexuses. Parasympathetic supply to the ascending colon is carried by the vagus nerves and would be lost.
GAS 345; GA 191

174 **B.** Adynamic ileus is paralysis of the bowel. Peristaltic activity ceases. Borborygmi (bowel sounds) are absent when this occurs, as in peritonitis. Radio-

graphs would indicate the presence of air under the diaphragm. Pain in the shoulder is due to air under the diaphragm from the perforated anterior duodenal wall; this air irritates afferent pain fibers of the diaphragm, carried by the right phrenic nerve to spinal nerve levels C3 to C5. Referral of pain to the shoulder occurs because somatic sensory fibers from the shoulder enter the spinal cord at similar levels. A posterior penetrating ulcer would be associated usually with profuse bleeding, mostly from branches of the gastroduodenal artery that supply the duodenal bulb, the first part of the duodenum. Acute appendicitis is not associated with shoulder pain and adynamic ileus. A perforated appendix, however, will produce symptoms of peritonitis.
GAS 389; GA 193

175 **A.** The middle colic artery is the principal source of arterial supply to the transverse colon. The right colic artery, an infrequent branch of the superior mesenteric artery, supplies the ascending colon. The ileocolic branch of the superior mesenteric artery supplies distal ileum, cecum, and ascending colon. The left colic artery provides blood supply to the descending colon.
GAS 333, 335; GA 147, 154, 160

176 **C.** The dermatome of spinal nerve level T10 crosses the level of the umbilicus; that of T7 is at the level of the xiphoid process. T8 and T9 dermatomes lie between the two preceding spinal nerve levels. T12 innervates the lowest portion of the rectus abdominis and overlying skin with motor and sensory supply, respectively. L1 distribution by iliohypogastric and ilioinguinal nerves supplies the suprapubic region, the pubic area, and anterior portions of the urogenital region. Pain from appendicitis is most often perceived at first in the periumbilical region, reflecting the level of embryologic spinal nerve supply to the appendix. When the appendix swells and/or ruptures and contacts the body wall, somatic sensory fibers of the adjacent body wall cause the apparent site of pain to shift to the lower right abdominal quadrant.
GAS 280; GA 187

177 **D.** Caput medusae is an end-stage characteristic of liver cirrhosis. The snakelike appearance of veins on the body wall results from anastomoses between tiny veins that accompany the ligamentum teres (that is within the falciform ligament) with veins of the body wall. The umbilical veins are expanded, due to portal hypertension. Esophageal varices result from portal-systemic anastomoses between the left gastric vein and submucosal esophageal veins. Ascites is formed by fluid transudate from thin-walled and dilated anastomotic vessels joining retroperitoneal intestinal veins and veins of the body wall. Internal hemorrhoids result from expansion of anastomoses between superior rectal tributaries to the inferior mesenteric vein and middle rectal branches of the internal iliac vein. Anastomoses between middle rectal veins and inferior rectal branches of the internal pudendal vein of the perineum result in external hemorrhoids.
GAS 316-318; GA 162

178 **A.** The iliopubic tract is a reflective band of aponeurotic tissue of the origin of the transversus abdominis, when visualized with the laparoscope. The lateral border of the inguinal triangle (of Hesselbach) is provided by the inferior epigastric artery and vein. The lateral border of the femoral ring is the femoral vein and connective tissue separating the vein from the femoral canal. The part of the inguinal ligament that attaches to the pectineal ligament is the lacunar ligament (of Gimbernat). The pectineal ligament becomes less dense and thinner as it is traced laterally from the femoral artery toward the iliopectineal portion of the inguinal ligament.
GAS 290-291; GA 290

179 **E.** Taeniae coli are a characteristic feature of the colon. Those of the cecum can be traced inferiorly to the base of the appendix, even when the appendix is retrocolic or retroileal in position, hidden thereby. The posterior cecal artery, although it provides origin to the appendicular artery, is very difficult to find quickly, especially in the presence of malrotation and much adipose tissue. The other structures listed do not lead easily to the location of the appendix.
GAS 308; GA 154, 156

PELVIS AND PERINEUM

1 A 4-month-old male infant is admitted to the pediatric clinic because he was passing urine near the anus rather than from the tip of the penis. Physical examination reveals that the patient has perineal hypospadias. Which of the following embryologic structures failed to fuse?

- ▢ **A.** Labioscrotal folds
- ▢ **B.** Cloacal membrane
- ▢ **C.** Urogenital folds
- ▢ **D.** Genital tubercle
- ▢ **E.** Urogenital membrane

2 A 2-day-old female infant is diagnosed with tracheoesophageal fistula. In addition, physical examination reveals an imperforate anus. An MRI examination reveals that the rectum, vagina, and colon are joined into a single channel. Which of the following structures is directly involved in this malformation?

- ▢ **A.** Labioscrotal folds
- ▢ **B.** Persistent cloaca
- ▢ **C.** Urogenital folds
- ▢ **D.** Genital tubercle
- ▢ **E.** Urogenital membrane

3 A 6-year-old boy is admitted to the hospital because of a palpable mass located external to the aponeurosis of the external oblique. Radiographic examination reveals that the mass is an ectopic testis, classified as interstitial. Failure of normal development of which of the following embryologic structures is responsible for ectopic testis?

- ▢ **A.** Gubernaculum
- ▢ **B.** Processus vaginalis
- ▢ **C.** Genital tubercle
- ▢ **D.** Seminiferous cords
- ▢ **E.** Labioscrotal swellings

4 A 2-month-old infant has epispadias and the bladder mucosa is exposed to the outside. Which of the following is the most likely cause of this condition?

- ▢ **A.** Failure of the primitive streak mesoderm to migrate around the cloacal membrane
- ▢ **B.** Failure of urethral folds to fuse
- ▢ **C.** Insufficient androgen stimulation
- ▢ **D.** Klinefelter syndrome
- ▢ **E.** Persistent allantois

5 A bifid ureter or paired unilateral ureters result from partial or complete division of which of the following embryologic structures?

- ▢ **A.** Ureteric bud/metanephric diverticulum
- ▢ **B.** Mesonephric duct
- ▢ **C.** Paramesonephric duct
- ▢ **D.** Metanephric mesoderm
- ▢ **E.** Pronephros

6 A 16-year-old woman is visiting her gynecologist for her first checkup. On ultrasound examination it is noted that the woman has a double uterus. Failure of which of the following processes is responsible for the double uterus?

- ☐ **A.** Fusion of the inferior parts of the paramesonephric ducts
- ☐ **B.** Fusion of the superior parts of the mesonephric ducts
- ☐ **C.** Development of the hymen
- ☐ **D.** Development of the sinovaginal bulbs
- ☐ **E.** Fusion of the inferior parts of the mesonephric ducts

7 A 6-year-old boy has a large intraabdominal mass in the midline just above the pubic symphysis. During surgery a cystic mass is found attached to the umbilicus and to the apex of the bladder. Which of the following is the most likely diagnosis?

- ☐ **A.** Hydrocele
- ☐ **B.** Meckel cyst
- ☐ **C.** Meckel diverticulum
- ☐ **D.** Omphalocele
- ☐ **E.** Urachal cyst

8 A 26-year-old pregnant woman visits her gynecologist for a routine checkup. Ultrasound examination reveals that the patient has a normal pregnancy but that she also has two uteri. What is the most likely embryologic explanation of this condition?

- ☐ **A.** A complete fusion of the paramesonephric ducts
- ☐ **B.** An incomplete fusion of the paramesonephric ducts
- ☐ **C.** Hydronephros
- ☐ **D.** Cryptorchidism
- ☐ **E.** Regression of the pronephros

9 A 35-year-old woman is admitted to the emergency department with severe left abdominal and back pain. Radiographic evaluation reveals that the left ureter is blocked with a kidney stone. Because the ureter is completely obstructed, an emergency surgical procedure must be performed. Which of the following landmarks is most reliable for the identification of the ureter?

- ☐ **A.** The left ureter is located anterior to the left common iliac artery.
- ☐ **B.** The left ureter is located medial to the left inferior epigastric artery.
- ☐ **C.** The left ureter is located anterior to the left gonadal artery.
- ☐ **D.** The left ureter is located anterior to the left renal vein.
- ☐ **E.** The left ureter is located anterior to the left inferior epigastric artery.

10 A 1-year-old infant is admitted to the pediatric clinic because he is passing urine on the underside of the penis as shown in Fig. 4-1. Which embryologic structure failed to fuse?

- ☐ **A.** Spongy urethra
- ☐ **B.** Labioscrotal folds
- ☐ **C.** Urethral folds
- ☐ **D.** Urogenital folds
- ☐ **E.** Genital tubercle

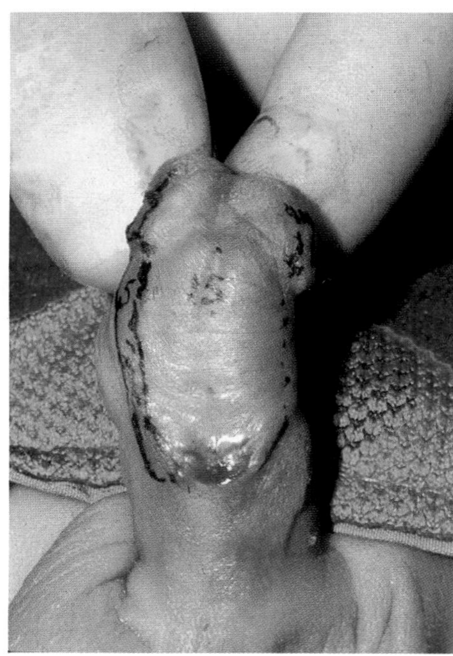

Fig. 4-1

11 A 4-month-old infant is admitted to the pediatric clinic because urine can be observed passing through an opening on the dorsum of the penis. Which of the following embryologic structures failed to fuse?

- ☐ **A.** Spongy urethra
- ☐ **B.** Labioscrotal folds
- ☐ **C.** Cloacal membrane
- ☐ **D.** Urogenital folds
- ☐ **E.** Genital tubercle

12 A 25-year-old male is admitted to the hospital with testicular pain. Physical examination reveals a swollen and inflamed right testis. CT scan examination reveals abnormal accumulation of fluid in the cavity of the tunica vaginalis (Fig. 4-2). Which of the following conditions will most accurately describe the signs observed in the patient?

- ▢ **A.** Varicocele
- ▢ **B.** Rectocele
- ▢ **C.** Cystocele
- ▢ **D.** Hydrocele
- ▢ **E.** Hypospadias

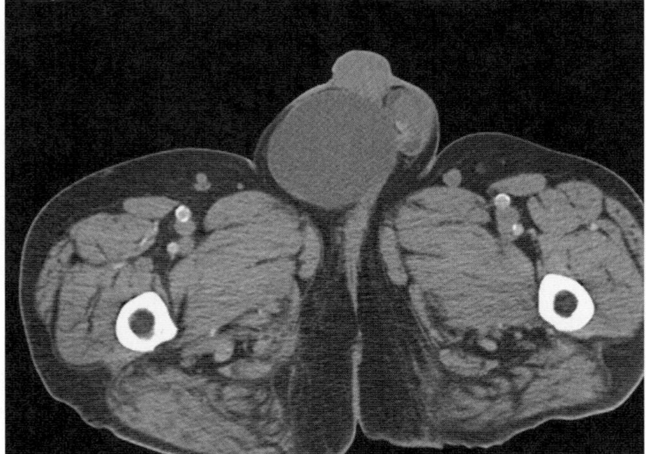

Fig. 4-2

13 A 54-year-old male is admitted to the hospital with severe back pain. Radiographic examination reveals carcinoma of the left kidney blocking the drainage of the testicular vein. Which of the following conditions will be most likely associated with these signs?

- ▢ **A.** Varicocele
- ▢ **B.** Rectocele
- ▢ **C.** Cystocele
- ▢ **D.** Hydrocele
- ▢ **E.** Hypospadias

14 A 54-year-old male is admitted to the hospital with severe back pain. Upon radiographic examination (Fig. 4-3) the scrotum resembles a "bag of worms." Which of the following conditions will be most likely associated with this radiographic picture?

- ▢ **A.** Varicocele
- ▢ **B.** Rectocele
- ▢ **C.** Cystocele
- ▢ **D.** Hydrocele
- ▢ **E.** Hypospadias

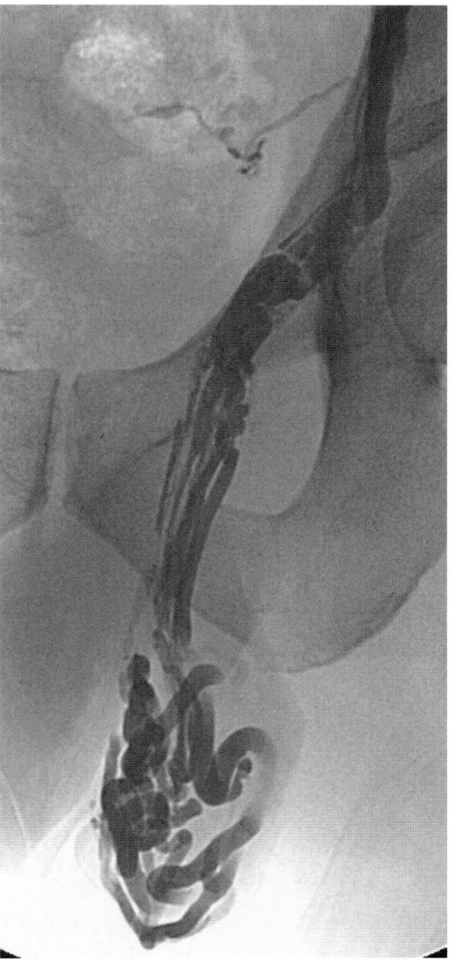

Fig. 4-3

15 A 16-year-old female is brought to the emergency department with severe abdominal pain and fever. Laboratory examination is remarkable for an elevated white blood cell count and a positive test for pregnancy. Colpocentesis is performed to ascertain the presence of blood in the pelvis from the ruptured ectopic pregnancy. Through which of the following structures does the needle need to be inserted?

- ▢ **A.** Through the perineal body into the vesicouterine space
- ▢ **B.** Through the posterior fornix into the rectouterine pouch
- ▢ **C.** Through the anterior fornix into the endocervical canal
- ▢ **D.** Through the introitus into the vestibular gland
- ▢ **E.** Though the perineal membrane into the urogenital diaphragm

16 A 46-year-old woman is admitted to the hospital with a noticeable bulge of tissue through her vaginal opening. During physical examination a rectocele is identified. Which of the following is most likely responsible for this condition?

- ☐ **A.** Compromised rectovaginal septum
- ☐ **B.** Weakened superficial and deep transverse perineal muscles
- ☐ **C.** Paralyzed ischiocavernosus muscle
- ☐ **D.** Loose sacrospinous ligament
- ☐ **E.** Ruptured sphincter urethra

17 A 68-year-old male is admitted to the hospital with painful urination and nocturia (urination during the night). MRI examination reveals enlargement and irregularity of the uvula of the urethra. This enlargement resulted in difficulty with urinary voiding and inadequate emptying of the bladder. Which of the following lobes of the prostate gland will most likely be hypertrophied?

- ☐ **A.** Anterior
- ☐ **B.** Median
- ☐ **C.** Lateral
- ☐ **D.** Posterior
- ☐ **E.** Lateral and Posterior

18 Radiographic studies of a 42-year-old woman reveal that she has a vulvar malignancy involving the clitoris. Removal of all affected lymph nodes would be indicated to avoid spread of this cancer. Which are the first lymph nodes to filter the lymphatic drainage of the involved area?

- ☐ **A.** Superficial and deep inguinal lymph nodes
- ☐ **B.** Internal iliac nodes
- ☐ **C.** Paraaortic lymph nodes
- ☐ **D.** Presacral lymph nodes
- ☐ **E.** Axillary lymph nodes

19 While performing a voiding cystourethrogram on a 45-year-old male, the urologist was too forceful when he inserted the catheter and accidentally damaged the wall of the membranous portion of the urethra in the deep perineal compartment (urogenital diaphragm). Which of the following structures would most likely be traumatized at this location?

- ☐ **A.** Bulbospongiosus muscle
- ☐ **B.** Sphincter urethra (compressor urethra)
- ☐ **C.** Corpus cavernosus penis (crus)
- ☐ **D.** Ischiocavernosus muscle
- ☐ **E.** Opening of the bulbourethral duct

20 A 22-year-old male complained to the urologist of pain that he experiences from bladder fullness after drinking large quantities of fluid. What is the location of the neural cell bodies responsible for pain sensation from the urinary bladder?

- ☐ **A.** Dorsal root ganglia of spinal cord levels S2, S3, and S4
- ☐ **B.** The intermediolateral cell column of spinal cord levels S2, S3, and S4
- ☐ **C.** The sensory ganglia of spinal nerves T5 to T9
- ☐ **D.** The preaortic ganglia at the site of origin of the testicular arteries
- ☐ **E.** Dorsal root ganglia of spinal levels T10 to L2

21 A 55-year-old woman complains of fecal incontinence. The most likely contributing factor to such a problem is atrophy, paralysis, or dysfunction of which of the following structures?

- ☐ **A.** Pubococcygeus muscle
- ☐ **B.** Iliococcygeus muscle
- ☐ **C.** Coccygeus muscle
- ☐ **D.** Pubovesicocervical fascia
- ☐ **E.** Urogenital diaphragm

22 A 45-year-old obese woman was admitted to the hospital because of "pains in her leg." Physical examination led to a diagnosis of "meralgia paresthetica." In her condition, excessive adipose tissue bulging over the inguinal ligament exerted traction upon it, compressing a nerve that passed through, or beneath, the ligament, just medial to the anterior superior iliac spine. Which of the following nerves was most likely affected in this patient?

- ☐ **A.** Femoral branch of the genitofemoral nerve
- ☐ **B.** Femoral nerve
- ☐ **C.** Iliohypogastric nerve
- ☐ **D.** Ilioinguinal nerve
- ☐ **E.** Lateral femoral cutaneous nerve

23 On digital examination of the vagina, the portion of the uterus that one anticipates palpating with the examining finger is the cervix and its external os. Which of the following is the most common position of the uterus?

- ☐ **A.** Anteflexed and retroverted
- ☐ **B.** Retroflexed and anteverted
- ☐ **C.** Anteflexed and anteverted
- ☐ **D.** Retroflexed and retroverted

24 A 42-year-old woman is admitted to the emergency department because of pelvic discomfort. During physical examination the gynecologist discovers that the patient has suffered complete uterine prolapse. Which of the following ligaments provides direct support to the uterus?

- ☐ **A.** Mesosalpinx and mesometrium
- ☐ **B.** Infundibulopelvic ligament
- ☐ **C.** Round ligament of the uterus
- ☐ **D.** Lateral cervical (cardinal) ligament
- ☐ **E.** Broad ligament of the uterus

25 A 34-year-old woman is admitted to the hospital due to severe lower abdominal pain. Radiographic examination reveals tumors in both of her ovaries. A biopsy is ordered and confirms the initial diagnosis of ovarian cancer. Which of the following lymph nodes are the first to receive lymph from the diseased ovaries?

- ☐ **A.** Superficial and deep inguinal lymph nodes
- ☐ **B.** External iliac nodes
- ☐ **C.** Paraartotic nodes at the level of the renal vessels
- ☐ **D.** Node of Cloquet
- ☐ **E.** Internal iliac nodes accompanying the uterine artery and vein

26 A 29-year-old pregnant woman is admitted to the hospital for her delivery. During a vaginal delivery the obstetrician performs a median episiotomy in which the area of the perineal body is cut deeply. Two weeks after the delivery the woman complains that she has had fecal incontinence since the delivery. Which of the following structures was also most likely damaged during the episiotomy?

- ☐ **A.** Superficial and deep transverse perineal muscles
- ☐ **B.** External anal sphincter
- ☐ **C.** Ischiocavernosus muscle
- ☐ **D.** Sacrospinous ligament
- ☐ **E.** Sphincter urethra

27 After having given birth to five children, a 41-year-old woman seeks correction of chronic urinary incontinence. While relating her history the patient reveals that she has leakage of urine with increased intraabdominal pressure. An MRI examination reveals injury to the pelvic floor that has altered the position of the neck of the bladder and the urethra. Which of the following structures has most probably been injured during the multiple deliveries?

- ☐ **A.** Tendinous arch of levator ani
- ☐ **B.** Coccygeus
- ☐ **C.** Tendinous arch of fascia pelvis
- ☐ **D.** Obturator internus
- ☐ **E.** Rectovaginal septum

28 A 58-year-old postmenopausal woman is diagnosed with carcinoma of the distal gastrointestinal tract. During surgery lymph nodes from the sacral, internal iliac, and inguinal lymph node groups were removed and sent for histopathologic examination. The pathology report revealed positive cancerous cells only at the inguinal lymph nodes. Which of the following parts of the gastrointestinal tract were most likely affected?

- ☐ **A.** Cutaneous portion of anal canal
- ☐ **B.** Distal rectum
- ☐ **C.** Mucosal zone of anal canal
- ☐ **D.** Pectinate line of anal canal
- ☐ **E.** Proximal rectum at the inferior valve (of Houston)

29 A 62-year-old man is admitted to the emergency department due to increasing difficulty in urinating over a period of several months. Physical examination reveals prostatic hypertrophy. After several unsuccessful attempts to catheterize the penile urethra, the urologist orders drainage of the urinary bladder by the least invasive procedure, avoiding entry into the peritoneal cavity or the injury of any major vessels or organs. Which of the following spaces needs to be traversed by the needle to reach the bladder?

- ☐ **A.** Ischioanal fossa
- ☐ **B.** Perineal body
- ☐ **C.** Retropubic space (of Retzius)
- ☐ **D.** Superficial perineal cleft
- ☐ **E.** Deep perineal pouch

30 A 13-year-old female is brought to the emergency department with a complaint of severe, deep pelvic discomfort. Physical examination reveals that the patient has an intact hymen. Incision of the hymen reveals hematocolpos. Which of the following conditions is associated with hematocolpos?

- ☐ **A.** Cyst of Bartholin gland
- ☐ **B.** Bleeding from an ectopic pregnancy
- ☐ **C.** Imperforate hymen
- ☐ **D.** Indirect inguinal hernia with cremasteric arterial bleeding
- ☐ **E.** Iatrogenic bleeding from the uterine veins

31 A 42-year-old woman is admitted to the emergency department with a complaint of dull, poorly localized pain in the deep pelvis. An MRI examination reveals a prolapsing of abdominal viscera, probably due to a tear of the rectovaginal septum. Which of the following conditions will most likely result from a defect in the rectovaginal septum?

- ☐ **A.** Cystocele
- ☐ **B.** Urethrocele
- ☐ **C.** Enterocele
- ☐ **D.** Urinary incontinence
- ☐ **E.** Prolapsed uterus

32 A 34-year-old woman is admitted to the hospital complaining of urinary incontinence. MRI examination reveals that one of the skeletal muscles of the pelvis has a significant tear. Which of the following muscles is the most significant in terms of maintaining continence?

- ☐ **A.** Pubococcygeus
- ☐ **B.** Obturator internus
- ☐ **C.** Piriformis
- ☐ **D.** Coccygeus
- ☐ **E.** Iliococcygeus

33 A 42-year-old woman is admitted to the emergency department with severe abdominal pain. MRI examination reveals a tumor at her left ovary. A frozen biopsy during the time of surgery reveals an ovarian carcinoma. Which of the following actions can be performed to reduce the pain from the ovarian carcinoma?

- ☐ **A.** Cut the infundibulopelvic ligament.
- ☐ **B.** Cut the pelvic sympathetic chain.
- ☐ **C.** Cut the cluneal nerves.
- ☐ **D.** Cut the pudendal nerve.
- ☐ **E.** Cut the broad ligament.

34 A 45-year-old man is admitted to the emergency department after a violent car crash. Physical examination reveals that the patient suffers from a “straddle” injury to the perineum. An MRI examination reveals that extravasating urine and blood from a torn bulbar urethra are present in the superficial perineal cleft. Which of the following fasciae provide boundaries for this space?

- ☐ **A.** Camper’s fascia and Scarpa’s fascia
- ☐ **B.** Perineal membrane and external perineal fascia of Gallaudet
- ☐ **C.** Colles’ fascia and external perineal fascia of Gallaudet
- ☐ **D.** Perineal membrane and the superior fascia of the urogenital diaphragm
- ☐ **E.** The urogenital diaphragm and the apex of the prostate gland

35 Several days after a 34-year-old woman was admitted to the hospital after her automobile collided with a lamppost, her urinary bladder gives evidence of paralysis. A CT scan reveals multiple fractures of her pelvis with a significant pelvic hematoma, either of which could have interrupted or injured the nerve supply of the organ. Which of the following nerves was most likely traumatized?

- ☐ **A.** Superior hypogastric
- ☐ **B.** Pelvic splanchnic
- ☐ **C.** Sacral splanchnic
- ☐ **D.** Lumbar splanchnic
- ☐ **E.** Pudendal

36 A 34-year-old woman is hospitalized because of an enlarged, painful abdomen. An ultrasound examination is performed and the presence of ascites (fluid) in the peritoneal cavity is confirmed. A needle is placed through the posterior vaginal fornix to drain the fluid. Which space must the needle enter to drain the fluid?

- ☐ **A.** Rectouterine pouch
- ☐ **B.** Pararectal fossa
- ☐ **C.** Paravesical space
- ☐ **D.** Uterovesical pouch
- ☐ **E.** Superficial perineal pouch

37 A 36-year-old male rodeo rider is admitted to the hospital after being thrown violently from a Brahma bull. An MRI scan reveals rupture of the penile urethra and deep (Bucks) fascia. Where is the most likely place that extravasated urine will flow?

- ☐ **A.** Ischioanal fossa
- ☐ **B.** Rectovesical pouch
- ☐ **C.** Deep perineal pouch
- ☐ **D.** Retropubic space
- ☐ **E.** Superficial perineal cleft

38 A 68-year-old man complains of pain upon urination. A CT scan and a biopsy provide evidence of an enlarged, cancerous prostate gland. Subsequently, he undergoes a radical prostatectomy. Postoperatively, he suffers from urinary incontinence because of paralysis of the external urethral sphincter. Which of the following nerves was injured during the operation?

- ☐ **A.** Pelvic splanchnic
- ☐ **B.** Sacral splanchnic
- ☐ **C.** Pudendal
- ☐ **D.** Superior gluteal
- ☐ **E.** Inferior gluteal

39 A 65-year-old male with a history of heavy smoking and hypercholesterolemia is diagnosed with severe atherosclerosis, affecting most of the arteries of his body. During the taking of the patient's history he complains also of impotence. Occlusion of which of the following arteries would most likely be the cause of this condition?

- ☐ **A.** External iliac
- ☐ **B.** Inferior epigastric
- ☐ **C.** Umbilical
- ☐ **D.** Internal pudendal
- ☐ **E.** Superficial and deep circumflex

40 A 58-year-old postmenopausal woman complains of pelvic discomfort and dull pain. Lymph nodes from the sacral, internal iliac, and inguinal lymph node groups are surgically removed for histopathologic examination. The pathology report reveals positive cancerous cells only in the inguinal lymph nodes. Which pelvic organ would most likely be involved in the cancer?

- ☐ **A.** The body of the uterus
- ☐ **B.** Distal rectum
- ☐ **C.** One or both of her ovaries
- ☐ **D.** Proximal rectum
- ☐ **E.** Anal canal superior to the pectinate line

41 A 34-year-old woman is admitted to the hospital due to severe lower abdominal pain. Radiographic examination reveals an ovarian tumor. Which of the following lymph nodes will most likely become invaded by cancerous cells?

- ☐ **A.** Superficial inguinal
- ☐ **B.** External iliac
- ☐ **C.** Lumbar/lateral aortic
- ☐ **D.** Deep inguinal
- ☐ **E.** Internal iliac

42 A 42-year-old female patient has a malignancy involving the vestibule of her vagina. Which are the first lymph nodes to filter the lymph drainage from this area and therefore the most likely to become involved in tumor spread?

- ☐ **A.** Superficial inguinal
- ☐ **B.** Internal iliac
- ☐ **C.** Lumbar/lateral aortic
- ☐ **D.** Presacral lymph
- ☐ **E.** Axillary lymph

43 A 34-year-old pregnant woman is prepared in the hospital for delivery. The gynecologist decides to perform a pudendal nerve block using a transvaginal approach. Which bony structure would be the most reliable as a landmark to block the pudendal nerve?

- ☐ **A.** Ischial spine
- ☐ **B.** Posterior inferior iliac spine
- ☐ **C.** Ischial tuberosity
- ☐ **D.** Posterior superior iliac spine
- ☐ **E.** Coccyx

44 A 55-year-old man complains of pain at his anus. Examination reveals external hemorrhoids. Which of the following nerves carries pain sensation from the anus?

- ☐ **A.** Sacral splanchnic
- ☐ **B.** Superior hypogastric
- ☐ **C.** Pelvic splanchnic
- ☐ **D.** Pudendal
- ☐ **E.** Ilioinguinal

45 A 42-year-old woman visits the outpatient clinic due to painful urination. A dipstick test reveals leukocytosis, which confirms the diagnosis of urinary tract infection. Which of the following is the best anatomic explanation for the fact that women are more susceptible to urinary tract infections than men?

- ☐ **A.** The vagina contains less bacterial flora than the penis.
- ☐ **B.** The prostate gland produces antibacterial prostatic fluids.
- ☐ **C.** The urethra is much shorter in females.
- ☐ **D.** The urethra is located within the vagina.
- ☐ **E.** The seminal vesicles produce fluids resistant to bacteria.

46 A 52-year-old woman visits the outpatient clinic due to a mass of tissue prolapsing through the vaginal introitus. Physical examination reveals that the patient has a cystocele. Loss of which of the following structures to the anterior part of the vagina is responsible for this problem?

- ☐ **A.** Pubovesical and vesicocervical fasciae
- ☐ **B.** Cardinal ligament
- ☐ **C.** Uterosacral ligament
- ☐ **D.** Levator ani muscle
- ☐ **E.** Median umbilical ligament

47 A 47-year-old woman with a family history of breast cancer mutations in the *BRCA1* and *BRCA2* genes has made a decision to have an elective hysterectomy as a prophylactic treatment. During ligation of the uterine artery which of the following adjacent structures must the surgeon be careful not to injure?

- ▢ **A.** Ureter
- ▢ **B.** Internal iliac artery
- ▢ **C.** Internal iliac lymph nodes
- ▢ **D.** Obturator nerve
- ▢ **E.** Lumbosacral trunk

48 A 32-year-old woman is admitted to the hospital with a complaint of painful spasms of her vagina. Physical examination reveals several involuntary contractions of the vaginal musculature. The patient also complains of painful intercourse. Which of the following conditions will most likely describe the signs of this patient?

- ▢ **A.** Vaginismus
- ▢ **B.** Pudendal nerve compression in the pudendal (Alcock) canal
- ▢ **C.** Disruption of the perineal body
- ▢ **D.** Endometriosis
- ▢ **E.** Fibroma of the uterus

49 A 46-year-old male is admitted to the emergency department after a car crash. An MRI examination reveals a hematoma of the perineum spreading to his abdominal wall beneath the superficial fascia. Where should the initial extravasation be located?

- ▢ **A.** Between the superior aspect of the urogenital diaphragm and the pelvic diaphragm
- ▢ **B.** Between the perineal membrane and the fascia of Gallaudet
- ▢ **C.** Between Camper's fascia and Scarpa's fascia
- ▢ **D.** Between Colles' fascia and Gallaudet's fascia
- ▢ **E.** Between Buck's fascia and the tunica albuginea

50 A 45-year-old woman is admitted to the hospital with lower abdominal and pelvic discomfort. Combined laparoscopic and MRI examinations reveal tears of the ligaments supporting the uterus with moderate uterine prolapse. Which of the following ligaments provides direct support to the uterus and thereby resists prolapse?

- ▢ **A.** Uterosacral
- ▢ **B.** Round ligament of the uterus
- ▢ **C.** Broad ligament
- ▢ **D.** Arcus tendineus fascia pelvis
- ▢ **E.** Levator ani muscle

51 A 68-year-old male is admitted to the hospital with dysuria, nocturia, urgency, and painful urination. MRI examination reveals enlargement and irregularity of the uvula of the urethra due to prostatic hypertrophy. Laboratory investigation reveals high levels of PSA (prostate-specific antigen) suggesting prostatic carcinoma, and a prostatectomy is performed. Which of the following lymph nodes should be removed during prostatectomy?

- ▢ **A.** Internal iliac and sacral
- ▢ **B.** External iliac
- ▢ **C.** Superficial inguinal
- ▢ **D.** Deep inguinal
- ▢ **E.** Gluteal

52 A 22-year-old male is admitted to the hospital with groin pain and blood in the semen. An MRI examination and biopsy reveal testicular cancer. Which of the following lymph nodes will be first involved in case of metastasis?

- ▢ **A.** Internal iliac
- ▢ **B.** External iliac
- ▢ **C.** Superficial inguinal
- ▢ **D.** Deep inguinal
- ▢ **E.** Paraaortic and lumbar

53 A 68-year-old male underwent a radical prostatectomy. Six months postoperatively the patient complains of being incapable of penile erection without the use of sildenafil (Viagra). Which of the following nerves was most probably damaged during the operation?

- ▢ **A.** Pudendal
- ▢ **B.** Perineal
- ▢ **C.** Pelvic splanchnic
- ▢ **D.** Sacral splanchnic
- ▢ **E.** Dorsal nerve to the penis

54 A 15-year-old is admitted to the emergency department 2 days after crashing his bicycle. MRI examination reveals severe edema of the boy's scrotum and abdominal wall and extravasated urine. Which of the following structures is most likely ruptured?

- ▢ **A.** Spongy urethra
- ▢ **B.** Preprostatic urethra
- ▢ **C.** Prostatic urethra
- ▢ **D.** Urinary bladder
- ▢ **E.** Ureter

55 A 35-year-old man is admitted to the surgery ward for correction of an inguinal hernia. During physical examination an indirect hernia is noted, together with an absent cremasteric reflex. Which of the following nerves carries the efferent component of the cremasteric reflex?

- ▢ **A.** Ilioinguinal nerve
- ▢ **B.** Genital branch of genitofemoral

- ▢ **C.** Iliohypogastric nerve
- ▢ **D.** Pudendal nerve
- ▢ **E.** Obturator nerve

56 A 19-year-old woman is admitted to the hospital with low blood pressure and intense pelvic pain. Physical examination reveals heavy blood loss during this menstrual period. Speculum examination reveals irritation of the cervix of the uterus. Which of the following nerves conveys sensory fibers from the cervix of the uterus?

- ▢ **A.** Pudendal
- ▢ **B.** Superior hypogastric
- ▢ **C.** Pelvic splanchnic
- ▢ **D.** Sacral splanchnic
- ▢ **E.** Lesser splanchnic

57 A 38-year-old woman visits her gynecologist for a routine Pap smear examination. During the collection of cells from her uterine cervix she feels a mild pain. Which of the following areas is most likely to experience "referral of pain" during this procedure?

- ▢ **A.** Perineum and lateral portion of the thigh
- ▢ **B.** Suprapubic region
- ▢ **C.** Umbilical region
- ▢ **D.** Inguinal region
- ▢ **E.** Epigastric region

58 A 35-year-old man is admitted to the hospital after being kicked in the groin while playing football. During physical examination it is noted that the left testicle of the patient is swollen. An MRI examination reveals coagulation of blood in the veins draining the testis. Into which of the following veins would a thrombus most likely pass first from the injured area?

- ▢ **A.** Inferior vena cava
- ▢ **B.** Left renal vein
- ▢ **C.** Left inferior epigastric
- ▢ **D.** Left internal pudendal
- ▢ **E.** Left iliac vein

59 A 32-year-old woman is admitted to the hospital due to a palpable mass superior to the inguinal ligament. It is demonstrated by physical examination that she suffers from an indirect inguinal hernia. Due to the severity of the hernia, an open hernia repair is performed. Which of the following structures would the surgeon expect to find in the canal?

- ▢ **A.** Round ligament of uterus
- ▢ **B.** Urachus
- ▢ **C.** Suspensory ligament of the ovary
- ▢ **D.** Uterine tube
- ▢ **E.** Mesosalpinx

60 A 32-year-old woman is admitted to the hospital with intense lower abdominal pain and an elevated temperature. Upon physical examination it is readily observed that the abdominal wall is tender to the touch. Blood tests reveal leukoytosis and a diagnosis is made of peritonitis. An exploratory laparotomy reveals a ruptured ectopic pregnancy. Which of the following is the most common site of an ectopic pregnancy?

- ▢ **A.** Over the internal cervical os
- ▢ **B.** Wall of the bowel
- ▢ **C.** Uterine tube
- ▢ **D.** Mesentery of the bowel
- ▢ **E.** Surface of the ovary

61 A 32-year-woman is admitted to the emergency department as a rape case. Fluids from her vagina are collected for DNA and fructose examination. Which of the following male organs is responsible for fructose production?

- ▢ **A.** Prostate gland
- ▢ **B.** Seminal vesicles
- ▢ **C.** Kidneys
- ▢ **D.** Testis
- ▢ **E.** Bulbourethral (Cowper) glands

62 A 1-year-old male infant is admitted to the pediatric clinic because his parents could not palpate his testicles in the scrotum. The pediatrician examines the infant and palpates the testes in the inguinal canal. Which of the following best describes this condition?

- ▢ **A.** Pseudohermaphroditism
- ▢ **B.** True hermaphroditism
- ▢ **C.** Cryptorchidism
- ▢ **D.** Congenital adrenal hyperplasia
- ▢ **E.** Chordee

63 A 38-year-old pregnant woman is admitted to the emergency department with severe vaginal bleeding. Ultrasound examination confirms the initial diagnosis of placenta previa. What is the site of implantation in placenta previa?

- ▢ **A.** Uterine (fallopian) tubes
- ▢ **B.** Cervix
- ▢ **C.** Mesentery of the abdominal wall
- ▢ **D.** Lower part of uterine body, overlapping the internal cervical os
- ▢ **E.** Fundus of the uterus

64 A 63-year-old male is admitted to the hospital with ascites, rectal bleeding, and an enlarged cirrhotic liver. He is overweight and has a history of alcohol abuse. Upon clinical examination it is found he is suffering from internal hemorrhoids. Which of the following best describes the nerves containing the pain fibers from his hemorrhoids?

- ▢ **A.** The pain fibers are carried by the inferior rectal nerve.
- ▢ **B.** The pain fibers are carried by the perineal nerve.
- ▢ **C.** The pain fibers are carried by the obturator nerve.
- ▢ **D.** The patient would not experience pain because this area is innervated by visceral afferent fibers.
- ▢ **E.** The patient would not experience well-localized pain because this area is innervated by pelvic splanchnic nerves.

65 A 34-year-old man is admitted to the emergency department after a traumatic landing into a swimming pool from a high diving platform. The patient has multiple traumas in his abdominal cavity. After a reconstructive operation of his abdominal organs the patient develops a high fever. Radiographic examination reveals that the lower portion of the descending colon and rectum has become septic and must be excised. Six months postoperatively the patient complains of impotence. Which of the following structures was most likely injured during the second operation?

- ▢ **A.** Pudendal nerve
- ▢ **B.** Sacral splanchnic nerves
- ▢ **C.** Pelvic splanchnic nerves
- ▢ **D.** Sympathetic chain
- ▢ **E.** Vagus nerve

66 A 32-year-old woman visits her gynecologist for a routine examination. The Pap smear reveals atypical cervical cells, indicating the possible existence of cervical cancer. Which of the following lymph nodes need to be biopsied to confirm the existence of initial metastasis from the suspected cancerous tumor?

- ▢ **A.** Internal iliac
- ▢ **B.** External iliac
- ▢ **C.** Superficial inguinal
- ▢ **D.** Deep inguinal
- ▢ **E.** Sacral

67 A 2-year-old male is admitted to the hospital with testicular pain. Physical examination reveals an enlarged scrotum. An otoscope is placed beneath the lateral side of the scrotum and the testis is transilluminated through the scrotal sac (Fig. 4-4). Which of the following best describes the signs observed in this patient?

- ▢ **A.** Varicocele
- ▢ **B.** Rectocele
- ▢ **C.** Cystocele
- ▢ **D.** Hydrocele
- ▢ **E.** Hypospadias

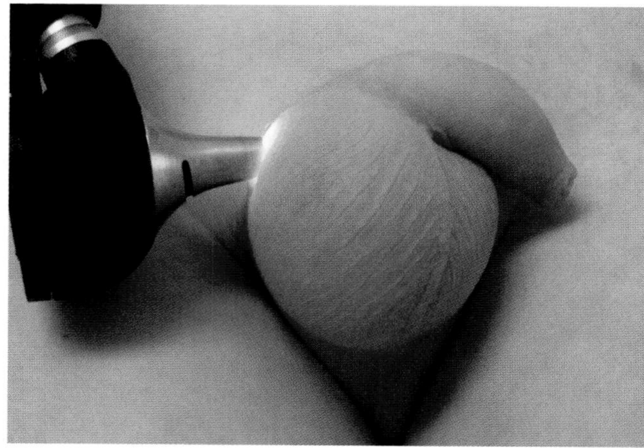

Fig. 4-4

68 A 34-year-old woman is admitted to the hospital with perineal pain. Laboratory blood tests reveal marked leukocytosis. Physical examination reveals abscesses in the anterior recess of the ischioanal fossa. A surgical procedure is performed to debride and drain the abscesses. Which of the following nerves will most likely need to be anesthetized to specifically numb the surgical area?

- ▢ **A.** Dorsal nerve to the clitoris
- ▢ **B.** Superficial perineal branch of perineal nerve
- ▢ **C.** Perineal nerve
- ▢ **D.** Inferior rectal nerve
- ▢ **E.** Pudendal nerve

69 A 34-year-old woman is admitted to the hospital with perineal pain. Laboratory blood tests reveal marked leukocytosis. Physical examination reveals perforation of the wall of the anal canal at the level of the anal valves. A horseshoe abscess extends from one ischioanal fossa to the other in the posterior recess. Which of the following nerves will most likely need to be anesthetized?

- ▢ **A.** Dorsal nerve to the clitoris
- ▢ **B.** Superficial perineal branch of perineal nerve
- ▢ **C.** Perineal nerve
- ▢ **D.** Inferior rectal nerve
- ▢ **E.** Pudendal nerve

70 A 35-year-old woman is undergoing a tension-free vaginal tape procedure to repair an inguinal hernia. Two days postoperatively the patient has a high fever and shows signs of hypovolemic shock. A radiographic examination reveals that a vessel crossing the pectineal (Cooper's) ligament as it descends into the pelvis was injured by a staple, confirming the presence of the so-called "arterial circle of death." Which of the following arteries is most likely injured?

- ▢ **A.** Obturator artery
- ▢ **B.** Aberrant obturator artery
- ▢ **C.** Superior vesicle artery
- ▢ **D.** Middle rectal
- ▢ **E.** Inferior vesicle

71 A 41-year-old male visits the outpatient urology clinic for a vasectomy procedure. Two months later the patient revisits the outpatient clinic complaining of pain in his testis. The diagnosis was made for postvasectomy pain syndrome. Which of the following nerves was most likely injured?

- ▢ **A.** Sympathetic fibers to ductus deferens
- ▢ **B.** Ilioinguinal
- ▢ **C.** Iliohypogastric
- ▢ **D.** Genital branch of genitofemoral
- ▢ **E.** Visceral afferent T10-L2

72 A 41-year-old woman is admitted to the obstetrics and gynecology department for a scheduled tubal ligation procedure. Two days postoperatively the patient has a high fever and shows signs of hypovolemic shock. A radiographic examination reveals a large hematoma adjacent to the external iliac artery. Which of the following vessels was most likely injured?

- ▢ **A.** Ovarian arteries
- ▢ **B.** Ascending branch of uterine arteries
- ▢ **C.** Descending branch of uterine arteries
- ▢ **D.** Superior vesicle artery
- ▢ **E.** Inferior vesicle artery

73 A 37-year-old woman is admitted to the hospital with pelvic pain. Radiographic examination reveals a benign tumor on the left ovary. An ovariectomy is performed and the ovarian vessels are ligated. Which of the following structures is most at risk of injury when the ovarian vessels are ligated?

- ▢ **A.** Uterine artery
- ▢ **B.** Vaginal artery
- ▢ **C.** Ureter
- ▢ **D.** Internal pudendal artery
- ▢ **E.** Pudendal nerve

74 A 23-year-old woman in her seventh month of pregnancy visits her gynecologist for a routine checkup. The patient is informed that a hormone called "relaxin" is responsible for the relaxation of the sacroiliac joint and pubic symphysis. Which of the following pelvic distances will most likely remain unaffected?

- ▢ **A.** Transverse diameter
- ▢ **B.** Interspinous distance
- ▢ **C.** True conjugate diameter
- ▢ **D.** Diagonal conjugate
- ▢ **E.** Oblique diameter

75 A 42-year-old woman is admitted to the hospital with a mass on her right ovary. An ovariectomy is performed and the lymphatics of the lateral pelvic wall are also removed. Four days postoperatively the patient complains of painful spasms of the adductor muscles of the thigh and sensory deficit in the distal medial thigh. Which of the following nerves is most likely injured?

- ▢ **A.** Genitofemoral
- ▢ **B.** Ilioinguinal
- ▢ **C.** Iliohypogastric
- ▢ **D.** Obturator
- ▢ **E.** Lumbosacral trunk

76 A 69-year-old man is admitted to the hospital for a scheduled radical prostatectomy. Six months postoperatively the patient visits the outpatient clinic complaining of impotence. Where are the nerve cell bodies located that are responsible for erection?

- ▢ **A.** Sacral parasympathetic nucleus
- ▢ **B.** Sacral sympathetic chain ganglia
- ▢ **C.** Inferior mesenteric ganglion
- ▢ **D.** Superior hypogastric plexus
- ▢ **E.** Intermediolateral column of L1, L2

77 A 34-year-old woman is at her third stage of delivery. The obstetrician is concerned that the pelvic canal is too narrow for a vaginal delivery. Which of the following dimensions is the most reliable determinant of the capacity for a vaginal birth?

- ▢ **A.** Transverse diameter
- ▢ **B.** Interspinous distance
- ▢ **C.** True conjugate diameter
- ▢ **D.** Diagonal conjugate
- ▢ **E.** Oblique diameter

78 A 32-year-old man visits the outpatient clinic and says he has had a painless mass at his right scrotum for several months. Ultrasonographic examination reveals a homogeneous hypoechoic intratesticular mass. Biopsy reveals a seminoma. Cancer of the testis metastasizes first to which of the following lymph nodes?

- ▢ **A.** Deep inguinal
- ▢ **B.** External iliac
- ▢ **C.** Internal iliac
- ▢ **D.** Lumbar
- ▢ **E.** Superficial inguinal

79 A 42-year-old woman is admitted to the hospital with severe uterine bleeding. Radiographic examination reveals uterine fibroids. A uterine artery embolization is performed. Which of the following arteries will supply collateral supply to the uterus?

- ▢ **A.** External iliac
- ▢ **B.** Inferior mesenteric
- ▢ **C.** Ovarian
- ▢ **D.** Internal pudendal
- ▢ **E.** Superior mesenteric

ANSWERS

1 A. Perineal hypospadias is due to a failure of fusion of labioscrotal folds so that the external urethral orifice is between the unfused halves of the scrotum. The cloacal membrane is formed from endoderm of the cloaca and ectoderm of the procotodeum and forms the future anus. The urogenital folds normally fuse along the ventral side of the penis to form the spongy urethra. Epispadias is a condition in which the urethra opens on the dorsal surface of the penis resulting from the genital tubercle developing more dorsally during development. The urogenital membrane is bounded by the urogenital folds and ruptures to form the urogenital orifice.
GAS 444-446; GA 224-225

2 B. Most anorectal anomalies result from abnormal development of the urorectal septum, ultimately resulting in nondivision of the cloaca into urogenital and anorectal parts. The common outlet of the intestinal, urinary, and reproductive tracts is specifically associated with a persistent cloaca. The labioscrotal folds are involved in forming the external urethral orifice only. The urogenital folds normally fuse along the ventral side of the penis to form the spongy urethra. Epispadias is an anomaly in the development of the genital tubercle and involves the urethral orifice. The urogenital membrane is bounded by the urogenital folds and ruptures to form the urogenital orifice.
GAS 312, 406, 438-440; GA 213-215

3 A. The gubernaculum arises in the upper abdomen from the lower end of the gonadal ridge and helps guide the testis in its descent to the inguinal region and then through the abdominal wall. Ectopic testes occur when a portion of the gubernaculum passes to an abnormal position or otherwise fails to descend or become fixed to the skin of the scrotum. The processus vaginalis is a tube of peritoneum that follows the same oblique course through the body wall as the testis, ventral to the gubernaculum. The distal part of the processus is retained as the tunica vaginalis. If part of the remainder of the processus remains patent, it can fill with fluid as a hydrocele of the testis or spermatic cord. The genital tubercle forms the primordial phallus and is associated with epispadias. The seminiferous cords form the primordia of the seminiferous tubules. The labioscrotal swellings approach each other and fuse to form the scrotum.
GAS 260, 263, 287, 453; GA 225

4 A. When the urinary bladder mucosa is open to the outside in the fetus or newborn, the condition is referred to as extrophy of the bladder. The extrophy results from failure of the primitive streak mesoderm to migrate around the cloacal membrane, and it occurs often in combination with epispadias. Penile hypospadias is characterized by a failure of fusion of the labioscrotal folds, with the external urethral orifice located between the two unfused halves of the scrotum. Androgens are responsible for development of the testes. Klinefelter syndrome is a condition in which the male has 47 XXY chromosomes. A persistent allantois is associated with a patent urachus and an allantoic cyst.
GAS 441, 453-455; GA 208, 210, 216, 218

5 A. The ureteric bud, or metanephric diverticulum, is an outgrowth from the mesonephric duct. It is the primordium of the ureter, renal pelvis, the calyces, and the collecting tubules. Incomplete division results in a divided kidney with a bifid ureter. Complete division results in a double kidney with a bifid ureter, or separate ureters.
GAS 441, 453; GA 210, 218-219

6 A. Failure of fusion of the inferior parts of the paramesonephric ducts results in a double uterus. A bicornuate uterus is the result of failure of fusion of the superior parts of the paramesonephric (Mülle-

rian) ducts. A failure of the sinovaginal bulbs to form the vaginal plate causes agenesis of the vagina. The mesonephric ducts are important embryologic structures involved in the development of male urogenital structures.
GAS 441, 453; GA 137, 210, 227-229

7 E. The persistence of the epithelial lining of the urachus can give rise to a urachal cyst. This swelling is found in the midline in the umbilical region. Hydrocele is fluid accumulation between the visceral and parietal layers of the tunica vaginalis of the testis. A Meckel diverticulum is located in the ileum of the small intestine. When it becomes inflamed, it can cause symptoms of appendicitis. A diverticulum can form a cyst (Meckel cyst). An omphalocele is the persistence of the herniation of the abdominal contents into the umbilical cord.
GAS 441, 453; GA 208, 210, 216, 218

8 B. A double uterus is caused by failure of inferior parts of the paramesonephric ducts. A complete fusion results in abnormal development of the uterine tubes because the uterine tubes form from the unfused portions of the cranial parts of the paramesonephric ducts. Hydronephros, swelling of the renal pelvis and calyces with urine, can result from the obstruction of the ureter by a renal stone. Cryptorchidism is a condition characterized by an undescended testis, in which the testis can be localized in the abdominal cavity or in any place along the path of testicular descent. The pronephros is part of the primordial urinary system and generally degenerates in the first four weeks of development.
GAS 455-457; GA 137, 210, 227-229

9 A. The ureters cross the pelvic brim anterior to the bifurcation of the common iliac artery bilaterally. Because of the proximity of this artery to the ureter, it is in danger of being damaged during surgery.
GAS 359-364; GA 218-219, 223

10 C. Hypospadias is a developmental defect in the urethra resulting in urine being expelled from the ventral side of the penis. This ectopic malformation may present when the urethral folds fail to completely fuse. Failure of fusion of the spongy urethra would result in epispadias. A failure of the labioscrotal folds to fuse will cause the external urethral orifice to be situated between the two scrotal halves. This is referred to as penile hypospadias. Failure of the urogenital folds to fuse would lead to agenesis of the external urethral folds.
GAS 444-453; GA 219, 222

11 A. Epispadias is a developmental defect in the spongy urethra resulting in urine being expelled from the dorsal aspect of the penis. A failure of the labioscrotal folds to fuse will cause the external urethral orifice to be situated between the two scrotal halves. This is referred to as penile hypospadias. Failure of the urogenital folds to fuse would lead to agenesis of the external urethral folds. The genital tubercle would not directly cause epispadias, as the tubercle still continues to develop, but it is located more dorsally.
GAS 444-453; GA 219, 222

12 D. Hydrocele results from an excess amount of fluid within a persistent processus vaginalis. Hydrocele can result from injury to the testis or by retention of a processus that fills with fluid in infants. The tunica vaginalis consists of parietal and visceral layers, the latter of which is closely attached to the testis and epididymis. The fluid buildup occurs within the cavity between these layers. A varicocele consists of varicosed veins of the pampiniform plexus and is associated with increased venous pressure in the testicular vein, followed by the accumulation and coagulation of venous blood.
GAS 504; GA 139, 224-225

13 A. Varicose veins occur with loss of elasticity within the walls of the vessels. As the veins weaken, they simultaneously dilate under pressure. A varicocele often occurs with a varicosity of the veins of the pampiniform venous plexus, resulting in a swelling of the veins. This condition can arise from a tumor in the left kidney, which occludes the testicular vein due to an anatomic constriction. A hydrocele is an accumulation of fluid within the cavity of the tunica vaginalis. Hypospadias occurs from failure of fusion of the urethral and labioscrotal folds, resulting in an external urethral opening on the ventral surface of the penis or in the perineum.
GAS 339-340, 504, 638-639; GA 139, 224-225

14 A. When veins lose their elasticity, they can become weak and often dilate. This causes the veins to become swollen and oftentimes tortuous, as a result of incompetent valves. The appearance of a "bag of worms" on the radiograph is characteristic of a varicosity of the pampiniform venous plexus. A hydrocele is an accumulation of fluid within the tunica vaginalis cavity. Hypospadias occurs from failure of fusion of the urethral and labioscrotal folds, resulting in an external urethral opening on the ventral surface of the penis or in the perineum.
GAS 339-340, 504; GA 139, 224-225

15 B. It is very likely that the ectopic pregnancy ruptured into the rectouterine pouch, also known as the pouch of Douglas. The most direct route to the rectouterine pouch is through the vaginal wall at the posterior vaginal fornix. It is unlikely that the pregnancy would have occurred in the vesicouterine space because the transfer of ova from the ovary to the fimbriae occurs on the posterior side of the broad ligament. Therefore, it would not be advisable to attempt initially to insert a needle into the vesicouterine space. Inserting a needle through the anterior fornix into the endocervical canal would lead one into the uterine cavity, with the probability of other undesirable consequences. The urogenital diaphragm is a closed space in the perineum. Entering a vestibular gland with a needle would not be near the location of ectopic pregnancy.
GAS 508; GA 208, 210, 231

16 A. A break or tear in the rectovaginal septum (fascia of Denonvilliers) can allow small intestine (in an enterocele) or rectum (in a rectocele) to herniate into the posterior vaginal wall, even to the point of protrusion through the vaginal introitus. The muscles listed are all in the anterior region of the perineum and have no association with an enterocele or rectocele. The sacrospinous ligament is unrelated to this condition.
GAS 454, 459; GA 208, 231

17 B. When the internal urethral orifice is obstructed, it is most likely due to an enlargement of the median (or middle) lobe of the prostate gland. The prostate gland is located at the base of the urinary bladder and is often described as possessing five ill-defined lobes, although this is not accepted by most urologists. The middle lobe consists of glandular tissue dorsal to the uvula of the urethral meatus of the urinary bladder, adjacent to the beginning of the urethra. This glandular tissue is most frequently involved in benign hypertrophy.
GAS 447, 451-452; GA 216, 218-223

18 A. The deep inguinal lymph nodes drain the glans clitoris and receive lymph also from superficial nodes. The internal iliac nodes drain the inferior pelvic structures, deep perineal structures, and sacral nodes. The paraaortic lymph nodes, or lumbar nodes, receive lymph from the common iliac nodes. The drainage of presacral lymph nodes can pass to the common or internal iliac nodes. Axillary nodes drain body wall structures above the T10 dermatome (or the umbilicus).
GAS 477; GA 254-256

19 B. If the membranous portion of the urethra is injured, urine and blood can leak upward into the retropubic space (of Retzius) limited inferiorly by the urogenital diaphragm and the muscle within (compressor urethra), which would be injured. The bulbospongiosus muscle and other perineal muscles, the corpus cavernosa penis, and the openings of the bulbourethral ducts are inferior and anterior to the region of injury.
GAS 444-447; GA 210, 220, 227

20 A. Conscious pain due to bladder fullness results from the excitation of stretch receptors in the bladder wall. These pain fibers are carried through the pelvic nerve plexuses and into the pelvic splanchnic nerves. The sensory fibers enter the dorsal root ganglia of spinal nerves S2, S3, and S4. Sensory fibers enter the spinal cord via these ganglia. The intermediomedial cell column of spinal cord levels S2, S3, and S4 contains parasympathetic soma. The levels T5 to T9, T10 to L2, and preaortic ganglia are well above where sensory fibers from the bladder are located.
GAS 441-444, 462-471; GA 238-240, 250-253

21 A. The pubococcygeus muscle, especially its most medial portion, the puborectalis, is of most importance in fecal continence. The levator ani consists of two major portions, the pubococcygeus and iliococcygeus, which help support pelvic viscera and resist increases in intraabdominal pressure. The puborectalis muscle is the most medial and inferior portion of the pubococcygeus. The puborectalis forms a loop around the rectoanal junction, and the integrity of this muscle is critical in maintenance of fecal continence. The coccygeus and pubovesicocervical fascia are not in direct contact with the rectum. Damage to the urogenital diaphragm can contribute to urinary incontinence but not fecal incontinence.
GAS 432-436; GA 214-215, 220

22 E. The lateral femoral cutaneous nerve (L2, L3) emerges from the lateral side of the psoas muscle and runs in front of the iliacus and through, or behind, the inguinal ligament and innervates the skin of the lateral aspect of the thigh to the level of the knee. This nerve has been constricted in this case of "Calvin Klein syndrome" (in this case from the patient's obesity, not too-tight jeans) causing pain, tingling, or burning sensations in the lateral thigh. The femoral branch of the genitofemoral nerve (L1, L2) supplies a small area of skin (over the femoral triangle), just inferior to the midpoint of the inguinal ligament. The femoral nerve (L2 to L4) is motor to the quadriceps and sartorius muscles and sensory to the anterior

thigh and the medial thigh and leg. The ilioinguinal supplies the suprapubic region; part of the genitalia and anterior perineum; and the upper, medial thigh. Cutaneous branches of the iliohypogastric nerve innervate skin of the anterolateral gluteal area and suprapubic region.
GAS 462-471; GA 238-240, 250-253

23 **C.** Normally the uterus is anteflexed at the junction of the cervix and the body and anteverted at the junction of the vagina and the cervical canal.
GAS 455-458; GA 227

24 **D.** The cardinal ligament, also known as Mackenrodt's ligament or transverse cervical ligament, is composed of condensations of fibromuscular tissues that accompany the uterine vessels. These bands of pelvic fascia provide direct support to the uterus. The other ligaments listed do not play a direct role in uterine stability.
GAS 455-458; GA 228-229

25 **C.** Ovarian lymph first drains into the paraaortic nodes at the level of the renal vessels. The superficial and deep inguinal nodes drain the body wall below the umbilicus, the lower limbs, and the cutaneous portion of the anal canal and parts of the perineum. The external iliac nodes receive the lymph from the inguinal nodes. The node of Cloquet is located in the femoral ring, adjacent to the external iliac vein and beneath the inguinal ligament. The node of Cloquet drains into the common iliac nodes. The internal iliac nodes accompany the uterine artery and vein, receiving lymph from much of the uterus but not the ovaries.
GAS 477; GA 254-256

26 **B.** The external anal sphincter is important for maintaining fecal continence. The external anal sphincter is located immediately posterior to the perineal body (central tendon) and would be susceptible to damage during a median episiotomy. The other structures listed play no role in maintaining fecal continence.
GAS 413, 436-438; GA 208, 210, 216-217

27 **C.** The tendinous arch of fascia pelvis is a dense band of connective tissue that joins the fascia of the levator ani to the feltlike pubocervical fascia that covers the anterior wall of the vagina. If this fascial band is torn, the ipsilateral side of the vagina falls, carrying with it the bladder and urethra, often leading to urinary incontinence. The tendinous arch of the levator ani is a thickened portion of the fascia of the obturator internus and provides part of the origin of the levator ani muscle, but it plays no direct role in incontinence. The coccygeus muscle supports and raises the pelvic floor but is not directly associated with urinary incontinence. The obturator internus is involved with lateral rotation of the thigh. If the rectovaginal septum is torn, the patient can be subject to the occurrence of rectocele or enterocele, as the lower portion of the GI tract prolapses into the posterior wall of the vagina.
GAS 413, 436-438, 454, 459; GA 213

28 **A.** Lymph from the cutaneous portion of the anal canal (below the pectinate line) drains into the inguinal nodes. Lymph from most parts of the rectum and from the mucosal zone of the anal canal (above the pectinate line) drains into the internal iliac nodes. Lymph from some parts of the rectum also drains into the sacral nodes.
GAS 477; GA 254-256

29 **C.** The retropubic space (of Retzius) is the extraperitoneal space between the pubic symphysis and the bladder. A needle placed over the pubic bone, through the body wall, and into the space of Retzius will enter the full bladder but avoids entry into the peritoneum and there is little risk of damaging major organs or vessels. Entry through the ischioanal fossa would not provide a direct route to the bladder. With entry through the superficial perineal cleft, perineal body, and deep perineal pouch there is a high risk of damaging important structures.
GAS 438-447; GA 210, 220, 227

30 **C.** Hematocolpos is characterized by filling of the vagina with menstrual blood. This commonly occurs due to the presence of an imperforate hymen. Bartholin gland ducts open into the vestibule of the vagina; therefore, a cyst in Bartholin gland would not cause hematocolpos. Blood from a ruptured ectopic pregnancy most often drains into the rectouterine pouch (of Douglas). Females often have a diminutive cremaster muscle and cremasteric artery and vein, but none of these is associated with hematocolpos. The cremasteric artery provides a small branch to the round ligament of the uterus (sometimes called "Samson's artery"), which must be kept in mind during a hysterectomy, with division of the round ligament. Bleeding from the uterine veins would not flow into the vagina.
GAS 508; GA 227, 231

31 **C.** An enterocele (herniation of small intestine into the posterior wall of the vagina) is caused by a tear of the rectovaginal septum, which weakens the pelvic floor. A urethrocele is characterized by prolapse of the

urethra into the vagina. It is usually associated with a cystocele (prolapse of the bladder into the urethra). Cystocele or urethrocele are associated with defects in the pubocervical fascia that covers the anterior wall of the vagina and assists in supporting the bladder. Urinary incontinence can result from weakening of the muscles that surround the urethra but would not be caused by a tear of the rectovaginal septum. Prolapse of the uterus is caused by weakening or tearing of the ligaments that support the uterus (especially the cardinal and/or uterosacral ligaments).
GAS 454, 459; GA 227, 231

32 **A.** Of the answer choices listed, the pubococcygeus is the muscle that is most directly associated with the arcus tendineus fascia pelvis and connective tissues of the vagina and the support of the bladder. The obturator internus, piriformis, and coccygeus do not form parts of the levator ani and provide no direct support to the urogenital organs, nor do they have any role in urinary incontinence. The iliococcygeus does form part of the levator ani, but it is located lateral to the pubococcygeus and therefore does not play a direct role in maintaining urinary continence.
GAS 432-436; GA 212-217

33 **A.** The ovarian vessels and nerves lie within the infundibulopelvic ligament (suspensory ligament of the ovary); therefore, cutting this ligament interrupts pain fibers from the ovary. Cutting the sympathetic chain might help to reduce some of the pain from the ovary, but the results of such a procedure are rather unpredictable, plus locating the lumbar sympathetic chain is more of a surgical challenge. The cluneal nerves are cutaneous nerves that innervate parts of the buttocks. They are not associated with the ovaries. The pudendal nerve innervates the perineum and does not carry afferent pain fibers from the ovary. The broad ligament contains only the uterovaginal vessels and nerve plexus and does not carry any nerve fibers from the ovary.
GAS 471-477; GA 228-229, 235

34 **C.** The superficial perineal space or cleft lies between the external perineal fascia of Gallaudet (fascia of inferior perineal muscles in the superficial perineal compartment) and the membranous layer of Colles' fascia. Camper's fascia is the superficial fatty layer of the anterior abdominal wall and the perineum; Scarpa's fascia is the deep membranous layer of the abdominal wall. The perineal membrane is the inferior fascia of the urogenital diaphragm that forms the inferior boundary of the deep perineal compartment. The superior fascia of the urogenital diaphragm bounds the inferior border of the anterior recess of the ischioanal fossa. There is no space between the urogenital diaphragm and the apex of the prostate gland.
GAS 478-482; GA 246, 248

35 **B.** The urinary bladder wall is formed by the detrusor muscle, and it receives both its motor and sensory innervation from parasympathetic nerve fibers transmitted by way of the pelvic splanchnic nerves from S2 to S4.
GAS 462-471; GA 258, 260

36 **A.** The rectouterine pouch (of Douglas) is the lowest point of the female peritoneal cavity. Therefore, fluid buildup within the peritoneal cavity accumulates here when the patient is standing or sitting. It is accessible transvaginally through the posterior fornix, with the patient positioned appropriately.
GAS 460-462; GA 210, 227

37 **E.** Because the penile urethra and deep (Bucks) fascia are both located in the superficial perineal pouch, rupture will occur here, with extravasation of fluids into the superficial perineal cleft. The ischioanal fossa is located posterior to the urogenital triangle, behind the area of injury. The other listed spaces are deep to the superficial compartment or within the pelvis and are not associated with the area of injury.
GAS 444-448, 478-481; GA 224-226

38 **C.** The perineal branch of the pudendal nerve is responsible for the innervation of the external urethral sphincter, and injury to this nerve can result in paralysis of the sphincter and urinary incontinence. Pelvic splanchnic and sacral splanchnic nerves are autonomic nerves that do not supply skeletal muscles in the urogenital region. The gluteal nerves innervate gluteal muscles.
GAS 462-471; GA 238-240, 250-253

39 **D.** The internal pudendal artery gives rise to both the dorsal artery and deep artery of the penis. The deep artery is the main supply for erectile tissue; therefore, significant atherosclerosis of the internal pudendal artery may result in impotence (erectile dysfunction).
GAS 471-476; GA 231-232, 236-237, 250, 252

40 **A.** Cancer present in the inguinal nodes can be indicative of cancer of the uterus at the level of the round ligaments, by which the cancer passes to the inguinal region. Uterine cancer must be especially suspected if the tissues of the lower limb, vulva, and anal canal appear normal. The pectinate line marks the end of the mucosal lining of the anal canal, below which

the canal is lined with nonkeratinized, stratified squamous epithelium. The pectinate line is also associated with the distal ends of the anal columns and anal valves. Lymphatic vessels inferior to the pectinate line of the anal canal will drain into the superficial inguinal nodes, but those above the pectinate line flow to internal iliac nodes. Lymph from the ovaries flows to the paraaortic nodes at the level of the kidneys. Lymph from the rectum flows to pelvic lymph nodes.
GAS 477, 496; GA 254-256

41 **C.** The lymphatic vessels of the ovaries join with lymphatics from the uterine tubes and the fundus of the uterus. These ascend to the right and left lumbar (caval/aortic) lymph nodes. These lymph nodes are the first to receive cancerous cells from the ovaries. Superficial inguinal nodes drain the lower limb, the anterior abdominal wall inferior to the umbilicus, and superficial perineal structures. The external iliac nodes drain the deep inguinal nodes that drain the clitoris and superficial inguinal nodes. The internal iliac nodes drain inferior pelvic structures and deep perineal structures.
GAS 477, 496; GA 254-256

42 **A.** The superficial inguinal nodes drain superficial perineal structures, including the superolateral uterine body near attachment of the round ligament, skin of the perineum (including the vulva), and the introitus of the vagina inferior to the hymen. The internal iliac nodes drain the middle and upper vagina, cervix, and body of the uterus. The lumbar/lateral aortic lymph nodes drain the ovaries. The axillary lymph nodes drain the upper limb and chest wall, including the breast.
GAS 477, 496; GA 254-256

43 **A.** The ischial spine is the correct bony landmark used to administer a pudendal nerve block. The pudendal nerve crosses the sacrospinous ligament, which attaches to the ischial spine. Accessing the ischial spine and thus the pudendal nerve is done most easily using a transvaginal approach. The posterior superior and inferior iliac spines are located on the posterior aspect of the pelvis and articulate with the lateral aspect of the sacrum. They do not relate to the course of the pudendal nerve. The ischial tuberosities are the most inferior aspect of the bony pelvis. The skin and soft tissues around the ischial tuberosities receive sensory supply from the pudendal nerve and perineal branches of the posterior femoral cutaneous nerve. Injections into the area around the tuberosities are less certain, however, than injections at the sacrospinous ligament and often fail to anesthetize the anal triangle well. The coccyx is a poor target for locating and anesthetizing the pudendal nerve.
GAS 421-428; GA 238-240, 250-253

44 **D.** Hemorrhoids are divided into two categories: internal and external. Pain due to external hemorrhoids is mediated by the pudendal nerve (somatosensory), which serves the majority of the perineum. The sacral splanchnic nerves are postganglionic sympathetic fibers from the sacral sympathetic chain, and the pelvic splanchnic nerves carry parasympathetic fibers and sensory fibers from within the pelvis. Superior hypogastric nerves are mixed nerves located anterior to the sacral promontory and do not mediate pain information from the perineum. The ilioinguinal nerve provides sensory innervation to the skin at the base of the penis; the scrotum; and upper, inner thigh.
GAS 340, 482; GA 217

45 **C.** The membranous urethra is shorter in women than in men. Because of its close proximity to the vestibule in women, it commonly leads to infections of the urinary tract. The vagina contains more bacterial flora than the penis. The prostate in the male produces a clear, alkaline fluid, but it has not been proved that it protects against bacterial infections. The uterus has no known antibacterial functions. The seminal vesicles produce a fructose-characterized fluid that provides nutrients to the sperm for the journey through the female genital tract.
GAS 444-448; GA 227, 231

46 **A.** The uterus is stabilized and anchored to the bladder by the pubovesical and vesicocervical fasciae on its anterior surface. During childbirth this connective tissue can be torn, allowing the bladder to herniate into the anterior vaginal wall, with prolapse possible through the vaginal introitus. The transverse cervical (cardinal) ligament is located within the base of the broad ligament and is a major ligament of the uterus but would offer no support if the bladder herniates through the vagina. The uterosacral ligament serves to anchor the uterus to the sacrum for support. Injury to the levator ani would not cause the bladder to herniate through the vagina. The median umbilical ligament contains the urachus and is located on the posterior aspect of the linea alba; the ligament is an embryologic remnant of the allantois.
GAS 453-458; GA 208, 210, 219, 227

47 **A.** During a hysterectomy, ligation of or injury to the ureter can happen relatively easily because it is the most susceptible structure due to its location. The ureter is located below the uterine vessels in the pel-

vic cavity approximately 1 cm lateral to the supravaginal cervix. The internal iliac artery bifurcates near the pelvic brim but is not in close proximity to the uterine vessels in the vicinity of the cervix. The obturator nerve travels along the pelvic sidewall and is not close to the site of ligation of the uterine vessels. The lumbosacral trunk is located on the lateral side of the sacrum and the pelvic sidewall, not in close proximity to the uterine vessels.
GAS 359-361, 415-416, 438-441, 508; GA 235

48 A. Vaginismus is a painful, psychosomatic gynecologic disorder; it is described as involving distension of the cavernous tissues and the bulbospongiosus and transverse perineal muscles, the stimulation of which triggers the involuntary spasms of the perivaginal and levator ani muscles. This can in turn lead to painful intercourse or dyspareunia.
GAS 457-458; GA 227-231

49 B. This is a classic example of extravasation of blood and urine from the superficial perineal pouch. This usually is a result of rupture of the spongy urethra. The extravasation of the fluid (urine) will begin to invade the layer between the Buck's fascia and dartos layer. This extravasation example is evident due to the fluid invading up to the abdomen between the subcutaneous tissues and muscle fascia. If the fluid collects between the other layers of the perineum, the clinical evidence will present differently in the perineum and abdominal area.
GAS 444-448, 479-481; GA 224-226

50 A. The uterosacral ligaments and the transverse cervical (cardinal) ligaments are the two main ligaments stabilizing the uterus. They help to inhibit the uterus from prolapsing into the vagina. The round ligament of the uterus is related to the descent of the ovaries in embryologic development and continues into the inguinal canal. The broad ligament is the peritoneal covering over the uterine tubes, uterus, and vessels. The arcus tendineus fascia pelvis joins the muscle fascia of the levator ani to the pubocervical fascia on the vagina and is not directly associated with the uterus or its ligaments. The levator ani muscles contribute to the floor of the pelvis and support all of the pelvic viscera indirectly; it does not, however, prevent prolapse of the uterus into the vagina.
GAS 454-455; GA 210, 229, 231

51 A. The internal iliac lymph nodes and sacral nodes would be involved in a pelvic lymphadenectomy, which often would be desired in surgical resection for prostate cancer. Sacral lymphatics can communicate with lymphatics within the vertebral canal and thus metastasize cranially. The external iliac nodes drain all of the anterosuperior pelvic structures, the lower limb and perineum, and the body wall to the level of the umbilicus. The superficial inguinal nodes drain all of the superficial structures below the umbilicus. The deep inguinal nodes drain the glans penis in the male.
GAS 477, 496; GA 254-256

52 E. The paraaortic and lumbar nodes at the level of the kidneys will most likely be infiltrated by metastasis of testicular cancer because testicular lymphatics run in close association with the testicular vessels and drain the testicles and epididymis. Testicular cancer is said to be a disease that is especially dangerous for young men. The internal iliac nodes drain the inferior pelvis and deep perineal structures. The external iliac nodes drain all anterosuperior pelvic structures. The superficial inguinal nodes drain all of the superficial structures below the umbilicus. Finally, the deep inguinal nodes receive more superficial vessels and drain the glans penis in males.
GAS 477, 496; GA 254-256

53 C. Penile erection is a parasympathetic mediated response that is delivered via the pelvic splanchnic nerves that pass through nerve bundles on the posterolateral aspect of the prostate gland. (In prostatectomy, these bundles should be left intact, if at all possible, to avoid impotence.) The pudendal nerve and its terminal branch, the dorsal nerve of the penis, carry the primary skeletal motor and sensory innervation to the external genitalia, and also sympathetic fibers. Sacral splanchnic nerves contain sympathetic fibers.
GAS 462-471, 490-492; GA 238-240, 250-253

54 A. Rupture of the spongy urethra leads to accumulation of fluid (edema) in the superficial perineal cleft. The continuity of Colles' fascia (superficial membranous layer of the superficial perineal fascia) with Scarpa's fascia of the abdominal wall allows for fluid spread upward upon the body wall. Rupture of the preprostatic urethra, prostatic urethra, or urinary bladder would lead to internal fluid accumulation within the pelvis because they are not located in the perineum. Damage to the ureter would manifest within the abdomen or pelvis, depending upon the level of rupture.
GAS 444-448, 478-481; GA 208, 210, 218-219, 222, 226

55 B. The cremasteric reflex afferents are carried by the iliolinguinal nerve; the motor (efferent) output is by the genitofemoral nerve. The sensory fibers of the genitofemoral nerve are to skin over the femo-

ral triangle. The ilioinguinal nerve is sensory to parts of the suprapubic region, anterior perineum, and inner thigh. The iliohypogastric nerve provides sensation for the abdominal wall and suprapubic area. The pudendal and obturator nerves do not travel through the inguinal canal and would not be damaged from the hernia. In addition, they play no role in the cremasteric reflex.
GAS 462-471, 490-492; GA 238-240, 250-253

56 **C.** Pain from the cervix is transmitted via the pelvic splanchnic nerves because the cervix is below the pelvic pain line. Pain above the pelvic pain line is carried via nerves that are primarily sympathetic in function. The superior hypogastric nerves carry pain fibers from the upper portions of the uterus. Sacral splanchnic nerves are principally sympathetic in function. The pudendal nerve contains skeletal motor, sensory, and sympathetic fibers and provides primary sensory innervation to external genitalia, including the lower third of the vagina.
GAS 462-471, 490-492; GA 238-240, 250-253

57 **A.** Pain from this area is mediated via parasympathetic responses and would thus travel to the S2 to S4 levels through the pelvic splanchnic nerves. The S2, S3, and S4 spinal cord levels also provide sensory innervation of the perineum and posterior thigh. The suprapubic and inguinal regions are supplied by ilioinguinal and iliohypogastric nerves (L1). The umbilical region receives sensory innervation from the T10 level. In the epigastric region the sensory innervation is provided by T7 to T10.
GAS 462-471, 490-492; GA 238-240, 250-253

58 **B.** The left testicular vein drains directly into the left renal vein, which then crosses over the midline to enter the inferior vena cava. The left inferior epigastric, left internal pudendal, and left iliac veins are not involved in the drainage of the testes.
GAS 474-477, 496; GA 138, 152, 183

59 **A.** During repair, the round ligament of the uterus may be seen within the inguinal canal, although it is often a small, fibrous strand that is easily overlooked. The remaining choices are not found in this region. The ovarian ligament connects the ovary to the uterus, whereas the suspensory (infundibulopelvic) ligament contains the ovarian vessels, nerves, and lymphatic. The uterine tubes are lateral projections of the uterus toward the ovaries. The mesosalpinx is a portion of the peritoneum of the broad ligament that attaches to the uterine tubes.
GAS 454-455; GA 227-229

60 **C.** The most common site of ectopic pregnancy is the uterine tube. Implantation at the internal cervical os would be within the uterus and lead to placenta previa. The other choices are less common sites of ectopic pregnancies.
GAS 508; GA 227-229

61 **B.** Seminal vesicles produce the alkaline constituent of the ejaculate. This includes fructose and choline. The prostate gland secretes prostaglandins, citric acid, and acid phosphatase. The kidneys are the site of urine production. The testes produce spermatozoa and sex hormones. The bulbourethral glands (Cowper's glands) produce mucous secretions that enter the penile bulb.
GAS 451-452; GA 220, 223, 226

62 **C.** In cryptorchidism, the testis has failed to descend into its proper location in the scrotum and may be found within the abdomen.
GAS 448-451; GA 224

63 **D.** By definition, the site of implantation in placenta previa overlaps the internal cervical os. Ectopic pregnancy in the uterine (Fallopian) tubes results in tubal pregnancy. The fundus of the uterus is the normal site of implantation. Implantation within the mesenteries of the abdomen will result in an abdominal pregnancy. The cervix is not a notable site of ectopic implantation.
GAS 508; GA 228-229

64 **D.** Internal hemorrhoids are located above the pectinate line. This tissue is derived from the hindgut and innervated by visceral nerves. Pain is usually not a symptom of internal hemorrhoids.
GAS 480-482; GA 217

65 **C.** The pelvic splanchnic nerves contain parasympathetic efferent fibers that mediate erection. These same nerves innervate the hindgut, the portions of the large intestine that were removed in this patient.
GAS 462-471, 490-492; GA 238-240, 250-253

66 **A.** The internal iliac nodes are the first in a chain of lymph nodes that receive lymph from the uterine cervix. Cancerous cells from the cervix are likely to involve the internal iliac nodes first. If these nodes do not have cancerous cells, this indicates that the tumor has not spread, at least through lymphatic channels.
GAS 477, 496; GA 254-256

67 **D.** As seen in the photograph, the swollen scrotum contains mostly a clear fluid. Since hydrocele is

the accumulation of fluid between the visceral and parietal layers of the tunica vaginalis, this condition best accounts for the findings in this patient.
GAS 448-451; GA 224-225

68 **C.** The perineal nerve would need to be anesthetized because it supplies the area described. The dorsal nerve to the clitoris pierces the perineal membrane and innervates the clitoris and not the anterior recess of the ischiorectal fossa. The superficial perineal branch of the perineal nerve supplies only the labia majora. The inferior rectal nerve innervates the skin around the anus and the external anal sphincter muscle. The pudendal nerve is the main nerve of the perineum and gives rise to all of the aforementioned nerves; therefore, anesthetizing it would result in widespread effects that would be superfluous to what is actually needed for drainage of the abscess.
GAS 462-471, 490-492; GA 238-240, 250-253

69 **D.** The inferior rectal nerve supplies the external anal sphincter muscle and the skin around the anus. Therefore this would be the best nerve to anesthetize for abscess drainage in this area. The dorsal nerve to the clitoris does not innervate the posterior recess of the perineum. The superficial perineal branch of the perineal nerve supplies the labia majora and would not need to be anesthetized in the event of a horseshoe anal abscess. The perineal nerve supplies all the perineal muscles and the labia majora, but for the area in question it does not have as direct a supply as the inferior rectal nerve. The pudendal nerve gives off all the branches above and thus anesthetizing it would result in additional unwanted effects.
GAS 462-471, 490-492; GA 238-240, 250-253

70 **B.** An aberrant obturator artery arising from the inferior epigastric arteries can be found in 20% to 30% of the population. Patients with this variation are more susceptible to inadvertent damage during certain surgeries if the surgeon is not aware of presence of the aberrant artery. The other arteries listed would be less likely to be injured because the surgeon would assume they are present and will thus take great care in making sure not to staple them.
GAS 246, 471-476, 492-494; GA 258, 260, 263, 276, 296, 298, 326

71 **E.** The afferents of the testis and most of the ductus accompany sympathetics to enter the chain at T10-L2, with cell bodies in the dorsal root ganglia of those spinal nerves. (That's why a kick in the testis seems to hurt so terribly in the upper belly.) The more proximal portion of the ductus has sensory fibers in the pelvic splanchnics. The ilioinguinal nerve is somatic and innervates the upper and medial thigh as well as the anterior scrotum and skin at the root of the penis, not the ductus deferens. The iliohypogastric nerve is an anterior abdominal wall nerve that innervates transverse and oblique abdominal muscles, supplies skin above the pubis, and has cutaneous supply to the lateral buttocks. The genital branch of the genitofemoral nerve supplies the cremaster muscle and the scrotum.
GAS 462-471, 490-492; GA 238-240, 250-253

72 **A.** The ovarian arteries arise from the abdominal aorta, descend retroperitoneally along the posterior abdominal wall, and cross just anterior to the external iliac vessels. The ovarian arteries are the most likely source of blood from a hematoma following a tubal ligation. The ascending and descending uterine arteries and superior and inferior vesicle arteries branch from the internal iliac arteries and are not likely to be the source of blood in this situation.
GAS 471-476, 492-494; GA 137, 182, 235

73 **C.** The ovarian vessels lie anterior to the ureter just proximal to the bifurcation of the aorta. The ureter is the structure that is at the most risk when ligating the ovarian vessels. The vaginal artery is a branch of the uterine artery. The uterine artery does anastomose with the ovarian vessels via the ascending uterine artery; however, it lies too far distally to be at risk during ligation of the ovarian vessels. The internal pudendal artery and pudendal nerve mostly lie in the perineum and are not at risk.
GAS 471-476, 492-494; GA 137, 182, 235

74 **C.** The conjugate diameter of the pelvis (anteroposterior) is not altered by relaxation of the pelvic joints. The transverse diameter is the longest distance extending from the middle of one pelvic brim to the other. The interspinous distance is the distance between the ischial spines and changes dramatically during pregnancy due to relaxation of the joints. The diagonal conjugate and oblique diameters are slightly increased during pregnancy due to the effects of the hormone relaxin.
GAS 421-433; GA 206-207

75 **D.** The obturator nerve innervates the major adductors of the thigh and the skin on the medial aspect of the distal thigh. Damage to the obturator nerve is the most likely cause for the sensory and motor deficit experienced by the patient. The genitofemoral nerve is motor to the cremaster muscle and sensory to the skin over the femoral triangle. The ilioinguinal nerve innervates the skin over the labium majus and upper,

inner thigh. The iliohypogastric nerve supplies skin over the anterolateral gluteal region and a strip to the area above the pubis. The lumbosacral trunk contains motor and sensory fibers from L4 and L5 and is the lumbar contribution to the lumbosacral plexus.
GAS 462-471, 490-492; GA 238-240, 250-253

76 A. The neural cell bodies responsible for erection are located in the sacral parasympathetic nucleus (intermediomedial cell column). The parasympathetic nervous system is responsible for producing an erection. The sacral sympathetic chain ganglia would not be responsible for the action of erection but rather the action of ejaculation. The inferior mesenteric ganglion would not contain parasympathetic neural cell bodies responsible for erection because they go to the hindgut. The superior hypogastric plexus contains few if any parasympathetic fibers and is not the primary location for the parasympathetic neural cell bodies. The intermediolateral column of L1 and L2 contains nerve cell bodies of preganglionic sympathetic neurons and therefore would not contribute to producing an erection.
GAS 462-471, 490-492; GA 238-240, 250-253

77 B. The interspinous distance is the distance between the ischial spines. The interspinous distance is usually the shortest distance, therefore being the most restricted area along the birth canal. The true conjugate diameter is the anteroposterior distance and does not change. The transverse diameter, oblique diameter, and diagonal conjugate diameter can change slightly during pregnancy, but the interspinous distance changes the most during birth; plus, it is more easily measured.
GAS 421-433; GA 206-207

78 D. Lymph vessels from the testicles follow the path of the testicular blood supply (abdominal aorta), and therefore lymph from the testicles drains into the lumbar nodes. The superficial inguinal lymph nodes drain lymph from the lower limb. The deep inguinal nodes drain lymph from the superficial inguinal nodes, the glans of the penis, and spongy urethra. The external iliac nodes drain lymph from anterosuperior pelvic structures and receive lymph from the deep inguinal nodes. Internal iliac nodes drain lymph from inferior pelvic structures and receive lymph from the sacral nodes.
GAS 477, 496; GA 254-256

79 C. Uterine artery embolization is performed to starve uterine fibroids of their blood supply resulting in a decrease in size of these benign tumors. Following the procedure, the uterus receives collateral blood supply from the ovarian artery (a direct branch of the abdominal aorta). The external iliac, inferior mesenteric, internal pudendal, and superior mesenteric arteries do not provide adequate collateral blood supply to the uterus.
GAS 471-476, 492-494; GA 234-235

5

LOWER LIMB

1 A 42-year-old man is admitted to the emergency department after his automobile hit a tree, and he is treated for a pelvic fracture and several deep lacerations. Physical examination reveals that dorsiflexion and inversion of the left foot and extension of the big toe are very weak. Sensation from the dorsum of the foot, skin of the sole, and the lateral aspect of the foot has been lost and the patellar reflex is normal. The foot is everted and plantar flexed. Which of the following structures is most likely injured?

- ☐ **A.** The lumbosacral trunk at linea terminalis
- ☐ **B.** L5 and S1 spinal nerves torn at the intervertebral foramen
- ☐ **C.** Fibular (peroneal) division of the sciatic nerve at the neck of the fibula
- ☐ **D.** Sciatic nerve injury at the "doorway to the gluteal region"
- ☐ **E.** Tibial nerve in popliteal fossa

2 A 23-year-old man is admitted to the emergency department with a deep, bleeding stab wound of the pelvis. After the bleeding has been arrested, an MRI examination gives evidence that the right ventral primary ramus of L4 has been transected. Which of the following problems will most likely be seen during physical examination?

- ☐ **A.** Reduction or loss of sensation from the medial aspect of the leg
- ☐ **B.** Loss of the Achilles tendon reflex
- ☐ **C.** Weakness of abduction of the thigh at the hip joint
- ☐ **D.** Inability to evert the foot
- ☐ **E.** Reduction or loss of sensation from the medial aspect of the leg and loss of Achilles tendon reflex

3 A 30-year-old male suffered a superior gluteal nerve injury in a motorcycle crash in which his right lower limb was caught beneath the bike. He is stabilized in the emergency department. Later he is examined and he exhibits a waddling gait and a positive Trendelenburg sign. Which of the following would be the most likely physical finding in this patient?

- ☐ **A.** Difficulty in standing from a sitting position
- ☐ **B.** The left side of the pelvis droops or sags when he attempts to stand with his weight supported just by the right lower limb.
- ☐ **C.** The right side of the pelvis droops or sags when he attempts to stand with his weight supported just by the left lower limb.
- ☐ **D.** Weakened flexion of the right hip
- ☐ **E.** Difficulty in sitting from a standing position

4 A 45-year-old male is treated at the hospital after he fell from his bicycle. Radiographic examination reveals fractures both of the tibia and the fibula. On physical examination the patient has a foot drop, but

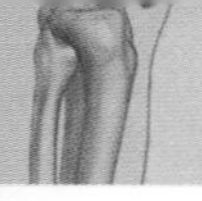

normal eversion (Fig. 5-1). Which of the following nerves is most likely injured?

- ▢ **A.** Tibial
- ▢ **B.** Common fibular (peroneal)
- ▢ **C.** Superficial fibular (peroneal)
- ▢ **D.** Saphenous
- ▢ **E.** Deep fibular (peroneal)

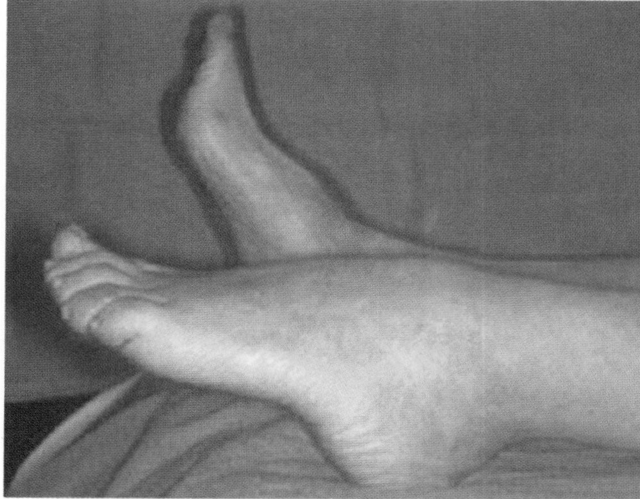

Fig. 5-1

5 A 49-year-old construction worker is admitted to the emergency department with a painful lump on the proximal medial aspect of his thigh. Radiographic and physical examinations reveal that the patient has a herniation of abdominal viscera beneath the inguinal ligament into the thigh. Through which of the following openings will a hernia of this type initially pass to extend from the abdomen into the thigh?

- ▢ **A.** Femoral ring
- ▢ **B.** Superficial inguinal ring
- ▢ **C.** Deep inguinal ring
- ▢ **D.** Fossa ovalis
- ▢ **E.** Obturator canal

6 A 37-year-old male is admitted to the hospital after an injury to his foot while playing flag football with friends on a Saturday morning. A series of radiographs demonstrates a fracture involving the talocrural (tibiotalar, ankle) joint. Which movements are the major ones to be affected by this injury?

- ▢ **A.** Plantar flexion and dorsiflexion
- ▢ **B.** Inversion and eversion
- ▢ **C.** Plantar flexion, dorsiflexion, inversion, and eversion
- ▢ **D.** Plantar flexion and inversion
- ▢ **E.** Dorsiflexion and eversion

7 After dividing the overlying superficial tissues and gluteal musculature in a 68-year-old female patient, the orthopedic surgeon carefully identified the underlying structures. The key landmark in the gluteal region, relied upon in explorations of this area, is provided by which of the following structures?

- ▢ **A.** Gluteus medius
- ▢ **B.** Obturator internus tendon
- ▢ **C.** Sciatic nerve
- ▢ **D.** Piriformis muscle
- ▢ **E.** Spine of the ischium

8 A 16-year-old male received a superficial cut on the lateral side of his foot while playing football and is admitted to the emergency department where the wound is sutured. Four days later the patient returns to the hospital with high fever and swollen lymph nodes. Which group of nodes will first receive lymph from the infected wound?

- ▢ **A.** Popliteal
- ▢ **B.** Vertical group of superficial inguinal
- ▢ **C.** Deep inguinal
- ▢ **D.** Horizontal group of superficial inguinal
- ▢ **E.** Internal iliac

9 A 45-year-old male presents at the local emergency clinic with the complaint of a painful knee and difficulty in walking. A CT scan examination reveals a very large cyst in the popliteal fossa compressing the tibial nerve. Which movement will most likely be affected?

- ▢ **A.** Dorsiflexion of the foot
- ▢ **B.** Flexion of the thigh
- ▢ **C.** Extension of the digits
- ▢ **D.** Extension of the leg
- ▢ **E.** Plantar flexion of the foot

10 A 19-year-old football player was hit on the lateral side of his knee just as he put that foot on the ground. Unable to walk without assistance, he is taken to the hospital. An MRI examination reveals a torn medial collateral ligament. Which structure would most likely also be injured due to its attachment to this ligament?

- ▢ **A.** Medial meniscus
- ▢ **B.** Anterior cruciate ligament
- ▢ **C.** Lateral meniscus
- ▢ **D.** Posterior cruciate ligament
- ▢ **E.** Tendon of the semitendinosus

11 A 49-year-old man underwent a coronary bypass graft procedure using the great (long) saphenous vein. Postoperatively the patient complains of pain and general

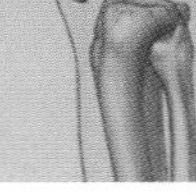

lack of normal sensation on the medial surface of the leg and foot on the limb from which the graft was harvested. Which nerve was most likely injured during surgery?

- ▢ **A.** Common fibular (peroneal)
- ▢ **B.** Superficial fibular (peroneal)
- ▢ **C.** Lateral sural
- ▢ **D.** Saphenous
- ▢ **E.** Tibial

12 A 22-year-old football player is admitted to the hospital with pain and swelling over the lateral aspect of the ankle. The emergency department doctor diagnoses an inversion sprain. Which ligament was most likely injured?

- ▢ **A.** Calcaneonavicular (spring)
- ▢ **B.** Calcaneofibular
- ▢ **C.** Long plantar
- ▢ **D.** Short plantar
- ▢ **E.** Deltoid

13 A 72-year-old woman is admitted to the hospital with a painful right foot. A CT scan examination reveals a thrombotic occlusion of the femoral artery in the proximal part of the adductor canal. Which artery will most likely provide blood supply to the leg through the genicular anastomosis?

- ▢ **A.** Medial circumflex femoral
- ▢ **B.** Descending branch of the lateral circumflex femoral
- ▢ **C.** First perforating branch of the deep femoral
- ▢ **D.** Inferior gluteal
- ▢ **E.** Descending genicular branch of femoral

14 A 75-year-old woman is admitted to the hospital after falling in her bathroom. Radiographic examination reveals an extracapsular fracture of the femoral neck. Which artery is most likely at risk for injury?

- ▢ **A.** Inferior gluteal
- ▢ **B.** First perforating branch of deep femoral
- ▢ **C.** Medial circumflex femoral
- ▢ **D.** Obturator
- ▢ **E.** Superior gluteal

15 A 56-year-old male with advanced bladder carcinoma suffers from difficulty while walking. Muscle testing reveals weakened adductors of the right thigh. Which nerve is most likely being compressed by the tumor to result in walking difficulty?

- ▢ **A.** Femoral
- ▢ **B.** Obturator
- ▢ **C.** Common fibular (peroneal)
- ▢ **D.** Tibial
- ▢ **E.** Sciatic

16 Upon removal of a leg cast, a 15-year-old boy complains of numbness of the dorsum of his right foot and inability to dorsiflex and evert his foot. Which is the most probable site of the nerve compression that resulted in these symptoms?

- ▢ **A.** Popliteal fossa
- ▢ **B.** Neck of the fibula
- ▢ **C.** Lateral compartment of the leg
- ▢ **D.** Anterior compartment of the leg
- ▢ **E.** Medial malleolus

17 A 32-year-old patient received a badly placed intramuscular injection to the posterior part of his gluteal region. The needle injured a motor nerve in the area. Later, he had great difficulty rising to a standing position from a seated position. Which muscle was most likely affected by the injury?

- ▢ **A.** Gluteus maximus
- ▢ **B.** Gluteus minimus
- ▢ **C.** Hamstrings
- ▢ **D.** Iliopsoas
- ▢ **E.** Obturator internus

18 During the preparation of an evening meal a female medical student dropped a sharp, slender kitchen knife. The blade pierced the first web space of her foot, resulting in numbness along adjacent sides of the first and second toes. Which nerve was most likely injured?

- ▢ **A.** Saphenous
- ▢ **B.** Deep fibular (peroneal)
- ▢ **C.** Superficial fibular (peroneal)
- ▢ **D.** Sural
- ▢ **E.** Common fibular (peroneal)

19 Following an injury suffered in a soccer match, a 32-year-old female is examined in a seated position in the orthopedic clinic. Holding the right tibia with both hands, the clinician can press the tibia backward under the distal part of her femur. The left tibia cannot be displaced in this way. Which structure was most likely damaged in the right knee?

- ▢ **A.** Anterior cruciate ligament
- ▢ **B.** Lateral collateral ligament
- ▢ **C.** Medial collateral ligament
- ▢ **D.** Medial meniscus
- ▢ **E.** Posterior cruciate ligament

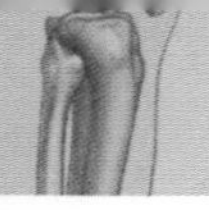

20 A 22-year-old woman is admitted to the emergency department after another vehicle collided with the passenger side of the convertible in which she was riding. Radiographic examination reveals an avulsion fracture of the greater trochanter. Which of the following muscles would continue to function normally if such an injury was incurred?

- ☐ **A.** Piriformis
- ☐ **B.** Obturator internus
- ☐ **C.** Gluteus medius
- ☐ **D.** Gluteus maximus
- ☐ **E.** Gluteus minimus

21 The news reported that the 58-year-old ambassador received a slashing wound to the upper medial thigh and died from exsanguination in less than 2 minutes. What was the most likely nature of his injury?

- ☐ **A.** The femoral artery was cut at the inguinal ligament.
- ☐ **B.** A vessel or vessels were injured at the apex of the femoral triangle.
- ☐ **C.** The femoral vein was transected at its junction with the saphenous vein.
- ☐ **D.** The medial circumflex femoral was severed at its origin.
- ☐ **E.** The deep femoral artery was divided at its origin.

22 A 72-year-old female suffered a hip dislocation when she fell down the steps to her garage. Which of the following structures is most significant in resisting hyperextension of the hip joint?

- ☐ **A.** Pubofemoral ligament
- ☐ **B.** Ischiofemoral ligament
- ☐ **C.** Iliofemoral ligament
- ☐ **D.** Negative pressure in the acetabular fossa
- ☐ **E.** Gluteus maximus muscle

23 A 75-year-old man is transported to the emergency department with severe pain of his right hip and thigh. A radiographic examination reveals avascular necrosis of the femoral head (Fig. 5-2). Which of the following conditions most likely occurred to produce avascular necrosis in this patient?

- ☐ **A.** Dislocation of the hip with tearing of the ligament of the head of the femur
- ☐ **B.** Intertrochanteric fracture of the femur
- ☐ **C.** Intracapsular femoral neck fracture
- ☐ **D.** Thrombosis of the obturator artery
- ☐ **E.** Comminuted fracture of the extracapsular femoral neck

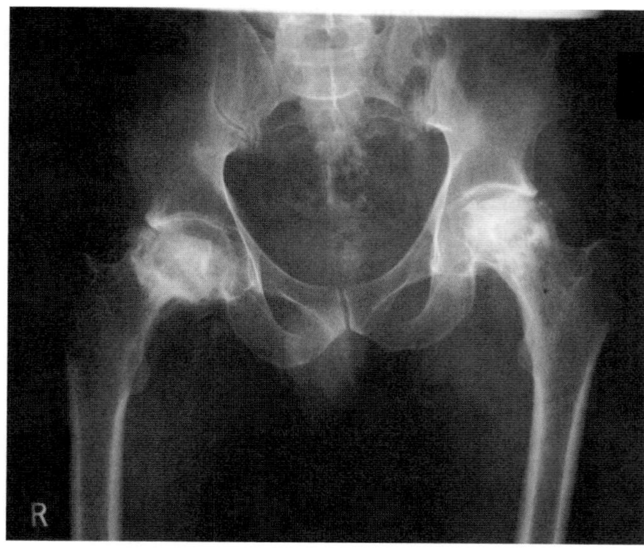

Fig. 5-2

24 A 58-year-old male farmer was accidentally struck with a scythe (a long, curved cutting blade) by another worker while they were cutting wheat. He was admitted to the county hospital with severe bleeding. During physical examination the doctor noted that the patient has foot drop, although sensation was present over the dorsum of the foot and the skin of the posterior calf. Which of the following nerves was injured?

- ☐ **A.** Femoral nerve
- ☐ **B.** Sciatic nerve
- ☐ **C.** Superficial fibular (peroneal) nerve
- ☐ **D.** Deep fibular (peroneal) nerve
- ☐ **E.** Common fibular (peroneal) nerve

25 A 45-year-old man is admitted to the emergency department after experiencing a sharp pain while lifting a box of books. He told the physician that he "felt the pain in my backside, the back of my thigh, my leg, and the side of my foot." During physical examination it is observed that his Achilles tendon jerk is weakened on the affected side. Which is the most likely cause of injury?

- ☐ **A.** Disk lesion at L3-4
- ☐ **B.** Disk lesion at L4-5
- ☐ **C.** Disk lesion at L5-S1
- ☐ **D.** Disk lesion at S1-2
- ☐ **E.** Gluteal crush syndrome of sciatic nerve or piriformis syndrome

26 A 55-year-old woman is admitted to the emergency department after an automobile crash. Physical examination reveals that the patient's foot is everted and she cannot invert it. A weakness in dorsiflexion and inversion of the foot is noted. Her ipsilateral patellar reflex is reduced in quality, although the Achilles tendon reflex is brisk. Knee extension is almost normal, as are all hip movements and knee flexion. Sensation is greatly reduced on the medial side of the leg. Which of the following nerves is most likely injured?

- ▢ **A.** Femoral nerve
- ▢ **B.** L4 spinal nerve
- ▢ **C.** L4 and L5 spinal nerves
- ▢ **D.** Common fibular (peroneal) nerve
- ▢ **E.** Tibial nerve

27 A 46-year-old woman stepped on a broken wine bottle on the sidewalk and the sharp glass entered the posterior part of her foot. The patient was admitted to the hospital, and a physical examination concluded that her lateral plantar nerve had been transected (cut through). Which of the following conditions will most likely be confirmed by physical examination?

- ▢ **A.** Loss of sensation over the plantar surface of the third toe
- ▢ **B.** Paralysis of the abductor hallucis
- ▢ **C.** Paralysis of the interossei and adductor hallucis
- ▢ **D.** Flexor hallucis brevis paralysis
- ▢ **E.** Flexor digitorum brevis paralysis

28 A 22-year-old male martial arts competitor was examined by the clinician because of pain and serious disability suffered from a kick to the side of his knee. Physical examination revealed a dark bruise just distal to the head of the fibula. Which of the following muscles will most likely be paralyzed?

- ▢ **A.** Tibialis anterior and extensor digitorum longus
- ▢ **B.** Tibialis posterior
- ▢ **C.** Soleus and gastrocnemius
- ▢ **D.** Plantaris and popliteus
- ▢ **E.** Flexor digitorum longus and flexor hallucis longus

29 A 61-year-old female immigrant had been diagnosed with spinal tuberculosis. The woman had developed a fluctuant, red, tender bulge on one flank, with a similar bulge in the groin on the same side. This presentation is likely due to spread of disease process within the fascia of a muscle with which of the following actions at the hip?

- ▢ **A.** Abduction
- ▢ **B.** Adduction
- ▢ **C.** Extension
- ▢ **D.** Flexion
- ▢ **E.** Internal rotation

30 In an accident during cleanup of an old residential area of the city, the Achilles tendon of a 32-year-old worker was cut through by the blade of a brush cutter. The patient is admitted to the hospital and a laceration of the Achilles tendon is diagnosed. Which of the following bones serves as an insertion for the Achilles tendon?

- ▢ **A.** Calcaneus
- ▢ **B.** Fibula
- ▢ **C.** Cuboid
- ▢ **D.** Talus
- ▢ **E.** Navicular

31 A 27-year-old female tennis pro injured her ankle during the quarterfinal match. A physical examination at the outpatient clinic revealed a severe inversion sprain of the ankle. Which of the following structures is most commonly damaged in such injuries?

- ▢ **A.** Medial plantar nerve
- ▢ **B.** Tibial nerve
- ▢ **C.** Anterior talofibular ligament
- ▢ **D.** Posterior talofibular ligament
- ▢ **E.** Deltoid ligament

32 A 41-year-old man is admitted to the emergency department with a swollen and painful foot. Radiographic examination reveals that the head of the talus has become displaced inferiorly, thereby causing the medial longitudinal arch of the foot to fall. What would be the most likely cause in this case?

- ▢ **A.** Tearing of the plantar calcaneonavicular (spring) ligament
- ▢ **B.** Fracture of the cuboid bone
- ▢ **C.** Interruption of the plantar aponeurosis
- ▢ **D.** Sprain of the anterior talofibular ligament
- ▢ **E.** Sprain of the deltoid ligament

33 During a football game a 21-year-old wide receiver was illegally blocked by a linebacker, who threw himself against the posterolateral aspect of the runner's left knee. As he lay on the ground, the wide receiver grasped his knee in obvious pain. Which of the following structures is frequently subject to injury from this type of force against the knee?

- ▢ **A.** Fibular collateral ligament
- ▢ **B.** Anterior cruciate ligament
- ▢ **C.** Lateral meniscus and posterior cruciate ligament
- ▢ **D.** Fibular collateral and posterior cruciate ligament
- ▢ **E.** All the ligaments of the knee will be affected.

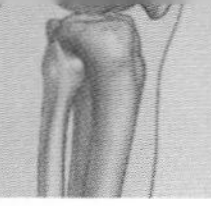

34 Arteriography of an 82-year-old female reveals a possible cause for her limb pain during her workout routines in the health spa. The artery that was occluded is one that should have been demonstrable passing between the proximal part of the space between the tibia and fibula. Which of the following arteries is most likely affected?

- ☐ **A.** Deep femoral
- ☐ **B.** Popliteal
- ☐ **C.** Posterior tibial
- ☐ **D.** Fibular (peroneal)
- ☐ **E.** Anterior tibial

35 A 43-year-old man visits the outpatient clinic with a painful, swollen knee joint. The patient's history reveals chronic gonococcal arthritis. A knee aspiration is ordered for bacterial culture of the synovial fluid. A standard suprapatellar approach is used, and the needle passes from the lateral aspect of the thigh into the region immediately proximal to and deep to the patella. Through which of the following muscles would the needle pass?

- ☐ **A.** Adductor magnus
- ☐ **B.** Short head of biceps femoris
- ☐ **C.** Rectus femoris
- ☐ **D.** Sartorius
- ☐ **E.** Vastus lateralis

36 A 34-year-old power lifter visits the outpatient clinic because he has difficulty walking. During physical examination it is observed that the patient has a problem unlocking the knee joint to permit flexion of the leg. Which of the following muscles is most likely damaged?

- ☐ **A.** Biceps femoris
- ☐ **B.** Gastrocnemius
- ☐ **C.** Popliteus
- ☐ **D.** Semimembranosus
- ☐ **E.** Rectus femoris

37 A 32-year-old male basketball player comes down hard on his ankle. He is admitted to the outpatient clinic, and radiographic examination reveals a Pott's fracture. What ligament is most likely injured?

- ☐ **A.** Calcaneofibular ligament
- ☐ **B.** Deltoid ligament
- ☐ **C.** Spring ligament
- ☐ **D.** Plantar ligament
- ☐ **E.** Long plantar ligament

38 A 23-year-old male is admitted to the emergency department with pain and cyanosis of his right lower limb. Doppler ultrasound studies reveal deficiency in development of his femoral artery, which appears to terminate midthigh. A thrombotic occlusion is seen in an unusual, rather tortuous, large vessel in the posterior compartment of the thigh, arising in the gluteal area and continuous inferiorly with a normal-appearing popliteal artery. It is decided that a vascular graft should be placed from the femoral artery to the popliteal artery. What is the identity of the aberrant artery?

- ☐ **A.** A large, fifth perforating branch of the femoral
- ☐ **B.** An ischiatic branch of the inferior gluteal artery
- ☐ **C.** Descending branch of the medial circumflex femoral
- ☐ **D.** Descending branch of the superior gluteal artery
- ☐ **E.** An enlarged descending lateral circumflex femoral artery

39 When he attempted to lift one side of his new electric automobile from the ground to demonstrate his strength, the 51-year-old male felt a sharp pain in his back and quickly dropped the vehicle. Upon examination it is observed that the patient has deficits in sensation on the dorsum and sole of his foot and marked weakness in abduction and lateral rotation of the lower limb. What was the nature of his injury?

- ☐ **A.** Piriformis syndrome, with entrapment of the sciatic nerve
- ☐ **B.** Disk lesion at L3-4
- ☐ **C.** Disk lesion at L4-5
- ☐ **D.** Disk lesion at L5-S1
- ☐ **E.** Posterior hip dislocation

40 A 43-year-old female is examined by a neurologist, to whom she complains of pain in her lower limb of 6 months' duration. She has pain in the gluteal area, thigh, and leg. The neurologist observes reduced sensation over the dorsum and lateral side of the involved foot and some weakness in foot dorsiflexion and eversion. A diagnosis of a piriformis entrapment syndrome is made, with compression of the fibular (peroneal) division of the sciatic nerve. Which of the following conditions did the neurologist also most likely find during her physical examination of the patient?

- ☐ **A.** Paralysis of plantar flexion
- ☐ **B.** Instability of the knee, due to paralysis of the quadriceps femoris

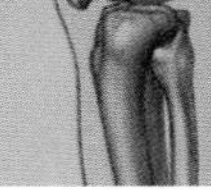

- ▢ **C.** Foot drop
- ▢ **D.** Spasm or clonic contractures of the adductor musculature of the thigh
- ▢ **E.** Loss of sensation in the gluteal area, by paralysis of anterior cluneal nerves

41 Three years following a 62-year-old's hip replacement, the man's CAT scans indicated that two of his larger hip muscles had been replaced by adipose tissue. The opinion is offered that his superior gluteal nerve could have been injured during the replacement procedure, and the muscles supplied by that nerve had atrophied and been replaced by fat. Which of the following muscles receives its innervation from the superior gluteal nerve?

- ▢ **A.** Tensor fasciae latae
- ▢ **B.** Rectus femoris
- ▢ **C.** Gluteus maximus
- ▢ **D.** Piriformis
- ▢ **E.** Quadratus femoris

42 A popliteal arterial aneurysm can be very fragile, bursting with great loss of blood and the potential loss of the leg if it is not dealt with safely and effectively. In a previous century, Dr. John Hunter discovered that if a primary artery of the thigh is temporarily compressed, blood flow in the popliteal artery can be reduced long enough to treat the aneurysm in the popliteal fossa surgically, with safety. What structure is indicated in Fig. 5-3 that is related to his surgical procedure?

- ▢ **A.** Sartorius
- ▢ **B.** Femoral vein
- ▢ **C.** Femoral artery
- ▢ **D.** Gracilis
- ▢ **E.** Adductor brevis

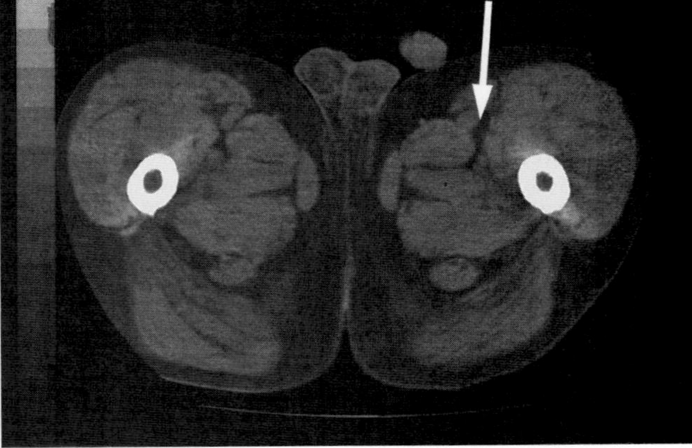

Fig. 5-3 From Weir J, Abrahams P: *Imaging Atlas of Human Anatomy,* ed 3, p 159, Philadelphia, 2003, Mosby.

43 A 49-year-old male worker fell from a ladder, with his weight impacting on the heels of his feet. Radiographic examination reveals comminuted calcaneal fractures. After the injury the contraction of which one of the following muscles could most likely increase the pain in the injured foot?

- ▢ **A.** Flexor digitorum profundus
- ▢ **B.** Gastrocnemius
- ▢ **C.** Tibialis posterior
- ▢ **D.** Tibialis anterior
- ▢ **E.** Fibularis (peroneus) longus

44 A 24-year-old female received a small-caliber bullet wound to the popliteal fossa from a drive-by assailant. The patient was admitted to the emergency department, where the surgeons recognized that the bullet had severed the tibial nerve. Such an injury would most likely result in which of the following?

- ▢ **A.** Inability to extend the leg at the knee
- ▢ **B.** Foot drop
- ▢ **C.** A dorsiflexed and everted foot
- ▢ **D.** A plantar flexed and inverted foot
- ▢ **E.** Total inability to flex the leg at the knee joint

45 An 82-year-old grandmother slipped on the polished floor in her front hall and was transported to the emergency department and admitted for examination with a complaint of great pain in her right lower limb. During physical examination it is observed by the resident that the right lower limb is laterally rotated and noticeably shorter than her left limb. Radiographic examination reveals an intracapsular fracture of the femoral neck. Which of the following arteries supplies the head of the femur in early childhood but no longer in a patient of this age?

- ▢ **A.** Superior gluteal
- ▢ **B.** Lateral circumflex femoral
- ▢ **C.** A branch of the obturator artery
- ▢ **D.** Inferior gluteal
- ▢ **E.** Internal pudendal

46 A 19-year-old patient is admitted to the orthopedic service with a complaint of severe pain in his very swollen and discolored foot. He states that he hurt the foot when jumping from his girlfriend's bedroom window to the concrete driveway below. Plain film radiographic studies reveal that the head of the talus has become displaced inferiorly, thereby causing the medial longitudinal arch of the foot to fall. What would be the most likely, serious problem in such a case?

- ▢ **A.** Tearing of the plantar calcaneonavicular (spring) ligament
- ▢ **B.** Fracture of the cuboid bone
- ▢ **C.** Interruption of the plantar aponeurosis
- ▢ **D.** Sprain of the anterior talofibular ligament
- ▢ **E.** Disruption of the distal tibiofibular ligament

47 A 29-year-old male police officer is examined in a neighborhood clinic, with a complaint of discomfort in the lateral thigh. During the taking of the patient's medical history the physician observes that the policeman is rather overweight and that he is wearing a heavy leather belt, to which numerous objects are attached, including his empty holster. After a thorough physical examination a tentative diagnosis is advanced of meralgia paresthetica. Which of the following nerves is most likely involved?

- ▢ **A.** Superior gluteal
- ▢ **B.** Femoral
- ▢ **C.** Obturator
- ▢ **D.** Fibular (peroneal) division of sciatic
- ▢ **E.** Lateral femoral cutaneous

48 The swollen and painful left foot of a 23-year-old female long-distance runner is examined in the university orthopedic clinic. She states that she stepped on an unseen sharp object while running through the park several days earlier. Emergent surgery is ordered to deal with her tarsal tunnel syndrome. The tarsal tunnel is occupied normally by tendons, vessels, and nerves that pass beneath a very strong band of tissue (the laciniate ligament) on the medial side of the ankle. What is the most anterior of the structures that pass through this tunnel?

- ▢ **A.** Flexor hallucis longus tendon
- ▢ **B.** Plantaris tendon
- ▢ **C.** Tibialis anterior tendon
- ▢ **D.** Tibialis posterior tendon
- ▢ **E.** Tibial nerve

49 A 42-year-old male sign painter is admitted to the emergency department after falling to the sidewalk from his ladder. Radiographic examination reveals a fracture of the proximal femur. Which of the following arteries supplies the proximal part of the femur?

- ▢ **A.** Deep circumflex iliac
- ▢ **B.** Acetabular branch of obturator
- ▢ **C.** Lateral circumflex femoral
- ▢ **D.** A branch of profunda femoris
- ▢ **E.** Medial circumflex femoral

50 A 22-year-old man is admitted to the emergency department after falling from his bicycle. Radiographic examination reveals a fracture of the tibia above the ankle. MRI and physical examination reveal that the tibial nerve is severed on the posterior aspect of the tibia. Which of the following signs will most likely be present during physical examination?

- ▢ **A.** Sensory loss of the dorsum of the foot
- ▢ **B.** Sensory loss on the sole of the foot
- ▢ **C.** Foot drop
- ▢ **D.** Paralysis of the extensor digitorum brevis
- ▢ **E.** Sensory loss of the entire foot

51 A 24-year-old man is admitted to the emergency department after a car collision. Radiographic examination reveals a fracture at the junction of the middle and lower thirds of the femur. An MRI examination provides evidence that the popliteal vessels were injured when the distal fragment of the fracture was pulled posteriorly. Which of the following muscles is most likely to displace the distal fracture fragment?

- ▢ **A.** Soleus
- ▢ **B.** Gastrocnemius
- ▢ **C.** Semitendinosus
- ▢ **D.** Gracilis
- ▢ **E.** Tibialis anterior

52 A 65-year-old man is admitted to the hospital after falling from his roof while cleaning leaves and pine needles from the gutters. Among other injuries suffered in his fall, radiographic examination reveals a fracture of the talus bone in one foot. Much of the blood supply of this bone can be lost in such an injury and can result in osteonecrosis. From what artery does this bone receive its primary vascular supply?

- ▢ **A.** Medial plantar
- ▢ **B.** Lateral plantar
- ▢ **C.** Dorsalis pedis
- ▢ **D.** Anterior tibial
- ▢ **E.** Posterior tibial

53 A 58-year-old female dancer presented to the orthopedic clinic with a complaint of great pain during her work because of bilateral bunions. She was referred to a podiatric surgeon who scheduled her for surgery. The protruding bony and soft tissues of the toe were excised, and a muscle was reflected from the lateral side of the proximal phalanx, together with a sesamoid bone, upon which the muscle also inserted. What muscle was this?

- ▢ **A.** Adductor hallucis
- ▢ **B.** Abductor hallucis

- ▢ **C.** First dorsal interosseous
- ▢ **D.** First lumbrical
- ▢ **E.** Quadratus plantae

54 A 34-year-old male long-distance runner complained to the team physician of swelling and pain of his shin. Skin testing in a physical examination showed normal cutaneous sensation of the leg. Muscular strength tests, however, showed marked weakness of dorsiflexion and impaired inversion of the foot. Which nerve serves the muscles involved in the painful swelling?

- ▢ **A.** Common fibular (peroneal)
- ▢ **B.** Deep fibular (peroneal)
- ▢ **C.** Sciatic
- ▢ **D.** Superficial fibular (peroneal)
- ▢ **E.** Tibial

55 A 7-year-old girl accidentally stepped on a sharp snail shell while walking to the beach. She was admitted to the hospital, where she received a tetanus shot, and the wound was cleaned thoroughly and sutured. One week later, during a return visit to her physician, it is seen that she has great difficulty in flexing her big toe, even though there is no inflammation present in the sole of the foot. Which nerve was most likely damaged by the piercing of the shell?

- ▢ **A.** Lateral plantar nerve
- ▢ **B.** Medial plantar nerve
- ▢ **C.** Sural nerve
- ▢ **D.** Superficial fibular (peroneal) nerve
- ▢ **E.** Deep fibular (peroneal) nerve

56 A 49-year-old man is admitted to the emergency department with a cold and pale foot. Physical examination reveals that the patient suffers from peripheral vascular disease; duplex ultrasound studies indicate possible occlusion of his popliteal artery, and the pulse of the posterior tibial artery is absent. What is the most common location for palpation of the pulse of the posterior tibial artery?

- ▢ **A.** Lateral to the muscular belly of the abductor hallucis
- ▢ **B.** Posteroinferior to the medial femoral condyle
- ▢ **C.** Groove midway between the lateral malleolus and the calcaneus
- ▢ **D.** Groove midway between the medial malleolus and the calcaneus
- ▢ **E.** Medially, between the two heads of the gastrocnemius

57 The young parents were concerned that their 14-month-old daughter had not yet begun walking. Their pediatrician reassured them, saying that one of the muscles of the leg, the fibularis (peroneus) tertius, had to complete its central neurologic development before the child could lift the outer corner of the foot and walk without stumbling over her toes. What is the most common nerve supply of this muscle?

- ▢ **A.** Sural
- ▢ **B.** Lateral plantar
- ▢ **C.** Deep fibular (peroneal)
- ▢ **D.** Superficial fibular (peroneal)
- ▢ **E.** Tibial

58 A 22-year-old woman is admitted with high fever and vaginal discharge. Physical and laboratory examinations reveal gonorrheal infection. A series of intramuscular antibiotic injections are ordered. Into which of the following parts of the gluteal region should the antibiotic be injected to avoid nerve injury?

- ▢ **A.** Anterior and superior to a line between the posterior superior iliac spine and the greater trochanter
- ▢ **B.** In the middle of a line between the anterior superior iliac spine and the ischial tuberosity
- ▢ **C.** Inferolateral to a line between the posterior superior iliac spine and the greater trochanter
- ▢ **D.** Inferomedial to a line between the posterior superior iliac spine and the greater trochanter
- ▢ **E.** Halfway between the iliac tuberosity and the greater trochanter

59 A 45-year-old intoxicated male was struck by a tour bus while walking in the middle of the street. The man was admitted to the emergency department and during physical examination was diagnosed with "scissor gait," in which an individual crosses one limb in front of the other, due to powerful hip adduction. Which of the following nerves was most likely involved in this condition?

- ▢ **A.** Tibial
- ▢ **B.** Obturator
- ▢ **C.** Inferior gluteal
- ▢ **D.** Superior gluteal
- ▢ **E.** Femoral

60 The baby was quite large, and the pelvis of the mother-to-be was somewhat narrow, causing her considerable difficulty and pain during the delivery. At her specific request, it was decided to inject local anesthetic into the perineum. The genitofemoral and ilioinguinal nerves were infiltrated anteriorly, and a deep injection was made medial to the ischial tuberosity to anesthetize the pudendal nerve, which supplies much of the perineum in most cases. A few minutes later, it became very obvious to those in attendance that the injection had not been effective enough in the central and posterior parts of the perineum. A separate injection was therefore inserted lateral to the ischial tuberosity. What other nerve(s) can provide much of the sensory supply to the perineum in some individuals?

- ▢ **A.** Posterior femoral cutaneous
- ▢ **B.** Inferior cluneal nerves
- ▢ **C.** Iliohypogastric nerve
- ▢ **D.** Inferior gluteal nerve
- ▢ **E.** Middle cluneal nerves

61 A 55-year-old man is admitted to the hospital for an iliofemoral bypass. The operation is performed successfully and the blood flow between the iliac and femoral arteries is restored. During rehabilitation which of the following arteries should be palpated to monitor good circulation of the lower limb?

- ▢ **A.** Anterior tibial
- ▢ **B.** Deep fibular (peroneal)
- ▢ **C.** Deep plantar
- ▢ **D.** Dorsalis pedis
- ▢ **E.** Dorsal metatarsal

62 A 55-year-old woman is bitten by a dog in the dorsum of the foot and is admitted to the emergency department. The wound is cleaned thoroughly, during which it is seen that no tendons have been cut, but the dorsalis pedis artery and the accompanying nerve have been injured. Which of the following conditions would be expected during physical examination?

- ▢ **A.** Clubfoot
- ▢ **B.** Foot drop
- ▢ **C.** Inability to extend the big toe
- ▢ **D.** Numbness between the first and second toes
- ▢ **E.** Weakness in inversion of the foot

63 A 31-year-old female presents to the department of surgery with a complaint of Bell's palsy, which had appeared a year earlier and had resulted in paralysis of muscles of one side of her face. The chief of plastic surgery recommends a nerve graft, taking a cutaneous nerve from the lower limb to replace the defective facial nerve. The surgery is successful. Six months after the procedure, there is restoration of function of previously paralyzed facial muscles. There is an area of skin on the back of the leg laterally and also on the lateral side of the foot that has no sensation. What nerve was used in the grafting procedure?

- ▢ **A.** Superficial fibular (peroneal)
- ▢ **B.** Tibial
- ▢ **C.** Common fibular (peroneal)
- ▢ **D.** Sural
- ▢ **E.** Saphenous

64 A 10-year-old girl is admitted to the emergency department after falling from a tree in which she was playing with her friends. Radiographic and physical examinations reveal Osgood-Schlatter disease (Fig. 5-4). Which of the following bony structures is chiefly affected?

- ▢ **A.** Medial condyle of tibia
- ▢ **B.** Posterior intercondylar area
- ▢ **C.** Intercondylar eminence
- ▢ **D.** Tibial tuberosity
- ▢ **E.** Anterolateral tibial tubercle (Gerdy's tubercle)

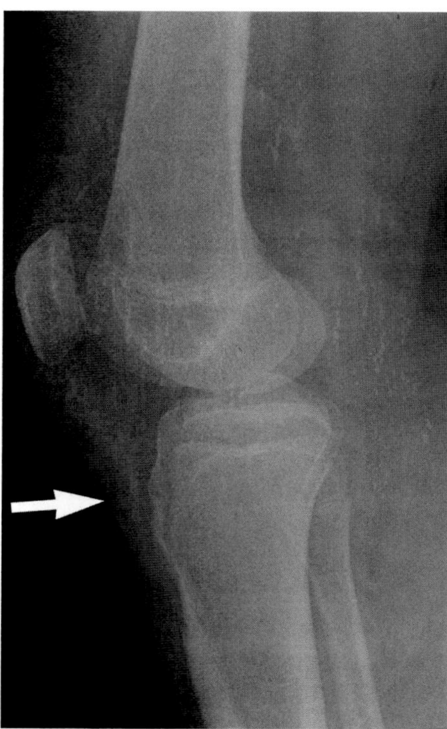

Fig. 5-4

65 An 81-year-old male is admitted to the emergency department with severe pain in his knees. The patient has a long history of osteoarthritis. Radiographic examination reveals degeneration of the joints of his lower limbs. The degeneration is more severe on the medial side of the knees, which causes his knees to be bowed outward when he stands upright. Which of the following terms best describes the condition of his knees?

- ▢ **A.** Genu varus
- ▢ **B.** Genu valgus
- ▢ **C.** Coxa varus

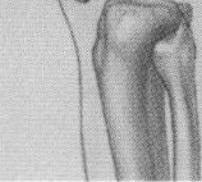

- ☐ **D.** Coxa valgus
- ☐ **E.** Hallux valgus

66 The patellar reflex appears to be markedly reduced in a 33-year-old diabetic female patient, due to deficient vascular supply of the nerves of her lower limb. The tendon of which of the following muscles is stretched during the patellar reflex?

- ☐ **A.** Quadriceps femoris
- ☐ **B.** Quadratus femoris
- ☐ **C.** Sartorius
- ☐ **D.** Pectineus
- ☐ **E.** Biceps femoris

67 A 52-year-old woman is admitted to the emergency department after severely injuring her right lower limb when she fell from a trampoline. Radiographic examination reveals a trimalleolar fracture of the ankle involving the lateral malleolus, medial malleolus, and the posterior process of the tibia. Which of the following bones will also most likely be affected?

- ☐ **A.** Navicular
- ☐ **B.** Calcaneus
- ☐ **C.** Cuneiform
- ☐ **D.** Cuboid
- ☐ **E.** Talus

68 A 72-year-old male visits the outpatient clinic with a complaint of great pain when walking. Physical examination reveals the problems in his feet as shown in Fig. 5-5. What is the most likely diagnosis?

- ☐ **A.** Coxa varus
- ☐ **B.** Coxa valgus
- ☐ **C.** Genu valgus
- ☐ **D.** Genu vara
- ☐ **E.** Hallux valgus

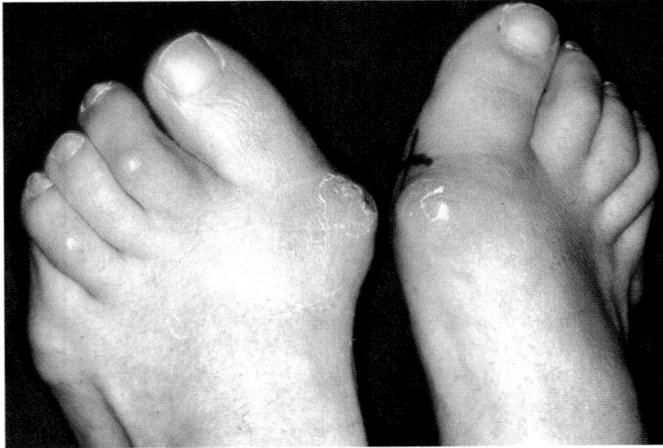

Fig. 5-5

69 A 63-year-old woman visits the outpatient orthopedic clinic with the complaint of pain in her foot for more than a year. Radiographic and physical examinations give evidence of constant extension at the metatarsophalangeal joints, hyperflexion at the proximal interphalangeal joints, and extension of distal interphalangeal joints (Fig. 5-6). Which of the following terms is most accurate to describe the signs of physical examination?

- ☐ **A.** Pes planus
- ☐ **B.** Pes cavus
- ☐ **C.** Hammer toes
- ☐ **D.** Claw toes
- ☐ **E.** Hallux valgus

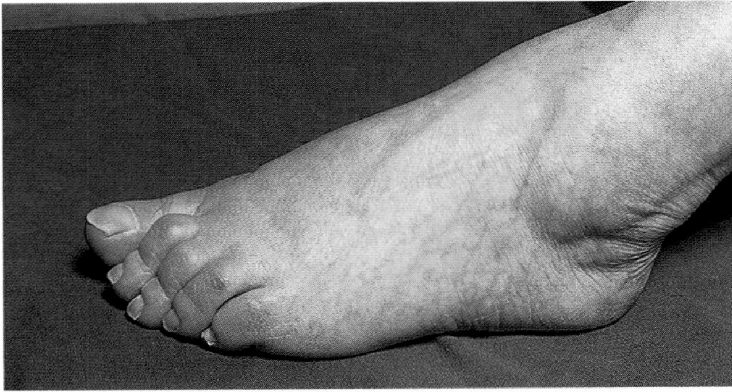

Fig. 5-6

70 A 58-year-old man is admitted to the hospital with pain in his lower limb for the past 2 months. Physical examination reveals point tenderness in the region of his greater sciatic foramen, with pain radiating down the posterior aspect of his thigh. An MRI examination reveals that the patient suffers from piriformis entrapment syndrome. He is directed to treatment by a physical therapist for stretching and relaxation of the muscle. Entrapment of which of the following nerves can mimic piriformis entrapment syndrome?

- ☐ **A.** L4
- ☐ **B.** L5
- ☐ **C.** S1
- ☐ **D.** S2
- ☐ **E.** S3

71 A 22-year-old woman is found in a comatose condition, having lain for an unknown length of time on the tile floor of the courtyard. She is found in possession of cocaine. The patient is transported to the hospital while EMT personnel receive instructions for treatment of drug overdose. During the physical examination the patient's gluteal region shows signs of ischemia. After regaining consciousness, she exhibits paralysis of knee flexion and dorsal and plantar flexion and sensory loss in the limb. What is the most likely diagnosis?

- A. Tibial nerve loss
- B. S1-2 nerve compression
- C. Gluteal crush injury
- D. Piriformis entrapment syndrome
- E. Femoral nerve entrapment

72 A 75-year-old man is admitted to the emergency department with severe pain at his right hip and thigh. An MRI examination reveals avascular necrosis of the femoral head (Fig. 5-7). Which of the following arteries is most likely injured, resulting in avascular necrosis?

- A. Deep circumflex iliac
- B. Acetabular branch of obturator
- C. Descending branch of lateral circumflex femoral
- D. Perforating branch of profunda femoris
- E. Ascending branch of medial circumflex femoral

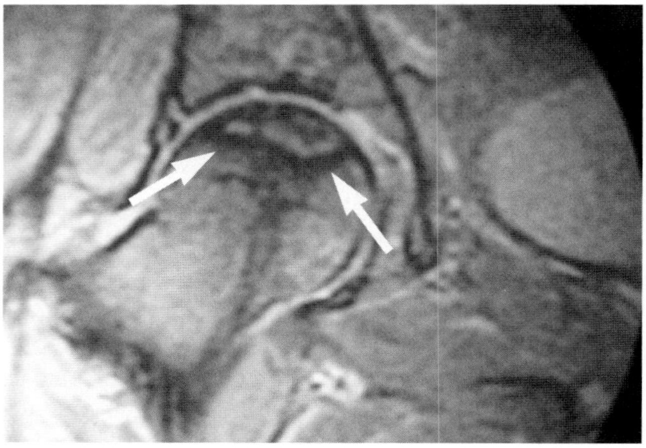

Fig. 5-7

73 A 27-year-old female had suffered a penetrating injury in the popliteal region by an object thrown from a riding lawnmower. She was admitted to the emergency department for removal of the foreign body. After making a midline incision in the skin of the popliteal fossa, the surgical resident observed a vein of moderate size in the superficial tissues. What vein would be expected at this location?

- A. Popliteal vein
- B. Perforating tributary to the deep femoral vein
- C. Great saphenous vein
- D. Lesser (short) saphenous vein
- E. Superior medial genicular vein

74 A 58-year-old diabetic patient is admitted to the hospital with a painful foot. Physical examination reveals that the patient suffers from peripheral vascular disease. There is no detectable dorsalis pedis arterial pulse, but the posterior tibial pulse is strong. Which of the following arteries will most likely provide adequate collateral supply from the plantar surface to the toes and dorsum of the foot?

- A. Anterior tibial
- B. Fibular (peroneal)
- C. Arcuate
- D. Medial plantar
- E. Lateral plantar

75 A 32-year-old man is admitted to the emergency department after an injury to his foot while playing football with his college friends. An MRI examination reveals multiple tendinous tears (Fig. 5-8). Which of the following bones is associated with the muscle tears?

- A. Navicular
- B. Cuboid
- C. Calcaneus
- D. Sustentaculum tali
- E. Talus

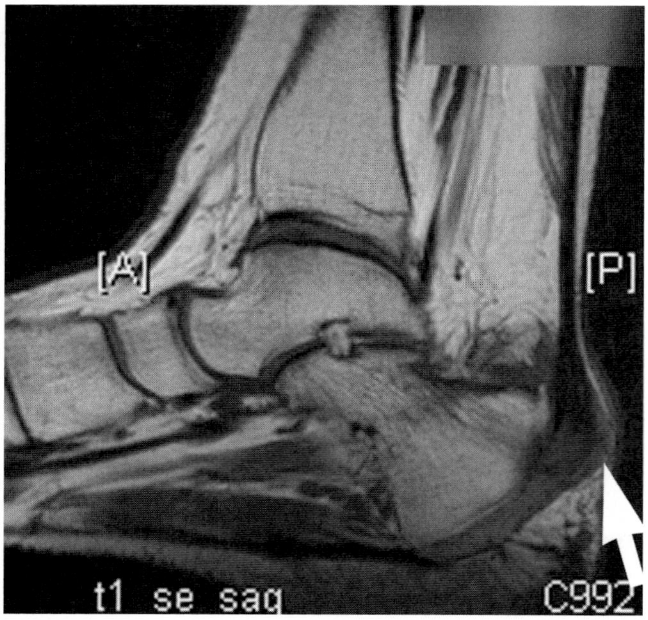

Fig. 5-8

76 An 18-year-old professional tennis player fell when she leaped for an overhead shot and landed with her foot inverted. Radiographic examination in the hospital revealed an avulsion fracture of the tuberosity of the fifth metatarsal. Part of the tuberosity is pulled off, producing pain and edema. Which of the following muscles is pulling on the fractured fragment?

- A. Fibularis (peroneus) longus
- B. Tibialis posterior

- ▢ **C.** Fibularis (peroneus) brevis
- ▢ **D.** Extensor digitorum brevis
- ▢ **E.** Adductor hallucis

77 A 58-year-old female employee of a housecleaning business visits the outpatient clinic with a complaint of constant, burning pain in her knees. Clinical examinations reveal a "housemaid's knee" condition (Fig. 5-9). Which of the following structures is most likely affected?

- ▢ **A.** Prepatellar bursa
- ▢ **B.** Infrapatellar bursa
- ▢ **C.** Posterior cruciate ligament
- ▢ **D.** Patellar retinacula
- ▢ **E.** Lateral meniscus

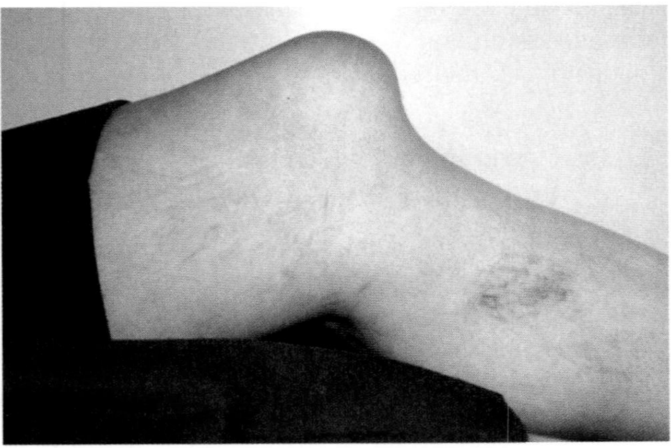

Fig. 5-9

78 A 42-year-old mother of three children visits the outpatient clinic complaining that her youngest son cannot walk yet. Radiographic and physical examinations reveal an unstable hip joint. Which of the following ligaments is responsible for stabilization of the hip joint in childhood?

- ▢ **A.** Iliofemoral
- ▢ **B.** Pubofemoral
- ▢ **C.** Ischiofemoral
- ▢ **D.** Ligament of the head of the femur
- ▢ **E.** Transverse acetabular ligament

79 A 45-year-old is admitted to the hospital after his left leg impacted a fence post when he was thrown from a powerful four-wheel all-terrain vehicle. Radiographic examination reveals posterior displacement of the tibia upon the femur. Which of the following structures was most likely injured?

- ▢ **A.** Anterior cruciate ligament
- ▢ **B.** Posterior cruciate ligament
- ▢ **C.** Lateral collateral ligament
- ▢ **D.** Lateral meniscus ligament
- ▢ **E.** Patellar ligament

80 A 55-year-old man visits the outpatient clinic complaining that he cannot walk more than 5 minutes without feeling severe pain in his feet. An image of the feet of this patient is shown in Fig. 5-10. What is the most common cause of this condition?

- ▢ **A.** Collapse of medial longitudinal arch, with eversion and abduction of the forefoot
- ▢ **B.** Exaggerated height of the medial longitudinal arch of the foot
- ▢ **C.** Collapse of long plantar ligament
- ▢ **D.** Collapse of deltoid ligament
- ▢ **E.** Collapse of plantar calcaneonavicular ligament

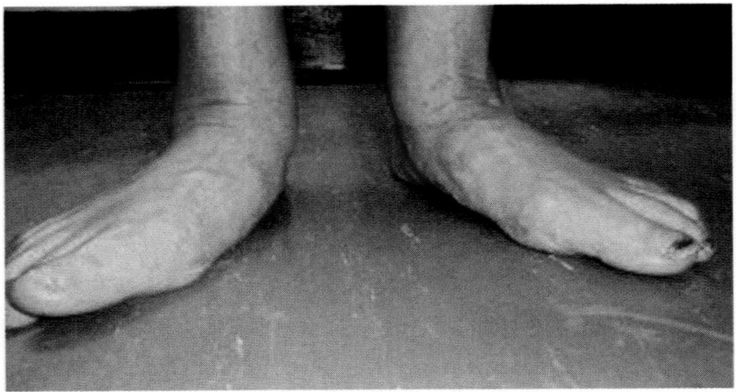

Fig. 5-10

81 A 55-year-old cowboy is admitted to the emergency department after he was knocked from his feet by a young longhorn steer. MRI examination reveals a large hematoma in the knee joint. Physical examination reveals that the patient suffers from the "unhappy triad" (of O'Donahue). Which of the following structures are involved in such an injury?

- ▢ **A.** Medial collateral ligament, medial meniscus, and anterior cruciate ligament
- ▢ **B.** Lateral collateral ligament, lateral meniscus, and posterior cruciate ligament
- ▢ **C.** Medial collateral ligament, lateral meniscus, and anterior cruciate ligament
- ▢ **D.** Lateral collateral ligament, medial meniscus, and anterior cruciate ligament
- ▢ **E.** Medial collateral ligament, medial meniscus, and posterior cruciate ligament

82 A 32-year-old man is admitted to the emergency department after a car collision. Radiographic examination reveals a distal fracture of the femur. The patient is in severe pain, and a femoral nerve block is admin-

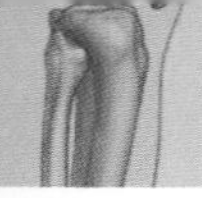

istered. What landmark is accurate for localizing the nerve for injection of anesthetics?

- ▢ **A.** 4 cm superolateral to the pubic tubercle
- ▢ **B.** 1.5 cm medial to the anterior superior iliac spine
- ▢ **C.** 1.5 cm lateral to the femoral pulse
- ▢ **D.** 1.5 cm medial to the femoral pulse
- ▢ **E.** Midway between the anterior superior iliac spine and pubic symphysis

83 A 39-year-old woman is admitted to the emergency department with a painful foot. Radiographic examination reveals Morton's neuroma. What is the most typical location of this neuroma?

- ▢ **A.** Between the third and fourth metatarsophalangeal joints
- ▢ **B.** Between the second and third metatarsophalangeal joints
- ▢ **C.** Between the first and second metatarsophalangeal joints
- ▢ **D.** Between the fourth and fifth metatarsophalangeal joints
- ▢ **E.** In the region of the second, third, and fourth metatarsophalangeal joints

84 A 34-year-old male distance runner visits the outpatient clinic with a complaint of pain he has suffered in his foot for the past week. The clinical examination indicates that the patient has an inflammation of the tough band of tissue stretching from the calcaneus to the ball of the foot. Which of the following conditions is most characteristic of these symptoms?

- ▢ **A.** Morton's neuroma
- ▢ **B.** Ankle eversion sprain
- ▢ **C.** Tarsal tunnel syndrome
- ▢ **D.** Plantar fasciitis
- ▢ **E.** Inversion sprain of the ankle

85 A 5-month-old baby boy is admitted to the pediatric orthopedic clinic. During physical examination it is noted that the baby has inversion and adduction of the forefoot relative to the hindfoot, and plantar flexion. Which of the following terms is diagnostic for the signs observed on physical examination?

- ▢ **A.** Coxa vara
- ▢ **B.** Talipes equinovarus
- ▢ **C.** Hallux valgus
- ▢ **D.** Hallux varus
- ▢ **E.** Plantar fasciitis

86 A 71-year-old man is admitted to the orthopedic clinic with difficulties walking. The patient has a past history of polio. Physical and radiographic examinations reveal extension at the metatarsophalangeal joints with flexion of both the proximal and distal interphalangeal joints. Which of the following descriptions is most appropriate for this patient's condition?

- ▢ **A.** Hallux valgus
- ▢ **B.** Pes planus
- ▢ **C.** Hammer toes
- ▢ **D.** Claw toes
- ▢ **E.** Pes cavus

87 A 62-year-old man is admitted unconscious to the emergency department. Radiographic examination and the available data indicate the likelihood of a transient ischemic attack. During physical examination the ankle jerk reflex is absent. Which of the following nerves is responsible for the reflex arc?

- ▢ **A.** Common fibular (peroneal)
- ▢ **B.** Superficial fibular (peroneal)
- ▢ **C.** Deep fibular (peroneal)
- ▢ **D.** Tibial
- ▢ **E.** Sciatic

88 Following the insertion of a prosthetic hip joint in a 72-year-old man, it was observed that the patient had greatly diminished sensation in the region of distribution of the posterior femoral cutaneous nerve. Which of the following is characteristic of this nerve?

- ▢ **A.** Cutaneous supply of the superior aspect of the gluteal region
- ▢ **B.** Arises from sacral spinal nerve levels S1, S2, S3
- ▢ **C.** Motor innervation of the obturator internus and gemelli muscles
- ▢ **D.** Injury results in meralgia paresthetica
- ▢ **E.** Provides origin of the sural cutaneous nerve

89 A 34-year-old woman has a direct blow to the patella by the dashboard of the vehicle during an automobile crash. The woman is admitted to the emergency department and radiographic examination reveals patellofemoral syndrome. This type of syndrome is characterized by lateral dislocation of the patella. Which of the following muscles requires strengthening by physical rehabilitation to prevent future dislocation of the patella?

- ▢ **A.** Vastus lateralis
- ▢ **B.** Vastus medialis
- ▢ **C.** Vastus intermedius

- ▢ **D.** Rectus femoris
- ▢ **E.** Patellar ligament

90 A 34-year-old man visits the outpatient clinic for an annual checkup. A radiographic examination of his knees is shown in Fig. 5-11. Physical examination reveals no pathology or pain to his knees. The patient has no past history of any knee problems. What is the most likely diagnosis?

- ▢ **A.** Enlarged prepatellar bursa
- ▢ **B.** Osgood-Schlatter disease
- ▢ **C.** Normal intercondylar eminence
- ▢ **D.** Bipartite patella
- ▢ **E.** Injury to lateral meniscus

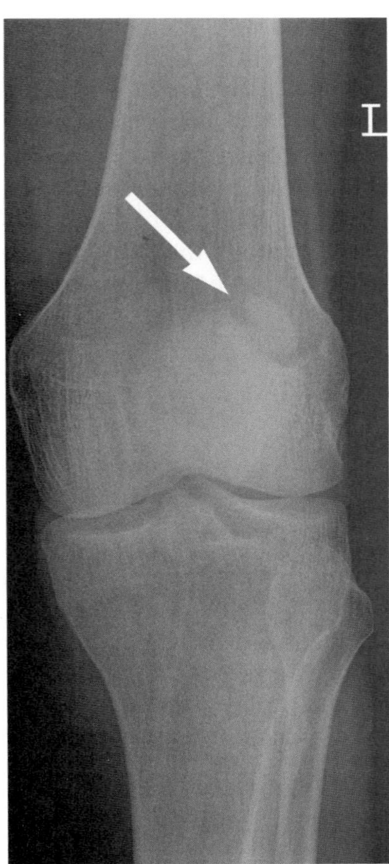

Fig. 5-11

91 A 48-year-old woman is admitted to the hospital with severe abdominal pain. Several imaging methods reveal that the patient suffers from intestinal ischemia. An abdominopelvic catheterization is ordered for antegrade angiography. A femoral puncture is performed (Fig. 5-12). What is the landmark for femoral artery puncture?

- ▢ **A.** Halfway between anterior superior iliac spine and pubic symphysis
- ▢ **B.** 4.5 cm lateral to the pubic tubercle
- ▢ **C.** Midpoint of the inguinal skin crease
- ▢ **D.** Medial aspect of femoral head
- ▢ **E.** Lateral to the fossa ovalis

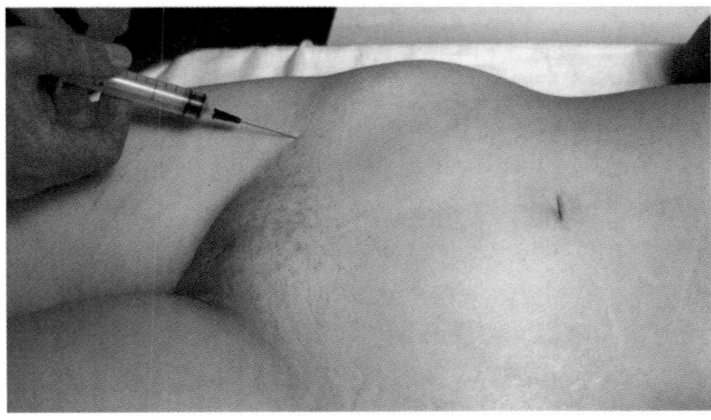

Fig. 5-12

92 A 23-year-old man is admitted to the emergency department after injuring his knee while playing football. During physical examination there is pain and swelling of the knee, in addition to locking of the knee. Radiographic examination reveals a bucket-handle meniscal tear (Fig. 5-13). Which of the following ligaments is most likely injured?

- ▢ **A.** Posterior cruciate
- ▢ **B.** Medial collateral
- ▢ **C.** Lateral collateral
- ▢ **D.** Anterior cruciate
- ▢ **E.** Coronary

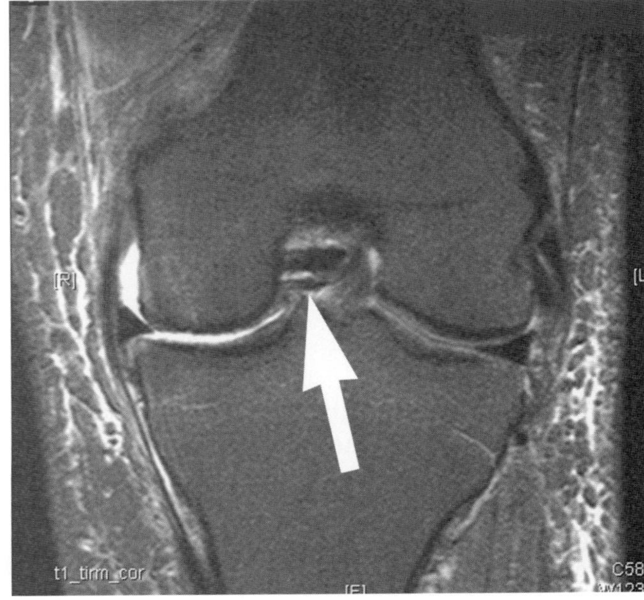

Fig. 5-13

93 The 27-year-old male triathlon competitor complained that he frequently experienced deep pains in one calf that almost caused him to drop out of a regional track-and-field event. Doppler ultrasound studies indicated, and surgical exposure confirmed, the existence of an accessory portion of the medial head of the gastrocnemius that was constricting the popliteal artery. Above the medial head of the gastrocnemius, the superior medial border of the popliteal fossa could be seen. Which of the following structures forms this border?

- ▢ **A.** Tendon of biceps femoris
- ▢ **B.** Tendons of semitendinosus and semimembranosus
- ▢ **C.** Tendon of plantaris
- ▢ **D.** Tendinous hiatus of adductor magnus
- ▢ **E.** Popliteus

94 The neurosurgeon had removed a portion of the dense tissue (dura mater) covering the brain of the patient when she removed the tumor that had invaded the skull. To replace this important tissue covering of the brain, she took a band of the aponeurotic tissue of the lateral aspect of the thigh, covering the vastus lateralis muscle. What muscle, supplied by the inferior gluteal nerve, inserts into this band of dense tissue as part of its insertion?

- ▢ **A.** Gluteus medius
- ▢ **B.** Gluteus minimus
- ▢ **C.** Gluteus maximus
- ▢ **D.** Tensor fasciae latae
- ▢ **E.** Rectus femoris

95 In the radiographs of the knee of a male 28-year-old basketball player, who had apparently suffered a tear in a medial ligament of the knee, the tubercle on the superior aspect of the medial femoral condyle could be seen more clearly than in most individuals. What muscle attaches to this tubercle?

- ▢ **A.** Semimembranosus
- ▢ **B.** Gracilis
- ▢ **C.** Popliteus
- ▢ **D.** Adductor magnus
- ▢ **E.** Vastus medialis

96 In preparing to isolate the proximal portion of the femoral artery, the vascular surgeon gently separated it from surrounding tissues. Posterior to the femoral sheath, what muscle forms the lateral portion of the floor of the femoral triangle?

- ▢ **A.** Adductor longus
- ▢ **B.** Iliopsoas
- ▢ **C.** Sartorius
- ▢ **D.** Pectineus
- ▢ **E.** Rectus femoris

97 A 37-year-old female had been suffering for months from piriformis entrapment syndrome, which was not relieved by physical therapy. Part of the sciatic nerve passed through the piriformis, and a decision was made for surgical resection of the muscle. When the area of entrapment was identified and cleared, a tendon could be seen emerging through the lesser sciatic foramen, at first hidden by two smaller muscles and several nerves and vessels destined for the region of the perineum. What tendon passes through this opening?

- ▢ **A.** Obturator internus
- ▢ **B.** Obturator externus
- ▢ **C.** Quadratus femoris
- ▢ **D.** Gluteus minimus
- ▢ **E.** Gluteus medius

98 A 34-year-old woman had a direct blow to the patella during a car collision. The woman is admitted to the emergency department and radiographic examination reveals patellofemoral syndrome. This type of syndrome is characterized by lateral dislocation of the patella. Which of the following muscles needs to be strengthened to prevent future dislocation of the patella?

- ▢ **A.** Vastus lateralis
- ▢ **B.** Vastus medialis
- ▢ **C.** Vastus intermedius
- ▢ **D.** Rectus femoris
- ▢ **E.** Patellar ligament

99 A 67-year-old woman has been suffering from osteoporosis for the past year. During her annual checkup, radiographic examination reveals an angle of 160° made by the axis of the femoral neck to the axis of the femoral shaft. Which of the following conditions is associated with these examination findings?

- ▢ **A.** Coxa vara
- ▢ **B.** Coxa valga
- ▢ **C.** Genu valgum
- ▢ **D.** Genu varum
- ▢ **E.** Hallux valgus

100 A 34-year-old male runner visits the outpatient clinic complaining of pain in his foot for the past week. Physical examination reveals inflammation of the tough band of tissue stretching from the calcaneus to the ball of the foot. Which of the following conditions is characteristic of these symptoms?

- ▢ **A.** Pott fracture
- ▢ **B.** Dupuytren fracture

- [ ] **C.** Tarsal tunnel
- [ ] **D.** Plantar fascitis
- [ ] **E.** Rupture of spring ligament

101 A 50-year-old man is admitted to the emergency department after a car crash. An MRI examination reveals an injured anterior cruciate ligament. Physical examination reveals a positive drawer sign. Which of the following signs is expected to be present during physical examination?

- [ ] **A.** The tibia can be slightly displaced anteriorly.
- [ ] **B.** The tibia can be slightly displaced posteriorly.
- [ ] **C.** The fibula can be slightly displaced posteriorly.
- [ ] **D.** The fibula can be slightly displaced anteriorly.
- [ ] **E.** The tibia and fibula can be slightly displaced anteriorly.

102 A 23-year-old male basketball player injured his foot during training and is admitted to the emergency department. An MRI examination reveals a hematoma in the medial malleolus. Upon physical examination the patient shows overeversion of his foot. Which of the following ligaments most likely has a tear?

- [ ] **A.** Plantar calcaneonavicular (spring)
- [ ] **B.** Calcaneofibular
- [ ] **C.** Long plantar
- [ ] **D.** Short plantar
- [ ] **E.** Deltoid

103 A 5-year-old boy is admitted to the emergency department after a car collision. Radiographic examination reveals a fracture of the head of the femur. An MRI examination reveals a large hematoma. Which of the following arteries is most likely injured?

- [ ] **A.** Deep circumflex iliac
- [ ] **B.** Acetabular branch of obturator
- [ ] **C.** Descending branch of lateral circumflex femoral
- [ ] **D.** Medial circumflex femoral
- [ ] **E.** Radicular branches of circumflex artery

104 A 72-year-old woman is admitted to the emergency department after an episode of stroke. During neurologic examination the patient shows no response to the ankle reflex test. Which of the following nerve roots is responsible for this reflex?

- [ ] **A.** L2
- [ ] **B.** L3
- [ ] **C.** L4
- [ ] **D.** L5
- [ ] **E.** S1

105 A 20-year-old male visits the family physician complaining of difficulty to flex and medially rotate his thigh while running and climbing. Which of the following muscles is most likely damaged in this individual?

- [ ] **A.** Rectus femoris
- [ ] **B.** Tensor fasciae latae
- [ ] **C.** Vastus intermedius
- [ ] **D.** Semimembranosus
- [ ] **E.** Sartorius

106 A 49-year-old man is admitted to the emergency department with a cold and pale foot. Physical examination reveals that the patient suffers from peripheral vascular disease and his popliteal artery is occluded and no pulse is felt upon palpation. What is the landmark to feel the pulse of the femoral artery?

- [ ] **A.** Adductor canal
- [ ] **B.** Femoral triangle
- [ ] **C.** Popliteal fossa
- [ ] **D.** Inguinal canal
- [ ] **E.** Pubic symphysis

107 A 49-year-old man is admitted to the emergency department complaining that he has difficulties walking. Physical examination reveals that the patient suffers from peripheral vascular disease. An ultrasound examination reveals an occlusion of his femoral artery at the proximal portion of the adductor canal. Which of the following arteries will most likely provide collateral circulation to the thigh?

- [ ] **A.** Descending branch of the lateral circumflex femoral
- [ ] **B.** Descending genicular
- [ ] **C.** Medial circumflex femoral
- [ ] **D.** First perforating branch of deep femoral
- [ ] **E.** Obturator artery

108 A 34-year-old man is pushing some heavy weights while doing squats. Unfortunately, while maxing out, he drops the weight and immediately grabs at his upper thigh, writhing in pain. The man is admitted to the emergency department and during physical examination is diagnosed with a femoral hernia. What reference structure would be found immediately lateral to the herniated structures?

- [ ] **A.** Femoral vein
- [ ] **B.** Femoral artery
- [ ] **C.** Pectineus muscle
- [ ] **D.** Femoral nerve
- [ ] **E.** Adductor longus muscle

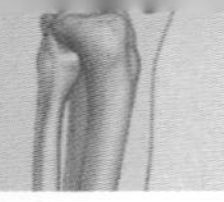

109 A 25-year-old man, an intravenous drug abuser, had been injecting himself with temazepam (a powerful intermediate-acting drug in the same group as Valium) and heroin for 5 years, leaving much residual scar tissue over points of vascular access. The patient is admitted to the emergency department for a detoxification program requiring an intravenous infusion. The femoral veins in his groin are the only accessible and patent veins for intravenous use. Which of the following landmarks is the most reliable to identify the femoral veins?

- ▢ **A.** The femoral vein lies medial to the femoral artery.
- ▢ **B.** The femoral vein lies within the femoral canal.
- ▢ **C.** The femoral vein lies lateral to the femoral artery.
- ▢ **D.** The femoral vein lies directly medial to the femoral nerve.
- ▢ **E.** The femoral vein lies lateral to the femoral nerve.

110 A 42-year-old male is bitten superficially on his posterior thigh by a dog. The superficial wound is sutured in the emergency department. Four days later the patient returns to the hospital with high fever and swollen lymph nodes. Which group of nodes will first receive lymph from the infected wound?

- ▢ **A.** External iliac
- ▢ **B.** Vertical group of superficial inguinal
- ▢ **C.** Deep inguinal
- ▢ **D.** Horizontal group of superficial inguinal
- ▢ **E.** Internal iliac

ANSWERS

1 **A.** The lumbosacral trunk consists of fibers from a portion of the ventral ramus of L4 and all of the ventral ramus of L5 and provides continuity between the lumbar and sacral plexuses. The deep fibular (peroneal) nerve receives supply from segments of L4, L5, and S1. It supplies the extensor hallicus longus, and extensor digitorum longus, the main functions of which are extension of the toes and dorsiflexion of the ankle. L5 is responsible for cutaneous innervation of the dorsum of the foot. Injury to L4 would affect foot inversion by the tibialis anterior. Injury to L4 in the lumbosacral trunk would not affect the patellar tendon reflex, for these fibers are delivered by the femoral nerve. Therefore, an injury to the lumbosacral trunk would result in all of the patient's symptoms. Nerve root injury at L5 and S1 would result in loss of sensation of the plantar aspect of the foot and motor loss of plantar flexion, with weakness of hip extension and abduction. The fibularis (peroneus) longus and brevis are supplied by the superficial fibular (peroneal) nerve, which is composed of fibers from segments L5, S1, and S2; these are responsible for eversion of the foot (especially S1). Transection of the fibular (peroneal) division of the sciatic nerve would result in loss of function of all the muscles of the anterior and lateral compartments of the leg. Injury to the sciatic nerve will affect hamstring muscles and all of the muscles below the knee. Injury to the tibial nerve causes loss of plantar flexion and impaired inversion.
GAS 463-464, 536; GA 186, 238-239, 283

2 **A.** The ventral ramus of L4 contains both sensory and motor nerve fibers. Injury from a stab wound could result in loss of sensation from the dermatome supplied by this segment. A dermatome is an area of skin supplied by a single spinal nerve; L4 dermatome supplies the medial aspect of the leg and foot. Loss of the Achilles tendon reflex relates primarily to an S1 deficit. The Achilles tendon reflex is elicited by tapping the calcaneus tendon, which results in plantar flexion. The obturator internus and gluteus medius and minimus are responsible for abduction of the thigh and are innervated by nerves L4, L5, and S1 (with L5 usually dominant). Nerves L5, S1, and S2 are responsible for eversion of the foot (S1 dominant).
GAS 38-39; GA 34, 346-347

3 **B.** Injury to the superior gluteal nerve results in a characteristic motor loss, with paralysis of gluteus medius and minimus. In addition to their role in abducting the thigh, the gluteus medius and minimus function to stabilize the pelvis: When the patient is asked to stand on the limb of the injured side, the pelvis descends on the opposite side, indicating a positive Trendelenburg test. The gluteal, or lurching, gait that results from this injury is characterized by the pelvis drooping to the unaffected side when the opposite leg is raised.

In stepping forward, the affected individual leans over the injured side when lifting the good limb off the ground. The uninjured limb is then swung forward. The gluteus maximus, supplied by the inferior gluteal nerve, is the main muscle responsible for allowing a person to rise to a standing position (extending the flexed hip). Spinal nerve roots L1 and L2 and the femoral nerve are responsible for hip flexion. Injury to the left superior gluteal nerve would result in sagging of the right side of the pelvis when the affected individual stands on the left limb. The hamstring muscles, responsible for flexing the leg at the knee joint to allow a person to sit down from a standing position, are innervated by the tibial branch of the sciatic nerve.
GAS 466, 467, 523, 524, 538, 539, 551-552; GA 238-240, 251, 282-283, 295

4 E. The deep fibular (peroneal) nerve is responsible for innervating the muscles of the anterior compartment of the leg, which are responsible for toe extension, foot dorsiflexion, and inversion. Injury to this nerve will result in foot drop and also loss of sensation between the first and second toes. Injury to the tibial nerve affects the posterior compartment muscles of the leg, which are responsible for plantar flexion and toe flexion, as well as the intrinsic muscles of the sole of the foot. The common fibular (peroneal) nerve splits into the superficial and deep fibular (peroneal) nerves, and these supply both the lateral and anterior compartments. The superficial fibular (peroneal) nerve innervates the fibularis longus and brevis muscles, which provide eversion of the foot. If the common fibular (peroneal) nerve were injured, eversion of the foot and plantar flexion would be lost in addition to dorsiflexion and inversion. The saphenous nerve, a continuation of the femoral nerve, is a cutaneous nerve that supplies the medial side of the leg and foot and provides no motor innervation.
GAS 595, 596, 597, 625-627; GA 326-327, 334-335

5 A. The femoral ring is the abdominal opening of the femoral canal. A femoral hernia passes through the femoral ring into the femoral canal deep and inferior to the inguinal ligament. It can appear as a bulging at the saphenous hiatus (fossa ovalis) of the deep fascia of the thigh, the hiatus through which the saphenous vein passes to the femoral vein. The superficial inguinal ring is the triangular opening in the aponeurosis of the external abdominal oblique and lies lateral to the pubic tubercle. The deep inguinal ring lies in the transversalis fascia lateral to the inferior epigastric vessels. Herniation into either of these two openings is associated with an inguinal hernia. The obturator canal, a bony opening between the superior and inferior ramus of the pubic bone, is the site of an obturator hernia.
GAS 291, 521, 547; GA 290

6 A. The talocrural (tibiotalar, ankle) joint is a hinge-type synovial joint between the tibia and talus. It permits dorsiflexion and plantar flexion, and fracture of this joint would affect these movements.
GAS 602, 604-606; GA 7, 273, 315-318

7 D. The piriformis muscle arises from the pelvic surface of the sacrum, passes through the greater sciatic notch, and inserts at the greater trochanter. It is considered the "key" to gluteal anatomy; the greater sciatic foramen is the "door." The gluteus medius lies posterior to the piriformis. The sciatic nerve emerges from the greater sciatic foramen, through the infrapiriformic space. The spine of the ischium separates the greater and lesser sciatic foramina.
GAS 409, 410, 430, 431, 536-537, 548, 549; GA 9, 212-215, 227, 244, 281-283, 285

8 A. The popliteal lymph nodes are the first to receive lymph from the foot. These nodes will then drain into the deep inguinal nodes and then to the external iliac nodes. The superficial inguinal and internal iliac nodes do not receive lymph from the foot.
GAS 542, 543; GA 12, 345

9 E. The tibial nerve is responsible for innervating the posterior compartment of the leg. These muscles are responsible for knee flexion, plantar flexion, and intrinsic muscle functions of the foot. Compression of this nerve can affect plantar flexion of the foot. Dorsiflexion of the foot would be compromised if the deep fibular (peroneal) nerve were compressed by this Baker cyst. Flexion of the thigh is a function of muscles supplied by lumbar nerves and the femoral nerve. The deep fibular (peroneal) nerve is also responsible for extension of the digits, whereas the femoral nerve is responsible for extension of the leg.
GAS 463, 465, 523, 524, 538, 594-597; GA 13, 294-295, 322, 341-342

10 A. The medial meniscus is firmly attached to the medial (tibial) collateral ligament. Damage to the medial collateral ligament often causes concomitant damage to the medial meniscus because of this relationship. The anterior cruciate ligament lies inside the knee joint capsule but outside the synovial cavity. It is taut during extension of the knee and may be torn when the knee is hyperextended. If this were damaged along with the medial meniscus and medial cruciate ligament, an "unhappy triad" (of O'Donahue)

injury would result. The lateral meniscus is not attached to the medial collateral ligament but receives muscular attachment to the popliteus muscle. The posterior cruciate ligament also lies outside of the synovial cavity and limits hyperflexion of the knee. The tendon of the semitendinosus forms one third of the pes anserinus, with the tendons of the sartorius and gracilis making up the other two thirds. The pes anserinus (goose foot) is located at the medial border of the tibial tuberosity, and a portion can be used for surgical repair of the anterior cruciate ligament.
GAS 576-578, 579; GA 303-305

11 D. The great saphenous vein is commonly used in coronary artery bypass grafts. Because branches of the saphenous nerve cross the vein in the distal part of the leg, the nerve can be torn out of the limb if the vein is stripped from the ankle to the knee. Stripping the vein in the opposite direction can protect the nerve and lessen the postoperative discomfort of patients. The saphenous nerve is responsible for cutaneous innervations on the medial surface of the leg and the medial side of the foot. Injury to this nerve will result in a loss of sensation and also can create chronic dysesthesias in the area. The common fibular (peroneal) nerve bifurcates at the neck of the fibula into the superficial and deep fibular (peroneal) nerves, which continue on to innervate the lateral and anterior compartments of the leg, respectively. These nerves are lateral and therefore not associated with the great saphenous vein. The lateral sural nerve is a cutaneous nerve that arises from the junction of branches from the common fibular (peroneal) nerve and tibial nerve and innervates the skin on the posterior aspect of the leg and lateral side of the foot. This nerve is often harvested for nerve grafts elsewhere in the body. The tibial nerve is a terminal branch of the sciatic nerve that continues deep in the posterior compartment of the leg.
GAS 452, 525, 541, 573, 624; GA 11, 254-255, 290, 296, 344

12 B. The calcaneofibular ligament is a round cord that passes posteroinferiorly from the tip of the lateral malleolus to the lateral surface of the calcaneus. A forced inversion of the foot can result in tearing of the calcaneofibular ligament and sometimes the anterior talofibular ligament as well. Both of these ligaments act to stabilize the foot and prevent an inversion injury. The long plantar ligament passes from the planter surface of the calcaneus to the groove on the cuboid and is important in maintaining the longitudinal arch of the foot. The short plantar ligament is located deep (superior) to the long plantar ligament and extends from the calcaneus to the cuboid and is also involved in maintaining the longitudinal arch of the foot. The deltoid (medial ligament of the ankle) attaches proximally to the medial malleolus and fans out to reinforce the joint capsule of the ankle.
GAS 606; GA 316-317, 332

13 B. The lateral circumflex femoral artery arises from the deep femoral (profunda femoris) artery of the thigh and sends a descending branch down the length of the femur to anastomose with the superior medial genicular artery and the superior lateral genicular artery. The medial circumflex femoral artery is responsible for supplying blood to the head and neck of the femur, and it does not anastomose with distal vessels at the knee. The first perforating artery sends an ascending branch that anastomoses with the medial circumflex femoral and the inferior gluteal artery in the buttock. The inferior gluteal artery is a branch of the internal iliac; it has important anastomotic supply to the hip joint. The typically small descending genicular branch of the femoral artery is given off just proximal to the continuation of the femoral artery as the popliteal.
GAS 533, 560-570; GA 282, 292, 295

14 C. The medial circumflex femoral artery is responsible for supplying blood to the head and neck of the femur by a number of branches that pass under the edge of the ischiofemoral ligament. This artery is most likely at risk for injury in an extracapsular fracture of the femoral neck. The inferior gluteal artery arises from the internal iliac and enters the gluteal region through the greater sciatic foramen, below the piriformis. The first perforating artery sends an ascending branch that anastomoses with the inferior gluteal artery in the buttock. The obturator artery arises from the internal iliac artery and passes through the obturator foramen. It commonly supplies the artery within the ligament of the head of the femur. The superior gluteal artery arises from the internal iliac artery and enters through the greater sciatic foramen above the piriformis.
GAS 533, 560, 561; GA 279, 282-283, 292, 294-295

15 B. The obturator nerve arises from the lumbar plexus and enters the thigh through the obturator canal. This nerve is responsible for innervation of the medial compartment of the thigh (adductor compartment). Injury to this nerve can result in weakened adduction and difficulty walking. The femoral nerve innervates muscles of the anterior compartment of the thigh that are responsible for hip flexion and leg extension. The sciatic nerve branches into the com-

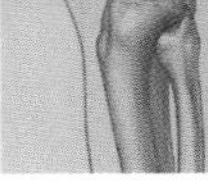

mon fibular (peroneal) and tibial nerves. The common fibular (peroneal) nerve branches into the deep and superficial branches of the fibular (peroneal) nerve responsible for innervation of the anterior and lateral compartments of the leg, respectively. The tibial nerve innervates the muscles of the posterior compartment of the thigh and leg, which are responsible for extension of the hip, flexion of the leg, and plantar flexion of the foot.
GAS 378, 379, 382, 463, 466, 524, 537-539; GA 13, 186-187, 238, 240, 251, 257, 283, 291, 296

16 **B.** The common fibular (peroneal) nerve winds around the neck of the fibula before dividing into superficial and deep branches that go on to innervate the lateral and anterior compartments of the leg, respectively. These compartments are responsible for dorsiflexion and eversion of the foot, and injury to these nerves would result in deficits in these movements. The tibial nerve lies superficially in the popliteal fossa. This nerve innervates the posterior compartment of the leg, so compression in this area would result in a loss of plantar flexion and weakness of inversion. The lateral compartment of the leg is innervated by the superficial fibular (peroneal) nerve and is mainly involved in eversion of the foot. The cutaneous branches of the superficial fibular (peroneal) nerve emerge through the deep fascia in the anterolateral aspect of the leg and supply the dorsum of the foot. The anterior compartment of the leg is innervated by the deep fibular (peroneal) nerve and is mainly involved in dorsiflexion of the foot. The medial malleolus is an inferiorly directed projection from the medial side of the distal end of the tibia. The tibial nerve runs near the groove behind the medial malleolus, and compression at this location would result in loss of toe flexion, adduction, abduction, and abduction of the great toe.
GAS 463, 465, 523, 524, 538, 573-574; GA 294-295, 322, 326

17 **A.** The gluteus maximus is innervated by the inferior gluteal nerve, and this muscle is responsible for extension and lateral rotation of the thigh. It is the primary muscle used to rise from a seated position. The gluteus minimus is innervated by the superior gluteal nerve and is responsible for abduction of the thigh. Hamstring muscles are innervated by the tibial portion of the sciatic nerve, and these are responsible for extension of the thigh and flexion of the leg. The iliopsoas muscle is innervated by L1 and L2 and the femoral nerve, and it flexes the thigh. The obturator internus is innervated by the nerve to the obturator internus and is a lateral rotator of the thigh.
GAS 545, 548, 549-551; GA 9, 241-242, 272, 281-282, 285, 287, 296

18 **B.** The medial branch of the deep fibular (peroneal) nerve accompanies the dorsalis pedis artery and innervates the skin between the contiguous sides of the first and second toes. The saphenous nerve is responsible for cutaneous innervation of the anteromedial aspect of the leg and foot. The superficial fibular (peroneal) nerve innervates most of the dorsum of the foot, with the exception of the area where sensation was lost (medial branch of deep fibular nerve). The common fibular (peroneal) nerve gives off a cutaneous branch, the sural nerve, which innervates the lateral aspect of the leg and lateral side of the foot.
GAS 596, 597, 599, 625-627; GA 326-327, 334-335

19 **E.** The posterior cruciate ligament is responsible for preventing the forward sliding of the femur on the tibia. The anterior cruciate ligament prevents posterior displacement of the femur on the tibia. The lateral collateral ligament limits extension and adduction of the leg. The medial meniscus acts as a shock absorber and cushions the articular surfaces of the knee joint.
GAS 557, 579-581; GA 303-305

20 **D.** The gluteus maximus inserts into the gluteal tuberosity and the iliotibial tract. Although the gluteus maximus would continue to contract at the regions of insertion, their orientation would be displaced by the fracture. The gluteus medius, gluteus minimus, obturator internus, and piriformis all insert on some aspect of the greater trochanter of the femur.
GAS 531; GA 276

21 **B.** The apex of the femoral triangle occurs at the junction of the adductor longus and sartorius muscles. The subsartorial (Hunter) canal begins at this location. Immediately deep to this anatomic point lie the femoral artery, femoral vein, deep femoral artery, and deep femoral vein, often overlying one another in that sequence. This has historically been a site of injuries with a meat cleaver. For this reason, injuries at this location are referred to as the "butcher's block" injury. Fatal loss of blood can occur in just a few minutes if pressure, or a tourniquet, is not applied immediately. The common iliac artery becomes the femoral artery at the inguinal ligament. The saphenous vein joins the femoral vein at the saphenous hiatus, or fossa ovalis. The medial circumflex femoral usually arises from the deep femoral artery about 3 to 5 inches inferior to the inguinal ligament, near the origin of the deep femoral artery from the common femoral. Serious blood loss

can occur with injury to any of these vessels, although injury to them is not so often fatal.
GAS 512-515, 545-547; GA 290

22 C. The iliofemoral ligament is the most important ligament reinforcing the joint anteriorly that would resist both hyperextension and lateral rotation at the hip joint. The pubofemoral ligament reinforces the joint inferiorly and limits extension and abduction. The ischiofemoral ligament reinforces the joint posteriorly and limits extension and medial rotation. Negative pressure in the acetabular fossa has nothing to do with resisting hyperextension of the hip joint but does help resist dislocation of the head of the femur. The gluteus maximus muscle extends and laterally rotates the thigh and does not particularly resist hyperextension.
GAS 534-536; GA 212, 279

23 C. An intracapsular femoral neck fracture causes avascular necrosis of the femoral head because the fracture damages the radicular branches of the medial and lateral circumflex arteries that pass beneath the ischiofemoral ligament and pierce the femoral neck. Until an individual reaches about 6 to 10 years of age, blood supply to the head of the femur is provided by a branch of the obturator artery that runs with the ligament of the head of the femur. Thereafter, the artery of the ligament of the head of the femur is insignificant. Intertrochanteric fracture of the femur would not damage the blood supply to the head of the femur but would cause complications because the greater trochanter is an attachment site for several gluteal muscles. During childhood the obturator artery provides the artery of the ligament of the head of the femur. Thrombosis of the obturator artery could result in muscular symptoms, although there are several collateral sources of blood supply in the thigh. Comminuted fracture of the extracapsular femoral neck would not ordinarily imperil the vascular supply.
GAS 533, 642; GA 275-276, 278

24 D. The farm instrument has injured the deep fibular (peroneal) branch of the common fibular (peroneal) nerve. It is vulnerable to injury as it arises from the common fibular (peroneal) at the neck of the fibula. The muscles denervated are largely dorsiflexors of the foot; hence, foot drop and steppage gait can occur. Sensation on the dorsum of the foot is still present; therefore, the superficial branch is mostly or entirely intact, although sensation between the first and second toes would be absent. Femoral nerve injury would result in loss of knee extension. Loss of the sciatic nerve would result in loss of both the tibial and common fibular (peroneal) nerves. Because plantar flexion is still functional, the tibial nerve has not been cut.
GAS 596, 597, 599, 624-627; GA 326-327, 334-335

25 C. The Achilles tendon reflex is a function of the triceps surae muscle, composed of insertion of the gastrocnemius and soleus muscles on the calcaneus. The innervation is provided primarily by spinal nerve S1. The S1 root leaves the vertebral column at the S1 foramen of the sacrum, but a herniated disk at the L5-S1 intervertebral space puts the S1 root under tension, resulting in pain and possible weakness or paralysis of S1-supplied muscles, especially the plantar flexors. A disk lesion at L3-4 would affect the L4 spinal nerve (affecting foot inversion and extension); a lesion at L4-5 would cause problems with L5 (hip abduction and knee flexion). A disk lesion at S1-2 in the sacrum is improbable, unless there was lumbarization of the S1 vertebra. The gluteal crush syndrome usually occurs when a patient has been lying unconscious and unmoving on a hard surface for an extended period of time.
GAS 523-524; GA 5

26 B. An injury to L4 would cause weakness in the patellar reflex and loss of cutaneous innervation to the medial side of the leg. Patellar reflex is used to test L2 to L4 nerve integrity. The motor side of the reflex is primarily derived from spinal nerves L2 and L3, whereas the sensory side of the arc is said to be principally from L4. The L4 spinal nerve supplies the L4 dermatome on the medial side of the leg and foot, by way of the saphenous nerve. It also supplies foot inversion, a function of the tibialis anterior and tibialis posterior muscles; the first is supplied by the deep fibular (peroneal) nerve, and the second supplied by the tibial nerve. Foot dorsiflexion is weakened because of partial denervation of the extensor digitorum longus, but L5 is still contributing to that function. The foot is everted because the S1-supplied (by the superficial fibular nerve) fibularis (peroneus) longus and brevis are unopposed. The Achilles reflex is also primarily supplied by S1. Hip movements are produced primarily by L5- and S1-supplied muscles, as is knee flexion.
GAS 522-523; GA 34, 346-347

27 C. The lateral plantar nerve innervates the interossei and adductor hallucis. These losses would be obvious when the patient attempts to abduct and adduct the toes. Sensation would be absent over the lateral side of the sole, the fifth and fourth toes, and half of the third toe. The medial plantar nerve provides sensation over the plantar surface of the first and second toes and half of the third toe as well as function of the so-called LAFF

muscles: first lumbrical abductor hallucis, flexor hallucis brevis, and flexor digitorum brevis.
GAS 623, 624; GA 327, 341-342

28 **A.** The common fibular (peroneal) nerve passes around the head of the fibula and gives off deep (L4-5) and superficial fibular (peroneal) nerve (L5, S1-2) branches. The two nerves supply the dorsiflexors and evertors of the foot, respectively. In this case, the tibialis anterior and extensor digitorum longus are the only muscles listed that are supplied by either of these nerve branches, and both are innervated by the deep fibular (peroneal) nerve. The fibularis (peroneus) brevis and longus are innervated by the superficial fibular (peroneal) nerve and are evertors of the foot. The tibial nerve supplies each of the other muscles listed.
GAS 463, 465, 523, 524, 538, 573-574; GA 294-295, 322, 326

29 **D.** Spinal tuberculosis can spread within the sheath of the psoas major to its insertion with the iliacus upon the lesser trochanter, presenting there also with painful symptoms. The iliopsoas muscle is the principal flexor of the hip joint. Abduction of the hips is performed by the gluteus medius and minimus with assistance from short lateral rotator muscles. Extension of the hip is a function of the gluteus maximus, together with the hamstring muscles. Internal rotation is performed by the abductor muscle group.
GAS 348-349, 353, 561, 562; GA 29, 42, 127, 137, 141, 173, 175-176, 254, 291

30 **A.** The Achilles tendon inserts upon the calcaneus bone. This tendon represents a combination of the tendons of gastrocnemius and soleus muscles. The tendon of the plantaris can insert with this tendon.
GAS 589, 590, 602; GA 5

31 **C.** In an inversion injury the most common ligament involvement comes from the anterior talofibular and calcaneofibular ligaments. The medial plantar nerve is medially located within the sole of the foot and might be injured by traction in an eversion injury, not an inversion injury. The posterior talofibular ligament is located posteriorly and is not usually injured in an inversion injury. The deltoid ligament is located medially and would be injured with an eversion injury; it is so strong, however, that eversion is more likely to fracture the medial malleolus rather than tear the deltoid ligament.
GAS 607-608, 646; GA 332

32 **A.** The plantar calcaneonavicular ligament (spring ligament) supports the head of the talus and maintains the longitudinal arch of the foot. A fracture of the cuboid bone would not disrupt the longitudinal arch of the foot. Interruption of the plantar aponeurosis is not the best answer because this aponeurosis provides only passive support, unlike the spring ligament. A sprain of the anterior talofibular ligament would result from an inversion injury of the ankle and would not disrupt the longitudinal arch of the foot. A sprain of the deltoid ligament results from eversion of the ankle joint and would not disrupt the longitudinal arch of the foot.
GAS 602, 609, 610; GA 317

33 **B.** This type of injury can result in the "unhappy triad" (of O'Donahue) injury, with damage to the medial collateral ligament (MCL), anterior cruciate ligament (ACL), and medial meniscus. A blow to the lateral side of the knee stretches and tears the MCL, which is attached to the medial meniscus. The ACL is tensed during knee extension and can tear subsequent to the rupture of the MCL. The remaining answer choices describe structures on the lateral surface of the knee, which are not usually injured by this type of trauma.
GAS 640-641; GA 331-332, 389, 395

34 **E.** The popliteal artery is the continuation of the femoral artery after it passes through the hiatus of the adductor magnus. The popliteal artery divides into the anterior and posterior tibial arteries. The anterior tibial artery passes between the tibia and fibula proximally in the posterior compartment of the leg, whereas the posterior tibial artery continues in the posterior compartment of the leg, to its division into medial and lateral plantar arteries. The posterior tibial artery provides origin for the fibular (peroneal) artery, which supplies the lateral compartment of the leg. The deep femoral artery provides origin for the three or four perforating branches that supply the posterior compartment of the thigh.
GAS 584, 585, 593-594; GA 10, 294-295, 307, 322, 326

35 **E.** The vastus lateralis muscle is located on the lateral aspect of the thigh. The distal portion of this muscle lies superficial to the proximal part of the lateral aspect of the joint capsule of the knee. When a needle is inserted superiorly and laterally to the patella, it penetrates the vastus lateralis muscle on its course to the internal capsule. The short head of biceps femoris has its origin on the posterior aspect of the femur, merges with the long head of the biceps femoris, and inserts on the head of the fibula. The rectus femoris passes longitudinally on the medial

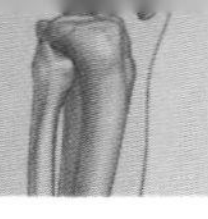

aspect of the femur and inserts on the tibial tuberosity, via the patellar tendon, or quadriceps tendon. A needle inserted laterally to the patella would not penetrate this muscle. The sartorius originates on the anterior superior iliac spine and forms part of the pes anserinus, which inserts on the medial aspect of the proximal part of the tibia. A needle inserted laterally to the patella would not penetrate this muscle.
GAS 561-563; GA 8, 272, 280-281, 285-288, 296, 307, 320, 323-324

36 C. When the popliteus contracts, it rotates the distal portion of the femur in a lateral direction. It also draws the lateral meniscus posteriorly, thereby protecting this cartilage as the distal femoral condyle glides and rolls backward, as the knee is flexed. This allows the knee to flex and therefore serves in unlocking the knee. The biceps femoris is a strong flexor of the leg and laterally rotates the knee when it is in a position of flexion. The gastrocnemius is a powerful plantar flexor of the foot. The semimembranous, similar to the biceps femoris, is a component of the hamstring muscles and is involved in extending the thigh and flexing the leg at the knee joint. The rectus femoris is the strongest quadriceps muscle in extending the leg at the knee.
GAS 589, 590; GA 9, 285, 321

37 B. Pott's fracture is a rather archaic term for a fracture of the fibula at the ankle. The term is often used to indicate a bimalleolar fracture of fibula and tibia, perhaps with a tear in the medial collateral ligament, allowing the foot to be deviated laterally. (The medial malleolus will often break before the deltoid ligament tears.) This fracture is also known as Dupuytren's fracture. The fracture results from abduction and lateral rotation of the foot in extreme eversion. There can also be breaking of the posterior aspect of the distal tibia. The spring ligament, also known as the plantar calcaneonavicular ligament, extends from the calcaneus to the navicular bone and is a part of the medial longitudinal arch. This ligament would not be affected in eversion or inversion of the ankle. The plantar ligament, which is composed of the long and short plantar ligaments, supports the lateral longitudinal arch of the foot and would therefore not be affected by inversion or eversion of the foot. The calcaneofibular ligament runs from the calcaneus to the fibula. It would be injured during inversion of the foot, not in eversion, as is the case in a Pott fracture.
GAS 608; GA 7, 272-273, 309

38 B. The original axial vessel of the lower limb is retained as the (usually tiny) ischiatic branch of the inferior gluteal artery. In some cases this vessel is retained as the primary proximal vessel to the limb, wherein there is hypoplastic development of the femoral artery. Aneurysms of the enlarged ischiatic artery in the gluteal region are relatively common, as is rupture of the vessel (with profuse bleeding) if they are exposed in the gluteal area. The profunda femoris or deep femoral branch of the femoral artery usually provides three perforating branches to the posterior compartment, but not a branch such as that described. The descending branch of the medial circumflex femoral anastomoses with the first perforator. The superior gluteal artery anastomoses with the inferior gluteal by a descending branch or branches. The descending branch of the lateral circumflex femoral is the descending genicular artery, which anastomoses with the superior lateral genicular branch of the popliteal artery.
GAS 473, 474-477, 533, 540, 541, 554; GA 182, 232, 282-283, 292, 294-295

39 C. Herniation of the intervertebral disk at L4-5 results typically in compression of the L5 spinal nerve. The L4 spinal nerve exits at the L4-5 intervertebral foramen, but the L5 spinal nerve is put under tension as it passes the herniation to reach the L5-S1 foramen. Piriformis entrapment of the fibular (peroneal) division of the sciatic nerve is relatively common, but the dermatome affected here appears to be confined to the L5 distribution to the skin of the foot and also includes the superior gluteal nerve, which supplies the large hip abductors. S1 would involve loss of sensation on the lateral side of the foot and potential weakness in hip extension and plantar flexion. A posterior dislocation of the hip would be unlikely in this injury but, even so, would not result in these deficits.
GAS 80, 82; GA 33-34

40 C. Entrapment compression of all or part of the sciatic nerve by the piriformis can mimic disk herniation, most commonly resembling compression of spinal nerve S1. This results in pain down the posterior aspect of the thigh and leg and the lateral side of the foot. In this case, loss of sensation over the dorsum of the foot and weakness of foot extension, in addition to eversion, indicate that more than S1 is involved. Foot drop would be anticipated with fibular (peroneal) nerve involvement. As noted also in a previous question, compression of the common fibular (peroneal) division of the sciatic nerve by the piriformis gives rise to the clinical condition known as piriformis entrapment. This condition is associated with point pain in the gluteal area, pain in the posterior part of the limb,

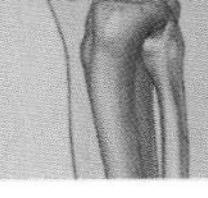

and possible weakness of muscles in the lateral and anterior compartments of the leg. It can be confused with herniated disk (L5) compression of S1 and sciatica. Paralysis of plantar flexion occurs with a lesion of the tibial division of the sciatic nerve or the tibial nerve. Paralysis of the quadriceps is associated with pathology of the femoral nerve. Clonic contraction of the adductors could result from obturator nerve problems. Anterior cluneal nerves (sensory to anterior gluteal region) arise from the iliohypogastric nerve.
GAS 118; GA 13, 238, 282-283, 294-296

41 **A.** The superior gluteal nerve innervates the gluteus medius, gluteus minimus, and tensor fasciae latae muscles. The tensor fasciae latae arises from the iliac crest, inserts into the iliotibial tract of the lateral aspect of the thigh, and assists in flexion of the hip. The rectus femoris is innervated by the femoral nerve; it flexes the hip and extends the knee, thus acting upon two major joints. It arises in part from the anterior inferior iliac spine and the rim of the acetabulum and inserts into the quadriceps tendon. The gluteus maximus is supplied by the inferior gluteal nerve. The piriformis and quadratus femoris are both short lateral rotators of the hip and are supplied by branches of the sacral plexus.
GAS 463, 466, 523, 524, 538, 539, 551-552; GA 238-240, 251, 282-283, 295

42 **A.** The sartorius is indicated by the arrow in the sectional image. This muscle forms the roof of the subsartorial canal (Hunter canal), with the adductor longus and vastus medialis forming other muscular borders. The femoral artery and vein, the saphenous nerve, the nerve to the vastus medialis, and the medial cutaneous nerve of the thigh all pass into this canal. The femoral artery leaves the canal by passing through the adductor magnus. The saphenous nerve emerges from the canal and from beneath the sartorius on the medial side of the lower limb proximally, thereafter providing sensory branches to the medial side of the lower limb and foot. Dr. Hunter mobilized the sartorius, thereby exposing the femoral artery (which continues as the popliteal artery beyond the adductor hiatus), which could be clamped while an aneurysmal popliteal artery was treated surgically.
GAS 561, 563, 564, 630; GA 8, 272, 280, 285-288, 290, 296, 320, 324

43 **B.** Contraction of the gastrocnemius on the broken calcaneus would increase the pain because the gastrocnemius inserts with the soleus upon that bone, via the calcaneal tendon, or tendo Achilles. The flexor digitorum profundus passes the ankle medially to enter the sole of the foot, where it inserts upon the distal phalanges. The tibialis posterior, likewise, passes under the medial malleolus, with complex insertions upon the navicular bone, cuneiform bones, metatarsal bones, and the cuboid bone. The tibialis anterior, a muscle of the anterior leg compartment, inserts upon the navicular bone and, with the tibialis posterior, is a strong invertor of the foot. The fibularis (peroneus) longus is a muscle of the lateral compartment of the leg. It passes under the lateral malleolus, entering the sole of the foot by crossing the lateral surface of the calcaneus, and inserts primarily into the medial cuneiform and base of the first metatarsal bone.
GAS 589, 590; GA 5, 8-9, 272, 280, 285, 287, 320, 323-324

44 **C.** A severe injury of the tibial nerve in the popliteal fossa would result in a dorsiflexed and everted foot because of the intact muscles of the extensor (anterior) and evertor (lateral) compartments of the leg. It would result also in some weakening of knee flexion because of loss of the gastrocnemius muscle, which flexes the knee and plantar flexes the foot. The hamstrings also flex the knee, so this function would not be lost. Plantar flexion at the ankle would be paralyzed with the loss of the gastrocnemius and soleus, in addition to the flexors of the toes, and inversion by the tibialis posterior. Foot drop results from loss of the anterior compartment, innervated by the deep fibular (peroneal) nerve.
GAS 584, 585; GA 13, 294-295, 322, 341-342

45 **C.** The obturator artery provides the artery within the ligament of the head of the femur (in about 60%), the artery that supplies the head of the femur, primarily during childhood, later becoming atretic. In the adult this artery supplies only the area of the fovea of the head of the femur. The ligament of the head of the femur arises from the acetabular notch, thereafter receiving the little artery. In some individuals the medial circumflex femoral gives origin to the artery of the head. In the adult the arterial supply of the neck and head is provided by intracapsular branches of the medial circumflex femoral and lateral circumflex femoral arteries that pierce the neck of the femur, with some supply also from the gluteal arteries. The lateral circumflex femoral artery arises from the deep femoral and supplies the vastus lateralis. The pudendal artery arises from the internal iliac and provides blood supply for the structures of the perineum. Quite often, when an older patient with osteoporosis has a hip fracture, the femoral neck may have broken, precipitating a fall, rather than the fall resulting in the hip fracture.
GAS 473, 474-477, 540, 541, 573; GA 220, 232, 234, 237, 250, 277, 279, 292

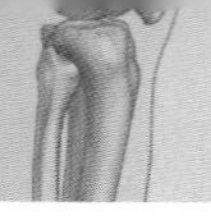

46 A. With sufficient downward force, the head of the talus can break through the plantar calcaneonavicular (spring) ligament, causing the medial longitudinal arch of the foot to fall, forcing the anterior part of the foot into abduction. The plantar calcaneonavicular ligament is attached between the sustentaculum tali of the calcaneus and the medial surface of the navicular bone, with the head of the talus lying directly upon the inner surface of the ligament. The cuboid bone is located lateral and anterior to the talus bone and would not be fractured. The plantar aponeurosis, a dense, wide band of tissue beneath the fascia of the sole, attaches to the calcaneus and ends distally in longitudinal bands to each of the toes. It stretches very little, even under very heavy loads, and would not break in this case. The anterior talofibular ligament is very often injured in "sprained ankle" but would not be directly involved here. The distal tibiofibular joint is a fibrous (and usually nonsynovial) type of joint between the tibia and fibula, not involved in the displacement of the talus bone.
GAS 518, 519, 614; GA 311

47 E. The lateral femoral cutaneous nerve leaves the pelvis laterally, about 2 cm medial to the anterior superior iliac spine, passing beneath, or through, the inguinal ligament. As a consequence of its site of exit, any tension upon or compression of the inguinal ligament can affect the nerve. If it is thus affected, the individual may feel burning sensations or pain along the lateral aspect of the thigh, which is the region of distribution of the nerve. Obesity, sudden weight loss, wearing a heavy gun belt, wearing trousers that are too tight (Calvin Klein syndrome), or having someone sitting on another's lap for an extended period of time can lead to meralgia paresthetica, the painful lateral thigh. The femoral nerve emerges from beneath the middle of the inguinal ligament and is not usually affected by similar traction or compression. The obturator nerve leaves the pelvis through the obturator canal and enters the thigh deeply in a protected location. It innervates the adductor muscles and supplies sensation on the medial aspect of the thigh. The fibular (peroneal) division of the sciatic nerve supplies the muscles of the anterior and lateral compartments of the leg and provides sensory fibers for the dorsum and lateral side of the foot. The superior gluteal nerve provides motor supply to the gluteus medius and minimus muscles.
GAS 465; GA 187

48 D. The tibialis posterior tendon is the most anterior of the structures that pass under the laciniate ligament (flexor retinaculum) on the medial side of the ankle to enter the sole of the foot. Increases of pressure within the tissues of the plantar aspect of the foot, usually due to increased fluid from hemorrhage, inflammatory processes, or infections, cause tarsal tunnel syndrome, comparable to carpal tunnel syndrome of the hand. The plantar aponeurosis and other fibrous and osseous tissues of the plantar surface cause this area to be relatively nondistensible; therefore, it takes little increase of fluid content to result in pressures adequate to restrict venous drainage and, thereafter, arterial inflow to the region. Fasciotomy of the medial skin and fascia of the foot and the posterior compartment of the leg can be required to reduce the pressure and allow healing to take place. The structures that pass beneath the flexor retinaculum are, from anterior to posterior: **T**endon of tibialis posterior; tendon of flexor **D**igitorum longus; posterior tibial **V**essels and **N**erve; tendon of flexor **H**allucis longus. (This is the basis of the mnemonic device: "Tom, Dick, and a Very Nervous Harry.") Neither the plantaris tendon nor the tibialis anterior tendon pass through this canal.
GAS 589-593, 612; GA 331-332

49 D. The second perforating branch of the profunda femoris (deep femoral) artery commonly provides the nutrient artery to the femur, a vessel that passes through a rather large foramen to enter the proximal part of the shaft. The deep circumflex branch of the external iliac passes around the medial aspect of the iliac crest, also supplying the lower lateral part of the anterior abdominal wall. The acetabular branch of the obturator artery supplies tissues in the hip socket, usually including a branch to the ligament of the head of the femur. The lateral circumflex femoral branch of the deep femoral artery supplies the vastus lateralis muscle. The medial circumflex femoral branch of the deep femoral artery supplies proximal adductor musculature and the region of the hip joint, including the neck and head of the femur.
GAS 570-571; GA 292

50 B. The tibial nerve divides into the medial and lateral plantar nerves on the medial side of the ankle. These two nerves provide sensation for the sole of the foot. Sensory supply to the dorsum of the foot is provided mostly by the superficial fibular (peroneal) nerve, with the deep fibular (peroneal) nerve providing sensation for the skin between the first and second toes. Foot drop would be caused by interruption of the common fibular (peroneal) nerve. Sensory loss to the lateral side of the foot results from loss of the sural nerve. Paralysis of the extensor digitorum brevis

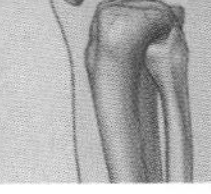

would be attributed to injury to the terminal motor branch of the deep fibular (peroneal) nerve.
GAS 625-626; GA 341-342

51 B. The gastrocnemius muscle arises from the femur just proximal to the femoral condyles. This strong muscle could displace the distal fragment of the broken femur posteriorly. In addition, the popliteal artery is the deepest structure in the popliteal fossa (right against the popliteal surface of the distal femur) and is susceptible to laceration in this scenario. The orthopedic surgeons always look for damage to the popliteal artery in a patient with a supracondylar fracture. The soleus arises from the tibia and would have no effect upon the femur. The semitendinosus arises from the ischial tuberosity and inserts medially on the proximal tibia, via the pes anserinus. The tibialis anterior arises from the tibia and inserts mostly onto the navicular bone.
GAS 589, 590; GA 5, 8-9, 272, 280, 285, 287, 320, 323-324

52 E. The posterior tibial artery provides most of the arterial supply for the neck and body of the talus bone. The fibular (peroneal) artery provides a small amount of vascular supply. The medial plantar and lateral plantar branches of the posterior tibial artery are distributed to tissues in the plantar surface of the foot. The dorsalis pedis is the continuation of the anterior tibial artery on the dorsum of the foot.
GAS 593-594, 605, 623-624; GA 10, 291-292, 307, 322, 335, 342

53 A. The adductor hallucis muscle inserts upon the lateral side of the proximal phalanx of the great toe, and also the lateral sesamoid bone, by way of its oblique and transverse heads. It is supplied by the lateral plantar nerve. The abductor hallucis inserts upon the medial side of the proximal phalanx and the medial sesamoid bone of the great toe. The sesamoid bones are within the tendon of the flexor hallucis brevis and assist it in its function at the first metatarsophalangeal joint. The abductor and flexor hallucis brevis are innervated by the medial plantar nerve. The first dorsal interosseous muscle and the first lumbrical both insert on the medial side of the extensor mechanism of the second toe. The quadratus plantae arises from the calcaneus and inserts on the tendon of the flexor digitorum longus muscle. The first lumbrical is supplied by the medial plantar nerve. The quadratus plantae, the lumbricals 2 to 4, and all interossei are innervated by the lateral plantar nerve.
GAS 620, 621; GA 340

54 B. The deep fibular (peroneal) nerve supplies the dorsiflexors of the foot, including the extensor hallucis longus and extensor digitorum longus. It also supplies the tibialis anterior, an invertor of the foot. This nerve has sensory distribution only to the skin between the first two toes. The common fibular (peroneal) nerve supplies not only the preceding muscles but also the evertors of the foot and provides sensation for most of the dorsum of the foot. The sciatic nerve innervates the muscles of the posterior thigh and all muscles of the leg and foot, in addition to providing sensory supply in those areas. The superficial fibular (peroneal) nerve innervates the evertors of the foot and provides sensation for the dorsum of the foot. The tibial nerve is the nerve for muscles of the posterior compartment of the leg and also of the plantar region and supplies sensation over the medial aspect of the leg posteriorly and the plantar surface of the foot and toes.
GAS 596, 597, 599, 625-627; GA 326-327, 334-335

55 B. The medial plantar nerve innervates the abductor hallucis and both flexor hallucis longus and brevis. This nerve also provides motor supply for the flexor digitorum brevis and the first lumbrical. The lateral plantar nerve innervates all other intrinsic muscles in the plantar region of the foot. The sural nerve is sensory to the lateral posterior leg and lateral side of the foot; it arises from a combination of branches of the tibial nerve and common fibular (peroneal) nerve. The deep fibular (peroneal) nerve supplies dorsiflexors, toe extensors, and invertors of the foot.
GAS 625-626; GA 327, 342-342

56 D. The posterior tibial artery passes under the medial malleolus, about halfway between that bony landmark and the heel, or the calcaneus. The medial edge of the plantar aponeurosis can be palpated just medial to the muscular belly of the abductor hallucis. The sural nerve and the short (lesser) saphenous vein pass around the lateral side of the foot, about halfway between the lateral malleolus and the calcaneus. The sartorius passes behind the medial femoral condyle to insert on the proximal, medial aspect of the tibia via the pes anserinus; usually no pulse can be felt clearly there. The popliteal artery passes between the two heads of the gastrocnemius, where the arterial pulse may be felt very deeply, medial to the midline.
GAS 593-594, 604, 622-623; GA 10, 291-292, 307, 322, 326, 334-335

57 C. The deep fibular (peroneal) nerve supplies the fibularis (peroneus) tertius muscle. Although its name might lead one to think that this muscle is in the lateral compartment with the other two fibularis

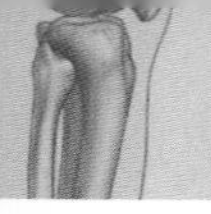

(peroneus) muscles, it is in the anterior, extensor compartment of the leg. It is named for its origin from the fibula. It inserts upon the dorsum of the base of the fifth (or fourth) metatarsal bone and assists in extension and eversion of the foot. The sural nerve is a cutaneous nerve, formed by contributions from the tibial and common fibular (peroneal) nerves; it supplies the posterior lateral leg and the lateral side of the foot. The lateral plantar nerve is a branch of the tibial nerve; it innervates the quadratus plantae, muscles of the little toe, the adductor hallucis, lumbricals 2 to 4, and all of the interossei. It is sensory to the lateral side of the sole and the lateral three and a half digits. The superficial fibular (peroneal) nerve supplies the fibularis (peroneus) longus and brevis and innervates the skin on most of the dorsum of the foot. The tibial nerve supplies the calf muscles and divides into the medial and lateral plantar nerves.
GAS 595-598; GA 326-327, 334-335

58 **A.** Gluteal injections should be given anterior and superior to a line drawn between the posterior superior iliac spine and the greater trochanter to avoid the sciatic nerve and other important nerves and vessels. Occasionally, one can encounter the lateral cutaneous branch of the iliohypogastric nerve, but this usually causes no serious problem. Certainly, one must stay anterior to a vertical line dropped from the highest point of the ilium. If the injected material is too near the sciatic nerve or other motor nerves, it can infiltrate the connective tissue sheath of the nerve, following the nerve, and result in major insult to the neural elements. The needle can cause trauma to this, or other nerves, likewise. Precautions to avoid the sciatic nerve are especially important in injecting the gluteal area in babies. The reduced dimensions are less "forgiving" in babies.
GAS 629; GA 201

59 **B.** The obturator nerve innervates the adductor muscles, including the gracilis, pectineus, and obturator externus. The tibial nerve supplies the calf muscles and intrinsic muscles in the plantar portion of the foot. The inferior gluteal nerve innervates the gluteus maximus; the superior gluteal nerve supplies the gluteus medius and minimus and tensor fasciae latae. The femoral nerve provides motor supply to the quadriceps femoris, sartorius, and, in some cases, the pectineus.
GAS 378, 379, 381, 463, 465-466, 524, 537-539, 574; GA 13, 186-187, 238, 240, 251, 257, 283, 291, 296

60 **A.** The perineal cutaneous branch of the posterior femoral cutaneous nerve provides a significant portion of the cutaneous innervation of the perineum in some individuals and can require separate anesthetic blockade in childbirth or perineal surgery, if other types of anesthesia are not used. The inferior cluneal branches of the posterior femoral cutaneous nerve supply the lower part of the gluteal skin. The lateral cutaneous branch of the iliohypogastric nerve provides sensation for the anterior superior aspect of the gluteal area. The inferior gluteal nerve innervates the gluteus maximus muscle. The middle cluneal nerves arise from the dorsal primary rami of S1 to S3 and supply skin over the middle of the gluteal region.
GAS 491-492; GA 251, 253

61 **D.** The dorsalis pedis is the continuation of the anterior tibial artery into the foot, as it passes the distal end of the tibia and the ankle joint. The pulse of the dorsalis pedis can be felt between the tendon of the extensor hallucis longus and the tendon of the extensor digitorum longus to the second toe. A strong pulse is a positive indicator of circulation through the limb. The fibular (peroneal) artery is a branch of the posterior tibial artery and passes in the calf between the flexor hallucis longus and tibialis posterior, making it difficult to palpate. The deep plantar artery, the extension of the first dorsal interosseous or lateral plantar arteries, passes deep to the aponeurotic tissues and central muscles of the foot, making palpation unlikely. The dorsal metatarsal branches of the dorsalis pedis pass under cover of the extensor digitorum longus and brevis tendons. Palpable pulses of the first or other dorsal metatarsal arteries can therefore be difficult to detect.
GAS 635; GA 10, 326, 334-335

62 **D.** Injury to the dorsalis pedis artery on the dorsum of the foot can also cause trauma to the terminal portion of the deep fibular (peroneal) nerve. In the proximal part of the foot, this could result in loss of sensation between the first and second toes and paralysis of the extensor digitorum brevis and the extensor hallucis brevis muscles. In the distal part of the foot, only the sensory loss might be apparent. Clubfoot is a congenital malformation observed in pediatric patients. This syndrome combines plantar flexion, inversion, and adduction of the foot. Neither extension of the big toe by the extensor hallucis longus nor paralysis of the tibialis anterior (weakness of foot inversion) would occur by this injury because both of these muscles are innervated by the deep fibular (peroneal) nerve much more proximally in the leg.
GAS 605, 623-624, 635; GA 10, 326, 334-335

63 **D.** The sural nerve is formed by contributions from the tibial nerve and a branch from the common

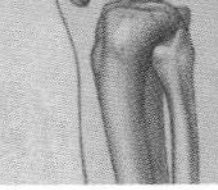

fibular (peroneal) nerve. It provides sensation for the lower lateral portion of the calf and continues beneath the lateral malleolus as the lateral cutaneous nerve of the foot. It is often used for nerve grafting procedures as well as biopsied for diagnostic purposes. When it is grafted to the "living end" of a cut motor or sensory nerve, the severed nerve processes within the "living" nerve grow into the sural nerve sheath, using it as a guide to the distal, surgically anastomosed nerve. Thus, axons from a branch of a functional motor nerve can grow to reinnervate paralyzed muscles. In this case, the surgeon would connect portions of the sural nerve to the functional facial nerve, tunnel it to the opposite side of the face, and join it surgically to the branches of the paralyzed nerve, where it would grow through the now-empty nerve sheaths (due to wallerian degeneration) to the muscles. Growth and reinnervation usually occur at a rate of 1 mm/day (or 1 inch/month) so the time estimated before reinnervation is based on the distance the regenerating fibers need to traverse. The tibial nerve supplies muscles and sensation to the calf and plantar surface of the foot. The common fibular (peroneal) nerve innervates the lateral and anterior compartment muscles and sensation to the dorsum of the foot. The saphenous nerve accompanies the great saphenous vein on the medial side of the leg and foot.
GAS 594, 595, 626, 627; GA 13, 295, 322, 327

64 D. Osgood-Schlatter disease is also called tibial tuberosity apophysitis and affects the area of the tibial tuberosity. It is not a disease but a problem of overuse, typically in boys of 12 to 14 years or girls 10 to 12 years of age. Very active boys and girls, usually during a growth spurt, are subject to the pain and swelling that occur at the site of attachment of the patellar ligament. The ligament can tear, resulting in a long period of healing following treatment. The medial femoral condyle is the area of attachment of the medial collateral ligament and medial meniscus of the knee joint. The posterior intercondylar eminence is the location of origin of the posterior cruciate ligament. The intercondylar eminence is a bony protuberance on the tibial plateau to which the cruciate ligaments and menisci are attached. The anterolateral tibial tubercle, or Gerdy's tubercle, is the attachment of the iliotibial band or tract; thus it connects the femur and tibia laterally.
GAS 558, 559, 630; GA 4, 6, 272, 284

65 A. The patient has bowlegs, or genu varus. The opposite of this is genu valgus, or knock-knee. The normal angle between the femoral shaft and femoral neck is between 120° and 135°. In coxa vara the angle between the shaft and neck of the femur is less than 120°. This can result from fractures, other injuries, or congenital softness of the bone of the femoral neck. This defect results in limb shortening and limping. In coxa valga there is an increase in femoral shaft-neck angulation, which can lead to hip subluxation or dislocation. Coxa valga results from weakness of the adductor musculature. Hallux valgus is commonly known as bunion. In this deformity the big toe points toward the little toe and may override the second toe; the base of the first metatarsal points medially, with a swollen bursal sac at the metatarsophalangeal joint. Excess bony growth of the distal protruding part of the metatarsal bone can also occur. Bunions occur only rarely in people who do not routinely wear shoes.
GAS 529; GA 275-276

66 A. The patellar ligament is a very heavy ligament that connects the patella to the tibial tuberosity; it provides the insertion of the quadriceps femoris tendon upon the tibia. The patella can be thought of as a bone (a sesamoid bone) that develops within the tendon of the quadriceps femoris muscle. When the reflex hammer strikes the patellar ligament, it stretches the ligament slightly for a brief time, resulting in reflex contraction of the quadriceps femoris muscles. This reflex arc is elicited by the femoral nerve (L4 sensory input component and L2, L3 motor output). The quadriceps femoris includes the rectus femoris and the vastus lateralis, intermedius, and medialis. The patella is the largest sesamoid bone in the body. A sesamoid bone is a bone that develops within a tendon. The quadratus femoris muscle of the gluteal area arises from the ischial tuberosity and inserts on the femur proximally. The sartorius arises from the anterior superior iliac spine and inserts on the proximal, medial aspect of the tibia as one of the three tendinous components of the pes anserinus (goose foot). The biceps femoris of the posterior thigh has a long head that arises from the ischial tuberosity and a short head that arises from the femur; they insert on the head of the fibula.
GAS 559, 563, 564, 578, 579, 630; GA 288, 300, 307

67 E. The talus can be rotated externally when the ankle sustains a trimalleolar fracture, also called a Henderson fracture. The fracture may be caused by eversion and posterior displacement of the talus. This injury involves the fracture of the distal fibula (lateral malleolus); the medial malleolus of the tibia; and the posterior portion, or lip, of the tibial plafond (the distal articular portion of the tibia, sometimes referred to as the posterior malleolus). The posterior part of the

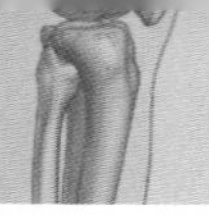

plafond is not truly a malleolus but acts this way in this type of twisting fracture of the ankle. The talus can be forced from its normal position in this fracture, adding to the instability of the ankle. The other bones listed are relatively far from the site of the fractures. The calcaneus resides beneath the talus and articulates distally with the cuboid bone. The head of the talus articulates also with the navicular bone. The navicular bone articulates distally with the three cuneiform bones.
GAS 606, 607; GA 6, 310-312, 314

68 **E.** Hallux valgus, or lateral displacement of the great toe, usually presents as pain over the prominent metatarsal head, due to rubbing from shoes, and it can be associated with deformity of the second toe, which then tends to override the great toe. Hallux valgus is commonly known as bunion. In this deformity the big toe points toward the little toe; the base of the first metatarsal points medially, with a swollen bursal sac at the metatarsophalangeal joint. Excess bony growth of the distal protruding part of the metatarsal bone can also occur. Bunions occur only rarely in people who do not routinely wear shoes. Genu varus is also referred to as bowlegs, or bandylegs, in which the knees are bowed outward. The opposite of this is genu valgus, or knock-knee. The normal angle between the femoral shaft and femoral neck is between 120° and 135°. In coxa vara the angle between the shaft and neck of the femur is less than 120°. This can result from fractures, other injuries, or congenital softness of the bone of the femoral neck. This defect results in limb shortening and limping. In coxa valga there is an increase in femoral shaft-neck angulation, which can lead to hip subluxation or dislocation. Coxa valga results from weakness of the adductor musculature.
GAS 598, 600, 610-611; GA 310-313

69 **C.** The patient's complaint is due to her case of hammer toes. Hammer toe can affect any toe but most commonly the second toe, then the third or fourth toes. It results most commonly from wearing shoes that are too short or shoes with heels that are too high. In hammer toe, the metatarsophalangeal joint is extended, the proximal interphalangeal joint is flexed, and the distal phalanx points downward, looking like a hammer. Hammer toe can occur as a result of a bunion. Calluses, or painful corns, can form on the dorsal surface of the joints. In claw toe, both the proximal and distal interphalangeal joints are strongly flexed, the result of muscle imbalance in the foot. Either hammer toe or claw toe can occur from arthritic changes. Pes cavus is the opposite of flat foot—the patient has a high, flexed plantar arch; it occurs as a result of hereditary motor and sensory neural problems. It is painful because of metatarsal compression.
GAS 604-606; GA 310-313

70 **C.** In piriformis entrapment, the sciatic nerve can be compressed when the piriformis is contracted, leading to painful sensations in the lower limb. These usually involve pain in the gluteal area, posterior thigh, and leg, most frequently resembling a disk lesion at L5-S1, with compression of the S1 spinal nerve. L4 compression would be rather unusual but would involve the quadriceps femoris knee extension, foot inversion, and sensory loss on the medial side of the leg. L5 compression would be indicated by weakness in hip abduction, knee flexion, and sensory loss on dorsal and plantar surfaces of the foot. S1 compression would weaken plantar flexion and foot eversion. Pudendal nerve entrapment would affect the perineal region. The fibular (peroneal) division of the sciatic nerve passes through the piriformis in some individuals, leading to L5, S1–S3 nerve compression.
GAS 118; GA 13, 238, 282-283, 294-296

71 **C.** Incapacitation and unconsciousness from use of cocaine and other powerful narcotics have led to numerous cases of the "gluteal crush syndrome." Compression of the gluteal region while supine for extended periods of time can lead to gluteal crush injury, in which the nerves and vessels of the gluteal area are compressed. This can result in loss of gluteal muscles and other soft tissues and sciatic nerve compression. The nerve compression can cause paralysis of knee flexors and muscles of the anterior and lateral compartments of the leg, with sensory loss in the posterior thigh and leg and sensory loss in the foot. Tibial nerve loss would not result in loss of dorsiflexion of the foot nor generalized sensory loss. Neither piriformis entrapment nor femoral nerve entrapment is associated with loss of gluteal musculature, nor loss of knee flexion or plantar flexion of the foot, nor do they lead to general sensory loss in the limb.
GAS 512, 513, 547-555; GA 280-282

72 **E.** In infants and children until about the age of 8 years, the head of the femur gets its arterial supply by a direct branch of the obturator artery (variably, the medial circumflex femoral). The arterial supply reaches the head of the femur at the fovea capitis by traveling along the ligament of the head of the femur. This source of supply is replaced later by vessels such as branches of the ascending branch of the medial circumflex femoral that pass into foramina of the neck of the femur within the capsule of the hip joint. Similar branches can arise from the lateral circumflex femoral and gluteal

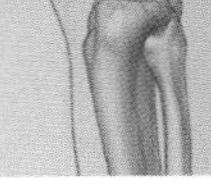

arteries. The deep circumflex iliac artery arises from the external iliac artery and supplies branches to the ilium, the iliacus muscle, and lower portions of the abdominal wall. The acetabular branch of the obturator artery often provides the branch to the head of the femur, an artery that normally regresses early in life, so that it supplies only the immediate area of the fovea capitis. The descending branch of the lateral circumflex femoral supplies the vastus lateralis muscle and participates in anastomoses at the knee. The second perforating branch of the deep femoral artery often supplies the nutrient artery of the shaft of the femur.
GAS 473-477, 532, 533, 540, 541, 572; GA 220, 232, 234, 237, 250, 277, 279, 292

73 D. The lesser (short) saphenous vein ascends up the middle of the calf from beneath the lateral malleolus, most commonly terminating at the popliteal fossa by piercing the deep fascia and joining the popliteal vein. The popliteal vein is the most superficial of major structures deep to the deep popliteal fascia. The perforating tributaries of the deep femoral vein drain to the deep femoral vein of the posterior compartment of the thigh, thereafter into the femoral vein. Superior medial genicular vein is a tributary to the popliteal vein.
GAS 525, 542, 584, 585, 624, 632; GA 11, 344

74 E. The lateral plantar artery provides origin to the deep plantar arterial arch. Medially, the vascular arch anastomoses with the distal portion of the dorsalis pedis by way of the deep plantar artery. The anterior tibial artery continues as the dorsalis pedis at the ankle joint. The fibular (peroneal) artery, by way of a perforating branch in some individuals, replaces the dorsal pedis. The arcuate artery, a branch of the dorsalis pedis, provides origin for the dorsal metatarsal arteries to the lateral toes.
GAS 622-623; GA 326, 334, 342

75 C. The bone to which the injured ligament attaches is the calcaneus. The navicular bone, located medially in the foot, articulates posteriorly with the head of the talus and anteriorly with the cuneiform bones. The cuboid bone of the lateral longitudinal arch articulates posteriorly with the calcaneus. The talus articulates with the tibia and fibula in the ankle joint mortise.
GAS 601, 603, 604, 607, 608; GA 7, 273, 310-312, 314

76 C. The fibularis (peroneus) brevis arises from the fibula and inserts upon the tuberosity at the base of the fifth metatarsal bone. Its attachment is often involved in an inversion fracture of the foot. This fracture can often be overlooked when it is combined with an inversion sprain of the ankle. The fibularis (peroneus) longus arises from the fibula, passes under the lateral malleolus, and then turns medially into the plantar surface of the foot, where it inserts upon the medial cuneiform and first metatarsal bones. The tibialis posterior arises from the tibia in the posterior compartment of the leg; it passes under the medial malleolus and inserts upon the navicular and metatarsal bones. The extensor digitorum brevis arises dorsally from the calcaneus and inserts upon the proximal phalanges of the lateral toes. The adductor hallucis arises from the lateral metatarsals and transverse tarsal ligament and inserts upon the proximal phalanx and lateral sesamoid bone of the big toe.
GAS 595, 596, 613, 634; GA 272, 316, 320, 323-325, 331

77 A. Excessive compression of the prepatellar bursa, as in working on bended knees, can result in pain and swelling of the prepatellar bursa, the so-called housemaid's knee. Prepatellar bursitis affects plumbers, carpet layers, and other people who spend a lot of time on their knees. The bursa normally enables the patella to move smoothly under the skin. The constant friction of these occupations irritates this small lubricating sac (bursa) located just in front of the patella, resulting in a deformable tense cushion of fluid. Treatment usually requires simple drainage, but this may need to be repeated and occasionally steroids introduced. Excessive irritation of the infrapatellar bursa in kneeling for frequent and long periods of time (as in prayer) can result in "parson's knee." The posterior cruciate ligament of the knee can be injured in sudden, strong flexion of the knee, with posterior displacement of the tibia upon the femur. The patellar retinacula are strong, tendinous bands of tissue that join the quadriceps tendon to the vastus lateralis and medialis muscles. The lateral meniscus is a cartilaginous structure between the lateral condyles of the femur and tibia.
GAS 577, 578; GA 306

78 D. The ligament of the head of the femur conveys a small blood vessel for supply of the head of the femur (primarily in childhood). The ligament is stretched during abduction and lateral rotation of the hip joint and has an important role in stabilizing an infant's hip joint before walking. It has the potential to increase stability of the joint in hip reconstruction in developmental hip dysplasia in the pediatric population. The strength of this ligament is comparable to the anterior cruciate ligament of the knee. The iliofemoral ligament (the "Y-shaped ligament of Bigelow") on the anterior aspect of the hip bone resists

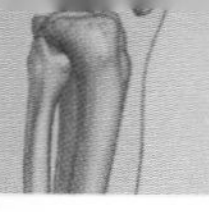

hyperextension of the hip joint. The pubofemoral ligament arises from the pubic bone and is located on the inferior side of the hip joint; it resists abduction of the joint. The ischiofemoral ligament is a triangular band of strong fibers that arises from the ischium and winds upward and laterally over the femoral neck, strengthening the capsule posteriorly. The transverse acetabular ligament attaches to the margins of the acetabular notch and provides origin for the ligament of the head of the femur. The transverse acetabular ligament is fibrous, not cartilaginous, but is regarded as part of the acetabular labrum.
GAS 533-534; GA 277-278

79 **B.** The posterior cruciate ligament tightens in flexion of the knee. It can be damaged by posterior displacement of the tibia upon the femur. With the patient seated, a rupture of the ligament can be demonstrated by the ability to push the tibia posteriorly under the femur. This is the posterior drawer sign. The anterior cruciate ligament resists knee hyperextension. The lateral collateral ligament is a thick, cordlike band that passes from the lateral femoral condyle to the head of the fibula. It is located external to the capsule of the knee joint. The lateral meniscus is a nearly circular band of fibrocartilage that is located laterally within the knee joint. It is less frequently injured than the medial meniscus because it is not attached to the joint capsule or other ligaments. The patellar ligament is the heavy, ligamentous band of insertion of the quadriceps muscle to the tibial tuberosity.
GAS 556-557, 579-581; GA 303-305

80 **A.** Flat foot (pes planus) is due to flattening of the medial longitudinal arch. Often congenital, it may be associated with minor structural anomalies of the tarsal bones. This condition can be seen in wet footprints in which the medial surface of the sole (normally raised in an arch) is visible. Treatment may include intensive foot exercises or arch supports worn in the shoes. Occasionally, surgery is needed in the form of arthrodesis (fusion of the tarsal bones). Pes cavus is a deformity of the foot characterized by a very high medial arch and hyperextension of the toes. The long plantar ligament is a passive ligament of the longitudinal arch. The long plantar ligament connects the calcaneus and cuboid bones. It can be involved with the plantar aponeurosis in plantar fascitis. The long plantar ligament converts the cuboid groove into a canal for the tendon of the fibularis (peroneus) longus. The deltoid ligament is a very strong ligament that interconnects the tibia with the navicular, calcaneus, and talus bones. The medial malleolus will usually fracture before this ligament will tear. The plantar calcaneonavicular, or spring, ligament is a key element in the medial longitudinal arch; it supports the head of the talus bone and thereby is subject to vertical forces exerted through the lower limbs. In the present case, the bilateral pes planus appears to be the result of gradual weakening and failure of the arches.
GAS 518, 519, 614; GA 311

81 **A.** The "unhappy triad" (of O'Donahue) is composed of the medial collateral ligament, medial meniscus, and anterior cruciate ligament. Sudden, forceful thrusts against the lateral side of the knee put tension on the medial collateral ligament, which can then rupture. The medial meniscus is attached to the medial collateral ligament so that it then tears. The anterior cruciate ligament resists hyperextension of the knee; thus, it is the third structure that breaks in the "unhappy triad" of the knee.
GAS 559, 576-577, 583, 646-647; GA 303-305

82 **C.** If the needle is inserted about 1.5 cm lateral to the maximal femoral pulse, it will intersect the femoral nerve in most cases. (Fluoroscopic or ultrasound guidance is advisable to avoid iatrogenic errors.) The deep inguinal ring is located about 4 cm superolateral to the pubic tubercle and very close to the origin of the inferior epigastric vessels from the external iliac artery and vein. The approximate site of exit of the lateral femoral cutaneous nerve from the abdomen is 1.5 cm medial to the anterior superior iliac spine. Injections 1.5 cm medial to the femoral artery pulse will enter the femoral vein. Midway between the anterior superior iliac spine and the pubic symphysis can vary approximately 1.5 cm either medial or lateral from the femoral artery.
GAS 630, 637; GA 290

83 **A.** Morton's neuroma most commonly involves compression (and possible enlargement) of an anastomosing branch that connects the medial and lateral plantar nerves between the third and fourth toes. The pain can be severe. The medial plantar nerve provides sensation for the medial three and a half toes; the lateral plantar nerve supplies the little toe and half of the fourth toe. The neural interconnection can be compressed between the transverse metatarsal ligament and the floor. Women are 10 times more likely than men to be afflicted with this problem, most likely due to wearing shoes that put excessive stress on the forefoot. In about 80% of cases the pain can be eased with different shoes or cortisone injections.
GAS 625-626; GA 327, 341-342

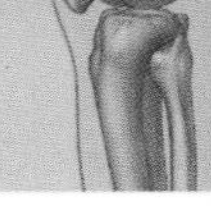

84 D. Inflammation of the plantar aponeurosis is referred to as plantar fasciitis. Plantar fasciitis is a common clinical condition that results from tearing or inflammation of the tough band of tissue stretching from the calcaneus to the ball of the foot (the plantar aponeurosis). It happens frequently to people who are on their feet a lot or engaged in athletics, especially in running and jumping. The pain of plantar fasciitis is usually most significant in the morning, just after you get up from bed and begin to walk. Rest, orthotics, night splints, and anti-inflammatory medications are employed in treatment. Morton's neuroma is a painful lesion of the neural interconnection of the medial and lateral plantar nerves between the third and fourth toes. An eversion sprain of the ankle can break the medial malleolus or tear the deltoid ligament. An inversion sprain commonly injures the fibulocalcaneal ligament or anterior talofibular ligament.
GAS 617; GA 336

85 B. The child has the problem of talipes equinovarus, or clubfoot. Clubfoot is a congenital malformation observed in about 1 in 1000 pediatric patients and first appears in the first trimester of pregnancy. This syndrome combines plantar flexion, inversion, and adduction of the foot. The heel is drawn upward by the tendo calcaneus and turned inward; the forefoot is also adducted, or turned inward. The foot usually is smaller than normal. In coxa vara, the angle between the femoral shaft and neck is reduced to less than 120°, often due to excessive activity of the adductor musculature. Hallux valgus is also known as bunion, in which the big toe points laterally. Hallux varus involves a medial deviation of the first metatarsal or big toe, sometimes the result of attempted correction of bunions. It can also result from arthritis or muscular problems.
GAS 512, 513, 600-627; GA 330-343

86 D. In claw toe, both the proximal and distal interphalangeal joints are strongly flexed, the result of muscle imbalance in the foot. With muscular imbalance, the extensors of the interphalangeal joints are overpowered by the long flexors. The metatarsophalangeal joint is extended, whereas in hammer toe it can be in a neutral position. Either hammer toe or claw toe can occur from arthritic changes. Hammer toe can affect any toe, but it most commonly affects the second toe, then the third or fourth toes. It results most commonly from wearing shoes that are too short or shoes with heels that are too high. In hammer toe, the metatarsophalangeal joint is extended, the proximal interphalangeal joint is flexed, and the distal phalanx may be dorsiflexed, or it may point downward, looking like a hammer. Hammer toe can occur as a result of a bunion. Calluses, or painful corns, can form on the dorsal surface of the joints. Hallux valgus is more commonly referred to as a bunion. The big toe is angulated toward the little toe and may override the second toe. The base of the first metatarsal bone is directed medially and is subject, painfully, to compression. Pes cavus is the opposite of flat foot; the patient has a high, flexed plantar arch. Pes cavus occurs as a result of hereditary motor and sensory neural problems. It is painful because of metatarsal compression.
GAS 518, 611; GA 313

87 D. The ankle jerk reflex, elicited by tapping the tendo Achilles with the reflex hammer, is mediated by the tibial nerve. The superficial fibular (peroneal) nerve supplies the foot evertor muscles of the lateral compartment of the leg and provides sensory supply for the dorsum of the foot. The deep fibular (peroneal) nerve innervates the foot extensor and invertor muscles in the anterior compartment of the leg and supplies skin between the first and second toes. The common fibular (peroneal) nerve combines the functions of the superficial and deep branches. The medial plantar nerve innervates the abductor and flexor muscles of the big toe, the first lumbrical muscle, and flexor digitorum brevis muscle and provides sensation for the medial plantar surface and three and a half toes.
GAS 592; GA 53

88 B. The posterior femoral cutaneous nerve arises from nerves S1 to S3. It provides inferior cluneal branches to the lower portion of the gluteal region and a perineal branch to the perineum and supplies sensation to the posterior thigh to the level of the popliteal fossa. Superior gluteal innervation arises from dorsal rami of L1 to L3. Meralgia paresthetica is the occurrence of pain or burning sensations on the lateral thigh, from compression of the lateral femoral cutaneous nerve. The sural nerve, sensory to the lower calf and lateral foot, arises from contributions from the tibial nerve and common fibular (peroneal) nerve. The posterior femoral cutaneous is a sensory nerve and does not innervate muscles.
GAS 463-468, 465, 538, 539, 552, 553, 584; GA 238, 257

89 B. The vastus medialis inserts upon the medial aspect of the patella and draws it medially, especially in the last quarter of extension—during which it is especially palpable in contraction. This muscle is referred to as the vastus medialus obliquus (VMO).

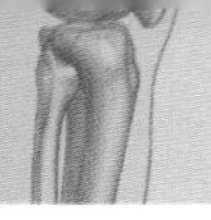

Increasing the strength of this muscle can lessen the lateral dislocation of the patella. The rectus femoris arises from the anterior inferior iliac spine and lip of the acetabulum and draws the patella vertically upward, as does the vastus intermedius.
GAS 561-563; GA 8, 272, 285-286, 288, 296, 307, 324

90 D. Bipartite patella is a normal variant of an unfused superolateral secondary ossification center, which can easily be mistaken for a fracture on a radiograph. The subcutaneous prepatellar bursa can become painfully enlarged with acute or chronic compression, as in crawling about on the knees. Osgood-Schlatter disease is painful involvement of the patellar ligament on the tibial tuberosity, commonly in children 10 to 14 years of age. The medial retinaculum is an expanded portion of the vastus medialis tendon toward the patella.
GAS 558, 616; GA 4, 6, 272, 284

91 D. Femoral artery puncture is one of the most common vascular procedures. The femoral artery can be localized often by simply feeling for the strongest point of the femoral pulse. The femoral artery can be accessed with fluoroscopic assistance at the medial edge of the upper portion of the head of the femur. It is easily localized by Doppler ultrasound if the pulse is poorly felt. It is here that catheters are passed into the femoral artery for catheterization of abdominopelvic and thoracic structures and for antegrade angiography. It is also a site where arterial blood can be obtained for gas analysis. The midinguinal point, halfway between the anterior superior iliac spine and the pubic symphysis, can be either medial or lateral to the femoral artery and is not a dependable landmark. A needle inserted at the level of the inguinal crease, or inferior to the femoral head, can enter the femoral artery distal to the origin of the deep femoral artery, presenting more risk for accidental vascular injury. Four centimeters lateral to the pubic tubercle overlies the deep inguinal ring, with potential entry to spermatic cord, femoral vein, or artery. The fossa ovalis is the opening in the deep fascia of the thigh for the termination of the great saphenous vein in the femoral vein.
GAS 630, 637; GA 290

92 D. Both the medial and lateral menisci are subject to rotational injuries and may be torn. The medial meniscus is much more liable to injury because it is attached to the fused deep layer of the medial collateral ligament and joint capsule. The lateral meniscus is separated from the fibular collateral ligament and is external to the capsule of the knee joint. Commonly seen in football players' knees, meniscal tears are usually diagnosed by MRI or by arthroscopy. The presenting symptoms of tearing may be pain and swelling, or locking of the knee. Locking of the knee suggests a bucket-handle tear, in which a partly detached cartilage wedges between the tibia and femur, inhibiting further movement. A bucket-handle tear is often associated with rupture of the anterior cruciate ligament. Sometimes a momentary click can be heard in flexion/extension movements of the knee. Meniscectomy is a successful operation, but currently there is greater emphasis on repairing small tears. Meniscal cysts can form secondary to meniscal tears and some of these can also be treated arthroscopically.
GAS 559, 576-577, 583, 646-647; GA 303-305

93 B. The tendons of the semitendinosus and semimembranosus provide the superior medial border of the popliteal fossa. The semitendinosus inserts with the pes anserinus on the proximal, medial tibia. The semimembranosus inserts on the tibia posteriorly. The biceps femoris forms the superior lateral border of the fossa, as the tendon passes to insertion on the fibula. The plantaris arises from the femur just above the lateral head of the gastrocnemius, passing distally to insert on the calcaneus via the tendo Achilles. The popliteus arises from the tibia and passes superiorly and laterally to insert on the lateral condyle of the femur, with a connection to the lateral meniscus.
GAS 584-585; GA 5, 308

94 C. The tensor fasciae latae (which is innervated by the superior gluteal nerve) and the iliotibial tract are dense, wide aponeurosis that receives the insertion of the tensor fasciae latae and about 75% of the gluteus maximus. The gluteus maximus is the only one of the muscles listed that is supplied by the inferior gluteal nerve; in fact, it is the only muscle innervated by the inferior gluteal nerve. Gluteus medius and minimus insert on the greater trochanter and are innervated by the superior gluteal nerve. The rectus femoris, supplied by the femoral nerve, inserts via the quadriceps tendon on the patella and tibial tuberosity.
GAS 544-545, 630-631; GA 8-9, 272, 280, 286, 296, 307

95 D. The tendinous distal portion of the adductor magnus inserts on the adductor tubercle on the upper border of the medial condyle of the femur. The femoral artery passes through the adductor hiatus proximal to this tendinous band, continuing as the popliteal artery. The semimembranosus inserts on the proximal, posterior portion of the tibia. The gracilis inserts with the

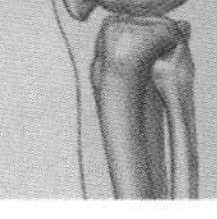

pes anserinus on the proximal, medial aspect of the tibia. The popliteus inserts on the distal lateral portion of the femur, just above the origin of the lateral head of gastrocnemius. The vastus medialis inserts with other quadriceps muscle components on the patella and then on to the tibial tuberosity.
GAS 563, 567; GA 289

96 **B.** The iliopsoas forms the lateral portion of the troughlike floor of the femoral triangle. The pectineus forms the medial portion of this floor. The adductor longus provides a medial border for the femoral triangle and meets the sartorius, the lateral border of the triangle, at the apex. The rectus femoris is a superficial contributor to the quadriceps femoris, lateral to the femoral triangle.
GAS 512-513, 545-547; GA 290

97 **A.** The tendon of the obturator internus leaves the pelvic cavity by passing through the lesser sciatic foramen, wrapping around the lesser sciatic notch. It is joined there by the superior and inferior gemelli and inserts with them on the upper portion of the greater trochanter. The obturator externus arises on the external surface of the pubic bone and obturator membrane and inserts on the greater trochanter. The quadratus femoris arises from the ischial tuberosity and inserts on the intertrochanteric line of the femur. The gluteus medius and minimus insert together on the lateral aspect of the greater trochanter.
GAS 409, 410, 429-431; GA 212, 244

98 **B.** The four muscles that comprise the quadriceps muscle continue distally as the patellar tendon. The patella is then attached to the tibia by the patellar ligament. The vastus lateralis and medialis also attach to the tibia via lateral and medial patellar retinacula, respectively. The lowest fibers of the vastus medialis take an oblique course to eventually attach to the patella, and this muscle is referred to clinically as the vastus medialis obliquus (VMO). The VMO has a relatively direct medial pull on the patella. Thus, weakness of the vastus medialis would lead to lateral dislocation of the patella because it would lose indirect medial stability through the medial patellar retinacula. Weakness of the vastus lateralis would lead to increased instability of the patella and eventually medial dislocation. The rectus femoris and vastus intermedius attach to the patellar tendon. Weakness of either or both would not lead to lateral or medial dislocation.
GAS 562-564; GA 285, 288, 323

99 **B.** Generally, the angle of inclination between the neck and shaft of the femur in older age decreases to around 120°. However, in pathologic conditions it can either increase or decrease from the predicted value. When the angle of inclination increases, it is referred to as coxa valga. Coxa vara on the other hand is a condition characterized by a decreased angle of inclination. Genu varum and genu valgum are deformities characterized by a decreased Q-angle and increased Q-angle, respectively. The Q-angle refers to the angle between the femur and tibia. Hallux valgus is a condition that presents with a lateral deviation of the large toe.
GAS 529-532, 556-558, 642, 646, 647; GA 6-7, 273, 275-278

100 **D.** Plantar fascitis is a common clinical condition that results from tearing or inflammation of the tough band of tissue stretching from the calcaneus to the ball of the foot (the plantar aponeurosis). It usually happens to people who are on their feet frequently or engaged in athletics, especially running and jumping. The pain of plantar fascitis is usually most significant in the morning, just after getting up from bed and beginning to walk. Rest, orthotics, night splints, and anti-inflammatory medications are employed in treatment. A Pott fracture is a bimalleolar fracture, specifically a fracture of the distal end of the fibula (lateral malleolus) and medial malleolus, with outward displacement of the foot. A Dupuytren fracture involves fracture of the distal fibula with dislocation of the foot. Each of these fractures occurs due to sudden and forceful eversion of the foot.
GAS 615; GA 336

101 **A.** When the anterior cruciate ligament is torn, the tibia can be slightly displaced anteriorly from the area of the knee joint by pulling firmly with both hands upon the leg, with the patient in a seated position. This is a positive anterior drawer sign.
GAS 583; GA 303-305

102 **E.** One important function of the deltoid ligament is the prevention of overeversion of the ankle. The ligament is so strong that excessive eversion can cause the medial malleolus to be pulled off (an avulsion fracture) rather than tearing the deltoid ligament.
GAS 605, 606; GA 316

103 **B.** In infants and children up to about 8 years of age, the head of the femur gets its arterial supply by a direct branch of the obturator artery (variably, the medial circumflex femoral). The arterial supply reaches the head of the femur at the fovea capitis by traveling along the ligament of the head of the femur. Probably due to repeated torsion on the ligament, and therefore on the artery, this artery occludes early in life. In turn,

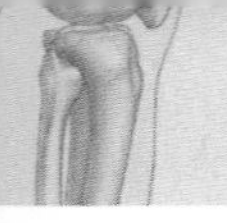

this source of supply is replaced by branches of the gluteal and femoral circumflex vessels.
GAS 473-477, 532, 540-541, 572; GA 220, 232, 234, 237, 250, 277, 279, 292

104 **E.** The ankle jerk reflex involves S1 and S2 levels. L2 to L4 are involved in the patellar reflex. L5 is not a component of a deep tendon reflex.
GAS 592; GA 53

105 **B.** The tensor fasciae lata assists in flexion of the thigh, as well as medial rotation and abduction. Damage to this muscle would adversely affect these motions. The rectus femoris performs hip flexion. The vastus intermedius does extension of the knee. The semimembranosus extends the hip and flexes and medially rotates the knee. The sartorius assists in flexion and lateral rotation of the hip, as well as medial rotation of the knee.
GAS 545, 548, 550, 551; GA 8, 272, 280-282, 285-287, 296

106 **B.** The femoral triangle is the best place to palpate the femoral pulse. It is bounded by the sartorius muscle laterally, adductor longus medially, and the inguinal ligament superiorly. It contains the femoral vein, artery, and nerve (from medial to lateral, respectively). The adductor canal lies deep between the anterior and medial compartments of the thigh and therefore cannot be palpated. The popliteal fossa is the fossa at the back of the knee and contains the popliteal artery and vein, tibial nerve, and common fibular (peroneal) nerve. The femoral pulse cannot be palpated here. The inguinal canal is in the pelvis and is in communication with the anterior abdominal wall. It contains the spermatic cord in males and round ligament of the uterus in females.
GAS 512, 513, 545, 546, 547; GA 290

107 **A.** If the femoral artery is occluded, the descending branch of the lateral circumflex femoral will provide collateral circulation to the thigh. The descending genicular artery is a branch of the femoral and therefore would also be occluded. The medial circumflex femoral artery is a proximal branch of the deep femoral artery and supplies part of the head of the femur. The first perforating branch of the deep femoral artery supplies a small portion of the muscles of the posterior thigh. Finally, the obturator artery supplies a very small artery and vascularizes only the most proximal part of the head of the femur and usually only during the early years of life.
GAS 532, 533, 569, 570; GA 10, 279, 294-295

108 **A.** In a femoral hernia, abdominal contents are forced through the femoral ring, which is just lateral to the lacunar ligament (of Gimbernant) and just medial to the femoral vein. The femoral vein would be found immediately lateral to the femoral hernia. This is correct in most cases because in the majority of people, the femoral vein is found more medial to both the femoral artery and nerve in the femoral triangle. The adductor longus muscle as well as the pectineus muscle would be found deep and medial to the hernia.
GAS 512, 513, 545, 546, 547; GA 290

109 **A.** The femoral vein lies medial to the femoral artery in the femoral sheath. The femoral sheath is broken into three compartments: lateral, intermediate, and medial. The lateral compartment contains the femoral nerve; the medial compartment encloses the femoral canal and consists of lymphatic tissue and a lymph node, plus areolar tissue. The intermediate contains the femoral vein.
GAS 547; GA 290

110 **B.** The superficial inguinal nodes are located near the saphenofemoral junction and drain the superior thigh region. The vertical group receives lymph from the superficial thigh, and the horizontal group receives lymph from the gluteal regions and the anterolateral abdominal wall. The deep inguinal lie deep to the fascia lata and receive lymph from deep lymph vessels (popliteal nodes). The external and internal iliac nodes first receive lymph from pelvic and perineal structures.
GAS 282, 283, 496, 542, 543, 544, 545, 554; GA 254-255, 345

6

UPPER LIMB

1 A 45-year-old woman is being examined as a candidate for cosmetic breast surgery. The surgeon notes that both of her breasts sag considerably. Which structure has most likely become stretched to result in this condition?

- ☐ **A.** Scarpa's fascia
- ☐ **B.** Pectoralis major muscle
- ☐ **C.** Pectoralis minor muscle
- ☐ **D.** Suspensory (Cooper's) ligaments
- ☐ **E.** Serratus anterior muscle

2 A 27-year-old man was admitted to the emergency department after an automobile collision in which he suffered a fracture of the lateral border of the scapula. Six weeks after the accident, physical examination reveals weakness in medial rotation and adduction of the humerus. Which nerve was most likely injured?

- ☐ **A.** Lower subscapular
- ☐ **B.** Axillary
- ☐ **C.** Radial
- ☐ **D.** Spinal accessory
- ☐ **E.** Ulnar

3 A 48-year-old female court stenographer is admitted to the orthopedic clinic with symptoms of carpal tunnel syndrome, with which she has suffered for almost a year. Which muscles most typically become weakened in this condition?

- ☐ **A.** Dorsal interossei
- ☐ **B.** Lumbricals III and IV
- ☐ **C.** Thenar
- ☐ **D.** Palmar interossei
- ☐ **E.** Hypothenar

4 A 45-year-old male arrived at the emergency department with injuries to his left elbow after he fell in a bicycle race. Radiographic and MRI examinations show a fracture of the medial epicondyle and a torn ulnar nerve. Which of the following muscles would be most likely to be paralyzed?

- ☐ **A.** Flexor digitorum superficialis
- ☐ **B.** Biceps brachii
- ☐ **C.** Brachioradialis
- ☐ **D.** Flexor carpi ulnaris
- ☐ **E.** Supinator

5 While walking to his classroom building, a first-year medical student slipped on the wet pavement and fell against the curb, injuring his right arm. Radiographic images showed a midshaft fracture of the humerus. Which pair of structures was most likely injured at the fracture site?

- ▢ **A.** Median nerve and brachial artery
- ▢ **B.** Axillary nerve and posterior humeral circumflex artery
- ▢ **C.** Radial nerve and deep brachial artery
- ▢ **D.** Suprascapular nerve and artery
- ▢ **E.** Long thoracic nerve and lateral thoracic artery

6 An 18-year-old male is brought to the emergency department after an injury while playing rugby. Imaging reveals a transverse fracture of the humerus about 1 inch proximal to the epicondyles. Which nerve is most frequently injured by the jagged edges of the broken bone at this location?

- ▢ **A.** Axillary
- ▢ **B.** Median
- ▢ **C.** Musculocutaneous
- ▢ **D.** Radial
- ▢ **E.** Ulnar

7 A 52-year-old band director suffered problems in her right arm several days after strenuous field exercises for a major athletic tournament. Examination in the orthopedic clinic reveals wrist drop and weakness of grasp but normal extension of the elbow joint. There is no loss of sensation in the affected limb. Which nerve was most likely affected?

- ▢ **A.** Ulnar
- ▢ **B.** Anterior interosseous
- ▢ **C.** Posterior interosseous
- ▢ **D.** Median
- ▢ **E.** Superficial radial

8 A 32-year-old woman is admitted to the emergency department after an automobile collision. Radiographic examination reveals multiple fractures of the humerus. Flexion and supination of the forearm are severely weakened. She also has loss of sensation on the lateral surface of the forearm. Which of the following nerves has most likely been injured?

- ▢ **A.** Radial
- ▢ **B.** Musculocutaneous
- ▢ **C.** Median
- ▢ **D.** Lateral cord of brachial plexus
- ▢ **E.** Lateral cutaneous nerve of the forearm

9 A 24-year-old medical student was bitten at the base of her thumb by her dog. The wound became infected and the infection spread into the radial bursa. The tendon(s) of which muscle will most likely be affected?

- ▢ **A.** Flexor digitorum profundus
- ▢ **B.** Flexor digitorum superficialis
- ▢ **C.** Flexor pollicis longus
- ▢ **D.** Flexor carpi radialis
- ▢ **E.** Flexor pollicis brevis

10 Laboratory studies in the outpatient clinic on a 24-year-old female included assessment of circulating blood chemistry. Which of the following arteries is most likely at risk during venipuncture at the cubital fossa?

- ▢ **A.** Brachial
- ▢ **B.** Common interosseous
- ▢ **C.** Ulnar
- ▢ **D.** Anterior interosseous
- ▢ **E.** Radial

11 A 22-year-old male is diagnosed with metastatic malignant melanoma of the skin over the xiphoid process. Which nodes receive most of the lymph from this area and are therefore most likely to be involved in metastasis of the tumor?

- ▢ **A.** Deep inguinal
- ▢ **B.** Vertical group of superficial inguinal
- ▢ **C.** Horizontal group of superficial inguinal
- ▢ **D.** Axillary
- ▢ **E.** Deep and superficial inguinal

12 A 49-year-old female who had suffered a myocardial infarction must undergo a bypass graft procedure using the internal thoracic artery. Which vessels will most likely continue to supply blood to the anterior part of the upper intercostal spaces?

- ▢ **A.** Musculophrenic
- ▢ **B.** Superior epigastric
- ▢ **C.** Posterior intercostal
- ▢ **D.** Lateral thoracic
- ▢ **E.** Thoracodorsal

13 A 22-year-old woman is admitted to the emergency department in an unconscious state. The nurse takes a radial pulse to determine the heart rate of the patient. This pulse is felt lateral to which tendon?

- ☐ **A.** Palmaris longus
- ☐ **B.** Flexor pollicis longus
- ☐ **C.** Flexor digitorum profundus
- ☐ **D.** Flexor carpi radialis
- ☐ **E.** Flexor digitorum superficialis

14 A 45-year-old male is admitted to the hospital after accidentally walking through a plate glass door in a bar while intoxicated. Physical examination shows multiple lacerations to the upper limb, with inability to flex the distal interphalangeal joints of the fourth and fifth digits. Which of the following muscles is most likely affected?

- ☐ **A.** Flexor digitorum profundus
- ☐ **B.** Flexor digitorum superficialis
- ☐ **C.** Lumbricals
- ☐ **D.** Flexor digitorum profundus and flexor digitorum superficialis
- ☐ **E.** Interossei

15 A 24-year-old man is admitted with a wound to the palm of his hand. He cannot touch the pads of his fingers with his thumb but can grip a sheet of paper between all fingers and has no loss of sensation on the skin of his hand. Which of the following nerves has most likely been injured?

- ☐ **A.** Deep branch of ulnar
- ☐ **B.** Anterior interosseous
- ☐ **C.** Median
- ☐ **D.** Recurrent branch of median
- ☐ **E.** Deep branch of radial

16 A 55-year-old male is examined in a neighborhood clinic after receiving blunt trauma to his right axilla in a fall. He has difficulty elevating the right arm above the level of his shoulder. Physical examination shows the inferior angle of his right scapula protrudes more than the lower part of the left scapula. The right scapula protrudes far more when the patient pushes against resistance. Which of the following neural structures has most likely been injured?

- ☐ **A.** The posterior cord of the brachial plexus
- ☐ **B.** The long thoracic nerve
- ☐ **C.** The upper trunk of the brachial plexus
- ☐ **D.** The site of origin of the middle and lower subscapular nerves
- ☐ **E.** Spinal nerve roots C7, C8, and T1

17 A mother tugs violently on her male child's hand to pull him out of the way of an oncoming car and the child screams in pain. Thereafter, it becomes obvious that the child cannot straighten his forearm at the elbow. When the child is seen in the emergency department, radiographic examination reveals a dislocation of the head of the radius. Which of the following ligaments is most likely directly associated with this injury?

- ☐ **A.** Anular
- ☐ **B.** Joint capsular
- ☐ **C.** Interosseous
- ☐ **D.** Radial collateral
- ☐ **E.** Ulnar collateral

18 After a forceps delivery of a male infant, the baby presents with his left upper limb adducted, internally rotated, and flexed at the wrist. The startle reflex is absent on the ipsilateral side. Which part of the brachial plexus was most likely injured during this delivery?

- ☐ **A.** Lateral cord
- ☐ **B.** Medial cord
- ☐ **C.** Roots of the lower trunk
- ☐ **D.** Root of the middle trunk
- ☐ **E.** Roots of the upper trunk

19 A 35-year-old patient has a small but painful tumor under the nail of the little finger. Which of the following nerves would have to be anesthetized for a painless removal of the tumor?

- ☐ **A.** Superficial radial
- ☐ **B.** Common palmar digital of median
- ☐ **C.** Common palmar digital of ulnar
- ☐ **D.** Deep radial
- ☐ **E.** Recurrent branch of median

20 A 25-year-old male athlete is admitted to the emergency department after a bad landing in the pole vault. Radiographic examination of his hand reveals a fractured carpal bone in the floor of the anatomic snuffbox (Fig. 6-1). Which bone has most likely been fractured?

- ☐ **A.** Triquetral
- ☐ **B.** Scaphoid
- ☐ **C.** Capitate

- D. Hamate
- E. Trapezoid

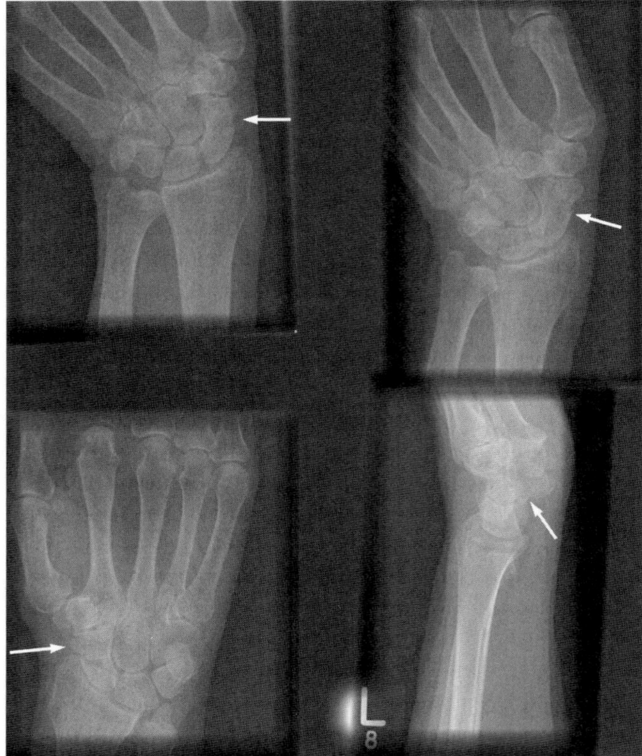

Fig. 6-1

21 A 36-year-old man is brought to the emergency department because of a deep knife wound on the medial side of his distal forearm. He is unable to hold a piece of paper between his fingers and has sensory loss on the medial side of his hand and little finger. Which nerve is most likely injured?

- **A.** Axillary
- **B.** Median
- **C.** Musculocutaneous
- **D.** Radial
- **E.** Ulnar

22 A 19-year-old man is brought to the emergency department after dislocating his shoulder while playing soccer. Following reduction of the dislocation, he has pain over the dorsal region of the shoulder and cannot abduct the arm normally. An MRI of the shoulder shows a torn muscle. Which of the following muscles is most likely to have been damaged by this injury?

- **A.** Coracobrachialis
- **B.** Long head of the triceps
- **C.** Pectoralis minor
- **D.** Supraspinatus
- **E.** Teres major

23 A 47-year-old female tennis professional is informed by her physician that she has a rotator cuff injury that will require surgery. Her physician explains that over the years of play a shoulder ligament has gradually caused severe damage to the underlying muscle. To which of the following ligaments is the physician most likely referring?

- **A.** Acromioclavicular ligament
- **B.** Coracohumeral ligament
- **C.** Transverse scapular ligament
- **D.** Glenohumeral ligament
- **E.** Coracoacromial ligament

24 A 69-year-old man has numbness in the middle three digits of his right hand and finds it difficult to grasp objects with that hand. He states that he retired 9 years earlier, after working as a carpenter for 50 years. He has atrophy of the thenar eminence (Fig. 6-2). Which of the following conditions is the most likely cause of the problems in his hand?

- **A.** Compression of the median nerve in the carpal tunnel
- **B.** Formation of the osteophytes that compress the ulnar nerve at the medial epicondyle
- **C.** Hypertrophy of the triceps muscle compressing the brachial plexus
- **D.** Osteoarthritis of the cervical spine
- **E.** Repeated trauma to the ulnar nerve

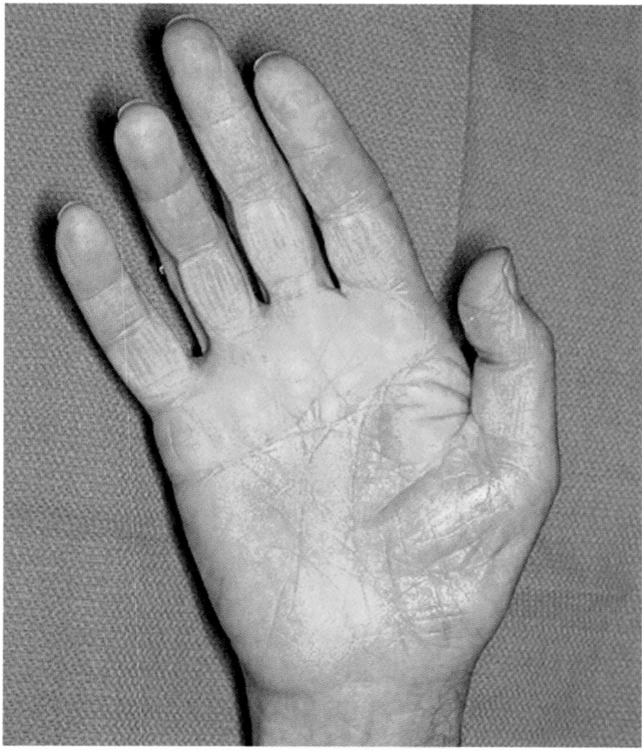

Fig. 6-2

25 A 13-year-old boy is brought to the emergency department after losing control during a motorbike race in which he was run over by several of the other racers. Physical examination reveals several cuts and bruises. He is unable to extend the left wrist, fingers, and thumb, although he can extend the elbow. Sensation is lost in the lateral half of the dorsum of the left hand. Which of the following nerves has most likely been injured to result in these signs, and in what part of the arm is the injury located?

- ▢ **A.** Median nerve, anterior wrist
- ▢ **B.** Median nerve, arm
- ▢ **C.** Radial nerve, midhumerus
- ▢ **D.** Ulnar nerve, midlateral forearm
- ▢ **E.** Ulnar nerve, midpalmar region

26 A 17-year-old male has weakness of elbow flexion and supination of the left hand after sustaining a knife wound in that arm in a street fight. Examination in the emergency department indicates that a nerve has been severed. Which of the following conditions will also most likely be seen during physical examination?

- ▢ **A.** Inability to adduct and abduct his fingers
- ▢ **B.** Inability to flex his fingers
- ▢ **C.** Inability to flex his thumb
- ▢ **D.** Sensory loss over the lateral surface of his forearm
- ▢ **E.** Sensory loss over the medial surface of his forearm

27 Following several days of 12-hour daily rehearsals of the symphony orchestra for a performance of a Wagnerian opera, the 52-year-old male conductor experienced such excruciating pain in the posterior aspect of his right forearm that he could no longer direct the musicians. When the maestro's forearm was palpated 2 cm distal to, and posteromedial to, the lateral epicondyle, the resulting excruciating pain caused the conductor to weep. Injections of steroids and rest were recommended to ease the pain. Which of the following injuries is most likely?

- ▢ **A.** Compression of the ulnar nerve by the flexor carpi ulnaris
- ▢ **B.** Compression of the median nerve by the pronator teres
- ▢ **C.** Compression of the median nerve by the flexor digitorum superficialis
- ▢ **D.** Compression of the superficial radial nerve by the brachioradialis
- ▢ **E.** Compression of the deep radial nerve by the supinator

28 A 54-year-old female marathon runner presents with pain in her right wrist that resulted when she fell with force on her outstretched hand. Radiographic studies indicate an anterior dislocation of a carpal bone (Fig. 6-3). Which of the following bones is most likely dislocated?

- ▢ **A.** Capitate
- ▢ **B.** Lunate
- ▢ **C.** Scaphoid
- ▢ **D.** Trapezoid
- ▢ **E.** Triquetrum

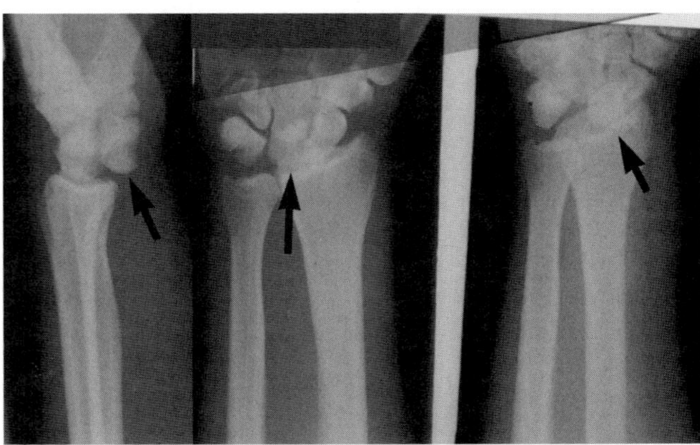

Fig. 6-3

29 A 45-year-old man is admitted to the hospital after a car crash. Radiographic examination reveals mild disk herniations of C7, C8, and T1. The patient presents with a sensory deficit of the C8 and T1 spinal nerve dermatomes. The dorsal root ganglia of C8 and T1 would contain cell bodies of sensory fibers carried by which of the following nerves?

- ▢ **A.** Medial antebrachial cutaneous nerve
- ▢ **B.** Long thoracic nerve
- ▢ **C.** Lateral antebrachial cutaneous nerve
- ▢ **D.** Deep branch of ulnar nerve
- ▢ **E.** Anterior interosseous nerve

30 A 23-year-old female maid was making a bed in a hotel bedroom. As she straightened the sheet by running her right hand over the surface with her fingers extended, she caught the end of the index finger in a fold. She experienced a sudden, severe pain over the base of the terminal phalanx. Several hours later when the pain had diminished, she noted that the end of her right index finger was swollen and she could not completely extend the terminal interphalangeal joint. Which one of the following structures within the digit was most likely injured?

- ▢ **A.** The proper palmar digital branch of the median nerve

- ☐ **B.** The vinculum longa
- ☐ **C.** The insertion of the tendon of the extensor digitorum onto the base of the distal phalanx
- ☐ **D.** The insertion of the flexor digitorum profundus tendon
- ☐ **E.** The insertion of the flexor digitorum superficialis tendon

31 A 45-year-old patient had fallen upon his outstretched hand, resulting in a Smith fracture of the distal end of the radius. The fractured bone displaced a carpal bone in the palmar direction, resulting in nerve compression within the carpal tunnel. Which of the following carpal bones will most likely be dislocated?

- ☐ **A.** Scaphoid
- ☐ **B.** Trapezium
- ☐ **C.** Capitate
- ☐ **D.** Hamate
- ☐ **E.** Lunate

32 A 15-year-old girl was brought to the emergency department with a tear of the tendons in the first dorsal compartment of the wrist from a severe bite by a pit bull dog. The injured tendons in this compartment would include which of the following muscles?

- ☐ **A.** Extensor carpi radialis longus and brevis
- ☐ **B.** Abductor pollicis longus and extensor pollicis brevis
- ☐ **C.** Extensor digitorum
- ☐ **D.** Extensor indicis proprius
- ☐ **E.** Extensor carpi ulnaris

33 As she fell from the uneven parallel bars, the 17-year-old female gymnast grasped the lower bar briefly with one hand but then fell painfully to the floor. An MRI examination reveals an injury to the medial cord of the brachial plexus. Which of the following spinal nerve levels would most likely be affected?

- ☐ **A.** C5, C6
- ☐ **B.** C6, C7
- ☐ **C.** C7, C8
- ☐ **D.** C7, C8, T1
- ☐ **E.** C8, T1

34 A 21-year-old female softball pitcher is examined in the emergency department after she was struck in the arm by a line drive (a ball hit very hard and low). Radiographic and MRI studies show soft tissue injury to the region of the spiral groove, with trauma to the radial nerve. Which of the following muscles would be intact after this injury?

- ☐ **A.** Flexor carpi ulnaris
- ☐ **B.** Extensor indicis
- ☐ **C.** Brachioradialis
- ☐ **D.** Extensor carpi radialis
- ☐ **E.** Supinator

35 Examination of a 21-year-old female athlete with an injury of the radial nerve in the spiral groove would typically demonstrate which of the following physical signs?

- ☐ **A.** Weakness of thumb abduction and thumb extension
- ☐ **B.** Weakness of thumb opposition
- ☐ **C.** Inability to extend the elbow
- ☐ **D.** Paralysis of pronation of the hand
- ☐ **E.** Paralysis of abduction and adduction of the arm

36 The 58-year-old convenience store operator had received a superficial bullet wound to the soft tissues on the medial side of the elbow in an attempted robbery. A major nerve was repaired at the site where it passed behind the medial epicondyle. Bleeding was stopped from an artery that accompanied the nerve in its path toward the epicondyle. Vascular repair was performed on this small artery because of its important role in supplying blood to the nerve. Which of the following arteries was most likely repaired?

- ☐ **A.** The profunda brachii
- ☐ **B.** The radial collateral artery
- ☐ **C.** The superior ulnar collateral artery
- ☐ **D.** The inferior ulnar collateral artery
- ☐ **E.** The anterior ulnar recurrent artery

37 A 60-year-old male butcher accidentally slashed his wrist with his butcher knife, partially dividing the ulnar nerve. Which of the following actions would most likely be lost as a result of this injury?

- ☐ **A.** Flexion of the proximal interphalangeal joint of the fifth digit (little finger)
- ☐ **B.** Extension of the thumb
- ☐ **C.** Adduction of the fifth digit
- ☐ **D.** Abduction of the thumb
- ☐ **E.** Opposition of the thumb

38 A 23-year-old male medical student fell asleep in his chair with Netter's *Atlas* wedged into his axilla. When he awoke in the morning, he was unable to extend the forearm, wrist, or fingers. Movements of the ipsilateral shoulder joint appear to be normal. Which of the following nerves was most likely compressed, producing the symptoms described?

- ▢ **A.** Lateral cord of the brachial plexus
- ▢ **B.** Medial cord of the brachial plexus
- ▢ **C.** Radial nerve
- ▢ **D.** Median nerve
- ▢ **E.** Lateral and medial pectoral nerves

39 The fact that the kidneys of a 32-year-old female patient were failing required that she be placed on dialysis. However, the search in her upper limb for a suitable vein was unexpectedly difficult. The major vein on the lateral side of the arm was too small; others were too delicate. Finally, a vein was found on the medial side of the arm that passed through the superficial and deep fascia to join veins beside the brachial artery. Which of the following veins was this?

- ▢ **A.** Basilic
- ▢ **B.** Lateral cubital
- ▢ **C.** Cephalic
- ▢ **D.** Medial cubital
- ▢ **E.** Medial antebrachial

40 A 29-year-old female had sustained a deep laceration in the proximal part of the forearm. After the wound is closed, the following functional deficits are observed by the neurologist on the service: The first three digits are in a position of extension and cannot be flexed. Digits 4 and 5 are partially flexed at the metacarpophalangeal joints and noticeably more flexed at the distal interphalangeal joints. Sensation is absent in the lateral side of the palm and the palmar surfaces of digits 1 to 3 and half of the fourth digit. Which of the following nerves has (have) most likely been injured?

- ▢ **A.** Median nerve
- ▢ **B.** Ulnar and median nerve
- ▢ **C.** Ulnar nerve
- ▢ **D.** Radial and ulnar nerve
- ▢ **E.** Radial nerve

41 A 35-year-old male wrestler is admitted to the emergency department with excruciating pain in his right shoulder and proximal arm. During physical examination the patient clutches the arm at the elbow with his opposite hand and is unable to move the injured limb. Radiographic studies show that the patient has a dislocation of the humerus at the glenohumeral joint. Which of the following conditions is the most likely?

- ▢ **A.** The head of the humerus is displaced anteriorly.
- ▢ **B.** The head of the humerus is displaced posteriorly.
- ▢ **C.** The head of the humerus is displaced inferiorly.
- ▢ **D.** The head of the humerus is displaced superiorly.
- ▢ **E.** The head of the humerus is displaced medially.

42 The 35-year-old female patient has a hard nodule about 1 cm in diameter slightly above and lateral to her right areola. A specific dye is injected into the tissue around the tumor, and an incision is made to expose the lymphatic vessels draining the area, for the lymphatic vessels take up the dye—which is visible to the eye. The vessels can then be traced to surgically expose the lymph nodes receiving the lymph from the tumor. Which of the following nodes will most likely first encounter the lymph from the tumor?

- ▢ **A.** Anterior axillary (pectoral) nodes
- ▢ **B.** Rotter interpectoral nodes
- ▢ **C.** Parasternal nodes along the internal thoracic artery and vein
- ▢ **D.** Central axillary nodes
- ▢ **E.** Apical or infraclavicular nodes

43 During a fight in a tavern, a 45-year-old male construction worker received a shallow stab wound from a broken beer bottle at a point near the middle of the left posterior triangle of his neck. Upon physical examination it is observed that the left shoulder is drooping lower than the right shoulder, and the superior angle of the scapula juts out slightly. Strength in turning the head to the right or left appears to be symmetric. Which of the following nerves is most likely injured?

- ▢ **A.** Suprascapular nerve in the supraspinous fossa
- ▢ **B.** The terminal segment of the dorsal scapular nerve
- ▢ **C.** The upper trunk of the brachial plexus
- ▢ **D.** The spinal accessory nerve in the posterior cervical triangle
- ▢ **E.** The thoracodorsal nerve in the axilla

44 A 44-year-old woman is diagnosed with radial nerve palsy. When muscle function is examined at the metacarpophalangeal (MCP), proximal interphalangeal (PIP), and distal interphalangeal (DIP) joints, what findings are most likely to be present?

- ▢ **A.** Inability to abduct the digits at the MCP joint
- ▢ **B.** Inability to adduct the digits at the MCP joint
- ▢ **C.** Inability to extend the MCP joints only
- ▢ **D.** Inability to extend the MCP, PIP, and DIP joints
- ▢ **E.** Inability to extend the PIP and DIP joints

45 A 27-year-old male painter is admitted to the hospital after falling from a ladder. Physical examination reveals that the patient is unable to abduct his arm more than 15° and cannot rotate the arm laterally. A radiographic examination reveals an oblique fracture of the humerus. He has associated sensory loss over the shoulder area. Which of the following injuries will most likely correspond to the symptoms of the physical examination?

- ☐ **A.** Fracture of the medial epicondyle
- ☐ **B.** Fracture of the glenoid fossa
- ☐ **C.** Fracture of the surgical neck of the humerus
- ☐ **D.** Fracture of the anatomic neck of the humerus
- ☐ **E.** Fracture of the middle third of the humerus

46 A 47-year-old female patient's right breast exhibited characteristics of peau d'orange; that is, the skin resembled orange peel. This condition is primarily a result of which of the following?

- ☐ **A.** Shortening of the suspensory ligaments by cancer in the axillary tail
- ☐ **B.** Blockage of cutaneous lymphatic vessels
- ☐ **C.** Contraction of the retinacula cutis of the areola and nipple
- ☐ **D.** Invasion of the pectoralis major by the cancer
- ☐ **E.** Ipsilateral (same side) inversion of the periareolar skin from ductular cancer

47 A 29-year-old female is examined in the emergency department after falling from her balcony. Radiographic examination reveals that she has suffered a broken clavicle, with associated internal bleeding. Which of the following vessels is most likely to be injured in clavicular fractures?

- ☐ **A.** Subclavian artery
- ☐ **B.** Cephalic vein
- ☐ **C.** Lateral thoracic artery
- ☐ **D.** Subclavian vein
- ☐ **E.** Internal thoracic artery

48 A 68-year-old female is examined by the senior resident in emergency medicine after her fall on a wet bathroom floor in the shopping center. Physical examination reveals a posterior displacement of the left distal wrist and hand. Radiographic examination reveals an oblique fracture of the radius. Which of the following is the most likely fracture involved in this case?

- ☐ **A.** Colles' fracture
- ☐ **B.** Scaphoid fracture
- ☐ **C.** Bennett's fracture
- ☐ **D.** Volkmann's ischemic contracture
- ☐ **E.** Boxer's fracture

49 A 34-year-old female skier was taken by ambulance to the hospital after she struck a tree on the ski slope. Imaging gives evidence of a shoulder separation. Which of the following typically occurs in this kind of injury?

- ☐ **A.** Displacement of the head of the humerus from the glenoid cavity
- ☐ **B.** Partial or complete tearing of the coracoclavicular ligament
- ☐ **C.** Partial or complete tearing of the coracoacromial ligament
- ☐ **D.** Rupture of the transverse scapular ligament
- ☐ **E.** Disruption of the glenoid labrum

50 A 22-year-old male construction worker is admitted to the hospital after he suffers a penetrating injury to his upper limb from a nail gun. Upon physical examination the patient is unable to flex the distal interphalangeal joints of digits 4 and 5. What is the most likely cause of his injury?

- ☐ **A.** Trauma to the ulnar nerve near the trochlea
- ☐ **B.** Trauma to the ulnar nerve at the wrist
- ☐ **C.** Median nerve damage proximal to the pronator teres
- ☐ **D.** Median nerve damage at the wrist
- ☐ **E.** Trauma to spinal nerve root C8

51 The shoulder of a 44-year-old deer hunter had been penetrated by a bolt released from a crossbow. The bolt had transected the axillary artery just beyond the origin of the subscapular artery. A compress is placed on the wound with deep pressure. After a clamp is placed on the bleeding artery, thought is given to the anatomy of the vessel. What collateral arterial pathways are available to bypass the site of injury?

- ☐ **A.** Suprascapular with circumflex scapular artery
- ☐ **B.** Dorsal scapular with thoracodorsal artery
- ☐ **C.** Posterior humeral circumflex artery with deep brachial artery
- ☐ **D.** Lateral thoracic with brachial artery
- ☐ **E.** Supreme thoracic artery with thoracoacromial artery

52 A 17-year-old male suffered the most common of fractures of the carpal bones when he fell on his outstretched hand. Which bone would this be?

- ☐ **A.** Trapezium
- ☐ **B.** Lunate

- C. Pisiform
- D. Hamate
- E. Scaphoid

53 A 54-year-old male cotton farmer visits the outpatient clinic because of a penetrating injury to his forearm with a baling hook. After the limb is anesthetized, the site of the wound is opened and flushed thoroughly to remove all debris. The patient is not able to oppose the tip of the thumb to the tip of the index finger, as in making the OK sign. He is able to touch the tips of the ring and little fingers to the pad of his thumb. What nerve has most likely been injured?

- A. Median
- B. Posterior interosseous
- C. Radial
- D. Recurrent median
- E. Anterior interosseous

54 Endoscopic examination of the shoulder of a 62-year-old female clearly demonstrated erosion of the tendon within the glenohumeral joint. What tendon was this?

- A. Glenohumeral
- B. Long head of triceps
- C. Long head of biceps
- D. Infraspinatus
- E. Coracobrachialis

55 The orthopedic surgeon exposed the muscle in the supraspinous fossa so that she could move it laterally, in repair of an injured rotator cuff. As she reflected the muscle from its bed, an artery was exposed crossing the ligament that bridges the notch in the superior border of the scapula. What artery was this?

- A. Subscapular
- B. Transverse cervical
- C. Dorsal scapular
- D. Posterior humeral circumflex
- E. Suprascapular

56 A 61-year-old man was hit by the cricket bat in the midhumeral region of his left arm. Physical examination reveals an inability to extend the wrist and loss of sensation on a small area of skin on the dorsum of the hand proximal to the first two fingers. What nerve supplies this specific region of the hand?

- A. Radial
- B. Posterior interosseous
- C. Lateral antebrachial cutaneous
- D. Medial antebrachial cutaneous
- E. Dorsal cutaneous of ulnar

57 A 45-year-old woman is admitted to the hospital with neck pain. An MRI examination reveals a herniated disk in the cervical region. Physical examination reveals weakness in wrist extension and paraesthesia on the back of her arm and forearm. Which of the following spinal nerves is most likely injured?

- A. C5
- B. C6
- C. C7
- D. C8
- E. T1

58 A 22-year-old male football player suffered a wrist injury while falling with force on his outstretched hand. When the anatomic snuffbox is exposed in surgery, an artery is visualized crossing the fractured bone that provides a floor for this space. What artery was visualized?

- A. Ulnar
- B. Radial
- C. Anterior interosseous
- D. Posterior interosseous
- E. Deep palmar arch

59 The right shoulder of a 78-year-old female had become increasingly painful over the past year. Abduction of the right arm caused her to wince from the discomfort. Palpation of the deltoid muscle by the physician produced exquisite pain. Imaging studies reveal intermuscular inflammation extending over the head of the humerus. What structure was inflamed?

- A. Subscapular bursa
- B. Infraspinatus muscle
- C. Glenohumeral joint cavity
- D. Subacromial bursa
- E. Teres minor muscle

60 A 55-year-old male metallurgist had been diagnosed with carpal tunnel syndrome. To begin the operation, an anesthetic injection into his axillary sheath was used instead of a general anesthesia. From which of the following structures does the axillary sheath take origin?

- A. Superficial fascia of the neck
- B. Superficial cervical investing fascia
- C. Buccopharyngeal fascia
- D. Clavipectoral fascia
- E. Prevertebral fascia

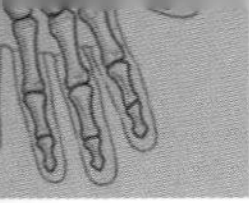

61 A 45-year-old woman is admitted to the hospital with neck pain. A CT scan reveals a tumor in the left side of her oral cavity. The tumor and related tissues are removed with a radical neck surgical procedure. Two months postoperatively the patient's left shoulder droops quite noticeably. Physical examination reveals distinct weakness in turning her head to the right and impairment of abduction of her left upper limb to the level of the shoulder. Which of the following structures was most likely injured during the radical neck surgery?

- ▢ **A.** Suprascapular nerve
- ▢ **B.** Long thoracic nerve
- ▢ **C.** Spinal accessory nerve
- ▢ **D.** The junction of spinal nerves C5 and C6 of the brachial plexus
- ▢ **E.** Radial nerve

62 A 23-year-old male basketball player is admitted to the hospital after injuring his shoulder during a game. Physical and radiographic examinations reveal total separation of the shoulder (Fig. 6-4). Which of the following structures has most likely been torn?

- ▢ **A.** Glenohumeral ligament
- ▢ **B.** Coracoacromial ligament
- ▢ **C.** Tendon of long head of biceps brachii
- ▢ **D.** Acromioclavicular ligament
- ▢ **E.** Transverse scapular ligament

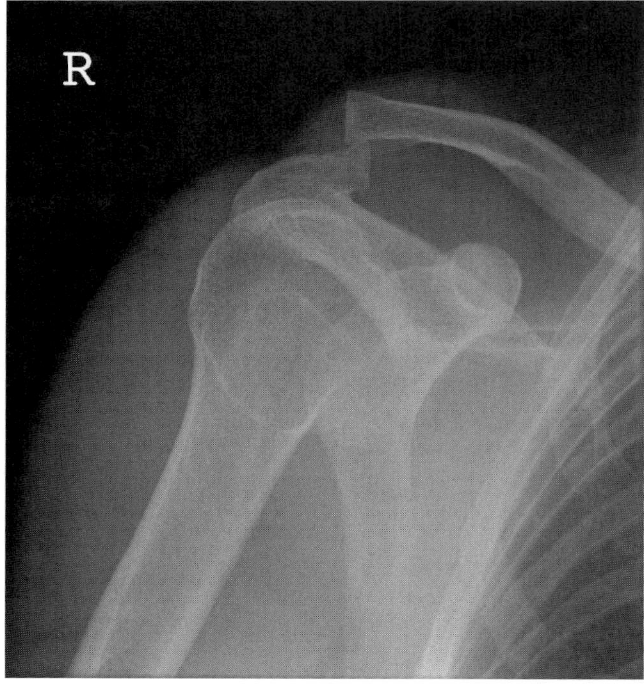

Fig. 6-4

63 A 35-year-old male body builder has enlarged his shoulder muscles to such a degree that the size of the quadrangular space is greatly reduced. Which of the following structures would most likely be compressed in this condition?

- ▢ **A.** Axillary nerve
- ▢ **B.** Anterior humeral circumflex artery
- ▢ **C.** Cephalic vein
- ▢ **D.** Radial nerve
- ▢ **E.** Subscapular artery

64 A 43-year-old woman visits the outpatient clinic with a neurologic problem. Diagnostically, she cannot hold a piece of paper between her thumb and the lateral side of her index finger without flexing the distal joint of her thumb. This is a positive Froment sign and a diagnosis of ulnar neuropathy. Weakness of which specific muscle causes this sign to appear?

- ▢ **A.** Flexor pollicis longus
- ▢ **B.** Adductor pollicis
- ▢ **C.** Flexor digiti minimi
- ▢ **D.** Flexor carpi radialis
- ▢ **E.** Extensor indicis

65 A 48-year-old female piano player visited the outpatient clinic with numbness and tingling in her left hand. A diagnosis was made of nerve compression in the carpal tunnel, and the patient underwent an endoscopic nerve release. Two weeks postoperatively the patient complained of a profound weakness in the thumb, with loss of thumb opposition. The sensation to the hand, however, was unaffected. Which of the following nerves was injured during the operation?

- ▢ **A.** The first common digital branch of the median nerve
- ▢ **B.** The second common digital branch of the median nerve
- ▢ **C.** Recurrent branch of median nerve
- ▢ **D.** Deep branch of the ulnar nerve
- ▢ **E.** Anterior interosseus nerve

66 A 19-year-old male had suffered a deep laceration to an upper limb when he stumbled and fell on a broken bottle. On examination of hand function it is observed that he is able to extend the metacarpophalangeal joints of all his fingers in the affected limb. He cannot extend the interphalangeal joints of the fourth and fifth digits, and extension of the interphalangeal joints of the second and third digits is very weak.

There is no apparent sensory deficit in the hand. Which of the following nerves has most likely been injured?

- ▢ **A.** Radial nerve at the elbow
- ▢ **B.** Median nerve at the wrist
- ▢ **C.** Ulnar nerve in midforearm
- ▢ **D.** Deep branch of ulnar nerve
- ▢ **E.** Recurrent branch of the median nerve

67 A 41-year-old woman is scheduled for a latissimus dorsi muscle flap to cosmetically augment the site of her absent left breast, postmastectomy. Part of the latissimus dorsi muscle is advanced to the anterior thoracic wall, based upon arterial supply provided in part by the artery that passes through the triangular space of the axilla. What artery is forming the vascular base of this flap?

- ▢ **A.** Circumflex scapular artery
- ▢ **B.** Dorsal scapular artery
- ▢ **C.** Transverse cervical artery
- ▢ **D.** Lateral thoracic artery
- ▢ **E.** Thoracoacromial artery

68 A 31-year-old male hockey player fell on his elbow and is admitted to the emergency department. Radiographic examination reveals a fracture of the surgical neck of the humerus, producing an elevation and adduction of the distal fragment. Which of the following muscles would most likely cause the adduction of the distal fragment?

- ▢ **A.** Brachialis
- ▢ **B.** Teres minor
- ▢ **C.** Pectoralis major
- ▢ **D.** Supraspinatus
- ▢ **E.** Pectoralis minor

69 A 74-year-old woman is admitted to the emergency department after stumbling over her pet dog. Radiographic examination reveals a fracture of the upper third of the right radius, with the distal fragment of the radius and hand pronated. The proximal end of the fractured radius deviates laterally. Which of the following muscles is primarily responsible for the lateral deviation?

- ▢ **A.** Pronator teres
- ▢ **B.** Supinator
- ▢ **C.** Pronator quadratus
- ▢ **D.** Brachioradialis
- ▢ **E.** Brachialis

70 A 12-year-old male had received a laceration in the palmar surface of the wrist while playing with a very sharp knife. The cut ends of a tendon could be seen within the wound in the exact midline of the wrist. Which tendon lies in this position in most people?

- ▢ **A.** Palmaris longus
- ▢ **B.** Flexor carpi radialis
- ▢ **C.** Abductor pollicis longus
- ▢ **D.** Flexor carpi ulnaris
- ▢ **E.** Flexor pollicis longus

71 A 22-year-old male medical student was seen in the emergency department with a complaint of pain in his hand. He confessed that he had hit a vending machine in the hospital when he did not receive his soft drink after inserting money twice. The medial side of the dorsum of the hand was quite swollen, and one of his knuckles could not be seen when he "made a fist." The physician made a diagnosis of a "boxer's fracture." What was the nature of the impatient student's injury?

- ▢ **A.** Fracture of the styloid process of the ulna
- ▢ **B.** Fracture of the neck of the fifth metacarpal
- ▢ **C.** Colles' fracture of the radius
- ▢ **D.** Smith's fracture of the radius
- ▢ **E.** Bennett's fracture of the thumb

72 Fine motor function in the right hand of a 14-year-old female with scoliosis since birth appeared to be quite reduced, including thumb opposition, abduction and adduction of the digits, and interphalangeal joint extension. Radiography confirmed that her severe scoliosis was causing marked elevation of the right first rib. Long flexor muscles of the hand and long extensors of the wrist appear to be functioning within normal limits. There is notable anesthesia of the skin on the medial side of the forearm; otherwise, sensory function in the limb is intact. Which of the following neural structures is most likely impaired?

- ▢ **A.** Median nerve
- ▢ **B.** Middle trunk of the brachial plexus
- ▢ **C.** Radial nerve
- ▢ **D.** Lower trunk of the brachial plexus
- ▢ **E.** T1 nerve root

73 A 23-year-old female had a painful injury to her hand in a dry ski-slope competition, in which she fell and caught her thumb in the matting. Radiographic and physical examinations reveal rupture of the ulnar collateral ligament of the metacarpophalangeal joint of the thumb. Lidocaine is injected into the area to relieve the pain, and she is scheduled for a surgical repair. From which of the following clinical problems is she suffering?

- ▢ **A.** De Quervain's syndrome
- ▢ **B.** Navicular bone fracture
- ▢ **C.** Boxer's thumb
- ▢ **D.** Gamekeeper's thumb
- ▢ **E.** Bennett's thumb

74 A 26-year-old male power lifter visits the outpatient clinic with a painful shoulder. Radiographic examination reveals tendinopathy of the long head of the biceps. Which of the following conditions will most likely be present during physical examination?

- ▢ **A.** Pain is felt in the anterior shoulder during forced contraction.
- ▢ **B.** Pain is felt in the lateral shoulder during forced contraction.
- ▢ **C.** Pain is felt during abduction and flexion of the shoulder joint.
- ▢ **D.** Pain is felt during extension and adduction of the shoulder joint.
- ▢ **E.** Pain is felt in the lateral shoulder during flexion of the shoulder joint.

75 A 43-year-old female tennis player visits the outpatient clinic with pain over the right lateral epicondyle of her elbow. Physical examination reveals that the patient has lateral epicondylitis. Which of the following tests should be performed during physical examination to confirm the diagnosis?

- ▢ **A.** Nerve conduction studies
- ▢ **B.** Evaluation of pain experienced during flexion and extension of the elbow joint
- ▢ **C.** Observing the presence of pain when the wrist is extended against resistance
- ▢ **D.** Observing the presence of numbness and tingling in the ring and little fingers when the wrist is flexed against resistance
- ▢ **E.** Evaluation of pain felt over the styloid process of radius during brachioradialis contraction

76 A male skier had a painful fall against a rocky ledge. Radiographic findings revealed a hairline fracture of the surgical neck of the humerus. The third-year medical student assigned to this patient was asked to determine whether there was injury to the nerve associated with the area of injury. Which of the following tests would be best for checking the status of the nerve?

- ▢ **A.** Have the patient abduct the limb while holding a 10-lb weight.
- ▢ **B.** Have the patient shrug the shoulders.
- ▢ **C.** Test for presence of skin sensation over the lateral side of the shoulder.
- ▢ **D.** Test for normal sensation over the medial skin of the axilla.
- ▢ **E.** Have the patient push against an immovable object like a wall and assess the position of the scapula.

77 A 27-year-old male had lost much of the soft tissue on the dorsum of his left hand in a motorcycle crash. Imaging studies show no other upper limb injuries. Because the left extensor carpi radialis longus and brevis tendons were lost, it was decided to replace those tendons with the palmaris longus tendons from both forearms because of those tendons' convenient location and relative unimportance. Postoperatively it is found that sensation is absent in both hands on the lateral palm and palmar surfaces of the first three digits; there is also paralysis of thumb opposition. What is the most likely cause of the sensory deficit and motor loss in both thumbs?

- ▢ **A.** Bilateral loss of spinal nerve T1 with fractures of first rib bilaterally
- ▢ **B.** Lower plexus (lower trunk) trauma
- ▢ **C.** Dupuytren contracture
- ▢ **D.** Left radial nerve injury in the posterior compartment of the forearm
- ▢ **E.** The palmaris longus was absent bilaterally; the nerve beneath it looked like a tendon.

78 A 15-year-old male received a shotgun wound to the ventral surface of the upper limb. Upon examination it is quickly observed that the patient exhibits a complete clawhand but can extend his wrist. What is the nature of this patient's injury?

- ▢ **A.** The ulnar nerve has been severed at the wrist.
- ▢ **B.** The median nerve has been injured in the carpal tunnel.
- ▢ **C.** The median and ulnar nerves are damaged at the wrist.
- ▢ **D.** The median and ulnar nerves have been injured at the elbow region.
- ▢ **E.** The median, ulnar, and radial nerves have been injured at midhumerus.

79 A 68-year-old woman fell when she missed the last step from her motor home. Radiographic examination at the local medical care center reveals a fracture of the distal radius. The distal fragment of the radius is angled forward. What name is commonly applied to this type of injury?

- ▢ **A.** Colles' fracture
- ▢ **B.** Scaphoid fracture
- ▢ **C.** Bennett's fracture
- ▢ **D.** Smith's fracture
- ▢ **E.** Boxer's fracture

80 It was reported by the sports media that the outstanding 27-year-old shortstop for the New York team would miss a number of baseball games. He was hit on a fingertip while attempting to catch a ball barehanded. A tendon had been torn. The team doctor commented that the ballplayer could not straighten the last joint of the long finger of his right hand, and the finger would require surgery. From what injury did the ballplayer suffer?

- ▢ **A.** Clawhand deformity
- ▢ **B.** Boutonnière deformity
- ▢ **C.** Swan-neck deformity
- ▢ **D.** Dupuytren contracture
- ▢ **E.** Mallet finger

81 A 31-year-old female figure skater is examined in the emergency department following an injury that forced her to withdraw from competition. When her male partner missed catching her properly from an overhead position, he grasped her powerfully, but awkwardly, by the forearm. Clinical examination demonstrated a positive Ochsner test, inability to flex the distal interphalangeal joint of the index finger on clasping the hands. In addition, she is unable to flex the terminal phalanx of the thumb and has loss of sensation over the thenar half of the hand. What is the most likely nature of her injury?

- ▢ **A.** Median nerve injured within the cubital fossa
- ▢ **B.** Anterior interosseous nerve injury at the pronator teres
- ▢ **C.** Radial nerve injury at its entrance into the posterior forearm compartment
- ▢ **D.** Median nerve injury at the proximal skin crease of the wrist
- ▢ **E.** Ulnar nerve trauma halfway along the forearm

82 A 19-year-old fell from a cliff when he was hiking in the mountains. He broke his fall by grasping a tree branch, but he suffered injury to the C8-T1 spinal nerve roots. Sensory tests would thereafter confirm the nature of his neurologic injury by the sensory loss in the part of the limb supplied by which of the following?

- ▢ **A.** Lower lateral brachial cutaneous nerve
- ▢ **B.** Musculocutaneous nerve
- ▢ **C.** Intercostobrachial nerve
- ▢ **D.** Medial antebrachial cutaneous nerve
- ▢ **E.** Median nerve

83 The mastectomy procedure on a 52-year-old female involved excision of the tumor and a removal of lymph nodes, including the pectoral, central axillary, and infraclavicular groups. Six months after her mastectomy, the patient complains to her personal physician of an unsightly deep hollow area inferior to the medial half of the clavicle, indicating a significant area of muscle atrophy and loss. She states that the disfigurement has taken place quite gradually since her mastectomy. Physical examination reveals no obvious motor or sensory deficits. What was the most likely cause of the patient's cosmetic problem?

- ▢ **A.** Part of the pectoralis major muscle was cut and removed in the mastectomy.
- ▢ **B.** The pectoralis minor muscle was removed entirely in the surgery.
- ▢ **C.** A branch of the lateral pectoral nerve was cut.
- ▢ **D.** The medial pectoral nerve was cut.
- ▢ **E.** The lateral cord of the brachial plexus was injured.

84 A 54-year-old female was found unconscious on the floor, apparently after a fall. She was admitted to the hospital, and during physical examination it was observed that she had absence of her brachioradialis reflex. Which spinal nerve is primarily responsible for this reflex in the majority of cases?

- ▢ **A.** C5
- ▢ **B.** C6
- ▢ **C.** C7
- ▢ **D.** C8
- ▢ **E.** T1

85 A 43-year-old man is admitted to the hospital, having suffered a whiplash injury when his compact auto was struck from behind by a sports utility vehicle. MRI examination reveals some herniation of a disk in the cervical region. Physical examination reveals that the patient has lost elbow extension; there is absence of his triceps reflex and loss of extension of the metacarpophalangeal joints on the ipsilateral side. Which of the following spinal nerves is most likely affected?

- ▢ **A.** C5
- ▢ **B.** C6
- ▢ **C.** C7

- D. C8
- E. T1

86 A 29-year-old patient has a dislocated elbow in which the ulna and medial part of the distal humerus have become separated. What classification of joint is normally formed between these two bones?

- A. Ball and socket
- B. Ginglymus
- C. Enarthrodial
- D. Synarthrosis
- E. Sellar

87 A 45-year-old woman motorcyclist, propelled over the handlebars of her bike by an encounter with a rut in the road, lands on the point of one shoulder. The woman is taken by ambulance to the emergency department. During physical examination the arm appears swollen, pale, and cool. Any movement of the arm causes severe pain. Radiographic examination reveals a fracture and a large hematoma, leading to diagnosis of Volkmann's ischemic contracture. At which of the following locations has the fracture most likely occurred?

- A. Surgical neck of humerus
- B. Radial groove of humerus
- C. Supracondylar line of humerus
- D. Olecranon
- E. Lateral epicondyle

88 A 55-year-old female choreographer had been treated in the emergency department after she fell from the stage into the orchestra pit. Radiographs revealed fracture of the styloid process of the ulna. Disruption of the triangular fibrocartilage complex is suspected. With which of the following bones does the ulna normally articulate at the wrist?

- A. Triquetrum
- B. Hamate
- C. Radius and lunate
- D. Radius
- E. Pisiform and triquetrum

89 A 67-year-old female had a bad fall while walking her dog the evening before. She states that she fell on her outstretched hand. Radiographs do not demonstrate any bony fractures. The clinician observes the following signs of neurologic injury: There is weakness of flexion of her wrist in a medial direction, there is a loss of sensation on the medial side of the hand, and there is clawing of the fingers. Where is the most likely place of nerve trauma?

- A. Behind the medial epicondyle
- B. Between the pisiform bone and the flexor retinaculum
- C. Within the carpal tunnel
- D. At the cubital fossa, between the ulnar and radial heads of origin of flexor digitorum superficialis
- E. At the radial neck, 1 cm distal to the humerocapitellar joint

90 An 18-year-old male suffered a significant laceration through the skin and underlying tissues at the distal crease of the wrist. The medical student rotating through the emergency department suspected (correctly) that the ulnar nerve was cut completely through at this location. Which of the following would most likely occur?

- A. The patient could not touch the tip of the thumb to the tips of the other digits.
- B. There would be loss of sensation on the dorsum of the medial side of the hand.
- C. The patient would be unable to flex the interphalangeal joints.
- D. There would be decreased ability to extend the interphalangeal joints.
- E. There would be no serious functional problem at all to the patient.

91 A 45-year-old man visits the outpatient clinic after a digit of his left hand was injured when a door was slammed on his hand. A superficial cut on his middle finger has been sutured, but functional deficits are observed in the finger: The proximal interphalangeal joint is pulled into constant flexion, whereas the distal interphalangeal joint is held in a position of hyperextension. What is the most likely diagnosis?

- A. Mallet finger
- B. Boutonnière deformity
- C. Dupuytren contracture
- D. Swan-neck deformity
- E. Silver fork wrist deformity

92 A 67-year-old housepainter visits the outpatient clinic complaining that his hands are getting progressively worse, becoming more and more painful and losing their function. On physical examination of the hands, there is flexion of the metacarpophalangeal joints, extension of the proximal interphalangeal joints, and slight flexion of the distal interphalangeal joints. What is the most likely diagnosis?

- A. Mallet finger
- B. Boutonnière deformity

- C. Dupuytren contracture
- D. Swan-neck deformity
- E. Silver fork wrist deformity

93 Several weeks after surgical dissection of her left axilla for the removal of lymph nodes for staging and treatment of her breast cancer, a 32-year-old woman was told by her general physician that she had "winging" of her left scapula when she pushed against resistance during her physical examination. She told the physician that she had also experienced difficulty lately in raising her right arm above her head when she was combing her hair. In a subsequent consult visit with her surgeon, she was told that a nerve was accidentally injured during the diagnostic surgical procedure and that this produced her scapular abnormality and inability to raise her arm normally. What was the origin of this nerve?

- A. The upper trunk of her brachial plexus
- B. The posterior division of the middle trunk
- C. Roots of the brachial plexus
- D. The posterior cord of the brachial plexus
- E. The lateral cord of the brachial plexus

94 A 72-year-old man consulted his physician because he had noticed a thickening of the skin at the base of his left ring finger during the preceding 3 months. As he described it, "There appears to be some hard tissue that is pulling my little and ring fingers into my palm." On examination of the palms of both hands, localized and firm ridges are observed in the palmar skin that extend from the middle part of the palm to the base of the ring and little fingers. What is the medical term for this sign?

- A. Ape hand
- B. Dupuytren
- C. Clawhand
- D. Wrist drop
- E. Mallet finger

95 A 24-year-old female basketball player is admitted to the emergency department after an injury to her shoulder. Radiographic examination reveals a shoulder dislocation. What is the most commonly injured nerve in shoulder dislocations?

- A. Axillary
- B. Radial
- C. Median
- D. Ulnar
- E. Musculocutaneous

96 A 45-year-old male is admitted to the hospital with a painful arm after a "strongest man in the world" contest. Physical examination gives evidence of a rupture of the long tendon of the biceps brachii (Fig. 6-5). Which of the following is the most likely location of the rupture?

- A. Intertubercular groove
- B. Midportion of the biceps muscle
- C. Junction with the short head of the biceps muscle
- D. Proximal end of the combined biceps muscle
- E. Bony insertion of the muscle

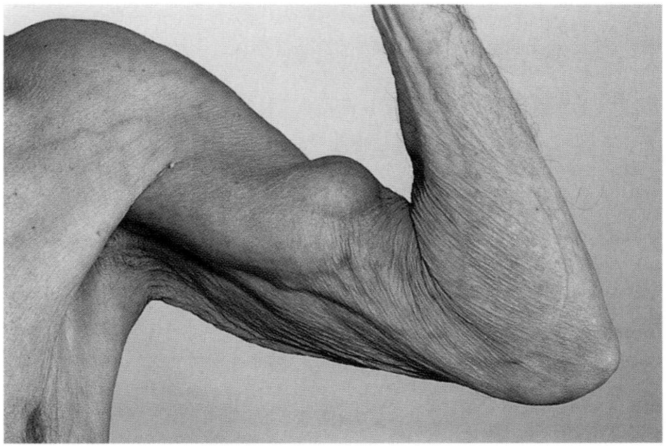

Fig. 6-5

97 After the orthopedic surgeon examined the MRI of the shoulder of a 42-year-old female he informed her that the supraspinatus muscle was injured and needed to be repaired surgically. Which of the following is true of the supraspinatus muscle?

- A. It inserts on the lesser tubercle of the humerus.
- B. It initiates adduction of the shoulder.
- C. It is innervated chiefly by the C5 spinal nerve.
- D. It is supplied by the upper subscapular nerve.
- E. It originates from the lateral border of the scapula.

98 A 5-year-old boy is admitted to the emergency department after falling from a tree. The parents are informed by the radiologist that their son's fracture is the most common fracture that occurs in children. Which of the following bones was broken?

- A. Humerus
- B. Radius
- C. Ulna
- D. Scaphoid
- E. Clavicle

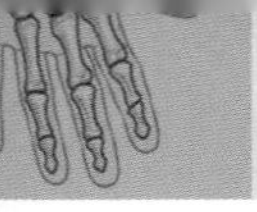

99 A 22-year-old woman visits the outpatient clinic with pain in her left upper limb. She has a long history of pain in this limb and difficulty with fine motor tasks of the hand. Physical examination reveals paraesthesia along the medial surface of the forearm and palm and weakness and atrophy of gripping muscles (long flexors) and the intrinsic muscles of the hand. The radial pulse is diminished when her neck is rotated to the ipsilateral side (positive Adson test). What is the most likely diagnosis?

- ☐ **A.** Erb-Duchenne paralysis
- ☐ **B.** Aneurysm of the brachiocephalic artery, with plexus compression
- ☐ **C.** Thoracic outlet syndrome
- ☐ **D.** Carpal tunnel syndrome
- ☐ **E.** Injury to the medial cord of the brachial plexus

100 Physical examination reveals weakness of medial deviation of the wrist (adduction), loss of sensation on the medial side of the hand, and clawing of the fingers. Where is the most likely place of injury?

- ☐ **A.** Compression of a nerve passing between the humeral and ulnar heads of origin of flexor carpi ulnaris
- ☐ **B.** Compression of a nerve passing at Guyon's canal between the pisiform bone and flexor retinaculum
- ☐ **C.** Compression of a nerve passing through the carpal tunnel
- ☐ **D.** Compression of a nerve passing between the ulnar and radial heads of origin of flexor digitorum superficialis
- ☐ **E.** Compression of a nerve passing deep to brachioradialis muscle

101 A 22-year-old pregnant woman was admitted emergently to the hospital after the baby had begun to appear at the introitus. The baby had presented in the breech position, and it had been necessary to exert considerable traction to complete the delivery. The newborn is shown in Fig. 6-6. Which of the following structures was most likely injured by the trauma of childbirth?

- ☐ **A.** Radial nerve
- ☐ **B.** Upper trunk of the brachial plexus
- ☐ **C.** Lower trunk of the brachial plexus
- ☐ **D.** Median, ulnar, and radial nerves
- ☐ **E.** Upper and lower trunks of the brachial plexus

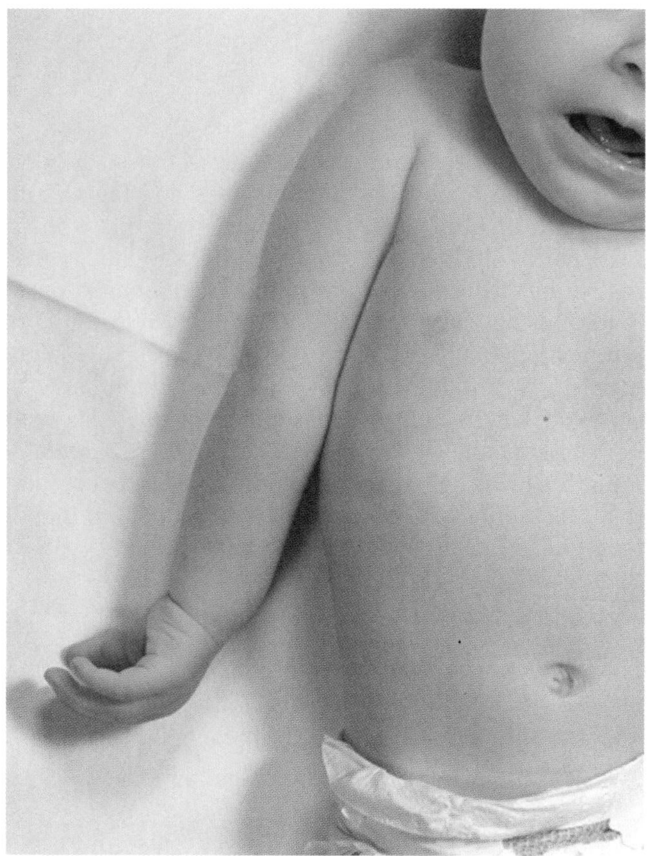

Fig. 6-6

102 A 17-year-old female student of martial arts entered the emergency department with a complaint of pain in her hand. Patient history reveals that she had been breaking concrete blocks with her hand. Examination reveals that the patient has weak abduction and adduction of her fingers but has no difficulty in flexing them. The patient also has decreased sensation over the palmar surfaces of the fourth and fifth digits. Which of the following best describes the nature of her injury?

- ☐ **A.** Compression of the median nerve in the carpal tunnel
- ☐ **B.** Fracture of the triquetrum, with injury to the dorsal ulnar nerve
- ☐ **C.** Dislocation of a bone in the proximal row of the carpus
- ☐ **D.** Fracture of the shaft of the fifth metacarpal
- ☐ **E.** Injury of the ulnar nerve in Guyon's canal

103 A 10-year-old male suffered a dog bite that entered the common flexor synovial sheath of his forearm. He was admitted to the hospital, where the wound was cleaned and dressed and he was treated further with rabies antiserum. Two days later the boy was suffering from an elevated temperature, and his palm and one digit were obviously swollen, causing him to cry with pain. Into which of the digits could the infection spread most easily, following the anatomy of the typical common flexor sheath?

- A. First
- B. Second
- C. Third
- D. Fourth
- E. Fifth

104 While sharpening his knife, a 23-year-old male soldier accidentally punctured the ventral side of the fifth digit at the base of the distal phalanx. The wound became infected, and within a few days the infection has spread into the palm, within the sheath of the flexor digitorum profundus tendons. If the infection were left untreated, into which of the following spaces could it most likely spread?

- A. Central compartment
- B. Hypothenar compartment
- C. Midpalmar space
- D. Thenar compartment
- E. Thenar space

105 A 36-year-old patient is admitted to the emergency department with a dull ache in the shoulder or axilla (Fig. 6-7). During physical examination the pain worsens by activity, and, conversely, rest and elevation relieve the pain. History reveals that the patient was hospitalized the past week and a central venous line was used. What is the most likely diagnosis?

- A. Axillary-subclavian vein thrombosis
- B. Compression of C5 to C8 spinal nerve
- C. Disk herniation of C4 to C8
- D. Impingement syndrome
- E. Injury to radial, ulnar, and median nerves

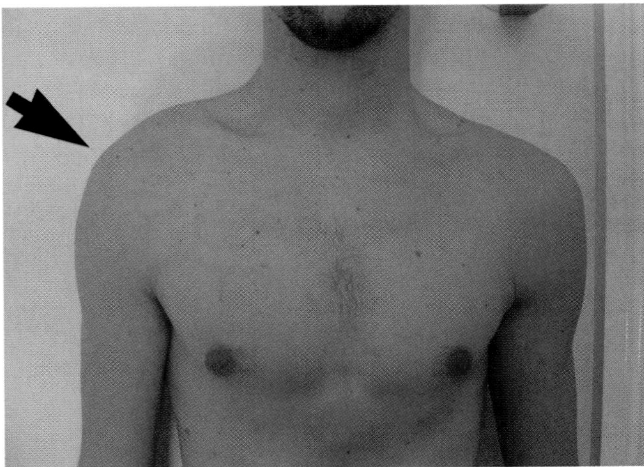

Fig. 6-7

106 A 22-year-old woman had suffered a severe knife wound to the upper lateral portion of her pectoral region, with entry of the knife at the deltopectoral groove. Pressure applied to the wound had prevented further profuse bleeding. In the emergency department, vascular clamps were applied to the axillary artery, proximal and distal to the site of injury—which had occurred between the second and third parts of the axillary artery. The vascular surgeon knew there was time to repair the wound of the artery because of the rich collateral pathway provided by the anastomoses between which of the following of arteries?

- A. Transverse cervical and suprascapular
- B. Posterior humeral circumflex and profunda brachii
- C. Suprascapular and circumflex scapular
- D. Supreme (superior) thoracic and thoracoacromial
- E. Lateral thoracic and suprascapular

107 In a penetrating wound to the forearm of a 24-year-old male, the median nerve is injured at the entrance of the nerve into the forearm. Which of the following would most likely be apparent when the patient's hand is relaxed?

- A. The MCP and IP joints of the second and third digits of the hand will be in a condition of extension.
- B. The third and fourth digits will be held in a slightly flexed position.
- C. The thumb will be flexed and slightly abducted.
- D. The first, second, and third digits will be held in a slightly flexed position.
- E. The MCP and IP joints of the second and third digits of the hand will be in a condition of flexion.

108 A 55-year-old male firefighter is admitted to the hospital after blunt trauma to his right axilla. Examination reveals winging of the scapula and partial paralysis of the right side of the diaphragm. Which of the following parts of the brachial plexus have been injured?

- A. Cords
- B. Divisions
- C. Roots
- D. Terminal branches
- E. Trunks

109 A 69-year-old man has numbness and pain in the middle three digits of his right hand at night. He retired

9 years ago after working as a carpenter for 30 years. He has atrophy of the thenar eminence (see Fig. 6-2 on page 172). Which of the following conditions will be the most likely cause of this atrophy?

- ▢ **A.** Compression of the median nerve in the carpal tunnel
- ▢ **B.** Formation of the osteophytes that compress the ulnar nerve at the ulnar condyle
- ▢ **C.** Hypertrophy of the triceps muscle compressing the brachial plexus
- ▢ **D.** Osteoarthritis of the cervical spine
- ▢ **E.** Repeated trauma to the ulnar nerve

110 A 54-year-old woman presents with pain in her right wrist that resulted when she fell forcefully on her outstretched hand. Radiographic studies indicate an anterior dislocation of a carpal bone of the proximal row (see Fig. 6-3 on page 180). Which of the following bones is most commonly dislocated?

- ▢ **A.** Capitate
- ▢ **B.** Lunate
- ▢ **C.** Scaphoid
- ▢ **D.** Pisiform
- ▢ **E.** Triquetrum

111 A 32-year-old male who is an expert target shooter reports pain in his right upper limb and slight tingling and numbness of all digits of the ipsilateral hand. However, the tingling and numbness of the fourth and fifth digits is the most severe. The man states that the problem usually occurs when he is firing his gun with his hand overhead. Radiographic studies reveal the presence of a cervical rib and accessory scalene musculature. Which of the following structures is most likely being compressed?

- ▢ **A.** Axillary artery
- ▢ **B.** Upper trunk of brachial plexus
- ▢ **C.** Subclavian artery
- ▢ **D.** Lower trunk of brachial plexus
- ▢ **E.** Brachiocephalic artery and lower trunk of brachial plexus

112 A 23-year-old woman arrives at the emergency department with a swollen, painful forearm. An MRI examination reveals a compartment syndrome originating at the interosseous membrane between the radius and ulna. Which of the following type of joint will most likely be affected?

- ▢ **A.** Synarthrosis
- ▢ **B.** Symphysis
- ▢ **C.** Synchondrosis
- ▢ **D.** Trochoid
- ▢ **E.** Ginglymus

113 While working out with weights, a 28-year-old woman experiences a severe pain in her chest. The pain is referred to the anterior chest wall and radiating to the mandible and her left arm. The woman felt dizzy and after 10 minutes she collapsed and was unconscious. A physician happened to be near the woman and immediately tried to feel her radial pulse. The radial artery lies between two tendons near the wrist, which are useful landmarks. Which of the following is the correct pair of tendons?

- ▢ **A.** Flexor carpi radialis and palmaris longus
- ▢ **B.** Flexor carpi radialis and brachioradialis
- ▢ **C.** Brachioradialis and flexor pollicis longus
- ▢ **D.** Flexor pollicis longus and flexor digitorum superficialis
- ▢ **E.** Flexor pollicis longus and flexor digitorum profundus

114 A 59-year-old woman is admitted to the hospital in a state of shock. During physical examination, several lacerations are noted in her forearm and her radial pulse is absent. Where is the most typical place to identify the radial artery immediately after crossing the radiocarpal joint?

- ▢ **A.** Between the two heads of the first dorsal interosseous muscles
- ▢ **B.** At the anatomic snuffbox
- ▢ **C.** Below the tendon of the flexor pollicis longus
- ▢ **D.** Between the first and second interosseous muscle
- ▢ **E.** Between the first interosseous muscle and the adductor pollicis longus

115 A 69-year-old woman visits the outpatient clinic with a complaint of numbness and tingling of her hand for the past 3 months. Physical examination reveals she has numbness and pain in the lateral three digits of her right hand that are relieved by vigorous shaking of the wrist. In addition, the abductor pollicis brevis, opponens pollicis, and the first two lumbrical muscles are weakened. Sensation was decreased over the lateral palm and the volar aspect of the first three digits. Which of the following nerves is most likely compressed?

- ▢ **A.** Ulnar
- ▢ **B.** Radial
- ▢ **C.** Recurrent median
- ▢ **D.** Median
- ▢ **E.** Posterior interosseous

116 A 32-year-old man is admitted to the emergency department after a severe car crash. Radiographic examination reveals multiple fractures of his right upper limb. A surgical procedure is performed and metallic plates are attached to various bony fragments to restore the anatomy. Five months postoperatively the patient visits the outpatient clinic. Upon physical examination the patient can abduct his arm and extend the forearm, but the sensation of the forearm and hand is intact; however, the hand grasp is very weak, and he cannot extend his wrist against gravity. Which of the following nerves was most likely injured during the surgical procedure?

- ☐ **A.** Posterior cord of the brachial plexus
- ☐ **B.** Radial nerve at the distal third of the humerus
- ☐ **C.** Radial and ulnar
- ☐ **D.** Radial, ulnar, and median
- ☐ **E.** Radial and musculocutaneous

117 A 52-year-old man is admitted to the emergency department after falling on wet pavement. Radiographic examination reveals fracture of the radius. An MRI study reveals a hematoma between the fractured radius and supinator muscle. Upon physical examination the patient has weakened abduction of the thumb and extension of the metacarpophalangeal joints of the fingers. Which of the following nerves is most likely affected?

- ☐ **A.** Anterior interosseous
- ☐ **B.** Posterior interosseous
- ☐ **C.** Radial nerve
- ☐ **D.** Deep branch of ulnar nerve
- ☐ **E.** Median nerve

118 A 34-year-old woman is admitted to the emergency department after a car crash. Radiographic studies show marked edema and hematoma of the arm, but there are no fractures. During physical examination the patient presents with inability to abduct her arm without first establishing lateral momentum of the limb, and inability to flex the elbow and shoulder. Which of the following portions of the brachial plexus is most likely injured?

- ☐ **A.** Superior trunk
- ☐ **B.** Middle trunk
- ☐ **C.** Inferior trunk
- ☐ **D.** Lateral cord
- ☐ **E.** Medial cord

119 A 22-year-old man is admitted to the hospital after a car collision. Radiographic examination reveals an oblique fracture of his humerus. Upon physical examination the patient is unable to extend his forearm. The damaged nerve was most likely composed of fibers from which of the following spinal levels?

- ☐ **A.** C5, C6
- ☐ **B.** C5, C6, C7
- ☐ **C.** C5, C6, C7, C8, T1
- ☐ **D.** C6, C7, C8, T1
- ☐ **E.** C7, C8, T1

120 A 56-year-old woman is admitted to the hospital after a severe car crash. A large portion of her chest wall needed to be surgically removed and replaced with a musculoosseous scapular graft involving the medial border of the scapula. Which of the following arteries will most likely recompensate the blood supply to the entire scapula?

- ☐ **A.** Suprascapular
- ☐ **B.** Dorsal scapular artery
- ☐ **C.** Posterior humeral circumflex artery
- ☐ **D.** Lateral thoracic
- ☐ **E.** Supreme thoracic artery

121 A 56-year-old woman visits the emergency department after falling on wet pavement. Radiographic examination reveals osteoporosis and a Colles' fracture. Which of the following carpal bones are often fractured or dislocated with a Colles' fracture?

- ☐ **A.** Triquetrum and scaphoid
- ☐ **B.** Triquetrum and lunate
- ☐ **C.** Scaphoid and lunate
- ☐ **D.** Triquetrum, lunate, and scaphoid
- ☐ **E.** Triquetrum and pisiform

122 A 3-year-old girl is admitted to the emergency department with severe pain. History taking reveals that the girl was violently lifted by her raised arm by her mother to prevent the girl from walking in front of a moving car. Which of the following is most likely the cause of the pain?

- ☐ **A.** Compression of median nerve
- ☐ **B.** Separation of the head of radius from its articulation with trochlea of humerus
- ☐ **C.** Separation of head of radius from its articulation with ulna and capitulum of humerus
- ☐ **D.** Separation of ulna from its articulation with trochlea of humerus
- ☐ **E.** Stretching of radial nerve as it passes behind medial epicondyle of humerus

123 A 61-year-old man was hit by a cricket bat in the midhumeral region of his left arm. Physical examination reveals normal elbow motion; however, he could not

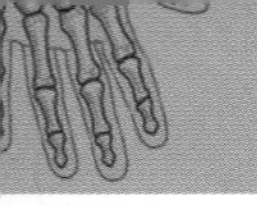

extend his wrist or his metacarpophalangeal joints and he reported a loss of sensation on a small area of skin on the dorsum of the hand proximal to the first two digits. Radiographic examination reveals a hairline fracture of the shaft of the humerus just distal to its midpoint. Which of the following nerves is most likely injured?

- ▢ **A.** Median
- ▢ **B.** Ulnar
- ▢ **C.** Radial
- ▢ **D.** Musculocutaneous
- ▢ **E.** Axillary

124 A 34-year-old man is admitted to the hospital after a car collision. Radiographic examination reveals a fracture at his wrist. Physical examination reveals paralysis of the muscles that act to extend the interphalangeal joints (Fig. 6-10). Which of the following nerves is most likely injured?

- ▢ **A.** Ulnar
- ▢ **B.** Recurrent branch of median
- ▢ **C.** Radial
- ▢ **D.** Musculocutaneous
- ▢ **E.** Anterior interosseous

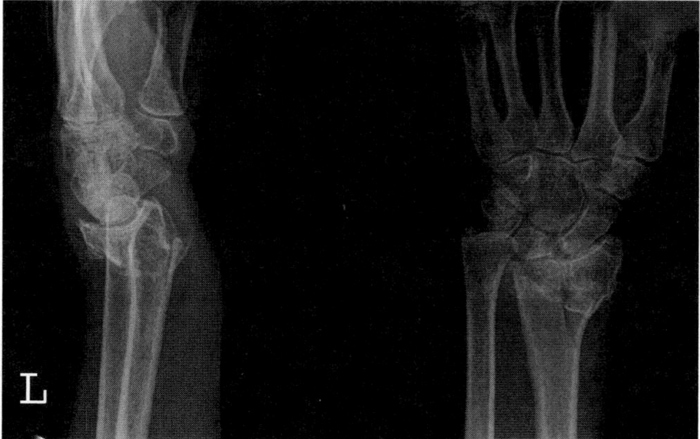

Fig. 6-10

125 A 45-year-old woman is admitted to the hospital with neck pain. An MRI examination reveals a herniated disk in the cervical region. Physical examination reveals weak triceps brachii muscles. Which of the following spinal nerves is most likely injured?

- ▢ **A.** C5
- ▢ **B.** C6
- ▢ **C.** C7
- ▢ **D.** C8
- ▢ **E.** T1

126 A 34-year-old woman is admitted to the hospital after a car collision. Physical examination reveals a mallet finger. Which of the following conditions is expected to be present during radiographic examination?

- ▢ **A.** A lesion of the ulnar nerve at the distal flexor crease of the wrist
- ▢ **B.** A separation of the extension expansion over the middle interphalangeal joint
- ▢ **C.** Compression of the deep ulnar nerve by dislocation of the lunate bone
- ▢ **D.** Avulsion fracture of the dorsum of the distal phalanx
- ▢ **E.** Fracture of the fourth or fifth metacarpal bone

127 A 42-year-old woman is admitted to the hospital with injury to the upper (superior) trunk of the brachial plexus. The diagnosis is Erb-Duchenne palsy. Which of the following conditions is expected to be present during physical examination?

- ▢ **A.** Winged scapula
- ▢ **B.** Inability to laterally rotate the arm
- ▢ **C.** Paralysis of intrinsic muscles of the hand
- ▢ **D.** Paraesthesia in the medial aspect of the arm
- ▢ **E.** Loss of sensation in the dorsum of the hand

128 A 41-year-old woman is admitted to the hospital after a car crash. Radiographic examination reveals a transverse fracture of the radius proximal to the attachment of the pronator teres muscle. The proximal portion of the radius is deviated laterally. Which of the following muscles will most likely be responsible for this deviation?

- ▢ **A.** Pronator teres
- ▢ **B.** Pronator quadratus
- ▢ **C.** Brachialis
- ▢ **D.** Supinator
- ▢ **E.** Brachioradialis

129 A 45-year-old woman is bitten by a dog on the lateral side of her hand. Two days later the woman develops fever and swollen lymph nodes. Which of the following group of lymphatics will most likely be involved?

- ▢ **A.** Central
- ▢ **B.** Humeral
- ▢ **C.** Pectoral
- ▢ **D.** Subscapular
- ▢ **E.** Parasternal

130 A 25-year-old woman is admitted to the emergency department after a car collision. Radiographic examination reveals a fracture at the spiral groove of the humerus. A cast is placed, and 3 days later the patient complains of severe pain over the length of her arm. During physical examination the arm appears swollen, pale, and cool. Radial pulse is absent, and any movement of the arm causes severe pain. Which of the following conditions will most likely characterize the findings of the physical examination?

- ▢ **A.** Venous thrombosis
- ▢ **B.** Thoracic outlet syndrome
- ▢ **C.** Compartment syndrome
- ▢ **D.** Raynaud's disease
- ▢ **E.** Injury of the radial nerve

131 A 22-year-old woman is admitted to the hospital after falling from a tree. Radiographic examination reveals fractured pisiform and hamate bones. Which of the following nerves will most likely be injured?

- ▢ **A.** Median
- ▢ **B.** Recurrent median
- ▢ **C.** Radial
- ▢ **D.** Anterior interosseous
- ▢ **E.** Deep ulnar

132 A 43-year-old man visits the outpatient clinic with a painful shoulder. Physical examination reveals a painful arc syndrome due to supraspinatus tendinopathy. Which of the following conditions will be present during physical examination?

- ▢ **A.** Painful abduction 0° to 15°
- ▢ **B.** Painful abduction 0° to 140°
- ▢ **C.** Painful abduction 70° to 140°
- ▢ **D.** Painful abduction 15° to 140°
- ▢ **E.** Painful abduction 40° to 140°

133 A 54-year-old woman is admitted to the hospital after falling from a tree with an outstretched hand. Radiographic examination reveals a wrist dislocation. Which of the following carpal bones will most likely be involved?

- ▢ **A.** Scaphoid-lunate
- ▢ **B.** Trapezoid-trapezium
- ▢ **C.** Hamate-lunate
- ▢ **D.** Pisiform-triquetrum
- ▢ **E.** Hamate-capitate

134 A 62-year-old man is admitted to the emergency department after falling on wet pavement. Radiographic examination reveals a carpometacarpal fracture at the base of the thumb. What is the term applied to the described fracture?

- ▢ **A.** Colles fracture
- ▢ **B.** Scaphoid fracture
- ▢ **C.** Bennett's fracture
- ▢ **D.** Smith's fracture
- ▢ **E.** Boxer's fracture

135 A 23-year-old woman is participating in a dry ski-slope competition. The woman is admitted to the emergency department after falling and catching her thumb in the matting. Radiographic and physical examinations reveal rupture of the ulnar collateral ligament of the metacarpophalangeal joint of the thumb. The thumb is extremely painful and an injection of lidocaine is performed. What is the most likely diagnosis in this case?

- ▢ **A.** Gamekeeper's thumb
- ▢ **B.** Scaphoid fracture
- ▢ **C.** Bennett's fracture
- ▢ **D.** Smith's fracture
- ▢ **E.** Boxer's fracture

136 A 54-year-old woman is found unconscious in her car. She is admitted to the hospital, and during physical examination she has absent biceps brachii reflex. What is the spinal level of the afferent component of this reflex?

- ▢ **A.** C5
- ▢ **B.** C6
- ▢ **C.** C7
- ▢ **D.** C8
- ▢ **E.** T1

137 A 54-year-old woman is found unconscious in her bed. She is admitted to the hospital, and during physical examination she has absence of her brachioradialis reflex. The ventral ramus of which spinal nerve is responsible for this reflex?

- ▢ **A.** C5
- ▢ **B.** C6
- ▢ **C.** C7
- ▢ **D.** C8
- ▢ **E.** T1

138 A 55-year-old woman is admitted to the emergency department after a car crash. Physical examination reveals severe pain in the flexor muscles of the forearm; fixed flexion position of the finger; and swelling, cyanosis, and anesthesia of the fingers. Which of the following is the most likely diagnosis?

- ▢ **A.** Colles' fracture
- ▢ **B.** Scaphoid fracture
- ▢ **C.** Bennett's fracture

- ▢ **D.** Volkmann's ischemic contracture
- ▢ **E.** Boxer's fracture

139 A 62-year-old man visits the outpatient clinic with pain in his hand after falling on the outstretched hand. Radiographic examination reveals a fracture of the pisiform bone and hematoma of the surrounding area. Which of the following nerves will most likely be affected?

- ▢ **A.** Ulnar
- ▢ **B.** Radial
- ▢ **C.** Median
- ▢ **D.** Deep ulnar
- ▢ **E.** Deep radial

140 A 32-year-old woman visits the outpatient clinic after injuring her elbow falling from her bicycle. Physical examination reveals a "benediction attitude" of the hand with the index and long fingers extended and the ring and little fingers flexed. Which of the following is the most likely diagnosis?

- ▢ **A.** Injury to median and radial nerves
- ▢ **B.** Injury to median nerve
- ▢ **C.** Injury to radial and ulnar nerves
- ▢ **D.** Injury to ulnar nerve
- ▢ **E.** Injury to median ulnar and radial nerves

141 A 54-year-old man is admitted to the emergency department with severe chest pain. Electrocardiographic evaluation reveals a myocardial infarction. Due to the severity of the infarction, a coronary artery bypass surgery using a radial artery graft is proposed. Which of the following tests should be performed during physical examination prior to the bypass graft operation?

- ▢ **A.** Allen test
- ▢ **B.** Triceps reflex
- ▢ **C.** Tinel test
- ▢ **D.** Brachioradialis reflex
- ▢ **E.** Biceps reflex

142 A 34-year-old man visits the outpatient clinic with a painful upper limb after a fall onto a concrete floor. Physical examination reveals that the patient has weak abduction and adduction of his fingers but has no difficulty in flexing them. The patient also has decreased sensation over the palmar surface of the fourth and fifth fingers. Which of the following diagnoses is most likely?

- ▢ **A.** Compression of the median nerve in the carpal tunnel
- ▢ **B.** Injury of the radial nerve from fractured humerus in the radial tuberosity
- ▢ **C.** Compression of the median nerve as it passes between the two heads of the pronator teres
- ▢ **D.** Compression of the radial nerve from the supinator
- ▢ **E.** Injury of the ulnar nerve by a fractured pisiform

ANSWERS

1 D. The suspensory ligaments of the breast, also known as Cooper's ligaments, are fibrous bands that run from the dermis of the skin to the deep layer of superficial fascia and are primary supports for the breasts against gravity. Ptosis of the breast is usually due to the stretching of these ligaments and can be repaired with plastic surgery. Scarpa's fascia is the deep membranous layer of superficial fascia of the anterior abdominal wall. The pectoralis major and pectoralis minor are muscles that move the upper limb and lie deep to the breast but do not provide any direct support structure to the breast. The serratus anterior muscle is involved in the movements of the scapula.
GAS 131, 137-138; GA 62

2 A. Lower subscapular nerves arise from the cervical spinal nerves 5 and 6. It innervates the subscapularis and teres major muscles. The subscapularis and teres major are both responsible for adducting and medially rotating the arm. A lesion of this nerve would result in weakness in these motions. The axillary nerve also arises from cervical spinal nerves 5 and 6 and innervates the deltoid and teres minor muscles. The deltoid muscle is large and covers the entire surface of the shoulder, and contributes to arm movement in any plane. The teres minor is a lateral rotator and a member of the rotator cuff group of muscles. The radial nerve arises from the posterior cord of the brachial plexus. It is the largest branch, and it innervates the triceps brachii and anconeus in the arm. The spinal accessory nerve is cranial nerve XI, and it innervates the trapezius muscle, which elevates and depresses the scapula. The ulnar nerve

arises from the medial cord of the brachial plexus and runs down the medial aspect of the arm. It innervates muscles of the forearm and hand.
GAS 676-682; GA 366, 369

3 C. The thenar muscles (and lumbricals I and II) are innervated by the median nerve, which runs through the carpal tunnel. The carpal tunnel is formed anteriorly by the flexor retinaculum and posteriorly by the carpal bones. Carpal tunnel syndrome is caused by a compression of the median nerve, due to reduced space in the carpal tunnel. The carpal tunnel contains the tendons of flexor pollicis longus, flexor digitorum profundus, and flexor digitorum superficialis muscles. The dorsal interossei, lumbricals III and IV, palmar interossei, and hypothenar muscles are all innervated by the ulnar nerve.
GAS 756-758, 764-765, 788; GA 8, 400

4 D. Fracture of the medial epicondyle often causes damage to the ulnar nerve due to its position in the groove behind the epicondyle. The ulnar nerve innervates one and a half muscles in the forearm—the flexor carpi ulnaris and the medial half of the flexor digitorum profundus. The nerve continues on to innervate muscles in the hand. The flexor digitorum superficialis is innervated by the median nerve and the biceps brachii by the musculocutaneous. The radial nerve innervates both the brachioradialis and supinator muscles.
GAS 724-730; GA 378, 390, 397-398

5 C. A midshaft humeral fracture can result in injury to the radial nerve and deep brachial artery because they lie in the spiral groove located in the midshaft. Injury to the median nerve and brachial artery can be caused by a supracondylar fracture that occurs by falling on an outstretched hand and partially flexed elbow. A fracture of the surgical neck of the humerus can injure the axillary nerve and posterior humeral circumflex artery. The suprascapular artery and nerve can be injured in a shoulder dislocation. The long thoracic nerve and lateral thoracic artery may be damaged during a mastectomy procedure.
GAS 713, 724; GA 361

6 B. A supracondylar fracture often results in injury to the median nerve. The course of the median nerve is anterolateral, and at the elbow it lies medial to the brachial artery on the brachialis muscle. The axillary nerve passes posteriorly through the quadrangular space, accompanied by the posterior circumflex humeral artery, and winds around the surgical neck of the humerus. Injury to the surgical neck may damage the axillary nerve. The musculocutaneous nerve pierces the coracobrachialis muscle and descends between the biceps and brachialis muscle. It continues into the forearm as the lateral antebrachial cutaneous nerve. The ulnar nerve descends behind the medial epicondyle in its groove and is easily injured and produces "funny bone" symptoms.
GAS 724-731; GA 361

7 C. The radial nerve descends posteriorly between the long and lateral heads of the triceps and passes inferolaterally on the back of the humerus between the medial and lateral heads of the triceps. It eventually enters the anterior compartment and descends to enter the cubital fossa, where it divides into superficial and deep branches. The deep branch of the radial nerve winds laterally around the radius and runs between the two heads of the supinator and continues as the posterior interosseous nerve, innervating extensor muscles of the forearm. Because this injury does not result in loss of sensation over the skin of the upper limb, it is likely that the superficial branch of the radial nerve is not injured. If the radial nerve were injured very proximally, the woman would not have extension of her elbow. The branches of the radial nerve to the triceps arise proximal to where the nerve runs in the spiral groove. The anterior interosseous nerve arises from the median nerve and supplies the flexor digitorum profundus, flexor pollicis longus, and pronator quadratus, none of which seem to be injured in this example. Injury to the median nerve causes a characteristic flattening (atrophy) of the thenar eminence.
GAS 750; GA 403

8 B. The musculocutaneous nerve supplies the biceps brachii and brachialis, which are the flexors of the forearm at the elbow. The musculocutaneous nerve continues as the lateral antebrachial cutaneous nerve, which supplies sensation to the lateral side of the forearm (with the forearm in the anatomic position). The biceps brachii is the most powerful supinator muscle. Injury to this nerve would result in weakness of supination and forearm flexion and lateral forearm sensory loss. Injury to the radial nerve would result in weakened extension and a characteristic wrist drop. Injury to the median nerve causes paralysis of flexor digitorum superficialis and other flexors in the forearm and results in a characteristic flattening of the thenar eminence. The lateral cord of the brachial plexus gives origin both to the musculocutaneous and lateral pectoral nerves. There is no indication of pectoral paralysis or weakness. Injury to the lateral cord can result in weakened flexion

and supination in the forearm, and weakened adduction and medial rotation of the arm. The lateral cutaneous nerve of the forearm is a branch of the musculocutaneous nerve and does not supply any motor innervation. Injury to the musculocutaneous nerve alone is unusual but can follow penetrating injuries.
GAS 720; GA 361, 369-371, 376, 390

9 **C.** Tenosynovitis can be due to an infection of the synovial sheaths of the digits. Tenosynovitis in the thumb may spread through the synovial sheath of the flexor pollicis longus tendon, also known as the radial bursa. The tendons of the flexor digitorum superficialis and profundus muscles are enveloped in the common synovial flexor sheath, or ulnar bursa. Neither the flexor carpi radialis nor flexor pollicis brevis tendons are contained in synovial flexor sheaths.
GAS 759-761; GA 397-399

10 **A.** The three chief contents of the cubital fossa are the biceps brachii tendon, brachial artery, and median nerve (lateral to medial). The common and anterior interosseous arteries arise distal to the cubital fossa; the ulnar and radial arteries are the result of the bifurcation of the brachial artery distal to the cubital fossa.
GAS 729; GA 361, 366-368, 380

11 **D.** Lymph from the skin of the anterior chest wall primarily drains to the axillary lymph nodes.
GAS 709; GA 12, 133

12 **C.** The anterior intercostal arteries are 12 small arteries, two in each of the upper six intercostal spaces at the upper and lower borders. The upper artery lying in each space anastomoses with the posterior intercostal arteries, whereas the lower one usually joins the collateral branch of the posterior intercostal artery. The musculophrenic artery supplies the pericardium, diaphragm, and muscles of the abdominal wall. It anastomoses with the deep circumflex iliac artery. The superior epigastric artery supplies the diaphragm, peritoneum, and the anterior abdominal wall and anastomoses with the inferior epigastric artery. The lateral thoracic artery runs along the lateral border of the pectoralis minor muscle and supplies the pectoralis major, pectoralis minor, and serratus anterior. The thoracodorsal artery accompanies the thoracodorsal nerve in supplying the latissimus dorsi muscle and lateral thoracic wall.
GAS 151-155; GA 68

13 **D.** The location for palpation of the radial pulse is lateral to the tendon of the flexor carpi radialis, where the radial artery can be compressed against the distal radius. The radial pulse can also be felt in the anatomic snuffbox between the tendons of the extensor pollicis brevis and extensor pollicis longus muscles, where the radial artery can be compressed against the scaphoid.
GAS 349-377; GA 374, 390, 397-398

14 **A.** The flexor digitorum profundus is dually innervated by the ulnar nerve to the medial phalanges and the median nerve for the lateral phalanges. Because of the superficial course of the ulnar nerve, it is vulnerable to laceration. Such an injury would result in an inability to flex the distal interphalangeal joints of the fourth and fifth digits. The flexor digitorum superficialis is innervated by the median nerve only, and the course of this nerve runs too deep to be affected by lacerations. The lumbricals function to flex the MP joints and assist in extending the IP joints. The interossei adduct and abduct the fingers.
GAS 736; GA 399, 402

15 **D.** The recurrent branch of the median nerve is motor to the muscles of the thenar eminence, which is an elevation caused by the abductor pollicis brevis, flexor pollicis brevis, and opponens pollicis. If the opponens pollicis is paralyzed, one cannot oppose the pad of the thumb to the pads of the other digits. The recurrent branch does not have a cutaneous distribution. Holding a piece of paper between the fingers is a simple test of adduction of the fingers. These movements are controlled by the deep branch of the ulnar nerve, which is not injured in this patient.
GAS 770, 773; GA 414, 417

16 **B.** "Winging" of the scapula occurs when the medial border of the scapula lifts off the chest wall when the patient pushes against resistance, such as a wall. The serratus anterior muscle holds the medial border of the scapula against the chest wall and is innervated by the long thoracic nerve. The serratus anterior assists in abduction of the arm above the horizontal plane.
GAS 690; GA 361

17 **A.** The anular ligament is a fibrous band that encircles the head of the radius, forming a collar that fuses with the radial collateral ligament and articular capsule of the elbow. The anular ligament functions to prevent displacement of the head of the radius from its socket. The joint capsule functions to allow free rotation of the joint and does not function in its stabilization. The interosseous membrane is a fibrous layer between the radius and ulna helping to hold these two bones together. The radial collateral ligament extends from the lateral epicondyle to the margins of the radial notch of the ulnar and the anular

ligament of the radius. The ulnar collateral ligament is triangular ligament and extends from the medial epicondyle to the olecranon of the ulna.
GAS 724-729; GA 388

18 E. The injury being described is also known as Erb-Duchenne paralysis or "waiter's tip-hand." This usually results from an injury to the upper trunk of the brachial plexus, presenting with loss of abduction, flexion, and lateral rotation of the arm. The superior trunk of the brachial plexus consists of spinal nerve roots C5-6.
GAS 700-709; GA 361, 369-371

19 C. The common palmar digital branch comes off the superficial branch of the ulnar nerve and supplies the skin of the little finger and the medial side of the ring finger. The superficial branch of the radial nerve provides cutaneous innervation to the radial (lateral) dorsum of the hand and the radial two and a half digits over the proximal phalanx. The common palmar digital branch of the median nerve innervates most of the lateral aspect of the palmar hand and the dorsal aspect of the second and third finger as well as the lateral part of the fourth digit. The deep radial nerve supplies the extensor carpi radialis brevis and supinator muscles and continues as the posterior interosseous nerve. The recurrent branch of the median nerve supplies the abductor pollicis brevis, flexor pollicis brevis, and opponens pollicis muscles.
GAS 744; GA 414

20 B. The anatomic snuffbox is formed by the tendons of the extensor pollicis brevis, the abductor pollicis longus, and the extensor pollicis longus. The floor is formed by the scaphoid bone, and it is here that one can palpate for a possible fractured scaphoid.
GAS 752-754; GA 392, 394, 422

21 E. The ulnar nerve innervates the palmar interossei, which adduct the fingers. This is the movement that would maintain the paper between the fingers. The axillary nerve does not innervate muscles of the hand. The median nerve supplies the first and second lumbricals, the opponens pollicis, abductor pollicis brevis, and the flexor pollicis brevis. None of these muscles would affect the ability to hold a piece of paper between the fingers. The musculocutaneous and radial nerves do not supply muscles of the hand.
GAS 661, 706, 720; GA 369-371, 390, 400, 417

22 D. The supraspinatus is one of the rotator cuff muscles. Its tendon is relatively avascular and is often injured when the shoulder is dislocated. This muscle initiates abduction of the arm, and damage would impair this movement. The coracobrachialis muscle, which runs from the coracoid process to the humerus, functions in adduction and flexion of the arm. The triceps' main function is to extend the elbow, and damage to its long head would not affect abduction. The pectoralis minor functions as an accessory respiratory muscle and to stabilize the scapula and is not involved in abduction. The teres major functions to adduct and medially rotate the arm.
GAS 678-680; GA 38-39, 361, 364

23 E. The coracoacromial ligament contributes to the coracoacromial arch, preventing superior displacement of the head of the humerus. Because this ligament is very strong, it will rarely be damaged; instead, the ligament can cause inflammation or erosion of the tendon of the supraspinatus muscle as the tendon passes back and forth under the ligament. The acromioclavicular ligament, connecting the acromion with the lateral end of the clavicle, is not in contact with the supraspinatus tendon. The coracohumeral ligament is located too far anteriorly to impinge upon the supraspinatus tendon. The glenohumeral ligament is located deep to the rotator cuff muscles and would not contribute to injury of the supraspinatus muscle. The transverse scapular ligament crosses the scapular notch and is not in contact with the supraspinatus tendon.
GAS 665; GA 354, 356

24 A. The median nerve supplies sensory innervation to the thumb, index, and middle fingers and also to the lateral half of the ring finger. The median nerve also provides motor innervation to muscles of the thenar eminence. Compression of the median nerve in the carpal tunnel explains these deficits in conjunction with normal functioning of the flexor compartment of the forearm because these muscles are innervated by the median nerve proximal to the carpal tunnel. The ulnar nerve is not implicated in these symptoms. It does not provide sensation to digits 1 to 3. Compression of the brachial plexus could not be attributed to pressure from the triceps because this muscle is located distal to the plexus. In addition, brachial plexus symptoms would include other upper limb deficits, rather than the focal symptoms described in this case. Osteoarthritis of the cervical spine would also lead to increasing complexity of symptoms.
GAS 764, 788; GA 406

25 C. The radial nerve innervates the extensor compartments of the arm and the forearm. It supplies the triceps brachii proximal to the spiral groove, so elbow extension is intact here. It also provides sensory in-

nervation to much of the posterior arm and forearm as well as the dorsal thumb, index, and middle fingers up to the level of the fingernails. Symptoms are described only in the distal limb due to the midhumeral location of the lesion. The median nerve innervates flexors of the forearm and thenar muscles and provides sensory innervation to the lateral palmar hand. The ulnar nerve supplies only the flexor carpi ulnaris and the medial half of the flexor digitorum profundus in the forearm. Additionally, its sensory distribution is to both the palmar and dorsal aspects of the medial hand. It does not supply extensor muscles.
GAS 713, 724; GA 361

26 **D.** The musculocutaneous nerve innervates the brachialis and biceps brachii muscles, which are the main flexors at the elbow. The biceps inserts on the radius and is an important supinator. Because the musculocutaneous nerve is damaged in this case, it leads to loss of sensory perception to the lateral forearm, which is supplied by the distal portion of the musculocutaneous nerve (known as the lateral antebrachial cutaneous nerve). Adduction and abduction of the fingers are mediated by the ulnar nerve and would not be affected in this instance. The flexor pollicis brevis flexes the thumb and is mainly innervated by the recurrent branch of the median nerve. Flexion of the fingers is performed by the long flexors of the fingers and lumbrical muscles, innervated by the median and ulnar nerves. Sensory innervation of the medial forearm is provided by the medial antebrachial cutaneous nerve, a branch of the medial cord of the brachial plexus.
GAS 744; GA 424-425

27 **E.** The deep radial nerve courses between the two heads of the supinator and is located just medial and distal to the lateral epicondyle. It can be irritated by hypertrophy of the supinator, which compresses the nerve, causing pain and weakness. The ulnar nerve courses laterally behind the medial epicondyle and continues anterior to the flexor carpi ulnaris. The median nerve passes into the forearm flexor compartment; the superficial radial nerve courses down the lateral aspect of the posterior forearm and would not cause pain due to pressure applied to the posterior forearm.
GAS 747; GA 390

28 **B.** The lunate is the most commonly dislocated carpal bone because of its shape and relatively weak ligaments anteriorly. Dislocations of the scaphoid and triquetrum are relatively rare. The trapezoid and capitate bones are located in the distal row of the carpal bones.
GAS 752-754; GA 392, 394, 422

29 **A.** The medial antebrachial cutaneous nerve carries sensory fibers derived from the C8 and T1 levels. The lateral antebrachial cutaneous nerve is the distal continuation of the musculocutaneous nerve, carrying fibers from the C5, C6, and C7 levels. The deep branch of the ulnar nerve and the anterior interosseous nerves carry predominantly motor fibers. The sensory fibers coursing in the radial nerve are derived from the C5 to C8 levels.
GAS 700-709; GA 361, 369-371

30 **C.** The contraction of the extensor mechanism produces extension of the distal interphalangeal joint. When it is torn from the distal phalanx, the digit is pulled into flexion by the flexor digitorum profundus. The proper palmar digital branches of the median nerve supply lumbrical muscles and carry sensation from their respective digits. Vincula longa are slender, bandlike connections from the deep flexor tendons to the phalanx that can carry blood supply to the tendons. The insertions of the flexor digitorum superficialis and profundus are on the flexor surface of the middle and distal phalanges, respectively, and act to flex the interphalangeal joints.
GAS 745-747; GA 378, 401

31 **E.** In a Smith fracture, the distal fragment of the radius deviates palmarward, often displacing the lunate bone. The other listed bones are unlikely to be displaced in a palmar direction by a Smith fracture.
GAS 752-754; GA 392, 394, 422

32 **B.** The abductor pollicis longus and extensor pollicis brevis are the occupants of the first dorsal compartment of the wrist. The extensor carpi radialis longus and brevis are in the second compartment. The extensor digitorum is in the third compartment, as is the extensor indicis proprius. The extensor carpi ulnaris is located in the sixth dorsal compartment.
GAS 748-749; GA 401-402, 412-413

33 **E.** The medial cord has been injured by traction on the lower trunk of the brachial plexus. The medial cord is the continuation of the inferior (lower) trunk of the brachial plexus, which is formed by C8 and T1. C5 and C6 are typically associated with the superior (upper) trunk level and thus the lateral cord. C7 forms the middle trunk. An injury to the posterior cord would usually involve the C7 spinal nerve. This is a typical Klumpke paralysis.
GAS 700-709; GA 361, 369-371

34 **A.** The flexor carpi ulnaris muscle is not innervated by the radial nerve but rather by the ulnar

nerve. The brachioradialis, extensor carpi radialis, and supinator muscles are all innervated by the radial nerve distal to the spiral groove.
GAS 737-739; GA 378, 390, 397, 398

35 **A.** Injury to the radial nerve in the spiral groove will paralyze the abductor pollicis longus and both extensors of the thumb. This injury will also lead to wrist drop (inability to extend the wrist). Weakness of grip would also occur, although this is not mentioned in the question. If the wrist is flexed, finger flexion and grip strength are weakened because the long flexor tendons are not under tension. Note how much your strength of grip is increased when your wrist is extended versus when it is flexed.
GAS 661, 709, 722-724; GA 366, 371

36 **C.** The superior ulnar collateral branch of the brachial artery accompanies the ulnar nerve in its path posterior to the medial epicondyle and is important in the blood supply of the nerve. The profunda brachii passes down the arm with the radial nerve. The radial collateral artery arises from the profunda brachii and anastomoses with the radial recurrent branch of the radial artery proximal to the elbow laterally. The inferior ulnar collateral artery arises from the brachial artery and accompanies the median nerve into the forearm. The anterior ulnar recurrent artery arises from the ulnar artery and anastomoses with the inferior ulnar collateral anterior to the elbow.
GAS 743, 767-769; GA 368

37 **C.** Adduction of the fifth digit is produced by contraction of the third palmar interosseous muscle. All of the interossei are innervated by the deep branch of the ulnar nerve. Flexion of the proximal interphalangeal joint is a function of the flexor digitorum superficialis, supplied by the median nerve. Opposition of the thumb is a function of the opponens pollicis, supplied by the recurrent branch of the median nerve.
GAS 729, 772-774; GA 414

38 **C.** The radial nerve is the most likely nerve compressed to cause these symptoms. This type of nerve palsy is often called "Saturday night palsy." One reason for this nickname is that people would supposedly fall asleep after being intoxicated on a Saturday night with their arm over the back of a chair, thereby compressing the nerve in the spiral groove. The radial nerve innervates all of the extensors of the elbow, wrist, and fingers. Paralysis of the lateral cord of the brachial plexus would result in loss of the musculocutaneous nerve and the pectoral nerves, which do not mediate extension of the forearm or hand. The medial cord of the brachial plexus branches into the median nerve and ulnar nerve. Neither of these nerves innervates muscles that control extension. The median nerve innervates flexors of the forearm and the thenar muscles. The lateral and median pectoral nerves do not extend into the arm and innervate the pectoralis major and minor muscles.
GAS 789-790; GA 366, 371

39 **A.** The basilic vein can be used for dialysis, especially when the cephalic vein is judged to be too small, as in this case. The basilic vein can be elevated from its position as it passes through the fascia on the medial side of the arm. The cephalic vein passes more laterally up the limb. The lateral cubital vein is a tributary to the cephalic vein, and the medial cubital vein joins the basilic vein—both rather superficial in position. The medial antebrachial vein courses up the midline of the forearm (antebrachium) ventrally.
GAS 663, 697, 720, 770; GA 350, 360, 377

40 **A.** The patient exhibits the classic "benediction attitude" of the thumb and fingers from injury to the median nerve proximally in the forearm. The thumb is somewhat extended (radial supplied abductor and extensors unopposed); digits 2 and 3 are extended (by intact interossei); digits 4 and 5 are partially flexed (by their intact flexor digitorum profundus). A lesion of the median nerve would result in weakened flexion of the PIP joints of all digits (flexor digitorum superficialis), loss of flexion of the interphalangeal joint of the thumb, the DIP joints of digits 2 and 3 (flexor digitorum profundus), and weakened flexion of the metacarpophalangeal joints of the second and third digits (first and second lumbricals). A lesion of both the ulnar and median nerves would cause weakness or paralysis of flexion of all of the digits. A lesion of the ulnar nerve would mostly cause weakness in flexion of the DIP of the fourth and fifth digits and would affect all of the interosseous muscles and the lumbricals of the third and fourth digits. A lesion of the radial nerve would cause weakness in extension of the wrist, thumb, and metacarpophalangeal joints.
GAS 724, 789-790; GA 371, 376

41 **C.** The head of the humerus is displaced inferiorly because in that location it is not supported by rotator cuff muscle tendons or the coracoacromial arch. It is also pulled anteriorly beneath the coracoid process by pectoralis and subscapularis muscles. It would not be displaced posteriorly because it is supported by the teres minor and infraspinatus muscle

tendons. It would not be displaced superiorly because the acromioclavicular ligament and supraspinatus reinforce in that direction. A medial dislocation is blocked by the subscapularis tendon.
GAS 667; GA 355

42 **A.** The anterior axillary (or anterior pectoral) nodes are the first lymph nodes to receive most of the lymph from the breast parenchyma, areola, and nipple. From there, lymph flows through central axillary, apical, and supraclavicular nodes in sequence. Rotter's nodes lie between the pectoral muscles and are, unfortunately, an alternate route in some patients, speeding the rate of metastasis. The parasternal nodes receive lymph from the medial part of the breast and lie along the internal thoracic artery and vein.
GAS 709; GA 63

43 **D.** The left spinal accessory nerve has been injured distal to the sternocleidomastoid muscle, resulting in paralysis of the trapezius, allowing the shoulder to droop and the superior angle to push out posteriorly. The sternocleidomastoid muscles are intact, as demonstrated by symmetry in strength in turning the head to the right and left. There is no indication of paralysis of the lateral rotators of the shoulder or elbow flexors (suprascapular nerve or upper trunk). Thoracodorsal nerve injury would result in paralysis of the latissimus dorsi, an extensor, and medial rotator of the humerus.
GAS 667, 973-974; GA 370

44 **C.** Inability to extend MCP joints. The tendons of the extensor digitorum and extensor digiti minimi, innervated by the radial nerve, are responsible for extension of the MCP, and to a much lesser degree, the PIP and DIP joints. Abduction and adduction of the MCP joints are functions of the interossei, all of which are innervated by the deep ulnar nerve. Extension of the PIP and DIP joints is performed by the lumbricals and interossei. The first two lumbricals are supplied by the median nerve; the other lumbricals and the interossei, by the deep branch of the ulnar nerve.
GAS 655; GA 395

45 **C.** Fracture of the surgical neck of the humerus often injures the axillary nerve, which innervates the deltoid and teres minor muscles. Abduction of the humerus between 15° and the horizontal is performed by the deltoid muscle. Lateral rotation of the humerus is mainly performed by the deltoid muscle, teres minor, and the infraspinatus. The deltoid and teres minor are both lost in this case. Fracture of the glenoid fossa would lead to drooping of the shoulder. Fracture of the anatomic neck of the humerus will similarly lead to a drooping of the shoulder but would not necessarily affect abduction of the humerus. It is also quite unusual. Fracture of the middle third of the humerus would most likely injure the radial nerve. The ulnar nerve would be potentially compromised in a fracture of the medial epicondyle of the humerus.
GAS 667, 668; GA 355

46 **B.** When cutaneous lymphatics of the breast are blocked by cancer, the skin becomes edematous, except where hair follicles cause small indentations of the skin, giving an overall resemblance to orange peel. Shortening of the suspensory ligaments or retinacula cutis leads to pitting of the overlying skin, pitting that is intensified if the patient raises her arm above her head. Invasion of the pectoralis major by cancer can result in fixation of the breast, seen upon elevation of the ipsilateral limb. Inversion of areolar skin with involvement of the ducts would also be due to involvement of the retinacula cutis.
GAS 709; GA 381

47 **D.** The subclavian vein traverses between the clavicle and first rib and is the most superficial structure to be damaged following a fracture of the clavicle. The subclavian artery runs deep to the subclavian vein, and though it is in the appropriate location, it would likely not be damaged because of its deep anatomic position. The cephalic vein is a tributary to the axillary vein after ascending on the lateral side of the arm. Its location within the body is too superficial and lateral to the site of injury. The lateral thoracic artery is a branch from the axillary artery that runs lateral to the pectoralis minor. It courses inferior and medial from its point of origin from the axillary artery, and it does not maintain a position near the clavicle during its descent. The internal thoracic artery arises from the first part of the subclavian artery before descending deep to the costal cartilages. Its point of origin from the subclavian artery is lateral to clavicular injury. Furthermore, its course behind the costal cartilages is quite medial to the clavicular fracture.
GAS 697, 952, 961, 973, 978; GA 37

48 **A.** Colles' fracture is a fracture of the distal end of the radius. The proximal portion of the radius is displaced anteriorly, with the distal bone fragment projecting posteriorly. The displacement of the radius from the wrist often gives the appearance of a dinner fork, thus a Colles' fracture is often referred to as a "dinner fork" deformity. A scaphoid fracture results from a fracture of the scaphoid bone and would thus not cause displace-

ment of the radius. This fracture usually occurs at the narrow aspect ("waist") of the scaphoid bone. Bennett's and boxer's fractures both result from fractures of the metacarpals (first and fifth, respectively). Volkmann's ischemic contracture is a muscular deformity that can follow a supracondylar fracture of the humerus, with arterial laceration into the flexor compartment of the forearm. Ischemia and muscle contracture, with extreme pain, accompany this fracture.
GAS 734; GA 392

49 **B.** In shoulder separation, either or both the acromioclavicular and coracoclavicular ligaments can be partially or completely torn through. The acromioclavicular joint can be interrupted and the distal end of the clavicle may deviate upward in a complete separation, while the upper limb droops away inferiorly, causing a "step off" that can be palpated and sometimes observed. Displacement of the head of the humerus is shoulder dislocation, not separation. The coracoacromial ligament is not torn in separation (but it is sometimes used in the repair of the torn coracoclavicular ligament). Disruption of the glenoid labrum often accompanies shoulder dislocation.
GAS 669; GA 354

50 **A.** The nail was fired explosively from the nail gun and then pierced the ulnar nerve near the coronoid process of the ulna trochlea of the humerus. Paralysis of the medial half of the flexor digitorum profundus would result (among other significant deficits), with loss of flexion of the distal interphalangeal joints of digits 4 and 5. Ulnar trauma at the wrist would not affect the interphalangeal joints, although it would cause paralysis of interossei, hypothenar muscles, etc. Median nerve damage proximal to the pronator teres would affect proximal interphalangeal joint flexion and distal interphalangeal joint flexion of digits 2 and 3 as well as thumb flexion. Median nerve injury at the wrist would cause loss of thenar muscles but not long flexors of the fingers. Trauma to spinal nerve root C8 would affect all long finger flexors.
GAS 729, 771; GA 376, 390

51 **C.** The injury has occurred just beyond the third part of the axillary artery. The only collateral arterial channel between the third part of the axillary artery and the brachial artery is that between the posterior humeral circumflex and the ascending branch of the profunda brachii—and this anastomotic path is often inadequate to supply the arterial needs of the limb. The posterior humeral circumflex arises from the third part of the axillary artery. It typically anastomoses with a variably small, ascending branch of the profunda brachii branch of the brachial artery. The suprascapular artery anastomoses with the circumflex scapular deep to the infraspinatus. The dorsal scapular artery (passing beneath the medial border of the scapula) has no anastomosis with thoracodorsal within the scope of the injury. The lateral thoracic artery has no anastomoses with the brachial artery. The supreme thoracic artery (from first part of axillary) has no helpful anastomoses with the thoracoacromial (second part of axillary).
GAS 683, 696, 697; GA 368

52 **E.** The scaphoid (or the older term, navicular) bone is the most commonly fractured carpal bone.
GAS 752-754; GA 392, 394, 422

53 **E.** The anterior interosseous nerve is a branch of the median nerve that supplies the flexor pollicis longus, the lateral half of the flexor digitorum profundus, and the pronator quadratus. If it is injured, flexion of the interphalangeal joint of the thumb will be compromised. The median nerve gives rise to the anterior interosseous nerve but is not a direct enough answer as injury to it would result in more widespread effects. The posterior interosseous nerve supplies extensors in the forearm, not flexors. The radial nerve gives rise to the posterior interosseous nerve and is not associated with the anterior interosseous nerve; therefore, it would not have any effect on the flexors of the forearm. The recurrent median nerve is also a branch of the median nerve but supplies the thenar eminence muscles, and its injury would result in problems with opposable motion of the thumb.
GAS 743, 751; GA 400

54 **C.** The tendon of the long head of the biceps brachii muscle passes through the glenohumeral joint, surrounded by synovial membrane. The glenohumeral is a ligament that attaches to the glenoid labrum. The long head of the triceps arises from the infraglenoid tubercle, beneath the glenoid fossa. The infraspinatus tendon passes posterior to the head of the humerus to insert on the greater tubercle. The coracobrachialis arises from the coracoid process and inserts on the humerus.
GAS 694, 715-716, 735; GA 370

55 **E.** The suprascapular artery passes over, and the suprascapular nerve passes under, the superior transverse scapular ligament. This ligament bridges the suprascapular notch in the upper border of the scapula. The artery and nerve then pass deep to the supraspinatus muscle, thereafter supplying it and then passing through the spinoglenoid notch to supply the

infraspinatus. The subscapular artery is a branch of the third part of the axillary artery; it divides into circumflex scapular and thoracodorsal branches. The transverse cervical artery courses anterior to this site. The dorsal scapular artery and nerve pass deep to the medial border of the scapula. The posterior humeral circumflex branch of the axillary artery passes through the quadrangular space with the axillary nerve.
GAS 696, 697; GA 366, 368

56 **A.** The patient has suffered injury to the radial nerve in the midhumeral region. The nerve that provides sensation to the dorsum of the hand proximal to the thumb and index finger is the superficial branch of the radial nerve. The posterior interosseous nerve supplies a strip of skin on the back of the forearm and wrist extensors. The lateral antebrachial cutaneous nerve is a continuation of the musculocutaneous nerve and supplies the lateral side of the forearm. The medial antebrachial cutaneous is a direct branch of the medial cord and supplies skin of the medial side of the forearm. The dorsal cutaneous branch of the ulnar nerve supplies the medial side of the dorsum of the hand.
GAS 772-774; GA 417

57 **C.** The seventh cervical nerve makes a major contribution to the radial nerve, and this nerve is the prime mover in wrist extension. The dermatome of C7 is in the region described.
GAS 700-709; GA 361, 369-371

58 **B.** As the radial artery passes from the ventral surface of the wrist to the dorsum, it crosses through the anatomic snuffbox, passing over the scaphoid bone. The ulnar artery at the wrist is located on the medial side of the wrist, passing from beneath the flexor carpi ulnaris to reach Guyon's canal between the pisiform bone and the flexor retinaculum. The anterior interosseous and posterior interosseous arteries arise from the common interosseous branch of the ulnar artery and pass proximal to distal in the forearm between the radius and ulna, in the flexor and extensor compartments, respectively. The deep palmar branch of the ulnar artery passes between the two heads of the adductor pollicis to anastomose with the radial artery in the palm.
GAS 759; GA 422

59 **D.** The patient is suffering from subacromial or subdeltoid bursitis. (If the pain on palpation is less when the arm has been elevated to the horizontal, the bursitis may be thought of as being more subacromial, that is, associated more with the supraspinatus tendon perhaps, for such a bursa may be drawn back under the acromion when the limb is abducted.) The subscapular bursa, beneath the subscapularis muscle, would not present as superficial pain. It can communicate with the glenohumeral joint cavity. Inflammation or arthritic changes within the glenohumeral joint present as more generalized shoulder pain than that present here. The teres minor muscle and tendon are located inferior to the point of marked discomfort.
GAS 670; GA 358

60 **E.** The axillary sheath is a fascial continuation of the prevertebral layer of the deep cervical fascia extending into the axilla. It encloses the nerves of the neurovascular bundle of the upper limb. Superficial fascia is loose connective tissue between the dermis and the deep investing fascia and contains fat, cutaneous vessels, nerves, lymphatics, and glands. The buccopharyngeal fascia covers the buccinator muscles and the pharynx mingles with the pretrachial fascia. The clavipectoral muscle invests the clavicle and pectoralis minor muscle. The axillary fascia is continuous with the pectoral and latissimus dorsi fascia and forms the hollow of the armpit.
GAS 700-709; GA 361, 369-371

61 **C.** The spinal accessory nerve arises from the ventral rootlets of C1 to C4 and ascends through the foramen magnum to then exit the cranial cavity through the jugular foramen. It innervates the sternocleidomastoid and trapezius muscles, which function in head rotation and raising of the shoulders. The suprascapular nerve receives fibers from C5-6 (occasionally from C4 if the plexus is "prefixed") and innervates the supraspinatus muscle, which is responsible for the first 15° of arm abduction. Erb point of the brachial plexus is at the union of C5-6 spinal nerves. The long thoracic nerve arises from plexus routes C5, 6, and 7, and supplies the serratus anterior.
GAS 700-706; GA 361, 369-371

62 **D.** The acromioclavicular ligament connects the clavicle to the coracoid process of the scapula. Separation of the shoulder (dislocation of the acromioclavicular [AC] joint) is associated with damage to the acromioclavicar ligament (capsule of the AC joint) and, in more severe injuries, disruption of the coracoclavicular ligaments (conoid and trapezoid portions). The glenohumeral ligament may be injured by an anterior dislocation of the humerus but is not likely to be injured by a separated shoulder. The coracoacromial ligament, transverse scapular ligament, and tendon of the long head of triceps brachii are not likely to be injured by separation of the shoulder.
GAS 669; GA 354, 363

63 A. The quadrangular space is bordered medially by the long head of the triceps, laterally by the surgical neck of the humerus, superiorly by the teres minor and subscapularis muscles, and inferiorly by the teres major muscle. Both the axillary nerve and posterior humeral circumflex vessels traverse this space. The other structures listed are not contained within the quadrangular space. The cephalic vein is located in the deltopectoral triangle, and the radial nerve is located in the triangular interval.
GAS 700-709; GA 361, 369-371

64 B. Froment's sign is positive for ulnar nerve palsy. More specifically it tests the action of the adductor pollicis muscle. The patient is asked to hold a sheet of paper between the thumb and a flat palm. The flexor pollicis longus is innervated by the anterior interosseous branch of the median nerve. The flexor digiti minimi is innervated by the deep branch of the ulnar nerve and would not be used to hold a sheet of paper between the thumb and palm. The flexor carpi radialis is innervated by the median nerve, and the extensor indicis is innervated by the radial nerve.
GAS 763-765; GA 410, 412

65 C. The recurrent branch of the median nerve innervates the thenar muscles (opponens pollicis, abductor pollicis brevis, and flexor pollicis brevis) and is not responsible for any cutaneous innervation. Damage to the palmar cutaneous branches of the median nerve or to the ulnar nerve would not cause weakness of opposition of the thumb for they are principally sensory in function. The deep branch of the ulnar nerve supplies the hypothenar muscles, adductor and abductor muscles of digits 2–5, and does not innervate the abductor policis brevis.
GAS 770-771; GA 414

66 D. Injury to the deep branch of the ulnar nerve results in paralysis of all interosseous muscles and the lumbrical muscles of digits 4 and 5. Extension of the metacarpophalangeal joints is intact, a function of the radial nerve. Interphalangeal extension of digits 4 and 5 is absent, due to the loss of all interosseous muscle and the lumbricals of digits 4 and 5. Some weak interphalangeal joint extension is still present in digits 2 and 3 because the lumbricals of these two fingers are innervated by the median nerve. The radial nerve and the median nerve appear to be intact in this case. If the ulnar nerve were injured in the midforearm region, there would be sensory loss in the palm and digits 4 and 5 and on the dorsum of the hand. The recurrent branch of the median nerve supplies the thenar muscles; it does not supply lumbricals. Moreover, paralysis of this nerve would have no effect on the interphalangeal joints.
GAS 770-771; GA 415

67 A. The circumflex scapular artery passes through the triangular space after arising from the subscapular artery. It provides superficial branches to the overlying latissimus dorsi, whereas its deep portion passes into the infraspinous fossa to anastomose with the suprascapular artery. The dorsal scapular artery passes between the roots of the brachial plexus and then deep to the medial border of the scapula. The transverse cervical artery arises from the thyrocervical trunk at the root of the neck and can provide origin for a dorsal scapular branch. The lateral thoracic and thoracoacromial arteries are branches of the second part of the axillary artery and provide no supply to the latissimus dorsi.
GAS 683, 684, 697; GA 368

68 C. The surgical neck of the humerus is a typical site of fractures. The fracture line lies above the insertions of the pectoralis major, teres major, and latissimus dorsi muscles. The supraspinatus muscle abducts the proximal fragment, whereas the distal fragment is elevated and adducted. The elevation results from contraction of the deltoid, biceps brachii, and coracobrachialis muscles. The adduction is due to the action of pectoralis major, teres major, and latissimus dorsi.
GAS 139-140, 659, 686-687; GA 374, 492

69 B. The fracture line of the upper third of the radius lies between the bony attachments of the supinator and the pronator teres muscles. The distal radial fragment and hand are pronated due to unopposed contraction of pronator teres and pronator quadratus muscles. The proximal fragment deviates laterally by the unopposed contraction of the supinator muscle. The brachioradialis inserts distally on the radius. The brachialis inserts on the coronoid process of the ulna and would not be involved in the lateral deviation of the radius.
GAS 736, 747-749; GA 390

70 A. The palmaris longus passes along the midline of the flexor surface of the forearm. The flexor carpi radialis is seen in the lateral portion of the forearm superficially, passing over the trapezium to insert at the base of the second metacarpal. The abductor pollicis longus tendon is laterally located in the wrist, where it helps form the lateral border of the anatomic snuffbox. The flexor carpi ulnaris tendon can be seen and palpated on the medial side of the wrist ventrally.

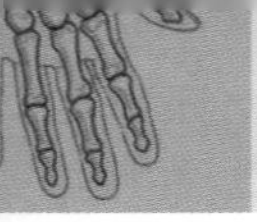

The flexor pollicis longus tendon passes deep through the carpal tunnel.
GAS 737-739; GA 374, 390, 398

71 B. The student had broken the neck of the fifth metacarpal when hitting the machine with his fist. This is the more common type of "boxer's fracture." Neither a fracture of the ulnar styloid nor a Colles' fracture nor a Smith fracture of the distal radius would present with the absence of a knuckle as observed here. Bennett's fracture involves dislocation of the carpometacarpal joint of the thumb. Indications are that the injury is on the medial side of the hand, not the wrist, nor the lateral side of the hand or wrist.
GAS 769; GA 392, 394

72 E. Scoliosis (severe, lateral curvature of the spine) in the patient is causing compression or stretching of the T1 spinal nerve root by the first rib as the nerve ascends to join C8 and form the lower trunk of the brachial plexus. T1 provides sensation for the medial side of the forearm, via the medial antebrachial cutaneous nerve from the medial cord of the brachial plexus. T1 is the principal source of motor supply to all of the intrinsic muscles in the palm. Its dysfunction affects all fine motor movements of the digits. Long flexors of the fingers are intact; therefore, the median nerve and ulnar nerve are not at fault. The extensors of the wrist are functional; therefore, the radial nerve is not paralyzed. The only sensory disturbance is that of the T1 dermatome.
GAS 700-709; GA 361, 369-371

73 D. Interestingly, "gamekeeper's thumb" was a term coined because this injury was most commonly associated with Scottish gamekeepers who, it is said, killed small animals such as rabbits by breaking their necks between the ground and the gamekeeper's thumb and index finger. The resulting valgus force on the abducted MCP joint caused injury to the ulnar collateral ligament. These days this injury is more commonly seen in skiers who land awkwardly with their hand braced on a ski pole, causing the valgus force on the thumb as is seen in this patient. Whereas the term "skier thumb" is sometimes used, "gamekeeper's thumb" is still in common usage.
GAS 755; GA 395

74 A. The long head of the biceps assists in shoulder flexion and during a tendinopathy would cause pain in the anterior compartment of the shoulder, where it originates at the supraglenoid tubercle. Also, forced contraction would cause more of a greater tension force on the tendon.
GAS 694, 715-716; GA 370

75 C. The common extensor tendon originates from the lateral epicondyle, and inflammation of this tendon is lateral epicondylitis, nicknamed "tennis elbow" because the tendon is often irritated during the backhand stroke in tennis. Because the extensors of the wrist originate as part of the common extensor tendon, extension of the wrist will exacerbate the pain of lateral epicondylitis.
GAS 691; GA 380

76 C. The axillary nerve passes dorsally around the surgical neck of the humerus (accompanied by the posterior humeral circumflex artery) and can be injured when the humerus is fractured at that location. The axillary nerve provides sensation to the skin over the upper, lateral aspect of the shoulder. Therefore, although the patient might not be able to abduct the arm because of the injury, a simple test of skin sensation can indicate whether there is associated nerve injury of the axillary nerve. Shrugging the shoulders can help assess trapezius function, thereby testing the spinal accessory nerve. Intact sensation of the skin on the medial aspect of the axilla or arm is an indication that the radial or intercostobrachial nerves are functional. Pushing against an immovable object tests the serratus anterior muscle and the long thoracic nerve.
GAS 667; GA 355

77 E. The surgeon took the distal segments of the median nerves from both forearms, mistakenly believing them to be palmaris longus tendons. Both of the structures lie in the midline of the ventral surface of the distal forearm and are often of similar appearance in color and diameter. The nerve is located deep to the tendon, when the tendon is present, but when the tendon is absent, the nerve appears to be where the tendon belongs. There is no evidence of rib fractures; even so, a fractured rib would not explain loss of sensation on the lateral portion of the palm. Lower plexus trauma (C8, T1) would result in paralysis of forearm flexor muscles and all intrinsic hand muscles and sensory loss over the medial dorsum of the hand, in addition to palmar sensory loss. Dupuytren's contracture is a flexion contracture of (usually) digits 4 and 5 from connective tissue disease in the palm. Radial nerve injury in the posterior forearm would affect metacarpophalangeal joint extension, thumb extension, etc., not palmar disturbances.
GAS 743-744; GA 400

78 **C.** Trauma both to the median and ulnar nerves at the wrist results in total clawing of the fingers. The metacarpophalangeal joints of all digits are extended by the unopposed extensors because the radial nerve is intact. All interossei and lumbricals are paralyzed because the deep branch of the ulnar nerve supplies all of the interossei; lumbricals I and II are paralyzed, for they are innervated by the median nerve; lumbricals III and IV are paralyzed, for they receive supply from the deep ulnar nerve. The interossei and lumbricals are responsible for extension of the interphalangeal joints. When they are paralyzed, the long flexor tendons pull the fingers into a position of flexion, completing the "claw" appearance. If the median nerve were intact, the clawing would be less noticeable in the index and long finger because the two lumbricals would still be capable of some degree of extension of those interphalangeal joints. If the median nerve alone is injured in the carpal tunnel, there would be loss of thenar opposition but not clawing. If the median and ulnar nerves are both transected at the elbow, the hand appears totally flat because of the loss of long flexors, in addition to intrinsic paralysis.
GAS 726; GA 400

79 **D.** Colles' fracture is a fracture of the distal radius with the distal fragment displaced dorsally. Smith's fracture involves the distal fragment displaced in a volar direction. Smith's fracture is sometimes referred to as a reverse Colles' fracture.
GAS 756; GA 392

80 **E.** The extensor tendons of the fingers insert distally on the distal phalanx of each digit. If the tendon is avulsed, or the proximal part of the distal phalanx is detached, the distal interphalangeal joint is pulled into total flexion by the unopposed flexor digitorum profundus. This result gives the digit the appearance of a mallet. In boutonnière deformity, the central portion of the extensor tendon expansion is torn over the PIP joint, allowing the tendon to move palmarward, causing the tendon to act as a flexor of the PIP joint. This causes the DIP joint to be hyperextended. Swan-neck deformity involves slight flexion of MCP joints, hyperextension of PIP joints, and slight flexion of DIP joints. This condition results most often from shortening of the tendons of intrinsic muscles, as in rheumatoid arthritis. Dupuytren contracture results from connective tissue disorder in the palm, usually causing irreversible flexion of digits 4 and 5. Clawhand occurs with lesions to the median and ulnar nerves at the wrist. In this clinical problem all intrinsic muscles are paralyzed, including the extensors of the interphalangeal joints. The MCP joint extensors, supplied by the radial nerve, and the long flexors of the fingers, supplied more proximally in the forearm by the median and ulnar nerves, are intact and are unopposed, pulling the fingers into the "claw" appearance.
GAS 760; GA 392, 394, 422

81 **A.** Because the median nerve is injured within the cubital fossa, the long flexors are paralyzed, including the flexor pollicis longus. Flexor pollicis longus would not be paralyzed if the median nerve were injured at the wrist. Lateral palm sensory loss confirms median nerve injury. If only the anterior interosseous nerve were damaged, there would be no cutaneous sensory deficit. The radial nerve supplies wrist extensors, long thumb abductor, and metacarpophalangeal joint extensors. The ulnar nerve does not supply sensation to the lateral palm.
GAS 651, 729, 731; GA 400

82 **D.** In a lesion of the lower trunk, or the C8 and T1 nerve roots, there is sensory loss on the medial forearm and the medial side of hand (dorsal and ventral). The medial cord is the extension of the lower trunk. The medial cord gives origin to the medial antebrachial cutaneous nerve, which supplies the T1 dermatome of the medial side of the antebrachium. The lower lateral brachial cutaneous nerve arises from the radial nerve, C5 and C6. The musculocutaneous nerve arises from the lateral cord, ending in the lateral antebrachial cutaneous nerve, with C5 and C6 dermatome fibers. The intercostobrachial nerve is the lateral cutaneous branch of the T2 ventral primary ramus and supplies skin on the medial side of the arm. The median nerve distributes C6 and C7 sensory fibers to the lateral part of the palm, thumb, index, long finger, and half of the ring finger.
GAS 743-745, 771-772; GA 384

83 **C.** The first branch of the lateral pectoral nerve is typically the only source of motor supply to the clavicular head of the pectoralis major. If it is injured (as in this case of an iatrogenic injury when the infraclavicular nodes were removed), this part of the muscle undergoes atrophy, leaving an infraclavicular cosmetic deficit. The remainder of the lateral pectoral nerve joins the medial pectoral nerve in a neural arch that provides motor supply to the remaining parts of the pectoralis major and the pectoralis minor. Physical examination reveals no obvious motor or sensory deficits. Loss of the medial pectoral nerve would have no effect on the clavicular head of pectoralis major and might not be discernible. Injury to the lateral cord would lead to loss not only of all of the lateral pectoral nerve but also the

musculocutaneous nerve, resulting in biceps and brachialis paralysis and lateral antebrachial sensory loss.
GAS 688, 702, 706; GA 370

84 B. The C6 spinal nerve is primarily responsible for the brachioradialis reflex. C5 and C6 are both involved in the biceps brachii reflex; C5 for motor, C6 for the sensory part of the reflex arc; C7 is the key spinal nerve in the triceps reflex.
GAS 700-709; GA 361, 369-371

85 C. C7 is the main spinal nerve that contributes to the radial nerve and innervates the triceps. Absence of the triceps reflex is usually indicative of a C7 radiculopathy or injury.
GAS 700-709; GA 361, 369-371

86 B. Ginglymus joint is the technical term to describe a hinge joint. It allows motion in one axis (flexion and extension in the case of the elbow) and is therefore a uniaxial joint. The other types of joints listed allow motion in more than one axis.
GAS 79-81; GA 372

87 C. A fracture of the humerus just proximal to the epicondyles is called a supracondylar fracture. This is the most common cause of a Volkmann ischemic fracture. The sharp bony fragment often lacerates the brachial (or other) artery, with bleeding into the flexor compartment. Diminution of arterial supply to the compartment results in the ischemia. Bleeding into the compartment causes greatly increased pressure, first blocking venous outflow from the compartment, then reducing the arterial flow into the compartment. The ischemic muscles then undergo unrelieved contracture. A humeral fracture is sometimes placed in a cast from shoulder to wrist, often concealing the ischemia until major tissue loss occurs. Cold, insensate digits and great pain are warnings of this compartmental problem, demanding that the cast be removed and the compartment opened ("released") for pressure reduction and vascular repair. Fracture of the surgical neck endangers the axillary nerve and posterior humeral circumflex artery, although not ischemic contracture. Fracture of the humerus in the spiral groove can injure the radial nerve and profunda brachii artery. Fracture of the olecranon does not result in Volkmann's contracture, although the triceps brachii can displace the distal fractured fragment of the ulna.
GAS 728; GA 355

88 D. Normally, the distal part of the ulna articulates only with the radius at the distal radioulnar joint at the wrist, a joint that participates in pronation/supination. The head of the ulna does not articulate with any of the carpal bones; instead, it is separated from the triquetrum and lunate bones by the triangular fibrocartilage complex between it and the radius. The pisiform articulates with the triquetrum. The carpal articulation of the radius is primarily that of the scaphoid (old name is navicular) bone. In addition to the scaphoid, the radius articulates also with the lunate.
GAS 713, 714, 731-733; GA 391

89 A. The force of the woman's fall on the outstretched hand was transmitted up through the forearm, sometimes resulting in dislocation of the olecranon at the elbow, putting traction on the ulnar nerve as it passes around the medial epicondyle of the humerus. Ulnar trauma at the elbow can cause weakness in medial flexion (adduction) at the wrist, from loss of the flexor carpi ulnaris. Ulnar nerve injury also results in sensory loss in the medial hand and paralysis of the interossei and medial two lumbricals, with clawing especially of digits 4 and 5. Injury of the ulnar nerve at the pisiform bone would not affect the flexor carpi ulnaris, nor would it produce sensory loss on the dorsum of the hand because the dorsal cutaneous branch of the ulnar branches off proximal to the wrist. Carpal tunnel problems affect median nerve function, which is not indicated here. The ulnar nerve passes medial to the cubital fossa between the heads of the flexor carpi ulnaris, not between the heads of the flexor digitorum superficialis. Injuries at the radial neck affect the site of division of the radial nerve, and its paralysis would not result in the clinical problems seen in this patient.
GAS 727-728; GA 386

90 D. The interossei are the most important muscles in extension of the interphalangeal (IP) joints because of the manner of their insertion into the extensor expansion of the fingers, which passes dorsal to the transverse axes of these joints. The lumbrical muscles assist in IP extension, in addition to flexing the metacarpophalangeal joints. Ulnar nerve injury at the wrist results in paralysis of all the interossei and the medial two lumbricals. Extensors of the MCP joints are innervated by the deep radial nerve. Unopposed extension of the MCP joints causes them to be held in extension whereas unopposed long flexors of the fingers (supplied by median and ulnar nerves proximally in the forearm) cause them to be flexed into the "claw" position. The lumbricals of digits 2 and 3 are still intact because they are supplied by the median nerve, so clawing is not seen as much on these digits. Loss of opposition would result from median or recurrent nerve paralysis. If the ulnar nerve

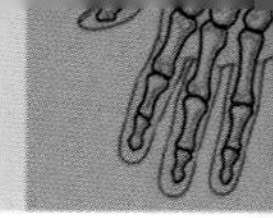

is cut at the wrist, its dorsal cutaneous branch to the dorsum of the hand is unaffected.
GAS 655, 755; GA 395

91 **B.** In boutonnière deformity, the central portion of the extensor tendon expansion is torn over the PIP joint, allowing the tendon to move palmarward, causing the tendon to act as a flexor of the PIP joint. This causes the DIP joint to be hyperextended. The tear in the extensor tendon is said to resemble a buttonhole ("boutonnière" in French), and the head of the proximal phalanx may stick through the hole.
GAS 732-755; GA 395

92 **D.** Swan-neck deformity involves slight flexion of MCP joints, hyperextension of PIP joints, and slight flexion of DIP joints. This condition results most often from shortening of the tendons of intrinsic muscles, as in rheumatoid arthritis. When asked to straighten the injured finger, the patient is unable to do so and the curvature of the finger somewhat resembles the neck of a swan.
GAS 732-755; GA 395

93 **C.** The long thoracic nerve was injured during the axillary dissection, resulting in paralysis of the serratus anterior. The serratus anterior is important in rotation of the scapula in raising the arm above the level of the shoulder. Its loss results in protrusion of the inferior angle ("winging" of the scapula), which is more obvious when one pushes against resistance. The long thoracic nerve arises from brachial plexus roots C5, C6, and C7. The upper trunk (C5, C6) supplies rotator and abductor muscles of the shoulder and elbow flexors. The posterior division of the middle trunk contains C7 fibers for distribution to extensor muscles; likewise, the posterior cord supplies extensors of the arm, forearm, and hand. The lateral cord (C5, C6, and C7) gives origin to the lateral pectoral nerve, the musculocutaneous nerve, and the lateral root of the median nerve. There is no sensory loss in the limb in this patient; injury to any of the other nerve elements listed here would be associated with specific dermatome losses.
GAS 700-709; GA 361, 369-371

94 **B.** Dupuytren contracture or deformity is a result of fibromatosis of palmar fascia, resulting in irregular thickening of the fascial attachments to the skin, which causes gradual contraction of the digits, especially digits 4 and 5. In 50% of cases, it is bilateral in occurrence. Ape hand, or flat hand, is a result of loss of the median and ulnar nerves at the elbow, with paralysis of all long flexors of the fingers and all intrinsic hand muscles. Clawhand results from paralysis of interphalangeal joint extension by interossei and lumbricals, innervated primarily by the ulnar nerve. Wrist drop occurs with radial nerve paralysis and loss of the extensors carpi radialis longus and brevis. Mallet finger results from detachment of the extensor mechanism from the distal phalanx of a finger and unopposed flexion of that distal interphalangeal joint.
GAS 758; GA 398

95 **A.** The axillary nerve is a direct branch of the posterior cord and wraps around the surgical neck of the humerus to innervate the teres minor and the deltoid muscles. With this anatomic arrangement, the axillary nerve is tightly "tethered" to the proximal humerus. When the head of the humerus is dislocated, it often puts traction on the axillary nerve.
GAS 674; GA 631

96 **A.** The long head of the biceps brachii muscles runs in the intertubercular groove on the proximal humerus as it changes direction and turns medially to attach to the supraglenoid tubercle of the scapula. This change in direction within an osseous structure predisposes the tendon to wear and tear, particularly in people who overuse the biceps muscle. This type of injury presents with a characteristic sign called the "Popeye sign."
GAS 694, 715-716, 735; GA 370

97 **C.** The supraspinatus muscle inserts on the greater tubercle of the humerus and is said to initiate abduction of the arm at the shoulder. It is supplied principally by spinal nerve C5. The subscapularis muscle is the only muscle that inserts on the lesser tubercle. The subscapularis muscle is innervated by the upper and lower subscapular nerves. The teres minor takes origin from the lateral border of the scapula; the teres major takes origin from the region of the inferior angle and the lateral border of the scapula.
GAS 678-679; GA 369

98 **E.** During a fall on an outstretched upper limb, the forces are conducted through the hand on up through the bones of the limb in succession. Often these bones do not fracture but rather pass the compressive forces proximally. The appendicular skeleton joins with the axial skeleton at the sternoclavicular joint. The forces are not sufficiently transferred to the sternum, causing the clavicle to absorb the force, resulting in fracture of this sigmoidal-shaped bone.
GAS 673; GA 4, 6-7, 56-57, 65, 108, 351

99 C. The patient is suffering from thoracic outlet syndrome, involving neural and vascular elements. This results from any condition that decreases the dimensions of the superior thoracic aperture. It could be a result of a cervical rib, accessory muscles, and/or atypical connective tissue bands at the root of the neck. In this case, symptoms involve the arm, forearm, and hand. Paraesthesia along the medial forearm and hand and atrophy of long flexors and intrinsic muscles point to a possible compression or traction problem of the lower trunk (C8, T1) rather than a lesion of either the median or ulnar nerve. The lateral palm has no sensory problem, which tends to rule out median nerve involvement. Changes in the radial pulse point to vascular compression. Erb-Duchenne paralysis of the upper trunk would affect proximal limb functions, such as arm rotation, abduction, etc. This lesion is on the left side, so the brachiocephalic artery could not be involved because it arises from the right side of the aortic arch; moreover, it would not compress the brachial plexus. Carpal tunnel syndrome would not explain the problems of the forearm and medial hand, or the long flexor atrophy. An isolated medial cord lesion would not explain the atrophy of all long flexors and intrinsic muscles and does not explain the radial pulse characteristics. The ischemic pain in the arm is due to vascular compression.
GAS 147; GA 370

100 A. The ulnar nerve enters the forearm by passing between the two heads of the flexor carpi ulnaris and descends between and innervates the flexor carpi ulnaris (for medial wrist deviation) and flexor digitorum profundus (medial half) muscles. Injuring the ulnar nerve results in clawhand. It enters the hand superficial to the flexor retinaculum and lateral to the pisiform bone, where it is vulnerable to damage. The ulnar nerve also enters Guyon's canal, but damage to it here would not present with the aforementioned symptoms. The median nerve enters the carpal tunnel and the radial nerve passes deep to the brachioradialis.
GAS 737; GA 398

101 B. During a breech delivery as described here, downward traction is applied to the shoulders and upper limbs as the baby is forcibly extracted from the birth canal. This exerts traction on the upper cord of the brachial plexus, often causing a traction injury from which the baby can often recover. If the roots of C5 and C6 are avulsed from the spinal cord, the injury is permanent.
GAS 700-709; GA 361, 369-371

102 E. Striking the concrete blocks with the medial side of her hand has injured the ulnar nerve in Guyon's canal. This is the triangular tunnel formed by the pisiform bone medially, the flexor retinaculum dorsally, and the deep fascia of the wrist ventrally. This injury would result in loss of sensation to the medial palm and the palmar surface of the medial one and a half digits and motor loss of the hypothenar muscles, the interossei, and the medial two lumbricals. The median nerve is not involved, for the thenar muscles and lateral palmar sensations are intact. The dorsal ulnar nerve arises proximal to the wrist, thus it would not be lost. Carpal dislocation is unlikely. If the lunate bone were dislocated, it would not cause compression of the ulnar nerve at the wrist. There is no indication of fifth metacarpal fracture, the so-called boxer's fracture.
GAS 744; GA 417

103 E. The common flexor sheath encloses the long flexor tendons of the fingers. This sheath is usually continuous with the flexor sheath of the little finger, which continues within the palm, having no connection with sheaths of the other digits, which do not extend into the palm.
GAS 755; GA 410

104 C. The infectious agent was introduced into the synovial sheath of the long tendons of the little (fifth) finger. Proximally, this sheath runs through the midpalmar space, and inflammatory processes typically rupture into this space unless aggressively treated with the appropriate antibiotics.
GAS 768; GA 410

105 A. Axillary-subclavian vein thrombosis is becoming much more common in recent years because of the extensive use of catheters in cancer patients and other chronic medical conditions. Effort-induced thrombosis is seen with strenuous use of the dominant arm with hyperabduction and external rotation of the arm or backward and downward rotation of the shoulder as in playing cricket, volleyball, or baseball or chopping wood. Because the symptoms of subclavian stenosis are fairly dramatic, most patients present promptly, usually within 24 hours. They complain of a dull ache in the shoulder or axilla, the pain worsened by activity. Conversely, rest and elevation often relieve the pain. Patients with catheter-associated axillary-subclavian deep vein thrombosis report similar symptoms at the arm or shoulder on the side with the indwelling catheter.
GAS 722; GA 377

106 C. The injury is at the second part of the axillary artery. The suprascapular artery is a branch of the thy-

rocervical trunk off the subclavian artery, proximal to the axillary artery. The subscapular artery is the major branch of the third part of the axillary artery, giving of the thorocodorsal and the circumflex scapular. In this case blood would be flowing from the circumflex scapular artery in a retrograde direction into the axillary artery, supplying blood distal to the injury.
GAS 695; GA 368

107 **A.** This proximal injury to the median nerve would paralyze all of the long flexors of the digits, except for the DIP flexors of digits 4 and 5, thereby swinging the "balance of power" to the muscles that extend the digits, all of which are innervated by the radial nerve. The intrinsic hand muscles can aid in flexion of the MCP joints, and they are innervated by the ulnar nerve. However, they are of insufficient size to compensate for the extensor forces exerted on fingers.
GAS 518, 611, 612; GA 395

108 **C.** The winged scapula results from a lesion of the long thoracic nerve, which supplies the serratus anterior muscle. This muscle is responsible for rotating the scapula upward, which occurs during abduction of the arm above the horizontal. The long thoracic nerve comes off the C5 to C7 roots of the brachial plexus. The diaphragm is supplied by the phrenic nerve, which comes off the spinal nerve roots C3 to C5.
GAS 700-709; GA 361, 369-371

109 **A.** The median nerve supplies sensory innervation to the thumb, index, and middle finger as well as to the lateral half of the ring finger. The median nerve also provides motor innervation to muscles of the thenar eminence. Compression of the median nerve in the carpal tunnel explains these deficits in conjunction with normal functioning of the flexor compartment of the forearm. The ulnar nerve is not implicated in these symptoms. Compression of the brachial plexus could not be attributed to pressure from hypertrophy of the triceps, it is located distal to the plexus. In addition, symptoms would include several upper limb deficits rather than the focal symptoms described in this instance. Osteoarthritis of the cervical spine would also lead to increasing complexity of symptoms.
GAS 764, 788; GA 406

110 **B.** The lunate bone is the most commonly dislocated bone. Displacement is always anteriorly. Dislocation of the lunate bone can precipitate the signs associated typically with carpal tunnel syndrome.
GAS 752-754; GA 392, 394, 422

111 **D.** A cervical rib (found at C7) typically causes thoracic outlet syndrome, which is a condition characterized by weak muscle tone in the hand and loss of radial pulse when the upper limb is abducted above the shoulder. The mechanism of injury with the gun being fired overhead suggests a lower trunk injury to the brachial plexus. The axillary artery supplies the shoulder muscles, and there is no loss of function to these muscles. The upper trunk of the brachial plexus also supplies innervation to the shoulder muscles, which are unaffected based on the patient's presenting abnormalities. The subclavian artery is located anterior to the brachial plexus until it separates the cords as it passes under the clavicle. The brachiocephalic artery and lower trunk of the brachial plexus is only partially correct; the brachiocephalic artery is not directly associated with the brachial plexus due to its location at the midline of the body behind the sternum.
GAS 700-709; GA 61, 369-371

112 **A.** A synarthrosis joint is a fibrous connection that allows minimal to no movement. In this case, virtually no movement is allowed by the interosseous membrane joint between the radius and ulna. Symphysis joints are permanent fibrocartilaginous fusions between two bones; pubic symphysis is an example. Synchondrosis is a temporary joint made of cartilage that transitions to bone typically after growth completes (i.e., epiphyseal plate). Trochoid joints are pivot joints, and the median atlantoaxial joint is an example. Ginglymus joints are hinge joints located at the interphalangeal junctions in the hand and foot (PIPs and DIPs).
GAS 731, 734-735; GA 396

113 **B.** The radial pulse is best located on the anterior forearm (antebrachium) just proximal to the wrist joint. At this point the radial artery travels on the distal radius between the flexor carpi radialis and brachioradialis tendons. The palmaris longus tendon travels more medially to the radial artery and above the flexor retinaculum. The flexor pollicis longus tendon is a deeper structure in the antebrachium and is also located medially to the radial artery.
GAS 785; GA 374, 390

114 **B.** The radial artery enters the palm through the anatomic snuffbox. The artery then moves on to pierce through the two heads of the first dorsal interosseous muscle and enter the deep aspect of the palm. The flexor pollicis longus tendon runs on the palmar aspect of the hand and the radial artery runs on the dorsal aspect of the hand before entering the

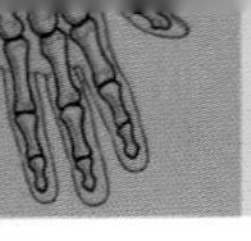

deep aspect of the palm, and therefore the radial artery does not run below this tendon. The radial artery does not run between the first and second interosseous muscle and therefore cannot be used as a landmark to identify the artery. Finally, the artery does not run between the first interosseous muscle and the adductor pollicis longus.
GAS 781; GA 422

115 **D.** The median nerve provides innervation to the flexor compartment of the forearm; cutaneous innervation of the second, third, and fourth digits and palmar and dorsum aspects of the hand; and innervation of four intrinsic hand muscles: first and second lumbricals, abductor pollicis brevis, opponens pollicis, and flexor pollicis brevis. The thenar compartment contains the muscle abductor pollicis brevis, opponens pollicis, and flexor pollicis brevis, and these muscles are innervated by the recurrent branch of the median nerve. The patient has weakening of the first two lumbricals and not simply the thenar muscles, so the median nerve is most likely to be compressed. Another indication that the median nerve is compressed is the vigorous shaking of the wrist. Because the median nerve traverses the carpal tunnel, carpal tunnel compression could lead to this action on part of the patient. The ulnar nerve provides innervation for part of the flexor digitorum profundus and flexor carpi ulnaris. These muscles are not weakened in this patient. The radial nerve provides cutaneous supply to the dorsum of the hand and forearm as well as extensor muscles of the forearm. The posterior interosseous nerve is a branch of the radial nerve and provides innervation of the extensor muscles in the forearm.
GAS 724-731; GA 361

116 **B.** Radial nerve at the distal third of the humerus. The patient can extend his forearm, which suggests that the triceps muscle is not weakened. Supination appears to be weak along with hand grasp and wrist drop. This would indicate that part of the radial nerve has been lost below the innervation of the triceps and above the branches to the supinator and extensors in the forearm. However, sensation on the forearm and hand is intact, indicating that the superficial branch of the radial nerve is intact. The superficial branch of the radial nerve divides from the deep radial nerve at the distal third of the humerus. The posterior cord of the brachial plexus is responsible for providing innervation of the axially and radial nerves. This patient does have some radial nerve innervation and no loss of axillary nerve function. The patient does not have weakened adduction of the wrist, indicating that the ulnar nerve is not injured. If both the radial and musculocutaneous nerves are injured, supination would not be possible as the supinator muscle and biceps provide supination of the forearm.
GAS 750; GA 376

117 **B.** The posterior interosseous nerve is an extension of the deep branch of the radial nerve. It is responsible for innervation of several muscles in the extensor compartment of the posterior aspect of the forearm, including extension of the metacarpophalangeal joints. The posterior interosseous nerve courses laterally around the radius and passes between the two heads of the supinator muscle and is thus likely to be compressed by a hematoma between the fractured radius and the supinator muscle. Though the radial nerve gives rise to the posterior interosseous nerve, this answer choice is too vague and would not indicate the precise injured branch of the radial nerve. Both the deep branch of the ulnar nerve and the median nerve traverse the medial and anteromedial aspect of the arm, respectively. These nerves primarily supply the flexor compartment of the arm. The anterior interosseous nerve is a branch of the median nerve and supplies the flexor digitorum profundus, flexor pollicis longus, and the pronator quadratus.
GAS 750; GA 403

118 **A.** The superior trunk of the brachial plexus includes C5 and C6, which give rise to the suprascapular nerve, which innervates the supraspinatus muscle. The supraspinatus muscle is the primary muscle involved in abduction of the arm from 0° to 15°. The deltoid muscle, supplied primarily by C5, abducts the arm from 15 degrees to 90 degrees. The middle trunk is just C7 and has nothing to do with the muscle involved in initial abduction of the arm. The inferior trunk is C8-T1 and does not supply the supraspinatus muscle; therefore, it is not the right answer. The cords are distal to the branching of the supraspinatus muscle; therefore, neither lateral cord nor medial cord is the correct answer.
GAS 700-709; GA 361, 369-371

119 **C.** The radial nerve acts to extend the forearm at the elbow. This nerve is derived from all the roots of the brachial plexus C5 to T1. None of the other answers include all the roots and are therefore incorrect.
GAS 700-709; GA 361, 369-371

120 **A.** The suprascapular artery arises as a major branch of the thyrocervical trunk from the subclavian artery. It has rich anastomoses with the circum-

flex scapular artery and could provide essential blood supply to the scapula. The dorsal scapular artery would be lost with the graft. None of the other vessels listed is in position to provide adequate supply to the scapula.
GAS 696, 697; GA 366, 368

121 **C.** The scaphoid and lunate carpal bones are in closest articulation with the radius, which is fractured in a Colles' fracture; therefore, they would most likely be disrupted or fractured. The other carpal bones listed do not have direct contact with the radius and have a more distal location; therefore, they would not be as likely to be injured with a Colles' fracture.
GAS 734; GA 392

122 **C.** This type of dislocation is common in children and results when the radius is dislocated and slips out from the anular ligament, which holds it in place, articulating with the ulna and the capitulum of the humerus. In adults the anular ligament has a good "grip" at the radial neck, but in young children the radial head is not fully developed, leading to an indistinct neck. Compression of the median nerve is not likely due to its medial position in the cubital fossa. The radius does not articulate with the trochlea of the humerus; the ulna articulates at this position. The ulna is not likely to be dislocated because it is more stable than the radius, which has only the anular ligament for its support. The radial nerve does not pass behind the medial epicondyle; rather, the ulnar nerve does this, so this is not the correct answer.
GAS 735; GA 391

123 **C.** Injury to the radial nerve can be caused by a blow to the midhumeral region since the nerve winds around the shaft of the humerus. The symptoms described include the loss of wrist and finger extension and a loss of sensation in an area of skin supplied by the radial nerve.
GAS 751; GA 380

124 **A.** The ulnar nerve innervates the dorsal and palmar interossei, which act to abduct and adduct the fingers and assist the lumbricals in their actions of flexing the metacarpophalangeal joints and extending the interphalangeal joints. The recurrent branch of the median nerve innervates the thenar muscle group that functions in the movement of the thumb. The radial and musculocutaneous nerves do not innervate any muscles in the hand. The anterior interosseous innervates the flexor pollicis longus and the pronator quadratus.
GAS 770-771; GA 417

125 **C.** The triceps brachii muscle is innervated by the radial nerve (primarily C7), which comes off C5 to T1 spinal nerves. Because the patient's only motor deficit involves the triceps brachii muscles, one can rule out C5 and C6, which supply fibers to the axillary, musculocutaneous, and upper subscapular nerves. Damage to either of these roots would result in additional motor deficits of the shoulder and flexor compartment of the arm. One can also rule out C8-T1 because these roots form the medial pectoral nerve and the medial brachial and antebrachial cutaneous nerves. Damage to these roots would result in loss of pectoral muscle function and cutaneous sensation over the medial surface of the upper limb.
GAS 700-709; GA 361, 369-371

126 **D.** Mallet finger, also known as baseball finger, is a deformity in which the finger will be permanently flexed at the distal interphalangeal joint, due to avulsion of the insertion of the extensor tendon at the distal phalanx.
GAS 760; GA 392, 394, 422

127 **B.** Injury to the superior trunk of the brachial plexus can damage nerve fibers going to the suprascapular, axillary, and musculocutaneous nerves. Damage to the suprascapular and axillary nerves causes impaired abduction and lateral rotation of the arm. Damage to the musculocutaneous nerve causes impaired flexion of the forearm. A winged scapula would be caused by damage to the long thoracic nerve. The long thoracic nerve is formed from spinal cord levels C5, C6, and C7, so the serratus anterior muscle would be weakened from the damage to C5 and C6, but the muscle would not be completely paralyzed. The intrinsic muscles of the hand are innervated by the ulnar and median nerves, which would most likely remain intact. Paraesthesia in the medial aspect of the arm would be caused by damage to the medial brachial cutaneous nerve (C8-T1; inferior trunk). Loss of sensation on the dorsum of the hand would be caused by damage to either the ulnar or radial nerves (C6 to T1).
GAS 700-709; GA 361, 369-371

128 **D.** The supinator muscle attaches to the radius proximally and when fractured would cause a lateral deviation. The pronator teres originates on the medial epicondyle and coronoid process of the ulna and inserts on the middle of the lateral side of the radius, pulling the radius medially below the fracture. Pronator quadratus originates on the anterior surface of the distal ulna and inserts on the anterior surface of the distal radius, pulling the radius medially. Brachioradialis originates on the lateral supracondylar ridge of

the humerus and inserts at the base of the radial styloid process, far below the fracture. Brachialis originates in the lower anterior surface of the humerus and inserts in the coronoid process and ulnar tuberosity, hence not causing an action on the radius.
GAS 715; GA 379

129 **A.** Lymph from the lateral side of the hand drains directly into humeral (epitrochlear) nodes then to the central (axillary) nodes. Pectoral nodes receive lymph mainly from the anterior thoracic wall, including most of the breast. Subscapular nodes receive lymph from the posterior aspect of the thoracic wall and scapular region. Parasternal nodes receive lymph from the lower medial quadrant of the breast.
GAS 710; GA 381

130 **C.** Compartment syndrome is characterized by increased pressure within a confined space by a fascial compartment, which impairs blood supply, resulting in paleness. Venous thrombosis would not cause pain but could cause death from a pulmonary embolism. Thoracic outlet syndrome affects nerves in the brachial plexus and the subclavian artery and blood vessels between the neck and the axilla, far above the cast. Raynaud's disease affects blood flow to the limbs when they are exposed to temperature changes or stress. The fracture at the radial groove probably resulted in a radial nerve injury but would not be responsible for these symptoms.
GAS 744; GA 381

131 **E.** The deep branch of the ulnar nerve arises at the level of the pisiform bone and passes between the pisiform and the hook of the hamate, hence the ulnar is the nerve most likely to be injured in this patient. The median nerve enters the forearm between the humeral and ulnar heads of the pronator teres muscle then becomes superficial near the wrist. The recurrent median enters the palm through the carpal tunnel. The radial nerve divides into superficial and deep branches when it enters the cubital fossa.
GAS 771; GA 417

132 **A.** The supraspinatus initiates abduction of the arm during the first 15° of abduction; palpation of the tendon during this phase would result in pain from a tendinopathy of the supraspinatus.
GAS 678; GA 361, 364

133 **A.** The hallmark fracture caused by a fall on an outstretched hand is a scaphoid-lunate fracture; the scaphoid and lunate are the two wrist bones most proximal to the styloid process of the radius. All the other wrist bones are less likely to be affected by this injury.
GAS 786; GA 392

134 **C.** Bennett's fracture is a carpometacarpal fracture at the base of the thumb. Smith's fracture is also called a reverse Colles' fracture and is caused when the distal fragment of the radius angles forward. Colles' fracture is also called "silver fork deformity" because the distal fragment is displaced posteriorly. Boxer's fractures of the necks of metacarpal bones are fractures to the fingers. A scaphoid fracture would be indicated by pain in the anatomical snuffbox.
GAS 756; GA 392

135 **A.** Interestingly, "gamekeeper's thumb" was a term coined because this injury was most commonly associated with Scottish gamekeepers who, it is said, killed small animals such as rabbits by breaking their necks between the ground and the gamekeeper's thumb and index finger. The resulting valgus force on the abducted MCP joint caused injury to the ulnar collateral ligament. These days this injury is more commonly seen in skiers who land awkwardly with their hand braced on a ski pole, causing the valgus force on the thumb as is seen in this patient. Whereas the term "skier thumb" is sometimes used, "gamekeeper's thumb" is still in common usage. Bennett fracture is a fracture at the base of the metacarpal of the thumb. Scaphoid fracture occurs after a fall on an outstretched hand, involving the scaphoid and lunate bone. Colles' fracture is also called silver fork deformity because the distal fragment of the radius is displaced posteriorly. Boxer's fracture is a fracture of the necks of the second and third (and sometimes the fifth) metacarpals. Smith's fracture is also called a reverse Colles' fracture and is caused when the distal radius is fractured and the distal radial fragment is angled forward.
GAS 755; GA 395

136 **B.** The biceps brachii reflex involves C5 and C6 spinal nerves. C5 provides the motor component; C6 the afferent side of the reflex arc.
GAS 700-709; GA 361, 369-371

137 **B.** The brachioradialis reflex is performed by tapping the tendon of the brachioradialis muscle. The reflex involves spinal nerves C5, C6, and C7. The major contribution is from C6.
GAS 700-709; GA 361, 369-371

138 **D.** Volkmann's contracture is a flexion deformity of the fingers and sometimes the wrist from an ischemic necrosis of the forearm flexor muscles. Bennett's fracture is a fracture at the base of the metacarpal of the thumb. Scaphoid fracture occurs after a fall on an outstretched hand and involves the scaphoid and lunate bones. Colles' fracture is also called silver fork deformity because the distal fragment of the radius is displaced posteriorly. Boxer's fracture is a fracture of the necks of the second and third (and sometimes the fifth) metacarpals. Smith's fracture is also called a reverse Colles' fracture and is caused when the distal radius is fractured, with the radial fragment angled forward.
GAS 762; GA 398

139 **D.** The ulnar nerve enters the forearm by passing between the two heads of the flexor carpi ulnaris and descends between and innervates the flexor carpi ulnaris and flexor digitorum profundus (medial half) muscles. It enters the hand superficial to the flexor retinaculum and lateral to the pisiform bone, where it is vulnerable to damage and provides the deep ulnar branch. The deep branch of the radial nerve arises proximally in the forearm.
GAS 771; GA 417

140 **B.** "Benediction attitude" of the hand with the index and long fingers straight and the ring and little fingers flexed is caused by an injury to the median nerve. The long flexors of the digits are supplied by the median nerve; the unopposed radial nerve and deep ulnar nerve supply the extensors of the digits 1–3, causing them to be in the extended position. Digits 4 and 5 are slightly flexed, because the flexors of the PIP joints are supplied by the ulnar nerve.
GAS 724; GA 371, 376

141 **A.** The Allen test involves compression of the radial and ulnar arteries at the wrist with the fingers flexed tightly. Pressure is then released on either vessel successively to determine the degree of supply to the hand by either vessel and the patency of the anastomoses between them. The usefulness of the radial artery for bypass can thereby be assessed. The other tests have nothing to do with the patency of the radial artery.
GAS 770; GA 400

142 **E.** The ulnar nerve enters the hand superficial to the flexor retinaculum and lateral to the pisiform bone and innervates all the interossei via the deep branch. These muscles are responsible for adduction and abduction of the fingers. Flexion of the fingers is spared because the flexor digitorum superficialis and most of the flexor digitorum profundus are innervated by the median nerve, which is unaffected by this injury. Had the median nerve been compressed in the carpal tunnel, one would have difficulty with motion of the thumb as a result of a lack of innervation of the thenar muscles. An injury of the radial nerve in the arm will result in extension deficit in the forearm and hand.
GAS 744; GA 417

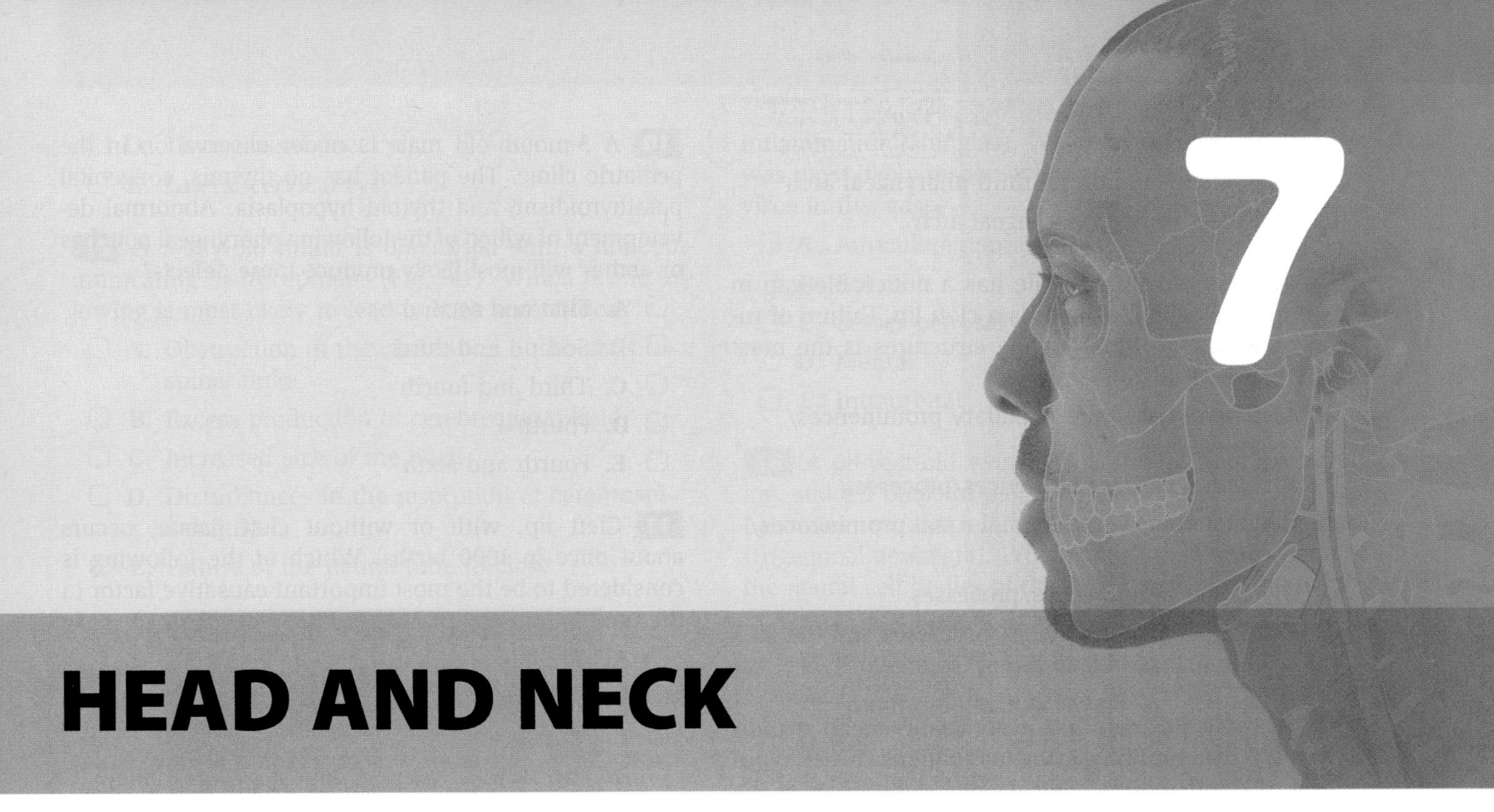

HEAD AND NECK

1 A 2-month-old male infant had a small pit at the anterior border of the sternocleidomastoid muscle, with mucus dripping intermittently from the opening. The pit extended to the tonsillar fossa as a branchial fistula. Which of the following embryologic structure(s) is (are) involved in this anomaly?

- ▢ **A.** Second pharyngeal arch
- ▢ **B.** Second pharyngeal pouch and groove
- ▢ **C.** Third pharyngeal pouch
- ▢ **D.** Thyroglossal duct
- ▢ **E.** Second pharyngeal pouch and cervical sinus

2 A 2-day-old infant was born with a cleft palate. The major portion of the palate develops from which of the following embryonic structures?

- ▢ **A.** Lateral palatine process
- ▢ **B.** Median palatine process
- ▢ **C.** Intermaxillary segment
- ▢ **D.** Median nasal prominences
- ▢ **E.** Frontonasal eminence

3 A 3-day-old infant has a small area of the right iris missing, and a diagnosis of coloboma of the iris is made. Which of the following is the most likely embryologic cause of the coloboma?

- ▢ **A.** Failure of the retinal/choroid fissure to close
- ▢ **B.** Abnormal neural crest formation
- ▢ **C.** Abnormal interactions between the optic vesicle and ectoderm
- ▢ **D.** Posterior chamber cavitation
- ▢ **E.** Weak adhesion between the inner and outer layers of the optic vesicle

4 Early closure of the fontanelles of the infant skull can result in compression of the brain, restricting brain growth. Which of the following fontanelles is located at the junction of sagittal and coronal sutures and at what age does this fontanelle typically close?

- ▢ **A.** Posterior fontanelle, which closes at about 2 years
- ▢ **B.** Mastoid fontanelle, which closes at about 16 months
- ▢ **C.** Lambdoid fontanelle, which closes at 8 months to 1 year
- ▢ **D.** Sphenoidal fontanelle, which closes at 3 years
- ▢ **E.** Anterior fontanelle, which closes at 18 months

5 A 3-year-old boy is admitted to the hospital because of a soft, anterior, midline cervical mass. When the patient is asked to protrude his tongue, the mass in the neck is observed to move upward. Which of the following is the most likely diagnosis?

- ▢ **A.** A thyroglossal duct cyst
- ▢ **B.** Defect in sixth pharyngeal arch

and loss of taste from the anterior two thirds of the tongue. Which of the following structures is most likely involved with the tumor?

- ☐ **A.** Auriculotemporal nerve
- ☐ **B.** Lesser petrosal nerve
- ☐ **C.** Facial nerve
- ☐ **D.** Inferior salivatory nucleus
- ☐ **E.** Pterygopalatine ganglion

22 A 17-year-old female was admitted to the hospital with a high fever. Following intravenous administration of antibiotics, a routine CT scan revealed a "thoracic outlet" syndrome. Which symptom would most likely result from this syndrome?

- ☐ **A.** Problems with respiration because of pressure on the phrenic nerve
- ☐ **B.** Reduced blood flow to the thoracic wall
- ☐ **C.** Reduced venous return from the head and neck
- ☐ **D.** Numbness in the upper limb
- ☐ **E.** Distention of the internal jugular vein

23 A 31-year-old female is admitted to the hospital after an automobile collision. A CT scan examination reveals a large hematoma inferior to the right jugular foramen. Physical examination reveals right pupillary constriction (miosis) and anhydrosis (loss of sweating) of the face. Which of the following ganglia is most likely affected by the hematoma?

- ☐ **A.** Submandibular
- ☐ **B.** Trigeminal (semilunar or Gasserian)
- ☐ **C.** Superior cervical
- ☐ **D.** Geniculate
- ☐ **E.** Ciliary

24 A 35-year-old male patient is admitted to the hospital with severe headaches. A CT scan evaluation reveals a tumor in the infratemporal fossa. Physical examination reveals loss of general sensation from the anterior two thirds of his tongue, but taste and salivation are intact. Which of the following nerves is most likely affected by the tumor?

- ☐ **A.** Lingual proximal to its junction with the chorda tympani
- ☐ **B.** Chorda tympani
- ☐ **C.** Inferior alveolar
- ☐ **D.** Lesser petrosal
- ☐ **E.** Glossopharyngeal

25 A 70-year-old man is admitted to the hospital with chronic headache and enlarged lymph nodes. A CT scan shows a tumor at the jugular foramen. Which of the following would be the most likely neurologic deficit?

- ☐ **A.** Loss of tongue movements
- ☐ **B.** Loss of facial expression
- ☐ **C.** Loss of sensation from the face and the scalp
- ☐ **D.** Loss of hearing
- ☐ **E.** Loss of gag reflex

26 A 40-year-old unconscious man is admitted to the emergency department after being hit in the head with a baseball. A CT scan examination reveals a fractured pterion and an epidural hematoma. Branches of which of the following arteries are most likely to be injured?

- ☐ **A.** External carotid
- ☐ **B.** Superficial temporal
- ☐ **C.** Maxillary
- ☐ **D.** Deep temporal
- ☐ **E.** Middle meningeal

27 An unconscious 48-year-old woman is admitted to the hospital. CT scan reveals a tumor in her brain. When she regains consciousness, her right eye is directed laterally and downward, with complete ptosis of her upper eyelid, and her pupil is dilated. Which of the following structures was most likely affected by the tumor to result in these symptoms?

- ☐ **A.** Oculomotor nerve
- ☐ **B.** Optic nerve
- ☐ **C.** Facial nerve
- ☐ **D.** Ciliary ganglion
- ☐ **E.** Superior cervical ganglion

28 A 55-year-old man is admitted to the hospital after an injury sustained at work in a factory. He presents with severe scalp lacerations, which were sutured. After three days the wound is inflamed, swollen, and painful. Between which tissue layers is the infection most likely located?

- ☐ **A.** The periosteum and bone
- ☐ **B.** The aponeurosis and the periosteum
- ☐ **C.** The dense connective tissue and the aponeurosis
- ☐ **D.** The dense connective tissue and the skin
- ☐ **E.** The dermis and the epidermis

29 A 36-year-old woman is admitted to the hospital with severe head injuries after a car crash. During neurologic examination her uvula is deviated to the right. Which nerve is most likely affected to result in this deviation?

- [ ] **A.** Left vagus
- [ ] **B.** Right vagus
- [ ] **C.** Right hypoglossal
- [ ] **D.** Left glossopharyngeal
- [ ] **E.** Right glossopharyngeal

30 A 22-year-old male is admitted to the emergency department and intubated. An endotracheal tube is passed through an opening between the vocal folds. What is the name of this opening?

- [ ] **A.** Piriform recess
- [ ] **B.** Vestibule
- [ ] **C.** Ventricle
- [ ] **D.** Vallecula
- [ ] **E.** Rima glottidis

31 A 55-year-old male has a complaint of left-sided maxillary tooth pain. A dental examination reveals no abnormalities of his teeth. During physical examination tapping on his right maxilla elicits sharp pain on the right side of his face. The patient reports that he has no allergies. Which of the following conditions will be the most likely diagnosis?

- [ ] **A.** Sphenoid sinusitis
- [ ] **B.** Anterior ethmoidal sinusitis
- [ ] **C.** Posterior ethmoidal sinusitis
- [ ] **D.** Maxillary sinusitis
- [ ] **E.** Frontal sinusitis

32 A 70-year-old man is admitted to the hospital with severe headaches. During physical examination he has difficulty coughing and swallowing. A CT scan shows a tumor affecting a cranial nerve. Which nerve is most likely affected?

- [ ] **A.** Mandibular
- [ ] **B.** Maxillary
- [ ] **C.** Glossopharyngeal
- [ ] **D.** Vagus
- [ ] **E.** Hypoglossal

33 A 7-year-old boy with a high fever is brought to the pediatrician. During physical examination the patient complains of pain in his ear. His throat appears red and inflamed, confirming the diagnosis of pharyngitis. Which of the following structures provided a pathway for the infection to spread to the tympanic cavity (middle ear)?

- [ ] **A.** Choanae
- [ ] **B.** Internal acoustic meatus
- [ ] **C.** External acoustic meatus
- [ ] **D.** Pharyngotympanic tube
- [ ] **E.** Pharyngeal recess

34 A 33-year-old woman is unconscious when she is admitted to the hospital after she fell, hitting her head. The physician in the emergency department performs a pupillary light reflex test. The integrity of which of the following nerves is being checked?

- [ ] **A.** Optic and facial
- [ ] **B.** Optic and oculomotor
- [ ] **C.** Maxillary and facial
- [ ] **D.** Ophthalmic and oculomotor
- [ ] **E.** Ophthalmic and facial

35 A 48-year-old male patient complains of diplopia (double vision). On neurologic examination he is unable to adduct his left eye and lacks a corneal reflex on the left side. Where is the most likely location of the lesion resulting in the symptoms?

- [ ] **A.** Inferior orbital fissure
- [ ] **B.** Optic canal
- [ ] **C.** Superior orbital fissure
- [ ] **D.** Foramen rotundum
- [ ] **E.** Foramen ovale

36 A 34-year-old male complains of hyperacusis (sensitivity to loud sounds). Injury to which of the following cranial nerves is responsible?

- [ ] **A.** Hypoglossal
- [ ] **B.** Facial
- [ ] **C.** Accessory
- [ ] **D.** Vagus
- [ ] **E.** Glossopharyngeal

37 A 34-year-old swimmer presents to your office with an external ear canal infection (otitis externa). The patient coughs during inspection of the external auditory meatus with a speculum. The cough results from the irritation of which nerve that innervates an area of the external auditory meatus?

- [ ] **A.** Vestibulocochlear
- [ ] **B.** Vagus
- [ ] **C.** Trigeminal
- [ ] **D.** Facial
- [ ] **E.** Accessory

38 A 29-year-old woman underwent a thyroidectomy. Postoperatively, the patient presented with hoarseness. Which of the following nerves was most likely injured during the operation?

- ▢ **A.** Internal laryngeal
- ▢ **B.** External laryngeal
- ▢ **C.** Recurrent laryngeal
- ▢ **D.** Superior laryngeal
- ▢ **E.** Glossopharyngeal

39 A 48-year-old man presents with a constricted right pupil that does not react to light. His left pupil and vision in both eyes are normal. These findings are most likely due to a lesion involving which of the following right-sided structures?

- ▢ **A.** Oculomotor nerve
- ▢ **B.** Superior cervical ganglion
- ▢ **C.** Nervus intermedius
- ▢ **D.** Edinger-Westphal nucleus
- ▢ **E.** Trigeminal (semilunar, Gasserian) ganglion

40 A 55-year-old woman is diagnosed with a tumor at the base of the skull, resulting in a decrease in tear production. Which of the following nerves is most likely injured?

- ▢ **A.** Chorda tympani
- ▢ **B.** Deep petrosal
- ▢ **C.** Greater petrosal
- ▢ **D.** Lesser petrosal
- ▢ **E.** Nasociliary

41 A 24-year-old man is admitted to the hospital after a street fight. Radiographic examination reveals an inferior (blow-out) fracture of the orbit. Orbital structures would most likely be found inferiorly in which of the following spaces?

- ▢ **A.** Ethmoidal sinus
- ▢ **B.** Frontal sinus
- ▢ **C.** Maxillary sinus
- ▢ **D.** Nasal cavity
- ▢ **E.** Sphenoidal sinus

42 A 35-year-old woman is hospitalized due to cavernous sinus thrombosis resulting from an infection on the face. Which of the following is the most direct route for spread of infection from the face to the cavernous sinus?

- ▢ **A.** Pterygoid venous plexus
- ▢ **B.** Superior ophthalmic vein
- ▢ **C.** Frontal venous plexus
- ▢ **D.** Basilar venous plexus
- ▢ **E.** Parietal emissary vein

43 A 7-year-old boy was suffering from a severe infection of the middle ear (otitis media), which spread to the mastoid air cells (mastoiditis). Surgery was required but resulted in the following: right corner of the mouth drooping, unable to close his right eye, food collection in his right oral vestibule. Which nerve was injured?

- ▢ **A.** Glossopharyngeal
- ▢ **B.** Vagus
- ▢ **C.** Facial
- ▢ **D.** Maxillary division of the trigeminal nerve
- ▢ **E.** Mandibular division of the trigeminal nerve

44 The arterial circle (of Willis) contributes greatly to cerebral arterial circulation when one primary artery becomes occluded by atherosclerotic disease. Which of the following vessels does not contribute to the circle?

- ▢ **A.** Anterior communicating artery
- ▢ **B.** Posterior communicating artery
- ▢ **C.** Middle cerebral artery
- ▢ **D.** Internal carotid artery
- ▢ **E.** Posterior cerebral artery

45 A 45-year-old woman is admitted to the hospital for severe ear pain. Physical examination reveals chronic infection of the mastoid air cells (mastoiditis). The infection can erode the thin layer of the bone between the mastoid air cells and the posterior cranial fossa and spread most commonly into which of the following venous structures?

- ▢ **A.** Superior sagittal sinus
- ▢ **B.** Inferior sagittal sinus
- ▢ **C.** Straight sinus
- ▢ **D.** Cavernous sinus
- ▢ **E.** Sigmoid sinus

46 A 63-year-old man with hearing loss in his left ear complains of a loss of taste and drooling from the left side of his mouth. A CT scan shows a tumor compressing the nerve entering the skull through which of the following openings?

- ▢ **A.** Foramen ovale
- ▢ **B.** Foramen rotundum
- ▢ **C.** Internal acoustic meatus
- ▢ **D.** Jugular foramen
- ▢ **E.** Superior orbital fissure

47 A 70-year-old man has a biopsy of a growth on his lower lip. The biopsy reveals a squamous cell carcinoma. Which lymph nodes will most likely be first involved in the spread of the cancer cells?

- ▢ **A.** Occipital
- ▢ **B.** Parotid
- ▢ **C.** Retropharyngeal
- ▢ **D.** Jugulodigastric
- ▢ **E.** Submental

48 A 54-year-old man is admitted to the hospital due to severe headaches. A CT examination reveals an internal carotid artery aneurysm inside the cavernous sinus. Which of the following nerves would be typically affected first?

- ▢ **A.** Abducens nerve
- ▢ **B.** Oculomotor nerve
- ▢ **C.** Ophthalmic nerve
- ▢ **D.** Maxillary nerve
- ▢ **E.** Trochlear nerve

49 A 24-year-old male had a third molar (wisdom tooth) extracted from his lower jaw. This resulted in the loss of general sense and taste sensation from the anterior two thirds of the tongue. This loss was most likely due to injury of which of the following nerves?

- ▢ **A.** Auriculotemporal
- ▢ **B.** Chorda tympani
- ▢ **C.** Lingual
- ▢ **D.** Mental
- ▢ **E.** Inferior alveolar

50 A 56-year-old woman is admitted to the hospital with rheumatoid arthritis of her temporomandibular joint (TMJ) and severe ear pain. An image from her radiographic examination is shown in Fig. 7-2. Which of the following nerves is most likely responsible for conducting the pain sensation?

- ▢ **A.** Facial
- ▢ **B.** Auriculotemporal
- ▢ **C.** Lesser petrosal
- ▢ **D.** Vestibulocochlear
- ▢ **E.** Chorda tympani

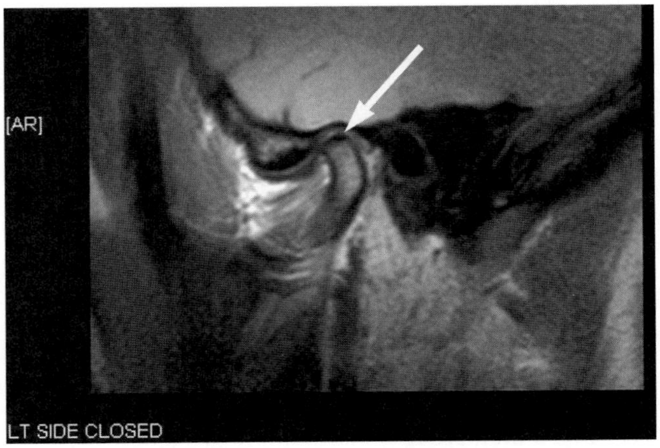

[AR]

LT SIDE CLOSED

Fig. 7-2

51 Where is the location of the postganglionic parasympathetic neural cell bodies that directly innervate the parotid gland?

- ▢ **A.** Trigeminal (semilunar, Gasserian) ganglion
- ▢ **B.** Inferior salivatory nucleus
- ▢ **C.** Superior cervical ganglion
- ▢ **D.** Otic ganglion
- ▢ **E.** Submandibular ganglion

52 The arachnoid villi allow cerebrospinal fluid to pass between which two of the following spaces?

- ▢ **A.** Choroid plexus and subdural space
- ▢ **B.** Subarachnoid space and superior sagittal sinus
- ▢ **C.** Subdural space and cavernous sinus
- ▢ **D.** Superior sagittal sinus and jugular vein
- ▢ **E.** Epidural and subdural space

53 A 22-year-old woman is admitted to the hospital with an injury to her eye. The corneal reflex is tested and found to be present. Which of the following nerves is responsible for the afferent limb of this reflex?

- ▢ **A.** Frontal
- ▢ **B.** Lacrimal
- ▢ **C.** Nasociliary
- ▢ **D.** Oculomotor
- ▢ **E.** Optic

54 A 21-year-old man was brought to the emergency department because of severe epistaxis (nosebleed) from the nasal septum. This area, knows as Kiesselbach's (or Little's) area, involves mostly anastomoses between which of the following arteries?

- ▢ **A.** Ascending palatine and ascending pharyngeal
- ▢ **B.** Posterior superior alveolar and accessory meningeal

- ☐ **C.** Lateral branches of posterior ethmoidal and middle meningeal
- ☐ **D.** Septal branches of the sphenopalatine and superior labial
- ☐ **E.** Descending palatine and tonsillar branches of the pharyngeal

55 An 11-year-old boy is examined by an ENT doctor for his swollen palatine tonsils. The palatine tonsils are located between the anterior and posterior tonsillar pillars. Which of the following muscles form these pillars?

- ☐ **A.** Levator veli palatini and tensor veli palatini
- ☐ **B.** Palatoglossus and palatopharyngeus
- ☐ **C.** Styloglossus and stylopharyngeus
- ☐ **D.** Palatopharyngeus and salpingopharyngeus
- ☐ **E.** Superior and middle pharyngeal constrictors

56 A 35-year-old female is under general anesthesia. Prior to laryngeal intubation the rima glottidis is opened by which pair of muscles?

- ☐ **A.** Posterior cricoarytenoids
- ☐ **B.** Lateral cricoarytenoids
- ☐ **C.** Thyroarytenoids
- ☐ **D.** Transverse arytenoids
- ☐ **E.** Cricothyroids

57 A 32-year-old female patient asks you what is the soft, thin ridge of tissue that she can feel running forward across the masseter muscle toward her upper lip. You reassure her that is perfectly normal. Which of the following is the most likely structure she is feeling?

- ☐ **A.** Facial artery
- ☐ **B.** Maxillary artery
- ☐ **C.** Parotid duct
- ☐ **D.** Marginal mandibular branch of facial nerve
- ☐ **E.** Facial vein

58 A 43-year-old man is diagnosed with laryngeal carcinoma. A surgical procedure is performed and the tumor is successfully removed from the larynx. The right ansa cervicalis is anastomosed with the right recurrent laryngeal nerve in order to reinnervate the muscles of the larynx and restore phonation. Which of the following muscles will most likely be paralyzed after this operation?

- ☐ **A.** Sternocleidomastoid
- ☐ **B.** Platysma
- ☐ **C.** Sternohyoid
- ☐ **D.** Trapezius
- ☐ **E.** Cricothyroid

59 A 67-year-old female is admitted to the emergency department with a severe swelling on the right side of her neck. An MRI examination reveals an abscess. The abscess is surgically removed from the middle of the posterior cervical triangle on the right side. During recovery the patient notices that her shoulder droops and she can no longer raise her right hand above her head to brush her hair. Which of the following nerves has most likely been iatrogenically injured?

- ☐ **A.** Accessory
- ☐ **B.** Ansa cervicalis
- ☐ **C.** Facial
- ☐ **D.** Hypoglossal
- ☐ **E.** Suprascapular

60 A 20-year-old man is admitted to the emergency department with a stab wound in the superior region of his neck. A radiographic examination reveals that the wound has not affected any major structures. Physical examination reveals that the patient has lost sensation from the skin over the angle of the jaw. Which of the following nerves is most likely injured?

- ☐ **A.** Supraclavicular
- ☐ **B.** Transverse cervical
- ☐ **C.** Great auricular
- ☐ **D.** Greater occipital
- ☐ **E.** Lesser occipital

61 A 6-year-old male child, whose medical history includes a complicated delivery, has a permanently tilted head posture, with the right ear near the right shoulder and the face turned upward and to the left. Which of the following muscles was most likely damaged during birth?

- ☐ **A.** Anterior scalene
- ☐ **B.** Omohyoid
- ☐ **C.** Sternocleidomastoid
- ☐ **D.** Trapezius
- ☐ **E.** Platysma

62 A 35-year-old woman is admitted to the emergency department after a violent automobile crash. The patient's upper airway is obstructed with blood and mucus, and a midline tracheotomy inferior to the thyroid isthmus is performed. Which of the following vessels are most likely to be present at the site of incision and will need to be cauterized?

- ☐ **A.** Middle thyroid vein and inferior thyroid artery
- ☐ **B.** Inferior thyroid artery and inferior thyroid vein

- C. Inferior thyroid vein and thyroidea ima artery
- D. Cricothyroid artery and inferior thyroid vein
- E. Left brachiocephalic vein and inferior thyroid artery

63 A 34-year-old woman is admitted to the hospital with a large mass at her thyroid gland. Ultrasound examination reveals a benign tumor. Twenty-four hours following a partial thyroidectomy, in which the inferior thyroid artery was also ligated, the patient speaks with a hoarse voice and has difficulty in breathing on exertion. Which of the following nerves was most likely injured during the surgical procedure?

- A. Internal branch of superior laryngeal
- B. Ansa cervicalis
- C. Ansa subclavia
- D. Recurrent laryngeal
- E. External branch of superior laryngeal

64 A 55-year-old woman is admitted to the hospital with difficulty swallowing. Physical examination reveals that the patient has episodes of severe headaches and frequently aspirates fluids when drinking them. A radiographic examination reveals a skull base tumor occupying the space behind the jugular foramen. Involvement of which of the following structures is most likely responsible for the findings in the patient?

- A. Ansa cervicalis
- B. Cervical sympathetic trunk
- C. External laryngeal nerve
- D. Hypoglossal nerve
- E. Vagus nerve

65 A 55-year-old woman is admitted to the hospital with severe hypertension. Laboratory examination reveals hypertension (190/110 mm Hg) and hypercholesterolemia (250 mg/dl). During physical examination the patient complains of headaches and dizziness. Radiographic examination reveals 90% occlusion of both common carotid arteries. A carotid endarterectomy is performed and large atherosclerotic plaques are removed. During a postoperative physical examination on the right side, it was noted that her tongue deviated toward the right when she was asked to stick it out. Which of the following nerves was most likely injured during the procedure?

- A. Right glossopharyngeal
- B. Right hypoglossal
- C. Left hypoglossal
- D. Left lingual
- E. Left vagus

66 A 34-year-old woman is admitted to the hospital with a large mass in her lower anterior neck. Ultrasonic examination reveals a benign tumor of her thyroid gland. Twenty-four hours following a partial thyroidectomy, it was noted that the patient frequently aspirates fluid into her lungs. Upon examination it was determined that the area of the piriform recess above the vocal fold of the larynx was anesthetized. Which of the following nerves was most likely iatrogenically injured?

- A. External branch of the superior pharyngeal
- B. Hypoglossal
- C. Internal branch of the superior laryngeal
- D. Lingual
- E. Recurrent laryngeal

67 A 38-year-old man is admitted to the hospital with a large mass in his lower anterior neck. Ultrasonic examination reveals a benign tumor of his thyroid gland. Twenty-four hours following a partial thyroidectomy, it was noted that the patient could not abduct the true vocal cords due to a nerve injury during the operation. Which of the following muscles was most likely dennervated?

- A. Posterior cricoarytenoid
- B. Lateral cricoarytenoid
- C. Thyroarytenoid
- D. Arytenoid
- E. Cricothyroid

68 A 46-year-old woman is admitted to the hospital with a large mass in her lower anterior neck. Ultrasonic examination reveals a benign tumor of her thyroid gland. During the procedure to remove the tumor the superior thyroid artery is identified and used as a landmark in order not to damage its small companion nerve. Which of the following nerves is most likely to accompany the superior thyroid artery?

- A. Cervical sympathetic trunk
- B. External branch of the superior laryngeal
- C. Inferior root of the ansa cervicalis
- D. Internal branch of the superior laryngeal
- E. Recurrent laryngeal

69 A 3-year-old girl ruptured her eardrum when she inserted a pencil into her external ear canal. She was urgently admitted to the emergency department. Physical examination revealed pain in her ear and a few drops of blood in the external auditory meatus. There was the concern that there might possibly have been an injury to the nerve that principally innervates the external surface of the tympanic membrane. Which of the following tests is most likely to be performed during physical examination to check for injury to this nerve?

- ☐ **A.** Check the taste in the anterior two thirds of the tongue.
- ☐ **B.** Check the sensation to the pharynx and palate.
- ☐ **C.** Check if there is paraesthesia at the TMJ.
- ☐ **D.** Check for sensation in the larynx.
- ☐ **E.** Check for sensation in the nasal cavity.

70 A 27-year-old woman is admitted to the emergency department after she was thrown from a motor scooter. Radiographic evaluation reveals a type I Lefort fracture and comminuted fracture of the mandible and TMJ. Despite reconstructive surgery, the patient develops hyperacusis (sensitivity to loud sounds) due to facial nerve paralysis. Which of the following muscles is most likely paralyzed?

- ☐ **A.** Posterior belly of digastric
- ☐ **B.** Stapedius
- ☐ **C.** Tensor tympani
- ☐ **D.** Stylohyoid
- ☐ **E.** Cricothyroid

71 A 43-year-old man is admitted to the emergency department with a fracture of the base of his skull. A thorough physical examination reveals that a number of structures have been injured, possibly including the right greater petrosal nerve. Which of the following conditions needs to be identified during physical examination to confirm the diagnosis of greater petrosal nerve injury?

- ☐ **A.** Partial dryness of the mouth due to lack of salivary secretions from the submandibular and sublingual glands
- ☐ **B.** Partial dryness of the mouth due to lack of salivary secretions from the parotid gland
- ☐ **C.** Dryness of the right cornea due to lack of lacrimal secretion
- ☐ **D.** Loss of taste sensation from the right anterior two thirds of the tongue
- ☐ **E.** Loss of general sensation from the right anterior two thirds of the tongue

72 A 12-year-old girl is admitted to the emergency department with a middle ear infection. Physical examination reveals a long history of chronic middle ear infections that have produced a lesion in the tympanic plexus in the middle ear cavity. Since the preganglionic parasympathetic fibers that pass through the plexus have been lost, which of the following conditions will be detectable during physical examination?

- ☐ **A.** Diminished mucus in the nasal cavity
- ☐ **B.** Diminished mucus on the soft palate
- ☐ **C.** Diminished saliva production by the parotid gland
- ☐ **D.** Diminished saliva production by the submandibular and sublingual glands
- ☐ **E.** Diminished tear production by the lacrimal gland

73 A 38-year-old patient is admitted to the dental clinic with acute dental pain. The attending dentist found penetrating dental caries (tooth decay) affecting one of the mandibular molar teeth. Which of the following nerves would the dentist need to anesthetize to remove the caries in that tooth?

- ☐ **A.** Lingual
- ☐ **B.** Inferior alveolar
- ☐ **C.** Buccal
- ☐ **D.** Mental
- ☐ **E.** Mylohyoid

74 A 59-year-old man is admitted to the emergency department with acute pain on his mandible. An MRI examination reveals an acute inflammation of the TMJ due to arthritis. Which of the following muscles will most likely be affected by the inflammatory process of the TMJ?

- ☐ **A.** Temporalis
- ☐ **B.** Medial pterygoid
- ☐ **C.** Masseter
- ☐ **D.** Lateral pterygoid
- ☐ **E.** Buccinator

75 A 56-year-old female complains of diplopia (double vision) when walking down stairs. A lesion of which of the following nerves is most likely responsible for this patient's complaint?

- ☐ **A.** Optic
- ☐ **B.** Oculomotor
- ☐ **C.** Abducens
- ☐ **D.** Trochlear
- ☐ **E.** Frontal

76 A 43-year-old male is admitted to the hospital complaining of diplopia (double vision) when walking down stairs. During physical examination of the extraocular muscles the patient experiences diplopia, and when he is asked to turn his right eye inward toward his nose and look down, he is able to look inward but not down. Which nerve is most likely involved?

- ▢ **A.** Abducens
- ▢ **B.** Nasociliary
- ▢ **C.** Oculomotor, inferior division
- ▢ **D.** Oculomotor, superior division
- ▢ **E.** Trochlear

77 A 44-year-old patient is admitted to the hospital with Raynaud's disease. A sympathetic blocking drug is administered in high doses. Which of the following conditions will be expected to occur as an adverse effect of the drug?

- ▢ **A.** Exophthalmos and dilated pupil
- ▢ **B.** Enophthalmos and dry eye
- ▢ **C.** Dry eye and inability to accommodate for reading
- ▢ **D.** Wide-open eyelids and loss of depth perception
- ▢ **E.** Ptosis and miosis

78 A 47-year-old woman is admitted to the hospital with signs of cavernous sinus thrombosis. Radiographic examination reveals a pituitary tumor involving the cavernous sinus, confirming the initial diagnosis (Fig. 7-3). During physical examination it is suspected that the right abducens nerve of the patient has been damaged by the tumor. In which direction will the physician most likely ask the patient to turn her right eye to confirm the abducens nerve damage, assuming she is unable to perform this task?

- ▢ **A.** Inward
- ▢ **B.** Outward
- ▢ **C.** Downward
- ▢ **D.** Down and out
- ▢ **E.** Down and in

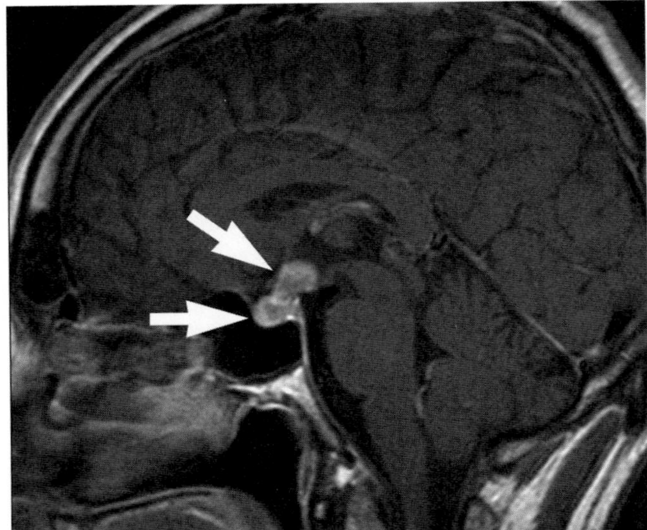

Fig. 7-3

79 An 8-year-old male is admitted to the hospital with a drooping right eyelid (ptosis). The initial diagnosis is Horner's syndrome (Fig. 7-4). Which of the following additional signs on the right side would confirm the diagnosis?

- ▢ **A.** Constricted pupil
- ▢ **B.** Dry eye
- ▢ **C.** Exophthalmos
- ▢ **D.** Pale, blanched face
- ▢ **E.** Sweaty face

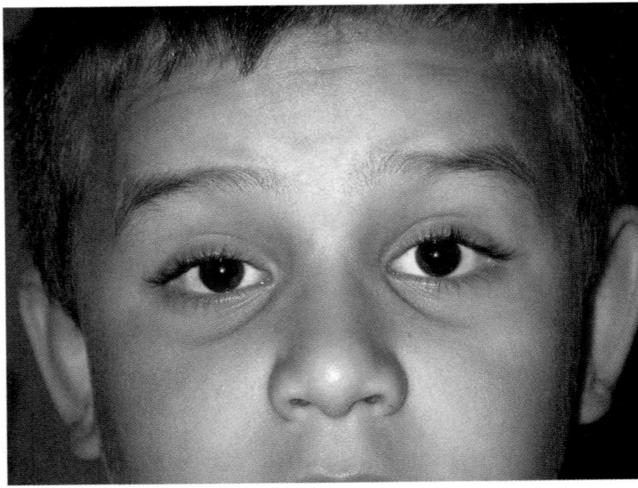

Fig. 7-4

80 A 32-year-old woman is admitted to the hospital with headaches and dizziness. During physical examination it is noted that the patient has partial ptosis (drooping eyelid). Which of the following muscles is most likely paralyzed?

- ▢ **A.** Orbicularis oculi, lacrimal part
- ▢ **B.** Orbicularis oculi, palpebral part
- ▢ **C.** Levator palpebrae superioris
- ▢ **D.** Superior oblique
- ▢ **E.** Superior tarsal (of Müller)

81 A 16-year-old boy is admitted to the hospital with fever, confused mental state, and drowsiness. During physical examination it is noted that the boy suffers from severe acne. Radiologic examination reveals cavernous sinus thrombosis. Which of the following routes of entry to the cavernous sinus would most likely be responsible for the infection and thrombosis?

- ▢ **A.** Carotid artery
- ▢ **B.** Mastoid emissary vein
- ▢ **C.** Middle meningeal artery
- ▢ **D.** Ophthalmic vein
- ▢ **E.** Parietal emissary vein

82 A 68-year-old man is admitted to the emergency department after an acute cerebral vascular accident (stroke). Radiographic studies reveal that the primary damage was to the anterior inferior cerebellar artery, resulting in a small hemorrhage of the artery at its origin from the main trunk. Which of the following nerves will most likely be immediately affected by the hemorrhage?

- ▢ **A.** Optic nerve
- ▢ **B.** Oculomotor nerve
- ▢ **C.** Trochlear nerve
- ▢ **D.** Trigeminal nerve
- ▢ **E.** Abducens nerve

83 A 5-year-old boy is admitted to the hospital with otitis media. Otoscopic examination reveals a bulging and inflamed eardrum. It is decided to incise the tympanic membrane to relieve the painful pressure and allow drainage of the infection associated with otitis media. Which of the following is the best location to make an opening (myringotomy) for drainage?

- ▢ **A.** The anterior superior quadrant of the eardrum
- ▢ **B.** The posterior superior quadrant of the eardrum
- ▢ **C.** Directly through the site of the umbo
- ▢ **D.** The posterior inferior quadrant of the eardrum
- ▢ **E.** A vertical incision should be made in the eardrum, from the 12 o'clock position of the rim of the eardrum to the 6 o'clock position of the rim.

84 A 56-year-old man is diagnosed with an extradural tumor in the posterior cranial fossa. When the patient protruded his tongue during physical examination, the tongue deviated to the right. Which of the following muscles and nerves are most likely injured?

- ▢ **A.** Right hypoglossal nerve and right genioglossus
- ▢ **B.** Left hypoglossal nerve and left genioglossus
- ▢ **C.** Right hyoglossus and left styloglossus
- ▢ **D.** Right geniohyoid and first cervical nerve
- ▢ **E.** Contralateral vagus and hypoglossal nerves

85 A 62-year-old man is admitted to the hospital with blurred vision. Physical examination reveals a long history of gradual loss of his visual field. The intraocular pressure is high, and a diagnosis of glaucoma is made. Which of the following spaces first receives the aqueous humor secreted by the epithelium of the ciliary body?

- ▢ **A.** Anterior chamber
- ▢ **B.** Posterior chamber
- ▢ **C.** Pupil
- ▢ **D.** Vitreous
- ▢ **E.** Lacrimal sac

86 A 17-year-old woman is admitted to the hospital with tonsillitis. A tonsillectomy is performed and the patient complains postoperatively of ear pain. Which of the following nerves was most likely injured during the surgical procedure?

- ▢ **A.** Auriculotemporal
- ▢ **B.** Lesser petrosal
- ▢ **C.** Vagus
- ▢ **D.** Glossopharyngeal
- ▢ **E.** Chorda tympani

87 A 49-year-old woman is admitted to the hospital with headaches and dizziness. Radiographic examination reveals a tumor in the jugular canal. Upon physical examination, when the right side of the pharyngeal wall is touched with a tongue depressor, the uvula deviates to the left and the left pharyngeal wall contracts upward. When the left pharyngeal wall is touched, the response is similar. Which of the following nerves is most likely to have been injured by the tumor?

- ▢ **A.** Right glossopharyngeal
- ▢ **B.** Left glossopharyngeal
- ▢ **C.** Right mandibular
- ▢ **D.** Left hypoglossal
- ▢ **E.** Right vagus

88 A 45-year-old man is admitted to the emergency department with severe dyspnea. During physical examination there is swelling in the floor of his mouth and pharynx so that his airway is nearly totally occluded. In addition, there is a swelling in his lower jaw and upper neck. His physical history indicates that one of his lower molars was extracted a week ago and he had been feeling worse every day since that event. Which of the following conditions will be the most likely diagnosis?

- ▢ **A.** Quinsy
- ▢ **B.** Torus palatinus
- ▢ **C.** Ankyloglossia
- ▢ **D.** Ranula
- ▢ **E.** Ludwig's angina

89 A 5-year-old girl is admitted to the hospital with an upper respiratory tract infection. During physical examination her sense of hearing appears to be poor. Her right ear is painful, and upon otoscopic examination a golden brown fluid can be observed through the tympanic membrane. Which is the most likely direct route for the spread of an infection from the upper respiratory tract to the middle ear cavity?

- ▢ **A.** Pharyngotympanic tube
- ▢ **B.** Choanae
- ▢ **C.** Nostrils
- ▢ **D.** Facial canal
- ▢ **E.** Internal acoustic meatus

90 A 54-year-old man is admitted to the hospital with severe pain in his nasal cavity. Radiographic examination reveals a carcinoma in his nasal cavity. In which of the following locations would the carcinoma block the hiatus of the maxillary sinus?

- ▢ **A.** Inferior meatus
- ▢ **B.** Middle meatus
- ▢ **C.** Superior meatus
- ▢ **D.** Nasopharynx
- ▢ **E.** Sphenoethmoidal recess

91 A 54-year-old male is diagnosed with an aneurysm of the basilar artery close to the cavernous sinus. An anterior approach to the sella turcica through the nasal cavity is performed. Through which of the following routes is the surgeon most likely to enter the cranial cavity?

- ▢ **A.** Cribriform plate
- ▢ **B.** Cavernous sinus
- ▢ **C.** Frontal sinus
- ▢ **D.** Maxillary sinus
- ▢ **E.** Sphenoidal sinus

92 A 10-year-old girl is admitted to the hospital with tonsillitis. A tonsillectomy is performed and the tonsils are removed. On physical examination one week later the patient has absence of the gag reflex on the left when the posterior part of the tongue is depressed. The sensory portion of which of the following nerves was most likely injured?

- ▢ **A.** Facial
- ▢ **B.** Glossopharyngeal
- ▢ **C.** Mandibular
- ▢ **D.** Maxillary
- ▢ **E.** Hypoglossal

93 A 56-year-old woman has just undergone a complete thyroidectomy. After she recovers from the anesthesia a hoarseness of her voice is noted that persists for 3 weeks. Subsequent examination shows a permanently adducted vocal fold on the right side. Surgical trauma to the innervation of which of the following muscles is most likely to be responsible for the position of the right vocal fold?

- ▢ **A.** Aryepiglottic
- ▢ **B.** Posterior cricoarytenoid
- ▢ **C.** Thyroarytenoid
- ▢ **D.** Transverse arytenoids
- ▢ **E.** Vocalis

94 A 45-year-old man with a complaint of ear pain and difficulty hearing is diagnosed with tonsillitis. Otoscopic examination reveals fluid in the middle ear cavity. Hypertrophy of which of the following structures would be most likely to compromise the drainage of the auditory tube?

- ▢ **A.** Lingual tonsil
- ▢ **B.** Palatine tonsil
- ▢ **C.** Pharyngeal tonsil
- ▢ **D.** Superior constrictor muscle
- ▢ **E.** Uvula

95 While at summer camp, a 10-year-old boy develops severe pharyngitis and swollen tonsils. Infection may spread from the nasopharynx to the middle ear cavity along the derivative of which embryonic pharyngeal pouch?

- ▢ **A.** First
- ▢ **B.** Second
- ▢ **C.** Third
- ▢ **D.** Fourth
- ▢ **E.** Sixth

96 You wake one morning to discover that your alarm has not worked and you are running late. Desperate to get to your biochemistry lecture in time, yet unbearably hungry, you quickly throw some bread in the toaster as you get ready. Despite the toast burning a little, you eat it quickly as you rush out the door. The burnt parts of the toast scratch the roof of your mouth, leaving you with a stinging sensation there. What nerve is collecting this sensation from the hard palate?

- ▢ **A.** Posterior superior alveolar nerve
- ▢ **B.** Inferior alveolar nerve
- ▢ **C.** Lingual nerve
- ▢ **D.** Greater palatine nerve
- ▢ **E.** Lesser palatine nerve

97 A 32-year-old woman underwent a thyroidectomy. Two months postoperatively, it was observed that the patient had lost the ability to notice the presence of foreign objects in the laryngeal vestibule. Which of the following nerves was most likely injured?

- ▢ **A.** Internal laryngeal nerve
- ▢ **B.** External laryngeal nerve
- ▢ **C.** Glossopharyngeal nerve
- ▢ **D.** Hypoglossal nerve
- ▢ **E.** Recurrent laryngeal nerve

98 A 4-year-old boy suffering from ankyloglossia is brought to the speech therapist. The examining physician recommends that the child be admitted for operation by a pediatric surgeon. Which of the following surgical procedures would be most appropriate for this condition?

- ▢ **A.** Removal of pterygomandibular raphe
- ▢ **B.** Resection of the pterygoid hamulus bilaterally
- ▢ **C.** Cutting the lingual frenulum
- ▢ **D.** Repair of the palate
- ▢ **E.** Removal of the central segment of the hyoid bone

99 An 8-year-old boy was suffering from a severe infection of the right middle ear. Within the course of a week, the infection had spread to the mastoid antrum and the mastoid air cells. The organisms did not respond to antibiotics, so the surgeon decided to perform a radical mastoid operation. Following the operation, it was noticed that the boy's face was distorted. The mouth was drawn upward to the left, and he was unable to close his right eye. Saliva tended to accumulate in his right cheek and dribble from the corner of his mouth. What structure was most likely damaged during the operation?

- ▢ **A.** Mandibular nerve
- ▢ **B.** Parotid duct
- ▢ **C.** Vagus nerve
- ▢ **D.** Facial nerve
- ▢ **E.** Glossopharyngeal nerve

100 An 8-year-old boy had an extensive mastoidectomy due to an infection that did not respond to antibiotics. Postoperatively he had Bell's palsy (facial paralysis), and one of the features was that saliva tended to accumulate in the vestibule of his oral cavity and dribble from the corner of his mouth. Which of the following muscles was paralyzed to allow this condition to occur?

- ▢ **A.** Zygomoaticus major
- ▢ **B.** Orbicularis oculi
- ▢ **C.** Buccinator
- ▢ **D.** Levator palpebrae superioris
- ▢ **E.** Orbicularis oris

101 A 32-year-old man is admitted to the emergency department with visual problems. Radiographic examination reveals a tumor of the adenohypophysis (anterior pituitary gland). Physical examination reveals a loss of the lateral halves of the fields of vision of both eyes (bitemporal hemianopia or "tunnel vision"). Which of the following structures was most likely compressed by the tumor?

- ▢ **A.** Optic nerve
- ▢ **B.** Optic chiasm
- ▢ **C.** Optic tract
- ▢ **D.** Oculomotor
- ▢ **E.** Abducens nerve

102 A 45-year-old female is admitted to the emergency department with visual problems when she walks down stairs. During physical examination the patient exhibits weakness of her downward medial gaze. Cerebral arteriography and CT images indicate that a nerve is being compressed by an arterial aneurysm just inferior to the tentorium cerebelli. Which of the following arteries and nerves is most likely being compressed?

- ▢ **A.** Internal carotid artery/abducens nerve
- ▢ **B.** Middle cerebral artery/oculomotor nerve
- ▢ **C.** Posterior cerebral artery/ophthalmic nerve
- ▢ **D.** Basilar artery/ophthalmic nerve
- ▢ **E.** Superior cerebellar artery/trochlear nerve

103 A 72-year-old woman is admitted to the emergency department with tenderness in the upper right thorax, painful to compression. During physical examination the patient presents with slight ptosis of her right eye. The right pupil is constricted more distinctly than the contralateral pupil. Which of the following is the most likely diagnosis?

- ▢ **A.** Raynaud's disease
- ▢ **B.** Frey syndrome
- ▢ **C.** Bell palsy
- ▢ **D.** Quinsy
- ▢ **E.** Pancoast tumor

104 A 32-year-old man is admitted to the hospital with severe headache and visual problems. The dilator pupillae muscle, the smooth muscle cell fibers of the superior tarsal muscle (of Müller, part of the levator palpebrae superioris), and the smooth muscle cells of the blood vessels of the ciliary body are supplied by efferent nerve fibers. Which of the following structures contains the neural cell bodies of these fibers?

- ▢ **A.** Pterygopalatine ganglion
- ▢ **B.** IML (lateral horn) C1 to C4

☐ **C.** Geniculate ganglion
☐ **D.** Nucleus solitarius
☐ **E.** Superior cervical ganglion

105 A 22-year-old male is admitted to the hospital after he was hit in the right eye with a frozen fish, thrown playfully by a friend while they were passing through the seafood section of the market. During physical examination considerable swelling and discoloration of the eyelids was observed. In addition, the patient could not turn his pupil laterally from forward gaze, indicating probable muscle entrapment. Which of the following bones was most likely fractured?

☐ **A.** Orbital plate of the frontal bone
☐ **B.** Lamina papyracea of the ethmoid bone
☐ **C.** Orbital plate of the maxilla
☐ **D.** Cribriform plate of the ethmoid bone
☐ **E.** Greater wing of the sphenoid bone

106 A 57-year-old man is admitted to the emergency department with dizziness and severe headaches. A CT scan evaluation reveals a tumor in the superior orbital fissure. Upon physical examination the patient's eyeball is fixed in an abducted position, slightly depressed, and the pupil is dilated. In addition, the superior palpebrae are ptotic. When the patient is asked to move the pupil toward the nose, the pupil rotates medially. Consensual corneal reflexes are normal. Which of the following nerves is most likely affected?

☐ **A.** Trochlear nerve
☐ **B.** Oculomotor nerve
☐ **C.** Abducens nerve and sympathetic nerve plexus accompanying the ophthalmic artery
☐ **D.** Ophthalmic nerve and short ciliary nerve
☐ **E.** Superior division of oculomotor nerve and the nasociliary nerve

107 An unconscious 57-year-old man is transported to the emergency department after falling from a tree. A CT scan evaluation reveals a fracture of the cribriform plate (Fig. 7-5). Which of the following conditions will most likely be present during the physical examination?

☐ **A.** Entrapment of the eyeball
☐ **B.** Anosmia
☐ **C.** Hyperacusis
☐ **D.** Tinnitus
☐ **E.** Deafness

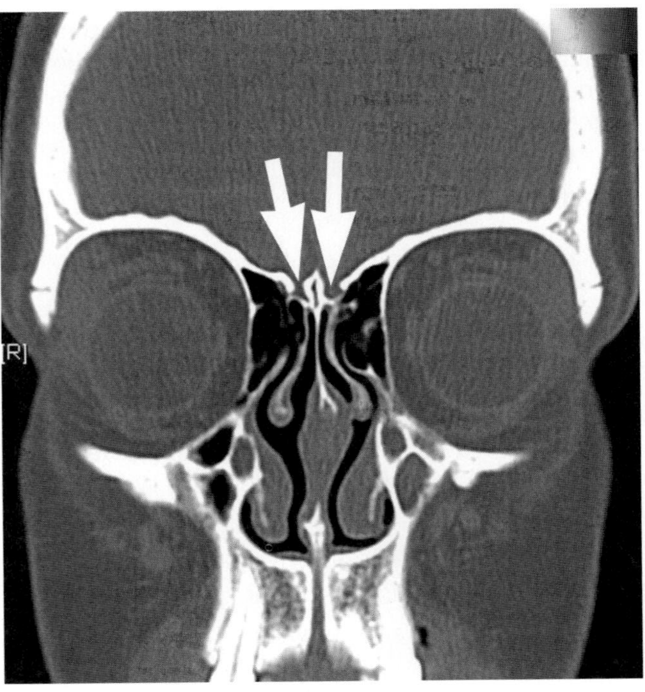

Fig. 7-5

108 A 45-year-old woman is admitted to the hospital with a swelling on the side of her face of 2 months' duration. Radiographic examination reveals a parotid gland tumor. An operative procedure is performed in which the tumor is removed from the parotid gland. Three months postoperatively the patient complains that her face sweats profusely when she tastes or smells food, and a diagnosis is made of Frey syndrome (gustatory sweating). Which of the following nerves was most likely injured during the procedure?

☐ **A.** Buccal
☐ **B.** Inferior alveolar
☐ **C.** Auriculotemporal
☐ **D.** Facial
☐ **E.** Lingual

109 A 54-year-old male is to undergo bilateral thyroidectomy. During this procedure there is the possibility of bilateral paralysis of muscles that can open the airway. If a particular nerve is injured bilaterally, there is significant risk of asphyxiation postoperatively unless the patient is intubated or the airway is opened surgically. Which of the following muscle pairs opens the airway?

☐ **A.** Cricothyroids
☐ **B.** Posterior cricoarytenoids
☐ **C.** Arytenoideus
☐ **D.** Thyroarytenoids
☐ **E.** Lateral cricoarytenoids

110 An 11-year-old boy with swollen palatine tonsils is examined by an otolaryngologist. Which of the following arteries supplies most of the blood to these tonsils and must be protected when its tonsillar branch is divided?

- ▢ **A.** Ascending pharyngeal
- ▢ **B.** Facial
- ▢ **C.** Lingual
- ▢ **D.** Descending palatine
- ▢ **E.** Superior thyroid

111 A 55-year-old man with severe ear pain visits the ENT doctor. During otoscopic examination the tympanic membrane is ruptured. Which of the following nerves is responsible for the sensory innervation of the inner surface of the tympanic membrane?

- ▢ **A.** Glossopharyngeal
- ▢ **B.** Auricular branch of facial
- ▢ **C.** Auricular branch of vagus
- ▢ **D.** Great auricular
- ▢ **E.** Lingual

112 A 45-year-old man was suffering from trigeminal neuralgia (tic douloureux). The pain was so severe that the patient had considered suicide as a way to escape the pain. Even light, gentle stimuli to the skin between the lower eyelid and the upper lip resulted in severe, agonizing pain. It was decided to lesion the nerve branch involved by injection of alcohol into the nerve. To reach the nerve, the needle will most likely need to be inserted through which of the following openings?

- ▢ **A.** Foramen ovale
- ▢ **B.** Foramen spinosum
- ▢ **C.** Infraorbital foramen
- ▢ **D.** Mandibular foramen
- ▢ **E.** Foramen magnum

113 A 32-year-old woman is undergoing a thyroidectomy. Two months postoperatively the patient suffers from loss of sensation within the larynx from the vocal folds upward to the entrance into the larynx, allowing for aspiration of liquids into the airway. Which of the following nerves is most likely injured?

- ▢ **A.** Internal laryngeal nerve
- ▢ **B.** External laryngeal nerve
- ▢ **C.** Glossopharyngeal nerve
- ▢ **D.** Hypoglossal nerve
- ▢ **E.** Recurrent laryngeal nerve

114 A 55-year-old man is admitted to the emergency department after slipping on wet pavement and falling. Physical examination reveals that the patient has a hematoma that formed in the danger zone of the scalp, spreading to the area of the eyelids. Which of the following layers is regarded as the "danger zone"?

- ▢ **A.** Loose, areolar layer
- ▢ **B.** Skin
- ▢ **C.** Galea aponeurotica
- ▢ **D.** Pericranium
- ▢ **E.** Subcutaneous layer

115 A 45-year-old woman is admitted to the hospital with severe headache. The patient is diagnosed with hypertension and arrhythmias. To reduce the patient's blood pressure, massage is initiated at a pressure point located deep to the anterior border of the sternocleidomastoid muscle at the level of the superior border of the thyroid cartilage. Which of the following structures is targeted by the massage?

- ▢ **A.** Carotid sinus
- ▢ **B.** Carotid body
- ▢ **C.** Thyroid gland
- ▢ **D.** Parathyroid gland
- ▢ **E.** Inferior cervical ganglion

116 A 59-year-old painter fell from the scaffolding and was admitted to the emergency department in an unconscious condition. An emergency tracheostomy is performed and brisk arterial bleeding suddenly occurs from the midline incision over the trachea. Which of the following vessels was most likely cut accidentally?

- ▢ **A.** Inferior thyroid branch of thyrocervical trunk
- ▢ **B.** Cricothyroid branch of the superior thyroid artery
- ▢ **C.** Thyroidea ima artery
- ▢ **D.** Middle thyroid vein
- ▢ **E.** Jugular arch connecting the anterior jugular veins

117 A 21-year-old male baseball player is brought to the emergency department after feeling severe dizziness. During physical examination the patient demonstrates lack of equilibrium and memory impairment. A 3-cm wound is noted in his scalp from an injury suffered in a game several weeks earlier. A lumbar puncture does not reveal blood in the cerebrospinal fluid. Which of the following is the most likely diagnosis?

- ▢ **A.** The middle meningeal artery was torn, resulting in epidural hematoma.
- ▢ **B.** There is a fracture in the pterion with injury to the adjacent vasculature.

- C. The injury resulted in the bursting of a preexisting aneurysm of the anterior communicating artery of the cerebral circle.
- D. A cerebral vein is torn.
- E. The cavernous sinus has a thrombus.

118 A 63-year-old man had his prostate gland tumor removed 2 years before his present admission to the hospital, complaining of various neurologic problems, including headache. Radiographic examination reveals that the cancer has spread from the pelvis to the posterior cranial fossa by way of the internal vertebral venous plexus (of Batson). During physical examination the patient's right shoulder droops noticeably lower than the left, he exhibits considerable weakness in turning his head to the left, and his tongue points to the right when he attempts to protrude it directly from his mouth. There are no other significant findings. Which of the following nerves are most likely affected?

- A. Right vagus, right accessory, and right hypoglossal nerves
- B. Left accessory, right glossopharyngeal, right vagus, and left hypoglossal nerves
- C. Left hypoglossal, right trigeminal, and left glossopharyngeal nerves
- D. Right accessory and right hypoglossal nerves
- E. Left facial, left accessory, right accessory, and vagus nerves

119 A 3-month-old male infant is admitted to the hospital because he cries continuously. During physical examination it is observed that the infant has a dry right eye. Upon the basis of imaging studies, the neuroophthalmologist diagnoses a lesion at the neural cell bodies of the preganglionic axons of the pterygopalatine ganglion. Which of the following structures contains the neural cell bodies of the preganglionic axons?

- A. Superior cervical ganglion
- B. Edinger-Westphal nucleus
- C. Superior salivatory nucleus
- D. Inferior salivatory nucleus
- E. Nucleus ambiguus

120 A 14-year-old female has been suffering from quinsy in the right side of her oropharynx. In surgical removal of the pathologic tissue, or for incision and drainage of the area, which of the following arteries will be at greatest risk?

- A. Lingual
- B. A branch of facial
- C. Superior laryngeal artery
- D. Ascending pharyngeal artery
- E. Descending palatine artery

121 A 17-year-old female visits the family dermatologist because of severe facial acne. During physical examination it was found that there was a rather obvious and painful lesion on the side of her nose. The patient was given antibiotics and warned not to press or pick at the large, inflamed swelling. If she were to squeeze, prick, or incise such a lesion in the area between the eye and the upper lip, or between the eye and the side of the nose, the infection could spread to the cavernous sinus. Which of the following pathways of spread of infection would be most typical?

- A. Nasal venous tributary to angular vein, to superior ophthalmic vein, then to cavernous sinus
- B. Retromandibular vein to supraorbital vein, then to inferior ophthalmic vein, then to cavernous sinus
- C. Dorsal nasal vein to superior petrosal vein, then inferior ophthalmic vein to cavernous sinus
- D. Facial vein to maxillary vein, then middle meningeal vein to cavernous sinus
- E. Transverse facial vein to superficial temporal vein to emissary vein to cavernous sinus

122 A 73-year-old male patient visits the outpatient clinic with a complaint of progressive, painless loss of vision. Radiographic examination reveals thrombophlebitis of the cavernous sinus. Through which of the following structures must a thrombus pass to cause the symptoms of this patient?

- A. Subarachnoid space
- B. Central artery of the retina
- C. Central vein of the retina
- D. Optic chiasm
- E. Ciliary ganglion

123 A 67-year-old man visits the outpatient clinic with complaints of deteriorating vision. A form of glaucoma is diagnosed in which the aqueous humor does not drain properly into the scleral venous sinus at the iridoscleral angle of the eyeball. The aqueous fluid is secreted by the epithelium of the ciliary body directly into which of the following spaces?

- A. Iridoscleral angle
- B. Posterior chamber
- C. Pupil
- D. Vitreous body
- E. Lacrimal sac

124 A 2-month-old female infant is hospitalized with hydrocephalus. Radiographic examination reveals cerebrospinal fluid between the compressed brain and overlying bones of the skull. Which of the following conditions will most likely lead to this type of clinical picture?

- ☐ **A.** Lack of filtration through arachnoid granulations
- ☐ **B.** Occlusion of cerebral aqueduct (of Sylvius)
- ☐ **C.** Blockage of the foramina of Luschka
- ☐ **D.** Congenital absence of the foramen of Magendie
- ☐ **E.** Closure of the interventricular foramina of Monro

125 A 54-year-old man was admitted to the emergency department after he was struck by an automobile. Radiographic examination revealed a fracture through the crista galli of the anterior cranial fossa, resulting in slow, local bleeding. Which of the following is the most likely source of bleeding?

- ☐ **A.** Middle meningeal artery
- ☐ **B.** The great cerebral vein of Galen
- ☐ **C.** Superior sagittal sinus
- ☐ **D.** Straight venous dural sinus
- ☐ **E.** Superior ophthalmic vein

126 During the routine ophthalmologic exam, the globe, the retina, and the cornea of each eye are tested. Which of the following nerves must be functioning properly if the patient is to be able to turn the eye laterally (abduction) without difficulty and without upward or downward deviation?

- ☐ **A.** Superior division of oculomotor, ophthalmic nerve, abducens nerve
- ☐ **B.** Trochlear nerve, abducens nerve, nasociliary nerve
- ☐ **C.** Inferior division of oculomotor, trochlear, abducens
- ☐ **D.** Oculomotor and ophthalmic nerves
- ☐ **E.** Superior division of oculomotor, trochlear, and abducens nerves

127 A 34-year-old female is admitted to the hospital because of hoarseness for the past 3 months. Radiographic examination reveals a cancerous growth in her larynx with no evidence of metastasis. In addition, the area in which the tumor is growing is characterized by very limited lymphatic drainage. Which of the following locations is most likely to contain a tumor with these characteristics?

- ☐ **A.** Anterior commissure of the vocal ligaments
- ☐ **B.** Interarytenoid fold
- ☐ **C.** Laryngeal ventricle
- ☐ **D.** Cricothyroid ligament
- ☐ **E.** Middle segment of the vocal cord

128 A 55-year-old man is admitted to the hospital with a complaint of severe headaches. A lumbar puncture reveals traces of blood in the cerebrospinal fluid. Which of the following conditions has most likely occurred in this patient?

- ☐ **A.** Fracture of the pterion with vascular injury
- ☐ **B.** A ruptured "berry" aneurysm
- ☐ **C.** Leakage of branches of the middle meningeal vein within the temporal bone
- ☐ **D.** A tear of the cerebral vein at the entrance to the superior sagittal sinus
- ☐ **E.** Occlusion of the internal carotid artery by a clot generated in the left atrium

129 A 55-year-old man is admitted to the neurosurgical clinic for a scheduled removal of a tumor in the left jugular canal. Postoperatively, the patient has no gag reflex when the ipsilateral pharyngeal wall is stimulated, although the pharynx moved upward, and a gag reflex resulted when the right pharyngeal wall was stimulated. The uvula was deviated to the right and the left vocal cord had drifted toward the midline. Which of the following structures will contain the neural cell bodies for the motor supply of the paralyzed muscles?

- ☐ **A.** Nucleus solitarius
- ☐ **B.** Trigeminal motor nucleus
- ☐ **C.** Dorsal motor nucleus
- ☐ **D.** Nucleus ambiguus
- ☐ **E.** Superior or inferior ganglia of vagus

130 A 65-year-old man is admitted to the emergency department after his head hit the dashboard in an automobile collision. Radiographic and physical examinations reveal that the inferior alveolar nerve is injured at its origin. Which of the following muscles would most likely be paralyzed as a result?

- ☐ **A.** Geniohyoid
- ☐ **B.** Hyoglossus
- ☐ **C.** Mylohyoid
- ☐ **D.** Stylohyoid
- ☐ **E.** Palatoglossus

131 A 64-year-old man is admitted to the hospital in an unconscious condition. A CT scan examination reveals that the patient has suffered a cerebral vascular accident (stroke), with a small hematoma produced by the superior cerebellar artery. Which of the following nerves will most likely be affected by the hematoma?

- ☐ **A.** Trochlear nerve
- ☐ **B.** Abducens nerve
- ☐ **C.** Facial nerve
- ☐ **D.** Vestibulocochlear nerve
- ☐ **E.** Glossopharyngeal nerve

132 A 65-year-old male is admitted to the hospital three weeks after a "small bump of his head" according to his narrative. He suffered the accidental bump from a low-hanging branch while driving his tractor through the apple orchard during harvesting season. During physical examination the patient displays mental confusion and poor physical coordination. Radiographic examination reveals leakage from a cerebral vein over the right cerebral hemisphere. From what type of bleeding is the patient most likely suffering?

- ☐ **A.** Subarachnoid bleeding
- ☐ **B.** Epidural bleeding
- ☐ **C.** Intracerebral bleeding into the brain parenchyma
- ☐ **D.** Subdural bleeding
- ☐ **E.** Bleeding into the cerebral ventricular system

133 A 27-year-old man is admitted to the hospital after a middleweight boxing match. During physical examination the strength and symmetry of strength in opening the jaws are tested. Which of the following muscles is the most important in jaw protrusion and depressing the mandible?

- ☐ **A.** Anterior portion of temporalis
- ☐ **B.** Lateral pterygoid
- ☐ **C.** Medial pterygoid
- ☐ **D.** Masseter
- ☐ **E.** Platysma

134 A 31-year-old mother visits the pediatric outpatient clinic with her 6-month-old baby complaining that her baby is not developing quickly and has no teeth. Which of the following teeth are expected to appear first?

- ☐ **A.** Superior medial incisors at 8 to 10 months of age
- ☐ **B.** Inferior medial incisors at 6 to 8 months of age
- ☐ **C.** Superior lateral incisors at 8 to 10 months of age
- ☐ **D.** Inferior lateral incisors at 12 to 14 months of age
- ☐ **E.** First molar at 6 to 8 months of age

135 A 56-year-old man visits the outpatient clinic with a complaint of severe headaches and ear pain. Radiographic examination reveals a tumor in the middle ear cavity, invading through the bony floor. Which of the following structures will most likely be affected?

- ☐ **A.** The cochlea and lateral semicircular canal
- ☐ **B.** The internal carotid artery
- ☐ **C.** The sigmoid venous sinus
- ☐ **D.** The internal jugular bulb
- ☐ **E.** The aditus ad antrum of the mastoid region and the facial nerve

136 A 52-year-old man is admitted to the emergency department with a bullet wound in the infratemporal fossa. During physical examination it is observed that the patient has lost unilateral sensation of hot, cold, pain, and pressure from the front part of the tongue, but taste and salivary function are preserved. Which of the following is the most likely diagnosis?

- ☐ **A.** The facial nerve was transected distal to the origin of the chorda tympani.
- ☐ **B.** Receptors for hot, cold, pain, and pressure are absent in the patient's tongue.
- ☐ **C.** The glossopharyngeal nerve has been injured in the pharynx.
- ☐ **D.** The superior laryngeal nerve was obviously severed by the bullet.
- ☐ **E.** The lingual nerve was injured at its origin near the foramen ovale.

137 A 12-year-old boy is admitted to the emergency department with signs of meningitis. To determine the specific type of meningitis, it is necessary to aspirate cerebrospinal fluid with a lumbar puncture for laboratory examination. However, before performing a lumbar puncture, it must be established that the cerebrospinal fluid pressure is not elevated. What condition in the eye would indicate that cerebrospinal fluid pressure is too elevated for a lumbar puncture to be performed?

- ☐ **A.** Papilledema
- ☐ **B.** Separation of the pars optica retinae anterior to the ora serrata
- ☐ **C.** The foveal centralis exhibits hemorrhage from medial retinal branches.
- ☐ **D.** Obvious opacity of the lens
- ☐ **E.** Pitting or compression of the optic disc

138 A 65-year-old woman is admitted to the hospital with signs of cavernous sinus thrombosis. Radiographic examination reveals an aneurysm of the internal carotid artery within the cavernous sinus. During physical examination what sign would one first expect to see if nerve compression has occurred within the cavernous sinus?

- ▢ **A.** Inability to gaze downward and medially on the affected side
- ▢ **B.** Complete ptosis of the superior palpebra
- ▢ **C.** Bilateral loss of accommodation and loss of direct pupillary reflex
- ▢ **D.** Ipsilateral loss of the consensual corneal reflex
- ▢ **E.** Ipsilateral paralysis of abduction of the pupil

139 A 54-year-old man is admitted to the emergency department with a fracture at the frontozygomatic suture. During physical examination the eyelid of the patient exhibits multiple lacerations and the sclera contains small fragments from his broken glasses. What site would be preferable for needle insertion to anesthetize the orbital contents and then the area of the eyelid injury?

- ▢ **A.** Into the sclera in the limbic region and also into the infraorbital foramen
- ▢ **B.** Into the lacrimal fossa and also beneath the lateral bulbar conjunctiva
- ▢ **C.** Into the supraorbital foramen and also into the lacrimal caruncle
- ▢ **D.** Through the upper eyelid deeply toward the orbital apex and also between the orbital septum and the palpebral musculature laterally
- ▢ **E.** Directly posteriorly through the anulus tendineus and superior orbital fissure

140 A 45-year-old male construction worker slips and falls on a nail protruding from a board. The nail penetrates the skin overlying the submental triangle lateral to the midline. Which of the following muscles would be the last to be penetrated?

- ▢ **A.** Platysma
- ▢ **B.** Mylohyoid
- ▢ **C.** Anterior belly of the digastric
- ▢ **D.** Geniohyoid
- ▢ **E.** Genioglossus

141 A 55-year-old woman has undergone facial surgery for the excision of a malignant parotid tumor. A week postoperatively, marked weakness is seen in the musculature of the patient's lower lip. Which of the following nerves was most likely injured during the parotidectomy?

- ▢ **A.** Marginal mandibular branch of facial
- ▢ **B.** Zygomatic branch of facial
- ▢ **C.** Mandibular division of the trigeminal nerve
- ▢ **D.** Buccal branch of facial
- ▢ **E.** Buccal nerve

142 A 15-year-old male is admitted to the emergency department with severe headache and hydrocephalus. Radiographic examination reveals a craniopharyngioma occupying the sella turcica, primarily involving the suprasellar space. Which of the following is the most likely cause of this tumor?

- ▢ **A.** Persistence of a small portion of the Rathke pouch
- ▢ **B.** Abnormal development of pars tuberalis
- ▢ **C.** Abnormal development of foramina of Monro
- ▢ **D.** Abnormal development of the alar plates that form the lateral wall of diencephalon
- ▢ **E.** Abnormal development of diencephalon

143 A 1-day-old infant presents with a telencephalic vesicle; the eyes are fused, and a single nasal chamber is present in the midline. In addition, the olfactory bulbs and tracts and the corpus callosum are hypoplastic. Which of the following is the most likely diagnosis?

- ▢ **A.** Holoprosencephaly
- ▢ **B.** Smith-Lemli-Opitz syndrome
- ▢ **C.** Schizencephaly
- ▢ **D.** Exencephaly
- ▢ **E.** Meningoencephalocele

144 A 1-day-old infant presents with meningohydroencephalocele. Which of the following bones is most commonly affected?

- ▢ **A.** Squamous part of temporal bone
- ▢ **B.** Petrous part of temporal bone
- ▢ **C.** Squamous part of occipital bone
- ▢ **D.** Sphenoid bone
- ▢ **E.** Ethmoid bone

145 A 1-day-old infant was born with the vault of the skull undeveloped, leaving the malformed brain exposed. A diagnosis of exencephaly is made. What is the embryologic cause of this condition?

- ▢ **A.** Toxoplasmosis infection
- ▢ **B.** Failure of closure of the cephalic part of the neural tube
- ▢ **C.** Ossification defect in the bones of the skull
- ▢ **D.** Caudal displacement of cerebellar structures
- ▢ **E.** Maternal alcohol abuse

146 A 6-month-old infant is admitted to the emergency department with hydrocephalus. Upon physical examination a spina bifida cystica is noted. Radiographic examination reveals a caudal displacement of the cerebellar structures through the foramen magnum. Which of the following is the most likely diagnosis?

- ☐ **A.** Arnold-Chiari malformation
- ☐ **B.** Holoprosencephaly
- ☐ **C.** Smith-Lemli-Opitz syndrome
- ☐ **D.** Schizencephaly
- ☐ **E.** Exencephaly

147 A 3-month-old infant was admitted to the hospital because of the parents' suspicion that the child was deaf. An MRI examination showed abnormal development of the membranous and bony labyrinths, leading the physician to the diagnosis of congenital deafness. Which of the following conditions can lead to congenital deafness?

- ☐ **A.** Infection with rubella virus
- ☐ **B.** Failure of the second pharyngeal arch to form
- ☐ **C.** Failure of the dorsal portion of first pharyngeal cleft
- ☐ **D.** Abnormal development of the auricular hillocks
- ☐ **E.** Failure of the dorsal portion of first pharyngeal cleft and second pharyngeal arch

148 A 3-month-old male infant is brought to the hospital by his parents because of white patches in his eyes. An ophthalmoscopic examination shows a congenital cataract. Which of the following conditions can cause a congenital cataract?

- ☐ **A.** Infection with rubella virus
- ☐ **B.** Choroid fissure fails to close
- ☐ **C.** Persistent hyaloid artery
- ☐ **D.** Toxoplasmosis infection
- ☐ **E.** Cytomegalovirus infection

149 A 1-day-old infant who exhibits absence of the ocular lens is admitted to the pediatric intensive care unit. Laboratory examination reveals a mutation in the *PAX6* gene. Which of the following conditions is the most likely diagnosis?

- ☐ **A.** Cyclopia
- ☐ **B.** Coloboma
- ☐ **C.** Anophthalmia
- ☐ **D.** Aphakia and aniridia
- ☐ **E.** Microphthalmia

150 A 2-month-infant presents with small and flat maxillary, temporal and zygomatic bones. In addition, the patient has anotia and a dermoid tumor in the eyeball. Which of the following conditions is the most likely diagnosis?

- ☐ **A.** Hemifacial microsomia
- ☐ **B.** Treacher Collins syndrome
- ☐ **C.** Robin Sequence
- ☐ **D.** DiGeorge syndrome
- ☐ **E.** Velocardiofacial syndrome

151 A 3-month-old infant is diagnosed with abnormal face, thymic hypoplasia, cleft palate, hypocalcemia, and a ventricular septal defect. Which of the following genes is defective?

- ☐ **A.** 22q11
- ☐ **B.** *SONIC HEDGEHOG*
- ☐ **C.** *PAX 2*
- ☐ **D.** *PAX 6*
- ☐ **E.** 47XXY

152 A 3-day-old male infant has a noticeably small mandible. A CT scan and physical examinations reveal hypoplasia of the mandible, underdevelopment of the bones of the face, downward-slanting palpebral fissures, defects of the lower eyelids, and deformed external ears. Abnormal development of which of the pharyngeal arches will most likely produce such symptoms?

- ☐ **A.** First arch
- ☐ **B.** Second arch
- ☐ **C.** Third arch
- ☐ **D.** Fourth arch
- ☐ **E.** Sixth arch

153 A 1-year-old infant is admitted to the hospital with fever. Radiographic examination reveals a sinus infection. Which of the following sinuses is present at this age?

- ☐ **A.** Frontal sinus
- ☐ **B.** Maxillary sinus
- ☐ **C.** Sphenoid sinus
- ☐ **D.** Middle ethmoidal air cells
- ☐ **E.** Posterior ethmoidal air cells

154 A newborn infant presents with severe brain abnormalities. The calvaria is defective and the brain is protruding from the cranium. A rudimentary brainstem and some functioning neural tissue are present. A diagnosis is made of meroencephaly. Which of the following is the most likely cause of this condition?

- ☐ **A.** Failure of the rostral neuropore to close in the fourth week
- ☐ **B.** Cytomegalovirus infection

- [ ] **C.** Failure of the hypophyseal diverticulum to develop
- [ ] **D.** Failure of the neural arch to develop
- [ ] **E.** Abnormal neural crest formation

155 A 55-year-old man is admitted to the emergency department with fever of 4 days' duration. Radiographic examination reveals the presence of an infection that is spreading from the retropharyngeal space to the posterior mediastinum. Between which of the following fascial layers are the infections most likely located?

- [ ] **A.** Between alar and prevertebral
- [ ] **B.** Between alar and pretracheal
- [ ] **C.** Between pretracheal and prevertebral
- [ ] **D.** Between buccopharyngeal and alar
- [ ] **E.** Between buccopharyngeal and prevertebral

156 A 24-year-old man is admitted to the hospital after a street fight. Radiographic examination reveals an inferior blow-out fracture of the orbit. Which of the following nerves is particularly vulnerable to this type of injury?

- [ ] **A.** Infraorbital
- [ ] **B.** Supratrochlear
- [ ] **C.** Frontal
- [ ] **D.** Inferior alveolar
- [ ] **E.** Optic

157 A 67-year-old man visits the outpatient clinic with hearing problems. During physical examination a Rinne test for hearing is performed by placing a tuning fork on his head to test for bone conduction. Upon what specific point should the tuning fork be placed to test conduction?

- [ ] **A.** Temporal bone
- [ ] **B.** Frontal bone
- [ ] **C.** Mastoid process
- [ ] **D.** External occipital protuberance
- [ ] **E.** Vertex of the head

158 A 55-year-old man is admitted to the emergency department with a complaint of pain when chewing over the previous 3 months. Physical examination reveals the patient suffers from odynophagia and some hoarseness in his speech. Radiographic examination reveals a tumor at the tracheoesophageal groove. Which of the following nerves is most likely affected by the tumor?

- [ ] **A.** Recurrent laryngeal
- [ ] **B.** Internal laryngeal
- [ ] **C.** Vagus
- [ ] **D.** External laryngeal
- [ ] **E.** Phrenic

159 A 34-year-old man is admitted to the emergency department after falling off his motorbike, suffering an injury to his head. The patient has multiple lacerations in the skin over the frontal bone. Which of the following veins could most likely provide a pathway of transmission of infection from the veins of the scalp to the underlying dural venous sinuses?

- [ ] **A.** Supratrochlear vein
- [ ] **B.** Diploic veins
- [ ] **C.** Anterior cerebral veins
- [ ] **D.** Superior sagittal sinus
- [ ] **E.** Supraorbital vein

160 A 65-year-old man is admitted to the emergency department after an episode of a transient ischemic attack. Radiographic examination reveals an aneurysm in the region between the posterior cerebral artery and superior cerebellar artery. Which of the following nerves will most likely be compressed from the aneurysm?

- [ ] **A.** Trochlear
- [ ] **B.** Abducens
- [ ] **C.** Oculomotor
- [ ] **D.** Vagus
- [ ] **E.** Optic

161 A 36-year-old female racquetball player is admitted to the hospital after being struck in the orbital region. Radiographic examination reveals a blow-out fracture of the medial wall of the orbit. Physical examination also reveals that the pupil of the affected eye cannot be turned laterally. Which of the following muscles is most likely injured or trapped?

- [ ] **A.** Lateral rectus
- [ ] **B.** Medial and inferior recti
- [ ] **C.** Medial rectus
- [ ] **D.** Medial rectus and superior oblique
- [ ] **E.** Inferior rectus

162 A 16-year-old female volleyball player is admitted to the hospital after being hit in the eye with a ball spiked at the net. Radiographic examination reveals a blow-out fracture of the inferior wall of the orbit. Physical examination also reveals that the pupil of her eye cannot be turned upward. Which of the following muscles is (are) most likely injured?

- [ ] **A.** Inferior rectus and inferior oblique
- [ ] **B.** Medial and inferior recti
- [ ] **C.** Inferior oblique

- ▢ **D.** Medial rectus, inferior rectus, and inferior oblique
- ▢ **E.** Inferior rectus

163 A 36-year-old man is admitted to the emergency department with a painful skin rash on the dorsum of his nose. Physical examination reveals that a herpetic lesion is affecting the dorsum of the nose and the eyeball. Which of the following nerves is most likely to be responsible for transmission of the virus to the eye?

- ▢ **A.** Nasociliary
- ▢ **B.** Supratrochlear
- ▢ **C.** Infraorbital
- ▢ **D.** Posterior ethmoidal
- ▢ **E.** Anterior ethmoidal

164 A 22-year-old man is admitted to the emergency department after he was beaten up in a street fight. Radiographic examination reveals that he has suffered a forehead fracture from a blow with a club, resulting in black and swollen eyes (Fig. 7-6). Because the patient is suffering from severe pain, an anesthetic solution is ordered to be injected into his orbit. Which of the following nerves is most likely to be anesthetized?

- ▢ **A.** Ophthalmic
- ▢ **B.** Infraorbital
- ▢ **C.** Anterior ethmoidal
- ▢ **D.** Frontal
- ▢ **E.** Optic

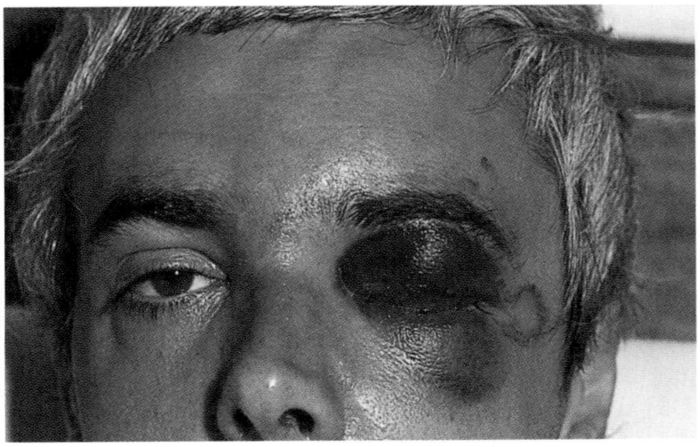

Fig. 7-6

165 A 34-year-old woman is admitted to the emergency department after her right cheekbone and bony orbit hit the dashboard in an automobile crash. Physical examination reveals that the patient has lost the ability for the affected eye to be directed downward when the pupil is in the adducted position. An MRI examination reveals a torn nerve. What is the most common location at which this nerve will be injured?

- ▢ **A.** As it pierces the dura of the tentorium cerebelli in the tentorial notch
- ▢ **B.** At the cavernous sinus
- ▢ **C.** At the sella turcica
- ▢ **D.** At the inferior orbital fissure
- ▢ **E.** At the superior orbital fissure

166 A 56-year-old woman is admitted to the hospital with eye pain. During physical examination the patient complains of excruciating pain when she performs any movement of the eye. An MRI examination reveals that the optic nerve is inflamed. What is the most likely explanation?

- ▢ **A.** The anular tendon (of Zinn) is inflamed.
- ▢ **B.** The inflammation has affected the nerves innervating the eye muscles.
- ▢ **C.** The muscles are contracting due to generalized inflammation.
- ▢ **D.** The nasociliary nerve is affected.
- ▢ **E.** The ophthalmic artery is constricted.

167 A 7-day-old infant is admitted to the pediatric intensive care unit with microphthalmia. Which of the following is the most likely cause of this condition?

- ▢ **A.** Infection with rubella virus
- ▢ **B.** Choroid fissure failed to close
- ▢ **C.** Persistent hyaloid artery
- ▢ **D.** Toxoplasmosis infection
- ▢ **E.** Epstein-Barr virus infection

168 A 2-month-old male infant is admitted to the hospital after falling from his stroller. During physical examination the infant shows signs of facial nerve injury. What is the most common place for facial nerve injury in an infant?

- ▢ **A.** At the stylomastoid foramen
- ▢ **B.** Posterior to the parotid gland
- ▢ **C.** Anterior to the parotid gland
- ▢ **D.** Proximal to the stylomastoid foramen
- ▢ **E.** Mandibular involvement of zygomatic and buccal branches

169 A 6-year-old boy is admitted to the hospital with high fever and pain over the parotid gland (Fig. 7-7). A diagnosis of parotiditis (mumps) is established, and the boy is sent back home. Which of the following nerves is responsible for painful sensations from the region of the parotid gland?

- ▢ **A.** Facial
- ▢ **B.** Auriculotemporal

- ▢ **C.** Lesser petrosal
- ▢ **D.** Lingual
- ▢ **E.** Chorda tympani

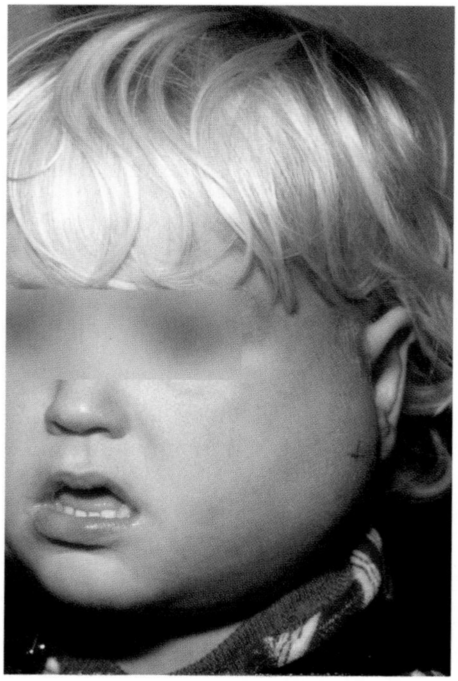

Fig. 7-7

170 A 55-year-old woman is admitted to the emergency department with ear pain, ringing in her ear (tinnitus), dizziness, and vertigo. Radiographic examination reveals indications of Ménière's disease. Which of the following structures is most likely affected by the edema that is associated with Ménière's disease?

- ▢ **A.** Middle ear
- ▢ **B.** Endolymphatic sac
- ▢ **C.** Semicircular canals
- ▢ **D.** Cochlea
- ▢ **E.** Helicotrema

171 A 55-year-old woman visits the outpatient clinic with a swelling in her neck. Radiographic and ultrasound examinations reveal a benign thyroid gland tumor. Three days after thyroidectomy the patient shows air bubbles in the CT of her brain. Which of the following is the most likely cause of the air bubbles in this case?

- ▢ **A.** Injury to inferior thyroid artery
- ▢ **B.** Injury to inferior and superior thyroid arteries
- ▢ **C.** Injury to superior thyroid artery and vein
- ▢ **D.** Injury to superior and middle thyroid veins
- ▢ **E.** Injury to superior, middle, and inferior thyroid veins

172 A 32-year-old man is admitted to the emergency department unconscious after a severe car crash. During an emergency cricothyroidostomy an artery is accidentally injured. Two days later the patient shows signs of aspiration pneumonia. Which of the following arteries was most likely injured?

- ▢ **A.** Superior thyroid
- ▢ **B.** Inferior thyroid
- ▢ **C.** Cricothyroid
- ▢ **D.** Superior laryngeal
- ▢ **E.** Suprahyoid

173 A 22-year-old woman is admitted to the emergency department unconscious after falling over the handlebars of her bicycle. An emergency tracheotomy is performed to insert a tracheotomy tube. What is the most common tracheal cartilage level at which a tracheotomy incision is performed?

- ▢ **A.** First to second
- ▢ **B.** Second to third
- ▢ **C.** Third to fourth
- ▢ **D.** Fourth to fifth
- ▢ **E.** Fifth to sixth

174 A 36-year-old woman is admitted to the hospital with severe head injuries after a car crash. During neurologic examination it is noted that her uvula is deviated to the right. Which of the following muscles is paralyzed?

- ▢ **A.** Left levator veli palatini
- ▢ **B.** Left tensor veli palatini
- ▢ **C.** Right levator veli palatini
- ▢ **D.** Right tensor veli palatini
- ▢ **E.** Right tensor veli palatini and left levator veli palatini

175 A 45-year-old man came to the outpatient clinic after stumbling and hitting his head on a table in a restaurant. During the neurologic examination photographs were taken of the patient's eyes as shown in Fig. 7-8. Which of the following nerves to the left eye was most likely injured?

- ▢ **A.** Trochlea
- ▢ **B.** Abducens
- ▢ **C.** Oculomotor
- ▢ **D.** Optic
- ▢ **E.** Oculomotor and abducens

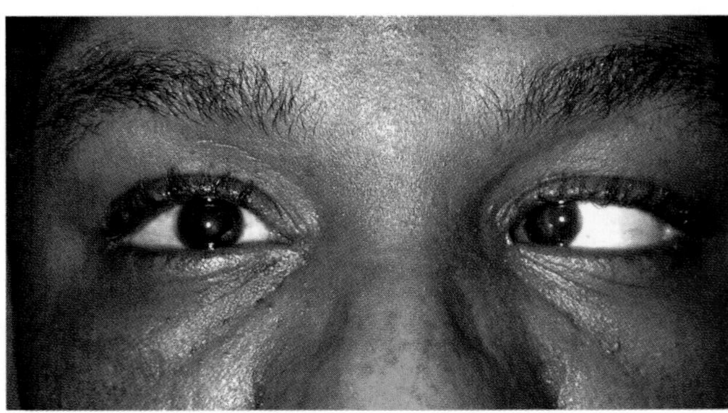

Fig. 7-8

176 A 32-year-old woman is admitted to the hospital after losing consciousness and collapsing in the middle of the street. A neurologic examination reveals absence of the accommodation reflex of her right eye. Which of the following is most likely involved in the pathology in this patient?

- ▢ **A.** Superior salivatory nucleus
- ▢ **B.** Superior cervical ganglion
- ▢ **C.** Nervus intermedius
- ▢ **D.** Edinger-Westphal nucleus
- ▢ **E.** Trigeminal ganglion

177 A 32-year-old man is admitted to the hospital with nausea, vomiting, and severe headache. An MRI examination reveals an acoustic neuroma as shown in Fig. 7-9. Which of the following nerves is most likely compressed by the tumor?

- ▢ **A.** Facial
- ▢ **B.** Oculomotor
- ▢ **C.** Vagus
- ▢ **D.** Hypoglossal
- ▢ **E.** Abducens

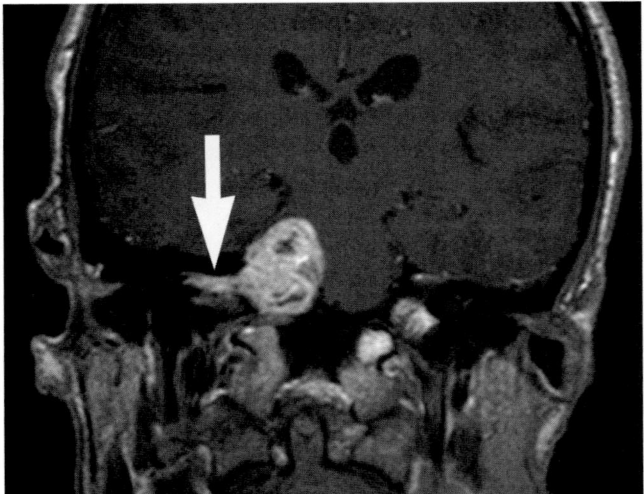

Fig. 7-9

178 A 3-year-old boy is brought to the outpatient clinic with a swelling in the side of his neck. Physical examination reveals a congenital mass of tissue anterior to the superior third of the sternocleidomastoid muscle (Fig. 7-10). The swelling is asymptomatic, nonpainful, and soft. Which of the following is the most likely diagnosis?

- ▢ **A.** Branchial cleft cyst
- ▢ **B.** Ruptured sternocleidomastoid muscle
- ▢ **C.** Lymph node inflammation
- ▢ **D.** Torticollis
- ▢ **E.** External carotid artery aneurysm

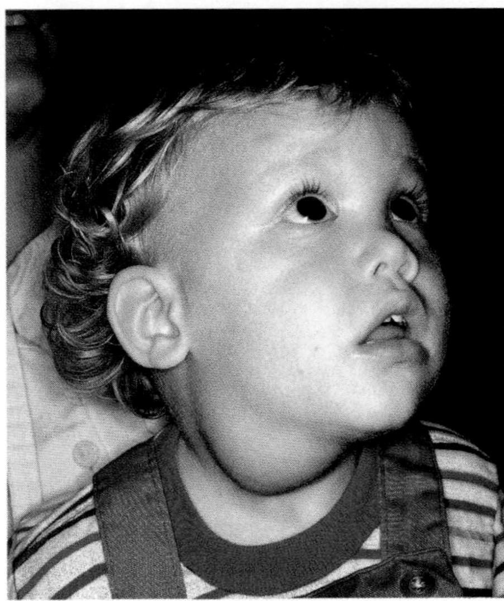

Fig. 7-10

179 A 68-year-old woman visits the outpatient clinic with a complaint of chronic dizziness and headaches. Cranial and cervical angiography (Fig. 7-11) reveals an occluded vessel. Which of the following vessels is most likely occluded?

- ▢ **A.** External carotid
- ▢ **B.** Internal carotid
- ▢ **C.** Common carotid
- ▢ **D.** Vertebral
- ▢ **E.** Superior thyroid

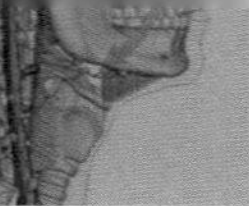

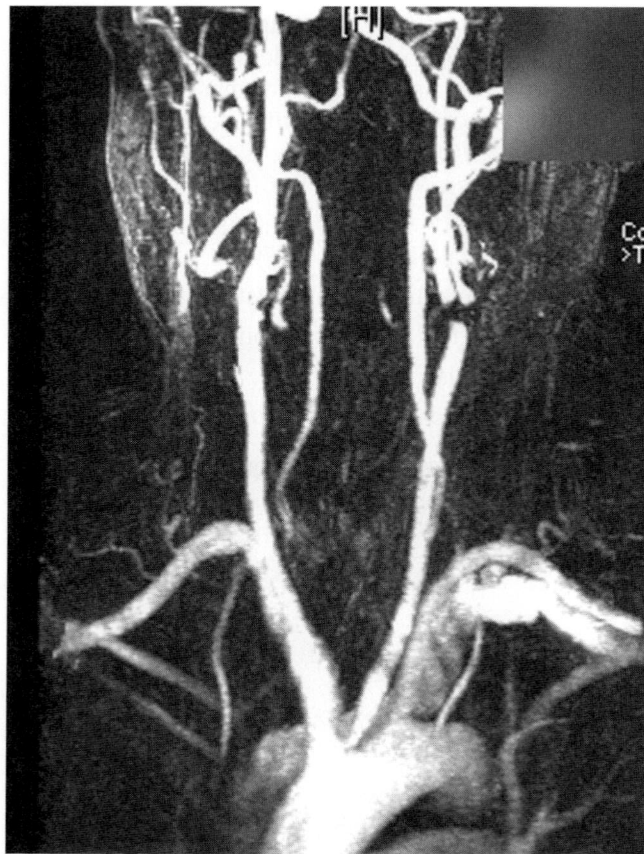

Fig. 7-11

180 A 9-year-old girl is admitted to the emergency department with a painful swelling behind her ear. An MRI examination reveals mastoiditis (Fig. 7-12). Which of the following structures is most likely to be affected by the inflammation?

- ▢ **A.** Transverse sinus
- ▢ **B.** Petrous part of the temporal bone
- ▢ **C.** Middle ear
- ▢ **D.** Occipital sinus
- ▢ **E.** Internal carotid artery

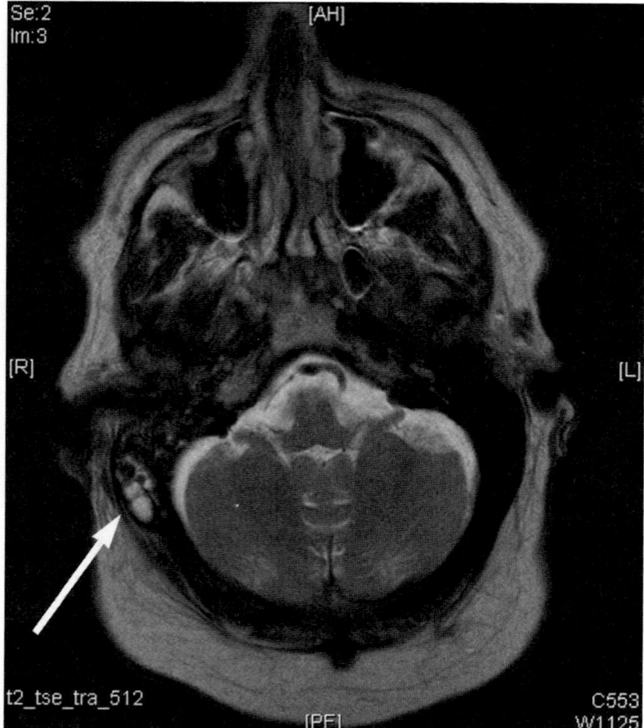

Fig. 7-12

181 A 34-year-old woman is admitted to the emergency department with a painful eye. Physical examination reveals a lump in the lower eyelid that consists of debris (Fig. 7-13). A diagnosis of a chalazion is made. Which of the following structures is (are) most likely blocked by the chalazion?

- ▢ **A.** Lacrimal ducts
- ▢ **B.** Tarsal glands
- ▢ **C.** Sclera
- ▢ **D.** Pupil
- ▢ **E.** Nasolacrimal duct

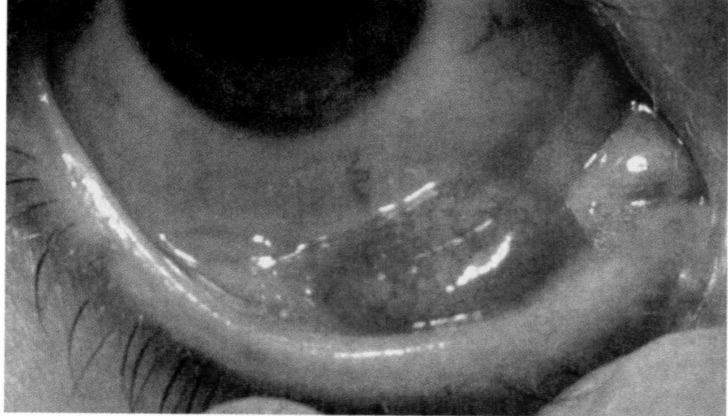

Fig. 7-13

182 A 45-year-old man is admitted to the hospital with breathing problems. During physical examination the patient shows signs of airway obstruction. A CT scan examination reveals a nasal polyp obstructing the airway (Fig. 7-14). Drainage from which of the following structures is also obstructed?

- ▢ **A.** Sphenoid sinus
- ▢ **B.** Maxillary sinus
- ▢ **C.** Ethmoidal sinus
- ▢ **D.** Frontal sinus
- ▢ **E.** Nasolacrimal duct

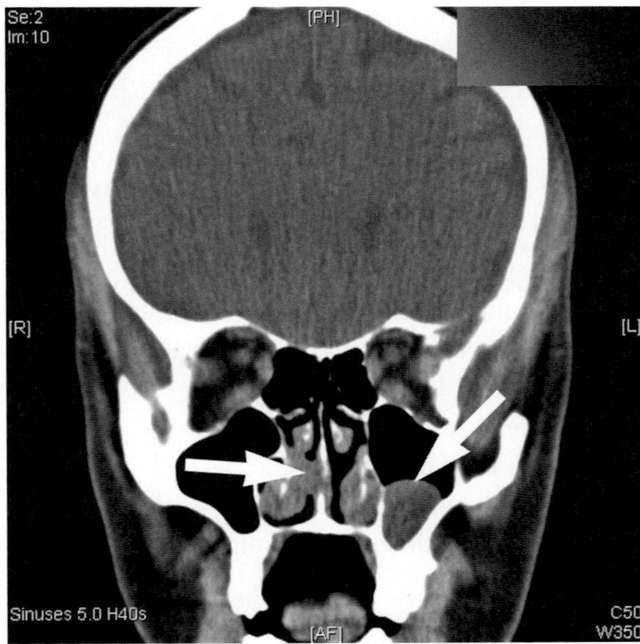

Fig. 7-14

183 A 58-year-old man is admitted to the emergency department with progressive unilateral hearing loss and ringing in the affected ear (tinnitus) of 4 months' duration. Radiographic examination reveals a tumor at the cerebellopontine angle. Which of the following nerves is most likely affected?

- ▢ **A.** Vagus
- ▢ **B.** Hypoglossal
- ▢ **C.** Vestibulocochlear
- ▢ **D.** Glossopharyngeal
- ▢ **E.** Trigeminal

184 A newborn infant is finally delivered with forceps after a difficult delivery. Upon physical examination of the newborn a cephalohematoma is noted from rupture of small periosteal arteries. Between which of the following layers of tissue does the blood accumulate?

- ▢ **A.** Between skin and dense connective tissue layer
- ▢ **B.** Between loose connective tissue layer and galea aponeurotica
- ▢ **C.** Between galea aponeurotica and pericranium
- ▢ **D.** Between pericranium and calvaria
- ▢ **E.** At the subcutaneous layer

185 An unconscious 54-year-old female is admitted to the hospital. A CT scan reveals a tumor in her brain, producing a tentorial herniation. When she regains consciousness, her right eye is directed laterally and downward, with complete ptosis of her upper eyelid and pupillary dilation. Which of the following lobes of the brain is affected by the tumor?

- ▢ **A.** Parietal
- ▢ **B.** Temporal
- ▢ **C.** Occipital
- ▢ **D.** Frontal
- ▢ **E.** Parietal and temporal

186 A 54-year-old man is admitted to the hospital with severe headaches. A CT scan reveals a tumor in his brain occupying a portion of the anterior cranial fossa. Which of the following is responsible for the sensation of pain from headache in this case?

- ▢ **A.** Meningeal branches of the maxillary nerve
- ▢ **B.** Meningeal branches of the mandibular nerve
- ▢ **C.** Meningeal branches of the ethmoidal nerve
- ▢ **D.** Tentorial nerve
- ▢ **E.** C2 and C3 fibers

187 A 55-year-old woman is admitted to the emergency department with chest angina. ECG examination reveals an acute myocardial infarction. A series of medications is administered to the patient, including sublingual nitroglycerin for reducing her blood pressure. Which of the following structures is most likely to be the route of absorption of this drug?

- ▢ **A.** Deep lingual vein
- ▢ **B.** Submandibular duct
- ▢ **C.** Sublingual duct
- ▢ **D.** Lingual vein
- ▢ **E.** Sublingual vein

188 A 35-year-old man is admitted to the hospital with severe pain in the area of his right submandibular gland. Radiographic examination reveals a tumor of the gland. An incision is made and the submandibular gland and its duct are removed. Which of the following nerves is most commonly injured in this type of procedure?

- ▢ **A.** Buccal
- ▢ **B.** Lingual
- ▢ **C.** Inferior alveolar
- ▢ **D.** Nerve to mylohyoid
- ▢ **E.** Glossopharyngeal

189 A 22-year-old man is admitted to the emergency department with a sinus infection. Radiographic examination reveals posterior ethmoidal cell infection. During physical examination the patient complains of progressive loss of vision. Which of the following structures is most likely affected?

- ▢ **A.** Ophthalmic artery
- ▢ **B.** Nasociliary nerve
- ▢ **C.** Anterior ethmoidal nerve
- ▢ **D.** Trochlear nerve
- ▢ **E.** Optic nerve

190 A 55-year-old male farmer is admitted to the emergency department after falling from the hayloft in his barn. Radiographic examination reveals a small, depressed fracture of the skull vertex and thrombosis of the superior sagittal sinus. A day later the patient loses consciousness. What is the most likely cause of his loss of consciousness?

- ▢ **A.** Obstruction of CSF resorption
- ▢ **B.** Obstruction of the cerebral aqueduct (of Sylvius)
- ▢ **C.** Laceration of the middle meningeal artery
- ▢ **D.** Fracture of the cribriform plate with CSF rhinorrhea
- ▢ **E.** Aneurysm of the middle cerebral artery

191 An 11-year-old boy visits the outpatient clinic with a history of recurrent infections of his tonsils. Which of the following lymph nodes is most likely to first become visibly enlarged during tonsillitis?

- ▢ **A.** Submandibular
- ▢ **B.** Parotid
- ▢ **C.** Jugulodigastric
- ▢ **D.** Submental
- ▢ **E.** Preauricular

192 A 45-year-old man is admitted to the emergency department with a red, painful eye. During physical examination it is noted that the conjunctiva of the affected eye is infected. Which of the following lymph node groups would be first involved if the infection spread?

- ▢ **A.** Submandibular
- ▢ **B.** Parotid
- ▢ **C.** Jugulodigastric
- ▢ **D.** Submental
- ▢ **E.** Preauricular

193 A 45-year-old woman visits the outpatient clinic with past history of dysphagia, nighttime fits of coughing, repeated chest infections, and a palpable swelling in her neck. Radiographic examination reveals the presence of a congenital pharyngeal pouch. Between which muscles is this pouch located?

- ▢ **A.** Between styloglossus and stylopharyngeus
- ▢ **B.** Between palatoglossal arch and median glossoepiglottic fold
- ▢ **C.** Between upper and middle pharyngeal constrictors
- ▢ **D.** Between the cricopharyngeal and thyropharyngeal portions of inferior pharyngeal constrictor
- ▢ **E.** Between the middle and inferior pharyngeal constrictors

194 A 5-year-old boy fell from a tree and was admitted to the emergency department unconscious. When an emergency tracheostomy was performed, profuse dark venous bleeding suddenly occurred from the midline incision over the trachea. Which of the following vessels was most likely accidentally cut?

- ▢ **A.** Superior thyroid vein
- ▢ **B.** Inferior thyroid vein
- ▢ **C.** Left brachiocephalic vein
- ▢ **D.** Middle thyroid vein
- ▢ **E.** Jugular arch connecting the anterior jugular veins

195 A 55-year-old woman visits the outpatient clinic complaining of loss of sensation in the posterior third of her tongue. Radiographic examination reveals Eagle's syndrome, in which the styloid process and stylohyoid ligament are elongated and calcified. Which of the following nerves is most likely affected by Eagle's syndrome in this patient?

- ▢ **A.** Vagus
- ▢ **B.** Facial
- ▢ **C.** Glossopharyngeal
- ▢ **D.** Hypoglossal
- ▢ **E.** Vestibulocochlear

196 A 62-year-old man visits the outpatient clinic complaining of spontaneous lacrimation during eating. Which of the following nerves has developed a lesion to cause this condition?

- ▢ **A.** Facial nerve proximal to the geniculate ganglion
- ▢ **B.** Greater petrosal nerve
- ▢ **C.** Lesser petrosal nerve
- ▢ **D.** Lacrimal nerve
- ▢ **E.** Chorda tympani

197 A 54-year-old woman is admitted to the emergency department after experiencing sudden problems with her vision for the preceding 5 days. Radiographic examination reveals that an aneurysm of one of the arteries at the base of the brain is compressing the optic chiasm. Which of the following arteries will most likely be involved?

- ▢ **A.** Middle cerebral
- ▢ **B.** Anterior communicating
- ▢ **C.** Anterior cerebral
- ▢ **D.** Superior cerebellar
- ▢ **E.** Posterior superior cerebellar

198 A 22-year-old woman visits the outpatient clinic with a sinus infection of two weeks' duration. Physical examination reveals that the patient has focal inflammation, with mucosal edema in the inferior nasal meatus. Drainage from which of the following structures is most likely to be obstructed by this inflammation and edema?

- ▢ **A.** Anterior ethmoidal air cells
- ▢ **B.** Frontonasal duct
- ▢ **C.** Maxillary sinus
- ▢ **D.** Middle ethmoidal air cells
- ▢ **E.** Nasolacrimal duct

199 A 40-year-old woman suffers severe head trauma in a car crash. After radiographic examination she is diagnosed with a fracture of the temporal bone resulting in a lesion of the facial nerve proximal to the origin of the chorda tympani in the posterior wall of the tympanic cavity. Which of the following functions would most likely remain intact in this patient?

- ▢ **A.** Control of muscles in lower half of face
- ▢ **B.** Control of secretions by submandibular gland
- ▢ **C.** Taste sensation from anterior two thirds of tongue
- ▢ **D.** Tear production by the lacrimal gland
- ▢ **E.** Voluntary closure of the eyelid

200 Cardiac pain is referred in some cases to the mandible and the region of the TMJ. Cutaneous sensation over the angle of the mandible is normally supplied by which of the following nerves?

- ▢ **A.** Cervical branch of facial
- ▢ **B.** Great auricular nerve
- ▢ **C.** Mandibular branch of trigeminal nerve
- ▢ **D.** Mandibular branch of facial nerve
- ▢ **E.** Transverse cervical nerve

201 A patient with enlarged cervical lymph nodes has a malignant tumor of the cecum. Which of the following lymph nodes of the neck is most frequently associated with malignant tumors of the gastrointestinal tract?

- ▢ **A.** Left inferior deep cervical
- ▢ **B.** Left supraclavicular
- ▢ **C.** Right inferior deep cervical
- ▢ **D.** Right supraclavicular
- ▢ **E.** Jugulodigastric

202 A 60-year-old man presents with a swelling in his neck. Physical examination and biopsy show a benign tumor in his piriform recess. The mucosa of the piriform recess must be anesthetized during the removal of the tumor. Which nerve supplies general sensation to the mucous membrane of the laryngeal vestibule and piriform recesses?

- ▢ **A.** External laryngeal
- ▢ **B.** Glossopharyngeal
- ▢ **C.** Hypoglossal
- ▢ **D.** Inferior laryngeal
- ▢ **E.** Internal laryngeal

203 A young couple hiking in a wilderness area discovered the body of a man apparently in his 20s. He appeared to have been dead a few days, but animal predation was minimal. A postmortem examination was performed by the county medical examiner, and no evidence of penetrating wounds (bullet, lacerations, etc.) was found. A plain radiograph showed a fractured hyoid bone, but the calvaria and other bones appeared to be intact. Which of the following is the most likely cause of death?

- ▢ **A.** Myocardial infarction (heart attack)
- ▢ **B.** A fall from a height that resulted in fatal internal bleeding
- ▢ **C.** Subdural hematoma
- ▢ **D.** Strangulation
- ▢ **E.** Ingestion of a poisonous substance

204 A 40-year-old woman presents with severe headaches and dizziness. An MRI reveals a brain tumor, and a biopsy confirms it as a melanoma. She dies 2 months later. Pigmented lesions are not seen on her skin or scalp at the time of diagnosis or during postmortem examination. Which of the following is the most likely source of the malignant melanoma cells?

- ▢ **A.** Superior sagittal sinus
- ▢ **B.** Sphenoidal sinus
- ▢ **C.** Retina of the eye
- ▢ **D.** Pituitary gland
- ▢ **E.** Thymus

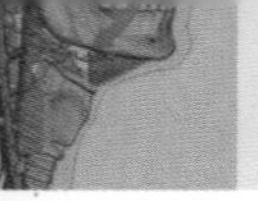

ANSWERS

1 E. The child in this problem suffers from a fistula that indicates an open malformation. This implies that the defect must be due to failure of closure for both an internal and an external structure. This excludes the second pharyngeal arch and third pharyngeal pouch from being the answers alone. A branchial fistula results from failure of closure of both the second pharyngeal pouch and the cervical sinus, the cervical sinus being the consolidation of the second through fourth pharyngeal clefts, external structures. The thyroglossal duct extends from the thyroid to the tongue and failure of its closure would not result in an external defect. The second pharyngeal groove merges with the third and fourth pharyngeal grooves to form the cervical sinus. Failure of closure of the second groove alone would not present with an open fistula.
GAS 954-955; GA 492-493

2 A. The largest part of the palate is formed by the secondary palate, which is embryologically derived from the lateral palatine processes. The median palatine process gives rise to the smaller primary palate, located anteriorly. The intermaxillary segment gives rise to the middle upper lip, premaxillary part of the maxilla, and the primary palate. The median nasal prominences merge with each other and the maxillary prominences to give rise to the intermaxillary segment. The frontonasal eminence gives rise to parts of the forehead, nose, and eyes.
GAS 1047-1054; GA 533-534

3 A. A coloboma of the iris is caused by failure of the retinal fissure to close during the sixth week. Abnormal neural crest formation would lead to abnormal development of choroid, sclera, and cornea because these are derived from neural crest cells. Abnormal interaction between the optic vesicle and ectoderm would lead to abnormal development of the entire eye because a lens placode may fail to develop or develop abnormally. The iris would not be affected by abnormal development of the posterior chamber. Weak adhesion between the layers of the optic vesicle leads to congenital retinal detachment.
GAS 898-901; GA 460-461

4 E. The anterior fontanelle is located at the junction of the sagittal and coronal sutures and closes at around 18 months of age. The posterior fontanelle is located at the junction of the sagittal suture and lambdoid suture, and it closes at around 2 to 3 months. The mastoid fontanelle is located at the junction of the squamous suture and the lambdoid suture, and it closes at the end of the first year. The sphenoidal fontanelle is located at the junction of the squamous suture and the coronal suture and closes at around 2 to 3 months. There is a lambdoid suture but not a lambdoid fontanelle.
GAS 812-821; GA 430-431

5 A. Thyroglossal duct cysts occur due to retention of a remnant of the thyroglossal duct along the path followed by the descending thyroid gland during development. The path begins from the foramen cecum of the tongue and descends in the midline to the final position of the thyroid. The sixth pharyngeal arch provides origin to muscles and cartilage of the neck and would produce a midline mass connected to the tongue. A branchial cyst or fistula would not be present in the midline. The first pharyngeal arch gives rise to muscles of mastication and the malleus and incus. The third pharyngeal arch provides origin to the stylopharyngeus muscle and hyoid bone.
GAS 964-968; GA 503-504

6 E. The most common cause of cleft lip is failure of fusion of the maxillary process and the intermaxillary segment. Defects located between the lateral nasal prominences and the maxillary processes would affect the development of the nasolacrimal duct. Failure of fusion of the medial nasal prominences would produce a median cleft lip, a rare congenital anomaly. The lateral and median nasal processes both arise from the nasal placodes and do not undergo subsequent fusion. The lateral nasal prominences do not fuse with each other.
GAS 813-816; GA 429-432

7 A. The listed symptoms are typical of first arch syndrome because the first arch normally gives rise to muscles of mastication, mylohyoid, anterior belly of the digastric, tensor tympani, tensor veli palatini, malleus, and incus. Abnormal development of the second arch would affect the muscles of facial expression, the stapes, and parts of the hyoid bone. Abnormal development of the third pharyngeal arch would affect only the stylopharyngeus and parts of the hyoid bone. Abnormal development of the fourth and sixth arch would affect various muscles and cartilages of the larynx and pharynx and would not produce the hypoplastic mandible characteristic of first arch syndrome.
GAS 925; GA 456-457

8 C. Obstructive hydrocephalus, in this case resulting from obstruction of the cerebral aqueduct, refers to a condition in which flow of cerebrospinal fluid (CSF) is obstructed within the ventricular system. This leads

to pressure increasing in the CSF above the obstruction, explaining the enlarged lateral and third ventricles. Nonobstructive hydrocephalus is due to either excessive CSF production or ineffective CSF reabsorption. This would lead to enlargement of all ventricular chambers. Anencephaly, also known as meroanencephaly, is a partial absence of the brain and is due to defective closure of the anterior neuropore. Holoprosencephaly is a failure of cleavage of the forebrain and would result in a single fused ventricle.
GAS 101, 834; GA 445

9 C. Both the inferior parathyroid glands and the thymus are derived from the third pharyngeal pouch. Therefore, an ectopic thymus is likely to be associated with ectopic parathyroid tissue, indicating abnormal development of the third pharyngeal pouch. The lingual tonsil develops from an aggregation of lymph nodules on the tongue and is not associated with development of the thymus. The submandibular gland develops from endodermal buds in the floor of the stomodeum and is not associated with development of the thymus. The thyroid gland arises from an outpocketing of the pharynx, descending along the route of the thyroglossal duct, and it is not associated with development of the thymus. Development of the lymph nodes is also not associated with development of the thymus.
GAS 206; GA 12, 102

10 C. The defect is likely in the development of third and fourth pharyngeal pouches because the superior parathyroid glands are derived from the fourth pouch, whereas the inferior parathyroid glands are derived from the third pouch. In addition, the third pouch gives rise to the thymus, and the parafollicular cells of the thyroid gland are derived from the fourth pharyngeal pouch. The first pouch gives rise to the tympanic membrane and cavity. The second pouch gives rise to the palatine tonsils and tonsillar sinus.
GAS 964, 967; GA 515, 517

11 C. Whereas all forms of clefts are considered to have a multifactorial etiology, cleft lip in particular seems to have a strong genetic factor. This has been determined using studies of twins. The other listed factors may or may not play a role in the development of a cleft lip, but genetics remains the most important causative factor.
GAS 813-816; GA 429-432

12 C. Absence of the thymus and inferior parathyroid glands would be due to defective development of the third pharyngeal pouch, their normal site of origin. The first pouch gives rise to the tympanic membrane and cavity. The second pouch gives rise to the palatine tonsils and tonsillar sinus. The fourth pharyngeal pouch gives rise to the superior parathyroid glands and the parafollicular cells of the thyroid gland. The fifth pharyngeal pouch contributes to the formation of the parafollicular cells of the thyroid gland.
GAS 206; GA 12, 102

13 D. The third pharyngeal arch gives rise to the greater cornu and lower part of the hyoid bone, in addition to the stylopharyngeus muscle. The maxillary prominence is important in the development of the cheeks and upper lip. The mandibular prominence is important in development of the mandible. The second pharyngeal arch gives rise to the lesser cornu and upper part of the hyoid bone. The fourth pharyngeal arches, while extensively involved in development of the cartilage and muscles of the larynx, play no part in the development of the hyoid bone.
GAS 803, 1034; GA 489, 504, 512-513

14 E. A lateral cervical cyst is caused by remnants of the cervical sinus and would present anterior to the sternocleidomastoid. A dermoid cyst is a cystic teratoma that often occurs near the lateral aspect of the eyebrow. A swollen lymph node is likely to present with pain. Accessory thyroid tissue is normally situated along the route of descent of the thyroglossal duct, either in the posterior tongue or along the midline of the neck. A cyst of the thyroglossal duct would be found in locations similar to where accessory thyroid tissue is found.
GAS 954, 955; GA 492-493

15 A. Noncommunicating hydrocephalus, also known as obstructive hydrocephalus, is due to an obstruction to flow of CSF within the ventricular system. Excess production of CSF or disturbed resorption of CSF gives rise to communicating or nonobstructive hydrocephalus. An increased size of the head can occur as a result of hydrocephalus but would not be a causative factor for hydrocephalus. Failure of the neural tube to close may lead to anencephaly or spina bifida, depending on the portion of the tube affected, but would not result in hydrocephalus.
GAS 101, 834; GA 445

16 C. A normal Apgar score indicates that the child appeared normal and healthy at birth, based on skin color, heart rate, reflexes, muscle tone, and breathing. An atretic external acoustic canal occurs due to failure of the meatal plug to canalize, an event that normally

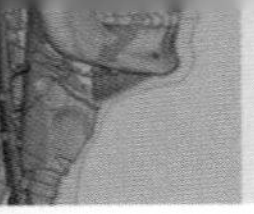

occurs in late fetal life. Failure of the otic pit to form results in an absent otic vesicle and absence of the membranous labyrinth. The first pharyngeal pouch gives rise to the tympanic membrane and cavity, and abnormal development would not affect the external acoustic meatus. Failure of the auricular hillocks to develop results in failure of the external ear to develop. A degenerated tubotympanic recess would not lead to an atretic external acoustic meatus.
GAS 796, 902-919; GA 472-474, 476

17 **D.** The chin and lower lip area are supplied by the mental nerve, a branch of the inferior alveolar nerve, which in turn is a branch of the mandibular division of the trigeminal nerve. The auriculotemporal nerve supplies the TMJ, the temporal region, the parotid gland, and the ear. The buccal nerve is sensory to the internal surface of the cheek. The lesser petrosal nerve is a parasympathetic nerve and would not be affected by herpes zoster, a disease of the dorsal root ganglia. The infraorbital nerve provides sensory innervation to the upper lip.
GAS 867-868, 933, 935, 1059-1060; GA 455, 483, 528

18 **B.** The semilunar ganglion, also known as the trigeminal or Gasserian ganglion, is the location of the sensory neuron cell bodies of the trigeminal nerve. Tic douloureux is a condition in which pain occurs over the area of distribution of trigeminal nerve branches. The geniculate ganglion is found on the facial nerve and receives sensory fibers for taste and transmits preganglionic parasympathetic fibers. Inferior glossopharyngeal ganglion is part of the glossopharyngeal nerve, not the trigeminal nerve, and is not the site of the cell bodies mediating the pain. The otic ganglion, located on the mandibular division of the trigeminal nerve, contains postganglionic parasympathetic cell bodies for parotid secretion. The pterygopalatine ganglion, located in the pterygopalatine fossa, also contains postganglionic parasympathetic cell bodies for lacrimation and mucosal secretion.
GAS 850-851, 932; GA 450-451, 487

19 **C.** The ophthalmic branch of the trigeminal nerve supplies sensory innervation to the eyeball, leading to pain upon damage. Pain in the hard palate and lower eyelid and anesthesia of the upper lip would be carried by the maxillary branch of the trigeminal nerve. Paraesthesia over the buccal portion of the face would be mediated by the maxillary division of the trigeminal nerve.
GAS 844, 852, 866-867; GA 444, 450-451, 455, 463, 465, 469, 483-484, 487

20 **D.** A tumor at the hypoglossal canal would compress the hypoglossal nerve and affect the genioglossus, a muscle it supplies. The palatoglossus is innervated by the vagus nerve, and the thyrohyoid is innervated by the ansa cervicalis (C1 to C3). The geniohyoid is supplied by C1, which runs with the hypoglossal nerve after it passes through the hypoglossal canal, and would therefore be unaffected. The mylohyoid is supplied by the nerve to mylohyoid, a branch of the mandibular nerve of the trigeminal nerve.
GAS 812, 822, 824-827, 848-851, 854; GA 436-437, 450-451, 494, 497, 531, 537

21 **C.** The superior salivatory nucleus is the autonomic nucleus for the facial nerve. Parasympathetic fibers carried by the greater petrosal branch of the facial nerve are responsible for supply of the lacrimal gland and sinuses, via the pterygopalatine ganglion. The geniculate ganglion contains the cell bodies for taste from the anterior two thirds of the tongue carried by the chorda tympani branch of the facial nerve. This branch also carries the parasympathetic supply for the submandibular and sublingual salivary glands. The auriculotemporal nerve provides sensory innervation to the temporal regions of the head, the TMJ, and general sensation from the ear. The inferior salivatory nucleus provides preganglionic parasympathetic fibers carried by the glossopharyngeal nerve that synapse in the otic ganglion, providing parotid stimulation. The pterygopalatine ganglion includes fibers that innervate only lacrimation and the nasal sinuses, but not taste on the anterior two thirds of the tongue.
GAS 807, 848-852, 863-864; GA 451, 458-459, 463, 473-474, 484, 537

22 **D.** Thoracic outlet syndrome is characterized by the presence of a cervical rib, accessory muscles, or connective tissue bands that constrict the limited dimensions of the thoracic outlet. The cervical rib is usually located on the C7 vertebra and can impinge on the brachial plexus, resulting in loss of some feeling to the upper limb. There would be no impingement on the phrenic nerve because it leaves C3 to C5 directly parallel with the vertebral column. The syndrome does not include reduction of blood flow to the thoracic wall because of extensive anastomoses between the vessels that supply blood to the anterior thoracic wall. Venous return from the head and neck is mainly through the internal jugular vein and would not be affected because of this vein's location near the midline of the body; thus, it would not be occluded or distended.
GAS 233; GA 6, 57-59

23 **C.** The superior cervical ganglion (SCG), which is the uppermost part of the sympathetic chain, supplies sympathetic innervation to the head and neck. The usual symptoms for SCG injury are miosis and anhydrosis in the head and neck region. Postganglionic sympathetic nerves usually run alongside the arteries leading into the head and neck region. The submandibular ganglion does not carry sympathetic nerves to areas of the head and neck. The trigeminal ganglion includes only cell bodies from afferent sensory nerves from the head. The geniculate ganglion includes cell bodies for taste sensation from the anterior two thirds of the tongue, carried by the facial nerve; it also transmits parasympathetic innervation to many sections of the head and face. The ciliary ganglion provides parasympathetic innervation to the eye and also has some sympathetic fibers coursing through but not synapsing; thus, it would not account for the symptoms of the face.
GAS 45, 882, 895, 980-981; GA 190, 496

24 **A.** The lingual nerve joins the chorda tympani in the infratemporal fossa, and a lesion to the lingual nerve before it joins the chorda tympani would account for the loss of general sensation, with no loss to the special sense of taste and saliva production. If the chorda tympani were injured, the patient would present with a loss of taste (anterior two thirds of tongue) and a decrease in saliva production because the submandibular and sublingual salivary glands would be dennervated. The inferior alveolar nerve provides sensory innervation to the mandibular teeth, but no such loss is present. The lesser petrosal nerve innervates postganglionic neurons supplying the parotid gland, but no loss of salivation is present. The glossopharyngeal nerve provides taste innervation to the posterior third of the tongue, but there is no deficit present in this patient.
GAS 937; GA 480, 484, 528-529, 532, 534

25 **E.** The jugular foramen is the route of exit for three nerves (glossopharyngeal, vagus, and accessory nerves) and one vein (internal jugular) from the cranial cavity. The glossopharyngeal nerve provides the sensory input for the gag reflex, whereas the vagus nerve provides the motor output. Nerve compression within this foramen would lead to a loss of both systems and thus no gag reflex. Tongue movements are supplied by the hypoglossal nerve, which exits the skull through the hypoglossal canal. The facial nerve innervates the muscles of the face and would not be affected by this injury. Loss of sensation from the face and scalp would be present only if there was involvement of the trigeminal nerve. Loss of hearing would be present with any compression of the vestibulocochlear nerve.
GAS 812, 821, 824-827, 852-853; GA 436-437

26 **E.** The middle meningeal artery is a branch of the maxillary artery and courses between the dura mater and skull close to the area of the pterion. Any fracture or impact trauma to this location typically results in a laceration of the middle meningeal artery resulting in an epidural hematoma. The external carotid artery ends behind the mandible by dividing into the maxillary and the superficial temporal arteries, and neither of these arteries directly affects the meninges of the brain. The deep temporal arteries do not penetrate the bony skull and thus would not contribute to an epidural hematoma.
GAS 814, 829, 845, 1066; GA 459, 483, 485

27 **A.** An injury to the oculomotor nerve would cause the eye to point downward and laterally due to the unopposed contractions of the trochlear and abducens nerves. The oculomotor nerve also provides innervation to the levator palpebrae superioris; thus, any injury would cause complete ptosis or drooping of the eyelid. The constriction of the pupil is provided by parasympathetic nerves via the oculomotor nerve. The optic nerve is responsible only for the sensory aspect of light via the retina in the eye. The facial nerve innervates the facial muscles, including the orbicularis oculi, which supplies the blink reflex. The ciliary ganglion could be damaged in this patient, but the loss of parasympathetic supply would not adequately explain the ptosis of the eyelid. The superior cervical ganglion provides sympathetic innervation to the head and neck, but no loss of sympathetics is evident in this patient.
GAS 855, 1075; GA 450-451, 465, 469, 536

28 **B.** The scalp is divided into five layers: skin, dense connective tissue, aponeurosis, loose connective tissue, and periosteum. Typically, infections will be located in the loose connective tissue because of the ease with which infectious agents spread via the many veins located in this region. This area is usually referred to as the "danger zone" of the scalp mainly because scalp infections here can be transmitted into the skull via emissary veins, then via diploic veins of the bone to the cranial cavity. The periosteum and bone are almost inseparable; thus, it is not likely to find infections between these layers. The areas between the dense connective tissue and aponeurosis and between the connective tissue and the skin layers do not include connecting veins but mainly superficial veins of the head. The skin pro-

bule) because the muscles of facial expression are paralyzed. There is a bony prominence over the facial nerve located on the medial wall of the middle ear. Because of its close proximity, the facial nerve can be damaged due to otitis media. The other nerves listed are not located in close proximity to the middle ear and, if injured, would not present with the symptoms described.
GAS 855, 872, 945; GA 451, 458-459, 463, 473-474, 484, 537

44 **C.** The arterial circle (of Willis) receives its blood supply from the internal carotid and vertebral arteries. The actual circle is formed by the bifurcation of the basilar, posterior cerebral, posterior communicating, internal carotid, anterior cerebral, and anterior communicating arteries. The middle cerebral artery is the lateral continuation of the internal carotid artery. Although it receives its blood supply from the arterial circle (of Willis), it does not actually form any part of the circle.
GAS 837-838; GA 452

45 **E.** The sigmoid venous sinus empties into the internal jugular vein and drains the cranial vault. It runs along the posterior cranial fossa near the suture between the temporal and occipital bones. The superior sagittal sinus lies within the superior aspect of the longitudinal fissure, between the two cerebral hemispheres. The inferior sagittal sinus runs inferior to the superior sagittal sinus within the falx cerebri and joins the great cerebral vein (of Galen) to form the straight sinus. The straight sinus drains the great cerebral vein (of Galen) into the confluence of sinuses. The cavernous sinus is located within the middle cranial fossa and receives the ophthalmic veins, the greater petrosal sinus, and other venous vessels.
GAS 842-844; GA 445

46 **C.** The tumor is compressing the facial nerve, which runs through the internal acoustic meatus along with the vestibulocochlear nerve, which provides sense of taste to the anterior two thirds of the tongue via the chorda tympani and also mediates all of the facial muscles, except the muscles of mastication. The mandibular branch of the trigeminal nerve courses through the foramen ovale and mediates motor to the muscles of mastication and sensory to the lower third of the face. The maxillary branch of the trigeminal passes through the foramen rotundum and is sensory to the middle third of the face. The jugular foramen has the glossopharyngeal, vagus, and accessory nerves coursing through it. Finally, the superior orbital fissure has the ophthalmic branch of the trigeminal nerve coursing through it, along with the oculomotor, trochlear, and abducens nerves.
GAS 855, 872; GA 451, 458-459, 463, 473-474, 484, 537

47 **E.** The submental lymph nodes drain roughly the anterior two thirds of the mouth and tongue, including the lower lips. The occipital nodes serve the inferoposterior aspect of the head. The parotid nodes lie anterior to the ear and serve the region of the lateral aspect of the eye, the parotid gland, and anterior ear. The retropharyngeal nodes lie posterior to the pharynx and drain the posterior aspect of the throat and pharynx. The jugulodigastric node is a large node posterior to the parotid gland and just below the angle of the mandible, and it receives lymph from much of the face and scalp.
GAS 872, 983-984, 1044, 1058; GA 458, 502-503

48 **A.** The abducens nerve would be affected first due to aneurysmal dilation of the internal carotid artery (ICA) because the nerve runs in closest proximity to the artery within the cavernous sinus. The other nerves running in the wall of the cavernous sinus are the oculomotor nerve, trochlear nerve, and both the maxillary and ophthalmic branches of the trigeminal nerve. Each of these nerves, however, courses along, or within, the lateral walls of the cavernous sinus and may not be immediately affected by an aneurysm of the ICA.
GAS 844; GA 445, 450, 452

49 **C.** The lingual nerve is the most likely nerve damaged because there is loss both of taste and general sensory supply to the anterior two thirds of the tongue, which is innervated by the lingual nerve, which at this point has been joined by the chorda tympani. The chorda tympani would be a likely choice; however, it carries only taste and does not mediate other general sensation to the tongue. The auriculotemporal nerve is a posterior branch of the mandibular division of the trigeminal nerve and innervates skin near the ear and temporal region. The mental nerve is the terminal branch of the inferior alveolar nerve and innervates the skin of the chin.
GAS 935; GA 480, 484, 528-529, 532, 534

50 **B.** The auriculotemporal nerve is a posterior branch of the mandibular division of the trigeminal nerve. It encircles the middle meningeal artery and courses medially to the TMJ and then ascends up near the auricle. Because this nerve supplies the TMJ and skin of the external auditory canal, pain from the joint can be referred to the ear as in this case. The facial nerve courses over the ascending ramus of

the mandible, passing superficial to the masseter muscle and below the TMJ through the parotid gland, and would not be involved in this problem. The lesser petrosal nerve courses through the middle cranial fossa and exits through the foramen ovale, where it joins the otic ganglion. The vestibulocochlear nerve exits the cranial cavity through the internal acoustic meatus and innervates structures in the inner ear. Finally, the chorda tympani is a branch of the facial nerve and joins the mandibular division of the trigeminal nerve anterior to the TMJ.
GAS 826-827, 904; GA 455, 483-485

51 D. The otic ganglion is the location of the postganglionic parasympathetic neural cell bodies innervating the parotid gland. The ganglion lies on the mandibular division of the trigeminal nerve near the foramen ovale. The trigeminal ganglion contains cell bodies for neurons innervating sensory aspects of the face. The inferior salivatory nucleus lies within the brainstem and contains preganglionic parasympathetic neurons whose axons pass within the lesser petrosal nerve to the otic ganglion for synapse in the supply of the parotid. The superior cervical ganglion has the cell bodies of postganglionic sympathetic fibers innervating sympathetic structures to the head. The submandibular ganglia contain the cell bodies of postganglionic parasympathetic fibers innervating the sublingual and submandibular salivary glands.
GAS 853, 864, 937; GA 484

52 B. The arachnoid villi are extensions of the arachnoid mater into the superior sagittal sinus. The villi allow for proper drainage of the CSF into the venous bloodstream from the subarachnoid space in which the CSF circulates. The villi are a crucial element in maintaining proper intracranial pressure and circulation of the CSF.
GAS 101, 834; GA 445

53 C. The afferent/sensory limb of the corneal (blink) reflex is carried by the nasociliary nerve. It is a branch of the ophthalmic division of the trigeminal nerve. The frontal and lacrimal nerves provide cutaneous supply to parts of the orbit and face, but they do not innervate the cornea. The facial nerve is the efferent limb of the corneal reflex and mediates the closing of both eyes in response to irritation of the cornea. The oculomotor nerve mediates the reopening of the eyes by contraction of the levator palpebrae superioris. The optic nerve also innervates the eye for the sense of vision and is the afferent limb of the pupillary light reflex.
GAS 894-897; GA 465, 469

54 D. Kiesselbach (also called Little) plexus is an anastomosis of four arteries on the anterior nasal septum. The four arteries are the anterior ethmoidal artery, sphenopalatine artery, superior labial artery, and greater palatine artery. The two largest contributors, however, are the septal branches of the sphenopalatine (from the maxillary artery) and superior labial arteries (branches of the facial artery, which in turn is a branch of the external carotid artery).
GAS 813, 814, 819-820, 1016, 1018, 1020; GA 507, 520

55 B. The palatine tonsils lie in tonsillar beds with muscular (covered with mucosa) anterior and posterior pillars forming the boundaries of the bed. These pillars are formed by the palatoglossal arch, anteriorly, and the palatopharyngeal arch, posteriorly. The anterior pillar, part of the palatoglossal arch, contains the palatoglossus muscle; the posterior pillar, provided by the palatopharyngeal arch, is formed by the palatopharyngeus muscle.
GAS 990, 992, 993, 1051; GA 12, 504-505, 520, 532-534

56 A. The posterior cricoarytenoid muscles lie on the superoposterior aspect of the lamina of the cricoid cartilage. When these muscles contract, they cause lateral rotation (abduction) of the vocal processes of the arytenoid cartilages, thereby opening the space between the vocal folds, the rima glottidis. The lateral cricoarytenoid is involved with adducting the arytenoid cartilage and closing the rima glottidis. The thyroarytenoid muscles lie alongside either vocal ligament and are also involved in adducting the vocal folds. The transverse arytenoid muscle connects both arytenoid cartilages and also aids in closing the rima glottidis. Finally, the cricothyroid muscle is located on the anterior aspect of the cricoid cartilage and aids in elongation and tensing of the vocal folds.
GAS 1006; GA 507, 513

57 C. The parotid duct, also known as the Stensen's duct, crosses the masseter muscle transversely and extends to the oral cavity. The facial artery can be palpated in the groove anterior to the mandibular angle. The facial vein lies anterior to the artery, passing toward the angle of the lips, but does not ascend in close proximity to the masseter. All of the other vessels are located more deeply and cannot be palpated.
GAS 863, 1044; GA 456-457

58 C. Because of the surgical division of the ansa cervicalis, the sternohyoid muscle will most likely be paralyzed following this tumor resection. The ansa

cervicalis innervates the strap muscles, including the sternohyoid, sternothyroid, and omohyoid muscles. The sternocleidomastoid is innervated by the accessory nerve, the spinal accessory nerve, and would not be involved with this surgery. The platysma is located most superficially on the neck and is innervated by cervical branch of the facial nerve. The trapezius muscle is also innervated by the spinal accessory nerve and plays no role in ansa cervicalis functions. Finally, the cricothyroid muscle is innervated by the external laryngeal branch of the vagus and would not be affected by the surgery.
GAS 964, 974; GA 496-497, 531

59 A. The spinal accessory nerve passes across the posterior triangle of the neck and innervates both the trapezius muscle and the sternocleidomastoid muscle for the respective side of the body. Upon surgical division of the nerve, the patient will lose the ability to raise the respective shoulder and will demonstrate weakness in turning the head to the opposite side. The trapezius will also lose tone and the shoulder will droop. The ansa cervicalis innervates strap muscles of the neck and, if cut, would not produce drooping of the shoulder. The facial nerve does not pass through any of the triangles of the neck; however, if it were divided, paralysis would result in the muscles of facial expression. The hypoglossal nerve innervates the intrinsic muscles of the tongue, plus the genioglossus, hyoglossus, and styloglossus and, if injured, would not result in any of the patient's symptoms.
GAS 973-974; GA 37, 450-451, 494, 537

60 C. Four nerves participate in providing cutaneous supply to the neck. The nerves are the supraclavicular, great auricular, transverse cervical, and the lesser occipital. The area over the angle of the jaw is innervated by the great auricular nerve. It ascends from spinal segments from C2 and C3 and innervates the skin over the angle of the jaw and posteroinferior to the auricle of the ear. The transverse cervical also originates from C2-3 spinal segments but passes anteriorly to innervate the anterior and lateral aspects of the neck. The lesser occipital nerve innervates skin in the area of the back of the neck and posterior occiput. The supraclavicular nerves originate from C3-4 and innervate the more inferior aspects of the neck, the upper deltoid region, and skin inferior to the clavicles.
GAS 974-975; GA 494, 496-497

61 C. Because of its size and vulnerable position during birth, the sternocleidomastoid muscle is injured more often than other muscles of the head and neck during birth. When acting alone, the action of this muscle is to turn the head to the opposite side and bend it toward the ipsilateral shoulder. When using both muscles, the head will flex toward the chest. Therefore, the most likely muscle to have been injured here is the left sternocleidomastoid muscle.
GAS 970-971; GA 492-493

62 C. The most likely structures one would encounter while performing a midline incision below the isthmus of the thyroid gland would be the inferior thyroid vein and the thyroidea ima artery. The inferior thyroid vein drains typically to the left brachiocephalic vein, which crosses superficially, just inferior to the isthmus. The thyroidea ima artery arises from the aortic arch, vertebral artery, or other source but is not a constant structure. The middle thyroid veins drain the thyroid gland to the internal jugular vein and are superior to the incision site. The inferior thyroid arteries branch from either subclavian artery and meet the thyroid gland at an oblique angle. They would not be ligated with a midline incision. The brachiocephalic veins are inferior to the site of incision.
GAS 967; GA 503-504, 515

63 D. The recurrent laryngeal nerve is the most likely nerve damaged during the surgery because it runs in close proximity to the inferior thyroid artery and is easily injured or transected with the artery if extreme care is not exercised during operative procedures. The recurrent laryngeal nerve innervates the majority of the vocal muscles that open and close the rima glottidis, in addition to providing sensory supply to the larynx below the vocal folds. Even relatively mild trauma to the nerve can result in hoarseness. The internal branch of the superior laryngeal nerve is not in close proximity to the inferior thyroid artery and pierces the thyrohyoid membrane to enter the pharynx. The ansa cervicalis lies lateral to the site of surgery and does not innervate any structures that, if paralyzed, would cause hoarseness.
GAS 967; GA 503-504, 515-517

64 E. The vagus nerve exits the skull at the jugular foramen and is responsible for motor innervation to the smooth muscles of the trachea, bronchi, and digestive tract, in addition to the muscles of the palate, pharynx, larynx, and superior two thirds of the esophagus. The ansa cervicalis innervates the strap muscles of the neck, with the exception of the thyrohyoid muscle. The cervical sympathetic trunk does not enter into the jugular foramen; it runs behind the carotid sheath, parallel with the internal carotid artery; its carotid branch accompanies the artery into the carotid canal and carries sympathetic fibers to deep areas of the head. Damage to the

external laryngeal nerve would result in paralysis of the cricothyroid muscle, presenting as an easily fatigued voice with hoarseness. Injury to the hypoglossal nerve would result in protrusion of the tongue toward the affected side and moderate dysarthria.
GAS 203, 211-213, 217, 345, 807, 849-851, 853-854; GA 537

65 B. The hypoglossal nerve provides motor innervation to the muscles of the tongue, with the exception of the palatoglossus. Injury to the hypoglossal nerve would result in deviation of the tongue toward the affected side when the tongue is protruded (in this case the right side), due mainly to the unilateral contraction of left genioglossus, and moderate dysarthria. Injury to the glossopharyngeal nerve would result in loss of taste in the posterior third of the tongue and a loss of soft palate sensation and gag reflex on the affected side. The inferior alveolar nerve supplies the tissues of the chin and lower teeth. The lingual nerve conveys parasympathetic preganglionic fibers to the submandibular ganglion and general sensation and taste fibers for the anterior two thirds of the tongue. Injury to the vagus nerve would cause sagging of the soft palate, deviation of the uvula to the unaffected side, hoarseness, and difficulty in swallowing and speaking.
GAS 855, 1041, 1043-1044; GA 450-451, 494, 497, 531, 537

66 C. During removal of the tumor, the internal branch of the superior laryngeal nerve was injured. Injury to this nerve results in loss of sensation above the vocal cords, at the entrance to the larynx, and loss of taste on the epiglottis. Loss of sensation in the laryngeal vestibule can precipitate aspiration of fluid into the larynx, trachea, and lungs. The pharyngeal nerve of the vagus supplies motor innervation to the muscles of the pharynx, except the stylopharyngeus (glossopharyngeal nerve). Injury to the hypoglossal nerve would result in protrusion of the tongue toward the affected side and moderate dysarthria. The lingual nerve conveys parasympathetic preganglionic fibers to the submandibular ganglion and general sensation and taste fibers for the anterior two thirds of the tongue. The recurrent laryngeal provides sensory fibers to the larynx below the vocal cords and motor fibers to all of the muscles of the larynx except for the cricothyroid.
GAS 996-1012; GA 495, 508, 514

67 A. The posterior cricoarytenoids are the only muscle of the larynx that abducts the vocal cords. The remaining answer choices are muscles that act in adduction of the vocal cords.
GAS 1006; GA 507, 513

68 B. The external branch of the superior laryngeal nerve courses together with the superior thyroid artery for much of its route. The cervical sympathetic trunk is located more laterally and quite posteriorly to this location. The inferior root of the ansa cervicalis is located more superficially in the anterior neck. The internal branch of the superior laryngeal nerve takes a route superior to that of the external branch and the superior thyroid artery and would be unlikely to be injured in this case. The recurrent laryngeal nerve terminates inferiorly, passing into the larynx in relation to the inferior thyroid artery or its branches.
GAS 996, 1012; GA 514

69 C. The external surface of the tympanic membrane is innervated primarily by the auriculotemporal nerve, a branch of the mandibular division of the trigeminal nerve. Damage to this nerve would additionally result in painful movements of the TMJ because this joint receives innervation from the same nerve. Taste in the anterior two thirds of the tongue is supplied by the facial nerve and would be unaffected in this injury. The sensory innervation of the nasal cavity is supplied by the ophthalmic and maxillary divisions of the trigeminal nerve and would be unaffected by injury to the tympanic membrane. Sensory innervation to the larynx is provided by the vagus nerve, whereas the pharynx receives sensory fibers from the glossopharyngeal and vagus nerves. The palate is supplied by the maxillary divisions of the trigeminal nerve and would be unaffected by this injury.
GAS 904; GA 455, 483-485

70 B. Both the stapedius and tensor tympani normally function to dampen movements of the middle ear ossicles, thereby muting sound and preventing hyperacusis. The stapedius would be the source of hyperacusis in this problem because it receives its innervation from the facial nerve. The tensor tympani receives motor innervation from the mandibular division of the trigeminal nerve. The posterior belly of the digastric and the stylohyoid receive innervation from the facial nerve, but their paralysis would not cause hyperacusis. Damaged innervation of the cricothyroid, which is supplied by the external branch of the superior laryngeal nerve, would not result in hyperacusis.
GAS 906, 910-911; GA 474

71 C. The greater petrosal nerve carries parasympathetic fibers that are involved in the innervation of the lacrimal gland, as well as the mucosal glands of the nose, palate, and pharynx. As a result, an injury to the right greater petrosal nerve would be expected to

result in decreased lacrimal secretions for the right eye. The sublingual and submandibular glands receive their parasympathetic fibers from the facial nerve via the chorda tympani and the lingual nerve. They would be unaffected by this lesion. The parotid gland receives its parasympathetic secretory innervation from the glossopharyngeal nerve via the lesser petrosal and auriculotemporal nerves and would be unaffected. Taste to the anterior tongue is provided by the facial nerve via the chorda tympani, and general sensation to the anterior tongue is provided by the mandibular division of the trigeminal nerve via the lingual nerve.
GAS 852, 917, 918, 945, 1016, 1029-1030, 1047; GA 463, 472, 487

72 C. Parasympathetic innervation of the parotid gland is provided by axons carried by the glossopharyngeal nerve that emerge from the tympanic plexus of the middle ear as the lesser petrosal nerve. These preganglionic parasympathetic fibers terminate by synapses in the otic ganglion, which supplies the secretory parasympathetic innervation to the parotid gland. Glandular secretions of the nasal cavity, soft palate, and lacrimal gland all receive parasympathetic innervation from the fibers of the greater petrosal nerve and would remain intact following a tympanic plexus lesion. Axons for secretory innervation to the sublingual and submandibular glands are carried by the facial nerve, then course through the chorda tympani, before synapsing in the submandibular ganglion, with postganglionic fibers eventually reaching the glands via the lingual nerve.
GAS 863-865; GA 456, 458-459, 480

73 B. The inferior alveolar branch of the mandibular division of the trigeminal nerve provides sensory innervation to the mandibular teeth and would require anesthesia to abolish painful sensation. The lingual nerve provides taste and sensation to the anterior two thirds of the tongue and carries general sensory fibers, taste fibers, and parasympathetic fibers. It does not provide sensory innervation to the teeth. The buccal nerve provides sensory innervation to the inner surface of the cheek. The mental nerve is the distal continuation of the inferior alveolar nerve as it exits the mental foramen of the mandible and does not affect the teeth. The nerve to the mylohyoid is a motor branch of the inferior alveolar nerve that supplies the mylohyoid and the anterior belly of the digastric.
GAS 937; GA 480, 483, 528

74 D. Part of the lateral pterygoid muscle has its insertion on the articular disk within the TMJ and would be most affected by the inflammation of this joint. The temporalis muscle inserts upon the coronoid process and retracts the jaw. The medial pterygoid muscle extends from the medial surface of the lateral pterygoid plate to the mandible and functions in elevation of the jaw. The masseter extends from the zygomatic arch to the lateral ramus of the mandible and elevates the jaw. The buccinator pulls back the angle of the mouth and flattens the cheek.
GAS 925, 930-931; GA 480-482, 484

75 D. The trochlear nerve innervates the superior oblique muscle, which acts to move the pupil downward and laterally. It is the only muscle that can depress the pupil when the eye is adducted. When an individual walks down stairs, this eye motion is initiated, and diplopia results if it is not functioning properly. The optic nerve provides vision, and a lesion of this nerve would not result in diplopia when an affected individual walks down the stairs, but rather diminished vision or blindness. The oculomotor nerve supplies the superior, inferior, and medial rectus as well as the inferior oblique. Overall, innervation from the oculomotor nerve results in upward and inward movements of the eye, and a lesion of this nerve would not induce diplopia in an individual walking down stairs. The abducens nerve innervates the lateral rectus muscle, which abducts the eye, and damage would not induce the diplopia presented in this problem. The frontal nerve is a branch of the ophthalmic division of the trigeminal nerve and provides sensory innervation to the forehead.
GAS 848, 850-851, 855; GA 450-451, 465, 536

76 E. The superior oblique muscle turns the pupil downward from the adducted position. Inability to perform this motion, in conjunction with diplopia when walking down stairs, indicates damage to the trochlear nerve. The abducens innervates the lateral rectus, resulting in abduction of the eye. The oculomotor nerve supplies the superior, inferior, and medial rectus as well as the inferior oblique. Overall, innervation from the oculomotor nerve results in upward and downward movements of the eye. Damage to this nerve would not induce diplopia when an affected individual walks down stairs. In addition, inability to gaze downward in the adducted position does not indicate oculomotor nerve damage. In this position the oculomotor nerve would be responsible for upward movement. The nasociliary nerve is a sensory nerve originating from the ophthalmic branch of the trigeminal nerve.
GAS 888-891; GA 464, 466

77 E. Ptosis and miosis occur in response to blocking of sympathetic innervation. Ptosis (drooping of the eyelid) results from lack of innervation of the superior tarsal muscle (of Müller), and miosis (pupillary constriction) results from unopposed parasympathetic innervation of the pupil. A dilated pupil would not occur because this requires the action of the sympathetically innervated dilator pupillae. Dry eye would occur due to lacrimal gland insufficiency, but because this is mediated by parasympathetic fibers, it would remain unaffected in this case. The same holds true for the parasympathetically mediated accommodation pathway. Depth perception involves the visual pathway and is not mediated by the sympathetic system.
GAS 45, 882, 895, 980-981; GA 190, 496

78 B. The right abducens nerve innervates the right lateral rectus, which mediates outward movement (abduction) of the right eye. Inward movement is accomplished by the medial rectus, supplied by the oculomotor nerve. Downward movement in the midline is accomplished by joint activation of the superior oblique and inferior rectus muscle. Downward movement of the pupil from the adducted position is a function of the superior oblique alone, which is supplied by the trochlear nerve. Down and out motion is mediated by the combined actions of the lateral rectus and inferior rectus, which are innervated by the abducens and oculomotor nerves. Downward movement of the pupil from a forward gaze is a result of combined actions of inferior rectus and superior oblique muscles, supplied by oculomotor and trochlear nerves, respectively.
GAS 849-852, 855; GA 450, 465, 536

79 A. Horner's syndrome involves interruption of sympathetic supply to the face. This results in ptosis (drooping eyelid), miosis (constricted pupil), and anhydrosis (lack of sweating) of the face. The eye is lubricated by the lacrimal gland, which secretes in response to parasympathetic stimulation, and would be unaffected. Exophthalmos (protrusion of the globe) is frequently caused by hyperthyroidism and is not present in Horner's syndrome. Loss of sympathetic innervation leads to unopposed vasodilatation of the vessels to the face, leading to flushing rather than paleness.
GAS 45, 882, 895, 980-981; GA 190, 496

80 E. The superior tarsal muscle (of Müller), innervated by sympathetics, assists in elevating the eyelids and holding them up. Damage would result in partial ptosis of the eyelid. The superior oblique, innervated by the trochlear nerve, moves the pupil downward from the adducted position (for example, as when your right eye gazes down toward your left foot). To test the trochlear nerve, ask the patient to look with each eye toward the tip of the nose. The orbicularis oculi, innervated by the facial nerve, is responsible for closure of the eye. The palpebral part closes the eyelids ordinarily; the lacrimal part contracts when the eye is closed more forcibly, resulting in increased tear movement across the globe (perhaps to flow down the cheeks). Damage to the levator palpebrae superioris, innervated by the oculomotor nerve, would result in complete, rather than partial, ptosis.
GAS 878, 881, 888-889, 892; GA 461

81 D. Cavernous sinus thrombosis can often result from squeezing pimples or other infectious processes located around the danger area of the face, which includes the area of the face directly surrounding the nose. This physical pressure has the potential to move infectious agents from the pimple into the ophthalmic vein, which then carries it to the cavernous sinus. The pterygoid venous plexus and ophthalmic vein both communicate with the cavernous sinus and therefore offer a route of travel for the spread of infection, but the path provided by the superior ophthalmic vein is a more direct route. Additionally, the superior ophthalmic vein receives blood supply from the supraorbital, supratrochlear, and angular veins that supply the area around the nose and lower forehead. (Venous blood in the head can flow in either direction because these veins do not possess valves.) The emissary veins communicate between the venous sinuses and the veins of the scalp and would therefore not be involved in the spread of infection between the nose and cavernous sinus. The middle meningeal artery courses between the dura and periosteum, whereas the carotid artery, specifically the internal carotid artery, traverses through the cavernous sinus and provides origin to the ophthalmic artery. As with the middle meningeal artery, the carotid artery would not offer a route of communication between the area of infection and the cavernous sinus.
GAS 871, 877, 886, 899; GA 459

82 E. The anterior inferior cerebellar artery (AICA) is a major supplier of the anterior inferior portion of the cerebellum. Nerves located in close proximity would likely be affected by hemorrhage of this artery. The optic, oculomotor, and trochlear nerves are all associated with the midbrain region and would likely not suffer any damage with a possible hemorrhage. The trigeminal nerve is situated in the pons and is thus located too far rostrally to be affected. The abducens nerve is situated at the pontomedullary junction

and is therefore most likely to be damaged following hemorrhage of the AICA.
GAS 837, 838; GA 452, 454

83 D. The posterior inferior quadrant of the eardrum is the only portion of the tympanic membrane that would allow for an incision with minimal or no damage to adjacent important structures. Incision in the anterior and posterior superior quadrants of the eardrum would likely damage the malleus, which is situated immediately superior and medially to the tympanic membrane. The umbo is situated in close proximity to the handle of the malleus and might be damaged during incision. A vertical incision through the eardrum would almost certainly damage the malleus of the middle ear. Damage to the malleus from surgical incision would interfere with the auditory conduction through the middle ear cavity, and this should be avoided to prevent conductive hearing loss.
GAS 904-906; GA 473, 476

84 A. The hypoglossal nerve innervates the muscles of the tongue and is therefore directly involved in alteration of shape and movement of the tongue. A lesion in this nerve would cause deviation of the tongue toward the injured side, which could be observed upon protrusion of the tongue. The genioglossus is the major muscle involved in protrusion of the tongue. The genioglossus muscles arise from the inside of the mandible and pass posteriorly to insert into the deep aspect of the tongue. When the genioglossi contract, they pull the tongue forward, and out of the mouth, in protrusion. If one genioglossus is paralyzed, it acts like a brake on one side of the tongue when the tongue is pulled forward, causing the tip of the tongue to point to the nonmoving side. The styloglossus muscle is responsible for retraction and elevation of the tongue.
GAS 1039-1041; GA 504, 530, 532-533

85 B. The posterior chamber receives ciliary body secretions first. The ciliary body produces aqueous humor and is located in the posterior chamber. Increased production of fluid from this site would cause an increase in intraocular pressure if drainage is inadequate. The iridoscleral angle of the anterior chamber is the location of drainage of the aqueous humor; therefore, a blockage of drainage in this location can cause increased intraocular pressure. The pupil is the connection between the anterior and posterior chamber; a collection of fluid does not occur here, for this is simply an aperture to allow light onto the retina. The vitreous body is not directly connected to the production of aqueous humor. The lacrimal sac is the upper dilated end of the nasolacrimal duct and opens up into the inferior meatus of the nasal cavity. The nasolacrimal duct has nothing to do with increased intraocular pressure.
GAS 898-899; GA 468

86 D. The glossopharyngeal nerve mediates general somatic sensation from the pharynx, the auditory tube, and from the middle ear. Painful sensations from the pharynx, including the auditory tube, can be referred to the ear by this nerve, as in this case of tonsillectomy. The auriculotemporal nerve supplies skin of the auricle and tympanic membrane and scalp. This nerve would not be involved directly or indirectly in the operation. The lesser petrosal nerve contains preganglionic parasympathetic fibers that run in the glossopharyngeal and tympanic nerves before synapsing in the otic ganglion. The vagus nerve mediates general somatic afferent supply to the auricle and external acoustic meatus; stimulation of the meatus can trigger a gag reflex or coughing reflex. The chorda tympani mediates taste for the anterior two thirds of the tongue.
GAS 912, 996-997; GA 450-451, 484, 495-496, 508, 531, 537

87 E. A tumor of the jugular canal would likely affect the glossopharyngeal, vagus, and accessory nerves as they exit the cranium through the jugular foramen. The uvula deviates toward the unaffected side of the pharyngeal muscles because of the pull of the unopposed levator veli palatini. In this case, the uvula deviates to the left, indicating that the left palatal muscles are unaffected whereas the right muscles are not working properly. The pharyngeal wall on the left side is also drawn upward by the nonparalyzed stylopharyngeus, supplied by the left glossopharyngeal nerve. The pharyngeal constrictor muscles, as well as muscles of the palate, are all innervated by the vagus nerve, except for the tensor veli palatini, which is supplied by the trigeminal nerve. The right mandibular nerve (of the mandibular division of trigeminal nerve) provides sensory innervation to the face and motor supply to the masticatory muscles and does not innervate the muscles of the pharynx. The left hypoglossal innervates the intrinsic and extrinsic muscles of the left side of the tongue. Compression or injury of this nerve would not lead to uvula deviation.
GAS 824, 826, 827; GA 436-437

88 E. An infection of the submandibular space is usually the result of a dental infection in the mandibular molar area in the floor of the mouth (Ludwig's

angina). If the patient is not treated with antibiotics promptly, the pharyngeal and submandibular swelling can lead to asphyxiation. Quinsy, also known as peritonsillar abscess, is a pus-filled inflammation of the tonsils that can occur due to tonsillitis. Ankyloglossia, which is also known as tongue-tie, is a congenital defect that results in a shortened lingual frenulum. The affected person will usually have a speech impediment. Torus palatinus is a benign bony growth on the hard palate; a torus mandibularis is a similar growth on the inside of the mandible. Such growths are usually benign and would not typically cause pain. A ranula is a mucocele found on the floor of the mouth, often resulting from dehydration in older individuals, with coagulation (inspissation) of salivary secretions. It can be caused by acute local trauma; however, they are usually asymptomatic.
GAS 797, 1030-1060; GA 504, 524-525, 527

89 **A.** The auditory (eustachian or pharyngotympanic) tube is a mucosal-lined tube that provides a direct connection from the nasopharynx to the middle ear cavity. A respiratory infection can travel from the upper respiratory tract to the oropharynx or nasopharynx and then on into the middle ear via the auditory tube. The choanae are paired openings from the nasal cavity into the nasopharynx and do not connect with the auditory tube or the middle ear. The facial canal and the internal acoustic meatus are passages for facial and vestibulocochlear nerves, respectively. Neither of these is a likely site for the spread of infection from the upper respiratory tract to the middle ear.
GAS 909, 938; GA 473-475, 504-507, 520, 524

90 **B.** The maxillary sinus drains via the middle meatus, specifically via the semilunar hiatus. The middle meatus and semilunar hiatus are located under the middle nasal concha. The inferior meatus drains the lacrimal secretions carried by the nasolacrimal duct, whereas the superior meatus drains the posterior ethmoidal and sphenoid sinuses. The nasopharynx and sphenoethmoidal recess are not situated in close proximity to the maxillary sinus and are therefore not involved in its drainage.
GAS 1014, 1015; GA 520

91 **E.** The sphenoidal sinus provides the most direct access to the pituitary gland, which is situated directly above this sinus. Neither the frontal sinus nor maxillary sinus has any direct communication with the interior of the cranial vault and would therefore not allow the surgeon a potential access point to the pituitary gland. The cribriform plate could offer a point of entry into the cranium; entry at that site would lead to damage of the olfactory cells and nerve, but it would also lead to entry into the subarachnoid space, with leakage of CSF and potential meningitis. The cribriform plates are also located too far anteriorly from the pituitary gland. The cavernous sinus is situated within the cranial vault and surrounds the pituitary gland; it is not a site for surgical entrance to the cranial cavity.
GAS 1019, 1020, 1022; GA 450, 504, 518-520

92 **B.** The gag reflex is composed of both an afferent and an efferent limb. These reflexes are mediated by the glossopharyngeal and vagus nerves, respectively. Together, the glossopharyngeal and vagus nerves are responsible for the contraction of the muscles of the pharynx involved in the gag reflex. In this case the glossopharyngeal nerve was injured when the tonsils were excised, resulting in the loss of the sensory side of the reflex. The mandibular and maxillary nerves are part of the trigeminal nerve and are thus largely associated with the sensory supply of the face, sinuses, and oral cavity. The hypoglossal nerve innervates most of the muscles of the tongue. The facial nerve is involved with taste of the anterior two thirds of the tongue; however, it does not mediate the gag reflex.
GAS 997; GA 450-451, 537

93 **B.** The recurrent laryngeal nerve is often at risk of being damaged during a thyroidectomy. Patients who have a transected or damaged recurrent laryngeal will often present with a characteristic hoarseness following surgery. The posterior cricoarytenoid is supplied by the recurrent laryngeal and would thus be impaired following damage to the nerve. The posterior cricoarytenoid is the only muscle responsible for abduction of the vocal cords, and paralysis of this muscle would result in a permanently adducted position of the involved vocal cord. The other muscles listed are all adductors of the vocal cords, and paralysis of these would not lead to closure of the airway.
GAS 967; GA 503-504, 515-517

94 **C.** The pharyngeal tonsil is situated in a slitlike space, the pharyngeal recess, in the nasopharynx behind the opening of the auditory (eustachian) tube, and a pharyngeal tonsil in this location can lead to blockage of the drainage of the auditory tube. The lingual tonsil is located in the posterior aspect of the tongue, whereas the palatine tonsil is contained within the tonsillar fossa between the palatoglossal and palatopharyngeal arches. An enlargement of the lingual tonsil or the palatine tonsil will

not occlude the auditory tube due to their location in the oropharynx. The superior pharyngeal constrictor would not be involved in occlusion of the auditory tube because it is located more posteriorly. The uvula is drawn upward during deglutition and prevents food from entering the nasopharynx; it does not block the auditory tube.
GAS 991-993; GA 12, 504-505, 520

95 **A.** Infection can spread from the nasopharynx to the middle ear by way of the auditory tube, which opens to both spaces. The first pharyngeal pouch is responsible for formation both of the auditory tube and middle ear cavity. The second pharyngeal pouch persists as the tonsillar sinus and tonsillar crypts. The third pharyngeal pouch develops into the inferior parathyroid gland and thymus, whereas the fourth pharyngeal pouch forms the remainder of the parathyroid glands and the ultimobranchial body. The sixth pharyngeal pouch is not well defined and would therefore not contribute to the development of the auditory tube.
GAS 918; GA 473-475, 504-507, 520, 524

96 **D.** The greater palatine nerve is responsible for innervation of the hard palate, or the hard part of the roof of the mouth. The lesser palatine nerve supplies the soft palate and palatine tonsil but is not involved in supply to the hard palate. The posterior superior alveolar nerve supplies multiple structures, including posterior portions of the gums, cheeks, and the upper posterior teeth. However, it is not involved in nerve supply to the hard palate. The inferior alveolar nerve has several branches, including the mental nerve, incisive branch, mylohyoid nerve, and inferior dental branch. These nerves do not supply the roof of the mouth and thus are not involved. The lingual nerve supplies taste and general sensation to the anterior two thirds of the tongue.
GAS 943, 1054, 1060; GA 529, 533-534

97 **A.** Damage to the internal laryngeal nerve would result in a general loss of sensation to the larynx above the vocal cords, leaving the patient with an inability to detect food or foreign objects in the laryngeal vestibule. The external laryngeal nerve and recurrent laryngeal nerve are both at risk during thyroidectomy. Damage to the recurrent laryngeal nerve would result in paralysis of all the laryngeal muscles except the cricothyroid; it would render the patient hoarse, with a loss of sensation below the vocal cords. Loss of the external laryngeal nerve would lead to paralysis of the cricothyroid muscle and vocal weakness. Injury to the hypoglossal nerve would result in weakness or paralysis of muscle movement of the tongue.
GAS 996, 1012; GA 514

98 **C.** Ankyloglossia (tongue-tie) is characterized by a lingual frenulum that extends all the way to the tip of the tongue. This condition can cause problems with speech, feeding, and oral hygiene as a result of the low range of motion of the tongue. Ankyloglossia can be treated surgically by cutting the lingual frenulum. None of the other procedures described would treat this condition.
GAS 1038; GA 534

99 **D.** Of the answer choices listed, the left facial nerve of the patient is the most likely to be damaged during the mastoidectomy. The facial nerve exits the skull via the stylomastoid foramen, just anterior to the mastoid process. A lesion of the facial nerve is likely to cause the symptoms described as a result of paralysis of the facial muscles. Depending upon the site of injury, the patient could also lose the chorda tympani branch of the facial nerve, leading to loss of taste from the anterior two thirds of the tongue ipsilaterally as well as loss of functions of the submandibular and sublingual salivary glands. The other nerves listed are not likely to be damaged during a mastoidectomy.
GAS 872; GA 436, 474

100 **C.** Normally the tonus of the buccinator muscle prevents the accumulation of saliva and foodstuffs in the oral vestibule. Although a lesion of the facial nerve would paralyze the other muscles listed, the buccinator is the most important muscle of the cheek.
GAS 1034-1035; GA 8, 456-457, 480, 506, 532

101 **B.** Compression of the optic chiasm can cause bitemporal hemianopia due to compression of nerve fibers coming from the nasal hemiretinas of both eyes. The optic chiasm is located in very close proximity above the pituitary gland. Compression of an optic nerve would cause complete blindness in the affected eye. Compression of an optic tract would cause homonymous hemianopia. Compression of the oculomotor nerve would cause the eye to deviate "out and down" (paralysis of the four extraocular muscles innervated by this nerve), ptosis (paralysis of levator palpebrae), and mydriasis (paralysis of constrictor pupillae). Compression of the abducens nerve would cause paralysis of the lateral rectus muscle, leading to medial deviation (adduction) of the eye.
GAS 1079; GA 447, 450-451

102 E. A lesion of the trochlear nerve causes weakness of downward medial gaze. As a result, patients with trochlear nerve lesions commonly have difficulty walking down stairs. The superior cerebellar artery branches from the basilar artery just before it bifurcates into the posterior cerebral arteries. The trochlear nerve emerges from the dorsal aspect of the midbrain and can easily be compressed by an aneurysm of the superior cerebellar artery as it wraps around the midbrain. Aneurysms of the other arteries mentioned are not likely to compress the trochlear nerve, and lesions of the nerves listed are not likely to cause problems walking down stairs.
GAS 855; GA 450-451, 465, 536

103 E. A Pancoast tumor is located in the pulmonary apex, usually in the right lung. (This is because inhaled gases tend to collect preferentially in the upper right lung, in part because of the manner of branching of the tertiary bronchi.) These tumors can involve the sympathetic chain ganglia and cause Horner's syndrome (slight ptosis and miosis). The other conditions listed are not likely to cause symptoms of Horner's syndrome. Raynaud's disease, a vascular disorder that affects the extremities, is caused by excessive tone of sympathetic vasoconstriction. Frey syndrome, a rare malady resulting from parotidectomy, is characterized by excessive facial sweating in the presence of food or when thinking about it. Bell's palsy is characterized by a lesion of the facial nerve, with weakness or paralysis of mimetic muscles. Quinsy is characterized by painful, pus-filled inflammation of the tonsils.
GAS 44-45, 214, 882, 895, 980-981; GA 190, 496

104 E. The dilator pupillae, superior tarsal muscle, and smooth muscle cells of blood vessels in the ciliary body all receive sympathetic innervation. The postsynaptic cell bodies of the sympathetic neurons that innervate these structures are located in the superior cervical ganglion. The intermediolateral cell column contains presynaptic sympathetic neurons, but it is located only at spinal cord levels T1 to L2. The other structures listed do not contain sympathetic cell bodies.
GAS 880-881, 887-889, 900-902; GA 461, 464, 468

105 B. A fracture of the lamina papyracea of the ethmoid bone is likely to entrap the medial rectus muscle, causing an inability to gaze medially. A fracture of the orbital plate of the frontal bone could perhaps entrap the superior oblique or superior rectus muscle, but this would be very unusual. A fracture of the orbital plate of the maxilla can entrap the inferior rectus or inferior oblique muscles, limiting upward gaze. A fracture of the cribriform plate could damage olfactory nerves and result in leakage of CSF (CSF rhinorrhea), with associated meningeal infection. A fracture of the greater wing of the sphenoid is not likely to entrap any extraocular muscles.
GAS 878, 1016-1017; GA 429, 437-438, 460, 486, 519

106 B. A lesion of the oculomotor nerve will cause the eye to remain in a "down and out" position. This is due to the actions of the unopposed lateral rectus (supplied by the abducens nerve) and the superior oblique (supplied by the trochlear nerve). The tertiary function of the superior oblique is to cause intorsion (internal rotation) of the eyeball, a function that is not usually seen unless the oculomotor nerve is paralyzed. The patient is also likely to present with a full or partial ptosis due to paralysis of the levator palpebrae muscle. The pupil will remain dilated because of loss of stimulation by parasympathetic fibers that innervate the constrictor pupillae muscle. Damage to the other nerves listed will not lead to the conditions described.
GAS 855, 1075; GA 450-451, 465, 469, 536

107 B. The axons of olfactory nerves run directly through the cribriform plate to synapse in the olfactory bulb. Damage to this plate can damage the nerve axons, causing anosmia (loss of the sense of smell). A fracture of the cribriform plate is not likely to entrap the eyeball. Hyperacusis can occur following paralysis of the stapedius muscle. A lesion of the vestibulocochlear nerve can cause tinnitus and/or deafness.
GAS 823; GA 437

108 C. Frey syndrome occurs following damage to parasympathetic axons in the auriculotemporal nerve. When these postganglionic cholinergic axons grow peripherally after parotid surgery, they establish synapses upon the cholinergic sweat glands, which are innervated normally only by sympathetic fibers. As the peripheral nerves make new connections, aberrant connections can be formed between the auriculotemporal nerve and other glands (not usually innervated by the auriculotemporal nerve). This results in flushing and sweating in response to the thought, smell, or taste of food, instead of the previous, normal salivary secretion by the parotid gland.
GAS 49, 864; GA 455, 483-485

109 B. The posterior cricoarytenoid muscle is the only abductor of the larynx that opens the rima glottidis and rotates the arytenoid cartilages laterally. All of the other listed muscles have adduction as part of

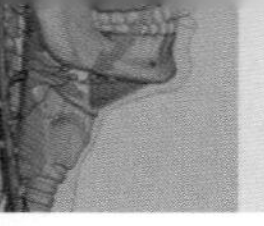

their function and thus are not required to maintain the airway.
GAS 1006; GA 507, 513

110 **B.** The palatine tonsils are highly vascular and are primarily supplied by the tonsillar branch of the facial artery; therefore, care is taken to preserve this artery while performing a tonsillectomy. The palatine tonsil also receives arterial supply from the ascending pharyngeal, the dorsal lingual, and the lesser palatine, but the supply from the facial artery is by far the most significant.
GAS 990, 992, 993, 1051; GA 12, 504, 532-534

111 **A.** The inner surface of the tympanic membrane is supplied by the glossopharyngeal nerve. The auricular branches of the facial and vagus nerves and the auriculotemporal branch of the trigeminal nerve innervate the external surface of the tympanic membrane. The great auricular nerve arises from C2 and C3 and supplies the posterior auricle and skin over the parotid gland. The lingual nerve does not have anything to do with sensory supply of the tympanic membrane.
GAS 904-906; GA 473, 476

112 **C.** The infraorbital branch of the maxillary division of the trigeminal nerve exits the front of the skull below the orbit through the infraorbital foramen. A needle inserted into the infraorbital foramen and directed posteriorly will pass through the foramen rotundum to reach the trigeminal ganglion and the beginning of the maxillary division of the trigeminal nerve. The mandibular division of the trigeminal nerve exits the skull through the foramen ovale. The middle meningeal artery exits the infratemporal fossa through the foramen spinosum to enter the cranial cavity. The inferior alveolar branch of the mandibular division passes into the mandibular foramen to then descend in the jaw to supply the mandibular teeth. The foramen magnum is where the spinal cord exits the skull and where the spinal accessory nerve ascends into the skull after arising from the cervical spinal cord and brainstem.
GAS 867, 886, 943, 944; GA 462, 487, 521, 528

113 **A.** If there is an injury to the internal laryngeal nerve, there is a loss of sensation above the vocal cords. In this case, for internal laryngeal injury to occur, one must conclude that the operative field extended above the position of the thyroid gland to the level of the thyrohyoid membrane. The external laryngeal nerve can be injured during a thyroidectomy, but its injury would result in paralysis of the cricothyroid muscle and weakened voice/hoarseness. Injury of the glossopharyngeal nerve would result in more widespread symptoms, including loss of sensation from the pharynx, posterior tongue, and middle ear. Injury to the hypoglossal nerve would cause deficits in motor activity of the tongue. Damage to the recurrent laryngeal nerve would result in paralysis of most laryngeal muscles, with possible respiratory obstruction, hoarseness, and loss of sensation below the vocal cords.
GAS 996, 1012; GA 514

114 **A.** The loose areolar connective tissue layer is known as the "danger zone" because hematoma can spread easily from this layer into the skull by means of emissary veins that pass into and through the bones of the skull. None of the other scalp layers listed is referred to as the "danger zone."
GAS 874; GA 442

115 **A.** The carotid sinus is a baroreceptor that can be targeted for carotid massage to decrease blood pressure. The carotid sinus receptors are sensitive to changes in pressure. For this reason, sustained compression of the carotid sinuses can lead to unconsciousness or death as the heart rate is reflexively reduced. The carotid body is a chemoreceptor, responsive to the balance of oxygen and carbon dioxide. Neither the thyroid gland nor the parathyroid gland has anything to do with acute control of blood pressure due to mechanical stimuli. The inferior cervical ganglion fuses with the first thoracic ganglion to form the stellate ganglion. It gives rise to the inferior cervical cardiac nerve and provides postganglionic sympathetic supply to the upper limb.
GAS 959; GA 452, 498

116 **C.** The thyroidea ima artery supplies the thyroid gland and ascends in the front of the trachea; therefore, it would be easily injured in an emergency tracheostomy with a midline incision over the trachea. The inferior thyroid branch of the thyrocervical trunk does not run along the front of the trachea in such a position that a midline incision could damage it. The cricothyroid branch of the superior thyroid artery passes across the cricothyroid ligament, well above the site of incision. Arterial bleeding would not result from damage to either the middle thyroid vein or the jugular venous arch.
GAS 210, 967; GA 500-501

117 **D.** A torn cerebral vein often results in a relatively slow-bleeding subdural hematoma. Such a hematoma can be involved in gradual compression

of the brain, resulting in confusion, dizziness, clumsiness, and memory loss. There would be no sign of blood in the CSF because the bleeding is into the subdural space, not the subarachnoid space. This would fit the description of symptoms in this case. Middle meningeal artery rupture results in an epidural hematoma, which is much more acute and often includes a brief period of unconsciousness followed by a lucid interval and can proceed to death if the bleeding is left untreated. Fracture of the pterion also can result in an epidural hematoma because the middle meningeal artery is the adjacent vasculature mentioned. Rupture of the anterior communicating artery would result in a subarachnoid hematoma, and there would be blood in the CSF upon lumbar puncture. In a cavernous sinus thrombosis there would be cranial nerve involvement due to compression of those nerves that run through or near the cavernous sinus, including the oculomotor, trochlear, trigeminal (maxillary and mandibular divisions), and abducens nerves.
GAS 834, 845-846; GA 445

118 **D.** Paralysis of the right accessory and hypoglossal nerves. Drooping of the right shoulder occurs as a result of paralysis of the trapezius as a result of injury to the right accessory nerve, which supplies that muscle. Loss of the right accessory nerve would also result in weakness in turning the head to the left, a function of the right sternocleidomastoid muscle, which is supplied by this nerve. The tongue deviation to the right is due to the unopposed activity of the left tongue muscles since the right hypoglossal nerve (which innervates the right tongue muscles) is affected. The other combinations of affected cranial nerves would not produce the specific symptoms described here.
GAS 855, 1040; GA 37, 450-451, 494, 497, 531, 537

119 **C.** The neural cell bodies whose axons synapse in the pterygopalatine ganglion are located in the superior salivatory nucleus, which is in the pons; this nucleus provides the GVE fibers of the facial nerve for lacrimal and salivary secretion. The superior cervical ganglion is a sympathetic ganglion containing postganglionic neurons and is not concerned with the pterygopalatine ganglion, which is a parasympathetic ganglion. The Edinger-Westphal nucleus is located in the midbrain and contains the cell bodies of the GVE fibers of the oculomotor nerve, which are responsible for constriction of the pupil via synapse in the ciliary ganglion and supply to the sphincter pupillae muscle and accommodation via the ciliary muscle. The inferior salivatory nucleus is located in the medulla and gives origin to GVE fibers of the glossopharyngeal nerve to the otic ganglion for secretion of saliva from the parotid gland.
GAS 853, 883-884, 917, 944; GA 463, 487

120 **B.** A branch of the facial artery would be of primary concern because its branches supply the oropharynx and it is the primary source of arterial supply to the palatine tonsil. The location of the lingual artery is inferior to the oropharynx and it would be less likely to be injured in the event of a surgical procedure. The superior laryngeal artery is also located lower and would not be subject to injury by surgery in the area of the oropharynx. The ascending pharyngeal artery arises in the carotid triangle from the external carotid artery and gives rise to pharyngeal, palatine, inferior tympanic, and meningeal branches. This vessel is located inferiorly to the site of surgery. Terminal branches of the descending palatine artery could be encountered at the upper pole of the palatine tonsil, but the main stem of the vessel would not be endangered in the surgical treatment here.
GAS 990, 992, 993; GA 12, 504, 532-534

121 **A.** Infection in the danger area of the face can lead to cavernous sinus thrombosis because infection spreads from the nasal venous tributary to the angular vein, then on to the superior ophthalmic vein, which passes into the cavernous sinus. None of the other routes listed would be correct for drainage from the danger area of the face.
GAS 871; GA 11, 458-459, 467, 485, 491

122 **C.** The thrombus may pass through the central vein of the retina to reach the cavernous sinus. The patient would suffer blindness because the central vein is the only vein draining the retina and if it is occluded, blindness will ensue. The subarachnoid space would not be associated with the blindness experienced. Thrombus of the central artery would not cause cavernous sinus thrombophlebitis. The optic chiasm is a neural structure that does not transmit thrombi. The ciliary ganglion is a parasympathetic ganglion; a thrombus in the cavernous sinus would not pass through it.
GAS 899; GA 467

123 **B.** Aqueous humor is secreted by the ciliary body into the posterior chamber of the eye. The humor flows through the pupil into the anterior chamber and then is filtered by a trabecular meshwork, then drained by the canal of Schlemm. The pupil is the opening in the iris, which leads from the posterior

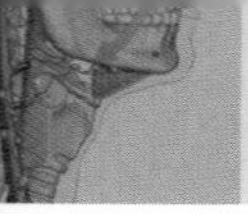

chamber to the anterior chamber. Vitreous humor, not aqueous humor, is found in the vitreous body. The lacrimal sac is involved with tears, not the secretion of aqueous humor.
GAS 898-899; GA 468

124 **A.** If there is CSF between the compressed brain and overlying skull bones, the problem must be a condition of communicating hydrocephalus, with inadequate drainage through the arachnoid granulations into the superior sagittal sinus. There is no evidence of obstruction of CSF flow somewhere in the ventricular system. The other choices listed are all examples of noncommunicating hydrocephalus that result from obstruction, not just overproduction or filtration problems.
GAS 101, 834; GA 445

125 **C.** The superior sagittal sinus would most likely be the source of the bleeding because it attaches anteriorly to the crista galli and because of the slow nature of the bleed. The middle meningeal artery would not be a good answer because its location is near the pterion on the temporal aspect of the skull but its bleeding would be profuse, not slow. The great cerebral vein (of Galen) is located posteriorly in the cranial cavity and is not in the right location for an injury of this type to disrupt it. The straight dural venous sinus is also posterior, receiving the draining of the inferior sagittal sinus and the great vein (of Galen). It drains posteriorly to the confluence of sinuses. The superior ophthalmic vein drains from the orbit to the cavernous sinus; further, it is located inferiorly to the crista galli and is not directly related to the superior sagittal sinus.
GAS 822, 842, 843, 1026-1027; GA 445

126 **C.** For proper movements of the eye to occur, all cranial nerves of the extraocular eye muscles are required (oculomotor, trochlear, and abducens nerves). The inferior division of the oculomotor innervates the inferior rectus, the medial rectus, and the inferior oblique. Lateral movement of the eye is initiated by the lateral rectus (abducens nerve), assisted thereafter by the superior oblique (trochlear nerve). The inferior rectus (inferior division of the oculomotor nerve) balances the upward deviation exerted by the superior rectus (superior division of the oculomotor nerve). The medial rectus (superior division of the oculomotor nerve) must relax to facilitate the lateral excursion. Answers A, B, and D all have branches of the trigeminal nerve, which have no role in motor movement of the eye. Finally, for answer E, the superior division innervates the superior rectus and the levator palpebrae; therefore, C is the best answer.
GAS 887-891; GA 464

127 **E.** The middle of the vocal cord would be the most likely location of the tumor because there is no direct lymph drainage from this region. All other locations mentioned are drained by the lymphatics. Areas above the vocal cords are drained by the superior deep cervical nodes, and areas below the vocal cords drain to the pretracheal nodes before draining into the inferior deep cervical nodes.
GAS 1011; GA 502-503

128 **B.** When a berry aneurysm ruptures, the blood flows into the subarachnoid space and therefore mixes with CSF; thus, blood would be present in the CSF when a lumbar puncture is performed. The pterion overlies the anterior branch of the middle meningeal vessels, and damage to these vessels would result in an epidural hematoma, with compression of the brain. Leakage of branches of the middle meningeal artery within the temporal bone would cause blood vessels within the bone to leak, without direct connection to the CSF fluid. A tear of the cerebral vein in the superior sagittal sinus would lead to a subdural hematoma, in which the blood collects in the subdural space, without entry to CSF. The occlusion of the internal carotid artery by way of clot would not lead to leakage of blood into the CSF.
GAS 840-841; GA 452

129 **D.** The nucleus ambiguus gives rise to efferent motor fibers of the vagus nerve, which supply the laryngeal and pharyngeal muscles. If supply to this region is interrupted, an individual loses the swallowing, cough, and gag reflexes. The nucleus solitarius is located in the brainstem and is responsible for receiving general visceral sensation and taste from the facial, glossopharyngeal, and vagus nerves. The trigeminal motor nucleus contains motor neurons that innervate muscles of mastication, the tensor tympani, tensor veli palatini, mylohyoid, and anterior belly of the digastric. The dorsal motor nucleus contains the cell bodies of preganglionic parasympathetic fibers of the vagus nerve innervating the heart muscle and smooth musculature and glands of the respiratory and intestinal tract. The superior ganglion of the vagus contains cell bodies of general somatic afferent fibers, and the inferior ganglion of the vagus is chiefly visceral afferent in function concerning sensations (with the exclusion of painful sensation) from the heart, lungs, larynx, and alimentary tract.
GAS 807, 849-851, 853-854; GA 450-451

130 C. Just before it passes into the mandible to supply the lower teeth and chin, the inferior alveolar nerve gives rise to the mylohyoid nerve, a motor nerve supplying the mylohyoid and anterior belly of the digastric. The geniohyoid muscle is innervated by motor fibers from spinal nerve C1 that run with the hypoglossal nerve. The hyoglossus muscle is innervated by the hypoglossal nerve. The stylohyoid muscle is innervated by the facial nerve. The palatoglossus muscle is innervated by the vagus nerve.
GAS 934-936; GA 480, 483, 528

131 A. The superior cerebellar artery arises near the termination of the basilar artery, passes immediately below the oculomotor nerve, and eventually winds around the cerebral peduncle, close to the trochlear nerve, as it continues on toward the upper surface of the cerebellum where it will divide into branches that anastomose with the inferior cerebellar arteries. The trochlear nerve passes between the posterior cerebral artery and the superior cerebellar artery, and therefore a hematoma of the superior cerebellar artery can easily injure the trochlear nerve, which runs alongside the internal carotid artery and then enters the orbit through the superior orbital fissure. The facial and vestibulocochlear nerves both enter the skull via the internal acoustic meatus (or internal auditory meatus) in the temporal bone and do not have an intimate relationship with the superior cerebellar artery. The glossopharyngeal nerve passes through the jugular foramen, and as it exits from the skull it passes forward between the internal jugular vein and internal carotid artery.
GAS 837, 838; GA 451-452, 454

132 D. Subdural bleeding usually results from tears in veins that cross the subdural space, between the dura and the arachnoid. This bleeding may cause a gradual increase in intracranial pressure and may result in leakage of venous blood over the right cerebral hemisphere with a variable rate of progression. A subarachnoid bleed is due to rupture of an artery into the subarachnoid space surrounding the brain, between the arachnoid membrane and the pia mater. Hydrocephalus may result if the subarachnoid bleeding or subsequent fibrosis create obstructions to CSF flow through the subarachnoid space or drainage of the CSF. Epidural bleeding results in most cases from tearing of the middle meningeal artery, and this rapidly expanding, space-occupying lesion can cause death within 12 hours. Intracerebral bleeding into the brain parenchyma is focal bleeding from a blood vessel into the brain parenchyma, most likely caused by hypertension and/or atherosclerosis. Typical symptoms include focal neurologic deficits, with abrupt onset of headache, nausea, and impairment of consciousness. Bleeding into the cerebral ventricular system may be due to trauma or hemorrhage of blood from nearby arteries, especially those related to the supply of the choroid plexus.
GAS 845-847; GA 445

133 B. The lateral pterygoid muscle is a muscle of mastication innervated by the lateral pterygoid nerve of the mandibular division of the trigeminal nerve. The lateral pterygoid acts to protrude the mandible and open the jaw. The anterior portion of temporalis is a muscle of mastication innervated by the deep temporal nerves of the mandibular division of the trigeminal nerve that elevates the mandible when contracted. The medial pterygoid muscle is a muscle of mastication innervated by the mandibular division of the trigeminal nerve. This muscle closes the jaw and works with the contralateral medial pterygoid in side-to-side (grinding) jaw movements. The masseter muscle is a muscle of mastication innervated by the mandibular division of the trigeminal nerve that specifically assists in chewing. The platysma is a thin muscle of facial expression that lies within the superficial fascia of the neck and lower face. It is innervated by the cervical branch of the facial nerve. The platysma produces a slight wrinkling of the surface of the skin of the neck in an oblique direction, depresses the lower jaw, and draws down the lower lip and angle of the mouth.
GAS 925, 930-931; GA 480-482, 484

134 B. The order of tooth eruption is a follows: inferior medial incisors (6 to 8 months), superior medial incisors (8 to 10 months), first molar (6 to 8 months), superior lateral incisors (8 to 10 months), and finally inferior lateral incisors (12 to 14 months).
GAS 1056-1057; GA 525-529

135 D. The sigmoid sinus collects venous blood from the transverse sinuses and empties it into a small cavity known as the jugular bulb, the inferior portion of which is located beneath the bony floor of the middle ear cavity. A paraganglioma is a tumor that may originate from paraganglia cells found in the middle ear and on the jugular bulb. Tumors that originate from the jugular bulb can grow to fill the entire bulb and may effectively block blood flow to the heart from that side of the brain. Blood flow from the brain is gradually diverted toward the opposite sigmoid sinus and jugular bulb, causing the opposite venous system to expand and accommodate increased blood flow. The cochlea and lateral semicircular ca-

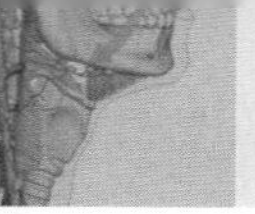

nals are located in the inner ear and are not directly affected by such a tumor. The internal carotid artery is related to the anterior wall of the middle ear cavity and is not likely to be affected by a tumor penetrating the middle ear. The sigmoid venous sinus collects venous blood beneath the temporal bone and follows a tortuous course to the jugular foramen where it becomes continuous with the internal jugular vein at the jugular bulb. The aditus ad antrum is the entrance to the mastoid antrum, which is the common cavity in the mastoid bone into which mastoid air cells open. Below the aditus ad antrum is an elevation of hollow bone, the pyramid of the stapes, which is occupied by the stapedius muscle.
GAS 842-844; GA 445

136 **E.** The lingual nerve supplies sensory innervation to the mucous membrane of the anterior two thirds of the tongue, taste sensation to the anterior part of the tongue, and parasympathetic fibers to the oral salivary glands. The chorda tympani branch of the facial nerve is responsible for carrying taste fibers from the anterior two thirds of the tongue and preganglionic parasympathetic fibers for the submandibular ganglion. Injury to the lingual nerve at its origin, before it joins with the chorda tympani, will result in loss of general sensation of the tongue, but with preservation of taste and salivary function. Injury to the glossopharyngeal nerve would result in loss of general sensory and taste fibers from the posterior third of the tongue and parasympathetic supply for the parotid gland. Injury to the superior laryngeal nerve, a branch of the vagus, would result in loss of sensation from the larynx above the vocal folds.
GAS 1040, 1043, 1045; GA 480, 484, 528-529, 532, 534

137 **A.** Papilledema is optic disc swelling ("edema of the papilla") that is caused by increased intracranial pressure and increased CSF pressure. If a lumbar puncture is performed in a patient with elevated CSF pressure and fluid is withdrawn from the lumbar cistern, the brain can become displaced caudally and the brainstem is pushed against the tentorial notch. This is a potentially fatal complication. Separation of the pars optica retinae anterior to the ora serrata, or retinal detachment, may result in vision loss or blindness. A hemorrhage from medial retinal branches may result in damage to the fovea centralis and can result in macular degeneration. Opacity of the lens (cataracts) will cause gradual yellowing and may reduce the perception of blue colors. Cataracts typically progress slowly to cause vision loss and are potentially blinding if untreated. Compression of the optic disc, resulting from increased intrabulbar pressure, will lead to an excessive accumulation of serous fluid in the tissue space.
GAS 894; GA 468

138 **E.** Within the cavernous sinus the abducens nerve is in intimate contact with the internal carotid artery. Therefore, an aneurysm of the internal carotid artery could quickly cause tension or compression on the abducens nerve. This would result in ipsilateral paralysis of abduction of the pupil. Inability to gaze downward and medially would be due to the trochlear nerve. Complete ptosis would be a result of a complete lesion in the oculomotor nerve, which is not apparent here. Bilateral loss of accommodation and loss of pupillary reflex would be the result of bilateral loss of the oculomotor nerve, which is not likely in this situation. Finally, ipsilateral loss of the consensual corneal reflex is a result of loss of both the ophthalmic division of the trigeminal nerve and the facial nerve, supplying the afferent and efferent limbs of the reflex, respectively.
GAS 844; GA 445, 450, 452

139 **D.** It is necessary to anesthetize the conjunctival covering of the sclera, which is supplied by the nasociliary branch of the ophthalmic nerve. To do that, the needle should be placed through the upper eyelid deeply toward the orbital apex to infiltrate the nasociliary nerve, and also between the orbital septum and the palpebral musculature laterally to anesthetize lateral sensory supply from the lacrimal nerve and (perhaps) twigs from the maxillary nerve. The lacrimal fossa, which is occupied by the lacrimal sac portion of the nasolacrimal duct, is too medial, whereas the supraorbital foramen is above the eye. Injections into either location would not result in anesthetizing of the sclera. Answers A and E both result in puncturing of the sclera and would most likely cause further damage to the eye.
GAS 894-897; GA 465, 469

140 **E.** During a puncture wound as described in this case, passing up from below the chin, the nail would first pierce the platysma, then the anterior belly of the digastric, then the mylohyoid, then the geniohyoid, and finally the genioglossus.
GAS 858, 862, 954-956, 1036-1038; GA 492, 504

141 **A.** The anterior division of the facial nerve passes through the parotid gland and is therefore at risk during surgery of the parotid gland. Since this patient's symptoms involved paralysis of the muscles of the lower lip, the branch of the facial nerve that supplies these muscles, the marginal mandibu-

lar branch, is the one that has suffered the iatrogenic injury.
GAS 865; GA 456, 458-459, 480

142 **A.** During embryologic development of the pituitary gland, an outgrowth from the roof of the pharynx (Rathke's pouch) grows cephalad and comprises the anterior lobe (pars distalis) of the pituitary gland. Since this gland normally occupies the sella turcica, it is most likely a tumor derived from the Rathke's pouch that is extending up into the sella turcica and the space just above it, the suprasellar space.
GAS 1079; GA 446-447, 450

143 **A.** In holoprosencephaly, loss of midline structures results in malformations of the brain and face. There is a single telencephalic vesicle, fused eyes, and a single nasal chamber. Also, there is often hypoplasia of the olfactory bulbs, olfactory tracts, and corpus callosum. Children with Smith-Lemli-Opitz syndrome have craniofacial and limb defects and 5% have holoprosencephaly. Schizencephaly is rare and is characterized by large clefts in the cerebral hemispheres, which in some cases cause a loss in brain tissue. Exencephaly is caused by failure of the cephalic part of the neural tube to close; therefore, the skull does not close, leaving the brain exposed. Meningohydroencephalocele is a deficit of the cranium involving the squamous part of the occipital bone and, in some cases, the posterior aspect of the foramen magnum. It can include the meninges if the herniation or protruding brain includes part of the ventricular system.
GAS 812-814; GA 430-431

144 **C.** Usually, deficits of the cranium involve the squamous part of the occipital bone and, in some cases, the posterior aspect of the foramen magnum. If the herniation or protruding brain includes part of the ventricular system (most likely the posterior horn of the lateral ventricles), then it is referred to as meningohydroencephalocele. The deficit in the squamous part of the occipital bone usually occurs at the posterior fontanelle of the skull.
GAS 815-817, 821, 826, 827; GA 429, 434-435

145 **B.** The rostral neuropore closes during the fourth week of development. If this does not occur, the forebrain primordium is abnormal and the calvaria or vault fails to develop. Toxoplasmosis infection during embryologic development leads to microcephaly, in which the brain and calvaria are small in size. These patients usually have mental retardation due to an undeveloped brain. An ossification defect in the bones of the skull is often a result of hydrocephalus. Caudal displacement of the cerebellar structures would not lead to an undeveloped calvaria or vault. Maternal alcohol abuse leads to intrauterine growth restriction, causing microcephaly and mental retardation.
GAS 812-818; GA 437

146 **B.** Holoprosencephaly is caused by failure of the prosencephalon to properly divide into two cerebral hemispheres. In severe cases, this is incompatible with life, but in less severe cases, such as the one presented here, babies have normal or near-normal brain development, sometimes with facial abnormalities. In this case the abnormal development of the forebrain has pushed some of the cerebellum caudally through the foramen magnum, probably due to the spina bifida cystica.
GAS 835-846; GA 446-450

147 **A.** Congenital deafness is due to a maldevelopment of the conducting system of the middle and external ear or neurosensory structures of the inner ear. Rubella infection during a critical time of ear development can lead to a malformed spiral organ (neurosensory hearing loss) or congenital fixation of the stapes, resulting in conducting hearing loss. Failure of the second pharyngeal arch to form would lead to an ear without a stapes bone. However, in congenital deafness, there is a fixation of the stapes. Failure of the dorsal portion of the first pharyngeal cleft would lead to undeveloped malleus and incus. These are not affected in congenital deafness, however. Abnormal development of the auricular hillocks does not lead to deafness but is a marker for other potential congenital anomalies.
GAS 902, 913-919; GA 472-473, 476

148 **A.** With congenital cataracts, the lens appears opaque and grayish white and blindness will result. Infection by teratogenic agents such as rubella virus (German measles) can cause congenital cataracts. This infection can affect the development of the lens, which has a critical period of development between the fourth and seventh week. Choroid fissure failure would lead to coloboma, a condition that can lead to a cleft and eye abnormalities but not congenital cataracts. A persistent hyaloid artery would not lead to a cataract but rather a freely moving, wormlike structure (as interpreted by the patient) projecting on the optic disc. Toxoplasmosis infection would lead to microcephaly and eventually mental retardation due to an undeveloped brain. Similarly, cytomegalovirus would cause microcephaly and mental retardation.
GAS 899; GA 461, 468

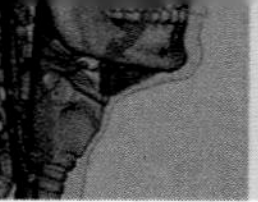

149 D. A mutation of the *PAX6* gene usually results in congenital aphakia (absence of lens) and aniridia (absence of iris). Cyclopia is a condition in which there is a single eye and is usually caused by a mutation of the *SONIC HEDGEHOG* gene *(SHH)*, leading to a loss of midline tissue and underdevelopment of the forebrain and frontonasal prominence. Coloboma occurs if the choroid fissure fails to fuse, which is usually caused by a mutation of the *PAX2* gene. Anophthalmia is a disorder in which there is a complete absence of the eye. In microphthalmia, the eye is small in development, typically less than two thirds its normal size. This condition usually results from an infection such as cytomegalovirus and toxoplasmosis.
GAS 898-902; GA 461-471

150 A. In hemifacial microsomia the craniofacial anomalies that usually occur involve small and flat maxillary, temporal, and zygomatic bones. Ear and eye anomalies also occur with this syndrome. Ear abnormalities include tumors and dermoids of the eyeball. Treacher Collins syndrome is normally characterized by malar hypoplasia (caused by undeveloped zygomatic bones), mandibular hypoplasia, down-slanted palpebral fissures, lower eyelid colobomas, and malformed ears. Robin Sequence is caused by an altered first arch structure, with the development of the mandible most affected. Infants with Robin Sequence normally have micrognathia, cleft palate, and glossoptosis. DiGeorge syndrome is a severe craniofacial defect that includes velocardiofacial syndrome and conotruncal anomalies face syndrome. It is characterized by cleft palate, cardiac defects, abnormal face, thymic hypoplasia, and hypocalcemia.
GAS 813; GA 430-431

151 A. Abnormal face, cardiac defects, thymic hypoplasia, cleft palate, and hypocalcemia are characteristics of DiGeorge syndrome. A deletion of the long arm of chromosome 22 (22q11) causes this developmental defect. A defect of the *SONIC HEDGEHOG* gene *(SHH)* can lead to cyclopia. *PAX2* and *PAX6* gene mutations lead to malformations of the eye. Specifically, *PAX2* mutations are responsible for coloboma, and *PAX6* mutations characterize congenital aphakia and aniridia. Turner syndrome (47XXY) is characterized by webbed neck and small stature.
GAS 206; GA 102

152 A. The first pharyngeal arch, which is often associated with the mandible, is responsible for development of Meckel's cartilage, malleus, incus, and mandible. Additionally, it is innervated by the trigeminal nerve, specifically the mandibular division that innervates the muscles of mastication. This patient presents with features characteristic of developmental defects in the first arch. The second pharyngeal arch gives rise to the stapes, styloid process, lesser cornu, Reichert's cartilage, and the upper half of the hyoid bone. It is innervated by the facial nerve. The third pharyngeal arch is responsible for formation of the greater cornu and the lower half of the hyoid bone and is innervated by the glossopharyngeal nerve. The fourth and sixth pharyngeal arches give rise to the laryngeal cartilages, in addition to being innervated by the vagus nerve.
GAS 848-849; GA 478-483

153 B. The maxillary sinus arises late in fetal development and is the only sinus present at birth. The frontal and sphenoid sinuses often develop at approximately 2 years of age from the anterior ethmoid air cells and the posterior ethmoid air cells, respectively.
GAS 797, 879, 1018, 1020, 1022; GA 487, 518, 525

154 A. Meroencephaly often results from a failure of the rostral neuropore to close during the fourth week of development. The calvaria is absent, with a resultant extrusion of the brain from the cranium. Defects are often found along the vertebral column as well. Cytomegalovirus infection is a major cause of microcephaly, in which both the brain and cranium are drastically reduced in size. However, there is no extrusion of the brain from the cranium. The hypophyseal diverticulum is associated with the pituitary gland and usually regresses to leave only a remnant stalk. Failure of this diverticulum to develop would not be associated with meroencephaly. Neural crest cells give rise to a variety of cell types, and abnormal formation would likewise not be associated with meroencephaly.
GAS 812, 818; GA 437

155 B. The retropharyngeal space extends from the inferior aspect of the skull to the posterior mediastinum. An infection or abscess in this space could thus travel toward the posterior mediastinum. The retropharyngeal space is enclosed between the visceral fascia covering the posterior wall of the pharynx and the alar layer of the prevertebral fascia. The alar fascia is formed from bilateral anterior extensions of the prevertebral fascia. Between the alar fascia and the more posterior prevertebral fascia covering the skeletal musculature is the so-called danger space of the neck. This space is continuous superiorly to the base of the skull and continues inferiorly through the posterior mediastinum to the level of the respiratory dia-

phragm. The alar fascia is continuous with the carotid sheath and provides the posterior boundary for the retropharyngeal space. Attachments of the alar fascia to the retropharyngeal fascia result in separation of the pretracheal space from the retropharyngeal space. The prevertebral fascia invests the vertebral column and the intrinsic muscles of the back. The pretracheal fascia encloses the trachea and larynx, whereas the buccopharyngeal fascia invests the superior pharyngeal constrictor and buccinator muscles.
GAS 949, 950, 985; GA 490

156 **A.** An inferior fracture of the orbit would likely damage the infraorbital nerve. A blow-out fracture often results in a displaced orbital wall, and in this case, the inferior wall. The infraorbital nerve leaves the skull immediately inferior to the inferior aspect of the orbit, via the infraorbital foramen. Thus, this nerve is the most likely to be damaged. The frontal nerve courses superiorly over the orbital contents before dividing into the supratrochlear and supraorbital nerves. The optic nerve is located behind the eyeball and travels posteriorly away from the orbit to enter the cranium. These nerves are therefore unlikely to be damaged.
GAS 867, 885-886, 943, 944; GA 462, 487, 521, 528

157 **C.** The Rinne test is often employed during physical examination to determine possible conduction hearing loss. A tuning fork is struck and placed on the mastoid process. It is then placed near the external ear until the patient can no longer detect vibrations. In a normal healthy patient the air conduction will be better than the bone conduction. The Rinne test is often used in conjunction with the Weber test to rule out sensoroneural hearing loss.
GAS 1062; GA 432, 434, 436, 475, 479, 492

158 **A.** The right and left recurrent laryngeal nerves loop around the right subclavian artery and the arch of the aorta, respectively. These nerves then travel superiorly in the tracheoesophageal groove to the larynx. Damage to the recurrent laryngeal as a result of surgical intervention or the presence of a tumor in the tracheoesophageal groove would render the patient hoarse. This hoarseness is due to a lack of innervation by the recurrent laryngeal nerve to most of the muscles of the larynx. Damage to the internal laryngeal nerve would cause a loss of sensation above the vocal cords, in addition to a loss of taste on the epiglottis. Damage to the external laryngeal, which can occur during thyroidectomy, will result in a loss of innervation to the cricothyroid muscle, with resultant vocal weakness. Patients with this lesion will often present with a fatigued voice. The vagus nerve gives rise to the recurrent laryngeal nerves; damage to this nerve, however, would result in numerous symptoms beyond just hoarseness.
GAS 214, 966, 967, 978-979, 1013, 1014, 1072; GA 82, 101, 104, 508, 514, 516

159 **B.** Diploic veins are responsible for communication between the veins of the scalp and the venous sinuses of the brain. Diploic veins are situated within the layers of bone of the skull and connect the emissary veins of the scalp to the venous sinuses located between two layers of dura. The diploe are of clinical significance in that the diploic veins within this layer provide a pathway of communication between the veins of the scalp and underlying venous sinuses of the brain, by means of emissary veins. The emissary veins and diploe provide a potential vascular pathway of infection. The supratrochlear and supraorbital veins are located superficially on the scalp, immediately superior to the upper eyelid, and do not communicate directly with the venous sinuses of the brain. The anterior cerebral vein is an intracranial vein and, as such, does not maintain a direct communication with the external veins of the scalp. The superior sagittal sinus receives blood from the cerebral, diploic, and emissary veins; however, it does not provide a pathway of communication to the veins of the scalp.
GAS 842; GA 442

160 **C.** The oculomotor nerve passes between the posterior cerebral artery (PCA) and the superior cerebellar artery near the junction of the midbrain and pons. The optic nerve arises near the circle of Willis close to the internal carotid artery. Its location would thus prevent compression following an aneurysm at the PCA and superior cerebellar artery. Although the trochlear nerve could be compressed by the superior cerebellar artery, it would not likely be damaged by an aneurysm of the PCA. The abducens nerve is located in the pons, and the vagus is situated near the postolivary sulcus in the medulla. Neither of these nerves is likely to be compressed by the arteries mentioned here due to their more distal location.
GAS 837-838; GA 451-452

161 **C.** A blow-out fracture of the medial wall of the orbit would likely render the medial rectus nonfunctional by entrapment of the muscle between the edges of the cracked medial wall. The medial rectus is responsible for adduction of the eye, but in this case the muscle acts as a tether or anchor on the eyeball, preventing lateral excursion (abduction) of the eye.

There is no nerve damage here, and the muscle is not paralyzed. The lateral rectus is responsible for abduction of the eye, and the inferior rectus rotates the eyeball downward. Damage to these muscles or their nerve supply would result in an inability to move the eye laterally and inferiorly, respectively.
GAS 887-891; GA 461-467

162 **A.** The inferior rectus and inferior oblique muscles are entrapped in the crack between the parts of the fractured orbital floor. Normally, the superior rectus and the inferior oblique are responsible for an upward movement of the eyeball. In this case, however, the broken orbital plate of the maxilla has snared or entrapped the inferior rectus and inferior oblique muscles, causing them to act as anchors on the eyeball, preventing upward movement of the eye. The muscles are not necessarily damaged, nor is there any nerve injury in this patient. Freeing the muscles from the bone will allow free movement of the eye again, barring any other injury. Damage to the medial and inferior recti would result in a laterally and superiorly deviated eye. The inferior oblique rotates the eye upward and laterally. Damage to this muscle would therefore cause the pupil to be directed somewhat downward. Damage to the medial rectus would result in lateral deviation of the eyeball. The inferior rectus is responsible for downward movement of the eye, and damage to this muscle would result in a superiorly deviated eyeball or an inability to gaze upward symmetrically with both eyes.
GAS 886-897; GA 461-467

163 **A.** A herpes rash on the dorsum of the nose is known as Hutchinson's sign. This indicates that the virus is located in cell bodies of the ophthalmic division of the trigeminal nerve. This nerve branches into nasociliary, frontal, and lacrimal branches. The nasociliary nerve has direct branches that carry sensory innervation from the eye. The nasociliary nerve also gives off the ethmoidal nerves that innervate the superior nasal mucosa, in addition to providing the origin of the dorsal nasal nerve. The supratrochlear nerve is a branch of the frontal nerve and carries sensory innervation from the skin superior to the orbit. The infraorbital nerve is a branch from the maxillary division of the trigeminal nerve and carries sensory innervation from the skin of the face between the orbit and the upper lips.
GAS 894-897; GA 465, 469

164 **A.** Anesthetics are injected into the submuscular layer of delicate (areolar) connective tissue, the layer that contains nerves of the eyelid. This space is continuous with the "danger zone" of the scalp. A blow to the forehead can result in a "black eye," with the passage of blood into the submuscular space. Infections can, likewise, pass within this space. One can insert a needle through the upper eyelid, near the orbital margin, and then direct it deeply toward the orbital apex. The anesthetic can there infiltrate the branches of the ophthalmic nerve, including its nasociliary branch, resulting in anesthesia of the area.
GAS 879-883; GA 461-462

165 **A.** Paralysis of the trochlear nerve results in loss of ability for the affected eye to be directed downward when the pupil is in the adducted position (the primary action of the superior oblique muscle). The patient must tilt her head toward the opposite side to allow the two pupils to converge on an object on the floor. Paralysis of the trochlear nerve is not unusual when a patient's head has hit the dashboard in an automobile crash—the delicate nerve is easily torn where it pierces the dura of the tentorium cerebelli in the tentorial notch because the brain and brainstem move forward and backward with the force of impact (a "coup-contrecoup" injury).
GAS 850-851, 855; GA 450-451, 465, 536

166 **A.** The dural covering of the optic nerve is connected to the anular tendon; therefore, when there is an inflammation of the optic nerve, contractions of the recti can evoke severe pain.
GAS 894; GA 450-451, 461, 465, 468, 536

167 **D.** Toxoplasmosis infection is caused by the parasite *Toxoplasma gondii*, which is associated with undercooked meat and the feces of cats. Whereas it is a relatively common infection, once you have been exposed, you have immunity. The biggest concern is when a pregnant woman is exposed who has not been previously exposed. Congenital malformation, microphthalmia being one of the more common, can occur if the infection is passed on to the fetus.
GAS 898-902; GA 468

168 **A.** At the point where the facial nerve exits the stylomastoid foramen it is most susceptible to shearing forces. In the absence of a skull fracture whereby the facial nerve can be damaged within the facial canal, the nerve is most commonly injured as it exits the stylomastoid foramen. In infants, in whom the mastoid process has not yet developed, the facial nerve lies unprotected, just beneath the skin.
GAS 776, 819, 820, 821, 868, 872; GA 436, 474

169 **B.** The auriculotemporal nerve leads into the parotid gland, and its compression in mumps can be

associated with severe pain. The compressive effects are due in large part to the continuity of the facial capsule of the parotid gland with the tough layer of superficial investing fascia of the neck, a layer that is almost non-distensible. When the gland swells, sensory fibers for pain are triggered rapidly, and can be referred to the ear. None of the other nerves listed supply the parotid gland.
GAS 864, 867-868, 874, 875; GA 455, 483-485

170 **B.** Hydrops (edema) results from accumulation of excessive fluid in the endolymphatic sac. Labyrinthine hydrops or endolymphatic hydrops is known as Ménière disease. This disease can result in hearing loss, roaring noises in the ear, and episodic dizziness (vertigo) associated with nausea and vomiting. About 10% of patients require surgical intervention for persistent, incapacitating vertigo; others are treated with diuretics, low salt intake, and reduction of stimulants like caffeine to lower the volume of body fluids and alleviate the symptoms of Ménière disease.
GAS 915, 916; GA 473-477

171 **D.** The superior thyroid vein is a tributary to the internal jugular vein; it accompanies the superior thyroid artery. The middle thyroid vein is typically a short, direct tributary to the internal jugular vein. The inferior thyroid vein usually drains vertically downward to one or both brachiocephalic veins. The superior and middle thyroid veins can be torn in thyroid surgery, perhaps admitting an air bubble (due to negative pressure in the veins) that can ascend in the internal jugular vein into the skull, with injurious or lethal results.
GAS 961, 966, 967; GA 516

172 **C.** The cricothyroid artery is a small branch of the superior thyroid artery. It anastomoses with the cricothyroid artery of the opposite side at the upper end of the median cricothyroid ligament, a common site for establishing an emergency airway. The cricothyroid artery can be pushed into the airway during a cricothyroidostomy. The vessel(s) can bleed directly into the trachea, bleeding that can go unnoticed by medical personnel, with potentially fatal aspiration of blood by the patient.
GAS 959, 960, 966; GA 452, 498, 516-517

173 **C.** An incision at the level of the third and fourth tracheal cartilages usually results in the fewest complications during a tracheostomy. The isthmus of the thyroid gland (a richly vascular structure) is usually at the level of the second tracheal cartilage and this incision is just inferior to that. However, other vascular structures such as a thyroidea ima artery or tributaries of the external jugular veins make a tracheostomy a surgical procedure to be performed with care.
GAS 806, 1009, 1065; GA 80

174 **A.** The uvula would move toward the intact right side. This is because the intact levator veli palatini would be unopposed by the opposite, paralyzed left levator veli palatini.
GAS 1051; GA 504-505, 507, 533

175 **B.** If the left abducens nerve is injured, there will be a loss of function of the left lateral rectus muscle so the patient will be unable to abduct his left eye. The trochlear nerve supplies the superior oblique muscle, which if injured would cause the patient to lose the ability to turn the pupil downward when it is in the adducted position. As an example, the affected patient could not turn the pupil to look downward to the left if the right trochlear nerve were paralyzed. This deficiency can make it difficult for individuals to descend stairs if they have trochlear nerve palsy. If the oculomotor nerve were injured, the pupil would be directed "down and out" due to unopposed actions of the lateral rectus and superior oblique, which are innervated by the abducens and trochlear nerves, respectively. If the optic nerve were injured, the patient would have blindness in the affected eye. If the oculomotor and abducens nerves were injured, the patient would have only the actions of the superior oblique muscle, and the eye would be directed downward and outward from the position of forward gaze.
GAS 849-852, 855, 894-895; GA 450, 465, 536

176 **D.** The accommodation reflex is performed by constriction of the pupil when trying to focus on a near object. This function is controlled by the parasympathetic nerve fibers carried in the oculomotor nerve from the Edinger-Westphal nucleus of the midbrain that synapse in the ciliary ganglion. Postganglionic axons act on the sphincter pupillae muscle to cause reduction in pupil diameter and on the ciliary muscle to cause relaxation of the suspensory ligament, allowing the lens to adopt a more spherical shape for near focusing. If there is a lack of accommodation, it means the action of the ciliary muscle is compromised. The ciliary muscle also gets parasympathetic innervation by postganglionic neurons evoked from the ciliary ganglion by GVE fibers of oculomotor nerve whose cell bodies are located in the Edinger-Westphal nucleus. The superior salivatory nucleus is involved with lacrimation and salivation, not the ciliary muscle and accommodation. The superior cervical ganglion is a sympathetic ganglion; its postgangli-

onic axons innervate the dilator pupillae muscle, which causes mydriasis, but not the miosis of accommodation. The trigeminal ganglion does not have parasympathetic fibers and does not innervate the ciliary muscle for accommodation.
GAS 807, 849, 850-851, 855, 1075; GA 450-451, 465, 469, 536

177 **A.** An acoustic neuroma (vestibular schwannoma or neurolemmoma) is a benign tumor of the vestibulocochlear nerve, which causes compression of VII nerve. This nerve leads from the inner ear to the brain. Although many such tumors will not grow or grow very slowly, growth can in some cases result ultimately in brainstem compression (as in this example), hydrocephalus, brainstem herniation, and death. It is diagnosed on MRI with gadolinium contrast as shown. Extension of the neuroma into the right internal auditory meatus can be seen on the coronal MRI (see arrow in Fig. 7-9). The exact cause of the tumor is unknown; most people with acoustic neuromas are diagnosed between the ages of 30 and 60. Due to advances in microsurgery, including intraoperative monitoring of facial and cochlear function, the risks of facial paralysis and hearing loss have been greatly reduced. Many acoustic neuromas can now be treated effectively with both surgery and targeted radiation therapy (gamma knife). The outcomes for those with small acoustic neuromas are better, whereas those with neuromas larger than 2.5 cm are likely to experience significant hearing loss postsurgery.
GAS 835; GA 450-451, 472-473, 476, 537

178 **A.** Pharyngeal (branchial) cleft cysts are the most common congenital cause of a neck mass. They are epithelial cysts that arise anterior to the superior third of the sternocleidomastoid muscle (1) from a failure of obliteration of the second branchial cleft in embryonic development. The second arch grows caudally and, ultimately, covers the third and fourth arches. The buried clefts become ectoderm-lined cavities that normally involute. Occasionally this process is arrested and the entrapped remnant forms an epithelium-lined cyst, in some cases with a sinus tract to the overlying skin. (2) Many branchial cleft cysts are asymptomatic; others may become tender, enlarged, or inflamed, or they may develop abscesses that rupture, resulting in a purulent draining sinus to the skin or pharynx. Surgery is indicated in these cases.
GAS 970-971; GA 492-493

179 **C.** The angiograph provided clearly shows that the radiopaque medium injected into the patient did not completely fill the common carotid artery. Portions of the internal and external carotid arteries are filled above the common carotid due to "back fill" provided by the collateral circulation. However, vascular supply to the brain is still compromised in this patient, leading to her symptoms.
GAS 806, 858-859; GA 458, 491, 498

180 **A.** Mastoiditis is an infection of the air cells within the mastoid process of the temporal bone, often caused by untreated acute otitis media. A known complication of mastoiditis is inflammation of the transverse sinus. Necrosis of the bone due to untreated infection will often affect the transverse sinus. The petrous part of the temporal bone is unlikely to experience inflammation. Infection in the middle ear is usually the preceding event to mastoiditis rather than occurring as a result of it. The occipital sinus is located far posteriorly to the mastoid process and is unlikely to be affected. Because of its position, the internal carotid artery will not be affected by this inflammation.
GAS 907, 909; GA 474-475

181 **B.** A chalazion is caused by an obstructed tarsal gland of the eyelid. Swellings of the lacrimal gland usually present on the upper lateral eyelid and are not indicative of a chalazion. A chalazion is not an infection within the eye, so this excludes sclera and pupil from being the correct answers. The nasolacrimal duct runs from the medially located lacrimal sacs to the inferior meatus of the nose and would be unaffected in the case of a chalazion.
GAS 881; GA 461

182 **B.** The nasal polyp also involved the maxillary sinus, located immediately laterally to the nasal cavity. The sphenoid sinus, located posterosuperiorly to the nasopharynx, is unlikely to be affected by a nasal polyp. The ethmoidal sinuses, located medially to the orbit and lateral to the nasal cavity, are also unlikely to be affected by a nasal polyp, although this possibility cannot be ruled out. The frontal sinuses located superomedially to the eyes are unlikely to be affected by the nasal polyp. The frontonasal ducts, the communication between the frontal sinus and the nasal cavity, are also unlikely to be affected.
GAS 797, 879, 1018, 1020, 1022; GA 487, 518, 525

183 **C.** A tumor at the cerebellopontine angle, such as an acoustic schwannoma, is most likely to affect first the vestibulocochlear nerve and then the facial nerve. This excludes the vagus, hypoglossal, glossopharyngeal, and trigeminal nerves from being the correct answers.
GAS 835; GA 472-477

184 D. Rupture of the periosteal arteries resulting in a cephalohematoma is defined as a collection of blood underneath the periosteum. On the head, it is located between the pericranium (periosteum of the skull) and the calvaria (skull). The galea aponeurotica, skin and areolar connective tissue are all located superficial to the site of bleeding and hematoma.
GAS 830; GA 461

185 B. The tentorial/uncal herniation described in this case is most likely to occur as a result of a temporal lobe tumor. The uncus is part of the temporal lobe, and when enlarged, it will be compressed against the foramen magnum. This results in the symptoms manifested by damage to the nearby oculomotor nerve. The uncus is not a part of the other named lobes.
GAS 824, 831; GA 444, 450

186 C. A tumor involving the meningeal branches of the ethmoidal nerves that originate from the ophthalmic division of the trigeminal nerve is likely to cause pain from pressure and nerve injury in the anterior cranial fossa. The maxillary and mandibular divisions of the trigeminal nerve provide sensory innervation to the middle and posterior aspects of the meninges, respectively. Spinal nerve C2 and C3 fibers do not provide meningeal innervation. The tentorial nerve, a branch of the ophthalmic division of the trigeminal nerve, supplies the tentorium and the supratentorial falx cerebri.
GAS 833; GA 483-484

187 A. The deep lingual vein is located most superficially on the underside of the tongue. It is therefore the most direct route for absorption of the administered nitroglycerin. The submandibular and sublingual ducts are excretory in function and do not function to absorb a drug, such as nitroglycerin. The lingual and sublingual vein are located more deeply within the floor of the mouth and do not provide the most direct route for absorption.
GAS 1042; GA 531, 534

188 B. The lingual nerve initially courses directly underneath the mucosa of the floor of the mouth and superficial to the submandibular gland, specifically the submandibular duct. This nerve is therefore at risk for ligation, division, or trauma during excision of the gland and duct. The lingual nerve is part of the mandibular division of the trigeminal nerve and carries fibers from the chorda tympani. These latter fibers supply taste to the anterior two thirds of the tongue and preganglionic parasympathetic axons involved in salivary gland secretion. Fibers of the trigeminal nerve supply general sensation to the anterior two thirds of the tongue. The lingual nerve passes deep both to the lateral pterygoid muscle and the ramus of the mandible and subsequently travels deep to the submandibular gland itself. The buccal nerve, also a branch of the mandibular division of the trigeminal nerve, supplies the mucosa of the cheek and is not in close proximity to the gland or duct. The inferior alveolar nerve, though close in proximity to the submandibular gland, travels deep to the lateral pterygoid muscle and later enters the mandibular canal to supply the lower teeth. The nerve to the mylohyoid, a branch of the inferior alveolar nerve, supplies the mylohyoid muscle and the anterior belly of the digastric. Neither of these nerves is at risk for damage during excision of the submandibular gland and duct.
GAS 1041, 1043, 1045; GA 480, 484, 528-529, 532, 534

189 A. The ophthalmic artery is a branch of the internal carotid artery and provides origin to the ocular and orbital vessels, including the central artery of the retina, which supplies the retina. The central artery of the retina is an end artery that has no anastomoses with other arterial sources; therefore, occlusion of this artery will result in loss of vision. The nasociliary nerve is a branch of the ophthalmic nerve. It is the general sensory nerve for the eye and is the afferent limb of the corneal blink reflex; it has no direct effect on vision. The anterior ethmoidal nerve is a branch of the nasociliary nerve and supplies the anterior ethmoid air cells, the nasal septum, and the lateral walls of the nasal cavity; it also supplies the skin on the bridge of the nose. The trochlear nerve is the fourth of the 12 cranial nerves and innervates the superior oblique muscle, one of the six extraocular muscles. The extraocular muscles function in the movement of the eyeball and not the perception of light. The optic nerve is the second of the 12 cranial nerves and is responsible for vision. A lesion of the optic nerve would lead to blindness; however, based on the location of the patient's infection, the optic nerve was not affected by the loss of arterial supply.
GAS 837, 838, 890, 892-893; GA 452, 485

190 A. CSF is mostly secreted from the choroid plexuses of the lateral, third, and fourth ventricles of the brain. The CSF enters the subarachnoid space from the fourth ventricle, via the foramina of Luschka and Magendie. The CSF then circulates in the subarachnoid space until it is finally resorbed back into the venous side of the circulation through the arachnoid granulations into the superior sagittal sinus. A thrombus of the superior sagittal sinus can to lead to an obstruction of CSF (communicating hydrocepha-

lus) in which all of the ventricles of the brain are enlarged and the intracranial pressure is increased.
GAS 834; GA 442-449

191 **C.** The jugulodigastric node, also known as the tonsillar lymph node, receives drainage from the tonsils, tongue, and pharynx. It is often enlarged during tonsillitis. The submandibular lymph nodes drain the back of the tongue, gums, upper lip, parts of the lower lip, and sides of the face. They drain into the deep cervical group of nodes. The parotid nodes are located superficially and deep to the parotid gland and drain aspects of the cheek, external acoustic meatus, the lateral aspects of the eyelids and posterior orbit. The submental nodes drain the tip of the tongue bilaterally, the lower lip, and floor of the mouth. Finally, the retropharyngeal lymph nodes drain the nasopharynx, nasal cavities, and auditory tubes.
GAS 983, 984, 995, 1044; GA 458, 502-503

192 **B.** The preauricular lymph nodes are also known as the deep parotid nodes. They are located deep to the parotid gland and drain lymph from the posterior orbit. The submandibular nodes drain the side of the cheek and lateral aspects of the nose and lips. The superficial parotid lymph nodes lie superficially to the parotid gland and drain the lateral angles of the eyelids, aspects of the nose, and the external acoustic meatus. The jugulodigastric nodes receive drainage from all of the superior nodes of the face and also drain the tonsils. The submental lymph nodes drain the tip of the tongue and chin.
GAS 872, 877, 878, 983, 984; GA 458, 502

193 **D.** The pharyngeal (Zenker) diverticulum is usually located between the cricopharyngeal and thyropharyngeal portions of the inferior pharyngeal constrictor. This is the most common site for development of a pharyngeal diverticulum due to the inherent weakness between the pharyngeal muscles in this location. Stasis of materials within this diverticulum can lead to inflammation, infection, and abscess. This site is also known as Killian's triangle.
GAS 987-989; GA 457, 504

194 **C.** The left brachiocephalic vein is the most likely vein punctured in the procedure because it extends across the trachea from the left side of the body, joining the right brachiocephalic vein to form the superior vena cava, which is located just to the right of the midline. The superior thyroid veins drain the superior aspects of the thyroid glands and join the internal jugular veins bilaterally and superiorly to the site of incision. The middle thyroid veins drain the middle portions of the thyroid glands and also terminate in the internal jugular veins laterally, superior to the incision site. The inferior thyroid veins drain the inferior aspects of the thyroid glands and descend bilaterally to the trachea to join the right and left brachiocephalic veins, respectively. Finally, the jugular arch connecting the anterior jugular veins is quite superficial and is not typically a source of concern if encountered surgically.
GAS 132, 206-207; GA 69, 76, 82, 95, 104, 516

195 **C.** The glossopharyngeal nerve enters the posterior oropharynx by coursing between the stylohyoid ligament and the stylopharyngeus muscle. Calcification of the stylohyoid ligament can readily affect this nerve by irritation or compression. The other nerves listed are not in close proximity to the styloid process or stylohyoid ligament. The glossopharyngeal nerve carries sensory nerve fibers from the posterior third of the tongue and the pharynx. A lesion of this nerve could cause loss of both general sensation and taste sensation from the posterior third of the tongue.
GAS 987, 1032-1034; GA 489, 506-507, 530

196 **A.** There is a lesion of the facial nerve proximal to the geniculate ganglion. At the geniculate ganglion the greater petrosal nerve branches from the facial nerve and ultimately runs to the pterygopalatine ganglion where preganglionic fibers synapse on postganglionic neurons that innervate the lacrimal gland. There is a disruption of the facial nerve proximal to this branch that allows the greater petrosal nerve to be stimulated by factors that would normally stimulate the submandibular and sublingual glands. These glands are innervated via the chorda tympani that comes off the facial nerve distal to the geniculate ganglion.
GAS 872; GA 451, 458-459, 463, 473-474, 484, 537

197 **B.** The anterior communicating artery, the portion of the arterial circle (of Willis), is directly superior to the optic chiasm, and an aneurysm of this artery would likely compress the chiasm, as in this patient.
GAS 837-841; GA 452, 454

198 **E.** The nasolacrimal duct is the only duct that normally drains into the inferior meatus of the nose and therefore would be affected by a focal inflammation in this region.
GAS 882-883, 884, 885, 1022; GA 462, 519-520

199 **D.** The greater petrosal nerve is a branch of the facial nerve that ultimately supplies the lacrimal gland. This branch comes off the facial nerve at the

geniculate ganglion proximal to the chorda tympani. The greater petrosal nerve is unlikely to be involved in a lesion of the facial nerve as described. The other listed functions of the facial nerve would be affected by the lesion.
GAS 882-884, 1069; GA 462-463

200 **B.** The great auricular nerve is derived from the ventral rami of the second and third cervical nerves and supplies the skin over the angle of the mandible up to the level of the TMJ.
GAS 973-975; GA 494, 496-497

201 **B.** The supraclavicular lymph node on the left side is associated with the thoracic duct. The thoracic duct receives lymph from below the diaphragm, including the gastrointestinal tract. Malignant cells that travel up the thoracic duct are known to involve the left supraclavicular lymph node.
GAS 138, 154, 205, 211, 215, 219-221, 372, 373, 374, 981-982; GA 12, 71, 118, 175, 503

202 **E.** The internal branch of the superior laryngeal nerve, often called the internal laryngeal nerve, supplies the mucosa of the larynx above the vocal folds (which includes the vestibule of the larynx) and the piriform recess. The external branch of the superior laryngeal nerve (external laryngeal nerve) is motor to the cricothyroid muscle. The inferior laryngeal nerve supplies the mucosa of the larynx below the vocal folds. The glossopharyngeal nerve supplies sensation to the posterior third of the tongue and to the pharynx. The hypoglossal nerve is motor.
GAS 996-1012; GA 514

203 **D.** A fractured hyoid bone is evidence of strangulation. A fall from a height and subdural hematoma would likely be accompanied by fractured bones. Whereas myocardial infarction or poison remain possibilities, the medical examiner would have a high index of suspicion for strangulation because of the fractured hyoid bone.
GAS 803, 1034; GA 489, 504, 512-513

204 **C.** Melanocytes in the pigmented layer of the retina are a potential source of malignant melanoma cells. The tumor spreads hematogenously directly to the brain and has a very poor prognosis. None of the other listed structures contains melanocytes.
GAS 901; GA 461, 468